DID YOU EVER PUZZLE OVER HOW TO:

spell abecedarian?

pluralize scarf?

form the possessive of Hercules?

break tit*il*lat*ing correctly?

Puzzle no more! *The New American Spelling Dictionary* will answer your questions—quickly and easily. Larger and more comprehensive than any other spelling reference on the market, this authoritative volume will be of immense value to those who know the meanings of words, but are in doubt about how to spell and divide them.

WILLIAM C. PAXSON is the author of seven books, including *The Mentor Guide to Punctuation, The Mentor Guide to Writing Term Papers,* and *The New American Dictionary of Confusing Words.* He lives in Sacramento, California.

THE
NEW AMERICAN
SPELLING
DICTIONARY

Easy Access
to More Than
45,000 Words,
Spelled and Divided

by

William C. Paxson

A SIGNET BOOK

SIGNET
Published by the Penguin Group
Penguin Books USA Inc., 375 Hudson Street,
New York, New York 10014, U.S.A.
Penguin Books Ltd, 27 Wrights Lane,
London W8 5TZ, England
Penguin Books Australia Ltd, Ringwood,
Victoria, Australia
Penguin Books Canada Ltd, 10 Alcorn Avenue,
Toronto, Ontario, Canada M4V 3B2
Penguin Books (N.Z.) Ltd, 182–190 Wairau Road,
Auckland 10, New Zealand

Penguin Books Ltd, Registered Offices:
Harmondsworth, Middlesex, England

First published by Signet,
an imprint of New American Library,
a division of Penguin Books USA Inc.

First Printing, October, 1992
10 9 8 7 6 5 4 3 2 1

 REGISTERED TRADEMARK—MARCA REGISTRADA

PRINTED IN THE UNITED STATES OF AMERICA

BOOKS ARE AVAILABLE AT QUANTITY DISCOUNTS WHEN USED TO PROMOTE
PRODUCTS OR SERVICES. FOR INFORMATION PLEASE WRITE TO PREMIUM MAR-
KETING DIVISION, PENGUIN BOOKS USA INC., 375 HUDSON STREET, NEW YORK,
NEW YORK 10014.

Contents

Acknowledgments

I am indebted to the editorial staff of New American Library.

Their help was invaluable to me, for no one person can be expected to bring under control all of the inconsistencies and variations in English spelling.

Introduction

This book is a spelling reference book. As a reference book, it is not a book to be read but instead is a book in which you look up the correct spelling and division of a word. It is a book that will be useful to students, writers, editors, typists, word processors, and compositors.

The first part is a spelling dictionary, an A-to-Z list of words used in American English. Content includes words in popular use, frequently seen scientific and technical terms, popular first names, and major place names of the world.

The spelling dictionary is followed by appendixes that contain supplemental spelling guidelines and useful tables.

Style and Content of Entries

Entries are listed in alphabetical order. Each entry shows the preferred spelling of that word or phrase and the suggested word division if it becomes necessary to break the word or phrase in your writing. Additional information is sometimes given for an entry, such as spelling variants, irregular or variant verb forms, unusual or variant plural forms, and notations pertaining to usage.

For example, the following entries show the pluralization of the words *no* and *no-no*:

no, *n. pl.* noes *or* nos
no-no, *n. pl.* no-no's *or* no-nos

In addition, many entries show verb forms that undergo major changes in spelling as they change tenses. These are some examples:

jew·el, *v.* jew·eled *or* jew·elled, jew·el·ing *or* jew·el·ling
know, *v.* knew, known, know·ing
shred, *v.* shred·ded, shred·ding
wobble, *v.* wob·bled, wob·bling

Still other entries give usage notes along with variant spellings:

junk·ie *or* junky (ADDICT), *n. pl.* jun·kies
junky (TRASHY), *adj.* junk·i·er, junk·i·est

Also shown are foreign words and phrases that have become popular in American English. Foreign expressions are not italicized as they might appear in print. The decision to italicize a word is based on factors such as type of writing, personal preference, and the style manual that the writer is using.

Spelling. For most entries only one spelling is shown. For some words, however, an additional spelling is shown. This additional spelling is a *spelling variant*. The variants are based upon how popular a spelling is in edited, professional writing.

A spelling variant is introduced with the word *or*, the abbreviation *occas.* (*occasionally*), or the word *rarely*. When variants are separated by *or*, either spelling is commonly seen. However, when variants separated by *or* are out of alphabetical order, there could be a *slight* preference for the first spelling. When separated by *occas.*, there is a *marked* preference for the first spelling. Use of *rarely* indicates that the variant is uncommon.

If you wish to simplify the variant-spelling terminology, do this: Whenever you are confronted with a choice of spelling variants, choose the first spelling listed. The first spelling is the one that is generally most acceptable to editors, teachers, and readers.

Spellings were based on *Webster's Ninth New Collegiate Dictionary* (Springfield, Massachusetts: Merriam-Webster, 1990). The secondary reference was *Webster's New World Dictionary of American English* (New York: Simon & Schuster, 1988).

Word division. Word division is shown so that you will know where to divide a word at the end of a line. A dot

(·) shows where the division may be made. With hyphen-ated words, the word may also be divided at the hyphen.

Therefore, a dictionary entry for *qual·i·fi·ca·tion* allows divisions that:

End on one line as	and continue on the next line as
qual-	ification
quali-	fication
qualifi-	cation
qualifica-	tion

Please note that this dictionary shows word division and not strict syllabication. Syllabication, or syllabifica-tion, is the dividing of a word into syllables.

Strict syllabication would divide *amiss* into two sylla-bles: *a·miss*. To divide *amiss* that way would end a line of type with an awkward *a-*. Instead, this dictionary rec-ommends against single-letter breaks. The preferred form is to spell on one line words such as *amiss*, *again*, and *over*.

A supplemental guide to word division appears in Ap-pendix 4.

Spellings not shown. To make the most use of space, the dictionary generally does not show spellings that are relatively standardized and usually well-known among users of English. Excluded from the dictionary are plu-rals formed by adding *s* (*car* becomes *cars*); plurals formed by adding *es* (*witness* becomes *witnesses*); and verbs that change their tenses solely by adding *d, ed*, or *ing* (*agree* becomes *agreed* and *agreeing, obey* becomes *obeyed* and *obeying*).

Abbreviations and Expressions
Used in the Dictionary

The following abbreviations and expressions are used in the dictionary:

adj. Adjective
adv. Adverb

Brit. British usage or spelling
conj. Conjunction
fem. Feminine
masc. Masculine
n. Noun
occas. (occasionally) Introduces an uncommon spelling variant
or Introduces a common spelling variant
pl. Plural
see also Directs you to another entry in the dictionary
sing. Singular
℠ Registered trademark
v. Verb, verb tense, or verb form
var. of (variant of) Introduces another, and sometimes less common, spelling

A

aard·vark

aard·wolf, *n. pl.*
aard·wolves

Aar·on

aback

aba·cus, *n. pl.*
aba·ci *or*
aba·cus·es

ab·a·lo·ne

aban·don

aban·doned

aban·don·ment

abase, *v.* abased,
abas·ing

abase·ment

abash

abash·ed·ly

abash·ment

abate, *v.* abat·ed,
abat·ing

abate·ment

ab·a·tis, *n. pl.*
ab·a·tis *or*
ab·a·tis·es

ab·at·toir

ab·ax·i·al

ab·ba·cy, *n. pl.*
ab·ba·cies

ab·bé
(CLERGYMAN)
(*see also* abbey)

ab·bess

ab·bey (CHURCH),
n. pl. ab·beys

ab·bot

ab·bre·vi·ate, *v.*
ab·bre·vi·at·ed,
ab·bre·vi·at·ing

ab·bre·vi·a·tion

ab·di·cate, *v.*
ab·di·cat·ed,
ab·di·cat·ing

ab·di·ca·tion

ab·di·ca·tor

ab·do·men

ab·dom·i·nal

ab·duct

ab·duc·tion

ab·duc·tor

abeam

abe·ce·dar·i·an

abed

Ab·er·deen

ab·er·rant

ab·er·ra·tion

abet, *v.* abet·ted,
abet·ting

abet·tor *or* abet·ter

abey·ance

ab·hor, *v.*
ab·horred,
ab·hor·ring

ab·hor·rence

ab·hor·rent

abide, *v.* abode *or*
abid·ed,
abid·ing

Ab·i·djan

Ab·i·lene

abil·i·ty, *n. pl.*
abil·i·ties

ab·ject

ab·jec·tion

ab·ject·ly

ab·ject·ness

ab·ju·ra·tion

ab·jure, *v.*
ab·jured,
ab·jur·ing

ab·late, *v.*
ab·lat·ed,
ab·lat·ing

ab·la·tion

1

ab·la·tive

ablaze

able, *adj.* abler, ablest

able-bod·ied

abloom

ab·lu·tion

ab·ne·gate, *v.* ab·ne·gat·ed, ab·ne·gat·ing

ab·ne·ga·tion

ab·nor·mal

ab·nor·mal·i·ty, *n.* *pl.* ab·nor·mal·i·ties

ab·nor·mal·ly

aboard

abode

aboil

abol·ish

abol·ish·ment

ab·o·li·tion

ab·o·li·tion·ism

ab·o·li·tion·ist

A-bomb

abom·i·na·ble

abom·i·na·bly

abom·i·nate, *v.* abom·i·nat·ed, abom·i·nat·ing

abom·i·na·tion

ab·orig·i·nal

ab·orig·i·nal·ly

ab·orig·i·ne

aborn·ing

abort

abor·tion

abor·tion·ist

abor·tive

abound

about

about-face

above

above·board

above·ground

ab·ra·ca·dab·ra

abrade, *v.* abrad·ed, abrad·ing

abra·sion

abra·sive

abra·sive·ly

abra·sive·ness

abreast

abridge, *v.* abridged, abridg·ing

abridg·ment *or* abridge·ment

abroad

ab·ro·gate, *v.* ab·ro·gat·ed, ab·ro·gat·ing

ab·ro·ga·tion

abrupt

abrupt·ly

abrupt·ness

ab·scess

ab·scis·sa, *n. pl.* ab·scis·sas (*occas.* ab·scis·sae)

ab·scis·sion

ab·scond

ab·scond·er

ab·sence

ab·sent

ab·sen·tee

ab·sen·tee·ism

ab·sent·ly

ab·sent·mind·ed

ab·sent·mind·ed·ly

ab·sent·mind·ed·ness

ab·sinthe (*occas.* ab·sinth)

ab·so·lute

ab·so·lute·ly

ab·so·lute·ness

ab·so·lu·tion

ab·so·lut·ism

ab·solve, *v.* ab·solved, ab·solv·ing

ab·sorb

ab·sorb·able

ab·sor·ben·cy, *n.* *pl.* ab·sor·ben·cies

ab·sor·bent (*occas.* ab·sor·bant)

ab·sorb·er

ab·sorb·ing

ab·sorp·tion

ab·sorp·tive

ab·stain

ab·ste·mi·ous

ab·ste·mi·ous·ly

ab·sten·tion

ab·sti·nence

ab·sti·nent

ab·stract

ab·strac·tion

ab·strac·tion·ism

ab·stract·ly
ab·stract·ness
ab·struse
ab·surd
ab·sur·di·ty, *n. pl.*
  ab·sur·di·ties
ab·surd·ly
ab·surd·ness
Abu Dha·bi
abun·dance
abun·dant
abun·dant·ly
abuse, *v.* abused,
  abus·ing
abu·sive
abu·sive·ly
abu·sive·ness
abut, *v.* abut·ted,
  abut·ting
abut·ment
abut·tals
abuzz
abys·mal
abys·mal·ly
abyss
abys·sal
aca·cia
ac·a·deme
ac·a·de·mi·a
ac·a·dem·ic
ac·a·dem·i·cal
ac·a·dem·i·cal·ly
ac·a·dem·i·cian
acad·e·my, *n. pl.*
  acad·e·mies
Aca·dia (NOVA

SCOTIA)(*see
  also* Arcadia)
acan·thus, *n. pl.*
  acan·thus·es
  (*occas.* acan·thi)
a cap·pel·la (*occas.*
  a ca·pel·la)
Aca·pul·co
ac·cede, *v.*
  ac·ced·ed,
  ac·ced·ing
ac·ce·le·ran·do
ac·cel·er·ant
ac·cel·er·ate, *v.*
  ac·cel·er·at·ed,
  ac·cel·er·at·ing
ac·cel·er·a·tion
ac·cel·er·a·tor
ac·cel·er·om·e·ter
ac·cent
ac·cen·tu·ate, *v.*
  ac·cen·tu·at·ed,
  ac·cen·tu·at·ing
ac·cen·tu·a·tion
ac·cept
ac·cept·abil·i·ty
ac·cept·able
ac·cept·ably
ac·cep·tance
ac·cess
ac·ces·si·bil·i·ty
ac·ces·si·ble
ac·ces·sion
ac·ces·so·rize, *v.*
  ac·ces·so·rized,
  ac·ces·so·riz·ing
ac·ces·so·ry, *n. pl.*
  ac·ces·so·ries
  (*occas.*

ac·ces·sa·ry, *pl.*
  ac·ces·sa·ries)
ac·ci·dence
ac·ci·dent
ac·ci·den·tal
ac·ci·den·tal·ly
  (*occas.*
  ac·ci·dent·ly)
ac·ci·dent-prone
ac·claim
ac·cla·ma·tion
ac·cli·mate, *v.*
  ac·cli·mat·ed,
  ac·cli·mat·ing
ac·cli·ma·ti·za·tion
ac·cli·ma·tize, *v.*
  ac·cli·ma·tized,
  ac·cli·ma·tiz·ing
ac·co·lade
ac·com·mo·date, *v.*
  ac·com·mo·dat·ed,
  ac·com·mo·dat·ing
ac·com·mo·da·tion
ac·com·pa·ni·ment
ac·com·pa·nist
ac·com·pa·ny, *v.*
  ac·com·pa·nied,
  ac·com·pa·ny·ing
ac·com·plice
ac·com·plish
ac·com·plish·ment
ac·cord
ac·cor·dance
ac·cor·dant
ac·cord·ing
ac·cord·ing·ly
ac·cor·di·on
ac·cost
ac·couche·ment

ac·count

ac·count·abil·i·ty

ac·count·able

ac·count·ably

ac·coun·tan·cy, *n.*
pl.
  ac·coun·tan·cies

ac·coun·tant

ac·count·ing

ac·cou·tre·ment *or*
  ac·cou·ter·ment

Ac·cra

ac·cred·it

ac·cred·i·ta·tion

ac·crete, *v.*
  ac·cret·ed,
  ac·cret·ing

ac·cre·tion

ac·cru·al

ac·crue, *v.*
  ac·crued,
  ac·cru·ing

ac·cul·tur·ate, *v.*
  ac·cul·tur·at·ed,
  ac·cul·tur·at·ing

ac·cul·tur·a·tion

ac·cu·mu·late, *v.*
  ac·cu·mu·lat·ed,
  ac·cu·mu·lat·ing

ac·cu·mu·la·tion

ac·cu·mu·la·tive

ac·cu·mu·la·tor

ac·cu·ra·cy

ac·cu·rate

ac·cu·rate·ly

ac·cu·rate·ness

ac·cursed *or*
  ac·curst

ac·cus·al

ac·cu·sa·tion

ac·cu·sa·tive

ac·cu·sa·to·ry

ac·cuse, *v.*
  ac·cused,
  ac·cus·ing

ac·cused, *n. pl.*
  ac·cused

ac·cus·er

ac·cus·ing·ly

ac·cus·tom

ac·cus·tomed

ace, *v.* aced, ac·ing

acer·bic

acer·bi·ty

ac·e·tate

ace·tic (ACID) (*see
  also* ascetic)

ac·e·tone

acet·y·lene

ache, *v.* ached,
  ach·ing

achieve, *v.*
  achieved,
  achiev·ing

achieve·ment

ach·ing

ach·ing·ly

ach·ro·mat·ic

acid

acid·head

acid·ic

acid·i·fi·ca·tion

acid·i·fy, *v.*
  acid·i·fied,
  acid·i·fy·ing

acid·i·ty, *n. pl.*
  acid·i·ties

acid·ly

acid·ness

ac·i·do·sis

acid·u·late, *v.*
  acid·u·lat·ed,
  acid·u·lat·ing

acid·u·lous

ac·know·ledge, *v.*
  ac·knowl·edged,
  ac·knowl·edg·ing

ac·knowl·edg·ment
  (*occas.*
  ac·knowl·edge·ment)

ac·me

ac·ne

ac·o·lyte

acorn

acous·tic

acous·ti·cal

acous·ti·cal·ly

acous·ti·cian

acous·tics

ac·quaint

ac·quain·tance

ac·quain·tance·ship

ac·qui·esce, *v.*
  ac·qui·esced,
  ac·qui·esc·ing

ac·qui·es·cence

ac·qui·es·cent

ac·quire, *v.*
  ac·quired,
  ac·quir·ing

ac·qui·si·tion

ac·quis·i·tive

ac·quis·i·tive·ly

ac·quis·i·tive·ness

ac·quit, *v.*

ac·quit·ted,
  ac·quit·ting
ac·quit·tal
ac·quit·tance
acre
acre·age
acre-foot
ac·rid
acrid·i·ty
Ac·ri·lan®
ac·ri·mo·ni·ous
ac·ri·mo·ni·ous·ly
ac·ri·mo·ni·ous·ness
ac·ri·mo·ny
ac·ro·bat
ac·ro·bat·ic
ac·ro·bat·i·cal·ly
ac·ro·bat·ics
ac·ro·nym
ac·ro·pho·bia
acrop·o·lis
across
across-the-board
acros·tic
ac·ry·late
acryl·ic
act
ac·tin·i·um
ac·tion
ac·tion·able
ac·tion·ably
ac·ti·vate, v.
  ac·ti·vat·ed,
  ac·ti·vat·ing
ac·ti·va·tion
ac·tive
ac·tive·ly

ac·tive·ness
ac·tiv·ism
ac·tiv·ist
ac·tiv·i·ty, n. pl.
  ac·tiv·i·ties
ac·tor
ac·tress
ac·tu·al
ac·tu·al·i·ty, n. pl.
  ac·tu·al·i·ties
ac·tu·al·ize, v.
  ac·tu·al·ized,
  ac·tu·al·iz·ing
ac·tu·al·iza·tion
ac·tu·al·ly
ac·tu·ar·i·al
ac·tu·ary
ac·tu·ate, v.
  ac·tu·at·ed,
  ac·tu·at·ing
ac·tu·a·tor
acu·ity
acu·men
acu·pres·sure
acu·punc·ture
acute, adj. acut·er,
  acut·est
acute·ly
acute·ness
adage
ada·gio, n. pl.
  ada·gios
Ad·am
ad·a·mant
ad·a·man·tine
ad·a·mant·ly
Adam's ap·ple
adapt (MAKE

SUITABLE (see
  also adept,
  adopt)
adapt·abil·i·ty
adapt·able
ad·ap·ta·tion
adap·ter (occas.
  adap·tor)
ad·dend
ad·den·dum, n. pl.
  ad·den·da
ad·der (SNAKE)
add·er (ONE WHO
  ADDS)
ad·dict
ad·dic·tion
ad·dic·tive
Ad·dis Aba·ba
ad·di·tion
ad·di·tion·al
ad·di·tion·al·ly
ad·di·tive
ad·dle, v. ad·dled,
  ad·dling
ad·dress
ad·dres·see
ad·duce, v.
  ad·duced,
  ad·duc·ing
Aden
ad·e·noid
ad·e·noid·al
adept (HIGHLY
  SKILLED) adj.
  (see also adapt,
  adopt)
ad·ept (AN
  EXPERT) n.
  adept·ly

adept·ness

ad·e·qua·cy, *n. pl.*
  ad·e·qua·cies

ad·e·quate

ad·e·quate·ly

ad·e·quate·ness

ad·here, *v.*
  ad·hered,
  ad·her·ing

ad·her·ence

ad·her·ent

ad·he·sion

ad·he·sive

ad·he·sive·ly

ad·he·sive·ness

ad hoc

ad ho·mi·nem

adi·a·bat·ic

adieu, *n. pl.* adieus
  or adieux

ad in·fi·ni·tum

ad in·ter·im

adi·os

ad·i·pose

ad·i·pos·i·ty

Ad·i·ron·dack

ad·it

ad·ja·cent

ad·ja·cent·ly

ad·jec·ti·val

ad·jec·ti·val·ly

ad·jec·tive

ad·join

ad·join·ing

ad·journ

ad·journ·ment

ad·judge, *v.*

ad·judged,
ad·judg·ing

ad·ju·di·cate, *v.*
  ad·ju·di·cat·ed,
  ad·ju·di·cat·ing

ad·ju·di·ca·tion

ad·junct

ad·ju·ra·tion

ad·jure, *v.*
  ad·jured,
  ad·jur·ing

ad·just

ad·just·abil·i·ty

ad·just·able

ad·just·ed

ad·just·er (*occas.*
  ad·just·or)

ad·just·ment

ad·ju·tant

ad·ju·tant gen·er·al,
  n. pl.
  ad·ju·tants
  gen·er·al

ad lib, *adv.*

ad-lib, *adj.*

ad-lib, *v.* ad-
  libbed, ad-lib·bing

ad li·bi·tum

ad·min·is·ter

ad·min·is·tra·ble

ad·min·is·trant

ad·min·is·trate, *v.*
  ad·min·is·trat·ed,
  ad·min·is·trat·ing

ad·min·is·tra·tion

ad·min·is·tra·tive

ad·min·is·tra·tive·ly

ad·min·is·tra·tor

ad·min·is·tra·trix, *n.*

pl.
ad·min·is·tra·tri·ces

ad·mi·ra·ble

ad·mi·ra·ble·ness

ad·mi·ra·bly

ad·mir·al

ad·mi·ral·ty, *n. pl.*
  ad·mi·ral·ties

ad·mi·ra·tion

ad·mire, *v.*
  ad·mired,
  ad·mir·ing

ad·mir·er

ad·mir·ing·ly

ad·mis·si·bil·i·ty

ad·mis·si·ble

ad·mis·sion

ad·mit, *v.*
  ad·mit·ted,
  ad·mit·ting

ad·mit·tance

ad·mit·ted·ly

ad·mix

ad·mix·ture

ad·mon·ish

ad·mon·ish·ment

ad·mo·ni·tion

ad·mon·i·to·ry

ad nau·se·am

ado

ado·be

ad·o·les·cence

ad·o·les·cent

adopt (CHOOSE)
  (*see also* adapt,
  adept)

adop·tion

adop·tive

ador·able

ador·ably

ad·o·ra·tion

adore, *v.* adored, ador·ing

adorn

adorn·ment

ad·re·nal

Adren·a·lin®

adren·a·line (EPINEPHRINE)

Adri·at·ic

adrift

adroit

adroit·ly

adroit·ness

ad·sorb

ad·sor·bate

ad·sor·bent

ad·sorp·tion

ad·sorp·tive

ad·u·late, *v.* ad·u·lat·ed, ad·u·lat·ing

ad·u·la·tion

adult

adul·ter·ant

adul·ter·ate, *v.* adul·ter·at·ed, adul·ter·at·ing

adul·ter·a·tion

adul·ter·er

adul·ter·ess

adul·ter·ous

adul·ter·ous·ly

adul·tery, *n. pl.* adul·ter·ies

adult·hood

ad·um·brate, *v.* ad·um·brat·ed, ad·um·brat·ing

ad·um·bra·tion

ad va·lo·rem

ad·vance, *v.* ad·vanced, ad·vanc·ing

ad·vanced

ad·vance·ment

ad·van·tage

ad·van·ta·geous

ad·van·ta·geous·ly

ad·van·ta·geous·ness

ad·vent

ad·ven·ti·tious

ad·ven·ti·tious·ly

ad·ven·ture, *v.* ad·ven·tured, ad·ven·tur·ing

ad·ven·tur·er

ad·ven·ture·some

ad·ven·tur·ess

ad·ven·tur·ous

ad·ven·tur·ous·ly

ad·ven·tur·ous·ness

ad·verb

ad·ver·bi·al

ad·ver·bi·al·ly

ad·ver·sar·i·al

ad·ver·sary, *n. pl.* ad·ver·sar·ies

ad·ver·sa·tive

ad·verse (HOSTILE, UNFAVORABLE TO PEOPLE) (*see also* averse)

ad·verse·ly

ad·verse·ness

ad·ver·si·ty, *n. pl.* ad·ver·si·ties

ad·vert

ad·ver·tise, *v.* ad·ver·tised, ad·ver·tis·ing

ad·ver·tise·ment

ad·ver·tis·er

ad·ver·tis·ing

ad·vice, *n.* (*see also* advise)

ad·vis·abil·i·ty

ad·vis·able

ad·vis·ably

ad·vise, *v.* ad·vised, ad·vis·ing (*see also* advice)

ad·vise·ment

ad·vis·er *or* ad·vi·sor

ad·vi·so·ry

ad·vo·ca·cy

ad·vo·cate, *v.* ad·vo·cat·ed, ad·vo·cat·ing

adz *or* adze, *n. pl.* ad·zes

Ae·ge·an

ae·gis

ae·o·lian

ae·on (*var. of* eon)

aer·ate, *v.* aer·at·ed, aer·at·ing

aer·a·tion

aer·a·tor

ae·ri·al

ae·ri·al·ist

ae·rie (NEST)
　(occas. ey·rie)
　(see also eerie)
aero
aero·bat·ics
aer·obe
aer·o·bic
aer·o·bics
aero·drome
aero·dy·nam·ic
aero·dy·nam·i·cal·ly
aero·dy·nam·ics
aero·naut
aero·nau·tic
aero·nau·ti·cal
aero·nau·tics
aero·sol
aero·space
aes·thete or es·thete
aes·thet·ic or es·thet·ic
aes·thet·i·cal
aes·thet·i·cal·ly
aes·thet·i·cism
aes·thet·ics or
　es·thet·ics
aes·ti·vate (var. of
　estivate)
aes·ti·va·tion (var.
　of estivation)
af·fa·bil·i·ty
af·fa·ble
af·fa·bly
af·fair
af·fect
　(INFLUENCE),
　v. (see also
　effect)
af·fec·ta·tion

af·fect·ed
af·fec·tion
af·fec·tion·ate
af·fec·tion·ate·ly
af·fec·tive
af·fi·ance, v.
　af·fi·anced,
　af·fi·anc·ing
af·fi·da·vit
af·fil·i·ate, v.
　af·fil·i·at·ed,
　af·fil·i·at·ing
af·fil·i·a·tion
af·fin·i·ty, n. pl.
　af·fin·i·ties
af·firm
af·fir·ma·tion
af·fir·ma·tive
af·fix
af·fla·tus
af·flict
af·flic·tion
af·flic·tive
af·flu·ence
af·flu·ent
af·ford
af·ford·able
af·fray
af·fright
af·front
af·ghan (SHAWL)
Af·ghan (NATIVE OF
　AFGHANISTAN)
af·ghani (MONEY)
Af·ghan·i·stan
afi·cio·na·do, n. pl.
　afi·cio·na·dos
afield

afire
aflame
af·la·tox·in
afloat
aflut·ter
afoot
afore·men·tioned
afore·said
afore·thought
a for·ti·o·ri
afraid
A-frame
afresh
Af·ri·ca
Af·ri·can
Af·ri·can·der or
　Af·ri·kan·der
　(CATTLE), (see
　also Afrikaner)
Af·ri·kaans
Af·ri·ka·ner
　(PEOPLE) (see
　also Africander)
Af·ro, n. pl. Af·ros
af·ter
af·ter·birth
af·ter·bur·ner
af·ter·care
af·ter·deck
af·ter·ef·fect
af·ter·glow
af·ter·hours
af·ter·life
af·ter·mar·ket
af·ter·math
af·ter·noon
af·ter-shave

af·ter·shock

af·ter·taste

af·ter·thought

af·ter·ward *or*
af·ter·wards

again

against

agape (GAPING),
adj., *adv.*

aga·pe (LOVE
FEAST), *n.*

ag·ate

ag·ate ware

aga·ve

age, *v.* aged, ag·ing
or age·ing

age·ism

age·ist

age·less

agen·cy, *n. pl.*
agen·cies

agen·da, *pl. of*
agen·dum

agen·dum, *n. pl.*
agen·da *or*
agen·das

agent

age-old

ag·gior·na·men·to,
n. pl.
ag·gior·na·men·tos

ag·glom·er·ate, *v.*
ag·glom·er·at·ed,
ag·glom·er·at·ing

ag·glom·er·a·tion

ag·glu·ti·nate, *v.*
ag·glu·ti·nat·ed,
ag·glu·ti·nat·ing

ag·glu·ti·na·tion

ag·gran·dize, *v.*
ag·gran·dized,
ag·gran·diz·ing

ag·gran·dize·ment

ag·gra·vate, *v.*
ag·gra·vat·ed,
ag·gra·vat·ing

ag·gra·va·tion

ag·gre·gate, *v.*
ag·gre·gat·ed,
ag·gre·gat·ing

ag·gre·ga·tion

ag·gres·sion

ag·gres·sive

ag·gres·sive·ly

ag·gres·sive·ness

ag·gres·sor

ag·grieve, *v.*
ag·grieved,
ag·griev·ing

aghast

ag·ile

agil·i·ty, *n. pl.*
agil·i·ties

ag·i·tate, *v.*
ag·i·tat·ed,
ag·i·tat·ing

ag·i·ta·tion

ag·i·ta·tor

agleam

aglit·ter

aglow

ag·nos·tic

ag·nos·ti·cism

ago

agog

ag·o·nize, *v.*
ag·o·nized,
ag·o·niz·ing

ag·o·niz·ing·ly

ag·o·ny, *n. pl.*
ag·o·nies

ag·o·ra (ASSEMBLY
PLACE), *n. pl.*
ag·o·ras *or*
ag·o·rae

ag·o·ra (MONEY), *n.*
pl. ago·rot

ag·o·ra·pho·bia

ag·o·ra·pho·bic

agrar·i·an

agree

agree·abil·i·ty

agree·able

agree·able·ness

agree·ably

agree·ment

ag·ri·busi·ness

ag·ri·cul·tur·al

ag·ri·cul·ture

ag·ri·cul·tur·ist

ag·ro·nom·ic

ag·ro·nom·i·cal

ag·ro·nom·i·cal·ly

agron·o·mist

agron·o·my

aground

Aguas·ca·lien·tes

ague

agu·ish

ahead

Ah·mad·abad *or*
Ah·med·abad

ahoy

aid (HELP), *n.*, *v.*

aide (ASSISTANT),
n.

aide-de-camp, *n.*
  pl. aides-de-
  camp
ai·ki·do
ail
ai·le·ron
ail·ment
aim·less
aim·less·ly
aim·less·ness
air
air bag
air base
air·borne
air·brush
air·burst
air·bus
air-con·di·tion, *v.*
air con·di·tion·er,
  n.
air-con·di·tion·ing,
  n.
air-cool, *v.*
air-cooled, *adj.*
air·craft
air·crew
air·drome
air·drop, *v.*
  air·dropped,
  air·drop·ping
air-dry, *v.* air-
  dried, air-dry·ing
air·fare
air·field
air·flow
air·foil
air force
air·frame

air·freight
air·head
air·ing
air·lift
air·line
air·lin·er
air·mail
air·man
air-mind·ed
air·plane
air pocket
air·port
air·ship
air·sick
air·sick·ness
air·space
air·speed
air·stream
air·strip
air·tight
air-to-air
air-to-sur·face
air·wave
air·way
air·wor·thi·ness
air·wor·thy
airy, *adj.*, air·i·er,
  air·i·est
aisle
ajar
akim·bo
akin
Ak·ron
Al·a·bama
Al·a·bam·ian *or*
  Al·a·bam·an

al·a·bas·ter
à la carte (*occas.* a
  la carte)
alac·ri·ty
à la mode (*occas.* a
  la mode)
alarm (*occas.*
  ala·rum)
alarm·ing
alarm·ing·ly
alarm·ist
alas
Alas·ka
Alas·kan
al·ba·core
Al·ba·nia
Al·ba·nian
Al·ba·ny
al·ba·tross
al·be·it
Al·ber·ta
al·bi·nism
al·bi·no, *n. pl.*
  al·bi·nos
al·bum
al·bu·men (EGG
  WHITE)
al·bu·min
  (PROTEIN)
al·bu·min·ous
Al·bu·quer·que
al·cal·de
al·ca·zar
al·che·mist
al·che·my, *n. pl.*
  al·che·mies
al·co·hol
al·co·hol·ic

al·co·hol·ism

al·cove

al·de·hyde

al·der

al·der·man, *n. pl.*
  al·der·men

al·der·wom·an, *n.
pl.*
  al·der·wom·an

ale

alee

ale·house

alert

alert·ly

alert·ness

Aleu·tian Is·lands

ale·wife, *n. pl.*
  ale·wives

Al·ex·an·dria

Al·ex·an·dri·an

al·fal·fa

al·fres·co

al·ga, *n. pl.* al·gae
  (*occas.* al·gas)

al·ge·bra

al·ge·bra·ic

al·ge·bra·i·cal·ly

Al·ge·ria

Al·ge·ri·an

Al·giers

al·go·rithm

alias

al·i·bi, *v.* al·i·bied,
  al·i·bi·ing

Ali·cia

alien

alien·able

alien·ate, *v.*
  al·ien·at·ed,
  al·ien·at·ing

alien·ation

alight, *v.* alight·ed
  (*occas.* alit),
  alight·ing

align

align·ment

alike

al·i·men·ta·ry

al·i·mo·ny, *n. pl.*
  al·i·mo·nies

alive

al·ka·li, *n. pl.*
  al·ka·lies *or*
  al·ka·lis

al·ka·line

al·ka·lin·i·ty, *n. pl.*
  al·ka·lin·i·ties

al·ka·loid

al·kyd

all

Al·lah

all-Amer·i·can

all-around

al·lay (RELIEVE),
  v. (*see also*
  allay, ally)

all-clear

al·le·ga·tion

al·lege, *v.* al·leged,
  al·leg·ing

al·leg·ed·ly

Al·le·ghe·ny *n. pl.*
  Al·le·ghe·nies

al·le·giance

al·le·gor·i·cal

al·le·go·ry, *n. pl.*
  al·le·go·ries

al·le·gret·to, *n. pl.*
  al·le·gret·tos

al·le·gro, *n. pl.*
  al·le·gros

al·le·lu·ia

al·le·mande

Al·len·town

al·ler·gen

al·ler·gen·ic

al·ler·gic

al·ler·gist

al·ler·gy, *n. pl.*
  al·ler·gies

al·le·vi·ate, *v.*
  al·le·vi·at·ed,
  al·le·vi·at·ing

al·le·vi·a·tion

al·ley (STREET), *n.
pl.* al·leys (*see
also* allay, ally)

al·ley·way

al·li·ance

al·lied

al·li·ga·tor

all-im·por·tant

all-in·clu·sive

all-in·clu·sive·ness

Al·li·son

al·lit·er·ate, *v.*
  al·lit·er·at·ed,
  al·lit·er·at·ing

al·lit·er·a·tion

al·lit·er·a·tive

al·lit·er·a·tive·ly

al·lo·cate, *v.*
  al·lo·cat·ed,
  al·lo·cat·ing

al·lo·ca·tion

all-or-noth·ing

al·lot, *v.* al·lot·ted, al·lot·ting

al·lot·ment

al·lot·tee

all-out

all·over (REPEATED PATTERN OR COLOR)

all over (FINISHED, EVERYWHERE)

al·low

al·low·able

al·low·ably

al·low·ance

al·loy

all-pur·pose

all ready (PREPARED, WAITING) (*see also* already)

all right (*occas.* al·right)

all-round

All Saints' Day

All Souls' Day

all·spice

all-star

all-ter·rain bike

all to·geth·er (IN UNISON) (*see also* altogether)

all ways (IN EVERY WAY) (*see also* always)

al·lude (REFER TO), *v.* al·lud·ed,

al·lud·ing (*see also* elude)

al·lure, *v.* al·lured, al·lur·ing

al·lure·ment

al·lur·ing·ly

al·lu·sion (INDIRECT REFERENCE) (*see also* elusion, illusion)

al·lu·sive (SUGGESTIVE) (*see also* elusive, illusive)

al·lu·sive·ly

al·lu·sive·ness

al·lu·vi·al

al·lu·vi·um

ally (SUPPORTER), *n. pl.* allies (*see also* allay, alley)

al·ly (UNITE), *v.* al·lied, al·ly·ing

al·ma-ma·ter

al·ma·nac

al·mighty

al·mond

al·mon·er

al·most

alms, *n. pl.* alms

alms·house

al·ni·co

al·oe

aloft

alo·ha

alone

along

along·shore

along·side

aloof

aloof·ly

aloof·ness

aloud

alp

al·paca

al·pen·stock

al·pha

al·pha·bet

al·pha·bet·ic

al·pha·bet·i·cal

al·pha·bet·iza·tion

al·pha·bet·ize, *v.* al·pha·bet·ized, al·pha·bet·iz·ing

al·pha·nu·mer·ic

al·pha·nu·mer·i·cal

al·pine

al·ready (BY THIS TIME) (*see also* all ready)

al·right (*var. of* all right)

al·so

al·so-ran

al·tar (TABLE), *n.* (*see also* alter)

al·tar·piece

al·ter (CHANGE), *v.* (*see also* altar)

al·ter·a·tion

al·ter·ca·tion

al·ter ego

al·ter·nate, *v.* al·ter·nat·ed, al·ter·nat·ing

al·ter·nate·ly

al·ter·na·tion

al·ter·na·tive

al·ter·na·tive·ly

al·ter·na·tor

al·though (*rarely* al·tho)

al·tim·e·ter

al·ti·tude

al·to, *n. pl.* al·tos

al·to·cu·mu·lus, *n. pl.* al·to·cu·mu·li

al·to·geth·er (ENTIRELY) (*see also* all together)

al·to·stra·tus, *n. pl.* al·to·stra·ti

al·tru·ism

al·tru·ist

al·tru·is·tic

al·tru·is·tic·al·ly

al·um

alu·mi·na

alu·mi·num

alum·na, *fem., n. pl.* alum·nae

alum·nus, *fem., masc., n. pl.* alum·ni

al·ve·o·lar

al·ways (FOREVER) (*see also* all ways)

amal·gam

amal·ga·mate, *v.* amal·ga·mat·ed, amal·ga·mat·ing

amal·ga·ma·tion

Aman·da

aman·u·en·sis, *n. pl* aman·u·en·ses

am·a·ranth

am·a·ran·thine

am·a·ret·to

Am·a·ril·lo

am·a·ryl·lis

amass

am·a·teur

am·a·teur·ish

am·a·teur·ish·ly

am·a·teur·ish·ness

am·a·tive

am·a·to·ry

amaze, *v.* amazed, amaz·ing

amaze·ment

amaz·ing·ly

Am·a·zon Riv·er

am·bas·sa·dor

am·bas·sa·do·ri·al

am·bas·sa·dress

am·ber

am·ber·gris

am·bi·dex·trous

am·bi·dex·trous·ly

am·bi·ence *or* am·bi·ance

am·bi·ent

am·bi·gu·i·ty, *n. pl.* am·bi·gu·ities

am·big·u·ous

am·big·u·ous·ly

am·big·u·ous·ness

am·bi·tion

am·bi·tious

am·bi·tious·ly

am·biv·a·lence

am·biv·a·lent

am·biv·a·lent·ly

am·ble, *v.* am·bled, am·bling

am·bro·sia

am·bro·sial

am·bu·lance

am·bu·lant

am·bu·la·to·ry

am·bu·lette

am·bus·cade

am·bush

ame·ba (*var. of* amoeba)

ame·bic (*var. of* amoebic)

ame·bic dys·en·tery

ame·lio·rate, *v.* ame·lio·rat·ed, ame·lio·rat·ing

ame·lio·ra·tion

ame·lio·ra·tive

amen

ame·na·ble

amend (CORRECT) (*see also* emend)

amend·ment

amen·i·ty, *n. pl.* amen·i·ties

Am·er·asian

Amer·i·ca

Amer·i·can

Amer·i·ca·na

Amer·i·ca·nism

Amer·i·can·iza·tion

Amer·i·can·ize, *v.*

Amer·i·can·ized,
  Amer·i·can·iz·ing

am·er·i·ci·um

Am·er·ind

Am·er·in·di·an

am·e·thyst

ami·a·bil·i·ty

ami·a·ble

ami·a·bly

am·i·ca·bil·i·ty

am·i·ca·ble

am·i·ca·bly

ami·cus cu·ri·ae, *n.*
  pl. ami·ci
  cu·ri·ae

amid *or* amidst

amid·ships

ami·go, *n. pl.*
  ami·gos

ami·no

Amish

amiss

am·i·ty, *n. pl.*
  am·i·ties

am·me·ter

am·mo

am·mo·nia

am·mo·ni·um

am·mu·ni·tion

am·ne·sia

am·ne·si·ac

am·ne·sic

am·nes·ty, *n. pl.*
  am·nes·ties

am·nio·cen·te·sis, *n.*
  pl.
  am·nio·cen·te·ses

amoe·ba *or* ame·ba

n. pl. amoe·bas
or amoe·bae

amoe·bic *or* ame·bic

amok

among (*occas.*
  amongst)

amon·til·la·do, *n.*
  pl.
  amon·til·la·dos

amor·al

amor·al·i·ty

amor·al·ly

am·o·rous

am·o·rous·ly

am·o·rous·ness

amor·phous

amor·phous·ly

amor·phous·ness

am·or·ti·za·tion

am·or·tize, *v.*
  am·or·tized,
  am·or·tiz·ing

amount

amour

am·per·age

am·pere

am·pere-hour

am·per·sand

am·phet·amine

am·phib·i·an

am·phib·i·ous

am·phib·i·ous·ly

am·phib·i·ous·ness

am·phi·the·ater

am·pho·ra, *n. pl.*
  am·pho·rae *or*
  am·pho·ras

am·ple, *adj.*

am·pler,
  am·plest

am·pli·dyne

am·pli·fi·ca·tion

am·pli·fi·er

am·pli·fy, *v.*
  am·pli·fied,
  am·pli·fy·ing

am·pli·tude

am·poule *or*
  am·pule (*occas.*
  am·pul)

am·pu·tate, *v.*
  am·pu·tat·ed,
  am·pu·tat·ing

am·pu·ta·tion

am·pu·tee

Am·ster·dam

am·u·let

amuse, *v.* amused,
  amus·ing

amuse·ment

amus·ing

amus·ing·ly

Amy

Ana·bap·tist

anach·ro·nism

anach·ro·nis·tic

an·a·con·da

anae·mia (*var. of*
  ane·mia)

anae·mic (*var. of*
  ane·mic)

an·aer·o·bic

an·aes·the·sia (*var. of* an·es·the·sia)

an·aes·the·tic (*var. of* an·es·the·tic)

ana·gram

Ana·heim

anal

an·al·ge·sia

an·al·ge·sic

an·a·log (MEASUREMENT) (*see also* analogue)

anal·o·gous

an·a·logue (SIMILARITY) (*see also* analog)

anal·o·gy, *n. pl.* anal·o·gies

anal·y·sis, *n. pl.* anal·y·ses

an·a·lyst

an·a·lyt·ic

an·a·lyt·i·cal

an·a·lyze, *v.* an·a·lyzed, an·a·lyz·ing

an·a·pest

an·a·pes·tic

an·ar·chic

an·ar·chism

an·ar·chist

an·ar·chis·tic

an·ar·chy

an·astig·mat·ic

anath·e·ma

anath·e·ma·tize, *v.* anath·e·ma·tized, anath·e·ma·tiz·ing

anat·o·mist

anat·o·mize, *v.* anat·o·mized, anat·o·miz·ing

anat·o·my, *n. pl.* anat·o·mies

an·ces·tor

an·ces·tral

an·ces·try

an·chor

an·chor·age

an·chor·man, *n. pl.* an·chor·men

an·chor·per·son

an·chor·wom·an, *n. pl.* an·chor·wom·en

an·cho·vy, *n. pl.* an·cho·vies *or* an·cho·vy

an·cient

an·cil·lary

an·dan·te

an·dan·ti·no, *n. pl.* an·dan·ti·nos

and·iron

An·dor·ra

An·dor·ran

An·drea

An·drew

an·dro·gen

an·drog·e·nous (PRODUCING ONLY MALE OFFSPRING)

an·drog·y·nous (MALE AND FEMALE IN ONE)

an·ec·dot·al

an·ec·dote

ane·mia (*occas.* anae·mia)

ane·mic (*occas.* anae·mic)

an·e·mom·e·ter

anem·o·ne

an·er·oid

an·es·the·sia

an·es·the·si·ol·o·gist

an·es·the·si·ol·o·gy

an·es·thet·ic

anes·the·tist

anes·the·tize, *v.* anes·the·tized, anes·the·tiz·ing

an·eu·rysm *or* an·eu·rism

anew

an·gel (SPIRIT) (*see also* angle)

An·ge·la

an·gel·ic

an·gel·i·cal

an·gel·i·cal·ly

an·ger

an·gi·na

an·gi·na pec·to·ris

an·gio·plas·ty

an·gle (CORNER, VIEWPOINT, METHOD), *n.* (*see also* angel)

an·gle (MOVE, TURN, FISH) *v.* an·gled, an·gling

an·gler

an·gle·worm

An·gli·can

an·gli·cize, v.
  an·gli·cized,
  an·gli·ciz·ing
An·glo-Amer·i·can
An·glo·phile
An·glo·phobe
An·glo-Sax·on
An·go·la
An·go·lan
An·go·ra
an·gos·tu·ra
an·gri·ly
an·gry, adj.
  an·gri·er,
  an·gri·est
angst
ang·strom
an·guish
an·gu·lar
an·gu·lar·i·ty, n. pl.
  an·gu·lar·i·ties
an·hy·drous
anile
an·i·mad·ver·sion
an·i·mad·vert
an·i·mal
an·i·mal·ism
an·i·mate, v.
  an·i·mat·ed,
  an·i·mat·ing
an·i·ma·tion
an·i·ma·tron·ics
an·i·mism
an·i·mist
an·i·mis·tic
an·i·mos·i·ty, n. pl.
  an·i·mos·i·ties
an·i·mus

an·ise
an·is·ette
An·ka·ra
an·kle
ank·let
an·nal·ist
an·nals
An·nap·o·lis
an·neal
an·nex
an·nex·ation
an·ni·hi·late, v.
  an·ni·hi·lat·ed,
  an·ni·hi·lat·ing
an·ni·hi·la·tion
an·ni·ver·sa·ry, n.
  pl.
  an·ni·ver·sa·ries
an·no Do·mi·ni
an·no·tate, v.
  an·no·tat·ed,
  an·no·tat·ing
an·no·ta·tion
an·no·ta·tor
an·nounce, v.
  an·nounced,
  an·nounc·ing
an·nounce·ment
an·nounc·er
an·noy
an·noy·ance
an·nu·al
an·nu·al·ize, v.,
  an·nu·al·ized,
  an·nu·al·iz·ing
an·nu·al·ly
an·nu·i·tant
an·nu·i·ty, n. pl.
  an·nu·i·ties

an·nul, v.
  an·nulled,
  an·nul·ling
an·nu·lar
an·nul·ment
an·nun·ci·ate
  (ANNOUNCE),
  v.
  an·nun·ci·at·ed,
  an·nun·ci·at·ing
  (see also
  enunciate)
an·nun·ci·a·tion
  (ANNOUNCEMENT,
  FESTIVAL) (see
  also
  enunciation)
an·nun·ci·a·tor
an·ode
an·od·ize, v.
  an·od·ized,
  an·od·iz·ing
an·o·dyne
anoint
anom·a·lous
anom·a·lous·ly
anom·a·lous·ness
anom·a·ly, n. pl.
  anom·a·lies
an·o·nym·i·ty, n. pl.
  an·o·nym·i·ties
anon·y·mous
anon·y·mous·ly
anon·y·mous·ness
anoph·e·les
an·orex·ia ner·vo·sa
an·orex·ic
an·other
an·ox·ia
an·swer

an·swer·able

ant·acid

an·tag·o·nism

an·tag·o·nist

an·tag·o·nis·tic

an·tag·o·nis·ti·cal·ly

an·tag·o·nize, *v.*
an·tag·o·nized,
an·tag·o·niz·ing

ant·arc·tic

Ant·arc·ti·ca

an·te, *v.* an·ted,
an·te·ing

ant·eat·er

an·te·bel·lum

an·te·ced·ent

an·te·cham·ber

an·te·date, *v.*
an·te·dat·ed,
an·te·dat·ing

an·te·di·lu·vi·an

an·te·lope, *n. pl.*
an·te·lope *or*
an·te·lopes

an·te me·ri·di·em

an·te·mor·tem

an·ten·na, *n. pl.*
an·ten·nae
(ANIMAL
APPENDAGES)
or an·ten·nas
(ELECTRONIC
DEVICES)

an·te·ri·or

an·te·room

an·them

an·ther

ant·hill

an·thol·o·gist

an·thol·o·gize, *v.*
an·thol·o·gized,
an·thol·o·giz·ing

an·thol·o·gy, *n. pl.*
an·thol·o·gies

An·tho·ny

an·thra·cite

an·thrax

an·thro·po·cen·tric

an·thro·poid
(RESEMBLING
MAN) (*see also*
arthropod)

an·thro·po·log·i·cal

an·thro·pol·o·gist

an·thro·pol·o·gy

an·thro·po·mor·phic

an·thro·po·mor·phism

anti

an·ti·air·craft

anti-Ameri·can

anti-Ameri·can·ism

an·ti·bac·te·ri·al

an·ti·bal·lis·tic
mis·sile

an·ti·bi·ot·ic

an·ti·bo·dy, *n. pl.*
an·ti·bo·dies

an·ti·bus·ing

an·tic

An·ti·christ

anti-Chris·tian

an·tic·i·pate, *v.*
an·tic·i·pat·ed,
an·tic·i·pat·ing

an·tic·i·pa·tion

an·tic·i·pa·to·ry

an·ti·cli·mac·tic

an·ti·cli·mac·ti·cal

an·ti·cli·max

an·ti·co·ag·u·lant

an·ti·con·vul·sant

an·ti·cy·clone

an·ti·de·pres·sant

an·ti·dote

an·ti·freeze

an·ti·gen

An·ti·gua

An·ti·guan

an·ti·grav·i·ty

an·ti·he·ro, *n. pl*
an·ti·he·roes

an·ti·his·ta·mine

an·ti-in·tel·lec·tu·al

an·ti·knock

an·ti·ma·cas·sar

an·ti·mis·sile

an·ti·mo·ny

an·ti·pas·to

an·ti·per·son·nel

an·ti·per·spi·rant

an·ti·phon

an·tiph·o·nal

an·tip·o·dal

an·ti·pode, *n. pl.*
an·tip·o·des

an·ti·pov·er·ty

an·ti·quar·i·an

an·ti·quark

an·ti·quate, *v.*
an·ti·quat·ed,
an·ti·quat·ing

an·ti·quat·ed

an·tique, *v.*

an·tiqued,
an·tiqu·ing

an·tiq·ui·ty, *n. pl.*
an·tiq·ui·ties

anti-Se·mit·ic

anti-Sem·i·tism

an·ti·sep·sis

an·ti·sep·tic

an·ti·sep·ti·cal·ly

an·ti·so·cial

an·tith·e·sis, *n. pl.*
an·tith·e·ses

an·ti·thet·ic

an·ti·thet·i·cal

an·ti·thet·i·cal·ly

an·ti·tox·in

an·ti·trust

an·ti·ven·in

ant·ler

ant·lered

An·to·nio

ant·onym

An·tron®

an·trum, *n. pl.*
an·tra

ant·sy, *adj.*,
ant·si·er,
ant·si·est

anus

an·vil

anx·i·ety, *n. pl.*
anx·i·eties

anx·ious

anx·ious·ly

anx·ious·ness

any·body

any·how

any·more

any·one

any·place

any·thing

any·time

any·way

any·where

any·wise

aor·ta, *n. pl.*
aor·tas *or*
aor·tae

aor·tic

apace

apart

apart·heid

apart·ment

ap·a·thet·ic

ap·a·thet·i·cal·ly

ap·a·thy

ape-man, *n. pl.*
ape-men

ape·ri·od·ic

aper·i·tif

ap·er·ture

apex, *n. pl.* apex·es
or api·ces

apha·sia

aph·elion, *n. pl.*
aph·elia

aphid, *n. pl.* aphids

aphis, *n. pl.*
aphi·des

aph·o·rism

aph·o·ris·tic

aph·ro·di·si·ac

aph·ro·di·si·a·cal

api·a·rist

api·ary, *n. pl.*
api·ar·ies

api·cal

apiece

aplomb

ap·nea *or* ap·noea

apoc·a·lypse

apoc·a·lyp·tic

apoc·a·lyp·ti·cal

apoc·ry·pha

apoc·ry·phal

apo·gee

apo·lit·i·cal

apol·o·get·ic

apol·o·get·i·cal·ly

ap·o·lo·gia

apol·o·gist

apol·o·gize, *v.*
apol·o·gized,
apol·o·giz·ing

ap·o·logue

apol·o·gy, *n. pl.*
apol·o·gies

ap·o·plec·tic

ap·o·plexy

apos·ta·sy, *n. pl.*
apos·ta·sies

apos·tate

a pos·te·ri·o·ri

apos·tle

apos·to·late

ap·os·tol·ic

apos·tro·phe

apos·tro·phize, *v.*
apos·tro·phized,
apos·tro·phiz·ing

apoth·e·cary, *n. pl.*
apoth·e·caries

ap·o·thegm

apo·the·o·sis, *n. pl.*
  apo·the·o·ses

Ap·pa·la·chia

Ap·pa·la·chian

ap·pall (*rarely*
  ap·pal), *v.*
  ap·palled,
  appall·ing

ap·pa·nage

ap·pa·ra·tus, *n. pl.*
  ap·pa·ra·tus·es
  or ap·pa·ra·tus

ap·par·el

ap·par·ent

ap·par·ent·ly

ap·par·ent·ness

ap·pa·ri·tion

ap·pas·sio·na·ta

ap·peal

ap·pear

ap·pear·ance

ap·pease, *v.*
  ap·peased,
  ap·peas·ing

ap·pease·ment

ap·pel·lant

ap·pel·late

ap·pel·la·tion

ap·pel·lee

ap·pend

ap·pend·age

ap·pen·dec·to·my,
  n. pl.
  ap·pen·dec·to·mies

ap·pen·di·ci·tis

ap·pen·dix, *n. pl.*
  ap·pen·dix·es *or*
  ap·pen·di·ces

ap·per·cep·tion

ap·per·tain

ap·pe·tite

ap·pe·tiz·er

ap·pe·tiz·ing

ap·pe·tiz·ing·ly

ap·plaud

ap·plause

ap·ple

apple cider

ap·ple·jack

apple-pie (NEAT),
  adj.

apple pie
  (PASTRY), *n.*

ap·pli·ance

ap·pli·ca·bil·i·ty

ap·pli·ca·ble

ap·pli·cant

ap·pli·ca·tion

ap·pli·ca·tor

ap·pli·qué

ap·ply, *v.* ap·plied,
  ap·ply·ing

ap·point

ap·poin·tee

ap·poin·tive

ap·point·ment

ap·por·tion

ap·por·tion·ment

ap·po·site
  (RELEVANT)
  (*see also*
  opposite)

ap·po·si·tion
  (POSITION) (*see
  also* opposition)

ap·pos·i·tive

ap·prais·al

ap·praise
  (EVALUATE),
  v. ap·praised,
  ap·prais·ing (*see
  also* apprise)

ap·prais·er

ap·pre·cia·ble

ap·pre·cia·bly

ap·pre·ci·ate, *v.*
  ap·pre·ci·at·ed,
  ap·pre·ci·at·ing

ap·pre·ci·a·tion

ap·pre·cia·tive

ap·pre·hend

ap·pre·hen·sion

ap·pre·hen·sive

ap·pren·tice, *v.*
  ap·pren·ticed,
  ap·pren·tic·ing

ap·pren·tice·ship

ap·prise (INFORM),
  v. ap·prised,
  ap·pris·ing (*see
  also* appraise)

ap·proach

ap·proach·abil·i·ty

ap·proach·able

ap·pro·ba·tion

ap·pro·pri·ate, *v.*
  ap·pro·pri·at·ed,
  ap·pro·pri·at·ing

ap·pro·pri·ate·ly

ap·pro·pri·ate·ness

ap·pro·pri·a·tion

ap·prov·al

ap·prove, *v.*
  ap·proved,
  ap·prov·ing

ap·prox·i·mate, *v.*

ap·prox·i·mat·ed,
  ap·prox·i·mat·ing
ap·prox·i·mate·ly
ap·prox·i·ma·tion
ap·pur·te·nance
ap·pur·te·nant
après-ski
apri·cot
April
April Fools' Day
a pri·o·ri
apron
ap·ro·pos
ap·ti·tude
apt·ly
apt·ness
aqua, *n. pl.* aquae
  or aquas
aqua·cade
aqua·ma·rine
aqua·naut
aqua·plane
Aquar·i·an
aquar·i·um, *n. pl.*
  aquar·i·ums *or*
  aquar·ia
Aquar·i·us
aquat·ic
aqua·vit
aq·ue·duct
aque·ous
aqui·fer
aq·ui·line
Ar·ab
ar·a·besque
Ara·bia
Ara·bi·an

Ar·a·bic
ar·a·bil·i·ty
ar·a·ble
arach·nid
Ar·al Sea
ar·bi·ter
ar·bi·trage
ar·bi·trag·eur *or*
  ar·bi·trag·er
ar·bit·ra·ment
ar·bi·trar·i·ly
ar·bi·trar·i·ness
ar·bi·trary
ar·bi·trate, *v.*
  ar·bi·trat·ed,
  ar·bi·trat·ing
ar·bi·tra·tion
ar·bi·tra·tor
ar·bor
ar·bo·re·al
ar·bo·re·tum, *n. pl.*
  ar·bo·re·tums *or*
  ar·bo·re·ta
ar·bor·vi·tae
arc (CURVE) (*see*
  also ark)
ar·cade
Ar·ca·dia (*Greece*)
  (*see also*
  Acadia)
Ar·ca·di·an
ar·cane
arch
ar·chae·o·log·i·cal
  or
  ar·che·o·log·i·cal
ar·chae·ol·o·gist *or*
  ar·che·ol·o·gist

ar·chae·ol·o·gy *or*
  ar·che·ol·o·gy
ar·cha·ic
ar·cha·i·cal·ly
arch·an·gel
arch·bish·op
arch·bish·op·ric
arch·dea·con
arch·di·o·cese
arch·duch·ess
arch·duke
arch·en·e·my, *n. pl.*
  arch·en·e·mies
ar·che·ol·o·gy (*var.*
  of archaeology)
Ar·cheo·zo·ic
  (*occas.*
  Ar·chaeo·zo·ic)
ar·cher
ar·chery
ar·che·type
arch·fiend
ar·chi·epis·co·pal
Ar·chi·me·des
Ar·chi·me·de·an
ar·chi·pel·a·go, *n.*
  pl.
  ar·chi·pel·a·goes
  or
  ar·chi·pel·a·gos
ar·chi·tect
ar·chi·tec·tur·al
ar·chi·tec·ture
ar·chi·val
ar·chive, *v.*
  ar·chived,
  ar·chiv·ing
ar·chiv·ist
arch·ly

arch·way

Arc·tic

ar·dent

ar·dent·ly

ar·dor

ar·du·ous

ar·du·ous·ly

ar·du·ous·ness

ar·ea

ar·ea·way

are·na

are·o·la, *n. pl.*
  are·o·lae *or*
  are·o·las

Ar·gen·tina

Ar·gen·tine

ar·gon

ar·go·naut

ar·go·sy, *n. pl.*
  ar·go·sies

ar·got

ar·gu·able

ar·gu·ably

ar·gue, *v.* ar·gued,
  ar·gu·ing

ar·gu·ment

ar·gu·men·ta·tion

ar·gu·men·ta·tive

ar·gyle (*occas.*
  ar·gyll)

aria

ar·id

arid·i·ty

ar·id·ness

Ar·ies

ari·o·so, *n. pl.*
  ari·o·sos (*occas.*
  ari·o·si)

arise, *v.* arose,
  aris·en, aris·ing

ar·is·toc·ra·cy, *n.*
  pl.
  ar·is·toc·ra·cies

aris·to·crat

aris·to·crat·ic

aris·to·crat·i·cal·ly

Ar·is·tot·le

Ar·is·to·te·lian *or*
  Ar·is·to·te·lean

arith·me·tic

ar·ith·met·i·cal

ar·ith·met·i·cal·ly

arith·me·ti·cian

Ar·i·zo·na

Ar·i·zo·nan

Ar·i·zo·ni·an

ark (BOAT) (*see*
  also arc)

Ar·kan·san

Ar·kan·sas

Ar·ling·ton

ar·ma·da

ar·ma·dil·lo, *n. pl.*
  ar·ma·dil·los

Ar·ma·ged·don

ar·ma·ment

ar·ma·ture

arm·band

arm·chair

Ar·me·nia
  (*formerly*
  Armenian Soviet
  Socialist
  Republic)

Ar·me·ni·an

Ar·me·ni·an
  So·vi·et

So·cial·ist
Re·pub·lic (*now*
  Armenia)

arm·hole

ar·mi·stice

arm·let

arm·lock

ar·moire

ar·mor

ar·mor·er

ar·mory, *n. pl.*
  ar·mor·ies

arm·pit

arm·rest

arm-twisting

arm wres·tling

ar·my, *n. pl.*
  ar·mies

ar·ni·ca

aro·ma

ar·o·mat·ic

ar·o·mat·i·cal·ly

around

arous·al

arouse, *v.* aroused,
  arous·ing

ar·peg·gio, *n. pl.*
  ar·peg·gios

ar·raign

ar·raign·ment

ar·range, *v.*
  ar·ranged,
  ar·rang·ing

ar·range·ment

ar·rant

ar·ray

ar·rears

ar·rest

ar·rhyth·mia

ar·riv·al

ar·rive, *v.* ar·rived,
  ar·riv·ing

ar·ro·gance

ar·ro·gant

ar·ro·gant·ly

ar·ro·gate, *v.*
  ar·ro·gat·ed,
  ar·ro·gat·ing

ar·row

ar·row·head

ar·row·root

ar·roy·o, *n. pl.*
  ar·roy·os

ar·se·nal

ar·se·nic

ar·son

ar·son·ist

art de·co

ar·te·ri·al

ar·te·ri·ole

ar·te·ri·o·scle·ro·sis

ar·te·ri·o·scle·ro·tic

ar·tery, *n. pl.*
  ar·ter·ies

ar·te·sian well

art·ful

art·ful·ly

art·ful·ness

ar·thrit·ic

ar·thri·tis, *n. pl.*
  ar·thrit·i·des

ar·thro·pod
  (SPIDERS,
  INSECTS, ETC.)
  (*see also*
  anthropoid)

ar·thro·scope

ar·thro·scop·ic

ar·thros·co·py

Ar·thur

Ar·thu·ri·an

ar·ti·choke

ar·ti·cle

ar·tic·u·lar

ar·tic·u·late, *v.*
  ar·tic·u·lat·ed,
  ar·tic·u·lat·ing

ar·tic·u·late·ly

ar·tic·u·late·ness

ar·tic·u·la·tion

ar·ti·fact

ar·ti·fice

ar·ti·fi·cer

ar·ti·fi·cial

ar·ti·fi·ci·al·i·ty

ar·ti·fi·cial·ly

ar·til·lery, *n. pl.*
  ar·til·ler·ies

art·i·ly

art·i·ness

ar·ti·san

art·ist (PERSON IN
  THE ARTS)

ar·tiste (SKILLED
  PERFORMER)

ar·tis·tic

ar·tis·ti·cal·ly

art·ist·ry

art·less

art·less·ly

art·less·ness

arty, *adj.* art·i·er,
  art·i·est

Ary·an

asail (SAILING)
  (*see also* assail)

as·bes·tos (*rarely*
  as·bes·tus)

as·cend

as·cen·dan·cy
  (*occas.*
  as·cen·den·cy)

as·cen·dant (*occas.*
  as·cen·dent)

as·cen·sion

as·cent (RISE) (*see
  also* assent)

as·cer·tain

as·cet·ic (SELF-
  DENYING) (*see
  also* acetic)

as·cet·i·cal

as·cet·i·cism

ascor·bic acid

as·cot

as·crib·able

as·cribe, *v.*
  as·cribed,
  as·crib·ing

asep·tic

asex·u·al

asex·u·al·ly

ashamed

asham·ed·ly

ash·en

ash·es

Ash·ley

ashore

ash·tray

ashy, *adj.* ash·i·er,
  ash·i·est

Asia

Asian

Asi·at·ic

aside

as·i·nine

as·i·nine·ly

as·i·nin·i·ty

askance (*rarely* askant)

askew

aslant

asleep

aso·cial

as·par·a·gus

as·par·tame

as·pect

as·pen

as·per·i·ty, *n. pl.* as·per·i·ties

as·per·sion

as·phalt *or* as·phalt·um

as·phyx·ia

as·phyx·i·ate, *v.* as·phyx·i·at·ed, as·phyx·i·at·ing

as·phyx·i·a·tion

as·pic

as·pi·dis·tra

as·pi·rant

as·pi·rate, *v.* as·pi·rat·ed, as·pi·rat·ing

as·pi·ra·tion

as·pi·ra·tor

as·pire, *v.* as·pired, as·pir·ing

as·pi·rin, *n. pl.*

as·pi·rin *or* as·pi·rins

as·sail (ATTACK) (*see also* asail)

as·sail·ant

as·sas·sin

as·sas·si·nate, *v.* as·sas·si·nat·ed, as·sas·si·nat·ing

as·sas·si·na·tion

as·sault

as·say (EVALUATE) (*see also* essay)

as·sem·blage

as·sem·ble, *v.* as·sem·bled, as·sem·bling

as·sem·bly, *n. pl.* as·sem·blies

as·sem·bly·man, *n. pl.* as·sem·bly·men

as·sem·bly·wom·an, *n. pl.* as·sem·bly·wom·en

as·sent (AGREE) (*see also* ascent)

as·sert

as·ser·tion

as·ser·tive

as·sess

as·sess·ment

as·ses·sor

as·set

as·sev·er·ate, *v.* as·sev·er·at·ed, as·sev·er·at·ing

as·sev·er·a·tion

as·si·du·ity, *n. pl.* as·si·du·ities

as·sid·u·ous

as·sid·u·ous·ly

as·sid·u·ous·ness

as·sign

as·sign·able

as·sig·na·tion

as·sign·ment

as·sim·i·late, *v.* as·sim·i·lat·ed, as·sim·i·lat·ing

as·sim·i·la·tion

as·sist

as·sis·tance

as·sis·tant

as·sis·tant·ship

as·size

as·so·ciate, *adj., n.*

as·so·ci·ate, *v.* as·so·ci·at·ed, as·so·ci·at·ing

as·so·ci·a·tion

as·so·cia·tive

as·so·nance

as·so·nant

as·sort

as·sort·ed

as·sort·ment

as·suage, *v.* as·suaged, as·suag·ing

as·sume, *v.* as·sumed, as·sum·ing

as·sump·tion

as·sur·ance

as·sure, *v.* as·sured, as·sur·ing

as·sured, *n. pl.*

as·sured *or*
as·sureds

as·sured·ly

As·syr·i·an

as·ta·tine

as·ter

as·ter·isk, *n. pl.*
as·ter·isks

as·ter·oid

asth·ma

asth·mat·ic

as·tig·mat·ic

astig·ma·tism

astir

as·ton·ish

as·ton·ish·ing

as·ton·ish·ing·ly

as·ton·ish·ment

as·tound

as·tound·ing

as·trad·dle

as·tral

astride

as·trin·gen·cy

as·trin·gent

as·tro·bi·ol·o·gist

as·tro·bi·ol·o·gy

as·tro·dome

as·tro·labe

as·trol·o·ger

as·tro·log·i·cal

as·trol·o·gy

as·tro·naut

as·tro·nau·tic

as·tro·nau·ti·cal

as·tro·nau·tics

as·tron·o·mer

as·tro·nom·i·cal

as·tron·o·my, *n. pl.*
as·tron·o·mies

as·tro·phys·i·cist

as·tro·phys·ics

As·tro·turf®

as·tute

asun·der

asy·lum

asym·met·ric

asym·met·ri·cal

asymp·tom·at·ic

at·a·vism

at·a·vis·tic

ate·lier

Ath·a·bas·ca

athe·ism

athe·ist

athe·is·tic

Ath·ens

ath·ero·scle·ro·sis

ath·ero·scle·rot·ic

ath·lete

ath·let·ic

ath·let·i·cal·ly

ath·let·ics

athwart

At·lan·ta

At·lan·tic Ocean

at·las

at·mo·sphere

at·mo·spher·ic

at·mo·spher·ics

atoll

at·om

atom·ic

atom·ics

at·om·ize, *v.*
at·om·ized,
at·om·iz·ing

at·om·iz·er

aton·al

ato·nal·i·ty

aton·al·ly

atone, *v.* atoned,
aton·ing

atone·ment

atop

atri·um, *n. pl.* atria
(*occas.*
atri·ums)

atro·cious

atro·cious·ly

atro·cious·ness

atroc·i·ty, *n. pl.*
atroc·i·ties

at·ro·phy, *v.*
at·ro·phied,
at·ro·phy·ing

at·ro·pine

at·tach

at·tach·able

at·ta·ché

at·tached

at·tach·ment

at·tack

at·tain

at·tain·abil·i·ty

at·tain·able

at·tain·der

at·tain·ment

at·tempt

at·tend

at·ten·dance

at·ten·dant

at·ten·dee

at·ten·tion

at·ten·tive

at·ten·u·ate, v.
at·ten·u·at·ed,
at·ten·u·at·ing

at·ten·u·a·tion

at·test

at·tes·ta·tion

at·tic

at·tire, v. at·tired,
at·tir·ing

at·ti·tude

at·ti·tu·di·nal

at·tor·ney, n. pl.
at·tor·neys

at·tor·ney-at-law,
n. pl.
at·tor·neys-at-law

at·tor·ney gen·er·al,
n. pl.
at·tor·neys
gen·er·al or
at·tor·ney
gen·er·als

at·tract

at·tract·able

at·trac·tion

at·trac·tive

at·trac·tive·ly

at·trac·tive·ness

at·trib·ut·able

at·tri·bute, n.

at·trib·ute, v.,
at·trib·ut·ed,
at·trib·ut·ing

at·tri·bu·tion

at·trib·u·tive

at·tri·tion

at·tune, v.
at·tuned,
at·tun·ing

atyp·i·cal

au·burn

au con·traire

au cou·rant

auc·tion

auc·tion·eer

auc·to·ri·al

au·da·cious

au·da·cious·ly

au·da·cious·ness

au·dac·i·ty, n. pl.
au·dac·i·ties

au·di·bil·i·ty

au·di·ble

au·di·bly

au·di·ence

au·dio

au·dio-
an·i·ma·tron·ics

au·dio·phile

au·dio·vi·su·al

au·dit

au·di·tion

au·di·tor

au·di·to·ri·um, n.
pl.
au·di·to·ri·ums
(occas.
au·di·to·ria)

au·di·to·ry

au·ger (TOOL) (see
also augur)

aught (ZERO,

NOTHING) (see
also ought)

aug·ment

aug·men·ta·tion

au gra·tin

au·gur (FORETELL)
(see also auger)

au·gu·ry, n. pl.
au·gu·ries

Au·gust

Au·gus·ta

auk

aunt

au·ra

au·ral

au·re·ate

au·re·ole or
au·re·o·la

Au·reo·my·cin℗

au re·voir

au·ri·cle

au·ric·u·lar

au·rif·er·ous

au·ro·ra, n. pl.
au·ro·ras or
au·ro·rae

au·ro·ra aus·tra·lis

au·ro·ra bo·re·al·is

aus·pice

aus·pi·cious

aus·pi·cious·ly

aus·pi·cious·ness

aus·tere

aus·tere·ly

aus·ter·i·ty, n. pl.
aus·ter·i·ties

Aus·tin

aus·tral, n. pl.

aus·tral·es
(*occas.* aus·trals)

Aus·tral·asia

Aus·tral·asian

Aus·tral·ia

Aus·tra·lian

Aus·tria

Aus·tri·an

au·teur

au·then·tic

au·then·ti·cal·ly

au·then·ti·cate, *v.*
au·then·ti·cat·ed,
au·then·ti·cat·ing

au·then·ti·ca·tion

au·then·tic·i·ty

au·thor

au·thor·ess

au·thor·i·tar·i·an

au·thor·i·ta·tive

au·thor·i·ty, *n. pl.*
au·thor·i·ties

au·tho·ri·za·tion

au·tho·rize, *v.*
au·tho·rized,
au·tho·riz·ing

au·thor·ship

au·tism

au·tis·tic

au·to

au·to·bahn

au·to·bi·og·ra·pher

au·to·bio·graph·i·cal

au·to·bi·og·ra·phy

au·to·clave, *v.*
au·to·claved,
au·to·clav·ing

au·toc·ra·cy, *n.*
au·toc·ra·cies

au·to·crat

au·to·crat·ic

au·to·crat·i·cal·ly

au·to-da-fé, *n. pl.*
au·tos-da-fé

au·to·er·o·tism *or*
au·to·erot·i·cism

au·to·gi·ro (*occas.*
au·to·gy·ro)

au·to·graph

Au·to·harp®

au·to·in·tox·i·ca·tion

au·to·mak·er

au·to·mate, *v.*
au·to·mat·ed,
au·to·mat·ing

au·to·mat·i·cal·ly

au·to·ma·tion

au·tom·a·ti·za·tion

au·tom·a·tize, *v.*
au·tom·a·tized,
au·tom·a·ti·zing

au·tom·a·ton, *n. pl.*
au·tom·a·tons *or*
au·tom·a·ta

au·to·mo·bile

au·to·mo·tive

au·ton·o·mous

au·ton·o·mous·ly

au·ton·o·my

au·to·pi·lot

au·top·sy, *n. pl.*
au·top·sies

au·top·sy, *v.*
au·top·sied,
au·top·sy·ing

au·tumn

au·tum·nal

aux·il·ia·ry, *n. pl.*
aux·il·ia·ries

avail

avail·abil·i·ty

avail·able

avail·ably

av·a·lanche

avant-garde

av·a·rice

av·a·ri·cious

av·a·ri·cious·ly

av·a·ri·cious·ness

avenge, *v.*
avenged,
aveng·ing

aveng·er

av·e·nue

aver, *v.* averred,
aver·ring

av·er·age, *v.*
av·er·aged,
av·er·ag·ing

averse (DISTASTE
FOR) (*see also*
adverse)

aver·sion

aver·sive

avert

avi·an

avi·ary, *n. pl.*
avi·ar·ies

avi·a·tion

avi·a·tor

avi·a·trix

av·id

avid·i·ty, *n. pl.*
avid·i·ties

av·id·ly

avi·on·ics

avo, *n. pl.* avos

av·o·ca·do, *n. pl.*
   av·o·ca·dos
   (*occas.*
   av·o·ca·does)

av·o·ca·tion

av·o·cet

avoid

avoid·able

avoid·ably

avoid·ance

av·oir·du·pois

avow

avow·al

avowed

avow·ed·ly

avun·cu·lar

await

awake, *v.* awoke
   (*occas.*
   awaked),
   awaked *or*

awo·ken,
   awak·ing

awak·en

award

aware

aware·ness

awash

away

aweigh

awe·some

awe·struck

aw·ful

aw·ful·ly

awhile

awhirl

awk·ward

awk·ward·ly

awk·ward·ness

awl

aw·ning

awry

ax *or* axe, *n. pl.*
   axes

ax *or* axe, *v.* axed,
   ax·ing

ax·i·al

ax·i·om

ax·i·om·at·ic

ax·is, *n. pl.* ax·es

ax·le

ax·le·tree

aza·lea

Azer·bai·jan
   (*formerly*
   Azerbaijan
   Soviet Socialist
   Republic)

Azer·bai·jan
   So·vi·et
   So·cial·ist
   Re·pub·lic (*now*
   Azerbaijan)

Azer·bai·jani

az·i·muth

Azores

Az·tec

azure

B

bab·bitt

bab·ble, *v.* bab·bled, bab·bling

Ba·bel

ba·boon

ba·bush·ka

ba·by, *n. pl.* ba·bies

ba·by, *v.* ba·bied, ba·by·ing

ba·by boom

ba·by boom·er

Bab·y·lon

Bab·y·lo·nia

Bab·y·lo·ni·an

ba·by-sit, *v.* ba·by-sat, ba·by-sit·ting

ba·by sit·ter

bac·ca·lau·re·ate

bac·ca·rat

bac·cha·nal

bac·cha·na·lia

bac·cha·na·li·an

bach·e·lor

bach·e·lor·hood

ba·cil·lus, *n. pl.* ba·cil·li

bac·i·tra·cin

back·ache

back·bench·er

back·bite, *v.* back·bit, back·bit·ten, back·bit·ing

back·bit·er

back·board

back·bone

back·date, *v.* back·dat·ed, back·dat·ing

back·door, *adj.*

back door, *n.*

back·drop

back·er

back·field

back·fire, *v.* back·fired, back·fir·ing

back-for·ma·tion

back·gam·mon

back·ground

back·hand

back·hand·ed

back·hoe

back·ing

back·lash

back·log, *v.* back·logged, back·log·ging

back·pack

back·rest

back·scat·ter·ing

back scratch·er

back·side

back·slap, *v.* back·slapped, back·slap·ping

back·slap·per

back·slide, *v.* back·slid, back·slid·ing

back·slid·er

back·space, *v.* back·spaced, back·spac·ing

back·spin

back·stage

back·stairs

back·stop, *v.* back·stopped, back·stop·ping

28

back·stretch

back·stroke, *v.*
back·stroked,
back·strok·ing

back talk

back·track

back·up, *adj., n.*

back up *v.*

back·ward *or*
back·wards

back·ward·ness

back·wash

back·wa·ter

back·woods

ba·con

bac·te·ria, *pl. of*
bac·te·ri·um

bac·te·ri·al

bac·te·ri·cid·al

bac·te·ri·o·log·ic

bac·te·ri·o·log·ic·al

bac·te·ri·ol·o·gist

bac·te·ri·ol·o·gy

bac·te·ri·um, *n. pl.*
bac·te·ria

badge

bad·ger

ba·di·nage

bad·lands

bad·ly

bad·min·ton

bad-mouth (*occas.*
bad·mouth)

bad·ness

Bae·de·ker

baf·fle, *v.* baf·fled,
baf·fling

bag, *v.* bagged,
bag·ging

bag·a·telle

Bag·dad (*var. of*
Baghdad)

ba·gel

bag·gage

Bag·gie⍟

bag·gy, *adj.*
bag·gi·er,
bag·gi·est

Bagh·dad *or*
Bag·dad

ba·gnio, *n. pl.*
ba·gnios

bag·pipe

bag·pip·er

ba·guette

Ba·ha·mas *or*
Ba·ha·ma
Islands

Ba·ha·mi·an *or*
Ba·ha·man

Bah·rain *or*
Bah·rein

Bah·raini *or*
Bah·reini

baht, *n. pl.* baht
(*occas.* bahts)

bail (MONEY) (*see
also* bale)

bai·liff

bai·li·wick

bail·ment

bails·man, *n. pl.*
bails·men

bail·out, *n.*

bail out, *v.*

bait

bai·za

baize

Ba·ja

bake, *v.* baked,
bak·ing

bak·er

bak·ery

bak·la·va
(DESSERT)
(*see also*
balaclava)

bak·sheesh

bal·a·cla·va (HEAD
COVERING) (*see
also* baklava)

bal·a·lai·ka

bal·ance, *v.*
bal·anced,
bal·anc·ing

Bal·boa (SPANISH
EXPLORER)

bal·boa (MONEY)

bal·co·ny, *n. pl.*
bal·co·nies

bal·der·dash

bald·ness

bale (BUNDLE), *v.*
baled, bal·ing
(*see also* bail)

bal·er

bale·ful

balk

Bal·kan

bal·kan·iza·tion

bal·kan·ize, *v.*
bal·kan·ized,
bal·kan·iz·ing

bal·ky, *adj.*
bal·ki·er,
bal·ki·est

ball (*see also* bawl)

bal·lad

bal·lad·eer

bal·last

ball bear·ing

bal·le·ri·na

bal·let

bal·let·o·mane

ball·game

bal·lis·tic

bal·loon

bal·loon·ist

bal·lot

ball·park

ball·room

bal·ly·hoo, *n. pl.*
    bal·ly·hoos

balmy, *adj.*
    balm·i·er,
    balm·i·est

ba·lo·ney
    (NONSENSE)
    (*see also*
    bologna)

bal·sa

bal·sam

Bal·tic

Bal·ti·more

bal·us·ter

bal·us·trade

bam·bi·no, *n. pl.*
    bam·bin·os *or*
    bam·bi·ni

bam·boo

bam·boo·zle, *v.*
    bam·boo·zled,
    bam·boo·zling

ban (MONEY), *n.*

pl. ba·ni (*see
    also* banns)

ban (PROHIBIT), *v.*
    banned,
    ban·ning

ba·nal

ba·nal·i·ty

ba·nana

band

ban·dage, *v.*
    ban·daged,
    ban·dag·ing

Band-aid®

ban·dan·na *or*
    ban·dana

band·box

ban·deau, *n. pl.*
    ban·deaux

ban·de·role *or*
    ban·de·rol

ban·dit

ban·dit·ry

band·lead·er

band·mas·ter

ban·do·lier *or*
    ban·do·leer

band·stand

band·wag·on

band·width

ban·dy, *v.*
    ban·died,
    ban·dy·ing

bane

bane·ful

Ban·ga·lore

Bang·kok

Ban·gla·desh

ban·gle

bang·tail

ban·ish

ban·ish·ment

ban·is·ter

ban·jo, *n. pl.*
    ban·jos (*occas.*
    ban·joes)

ban·jo·ist

bank·book

bank·er

bank·ing

bank·roll

bank·rupt

bank·rupt·cy, *n. pl.*
    bank·rupt·cies

Ban·lon®

ban·ner

ban·nock

banns
    (ANNOUNCEMENT)
    (*see also* ban)

ban·quet (FEAST)

ban·quette
    (BENCH)

ban·shee

ban·tam

ban·tam·weight

ban·ter

Ban·tu, *n. pl.*
    Ban·tu *or*
    Ban·tus

ban·yan

ban·zai

bap·tism

bap·tis·mal

Bap·tist

bap·tis·tery *or*
    bap·tis·try

bap·tize, *v.*

bap·tized,
bap·tiz·ing

bar, *v.* barred,
bar·ring

Bar·ba·di·an

Bar·ba·dos

Bar·ba·ra

bar·bar·ian

bar·bar·ian·ism

bar·bar·ic

bar·bar·i·cal·ly

bar·ba·rism

bar·bar·i·ty, *n. pl.*
bar·bar·i·ties

bar·ba·rous

bar·ba·rous·ly

bar·ba·rous·ness

bar·be·cue, *v.*
bar·be·cued,
bar·be·cu·ing

bar·bel (FISH)

bar·bell (WEIGHT)

bar·ber

bar·ber·shop

bar·ber·ry

bar·bi·tal

bar·bi·tu·rate

Bar·bu·da

bar·ca·role *or*
bar·ca·rolle

Bar·ce·lo·na

bar-code (*occas.*
barcode *or* bar
code) *n.*, *v.* bar·
cod·ed, bar·
cod·ing

bard

bare (NAKED), *adj.*

bar·er, bar·est
(*see also* bear)

bare (UNCOVER),
v. bared, bar·ing
(*see also* bear)

bare·back

bare·faced

bare·foot

bare·hand·ed

bare·head·ed

bare·leg·ged

bare·ly

bar·gain

barge, *v.* barged,
barg·ing

barge·man, *n. pl.*
barge·men

bar·hop, *v.*
bar·hopped,
bar·hop·ping

bari·tone

bar·i·um

bar·keep·er

bark·er

bar·ley

bar·maid

bar·man, *n. pl.*
bar·men

bar mitz·vah

bar·na·cle

barn·storm

barn·yard

baro·graph

ba·rom·e·ter

baro·met·ric

bar·on

bar·on·age

bar·on·ess

bar·on·et

bar·on·et·cy

ba·ro·ni·al

bar·ony

Ba·roque

bar·rack

bar·ra·cu·da, *n. pl.*
bar·ra·cu·da *or*
bar·ra·cu·das

bar·rage

bar·rat·ry, *n. pl.*
bar·rat·ries

bar·rel, *v.* bar·reled
or bar·relled,
bar·rel·ing *or*
bar·rel·ling

bar·ren

bar·ren·ness

bar·rette (HAIR
CLIP) (*see also*
beret)

bar·ri·cade, *v.*
bar·ri·cad·ed,
bar·ri·cad·ing

bar·ri·er

bar·rio, *n. pl.*
bar·ri·os

bar·ris·ter

bar·room

bar·row

bar·tend·er

bar·ter

bas·al (OF THE BASE)
(*see also* basil)

ba·salt

ba·sal·tic

bas·cule

base
(FOUNDATION),

adj. bas·er, bas·est (*see also* bass)

base (REST ON), *v.* based, bas·ing

base·ball

base·board

base·born

base·less

base·ly

base·ment

base·ness

ba·sen·ji

bash·ful

bash·ful·ly

bash·ful·ness

ba·sic

ba·si·cal·ly

ba·sil (HERB) (*see also* basal)

ba·sil·i·ca

bas·i·lisk

ba·sin

bas·i·net (HELMET) (*see also* bassinet)

ba·sis, *n. pl.* ba·ses

bask

bas·ket

bas·ket·ball

bas·ket·ry

bas·ket·work

bas mitz·vah *or* bat mitz·vah

Basque

bas-re·lief

bass (FISH), *n. pl.*

bass *or* bass·es (*see also* base)

bass (VOICE), *n. pl.* bass·es (*see also* base)

bas·set

bas·si·net (INFANT BED) (*see also* basinet)

bas·so, *n. pl.* bas·sos *or* bas·si

bas·soon

bass·wood

bas·tard

bas·tard·ize, *v.* bas·tard·ized, bas·tard·iz·ing

baste, *v.* bast·ed, bast·ing

bas·tille

bas·ti·na·do, *n. pl.* bas·ti·na·does *or* bas·ti·nades

bas·tion

bas·tioned

bat, *v.* bat·ted, bat·ting

bat·boy

batch

bate, *v.* bat·ed, bat·ing

ba·teau, *n. pl.* ba·teaux

bath, *n.*

bathe, *v.* bathed, bath·ing

bath·er

ba·thet·ic

bath·house

Bath·i·nette™

ba·thos

bath·robe

bath·room

bath·tub

bath·wa·ter

bathy·scaphe (*occas.* bathy·scaph)

bathy·sphere

ba·tik

bat·man, *n. pl.* bat·men

bat mitz·vah (*var.* of bas mitzvah)

ba·ton

Bat·on Rouge

bat·tal·ion

bat·ten

bat·ter

bat·tery, *n. pl.* bat·ter·ies

bat·tle, *v.* bat·tled, bat·tling

bat·tle-ax, *n. pl.* bat·tle-ax·es

bat·tle·field

bat·tle·ment

bat·tle·ship

bau·ble

baud (MEASUREMENT), *n. pl.* baud *or* bauds (*see also* bawd)

baux·ite

bawd (LOOSE WOMAN) (*see also* baud)

bawd·i·ly

bawd·i·ness

bawdy, *adj.*
  bawd·i·er,
  bawd·i·est

bawdy·house

bawl (CRY) (*see also* ball)

bay·ber·ry, *n. pl.*
  bay·ber·ries

bay leaf, *n. pl.* bay leaves

bay·o·net, *v.*
  bay·o·net·ed
  (*occas.*
  bay·o·net·ted),
  bay·o·net·ing
  (*occas.*
  bay·o·net·ting)

bay·ou, *n. pl.*
  bay·ous

bay·wood

ba·zaar (MARKET) (*see also* bizarre)

ba·zoo·ka

beach

beach·comb·er

beach·head

bea·con (LIGHT) (*see also* beckon)

bead

bead·ing

bea·dle

beady, *adj.*
  bead·i·er,
  bead·i·est

bea·gle

bea·ker

be-all

beam·ing

bean·bag

bean·ery, *n. pl.*
  bean·er·ies

bean·ie

bean·stalk

bear (ANIMAL), *n. pl.* bears *or* bear (*see also* bare)

bear (CARRY, ENDURE), *v.* bore, borne (*occas.* born), bear·ing (*see also* bare)

bear·able

bear·ably

beard·less

bear·er

bear·hug

bear·ish

bear·ish·ly

bear·ish·ness

bear·ing

bé·ar·naise sauce

bear·skin

beast·ly, *adj.*
  beast·li·er,
  beast·li·est

beat, *v.* beat, beat·en, beat·ing

be·a·tif·ic

be·at·i·fi·ca·tion

be·at·i·fy, *v.*
  be·at·i·fied,
  be·at·i·fy·ing

be·at·i·tude

beat·nik

beau, *n. pl.* beaux *or* beaus

beau monde

beau·te·ous

beau·te·ous·ly

beau·te·ous·ness

beau·ti·cian

beau·ti·fi·ca·tion

beau·ti·fi·er

beau·ti·ful

beau·ti·ful·ly

beau·ti·fy, *v.*
  beau·ti·fied,
  beau·ti·fy·ing

beau·ty, *n. pl.*
  beau·ties

bea·ver

be·calm

be·cause

beck·on (CALL) (*see also* beacon)

be·cloud

be·come, *v.*
  be·came,
  be·come,
  be·com·ing

be·com·ing·ly

bed, *v.* bed·ded, bed·ding

bed-and-break·fast

be·daz·zle, *v.*
  be·daz·zled,
  be·daz·zling

be·daz·zle·ment

bed·bug

bed·clothes

bed·ding

be·deck

be·dev·il, *v.*
be·dev·iled *or*
be·dev·illed,
be·dev·il·ing *or*
be·dev·il·ling

bed·fel·low

bed·lam

bed·ou·in *or*
bed·u·in, *n. pl.*
bed·ou·in *or*
bed·ou·ins *or*
bed·u·in *or*
bed·u·ins

bed·pan

be·drag·gle, *v.*
be·drag·gled,
be·drag·gling

bed·rid·den

bed·rock

bed·roll

bed·room

bed·side

bed·sore

bed·spread

bed·stead

bed·time

beech

beech·nut

beef, *n. pl.* beefs
(*rarely* beeves)

beef·steak

beefy, *adj.*
beef·i·er,
beef·i·est

bee·hive

bee·keep·er

bee·keep·ing

bee·line

beep·er

beer

beery, *adj.*
beer·i·er,
beer·i·est

bees·wax

beet

bee·tle

be·fall, *v.* be·fell,
be·fal·len,
be·fall·ing

be·fit, *v.* be·fit·ted,
be·fit·ting

be·fog, *v.*
be·fogged,
be·fog·ging

be·fore

be·fore·hand

be·friend

be·fud·dle, *v.*
be·fud·dled,
be·fud·dling

beg *v.* begged,
beg·ging

be·get, *v.* be·got
(*occas.*
be·gat),
be·got·ten *or*
begot,
be·get·ting

beg·gar

beg·gar·li·ness

beg·gar·ly

be·gin, *v.* be·gan,
be·gun,
be·gin·ning

be·gin·ner

be·gone

be·go·nia

be·grime, *v.*
be·grimed,
be·grim·ing

be·grudge, *v.*
be·grudged,
be·grudg·ing

be·guile, *v.*
be·guiled,
be·guil·ing

be·guine

be·gum

be·half

be·have, *v.*
be·haved,
be·hav·ing

be·hav·ior

be·hav·ior·al

be·hav·ior·ism

be·hav·ior·ist

be·head

be·he·moth

be·hest

be·hind

be·hold, *v.* be·held,
be·hold·ing

be·hold·en

be·hold·er

be·hoove, *v.*
be·hooved,
be·hoov·ing

beige

Bei·jing

be·ing

Bei·rut

be·jew·el, *v.*
be·jew·eled *or*
be·jew·elled,
be·jew·el·ing *or*
be·jew·el·ling

be·la·bor

Be·lar·us (*formerly*
　Belorussia *or*
　Byelorussia)

Be·la·rus·sian

be·lat·ed

be·lat·ed·ly

be·lat·ed·ness

be·lay

belch

be·lea·guer

Bel·fast

bel·fry, *n. pl.*
　bel·fries

Bel·gian (FROM
　BELGIUM)

Bel·gium
　(COUNTRY)

Bel·grade

be·lie, *v.* be·lied,
　be·ly·ing

be·lief

be·liev·abil·i·ty

be·liev·able

be·lieve, *v.*
　be·lieved,
　be·liev·ing

be·liev·er

be·lit·tle, *v.*
　be·lit·tled,
　be·lit·tling

Be·lize

bel·la·don·na

bell·boy

belles let·tres

bell·hop

bel·li·cose

bel·li·cos·i·ty

bel·lig·er·ence

bel·lig·er·en·cy

bel·lig·er·ent

bel·low

bel·lows

bell·weth·er

bel·ly, *n. pl.*
　bel·lies

bel·ly, *v.* bel·lied,
　bel·ly·ing

bel·ly·ache

bel·ly·but·ton

bel·ly-flop, *v.*
　bel·ly-flopped,
　bel·ly-flop·ping

bel·ly·ful

be·long

be·long·ing

Be·lo·rus·sia *or*
　Bye·lo·rus·sia
　(*now* Belarus)

be·loved

be·low

belt·way

be·moan

be·muse, *v.*
　be·mused,
　be·mus·ing

Ben·a·dryl®

bench mark

bend, *v.* bent,
　bend·ing

be·neath

ben·e·dict

ben·e·dic·tion

ben·e·fac·tion

ben·e·fac·tor

ben·e·fac·tress

ben·e·fice

be·nef·i·cence

be·nef·i·cent

ben·e·fi·cial

ben·e·fi·cial·ly

ben·e·fi·cia·ry, *n.*
　pl.
　ben·e·fi·cia·ries

ben·e·fit, *v.*
　ben·e·fit·ed
　(*occas.*
　ben·e·fit·ted),
　ben·e·fit·ing
　(*occas.*
　ben·e·fit·ting)

be·nev·o·lence

be·nev·o·lent

Ben·gal

Ben·gali

be·night·ed

be·nign

be·nig·nant

be·nig·ni·ty

be·nign·ly

Ben·ja·min

ben·thic

ben·thos

be·numb

Ben·ze·drine®

ben·zene
　(AROMATIC
　COMPOUND)

ben·zine
　(SOLVENT)

ben·zo·ic acid

ben·zo·in

ben·zol

be·queath

be·quest

be·rate, *v.*

be·rat·ed,
be·rat·ing

ber·ceuse

be·reave, *v.*
be·reaved *or*
be·reft,
be·reav·ing

be·reave·ment

be·ret (HAT) (*see
also* barrette)

Be·ret·ta
(WEAPON)
(*see also* biretta)

beri·beri

berke·li·um

Ber·lin

Ber·mu·da

Ber·mu·di·an *or*
Ber·mu·dan

ber·ry, *n. pl.*
ber·ries

ber·serk

berth (SHIP'S
PLACE) (*see
also* birth)

ber·yl

be·ryl·li·um

be·seech, *v.*
be·sought *or*
be·seeched,
be·seech·ing

be·set, *v.* be·set,
be·set·ting

be·side (NEXT TO),
prep.

be·sides (ALSO,
EXCEPT, ELSE),
adv., adj., prep.

be·siege, *v.*
be·sieged,
be·sieg·ing

be·sieg·er

be·smirch

be·sot, *v.*
be·sot·ted,
be·sot·ting

bes·tial

bes·ti·al·i·ty, *n. pl.*
bes·ti·al·i·ties

bes·ti·ary, *n. pl.*
bes·ti·ar·ies

be·stir, *v.*
be·stirred,
be·stir·ring

be·stow

best-sell·er

best-sell·ing

bet, *v.* bet (*occas.*
bet·ted),
bet·ting

be·ta

bête noire, *n. pl.*
bêtes noires

Beth·le·hem

be·tray

be·tray·al

be·tray·er

be·troth

be·troth·al

be·trothed

bet·ter (MORE
EXCELLENT)
(*see also* bettor)

bet·ter·ment

bet·tor (ONE WHO
BETS) (*see also*
better)

be·tween

bev·el, *v.* be·veled
or be·velled,

be·vel·ing *or*
be·vel·ling

bev·er·age

bevy, *n. pl.* bev·ies

be·wail

be·ware

be·wil·der

be·wil·der·ment

be·witch

be·yond

be·zel

Bhu·tan

Bhu·tan·ese, *n. pl.*
Bhu·tan·ese

bi·an·nu·al

bi·an·nu·al·ly

bi·as, *n. pl.* bi·as·es

bi·as, *v.* bi·ased *or*
bi·assed,
bi·as·ing *or*
bi·as·sing

bi·ath·lon

bi·ax·i·al

Bi·ble (RELIGIOUS
BOOK)

bi·ble
(AUTHORITATIVE
PUBLICATION)

Bi·ble Belt

bib·li·cal

bib·li·og·ra·pher

bib·li·o·gra·phic

bib·li·o·gra·phic·al

bib·li·og·ra·phy, *n.
pl.*
bib·li·og·ra·phies

bib·li·o·phile

bib·u·lous

bib·u·lous·ly

bib·u·lous·ness

bi·cam·er·al

bi·car·bon·ate

bi·cen·te·nary, *n. pl.*
bi·cen·te·nar·ies

bi·cen·ten·ni·al

bi·ceps, *n. pl.*
bi·ceps (*rarely*
bi·ceps·es)

bi·chlo·ride

bick·er

bi·cus·pid

bi·cy·cle, *v.*
bi·cy·cled,
bi·cy·cling

bi·cy·clist

bid, *v.* bade *or* bid,
bid·den *or* bid
(*occas.* bade),
bid·ding

bid·da·ble

bid·der

bid·dy, *n. pl.*
bid·dies

bide, *v.* bode *or*
bid·ed, bid·ed,
bid·ing

bi·det

bi·en·ni·al

bi·en·ni·al·ly

bi·en·ni·um, *n. pl.*
bi·en·ni·ums *or*
bi·en·nia

bier

bi·fo·cals

bi·fur·cate, *v.*
bi·fur·cat·ed,
bi·fur·cat·ing

bi·fur·ca·tion

big, *adj.* big·ger,
big·gest

big·a·mist

big·a·mous

big·a·mous·ly

big·a·my *n. pl.*
big·a·mies

big·heart·ed

big·heart·ed·ly

big·heart·ed·ness

bight

big-league

big·mouthed

big·ness

big·ot

big·ot·ed

big·ot·ry, *n. pl.*
big·ot·ries

big·wig

bi·jou, *n. pl.*
bi·jous *or*
bi·joux

bike, *v.* biked,
bik·ing

bik·er

bike·way

bi·ki·ni

bi·lat·er·al

bi·lat·er·al·ly

bile

bilge

bi·lin·gual

bil·ious

bil·ious·ness

bill·board

bil·let

bil·let-doux, *n. pl.*
bil·lets-doux

bill·fold

bil·liards

bill·ing

bil·lings·gate

bil·lion

bil·lion·aire

bil·lionth

bil·low

bil·lowy

bil·ly goat

bim·bo, *n. pl.*
bim·bos

bi·met·al

bi·met·al·lic

bi·met·al·lism

bi·mod·al

bi·month·ly

bi·na·ry

bin·au·ral

bind, *v.* bound,
bind·ing

bind·er

bind·ery, *n. pl.*
bind·er·ies

binge, *v.* binged,
binge·ing

bin·go, *n.* bin·gos

bin·na·cle

bin·oc·u·lar

bi·no·mi·al

bio·as·tro·nau·tics

bio·chem·i·cal

bio·chem·ist

bio·chem·ist·ry

bio·de·grad·abil·i·ty

bio·de·grad·able

bio·eth·ics

bio·feed·back

bio·geo·graph·ic

bio·ge·og·ra·phy

bi·og·ra·pher

bio·graph·i·cal

bi·og·ra·phy, *n. pl.*
  bi·og·ra·phies

bio·log·i·cal

bi·ol·o·gist

bi·ol·o·gy

bio·mass

bio·med·i·cal

bio·med·i·cine

bi·on·ics

bio·phys·ics

bi·op·sy, *n. pl.*
  bi·op·sies

bio·rhythm

bio·sphere

bio·syn·thet·ic

bio·syn·thet·i·cal·ly

bio·syn·the·sis

bi·o·ta

bi·o·tic

bi·par·ti·san

bi·par·ti·san·ship

bi·par·tite

bi·ped

bi·plane

bi·ra·cial

bird·bath

bird·brain

bird·house

bird·ie, *v.* bird·ied,
  bird·ie·ing

bird·lime

bird·seed

bird's-eye

bird-watch, *v.*

bird·watch·er, *n.*

bi·ret·ta (HAT)(*see
  also* Beretta)

Bir·ming·ham

birth (BRINGING
  FORTH) (*see
  also* berth)

birth·day

birth·mark

birth·place

birth·rate

birth·right

birth·stone

bis·cuit

bi·sect

bi·sex·u·al

bish·op

bish·op·ric

Bis·marck

bis·muth

bi·son, *n. pl.* bi·son

bisque

bis·tro, *n. pl.*
  bis·tros

bitch, *n. pl.* bitches

bitchy, *adj.*
  bitch·i·er,
  bitch·i·est

bite, *v.* bit, bit·ten
  (*occas.* bit),
  bit·ing

biter (ONE WHO
  BITES)

bit·ter (TASTE,

FEELING) (*see
  also* bitters)

bit·ter·ly

bit·tern

bit·ter·ness

bit·ters (KIND OF
  ALE OR
  FLAVORING)

bit·ter·sweet

bi·tu·men

bi·tu·mi·nous

bi·valve

biv·ouac, *v.*
  biv·ouacked,
  biv·ouack·ing

bi·week·ly

bi·zarre (STRANGE)
  (*see also*
  bazaar)

bi·zarre·ly

bi·zarre·ness

bi·zon·al

blab, *v.* blabbed,
  blab·bing

blab·ber·mouth

black·a·moor

black·ball

black·ber·ry, *n. pl.*
  black·ber·ries

black·bird

black·board

black·en

black·guard

black·head

black·jack

black·list

black·ly

black·mail

black·ness

black·out

black·smith

black·top, v.
black·topped,
black·top·ping

blad·der

blade

blame, v. blamed,
blam·ing

blame·less

blame·wor·thy

bland

blan·dish

blan·dish·ment

bland·ly

bland·ness

blank

blan·ket

blank·ly

blank·ness

blare, v. blared,
blar·ing

blar·ney

bla·sé (JADED)
(occas. blase)
(see also blaze)

blas·pheme, v.
blas·phemed,
blas·phem·ing

blas·phe·mous

blas·phe·mous·ly

blas·phe·mous·ness

blas·phe·my, n. pl.
blas·phe·mies

blast

blast-off, n.

blast off, v.

bla·tan·cy, n. pl.
bla·tan·cies

bla·tant

blath·er

blaze (FIRE, MARK)
(see also blasé)

blaze, v. blazed,
blaz·ing

blaz·er (COAT)

bla·zon (DISPLAY)

bleach

bleach·ers

bleak·ly

bleak·ness

bleary, adj.
blear·i·er,
blear·i·est

bleed, v. bled,
bleed·ing

blem·ish

bless, v. blessed
(occas. blest),
bless·ing

bless·ed·ness

blight

blind·fold

blind side, n.

blind·side, v.
blind·sid·ed,
blind·sid·ing

blink·er

blintze or blintz, n.
pl. blintzes

bliss·ful

bliss·ful·ly

bliss·ful·ness

blis·ter

blithe·ly

blithe·some

blithe·some·ly

blitz

blitz·krieg

bliz·zard

bloat

bloat·er

blob, v. blobbed,
blob·bing

bloc

block

block·ade, v.
block·ad·ed,
block·ad·ing

block·age

block·bust·er

block·head

block·house

blond, adj., n.
(masc. or fem.)

blonde, adj., n.
(fem. only)

blood·cur·dling

blood·hound

blood·i·ly

blood·i·ness

blood·less

blood·mo·bile

blood·shed

blood·shot

blood·stain

blood·stream

blood·suck·er

blood·thirst·i·ly

blood·thirst·i·ness

blood·thirsty

bloody, adj.
blood·i·er,
blood·i·est

bloody, v.
blood·ied,
blood·y·ing

bloop·er

blos·som

blot, v. blot·ted,
blot·ting

blotch

blot·ter

blouse, v. bloused,
blous·ing

blow, v. blew,
blown, blow·ing

blow·by

blow-by-blow

blow-dry, v.
blow·dried,
blow-dry·ing

blow·gun

blow·out

blow·pipe

blowsy (occas.
blowzy)

blow·torch

blub·ber

blub·bery

blu·cher

blud·geon

blue, adj. blu·er,
blu·est

blue·bell

blue·ber·ry, pl.
blue·ber·ries

blue·bird

blue-col·lar, adj.

blue·grass

blue·jeans

blue·nose

blue-pen·cil, v.
blue-pen·ciled
or blue-
pen·cilled, blue-
pen·cil·ling or
blue-pen·cil·ling

blue·print

blue·stock·ing

bluff

bluff·er

blu·ing or blue·ing

blu·ish

blun·der

blun·der·buss

blunt·ly

blunt·ness

blur, v. blurred,
blur·ring

blur·ry

blush

blus·ter

blus·tery

boa

boa con·stric·tor

boar (PIG) (see also
Boer, bore)

board·er

board·ing·house

board·walk

boast·ful

boast·ful·ly

boast·ful·ness

boat·hook

boat·man, n. pl.
boat·men

boat·swain

bob, v. bobbed,
bob·bing

bob·bin

bob·ble, v.
bob·bled,
bob·bling

Bob·by (PERSON'S
NAME), n. pl.
Bob·bys

bob·by (BRITISH
POLICE
OFFICER), n. pl.
bob·bies

bobby pin

bob·by-sox·er

bob·cat

bob·o·link

bob·sled, v.
bob·sled·ded,
bob·sled·ding

bob·white

boc·cie or boc·ci or
boc·ce

bo·da·cious

bo·da·cious·ly

bode, v. bod·ed,
bod·ing

bod·ice

bod·i·less

bod·i·ly

bod·kin

body, n. pl. bod·ies

body·guard

body-scan·ner

body·suit

Boer (SOUTH
AFRICAN) (see
also boar, bore)

bog, v. bogged,
bog·ging

bo·gey, n. pl.
bo·geys

bo·gey·man, *n. pl.*
bo·gey·men

bog·gle, *v.*
bog·gled,
bog·gling

bog·ie (GOLF)

Bo·go·tá or
Bo·go·ta

bo·gus

Bo·he·mia

Bo·he·mi·an

bo·he·mi·an
(UNCONVENTIONAL
PERSON)

boil·er

boil·er·mak·er

boil·er·plate

Boi·se

bois·ter·ous

bois·ter·ous·ly

bois·ter·ous·ness

bold·face
(PRINTING
TYPE), *n.*

bold-faced (SET IN
BOLDFACE),
adj.

bold-faced
(FORWARD
MANNER), *adj.*

bold·ly

bold·ness

bo·le·ro, *n. pl.*
bo·le·ros

Bo·li·var (So. Am.
liberator

bo·li·var (MONEY),
n. pl.
bo·li·va·res *or*
bo·li·vars

Bo·liv·ia

Bo·liv·i·an

bo·lo, *n. pl.* bo·los

bo·lo·gna
(SAUSAGE) (*see
also* baloney)

Bol·she·vik, *n. pl.*
Bol·she·viks
(*occas.*
Bol·she·vi·ki)

Bol·she·vism

bol·ster

bo·lus

bom·bard

bom·bar·dier

bom·bard·ment

bom·bast

bom·bas·tic

Bom·bay

bom·ba·zine

bomb·er

bomb·proof

bomb·shell

bomb·sight

bo·na fide, *adj.*

bo·na fi·des, *n.*

bo·nan·za

bon·bon

bond·age

bond·hold·er

bonds·man, *n. pl.*
bonds·men

bone, *v.* boned,
boning

bone-dry

bone·fish

bone·less

bon·er

boney (*var. of*
bony)

bon·fire

bon·go, *n. pl.*
bon·gos (*occas.*
bon·goes)

bon·ho·mie

bo·ni·to, *n. pl.*
bo·ni·tos *or*
bo·ni·to

bon·jour

bon mot, *n. pl.*
bons mots *or*
bon mots

bon·net

bon·ny, *adj.*
bon·ni·er,
bon·ni·est

bon·sai, *n. pl.*
bon·sai

bo·nus

bon vi·vant, *n. pl.*
bons vi·vants *or*
bon vi·vants

bon voy·age

bony (*occas.*
bon·ey), *adj.*
bon·i·er, bon·i·est

boo-boo *n. pl.*
boo-boos

boo·by

boo·by hatch

boo·by prize

boo·by trap, *n.*
boo·by-trap, *v.*
booby-trapped,
booby-trap·ping

boo·dle

boo·gie-woo·gie

book·case

book·end

book·ie

book·ish

book·ish·ly

book·ish·ness

book·keep·er

book·keep·ing

book·let

book·mak·er

book·mak·ing

book·mark

book·mo·bile

book·plate

book·sell·er

book·shelf

boo·mer·ang

boon·docks

boon·dog·gle

boor·ish

boor·ish·ly

boor·ish·ness

boost·er

boot·black

boo·tee *or* boo·tie
(BABY SHOE)
(*see also* booty)

booth, *n. pl.*
booths

boot·leg, *v.*
boot·legged,
boot·leg·ging

boot·strap

boo·ty (LOOT), *n.
pl.* boo·ties (*see
also* bootee)

booze, *v.* boozed,
booz·ing

boozy, *adj.*

booz·i·er,
booz·i·est

bo·rax

Bor·deaux, *n. pl.*
Bor·deaux

bor·del·lo, *n. pl.*
bor·del·los

bor·der

bor·der·land

bor·der·line

bore, *n.* (CALIBER,
DULL PERSON
OR THING) (*see
also* boar, Boer)

bore, *v.* bored,
bor·ing

bo·re·al

bore·dom

bor·er

bo·ric

bor·ing

bor·ing·ly

bor·ing·ness

born

born-again

Bor·neo

bo·ron

bor·ough (URBAN
AREA) (*see also*
burro, burrow)

bor·row

borscht *or* borsch

bor·zoi

bo·s'n *or* bo·'s'n *or*
bo·sun *or*
bo·'sun (*var. of*
boatswain)

bo·som

bo·somed

bo·somy

boss·i·ness

bossy, *adj.*
boss·i·er,
boss·i·est

Bos·ton

Bos·to·ni·an

bo·tan·i·cal

bot·a·nist

bot·a·ny, *n. pl.*
bot·a·nies

botch

both·er

both·er·some

Bot·swa·na

bot·tle, *v.* bot·tled,
bot·tling

bot·tle·brush

bot·tle·neck

bot·tom

bot·tom·less

bot·tom·most

bot·u·lism

bou·doir

bouf·fant

bough

bouil·la·baisse

bouil·lon (SOUP)
(*see also* bullion)

boul·der

bou·le·vard

bounce, *v.*
bounced,
bounc·ing

bounc·er

bound

bound·a·ry, *n. pl.*
bound·a·ries

bound·less

boun·te·ous

boun·te·ous·ly

boun·te·ous·ness

boun·ti·ful

boun·ti·ful·ly

boun·ti·ful·ness

boun·ty, n. pl.
boun·ties

bou·quet

bour·bon

bour·geois, n. pl.
bour·geois

bour·geoi·sie

bourse

bou·tique

bou·ton·niere

bo·vine

bow

bowd·ler·ize, v.
bowd·ler·ized,
bowd·ler·iz·ing

bow·el

bow·er

bow·ery, n. pl.
bow·er·ies

bowl·ful

bow·leg·ged

bowl·er

bowl·ing

bow·man, n. pl.
bow·men

bow·sprit

bow·string

box·car

box·er

box·ing

box·wood

boy·cott

boy·friend

boy·hood

boy·ish

boy·sen·ber·ry, n.
pl.
boy·sen·ber·ries

bo·zo, n. pl. bo·zos

brace, v. braced,
brac·ing

brace·let

bra·ce·ro, n. pl.
bra·ce·ros

brack·et

brack·ish

brack·ish·ness

Brad·ley

brag, v. bragged,
brag·ging

brag·ga·do·cio, n.
pl.
brag·ga·do·cios

brag·gart

Brah·ma

Brah·man (HINDU
PRIEST)
(occas.
Brahmin) (see
also Brahmin)

Brah·ma·pu·tra

Brah·min (New
England
aristocrat) (see
also Brahman)

braid

braille

brain·child

brain·less

brain·storm

brain·wash·ing

brainy, adj.
brain·i·er,
brain·i·est

braise (COOK) v.
braised,
brais·ing (see
also braze)

brake (STOP) v.
braked,
brak·ing (see also
break)

brake·man, n. pl.
brake·men

bram·ble

bran·dish

brand-new

Bran·don

bran·dy, n. pl.
bran·dies

brash

Bra·si·lia

bras·se·rie
(RESTAURANT)

bras·siere
(CLOTHING)
(see also brazier)

brassy, adj.
brass·i·er,
brass·i·est

brat

brat·ti·ness

brat·ty

brat·wurst

braun·schweig·er

bra·va·do, n. pl.
bra·va·does or
bra·va·dos

brave, *adj.* brav·er, brav·est

brave, *v.* braved, brav·ing

brave·ly

brav·ery, *n. pl.* brav·er·ies

bra·vo, *n. pl.* bra·vos *or* bra·voes

bra·vu·ra

brawl

brawl·er

brawny, *adj.* brawn·i·er, brawn·i·est

braze (JOIN METALS), *v.* brazed, braz·ing (*see also* braise)

bra·zen

bra·zen·ly

bra·zen·ness

bra·zier (PAN) (*see also* brassiere)

Bra·zil

Bra·zil·ian

Braz·za·ville

breach (BREAKING POINT) (*see also* breech)

bread-and-but·ter

bread·bas·ket

bread·board

breadth

bread·win·ner

break (FRACTURE), *v.* broke, broken,

break·ing (*see also* brake)

break·able

break·age

break·away

break·down

break·er

break-ev·en, *adj.*

break even, *v.*

break·fast

break·front

break-in, *n.*

break in, *v.*

break·out, *n.*

break out, *v.*

break·through, *n.*

break through, *v.*

break·wa·ter

breast·bone

breast-feed, *v.* breast-fed, breast-feed·ing

breast·plate

breast·stroke, *v.* breast·stroked, breast·strok·ing

breast·work

breath, *n.* (*see also* breathe)

Breath·a·ly·zer®

breathe, *v.* breathed, breathing (*see also* breath)

breath·er

breath·less

breath·less·ly

breath·less·ness

breath·tak·ing

breech (BACK END) (*see also* breach)

breech·block

breech·clout *or* breech·cloth

breech·es *or* britch·es (TROUSERS)

breech·load·er

breed, *v.* bred, breed·ing

breed·er

breeze·way

breezy, *adj.* breez·i·er, breez·i·est

breth·ren

bre·vet, *v.* bre·vet·ted *or* bre·vet·ed, bre·vet·ting *or* bre·vet·ing

bre·via·ry, *n. pl.* bre·via·ries

brev·i·ty

brew·ery, *n. pl.* brew·er·ies

Bri·an

bri·ar (PIPE) (*see also* brier)

bribe, *v.* bribed, brib·ing

brib·ery, *pl.* brib·er·ies

bric-a-brac

brick·bat

brick·lay·er

brid·al

bride·groom

brides·maid

bridge, v. bridged,
  bridg·ing

bridge·head

bridge·work

bri·dle, v. bri·dled,
  bri·dling

brief·case

bri·er (ROOT,
  PLANT) (see
  also briar)

bri·gade

brig·a·dier

brig·and

brig·an·dine
  (ARMOR)

brig·an·tine (SHIP)

bright·en

bright·ly

bright·ness

bril·liance

bril·lian·cy

bril·liant

bril·lian·tine

Brillo®

brim, v. brimmed,
  brim·ming

brim·ful

brim·stone

brin·dled

bring, v. brought,
  bring·ing

brink·man·ship
  (occas.
  brinks·man·ship)

briny, adj.
  brin·i·er,
  brin·i·est

bri·oche

bri·quette or
  bri·quet

bris·ket

brisk·ly

brisk·ness

bris·tle, v. bris·tled,
  bris·tling

bris·tly, adj.
  brist·li·er,
  brist·li·est

Brit·ain (ISLAND)
  (see also
  Briton)

Bri·tan·nic

britch·es (var. of
  breeches)

Brit·ish

Brit·on (PERSON)
  (see also
  Britain)

brit·tle

broach (n., TOOL;
  v., OPEN UP)
  (see also brooch)

broad·band

broad·cast, v.
  broad·cast
  (occas.
  broad·cast·ed),
  broad·cast·ing

broad·cloth

broad·en

broad-mind·ed

broad-mind·ed·ly

broad-mind·ed·ness

broad·side

broad·sword

bro·cade

broc·coli

bro·chette

bro·chure

bro·gan

brogue

broil·er

bro·ken

bro·ken-heart·ed

bro·ker

bro·ker·age

bro·mide

bro·mid·ic

bro·mine

Bro·mo Selt·zer®

bron·chi·al

bron·chi·tis

bron·chus, n. pl.
  bron·chi

bron·co (occas.
  bron·chos), n.
  pl. bron·cos or
  bron·chos

bron·co·bust·er

brooch (JEWELRY)
  (see also
  broach)

brood·er

brook·let

Brook·lyn

broom·stick

broth·el

broth·er

broth·er·hood

brother-in-law, n.
  pl. brothers-in-
  law

broth·er·li·ness

broth·er·ly

brougham

brou·ha·ha

brow·beat, *v.*
  brow·beat,
  brow·beat·en,
  brow·beat·ing

brown-bag, *v.*
  brown-bagged,
  brown-bag·ging

brown bag·ger

brown·ie

brown·stone

browse, *v.*
  browsed,
  brows·ing

bru·in

bruise, *v.* bruised,
  bruis·ing

bruis·er

Bru·nei

bru·net, *adj., n.*
  (*masc.* or *fem.*)

bru·nette, *adj., n.*
  (*fem.* only)

brush·off

brush·wood

brusque

brusque·ly

brusque·ness

Brus·sels or
  Bru·xelles

brus·sels sprout

bru·tal

bru·tal·i·ty

bru·tal·ize, *v.*
  bru·tal·ized,
  bru·tal·iz·ing

bru·tal·ly

brut·ish

brut·ish·ly

brut·ish·ness

bub·ble, *v.*
  bub·bled,
  bub·bling

bub·bly, *adj.*
  bub·bli·er,
  bub·bli·est

bu·bon·ic

buc·ca·neer

Bu·cha·rest

buck·a·roo

buck·board

buck·et

buck·et·ful, *n. pl.*
  buck·et·fuls or
  buck·ets·ful

buck·le, *v.*
  buck·led,
  buck·ling

buck·ler

buck·ram

buck·saw

buck·shot

buck·skin

buck·tooth, *n. pl.*
  buck·teeth

buck·wheat

bu·col·ic

bud, *v.* bud·ded,
  bud·ding

Bu·da·pest

Bud·dha

Bud·dhism

Bud·dhist

bud·dy, *n. pl.*
  bud·dies

bud·dy, *v.*
  bud·died,
  bud·dy·ing

budge, *v.* budged,
  budg·ing

bud·get

Bue·nos Ai·res

buf·fa·lo, *n. pl.*
  buf·fa·lo or
  buf·fa·loes
  (*occas.*
  buf·fa·los)

buf·fer

buf·fet

buf·foon

buf·foon·er·y

bug, *v.* bug·ged,
  bug·ging

bug·a·boo

bug·bear

bug·gy (INFESTED),
  adj. bug·gi·er,
  bug·gi·est

bug·gy
  (CARRIAGE), *n.*
  pl. bug·gies

bu·gle, *v.* bu·gled,
  bu·gling

bu·gler

build, *v.* built,
  build·ing

build·er

built-in

bul·bous

bul·bous·ly

Bul·gar·ia

Bul·gar·i·an

bulge, *v.* bulged,
  bulg·ing

bu·li·ma·rex·ic

bu·lim·ia

bu·lim·ic

bulk·head

bulk·i·ly

bulk·i·ness

bulky, *adj.*
bulk·i·er,
bulk·i·est

bull·dog, *v.*
bull·dogged,
bull·dog·ging

bull·doze,
*v.*bull·dozed,
bull·doz·ing

bull·doz·er

bul·let

bul·le·tin

bul·let·proof

bull·fight

bull·finch

bull·frog

bull·head·ed

bull·head·ed·ly

bull·head·ed·ness

bul·lion (GOLD OR
SILVER) (*see
also* bouillon)

bull·ish

bul·lock

bull·pen

bull's-eye, *n. pl.*
bull's-eyes

bul·ly, *n. pl.*
bul·lies

bul·ly, *v.* bul·lied,
bul·ly·ing

bul·rush (*occas.*
bull·rush), *n.
pl.* bul·rush·es

bul·wark

bum, *v.* bummed,
bum·ming

bum·ble·bee

bum·mer

bump·er

bumper-to-bumper

bump·i·ly

bump·i·ness

bump·kin

bump·tious

bump·tious·ly

bump·tious·ness

bumpy, *adj.*
bump·i·er,
bump·i·est

bun·co *or* bun·ko,
n. pl. bun·cos
or bun·kos

bun·dle, *v.*
bun·dled,
bun·dling

bun·ga·low

bung·hole

bun·gle, *v.*
bun·gled,
bun·gling

bun·gler

bun·ion

bun·ker

bun·kum *or*
bun·combe

bun·ny, *n. pl.*
bun·nies

bun·ting

buoy

buoy·an·cy

buoy·ant

buoy·ant·ly

bur·den

bur·den·some

bu·reau, *n. pl.*
bu·reaus (*occas.*
bu·reaux)

bu·reau·cra·cy, *n. pl.*
bu·reau·cra·cies

bu·reau·crat

bu·reau·crat·ese

bu·reau·crat·ic

bur·geon

bur·ger
(SANDWICH)
(*see also*
burgher)

bur·gess

bur·gher (PERSON)

bur·glar

bur·glar·ize, *v.*
bur·glar·ized,
bur·glar·iz·ing

bur·gla·ry, *n. pl.*
bur·gla·ries

bur·go·mas·ter

Bur·gun·dy (WINE,
REGION), *n. pl.*
Bur·gun·dies

bur·gun·dy
(COLOR)

bur·i·al

Bur·ki·na Fa·so

bur·lap

bur·lesque, *v.*
bur·lesqued,
bur·lesqu·ing

bur·ley (TOBACCO)
(*see also* burly)

Bur·ling·ton

bur·ly (BIG,
STRONG), *adj.*
burl·i·er,

burl·i·est (*see also* burley)

Bur·ma

Bur·man

Bur·mese, *n. pl.* Bur·mese

burn, *v.* burned *or* burnt, burn·ing

burn·er

bur·nish

bur·noose *or* bur·nous, *n. pl.* bur·noos·es, bur·nous·es

burn·out

burr

bur·ri·to, *n. pl.* bur·ri·tos

bur·ro (ANIMAL), *n. pl.* bur·ros (*see also* borough, burrow)

bur·row (HOLE), *n., v.* (*see also* borough, burro)

bur·sar

bur·si·tis

burst, *v.* burst (*rarely* burst·ed), burst·ing

Bu·run·di

Bu·run·di·an

bury, *v.* bur·ied, bury·ing

bus (VEHICLE), *n. pl.* bus·es *or* bus·ses (*see also* buss)

bus, *v.* bused *or*

bussed, bus·ing *or* bus·sing

bus·boy

bush·el

bush·ing

bush·whack

bus·i·ly

busi·ness

busi·ness·like

busi·ness·man, *n. pl.* busi·ness·men

busi·ness·per·son

busi·ness·wom·an, *n. pl.* busi·ness·wom·en

bus·kin

buss (KISS) (*see also* bus)

bus·tle, *v.* bus·tled, bus·tling

busy, *adj.* bus·i·er, bus·i·est

busy, *v.* bus·ied, busy·ing

busy·body

but, *conj.*

bu·tane

butch·er

butch·ery, *n. pl.* butch·er·ies

but·ler

butt

butte

but·ter

but·ter·cup

but·ter·fat

but·ter·fin·gered

but·ter·fin·gers

but·ter·fly, *n. pl.* but·ter·flies

but·ter·milk

but·ter·nut

but·ter·scotch

but·tery, *n. pl.* but·ter·ies

but·tocks

but·ton

but·ton·hole

but·ton·hook

but·tress

Bu·tyl® (RUBBER)

bux·om

buy, *v.* bought, buy·ing

buy·back

buy·er

buz·zard

buzz·er

buzz·word

by-and-by

bye-bye

by·gone

by·law

by·line

by·pass

by·path

by·play

by-product

by·stand·er

byte

by·way

by·word

Byz·an·tine

C

ca·bal, *v.* ca·balled,
  ca·bal·ling

ca·bal·le·ro, *n. pl.*
  ca·bal·le·ros

ca·bana

cab·a·ret

cab·bage

cab·bie *or* cab·by,
  n. pl. cab·bies

cab·driv·er

ca·ber·net
  sau·vi·gnon

cab·in

cab·i·net

cab·i·net·mak·er

cab·i·net·mak·ing

cab·i·net·work

ca·ble, *v.* ca·bled,
  ca·bling

cab·le·gram

cab·man, *n. pl.*
  cab·men

ca·bood·le

ca·boose

cab·ri·o·let

cab·stand

ca·cao (TREE,
  BEAN), *n. pl.*
  ca·caos (*see also*
  coca, cocoa)

cac·cia·to·re

cache, *v.* cached,
  cach·ing

ca·chet

cack·le, *v.* cack·led,
  cack·ling

ca·coph·o·nous

ca·coph·o·nous·ly

ca·coph·o·ny, *n.*
  pl. ca·coph·o·nies

cac·tus, *n. pl.* cac·ti
  (*occas.*
  cac·tus·es *or*
  cac·tus)

ca·dav·er

ca·dav·er·ous

ca·dav·er·ous·ly

cad·die *or* cad·dy
  (GOLF), *n. pl.*
  cad·dies (*see also*
  caddy)

cad·die *or* cad·dy
  (GOLF), *v.*
  cad·died,
  cad·dy·ing (*see*
  also caddy)

cad·dish

cad·dish·ness

cad·dy (SMALL
  CONTAINER),
  n. pl. cad·dies
  (*see also*
  caddie)

ca·dence

ca·den·za

ca·det

cadge (BEG), *v.*
  cadged,
  cadg·ing (*see also*
  cage)

cad·mi·um

ca·dre

ca·du·ce·us, *n. pl.*
  ca·du·cei

Cae·sar·e·an *or*
  Cae·sar·i·an

cae·su·ra, *n. pl.*
  cae·su·ras *or*
  cae·su·rae

ca·fé (*occas.* ca·fe)

ca·fé au lait

caf·e·te·ria

caf·fein·at·ed

caf·feine

caf·tan

cage (ENCLOSE), *v.*

49

cag·ing (*see also* cadge)

ca·gey (*occas.* cagy), *adj.* ca·gi·er, ca·gi·est

ca·gi·ly

ca·gi·ness (*occas.* ca·gey·ness)

ca·hoots

cai·man, *n. pl.* cai·mans *or* cay·mans (*see also* Cayman Islands)

Cai·ro

cais·son

ca·jole, *v.* ca·joled, ca·jol·ing

ca·jole·ment

ca·jol·ery

Ca·jun (*occas.* Ca·jan)

cake, *v.* caked, cak·ing

cake·walk

cal·a·bash

cal·a·boose

cal·a·mari

cal·a·mine

ca·lam·i·tous

ca·lam·i·tous·ly

ca·lam·i·tous·ness

ca·lam·i·ty, *n. pl.* ca·lam·i·ties

cal·ci·fi·ca·tion

cal·ci·fy, *v.* cal·ci·fied, cal·ci·fy·ing

cal·ci·mine, *v.*

cal·ci·mined, cal·ci·min·ing

cal·ci·na·tion

cal·cine, *v.* cal·cined, cal·cin·ing

cal·ci·um

cal·cu·la·ble

cal·cu·late, *v.* cal·cu·lat·ed, cal·cu·lat·ing

cal·cu·la·tion

cal·cu·la·tor

cal·cu·lus

Cal·cut·ta

cal·dron (*occas.* caul·dron)

cal·en·dar (DATES) (*see also* calender, colander)

cal·en·der (PRESS) (*see* calendar, colander)

calf, *n. pl.* calves (*occas.* calfs) (*see also* calve)

calf·skin

Cal·ga·ry

cal·i·ber *or* cal·i·bre

cal·i·brate, *v.* cal·i·brat·ed, cal·i·brat·ing

cal·i·bra·tion

cal·i·co, *n. pl.* cal·i·coes *or* cal·i·cos

Cal·i·for·nia

Cal·i·for·nian

cal·i·for·ni·um

cal·i·per *or* cal·lip·er

ca·liph

ca·liph·ate

cal·is·then·ics

call·back, *n.*

call back, *v.*

call·boy (BELLHOP)

call·er

call girl (PROSTITUTE)

cal·lig·ra·pher

cal·lig·ra·phy, *n. pl.* cal·lig·ra·phies

call·ing

cal·li·o·pe

cal·lous (UNFEELING) (*see also* callus)

cal·lous·ly

cal·lous·ness

cal·low

cal·lus (SKIN) (*see also* callous)

calm·ly

calm·ness

cal·o·mel

ca·lo·ric

ca·lo·ri·cal·ly

ca·lo·rie (*rarely* cal·o·ry)

cal·o·rim·e·ter

cal·u·met

ca·lum·ni·ate, *v.* ca·lum·ni·at·ed, ca·lum·ni·at·ing

ca·lum·ni·a·tion

ca·lum·ni·a·tor

ca·lum·ni·ous

ca·lum·ni·ous·ly

cal·um·ny, *n. pl.*
  cal·um·nies

Cal·va·ry (PLACE),
  (*see also*
  cavalry)

calve (TO BIRTH),
  v. calved, calv·ing
  (*see also* calf)

Cal·vin·ism

Cal·vin·is·tic

ca·lyp·so, *n. pl.*
  ca·lyp·sos
  (*occas.*
  ca·lyp·soes)

ca·lyx, *n. pl.*
  ca·lyx·es *or*
  ca·ly·ces

cal·zo·ne, *n. pl.*
  cal·zo·ne *or*
  cal·zo·nes

ca·ma·ra·de·rie

cam·ber

cam·bi·um

Cam·bo·dia

Cam·bo·di·an

Cam·bri·an

cam·bric

Cam·bridge

cam·cord·er

Cam·den

cam·el

ca·mel·lia

Cam·em·bert

cam·eo, *n. pl.*
  cam·eos

cam·era

Cam·e·roon

Cam·e·roon·i·an

cam·i·sole

cam·ou·flage, *v.*
  cam·ou·flaged,
  cam·ou·flag·ing

cam·paign

cam·pa·nile

Cam·pe·che

camp·er

camp·fire

camp·ground

cam·phor

cam·phor·ate, *v.*
  cam·phor·at·ed,
  cam·phor·at·ing

camp·o·ree

camp·stool

cam·pus

cam·shaft

can, *v.* canned,
  can·ning

Can·a·da

Ca·na·di·an

ca·naille

ca·nal, *v.* ca·nalled
  or ca·naled,
  ca·nal·ling *or*
  ca·nal·ing

can·a·li·za·tion

ca·nal·ize, *v.*
  ca·nal·ized,
  ca·nal·iz·ing

can·a·pé (HORS
  D'OEUVRE) (*see
  also* canopy)

ca·nard

ca·nary, *n. pl.*
  ca·nar·ies

ca·nas·ta

can·can

can·cel, *v.*
  can·celed *or*
  can·celled,
  can·cel·ing *or*
  can·cel·ling

can·cel·la·tion
  (*occas.*
  can·ce·la·tion)

can·cer

can·cer·ous

can·cer·ous·ly

can·de·la·bra, *n. pl.*
  of candelabrum

can·de·la·brum, *n.*
  pl. can·de·la·bra
  (*occas.*
  can·de·la·brums)

can·des·cence

can·des·cent

Can·dice

can·did

can·di·da·cy, *n. pl.*
  can·di·da·cies

can·di·date

can·died

can·dle, *v.*
  can·dled,
  can·dling

can·dle·light

Can·dle·mas

can·dle·pin

can·dle·stick

can·dle·wick

can·dor

can·dy, *n. pl.*
  can·dies

can·dy, *v.* can·died,
  can·dy·ing

cane·brake

ca·nine

can·is·ter (*occas.* can·nis·ter)

can·ker

can·ker·ous

can·ker·worm

can·na·bas

can·nel·lo·ni (PASTA) (*see also* cannoli)

can·nery, *n. pl.* can·ner·ies

can·ni·bal

can·ni·bal·ism

can·ni·bal·is·tic

can·ni·bal·ize, *v.* can·ni·bal·ized, can·ni·bal·iz·ing

can·ni·ly

can·ni·ness

can·noli (PASTRY) (*see also* cannelloni)

can·non (ARTILLERY), *n. pl.* cannons *or* cannon (*see also* canon)

can·non·ade, *v.* can·non·ad·ed, can·non·ad·ing

can·non·ball

can·non·eer

can·not

can·ny, *adj.* can·ni·er, can·ni·est

ca·noe, *v.* ca·noed, ca·noe·ing

can·on (LAW) (*see also* cannon)

ca·non·i·cal

can·on·i·za·tion

can·on·ize, *v.* can·on·ized, can·on·iz·ing

can·o·py (COVERING), *n. pl.* can·o·pies (*see also* canapé)

can·o·py, *v.* can·o·pied, can·o·py·ing

can't (*contraction of* cannot)

can·ta·bi·le

can·ta·loupe (*occas.* can·ta·loup)

can·tan·ker·ous

can·tan·ker·ous·ly

can·tan·ker·ous·ness

can·ta·ta

can·teen

can·ter

can·ti·cle

can·ti·le·ver

can·ti·na

can·to, *n. pl.* can·tos

Can·ton (CITY NAME)

can·ton (TERRITORIAL SUBDIVISION)

can·ton·al

Can·ton·ese

can·ton·ment

can·tor

can·vas (*occas.* can·vass) (CLOTH), *n. pl.* can·vas·es (*see also* canvass)

can·vas·back

can·vass (*occas.* can·vas) (POLL), *n. pl.* can·vas·ses (*see also* can·vas)

can·yon

cap, *v.* capped, cap·ping

ca·pa·bil·i·ty

ca·pa·ble

ca·pa·bly

ca·pa·cious

ca·pa·cious·ly

ca·pa·cious·ness

ca·pac·i·tance

ca·pac·i·tor

ca·pac·i·ty, *n. pl.* ca·pac·i·ties

ca·par·i·son

ca·per

cape·skin

Cape Town

Cape Verde

cap·il·lar·i·ty, *n. pl.* cap·il·lar·i·ties

cap·il·lary, *n. pl.* cap·il·lar·ies

cap·i·tal (CITY, MONEY) (*see also* capitol)

cap·i·tal-in·ten·sive

cap·i·tal·ism

cap·i·tal·ist

cap·i·tal·is·tic

cap·i·tal·is·ti·cal·ly

cap·i·tal·iza·tion

cap·i·tal·ize, v.
  cap·i·tal·ized,
  cap·i·tal·iz·ing

cap·i·tal·ly

cap·i·ta·tion

cap·i·tol
  (BUILDING)
  (see also capital)

ca·pit·u·late, v.
  ca·pit·u·lat·ed,
  ca·pit·u·lat·ing

ca·pit·u·la·tion

cap·let

ca·pon

cap·puc·ci·no, n. pl.
  cap·puc·ci·noes

ca·pric·cio, n. pl.
  ca·pric·cios

ca·price

ca·pri·cious

ca·pri·cious·ly

ca·pri·cious·ness

Cap·ri·corn

cap·ri·ole

cap·size, v.
  cap·sized,
  cap·siz·ing

cap·stan

cap·su·lar

cap·su·late

cap·su·lat·ed

cap·sule

cap·tain

cap·tain·cy, n. pl.
  cap·tain·cies

cap·tion

cap·tious

cap·tious·ly

cap·tious·ness

cap·ti·vate, v.
  cap·ti·vat·ed,
  cap·ti·vat·ing

cap·ti·va·tion

cap·tive

cap·tiv·i·ty, n. pl.
  cap·tiv·i·ties

cap·tor

cap·ture, v.
  cap·tured,
  cap·tur·ing

Ca·pu·chin (MONK)

ca·pu·chin (HOOD,
  MONKEY)

Ca·ra·cas

ca·rafe

car·a·mel (CANDY,
  FLAVOR) (see
  also Carmel)

car·a·pace

car·at (WEIGHT)
  (see also caret,
  carrot, karat)

car·a·van

car·a·vel

car·a·way

car·bide

car·bine

car·bo·hy·drate

car·bol·ic acid

car·bon

car·bo·na·ceous

car·bon·ate, v.
  car·bon·at·ed,
  car·bon·a·ting

car·bon·a·tion

car·bon·ic

car·bon·if·er·ous

car·bon·iza·tion

car·bon·ize, v.
  car·bon·ized,
  car·bon·iz·ing

Car·bo·run·dum℗

car·bun·cle

car·bu·re·tor

car·cass

car·cin·o·gen

car·cin·o·gen·ic

car·cin·o·ge·nic·i·ty

car·ci·no·ma, n. pl.
  car·ci·no·mas or
  car·ci·no·ma·ta

card·board

card-car·ry·ing

car·di·ac

car·di·gan

car·di·nal

car·di·nal·i·ty

car·dio·gram

car·dio·graph

car·di·og·ra·phy

car·di·o·lo·gy

car·di·o·vas·cu·lar

care, v. cared,
  car·ing

care·giv·er

ca·reen

ca·reer

ca·reer·ist

care·free

care·ful

care·ful·ly

care·ful·ness
care·less
care·less·ly
care·less·ness
ca·ress
car·et (EDITING
  MARK) (see also
  carat, carrot,
  karat)
care·tak·er
care·worn
car·fare
car·go, n. pl.
  car·goes or
  car·gos
car·hop
Car·ib·be·an
car·i·bou, n. pl.
  car·i·bou or
  car·i·bous
car·i·ca·ture
car·i·ca·tur·ist
car·ies (TOOTH
  DECAY) (see
  also carries)
car·il·lon
car·load
Car·mel (CITY,
  MOUNT) (see
  also caramel)
Car·mel·ite
car·mine
car·nage
car·nal
car·nal·i·ty
car·nal·ly
car·na·tion
car·nau·ba
car·ne·lian

car·ni·val
car·ni·vore
car·niv·o·rous
car·niv·o·rous·ly
car·niv·o·rous·ness
car·ol, v. car·oled
  or car·olled,
  car·ol·ing or
  car·ol·ling
Car·o·lina
Car·o·line
car·om
ca·ro·tene
ca·rot·id
ca·rous·al (PARTY)
  (see also
  carousel)
ca·rouse, v.
  ca·roused,
  ca·rous·ing
ca·rou·sel (MERRY-
  GO-ROUND)
  (see also
  carousal)
car·pal (BONE)
car·pel (LEAF)
car·pen·ter
car·pen·try
car·pet
car·pet·bag, v.
  car·pet·bagged,
  car·pet·bag·ging
car·pet·bag·ger
car·pet·ing
car·port
car·rel
car·riage
car·ri·er

car·ries (TOTES)
  (see also caries)
car·ri·on
car·rot
  (VEGETABLE)
  (see also carat,
  caret, karet)
car·ry, v. car·ried,
  car·ry·ing
car·ry·all
car·ry-on, adj., n.
car·ry on, v.
car·ry-over, n.
car·ry over, v.
car·sick
Car·son City
car·tage
carte blanche
car·tel
car·ti·lage
car·ti·lag·i·nous
car·to·gram
car·tog·raph·er
car·to·graph·ic
car·tog·ra·phy
car·ton (BOX)
car·toon
  (DRAWING)
car·toon·ist
car·tridge
cart·wheel
carve, v. carved,
  carv·ing
car·vel, see caravel
carv·er
carv·ing
ca·sa·ba (MELON)

(see also
cassava)

Ca·sa·blan·ca

Ca·sa·no·va

Cas·bah

cas·cade, v.
cas·cad·ed,
cas·cad·ing

ca·sein

case·load

case·mate

case·ment

case·work

cash-and-car·ry

ca·shew

ca·shier

cash·mere

cas·ing

ca·si·no, n. pl.
ca·si·nos

cas·ket

Cas·pi·an Sea

cas·sa·va (ROOT)
(see also
casaba)

cas·se·role

cas·sette

cas·sock

casson, see caisson

cast, v. cast,
cast·ing

cas·ta·net

cast·a·way

caste

cas·tel·lat·ed

cast·er (ROLLER)
(see also castor)

cas·ti·gate, v.

cas·ti·gat·ed,
cas·ti·gat·ing

cas·ti·ga·tion

cast·ing

cast iron

cas·tle

cast-off, adj.

cast·off, n.

cast off, v.

Cas·tor (STAR)

cas·tor (BEAN,
MUSK) (see also
caster)

cas·trate, v.
cas·trat·ed,
cas·trat·ing

cas·tra·tion

ca·su·al

ca·su·al·ly

ca·su·al·ness

ca·su·al·ty, n. pl.
ca·su·al·ties

ca·su·ist

ca·su·ist·ic

ca·su·is·tic·al

ca·su·ist·ry, n. pl.
ca·su·ist·ries

ca·sus bel·li, n. pl.
ca·sus bel·li

cat·a·clysm

cat·a·clys·mal

cat·a·clys·mic

cat·a·comb

cat·a·falque

Cat·a·lan

cat·a·lep·sy, n. pl.
cat·a·lep·sies

cat·a·lep·tic

cat·a·log, or
cat·a·logue, v.
cat·a·loged or
cat·a·logued,
cat·a·log·ing or
cat·a·logu·ing

cat·a·log·er or
cat·a·logu·er

ca·tal·pa

ca·tal·y·sis, n. pl.
ca·tal·y·ses

cat·a·lyst

cat·a·lyt·ic

cat·a·ma·ran

cat·a·pult

cat·a·ract

cata·to·nia

cata·ton·ic

ca·tarrh

ca·tarrh·al

ca·tas·tro·phe

cat·a·stroph·ic

cat·a·stroph·i·cal·ly

cat·call

catch, v. caught,
catch·ing

catch·all

catch·er

catch·ment

catch·pen·ny

catch-up, adj., n.

catch up, v.

catch·word

catchy, adj.
catch·i·er,
catch·i·est

cat·e·chism

cat·e·chist

cat·e·chize, *v.*
  cat·e·chized,
  cat·e·shiz·ing

cat·e·chu·men

cat·e·gor·ic

cat·e·gor·i·cal

cat·e·gor·i·cal·ly

cat·e·go·ri·za·tion

cat·e·go·rize, *v.*
  cat·e·go·rized,
  cat·e·go·riz·ing

cat·e·go·ry, *n. pl.*
  cat·e·go·ries

ca·ter

ca·ter-cor·ner,
  ca·ter-
    cor·nered *or*
  cat·ty-cor·ner,
  cat·ty-cor·nered
  or kit·ty-
  cor·ner, kit·ty-
  cor·nered

ca·ter·er

cat·er·pil·lar

cat·er·waul

cat·fish

cat·gut

ca·thar·sis

ca·thar·tic

ca·the·dral

Cath·er·ine

cath·e·ter

cath·ode

ca·thod·ic

Cath·o·lic
  (CHURCH)

cath·o·lic
  (UNIVERSAL)

Ca·thol·i·cism

cath·o·lic·i·ty

cat·kin

cat·like

cat·nap, *v.*
  cat·napped,
  cat·nap·ping

cat·nip

cat-o'-nine-tails, *n.*
  pl. cat-o'-nine-
  tails

cat·sup (*var. of*
  ketchup)

cat·tail

cat·ti·ly

cat·ti·ness

cat·tle

cat·ty

catty-corner, *see*
  cater-corner

cat·walk

Cau·ca·sian

Cau·ca·soid

cau·cus

cau·dal

caul·dron (*var. of*
  caldron)

cau·li·flow·er

caulk

caus·al

cau·sal·i·ty

caus·al·ly

cau·sa·tion

caus·a·tive

cause, *v.* caused,
  caus·ing

cause cé·lè·bre, *n.*
  pl. caus·es
  cé·lè·bres

cau·se·rie

cause·way

caus·tic

caus·ti·cal·ly

cau·ter·iza·tion

cau·ter·ize, *v.*
  cau·ter·ized,
  cau·ter·iz·ing

cau·tion

cau·tion·ary

cau·tious

cau·tious·ly

cau·tious·ness

cav·al·cade

cav·a·lier

cav·al·ry
  (MOUNTED
  SOLDIERS), *n.*
  pl. cav·al·ries,
  (*see also*
  Calvary)

ca·ve·at

ca·ve·at emp·tor

cave-in, *n.*

cave in *v.*

cave·man, *n. pl.*
  cave·men

cave·wom·an, *n. pl.*
  cave·wom·en

cav·ern

cav·ern·ous

cav·ern·ous·ly

cav·i·ar *or* cav·i·are

cav·il, *v.* ca·viled *or*
  ca·villed,
  ca·vil·ing *or*
  ca·vil·ling

ca·vi·ta·tion

cav·i·ty, *n. pl.*
  cav·i·ties

ca·vort

cay·enne

Cay·man Is·lands

cay·use

cease, *v.* ceased,
  ceas·ing

cease-fire, *n.*

cease fire, *v.*

cease·less

ce·cum, *n. pl.* ce·ca

ce·dar

Ce·dar Rap·ids

cede, *v.* ced·ed,
  ced·ing

ce·di

ce·dil·la

ceil·ing

cel·an·dine

Cel·e·bes

cel·e·brant

cel·e·brate, *v.*
  cel·e·brat·ed,
  cel·e·brat·ing

cel·e·bra·tion

cel·e·bri·ty, *n. pl.*
  cel·e·bri·ties

ce·ler·i·ty

cel·ery

ce·les·ta

ce·les·tial

ce·li·ac

cel·i·bacy

cel·i·bate

cel·lar

cel·lar·age

cel·lar·ette *or*
  cel·lar·et

cell·block

cel·list

cel·lo, *n. pl.* cel·los

cel·lo·phane

cel·lu·lar

cel·lu·lite

cel·lu·loid

cel·lu·lose

Cel·si·us

Cel·tic

ce·ment

ce·men·ta·tion

cem·e·tery, *n. pl.*
  cem·e·ter·ies

cen·o·bite

cen·o·bit·ic

ceno·taph

Ce·no·zo·ic

cen·ser
  (CONTAINER)

cen·sor (PERSON),
  n. (*see also*
  sensor)

cen·sor
  (SUPPRESS), *v.*

cen·so·ri·al

cen·so·ri·ous

cen·so·ri·ous·ly

cen·so·ri·ous·ness

cen·sor·ship

cen·sur·able

cen·sure, *v.*
  cen·sured,
  cen·sur·ing

cen·sur·er

cen·sus

cent

cen·taur

cen·ta·vo, *n. pl.*
  cen·ta·vos

cen·te·nar·i·an

cen·te·na·ry, *n. pl.*
  cen·te·na·ry

cen·ten·ni·al

cen·ten·ni·al·ly

cen·ter

cen·ter·board

cen·tered

cen·ter·fold

cen·ter·piece

cen·tes·i·mal

cen·tes·i·mo, *n. pl.*
  cen·tes·i·mos *or*
  cen·tes·i·mi

cen·ti·grade

cen·ti·gram

cen·time

cen·ti·meter

cen·ti·mo, *n. pl.*
  cen·ti·mos

cen·ti·pede

cen·to, *n. pl.*
  cen·to·nes

cen·tral

cen·tral·iza·tion

cen·tral·ize, *v.*
  cen·tral·ized,
  cen·tral·iz·ing

cen·trif·u·gal

cen·tri·fuge

cen·trip·e·tal

cen·trist

cen·tu·ri·on

cen·tu·ry, *n. pl.*
  cen·tu·ries

ce·phal·ic

ce·ram·ic

ce·ra·mist *or*
  ce·ram·i·cist

ce·re·al

cer·e·bel·lum, *n. pl.*
  cer·e·bel·lums
  or cer·e·bel·la

ce·re·bral

cer·e·bra·tion

cer·e·brum

cer·e·mo·ni·al

cer·e·mo·ni·al·ly

cer·e·mo·ni·ous

cer·e·mo·ni·ous·ly

cer·e·mo·ni·ous·ness

cer·e·mony, *n. pl.*
  cer·e·mo·nies

ce·rise

ce·ri·um

cer·met

cer·tain

cer·tain·ly

cer·tain·ty

cer·tif·i·cate, *v.*
  cer·tif·i·cat·ed,
  cer·tif·i·cat·ing

cer·ti·fi·ca·tion

cer·ti·fy, *v.*
  cer·ti·fied,
  cer·ti·fy·ing

cer·ti·tude

ce·ru·le·an

cer·vi·cal

cer·vix, *n. pl.*
  cer·vi·ces *or*
  cer·vi·xes

ce·sar·e·an *or*
  ce·sar·i·an

ce·si·um

ces·sa·tion (STOP)

ces·sion (GIVING
  UP) (*see also*
  session)

cess·pool

ces·ta

Cey·lon

Cey·lon·ese

Cha·blis, *n. pl.*
  Cha·blis

cha·cha

Chad

Chad·ian

chafe (RUB), *v.*
  chafed, chaf·ing

chaff (HUSKS), *n.*

chaf·finch

cha·grin

chair·lift

chair·man, *n. pl.*
  chair·men

chair·per·son

chair·wom·an, *n.
  pl.*
  chair·wom·en

chaise lounge

chal·ced·o·ny, *n. pl.*
  chal·ced·o·nies

Chal·de·an

cha·let

chal·ice (CUP) (*see
  also* challis)

chalk·board

chalky

chal·lenge, *v.*

chal·lenged,
  chal·leng·ing

chal·lis (FABRIC)
  (*see also*
  chalice)

cham·ber

cham·ber·lain

cham·ber·maid

cham·bray

cha·me·leon

cham·fer

cham·ois, *n. pl.*
  cham·ois
  (*occas.*
  cham·oix)

cham·pagne

cham·pi·on

cham·pi·on·ship

Cham·plain

chance, *v.*
  chanced,
  chanc·ing

chan·cel

chan·cel·lery *or*
  chan·cel·lory, *n.
  pl.*
  chan·cel·ler·ies
  or
  chan·cel·lor·ies

chan·cel·lor

chan·cery, *n. pl.*
  chan·cer·ies

chan·cre

chancy, *adj.*
  chanc·i·er,
  chanc·i·est

chan·de·lier

chan·delle

chan·dler

chan·dler·y, *n. pl.*
  chan·dler·ies

change, *v.*
  changed,
  chang·ing

change·abil·i·ty

change·able

change·able·ness

change·less

change·ling

chang·er

chan·nel, *v.*
  chan·neled *or*
  chan·nelled,
  chan·nel·ing *or*
  chan·nel·ling

chan·nel·iza·tion

chan·nel·ize, *v.*
  chan·nel·ized,
  chan·nel·iz·ing

chan·son

chan·teuse

chan·tey *or* chan·ty
  (SONG), *n. pl.*
  chan·teys *or*
  chan·ties (*see
  also* shanty)

Cha·nu·kah (*var. of*
  Hanukkah)

cha·os

cha·ot·ic

cha·ot·i·cal·ly

chap, *v.* chapped,
  chap·ping

chap·ar·ral

chap·book

cha·peau, *n. pl.*
  cha·peaus *or*
  cha·peaux

chap·el

chap·er·on *or*
  chap·er·one, *v.*
  chap·er·oned,
  chap·er·on·ing

chap·lain

chap·let

chap·ter

char, *v.* charred,
  char·ring

char·ac·ter

char·ac·ter·is·tic

char·ac·ter·is·ti·cal·ly

char·ac·ter·iza·tion

char·ac·ter·ize, *v.*
  char·ac·ter·ized,
  char·ac·ter·iz·ing

cha·rade

char·coal

Char·don·nay *or*
  char·don·nay

charge, *v.* charged,
  charg·ing

charge·able

charge card

char·gé d'af·faires,
  n. pl. char·gés
  d'af·faires

char·ger

chari·ly

chari·ness

char·i·ot

char·i·o·teer

cha·ris·ma (*occas.*
  charism), *n. pl.*
  cha·ris·ma·ta
  (*occas.*
  charisms)

char·is·mat·ic

char·i·ta·ble

char·i·ta·ble·ness

char·i·ty, *n. pl.*
  char·i·ties

char·la·tan

Charles

Charles·ton

char·ley horse

Char·lotte
  (PERSON'S
  NAME)

char·lotte
  (DESSERT)

char·lotte russe

charm·er

charm·ing

char·nel

char·ter

char·treuse

char·wom·an, *n. pl.*
  char·wom·en

chary, *adj.*
  char·i·er,
  char·i·est

chase, *v.* chased,
  chas·ing

chas·er

chasm

chas·sis, *n. pl.*
  chas·sis

chaste

chas·ten

chas·tise, *v.*
  chas·tised,
  chas·tis·ing

chas·tise·ment

chas·ti·ty

cha·su·ble

chat, *v.* chat·ted,
  chat·ting

châ·teau, *n. pl.*
  châ·teaus *or*
  châ·teaux

cha·teau·bri·and

chat·e·laine

Chat·ta·noo·ga

chat·tel

chat·ter

chat·ter·box

chat·ty, *adj.*
  chat·ti·er,
  chat·ti·est

chauf·feur

chau·vin·ism

chau·vin·ist

chau·vin·is·tic

chau·vin·is·ti·cal·ly

cheap
  (INEXPENSIVE)
  (*see also* cheep)

cheap·en

cheap·skate

cheat·er

check·book

check·er

check·ered

check·er·board

check·ers

check·list

check·mate, *v.*
  check·mat·ed,
  check·mat·ing

check·off, *n.*

check off, *v.*

check·out, *n.*

check out, *v.*

check·point

check·room

check·up, *n.*

check up, *v.*

ched·dar

cheek·bone

cheek·i·ly

cheek·i·ness

cheeky, *adj.*
  cheek·i·er,
  cheek·i·est

cheep (SOUND)
  (*see also* cheap)

cheer·ful

cheer·ful·ly

cheer·ful·ness

cheer·i·ly

cheer·i·ness

cheer·lead·er

cheer·less

cheer·less·ly

cheer·less·ness

cheery

cheese·burg·er

cheese·cake

cheese·cloth

cheesy, *adj.*
  chees·i·er,
  chees·i·est

chee·tah

chef d'oeu·vre, *n.*
  pl. chefs
  d'oeu·vre

Chel·sea

chem·i·cal

chem·i·cal·ly

chem·i·lu·mi·nes·cence

chem·i·lu·mi·nes·cent

che·mise

chem·ist

chem·is·try, *n. pl.*
  chem·is·tries

che·mo·ther·a·py,
  n. pl.
  che·mo·ther·a·pies

che·nille

che·nin blanc

cher·ish

Cher·o·kee, *n. pl.*
  Cher·o·kee *or*
  Cher·o·kees

che·root

cher·ry, *n. pl.*
  cher·ries

cher·ry bomb

cher·ry picker

cher·ry·stone

Che·ryl

cher·ub, *n. pl.*
  cher·u·bim *or*
  cher·ubs

Ches·a·peake

Chesh·ire

chess·board

ches·ter·field

chest·nut

chesty, *adj.*
  chest·i·er,
  chest·i·est

che·va·lier

chev·i·ot

chev·ron

chewy

Chey·enne

Chi·an·ti

Chi·a·pas

chiar·oscu·ro, *n. pl.*
  chiar·oscu·ros

chic

Chi·ca·go

chi·ca·ner·y, n. pl.
chi·ca·ner·ies

Chi·ca·no

chi·chi

chick

chick·a·dee

chick·en

chick·en·heart·ed

chick·en·pox

chick·pea

chick·weed

chic·o·ry

chide, v. chid or
chid·ed, chid or
chid·den or
chid·ed,
chid·ing

chief·ly

chief·tain

chif·fon

chif·fo·nier

chig·ger

chi·gnon

Chi·hua·hua

chil·blain

child, n. pl.
chil·dren

child·bear·ing

child·birth

child·hood

child·ish

child·like

Chi·le

chile, see chili

Chil·ean

chili or chile or
chil·li, n. pl.

chil·ies or chil·es
or chil·lies

Chili con car·ne

chili sauce

chill·er

chill·i·ness

chilly, adj.
chill·i·er,
chill·i·est

chime, v. chimed,
chim·ing

chi·me·ra (occas.
chi·mae·ra)

chi·me·ric

chi·me·ri·cal

chi·mi·chan·ga

chim·ney, n. pl.
chim·neys

chim·pan·zee

chin, v. chinned,
chin·ning

Chi·na

Chi·na·town

chin·chil·la

Chi·nese, n. pl.
Chi·nese

chi·no, n. pl.
chi·nos

chintz

chintzy, adv.
chintz·i·er,
chintz·i·est

chip, v. chipped,
chip·ping

chip·munk

chip·per

chi·rog·ra·pher

chi·ro·graph·ic

chi·rog·ra·phy

chi·ro·man·cy

chi·rop·o·dist

chi·rop·o·dy

chi·ro·prac·tic

chi·ro·prac·tor

chis·el, v. chis·eled
or chis·elled,
chis·el·ing or
chis·el·ling

chis·el·er or
chis·el·ler

chit·chat

chit·ter·lings or
chit·lins

chi·val·ric

chiv·al·rous

chiv·al·rous·ly

chiv·al·rous·ness

chiv·al·ry

chlo·ral

chlor·dane

chlo·ric

chlo·ride

chlo·ri·nate, v.
chlo·ri·nat·ed,
chlo·ri·nat·ing

chlo·ri·na·tion

chlo·rine

chlo·ro·form

chlo·ro·phyll

chock·a·block

chock-full or
chock·full

choc·o·hol·ic

choc·o·late

choir

choir·boy

choir loft

choir·mas·ter

choke, v. choked,
  chok·ing

choke·ber·ry, n. pl.
  choke·ber·ries

chok·er

cho·ler (ANGER)

chol·era (DISEASE)

cho·ler·ic

cho·les·ter·ol

choose, v. chose,
  chos·en, choos·ing

choos·er

choosy or
  choo·sey, adj.
  choos·i·er,
  choos·i·est

chop, v. chopped,
  chop·ping

chop·house

chop·per

chop·pi·ly

chop·pi·ness

chop·py, adj.
  chop·pi·er,
  chop·pi·est

chop·stick

chop su·ey

cho·ral (OF A
  CHOIR)

cho·rale (HYMN,
  GROUP OF
  SINGERS)

cho·ral·ly

chord (MUSIC) (see
  also cord)

chore

cho·rea

cho·reo·graph

cho·re·og·raph·er

cho·reo·graph·ic

cho·reo·graph·i·cal·ly

cho·re·og·ra·phy, n.
  pl.
  cho·re·og·ra·phies

cho·ris·ter

cho·ri·zo, n. pl.
  cho·ri·zos

chor·tle, v.
  chor·tled,
  chor·tling

cho·rus

cho·sen

chow chow (DOG)

chow·chow
  (RELISH)

chow·der

chow·der·head

chow mein

chrism

chris·ten

Chris·ten·dom

chris·ten·ing

Chris·tian

Chris·tian·i·ty

Chris·tian·ize, v.
  Chris·tian·ized,
  Chris·tian·iz·ing

Chris·ti·na

Chris·tine

Christ·mas

Christ·mas·tide

Chris·to·pher

chro·mat·ic

chro·ma·tic·i·ty

chro·mato·graph·ic

chro·mato·graph·i·cal·ly

chro·ma·tog·ra·phy

chrome

chro·mic

chro·mite

chro·mi·um

chro·mo·som·al

chro·mo·some

chron·ic

chron·i·cal·ly

chron·i·cle, v.
  chron·i·cled,
  chron·i·cling

chron·i·cler

chro·no·graph

chro·no·log·i·cal

chro·nol·o·gist

chro·nol·o·gy, n. pl.
  chro·nol·o·gies

chro·nom·e·ter

chrys·a·lis, n. pl.
  chry·sal·i·des or
  chrys·a·lis·es

chry·san·the·mum

chrys·o·lite

chub·bi·ness

chub·by, adj.
  chub·bi·er,
  chub·bi·est

chuck·hole

chuck·le, v.
  chuck·led,
  chuck·ling

chug, v. chugged,
  chug·ging

chuk·ka (BOOT)

chuk·ker (POLO) or
  chuk·kar or
  chuk·ka

chum, v.

chummed,
chum·ming

chum·mi·ly

chum·mi·ness

chum·my, *adj.*
chum·mi·er,
chum·mi·est

chunky, *adj.*
chunk·i·er,
chunk·i·est

church·go·er

church·less

church·ly

church·man, *n. pl.*
church·men

church·war·den

church·wom·an, *n. pl.*
church·wom·en

church·yard

churl

churl·ish

churl·ish·ly

churl·ish·ness

churn

chute

chut·ney, *n. pl.*
chut·neys

chutz·pah (*occas.*
chutz·pa)

ci·ca·da, *n. pl.*
ci·ca·das (*occas.*
ci·ca·dae)

cic·a·trix *n. pl.*
cic·a·tri·ces

ci·ce·ro·ne

ci·der

ci·gar

cig·a·rette (*occas.*
cig·a·ret)

Cin·cin·nati

cinc·ture

cin·der

cin·e·ma

cin·e·mat·ic

cin·e·mat·o·graph

cin·e·ma·tog·raph·er

cin·e·mat·o·graph·ic

cin·e·ma·tog·ra·phy

cin·er·ar·i·um, *n.
pl.* cin·er·ar·ia

cin·na·bar

cin·na·mon

ciop·pi·no

ci·pher

cir·ca

cir·ca·di·an

cir·cle, *v.* cir·cled,
cir·cling

cir·clet

cir·cuit

cir·cu·i·tous

cir·cu·i·tous·ly

cir·cu·i·tous·ness

cir·cuit·ry, *n. pl.*
cir·cuit·ries

cir·cu·ity

cir·cu·lar

cir·cu·lar·i·ty

cir·cu·lar·iza·tion

cir·cu·lar·ize, *v.*
cir·cu·lar·ized,
cir·cu·lar·iz·ing

cir·cu·late, *v.*
cir·cu·lat·ed,
cir·cu·lat·ing

cir·cu·la·tion

cir·cu·la·to·ry

cir·cum·am·bu·late,
v.
cir·cum·am·bu·lat·ed,
cir·cum·am·bu·lat·ing

cir·cum·cise, *v.*
cir·cum·cised,
cir·cum·cis·ing

cir·cum·ci·sion

cir·cum·fer·ence

cir·cum·flex

cir·cum·lo·cu·tion

cir·cum·lu·nar

cir·cum·nav·i·gate,
v.
cir·cum·nav·i·gat·ed,
cir·cum·nav·i·gat·ing

cir·cum·nav·i·ga·tion

cir·cum·po·lar

cir·cum·scribe, *v.*
cir·cum·scribed,
cir·cum·scrib·ing

cir·cum·scrip·tion

cir·cum·spect

cir·cum·spec·tion

cir·cum·stance, *v.*
cir·cum·stanced,
cir·cum·stanc·ing

cir·cum·stan·tial

cir·cum·stan·tial·ly

cir·cum·vent

cir·cum·ven·tion

cir·cus

cir·rho·sis, *n. pl.*
cir·rho·ses

cir·rhot·ic

cir·ro·cu·mu·lus

cir·ro·stra·tus

cir·rus

cis·lu·nar

Cis·ter·cian (MONK)

cis·tern (WELL)

cit·a·del

ci·ta·tion

cite, v. cit·ed, cit·ing

cit·i·fied

cit·i·zen

cit·i·zen·ry, n. pl. cit·i·zen·ries

cit·i·zen·ship

ci·trate

cit·ric acid

cit·ron

cit·ro·nel·la

cit·rus

city, n. pl. cit·ies

city-state

city·wide

civ·et

civ·ic

civ·ics

civ·il

ci·vil·ian

ci·vil·i·ty, n. pl. ci·vil·i·ties

civ·i·li·za·tion

civ·i·lize, v. civ·i·lized, civ·i·liz·ing

civ·il·ly

claim·ant

clair·voy·ance

clair·voy·ant

clam·bake

clam·ber

clam·mi·ly

clam·mi·ness

clam·my, adj. clam·mi·er, clam·mi·est

clam·or

clam·or·ous

clam·or·ous·ly

clam·or·ous·ness

clam·shell

clan·des·tine

clan·des·tine·ly

clang·or

clang·or·ous

clang·or·ous·ly

clan·nish

clans·man, n. pl. clans·men

clans·wom·an, n. pl. clans·wom·en

clap, v. clapped, clap·ping

clap·board

clap·per

clap·trap

claque (ADMIRING FOLLOWERS) (see also clique)

claret

clar·i·fi·ca·tion

clar·i·fy, v. clar·i·fied, clar·i·fy·ing

clar·i·net

clar·i·net·ist or clar·i·net·tist

clar·i·on

clar·i·ty

clas·sic

clas·si·cal

clas·si·cal·ly

clas·si·cism

clas·si·cist

clas·si·fi·able

clas·si·fi·ca·tion

clas·si·fy, v. clas·si·fied, clas·si·fy·ing

class·mate

class·room

classy, adj. class·i·er, class·i·est

clat·ter

clause

claus·tro·pho·bia

claus·tro·pho·bic

clav·i·chord

clav·i·cle

cla·vier

clay·ey

Clay·ma·tion℠

clay·more

clean-cut

clean·er

clean·li·ness

clean·ly, adj. clean·li·er, clean·li·est

clean·ness

cleanse, v. cleansed, cleans·ing

cleans·er

clean·shav·en

clear·ance

clear-cut

clear·eyed

clear·head·ed

clear·head·ed·ly

clear·head·ed·ness

clear·ing

clear·ing·house

cleav·age

cleave (CLING), v.
cleaved or clove
(occas. clave),
cleaved,
cleav·ing

cleave (SPLIT), v.
cleaved
(occas. cleft or
clove), cleaved
(occas. cleft or
clo·ven),
cleav·ing

cleav·er

cle·ma·tis

clem·en·cy, n. pl.
clem·en·cies

clem·ent

clere·sto·ry, n. pl.
clere·sto·ries

cler·gy, n. pl.
cler·gies

cler·gy·man, n. pl.
cler·gy·men

cler·gy·wom·an, n.
pl.
cler·gy·wom·en

cler·ic

cler·i·cal

cler·i·cal·ism

Cleve·land

clev·er

clev·er·ly

clev·er·ness

clew or clue
(YARN) (see
also clue)

cli·ché (occas.
cli·che)

cli·ent

cli·en·tele

cliff dwel·ler

cliff-hanger

cli·mac·tic (OF A
CLIMAX) (see
also climatic)

cli·mate

cli·mat·ic
(WEATHER) (see
also climactic)

cli·ma·to·log·i·cal

cli·ma·tol·o·gist

cli·ma·tol·o·gy

cli·max

climbed

climb·er

cling, v. clung,
cling·ing

clin·ic

clin·i·cal

clin·i·cal·ly

cli·ni·cian

clin·ker

clip, v. clipped,
clip·ping

clip·board

clip·per

clip·ping

clip·sheet

clique (EXCLUSIVE
GROUP) (see
also claque)

cli·to·ral or cli·tor·ic

cli·to·ris, n. pl.
cli·to·ri·des

cloche

clock·wise

clock·work

clod·hop·per

clog, v. clogged,
clog·ging

cloi·son·né

clois·ter

clone, v. cloned,
clon·ing

close, adj. clos·er,
clos·est

close, v. closed,
clos·ing

closed-cap·tioned

closed-end

close·fist·ed

close·fit·ting

close-knit

close·ly

close·mouthed

close·ness

clos·et

close-up

clos·ing, n.

clo·sure (CLOSING)
(see also
cloture)

clot, v. clot·ted,
clot·ting

cloth (FABRIC) (see
also clothe)

clothe (TO DRESS), *v.* clothed *or* clad, cloth·ing (*see also* cloth)

clothes·horse

clothes·line

clothes·pin

cloth·ier

cloth·ing

clo·ture (END OF DEBATE) (*see also* closure)

cloud·burst

cloud·i·ly

cloud·i·ness

cloudy, *adj.* cloud·i·er, cloud·i·est

clo·ver

clo·ver·leaf, *n. pl.* clo·ver·leafs *or* clo·ver·leaves

clown·ish

club, *v.* clubbed, club·bing

club·foot, *n. pl.* club·feet

club·house

clue (EVIDENCE) (*see also* clew)

clum·si·ly

clum·si·ness

clum·sy, *adj.* clum·si·er, clum·si·est

clus·ter

clutch

clut·ter

coach·man, *n. pl.* coach·men

co·ad·ju·tant

co·ad·ju·tor

co·ag·u·lant

co·ag·u·late, *v.* co·ag·u·lat·ed, co·ag·u·lat·ing

co·ag·u·la·tion

co·ag·u·lum

Coa·hui·la

co·alesce, *v.* co·alesced, co·alesc·ing

co·ales·cence

co·ales·cent

coal·field

co·ali·tion

coarse (ROUGH), *adj.* coars·er, coars·est (*see also* course)

coarse·ly

coarse·ness

coast·al

coast·er

coast·guard

coast·line

coat·ing

coat·tail

co·au·thor

coax

co·ax·i·al

co·balt

cob·ble, *v.* cob·bled, cob·bling

cob·ble·stone

co·bra

cob·web

co·ca (SHRUB, LEAF) (*see also* cacao, cocoa)

Co·ca-Co·la℗

co·caine

coc·cus, *n. pl.* coc·ci

coc·cyx, *n. pl.* coc·cy·ges *or* coc·cyx·es

co·chi·neal

co·chlea, *n. pl.* co·chle·as *or* co·chle·ae

cock·ade

cock·a·too, *n. pl.* cock·a·toos

cock·crow

cock·er·el

cock·er span·iel

cock·eyed

cock·fight

cock·i·ly

cock·i·ness

cock·le, *v.* cock·led, cock·ling

cock·le·shell

cock·ney, *n. pl.* cock·neys

cock·pit

cock·roach, *n. pl.* cock·roach·es

cocks·comb (FLOWER) (*see also* coxcomb)

cock·sure

cock·tail

cocky, *adj.*

cock·i·er,
cock·i·est

co·coa (POWDER,
DRINK) (see
also cacao, coca)

co·co·nut

co·coon

co·da

cod·dle, v.
cod·dled,
cod·dling

code, v. cod·ed,
cod·ing

co·deine

co·dex, n. pl.
co·di·ces

cod·fish

cod·ger

cod·i·cil

cod·i·fi·ca·tion

cod·i·fy, v.
cod·i·fied,
cod·i·fy·ing

cod·piece

coed

co·ed·u·ca·tion

co·ed·u·ca·tion·al

co·ef·fi·cient

co·equal

co·erce, v.
co·erced,
co·erc·ing

co·er·cion

co·er·cive

co·eval

co·evo·lu·tion

co·ex·ist

co·ex·is·tence

co·ex·ten·sive

cof·fee break

cof·fee cake

cof·fee·house

cof·fee·pot

cof·fer

cof·fer·dam

cof·fin

co·gen·cy

co·gen·er·a·tion

co·gent

cog·i·tate, v.
cog·i·tat·ed,
cog·i·tat·ing

cog·i·ta·tion

co·gnac

cog·nate

cog·ni·tion

cog·ni·tive

cog·ni·zance

cog·ni·zant

cog·no·men

cog·wheel

co·hab·it

co·hab·it·ant

co·hab·i·ta·tion

co·heir

co·here, v.
co·hered,
co·her·ing

co·her·ence

co·her·ent

co·her·ent·ly

co·he·sion

co·he·sive

co·he·sive·ly

co·he·sive·ness

co·hort

coif·feur (MALE
HAIRDRESSER)

coif·fure (HAIR
STYLE), v.
coif·fured,
coif·fur·ing

coin·age

co·in·cide, v.
co·in·cid·ed,
co·in·cid·ing

co·in·ci·dence

co·in·ci·dent

co·in·ci·den·tal

co·in·ci·den·tal·ly

coin-op·er·at·ed

co·in·sur·ance

co·in·sure, v.
co·in·sured,
co·in·sur·ing

co·in·sur·er

co·ition

co·itus

co·la

col·an·der (SIEVE)
(see also
calendar,
calender)

cold, adj. cold·er,
cold·est

cold-blood·ed

cold·ly

cold·ness

Cole·man® (LAMP,
LANTERN,
STOVE)

cole·slaw

col·ic

col·icky

Co·li·ma

col·i·se·um
(STADIUM) (*see
also* Colosseum)

co·li·tis

col·lab·o·rate, *v.*
col·lab·o·rat·ed,
col·lab·o·rat·ing

col·lab·o·ra·tion

col·lab·o·ra·tor

col·lage (ART,
ASSEMBLY) (*see
also* college)

col·lapse, *v.*
col·lapsed,
col·laps·ing

col·laps·ible

col·lar

col·lar·bone

col·lard

col·late, *v.*
col·lat·ed,
col·lat·ing

col·lat·er·al

col·la·tion

col·la·tor

col·league

col·lect

col·lect·ed

col·lect·ible *or*
col·lect·able

col·lec·tion

col·lec·tive

col·lec·tive·ly

col·lec·tiv·ism

col·lec·tiv·is·tic

col·lec·tiv·iza·tion

col·lec·tiv·ize, *v.*
col·lec·tiv·ized,
col·lec·tiv·iz·ing

col·lec·tor

col·leen

col·lege (SCHOOL)
(*see also*
collage)

col·le·gi·al·ity

col·le·gian

col·le·gi·ate

col·le·gi·um, *n. pl.*
col·le·gia *or*
col·le·gi·ums

col·lide, *v.*
col·lid·ed,
col·lid·ing

col·lid·er

col·lie

col·lier

col·liery, *n. pl.*
col·lier·ies

col·li·sion

col·lo·ca·tion

col·lo·di·on

col·loid

col·loi·dal

col·lo·qui·al

col·lo·qui·al·ism

col·lo·qui·al·ly

col·lo·qui·um, *n. pl.*
col·lo·qui·ums
or col·lo·quia

col·lo·quy, *n. pl.*
col·lo·quies

col·lu·sion

col·lu·sive

Co·logne (CITY)

co·logne
(PERFUME)

Co·lom·bia

(COUNTRY) (*see
also* Columbia)

Co·lom·bi·an

Co·lón (CITY)

co·lon (INTESTINE,
POETRY), *n. pl.*
co·lons *or* co·la

co·lon
(PUNCTUATION
MARK), *n. pl.*
co·lons

co·lon (MONEY), *n.
pl.* co·lo·nes

col·o·nel

co·lo·ni·al

co·lo·ni·al·ism

co·lo·nist

col·o·ni·za·tion

col·o·nize, *v.*
col·o·nized,
col·o·niz·ing

col·o·niz·er

col·on·nade

col·o·ny, *n. pl.*
col·o·nies

col·o·phon

col·or

Col·o·ra·dan

Col·o·ra·do

col·or·a·tion

col·or·a·tu·ra

col·or·blind

col·or·cast

col·ored

col·or·fast

col·or·fast·ness

col·or·ful

col·or·iza·tion

col·o·rize, v.
  col·o·rized,
  col·o·riz·ing

col·or·less

co·los·sal

Col·os·se·um
  (ROMAN
  AMPHITHEATER)
  (see also
  coliseum)

co·los·sus

co·los·to·my, n. pl.
  co·los·to·mies

colt·ish

Co·lum·bia (CITY,
  DISTRICT,
  RIVER) (see also
  Colombia)

Co·lum·bi·an

col·um·bine

Co·lum·bus

col·umn

co·lum·nar

col·um·nist

co·ma

co·ma·tose

com·bat, v.
  com·bat·ed or
  com·bat·ted,
  com·bat·ing or
  com·bat·ting

com·bat·ant

com·bat·ive

comb·er

com·bi·na·tion

com·bine, v.
  com·bined,
  com·bin·ing

comb·ings

com·bo, n. pl.
  com·bos

com·bus·ti·ble

com·bus·tion

come, v. came,
  come, com·ing

come·back, n.

come back, v.

co·me·di·an (masc.
  or fem.) (see
  also
  comedienne)

co·me·dic

co·me·di·enne
  (fem. only)

come·down, n.

come down, v.

com·e·dy, n. pl.
  com·e·dies

come·li·ness

come·ly, adj.
  come·li·er,
  come·li·est

come-on, n.

come on, v.

co·mes·ti·ble

com·et

come·up·pance

com·fit

com·fort

com·fort·able

com·fort·ably

com·fort·er

com·fy, adj.
  com·fi·er,
  com·fi·est

com·ic

com·i·cal

com·ic strip

com·i·ty, n. pl.
  com·i·ties

com·ma

com·mand

com·man·dant

com·man·deer

com·man·der

com·mand·ment

com·man·do, n. pl.
  com·man·dos or
  com·man·does

com·mem·o·rate, v.
  com·mem·o·rat·ed,
  com·mem·o·rat·ing

com·mem·o·ra·tion

com·mem·o·ra·tive

com·mence, v.
  com·menced,
  com·menc·ing

com·mence·ment

com·mend

com·mend·able

com·men·da·tion

com·men·su·ra·bil·i·ty

com·men·su·ra·ble

com·men·su·rate

com·ment

com·men·tary, n.
  pl.
  com·men·tar·ies

com·men·ta·tor

com·merce

com·mer·cial

com·mer·cial·ism

com·mer·cial·iza·tion

com·mer·cial·ize, v.
  com·mer·cial·ized,
  com·mer·cial·iz·ing

com·min·gle, v.

com·min·gled,
com·min·gling

com·mis·er·ate, *v.*
  com·mis·er·at·ed,
  com·mis·er·at·ing

com·mis·er·a·tion

com·mis·sar

com·mis·sar·i·at

com·mis·sary, *n. pl.*
  com·mis·sar·ies

com·mis·sion

com·mis·sion·er

com·mit, *v.*
  com·mit·ted,
  com·mit·ting

com·mit·ment

com·mit·tal

com·mit·tee

com·mit·tee·man,
  n. pl.
  com·mit·tee·men

com·mit·tee·wom·an,
  n. pl.
  com·mit·tee·wom·en

com·mode

com·mo·di·ous

com·mo·di·ous·ly

com·mo·di·ous·ness

com·mod·i·ty, *n. pl.*
  com·mod·i·ties

com·mo·dore

com·mon

com·mon·al·i·ty
  (SIMILARITY,
  COMMONNESS),
  n. pl.
  com·mon·al·i·ties

com·mon·al·ty
  (GROUP,
  COMMON

PEOPLE), *n. pl.*
  com·mon·al·ties

com·mon·er

com·mon law, *n.*

com·mon-law
  mar·riage

com·mon·ly

com·mon·ness

com·mon·place

com·mon sense, *n.*

com·mon·sense,
  adj.

com·mon·sen·si·cal

com·mon·weal
  (PUBLIC GOOD)

com·mon·wealth
  (REPUBLIC,
  POLITICAL UNIT)

Com·mon·wealth
  of In·de·pen·dent
  States (*formerly*
  Union of Soviet
  Socialist
  Republics)

com·mo·tion

com·mu·nal

com·mune, *n.*

com·mu·nal

com·mune, *n.*

com·mune, *v.*
  com·muned,
  com·mun·ing

com·mu·ni·ca·ble

com·mu·ni·cant

com·mu·ni·cate, *v.*
  com·mu·ni·cat·ed,
  com·mu·ni·cat·ing

com·mu·ni·ca·tion

com·mu·ni·ca·tive

Com·mu·nion

(CHURCH
  SACRAMENT)

com·mu·nion
  (SHARING)

com·mu·ni·qué

com·mu·nism

com·mu·nist

com·mu·nis·tic

com·mu·nis·ti·cal·ly

com·mu·ni·ty, *n. pl.*
  com·mu·ni·ties

com·mu·nize, *v.*
  com·mu·nized,
  com·mu·niz·ing

com·mut·able

com·mu·ta·tion

com·mu·ta·tor

com·mute, *v.*
  com·mut·ed,
  com·mut·ing

com·mut·er

com·pact

com·pact·ly

com·pact·ness

com·pac·tor

com·pan·ion

com·pan·ion·able

com·pan·ion·ship

com·pan·ion·way

com·pa·ny, *n. pl.*
  com·pa·nies

com·pa·ra·ble

com·par·a·tive

com·par·a·tive·ly

com·par·a·tive·ness

com·pare, *v.*
  com·pared,
  com·par·ing

com·par·i·son

com·part·ment

com·part·men·tal·ize, v.
com·part·men·tal·ized, com·part·men·tal·iz·ing

com·pass

com·pas·sion

com·pas·sion·ate

com·pat·i·bil·i·ty

com·pat·i·ble

com·pa·tri·ot

Com·pa·zine®

com·pel, v.
com·pelled, com·pel·ling

com·pen·di·um, n. pl.
com·pen·di·ums or com·pen·dia

com·pen·sate, v.
com·pen·sat·ed, com·pen·sat·ing

com·pen·sa·tion

com·pen·sa·to·ry

com·pete, v.
com·pet·ed, com·pet·ing

com·pe·tence

com·pe·ten·cy, n. pl.
com·pe·ten·cies

com·pe·tent

com·pe·ti·tion

com·pet·i·tive

com·pet·i·tor

com·pi·la·tion

com·pile, v.

com·piled, com·pil·ing

com·pil·er

com·pla·cence

com·pla·cen·cy

com·pla·cent (SATISFIED) (see also complaisant)

com·plain

com·plain·ant

com·plaint

com·plai·sance

com·plai·sant (OBLIGING) (see also complacent)

com·ple·ment (COMPLETE) (see also compliment)

com·ple·men·ta·ry

com·plete, v.
com·plet·ed, com·plet·ing

com·plete·ness

com·ple·tion

com·plex

com·plex·ion

com·plex·i·ty, n. pl.
com·plex·i·ties

com·pli·ance

com·pli·an·cy

com·pli·ant

com·pli·cate, v.
com·pli·cat·ed, com·pli·cat·ing

com·pli·ca·tion

com·plic·i·ty

com·pli·er

com·pli·ment (FLATTERY) (see also complement)

com·pli·men·ta·ry

com·ply, v.
com·plied, com·ply·ing

com·po·nent

com·port

com·port·ment

com·pose, v.
com·posed, com·pos·ing

com·pos·er

com·pos·ite

com·po·si·tion

com·pos·i·tor

com·post

com·po·sure

com·pote

com·pound

com·pre·hend

com·pre·hen·si·bil·i·ty

com·pre·hen·si·ble

com·pre·hen·sion

com·pre·hen·sive

com·pre·hen·sive·ly

com·pre·hen·sive·ness

com·press

com·pressed

com·pres·sion

com·pres·sor

com·prise, v.
com·prised, com·pris·ing

com·pro·mise, v.
com·pro·mised, com·pro·mis·ing

comp·trol·ler
com·pul·sion
com·pul·sive
com·pul·sive·ly
com·pul·sive·ness
com·pul·so·ry
com·punc·tion
com·pu·ta·tion
com·pute, *v.*
  com·put·ed,
  com·put·ing
com·put·er
com·put·er·ese
com·put·er·iza·tion
com·put·er·ize, *v.*
  com·put·er·ized,
  com·put·er·iz·ing
com·rade
com·rade·ly
com·rade·ship
con, *v.* conned,
  con·ning
con amo·re
con brio
con·cat·e·na·tion
con·cave, *v.*
  con·caved,
  con·cav·ing
con·cav·i·ty
con·ceal
con·ceal·ment
con·cede, *v.*
  con·ced·ed,
  con·ced·ing
con·ceit
con·ceit·ed
con·ceiv·able
con·ceiv·ably

con·ceive, *v.*
  con·ceived,
  con·ceiv·ing
con·cel·e·brant
con·cel·e·brate, *v.*
  con·cel·e·brat·ed,
  con·cel·e·brat·ing
con·cen·trate, *v.*
  con·cen·trat·ed,
  con·cen·trat·ing
con·cen·tra·tion
con·cen·tric
con·cen·tric·al·ly
con·cen·tric·i·ty
con·cept
con·cep·tion
con·cep·tual
con·cep·tu·al·iza·tion
con·cep·tu·al·ize, *v.*
  con·cep·tu·al·ized,
  con·cep·tu·al·iz·ing
con·cep·tu·al·ly
con·cern, *v.*
  con·cerned,
  con·cern·ing
con·cert
con·cert·ed
con·cer·ti·na
con·cert·mas·ter *or*
  con·cert·meis·ter
con·cer·to, *n. pl.*
  con·cer·ti *or*
  con·cer·tos
con·ces·sion
con·ces·sion·naire
conch, *n. pl.*
  conchs *or*
  conch·es
con·ci·erge
con·cil·i·ate, *v.*

con·cil·i·at·ed,
  con·cil·i·at·ing
con·cil·i·a·tion
con·cil·ia·to·ry
con·cise
con·cise·ly
con·cise·ness
con·ci·sion
con·clave
con·clude, *v.*
  con·clud·ed,
  con·clud·ing
con·clu·sion
con·clu·sive
con·clu·sive·ly
con·clu·sive·ness
con·coct
con·coc·tion
con·com·i·tant
con·cord
con·cor·dance
con·cor·dant
  (AGREEING), *adj.*
con·cor·dat
  (ECCLESIASTICAL
  AGREEMENT),
  n.
con·course
con·crete
con·cu·bi·nage
con·cu·bine
con·cu·pis·cence
con·cur, *v.*
  con·curred,
  con·cur·ring
con·cur·rence
con·cur·rent
con·cur·rent·ly

con·cus·sion

con·demn (DOOM)
(see also
contemn)

con·dem·na·tion

con·dem·na·to·ry

con·den·sa·tion

con·de·scend

con·de·scend·ing·ly

con·de·scen·sion

con·dense, v.
con·densed,
con·dens·ing

con·dens·er

con·di·ment

con·di·tion

con·di·tion·al

con·di·tion·al·ly

con·di·tioned

con·do
(CONDOMINIUM),
n. pl. con·dos

con·do·lence

con·dom

con·do·min·i·um

con·done, v.
con·doned,
con·don·ing

con·dor

con·du·cive

con·du·cive·ness

con·duct

con·duc·tance

con·duc·tion

con·duc·tive

con·duc·tiv·i·ty

con·duc·tor

con·duit

co·ney, n. pl.
co·neys

con·fab·u·la·tion

con·fec·tion

con·fec·tion·er

con·fec·tion·ery, n.
pl.
con·fec·tion·er·ies

con·fed·er·a·cy, n.
pl.
con·fed·er·a·cies

con·fed·e·rate, v.
con·fed·e·rat·ed,
con·fed·e·rat·ing

con·fed·er·a·tion

con·fer, v.
con·ferred,
con·fer·ring

con·fer·ee

con·fer·ence

con·fess

con·fess·ed·ly

con·fes·sion

con·fes·sion·al

con·fes·sor

con·fet·ti

con·fi·dant
(FRIEND) (see
also confident)

con·fide, v.
con·fid·ed,
con·fid·ing

con·fi·dence

con·fi·dent (SURE)
(see also
confidant)

con·fi·den·tial

con·fi·den·tial·ly

con·fi·dent·ly

con·fid·ing

con·fig·u·ra·tion

con·fine, v.
con·fined,
con·fin·ing

con·fine·ment

con·firm (VERIFY)
(see also
conform)

con·fir·ma·tion
(VERIFICATION)
(see also
conformation)

con·fir·ma·to·ry

con·firmed

con·fis·cate, v.
con·fis·cat·ed,
con·fis·cat·ing

con·fis·ca·tion

con·fis·ca·to·ry

con·fla·gra·tion

con·flict

con·flu·ence

con·flu·ent

con·form (MAKE
SIMILAR,
OBEY) (see also
confirm)

con·form·able

con·for·mance

con·for·ma·tion
(ARRANGEMENT)
(see also
confirmation)

con·form·ist

con·for·mi·ty

con·found

con·fra·ter·ni·ty, n.
pl.
con·fra·ter·ni·ties

con·frere

con·front

con·fron·ta·tion

Con·fu·cian·ism

Con·fu·cius

con·fuse, *v.*
  con·fused,
  con·fus·ing

con·fus·ed·ly

con·fu·sion

con·fute, *v.*
  con·fut·ed,
  con·fut·ing

con·ga

con·geal

con·ge·nial

con·gen·i·tal

con·ger

con·ge·ries

con·gest

con·ges·tion

con·ges·tive

con·glom·er·ate, *v.*
  con·glom·er·at·ed,
  con·glom·er·at·ing

con·glom·er·a·tion

Con·go

Con·go·lese

con·grat·u·late, *v.*
  con·grat·u·lat·ed,
  con·grat·u·lat·ing

con·grat·u·la·tion

con·grat·u·la·to·ry

con·gre·gate, *v.*
  con·gre·gat·ed,
  con·gre·gat·ing

con·gre·ga·tion

con·gre·ga·tion·al

con·gre·ga·tion·al·ism

con·gre·ga·tion·al·ist

con·gress

con·gres·sion·al

con·gress·man, *n.*
  pl.
  con·gress·men

con·gress·wom·an,
  n. pl.
  con·gress·wom·en

con·gru·ence

con·gru·en·cy

con·gru·ent

con·gru·ity, *n. pl.*
  con·gru·i·ties

con·gru·ous

con·gru·ous·ly

con·gru·ous·ness

con·ic

con·i·cal

co·ni·fer

co·nif·er·ous

con·jec·tur·al

con·jec·ture, *v.*
  con·jec·tured,
  con·jec·tur·ing

con·join

con·joint

con·ju·gal

con·ju·gate, *v.*
  con·ju·gat·ed,
  con·ju·gat·ing

con·ju·ga·tion

con·junct

con·junc·tion

con·junc·tive

con·junc·ti·vi·tis

con·junc·ture

con·jure, *v.*

con·jured,
con·jur·ing

con·jur·er *or*
con·jur·or

con mo·to

con·nect

con·nect·ed

Con·nect·i·cut

con·nec·tion

con·nec·tive

con·nec·tor (*occas.*
  con·nec·ter)

con·nip·tion

con·niv·ance

con·nive, *v.*
  con·nived,
  con·niv·ing

con·nois·seur

con·no·ta·tion

con·no·ta·tive

con·note, *v.*
  con·not·ed,
  con·not·ing

con·nu·bi·al

con·quer

con·quer·or

con·quest

con·quis·ta·dor, *n.*
  pl.
  con·quis·ta·do·res
  or
  con·quis·ta·dors

con·san·guin·e·ous

con·san·guin·i·ty, *n.*
  pl.
  con·san·guin·i·ties

con·science

con·sci·en·tious

con·sci·en·tious·ly

con·sci·en·tious·ness

con·scious

con·scious·ly

con·scious·ness

con·scious·ness-
  rais·ing

con·script

con·scrip·tion

con·se·crate, *v.*
  con·se·crat·ed,
  con·se·crat·ing

con·se·cra·tion

con·sec·u·tive

con·sec·u·tive·ly

con·sec·u·tive·ness

con·sen·su·al

con·sen·sus

con·sent

con·se·quence

con·se·quent

con·se·quen·tial

con·se·quent·ly

con·ser·van·cy, *n.*
  pl.
  con·ser·van·cies

con·ser·va·tion

con·ser·va·tion·ist

con·ser·va·tism

con·ser·va·tive

con·ser·va·tive·ly

con·ser·va·tor

con·ser·va·to·ry, *n.*
  pl.
  con·ser·va·to·ries

con·serve, *v.*
  con·served,
  con·serv·ing

con·sid·er

con·sid·er·able

con·sid·er·ably

con·sid·er·ate

con·sid·er·a·tion

con·sid·ered

con·sid·er·ing

con·sign

con·sign·ee

con·sign·ment

con·sign·or

con·sist

con·sis·tence

con·sis·ten·cy, *n.*
  pl.
  con·sis·ten·cies

con·sis·tent

con·sis·to·ry

con·so·la·tion

con·sole, *v.*
  con·soled,
  con·sol·ing

con·sol·i·date, *v.*
  con·sol·i·dat·ed,
  con·sol·i·dat·ing

con·sol·i·da·tion

con·som·mé

con·so·nance

con·so·nant

con·so·nan·tal

con·sort

con·sor·tium, *n. pl.*
  con·sor·tia
  (*occas.*
  con·sor·tiums)

con·spic·u·ous

con·spic·u·ous·ly

con·spir·a·cy, *n. pl.*
  con·spir·a·cies

con·spir·a·tor

con·spir·a·to·ri·al

con·spire, *v.*
  con·spired,
  con·spir·ing

con·sta·ble

con·stab·u·lary, *n.*
  pl.
  con·stab·u·lar·ies

con·stan·cy

con·stant

con·stant·ly

con·stel·la·tion

con·ster·na·tion

con·sti·pate, *v.*
  con·sti·pat·ed,
  con·sti·pat·ing

con·sti·pa·tion

con·stit·u·en·cy, *n.*
  pl.
  con·stit·u·en·cies

con·stit·u·ent

con·sti·tute, *v.*
  con·sti·tut·ed,
  con·sti·tut·ing

con·sti·tu·tion

con·sti·tu·tion·al

con·sti·tu·tion·al·i·ty

con·sti·tu·tion·al·ly

con·strain

con·strained

con·straint

con·strict

con·stric·tion

con·stric·tive

con·stric·tor

con·struct

con·struc·tion

con·struc·tion·ist
con·struc·tive
con·struc·tor
con·strue, *v.*
  con·strued,
  con·stru·ing
con·sub·stan·ti·ate,
  v.
  con·sub·stan·ti·at·ed,
  con·sub·stan·ti·at·ing
con·sub·stan·ti·a·tion
con·sul
con·sul·ar
con·sul·ate
con·sult
con·sul·tant
con·sul·ta·tion
con·sul·ta·tive
con·sume, *v.*
  con·sumed,
  con·sum·ing
con·sum·er
con·sum·er·ism
con·sum·er·ist
con·sum·mate, *v.*
  con·sum·mat·ed,
  con·sum·mat·ing
con·sum·ma·tion
con·sump·tion
con·sump·tive
con·tact
con·ta·gion
con·ta·gious
con·ta·gious·ly
con·ta·gious·ness
con·tain
con·tain·er
con·tain·er·iza·tion

con·tain·er·ize, *v.*
  con·tain·er·ized,
  con·tain·er·iz·ing
con·tain·ment
con·tam·i·nant
con·tam·i·nate, *v.*
  con·tam·i·nat·ed,
  con·tam·i·nat·ing
con·tam·i·na·tion
con·temn
  (DESPISE) (*see
  also* condemn)
con·tem·plate, *v.*
  con·tem·plat·ed,
  con·tem·plat·ing
con·tem·pla·tion
con·tem·pla·tive
con·tem·po·ra·ne·ous
con·tem·po·rary, *n.
pl.*
  con·tem·po·rar·ies
con·tempt
con·tempt·ible
con·temp·tu·ous
con·tend
con·tend·er
con·tent
con·tent·ed
con·ten·tion
con·ten·tious
con·ten·tious·ly
con·tent·ment
con·ter·mi·nous *or*
  co·ter·mi·nous
con·test
con·tes·tant
con·text
con·tex·tu·al

con·ti·gu·ity, *n. pl.*
  con·ti·gu·i·ties
con·tig·u·ous
con·tig·u·ous·ly
con·tig·u·ous·ness
con·ti·nence
  (RESTRAINT)
con·ti·nent
  (SHOWING
  RESTRAINT),
  adj.
con·ti·nent (LAND
  MASS), *n.*
con·ti·nen·tal
con·tin·gen·cy, *n.
pl.*
  con·tin·gen·cies
con·tin·gent
con·tin·u·al
con·tin·u·al·ly
con·tin·u·ance
con·tin·u·a·tion
con·tin·ue, *v.*
  con·tin·ued,
  con·tin·u·ing
con·ti·nu·ity, *n. pl.*
  con·ti·nu·ities
con·tin·u·ous
con·tin·u·ous·ly
con·tin·u·ous·ness
con·tin·u·um, *n. pl.*
  con·tin·ua *or*
  con·tin·u·ums
con·tort
con·tor·tion
con·tor·tion·ist
con·tour
con·tra·band
con·tra·cep·tion

con·tra·cep·tive
con·tract
con·trac·tile
con·trac·tion
con·trac·tor
con·trac·tu·al
con·trac·tu·al·ly
con·tra·dict
con·tra·dic·tion
con·tra·dic·to·ry
con·tra·dis·tinc·tion
con·trail
con·tra·in·di·cate, v.
  con·tra·in·di·cat·ed,
  con·tra·in·di·cat·ing
con·tral·to, n. pl.
  con·tral·tos
con·trap·tion
con·tra·pun·tal
con·trar·i·ly
con·trar·i·ness
con·trar·i·wise
con·trary
con·trast
con·tra·vene, v.
  con·tra·vened,
  con·tra·ven·ing
con·tra·ven·tion
con·tre·temps
con·trib·ute, v.
  con·trib·ut·ed,
  con·trib·ut·ing
con·tri·bu·tion
con·trib·u·tor
con·trib·u·to·ry
con·trite
con·trite·ly

con·trite·ness
con·tri·tion
con·triv·ance
con·trive, v.
  con·trived,
  con·triv·ing
con·triv·er
con·trol, v.
  controlled,
  con·trol·ling
con·trol·la·ble
con·trol·ler
con·tro·ver·sial
con·tro·ver·sy, n.
  pl.
  con·tro·ver·sies
con·tro·vert
con·tro·vert·ible
con·tu·ma·cious
con·tu·ma·cy, n. pl.
  con·tu·ma·cies
con·tu·me·li·ous
con·tu·me·ly
con·tu·sion
co·nun·drum
con·va·lesce, v.
  con·va·lesced,
  con·va·lesc·ing
con·va·les·cence
con·va·les·cent
con·vec·tion
con·vene, v.
  con·vened,
  con·ven·ing
con·ve·nience
con·ve·nient
con·vent
con·ven·tion
con·ven·tion·al

con·ven·tion·al·i·ty
con·ven·tion·al·ly
con·ven·tion·eer
con·verge, v.
  con·verged,
  con·verg·ing
con·ver·gence
con·ver·gent
con·ver·sant
con·ver·sa·tion
con·ver·sa·tion·al
con·ver·sa·tion·al·ly
con·ver·sa·tion·al·ist
con·verse, v.
  con·versed,
  con·vers·ing
con·verse·ly
con·ver·sion
con·vert
con·vert·ible
con·vert·or or
  con·vert·er
con·vex
con·vex·i·ty, n. pl.
  con·vex·i·ties
con·vey (MOVE,
  SUGGEST) (see
  also convoy)
con·vey·ance
con·vey·er or
  con·vey·or
con·vict
con·vic·tion
con·vince, v.
  con·vinced,
  con·vinc·ing
con·viv·ial
con·viv·i·al·i·ty
con·viv·ial·ly

con·vo·ca·tion

con·voke, v.
  con·voked,
  con·vok·ing

con·vo·lute, v.
  con·vo·lut·ed,
  con·vo·lut·ing

con·vo·lu·tion

con·voy (n.,
  GROUP; v.,
  ACCOMPANY)
  (see also convey)

con·vulse, v.
  con·vulsed,
  con·vuls·ing

con·vul·sion

con·vul·sive

cook·book

cook·er·y, n. pl.
  cook·er·ies

cook·ie (occas.
  cooky), n. pl.
  cook·ies (see also
  kooky)

cook·out

cook·ware

cool·ant

cool·er

cool·head·ed

coo·lie
  (LABORER), n.

cool·ly or cooly (IN
  A COOL
  MANNER), adv.

cool·ness

coon·skin

coop (CAGE) (see
  also coupé)

co-op
  (COOPERATIVE)
  (occas. coop)

coo·per

coo·per·age

co·op·er·ate, v.
  co·op·er·at·ed,
  co·op·er·at·ing

co·op·er·a·tion

co·op·er·a·tive

co-opt

co·or·di·nate, v.
  co·or·di·nat·ed,
  co·or·di·nat·ing

co·or·di·na·tion

co·or·di·na·tor

coot

cop, v. copped,
  cop·ping

co·part·ner

cope, v. coped,
  cop·ing

Co·pen·hag·en

copi·er

co·pi·lot

cop·ing

co·pi·ous

co·pi·ous·ly

co·pi·ous·ness

cop·per

cop·per·head

co·pra

cop·u·la

cop·u·late, v.
  cop·u·lat·ed,
  cop·u·lat·ing

cop·u·la·tion

cop·u·la·tive

copy, n. pl. cop·ies

copy, v. cop·ied,
  copy·ing

copy·book

copy·cat

copy·desk

copy edit or
  copy·edit

copy ed·i·tor

copy·hold·er

copy·ist

copy·read·er

copy·right

copy·writ·er

coq au vin

co·quet or
  co·quette
  (FLIRT), v.
  co·quet·ted,
  co·quet·ting, (see
  also coquette)

co·que·try, n. pl.
  co·que·tries

co·quette
  (FLIRTATIOUS
  WOMAN) (see
  also coquet)

co·quett·ish

cor·al (COLOR,
  MARINE
  SKELETON) (see
  also corral)

cord (STRING,
  WOOD MEASURE-
  MENT) (see also
  chord)

cord·age

cor·dial

cor·di·al·i·ty

cor·dial·ly

cor·dil·le·ra

cord·less

Cór·do·ba or

Cor·do·va
(PROVINCE,
CITY)

cor·do·ba (MONEY)

cor·don

cor·do·van

cor·du·roy

core

co·res·pon·dent
(LAW), (see also
correspondent)

Cor·ey

Cor·fam℠

co·ri·an·der

cork

cork·age

cork·er

cork·screw

cor·mo·rant

corn·cob

corn·crib

cor·nea

cor·ne·al

cor·ner

cor·ner·back

cor·nered

cor·ner·stone

cor·net (MUSICAL
INSTRUMENT)
(see also
coronet)

corn·flow·er

corn·husk·er

corn·husk·ing

cor·nice

Cor·nish hen

corn·meal

corn·stalk

corn·starch

cor·nu·co·pia

corny, adj.
corn·i·er,
corn·i·est

co·rol·la

cor·ol·lary, n. pl.
cor·ol·lar·ies

co·ro·na

cor·o·nary, n. pl.
co·o·nar·ies

cor·o·na·tion

cor·o·ner

cor·o·net (CROWN),
(see also
cornet)

cor·po·ral

cor·po·rate

cor·po·ra·tion

cor·po·re·al

corps (GROUP OF
PEOPLE), n. pl.
corps (see also
corpse)

corps de bal·let, n.
pl. corps de
bal·let

corpse (dead
body), n. pl.
corpses (see also
corps)

cor·pu·lence

cor·pu·lent

cor·pus, n. pl.
cor·po·ra

Cor·pus Chris·ti

cor·pus·cle

cor·pus·cle

cor·pus de·lic·ti

cor·ral

(ENCLOSURE)
(see also coral)

cor·ral (ENCLOSE),
v. cor·ralled,
cor·ral·ling

cor·rect

cor·rec·tion

cor·rec·tive

cor·rect·ly

cor·rect·ness

cor·re·late, v.
cor·re·lat·ed,
cor·re·lat·ing

cor·re·la·tion

cor·rel·a·tive

cor·res·pond

cor·res·pon·dence

cor·res·pon·dent
(LETTER
WRITER) (see
also
corespondent)

cor·ri·dor

cor·ri·gen·dum, n.
pl. cor·ri·gen·da

cor·rob·o·rate, v.
cor·rob·o·rat·ed,
cor·rob·o·rat·ing

cor·rob·o·ra·tion

cor·rob·o·ra·tive

cor·rob·o·ra·to·ry

cor·rode, v.
cor·rod·ed,
cor·rod·ing

cor·ro·sion

cor·ro·sive

cor·ro·sive·ly

cor·ro·sive·ness

cor·ru·gate, v.

cor·ru·gat·ed,
cor·ru·gat·ing

cor·rupt

cor·rupt·ible

cor·rup·tion

cor·sair

cor·set

Cor·si·ca

cor·tege (*occas.*
cor·tège)

cor·tex, *n. pl.*
cor·ti·ces *or*
cor·tex·es

cor·ti·cal

cor·ti·sone

co·run·dum

cor·vette

co·se·cant

co·sign

co·sig·na·to·ry, *n.
pl.*
co·sig·na·to·ries

co·sine

cos·met·ic

cos·me·ti·cian

cos·me·tol·o·gist

cos·me·tol·o·gy

cos·mic

cos·mog·o·ny, *n. pl.*
cos·mog·o·nies

Cos·mo·line™

cos·mo·log·i·cal

cos·mol·o·gy, *n. pl.*
cos·mol·o·gies

cos·mo·naut

cos·mo·pol·i·tan

cos·mop·o·lite

cos·mos

cos·sack

co·star, *v.*
co·starred,
co·star·ring

Cos·ta Ri·ca

Cos·ta Ri·can

cost-ben·e·fit

cost-ef·fec·tive

cost-ef·fec·tive·ness

cost·li·ness

cost·ly, *adj.*
cost·li·er,
cost·li·est

cos·tume, *v.*
cos·tumed,
cos·tum·ing

cos·tum·er

co·tan·gent

co·te·rie

co·ter·mi·nous *or*
con·ter·mi·nous

co·til·lion (*occas.*
co·til·lon)

Cots·wold

cot·tage

cot·tage cheese

cot·ter

cot·ton

cot·ton·seed

cot·ton·tail

cot·ton·wood

cot·y·le·don

cou·gar, *n. pl.*
cou·gars (*occas.*
cou·gar)

cough

cou·lomb

coun·cil (GROUP
OF PEOPLE),

(*see also*
counsel)

coun·cil·lor *or*
coun·cil·or
(COUNCIL
MEMBER),
(*see also*
counselor)

coun·cil·man, *n. pl.*
coun·cil·men

coun·cil·wom·an, *n.
pl.*
coun·cil·wom·en

coun·sel (ADVICE,
LAWYER) (*see
also* council)

coun·sel (ADVISE),
v. coun·seled,
or coun·selled,
coun·sel·ing *or*
coun·sel·ling

coun·sel·or *or*
coun·sel·lor
(ADVISER,
LAWYER) (*see
also* councillor)

coun·sel·or-at-law,
n. pl.
coun·sel·ors-at-
law

count·able

count·down, *n.*

count down, *v.*

coun·te·nance

count·er

coun·ter·act

coun·ter·ac·tive

coun·ter·at·tack

coun·ter·bal·ance,
v.
coun·ter·bal·anced,
coun·ter·bal·anc·ing

coun·ter·charge, *v.*
coun·ter·charged,
coun·ter·charg·ing

coun·ter·claim

coun·ter·clock·wise

coun·ter·cul·ture

coun·ter·es·pi·o·nage

coun·ter·feit

coun·ter·feit·er

coun·ter·in·sur·gen·cy

coun·ter·in·tel·li·gence

coun·ter·mand

coun·ter·mea·sure

coun·ter·of·fen·sive

coun·ter·of·fer

coun·ter·pane

coun·ter·part

coun·ter·plan

coun·ter·point

coun·ter·poise

coun·ter·pro·duc·tive

coun·ter·pro·pos·al

coun·ter·rev·o·lu·tion

coun·ter·sign

coun·ter·sig·na·ture

coun·ter·sink

coun·ter·weight

count·ess

count·less

coun·tri·fied

coun·try, *n. pl.*
coun·tries

coun·try·man, *n.
pl.*
coun·try·men

coun·try·side

coun·try·wom·an,

n. pl.
coun·try·wom·en

coun·ty, *n. pl.*
coun·ties

coup de grace, *n.
pl.* coups de
grace

coup d'état, *n. pl.*
coups de·état

coupé *or* coupe
(CAR) (*see also*
coop)

cou·ple, *v.*
cou·pled,
cou·pling

cou·plet

cou·pling

cou·pon

cour·age

cou·ra·geous

cou·ra·geous·ly

cou·ra·geous·ness

cou·ri·er

course (WAY), *n.*
(*see also*
coarse)

course (RUN), *v.*
coursed,
cours·ing

cour·te·ous

cour·te·ous·ly

cour·te·san

cour·te·sy
(POLITENESS),
n. pl. cour·te·sies
(*see also* curtsy)

court·house

court·ier

court·li·ness

court·ly, *adj.*

court·li·er,
court·li·est

court-mar·tial, *n.
pl.* courts-
mar·tial (*occas.*
court-mar·tials)

court-mar·tial, *v.*
court-
mar·tialed
(*occas.* court-
mar·tialled),
court-
mar·tial·ing
(*occas.* court-
mar·tial·ling)

Court·ney

court·room

court·ship

court·yard

cous·cous

cous·in

cov·en

cov·e·nant

cov·er

cov·er·age

cov·er·all

cov·er·let

co·vert

cov·er-up, *n.*

cover up, *v.*

cov·et

cov·et·ous

cov·et·ous·ly

cov·et·ous·ness

cov·ey

cow·ard

cow·ard·ice

cow·ard·li·ness

cow·bell

cow·boy

cow·catch·er

cow·er

cow·hide

cow·lick

cowl·ing

co-work·er

cow·poke

cow·punch·er

cow·slip

cox·comb (FOOL)
(see also
cockscomb)

cox·swain

coy·ly

coy·ness

coy·o·te, n. pl.
coy·o·tes or
coy·o·te

coz·en

co·zi·ly

co·zi·ness

co·zy, adj. co·zi·er,
co·zi·est

crab, v. crabbed,
crab·bing

crab·bed, adj.

crab·by

crack·down, n.

crack down, v.

crack·er

crack·er·jack
(occas.
crack·a·jack)

crack·le, v.
crack·led,
crack·ling

crack·pot

crack-up, n.

crack up, v.

cra·dle, v. cra·dled,
cra·dling

craft·i·ly

craft·i·ness

crafts·man, n. pl.
crafts·men

crafts·per·son

crafty, adj.
craft·i·er,
craft·i·est

cram, v. crammed,
cram·ming

cramped

cram·pon

cran·ber·ry, pl.
cran·ber·ries

crane, v. craned,
cran·ing

cra·ni·al

cra·ni·um, n. pl.
cra·ni·ums or
cra·nia

crank·case

crank·i·ly

crank·i·ness

crank·shaft

cranky, adj.
crank·i·er,
crank·i·est

cran·ny, n. pl.
cran·nies

crap·shoot

crap·shoot·er

crash dive, n.

crash-dive, v.
crash-dived,
crash-div·ing

crash-land or
crash·land

crash land·ing

crass·ly

cra·ter

cra·vat

cra·ven

crave, v. craved,
crav·ing

craw·dad

craw·fish

crawl·er

crawly

cray·fish

cray·on

craze, v. crazed,
cra·zing

cra·zi·ly

cra·zi·ness

cra·zy, adj.
craz·i·er,
craz·i·est

cra·zy, n. pl.
cra·zies

cra·zy bone

cra·zy quilt

creak

creaky, adj.
creak·i·er,
creak·i·est

cream·ery, n. pl.
cream·er·ies

creamy, adj.
cream·i·er,
cream·i·est

cre·ate, v.
cre·at·ed,
cre·at·ing

cre·ation

cre·ation·ism

cre·ative

cre·ativ·i·ty

cre·ator

crea·ture

crèche

cre·dence

cre·den·tial

cre·den·za

creed

cred·i·bil·i·ty

cred·i·ble

cred·it

cred·it·able

cred·it·ably

cred·i·tor

cre·do, *n. pl.*
  cre·dos

cre·du·li·ty

cred·u·lous

cred·u·lous·ly

cred·u·lous·ness

creel

creep, *v.* crept,
  creep·ing

creep·er

creepy, *adj.*
  creep·i·er,
  creep·i·est

cre·mains

cre·mate, *v.*
  cre·mat·ed,
  cre·mat·ing

cre·ma·tion

cre·ma·to·ry, *n. pl.*
  cre·ma·to·ries

crème de la crème

Cre·ole (PERSON)

cre·ole (FOOD)

cre·o·sote

crepe *or* crêpe

crêpe su·zette, *n.
pl.* crêpes
su·zette *or* crêpe
su·zettes

cre·pus·cu·lar

cre·scen·do, *n. pl.*
  cre·scen·dos *or*
  cre·scen·does

cres·cent

crest·fall·en

cre·ta·ceous

Crete

cre·tin

cre·tonne

cre·vasse (DEEP
  GORGE OR
  BREAK)

cre·vice (NARROW
  OPENING)

crew·el

crew·el·work

crib, *v.* cribbed,
  crib·bing

crib·bage

crick·et

cri·er

crim·i·nal

crim·i·nal·i·ty

crim·i·nal·ly

crim·i·nol·o·gist

crim·i·nol·o·gy

crim·son

cringe, *v.* cringed,
  cring·ing

crin·kle, *v.*

crin·kled,
  crin·kling

crin·kly, *adj.*
  crink·li·er,
  crink·li·est

crin·o·line

crip·ple, *v.*
  crip·pled,
  crip·pling

cri·sis, *n. pl.* cri·ses

crisp·ly

crisp·ness

crispy, *adj.*
  crisp·i·er,
  crisp·i·est

criss·cross

cri·te·ri·on, *n. pl.*
  cri·te·ria

crit·ic

crit·i·cal

crit·i·cal·ly

crit·i·cism

crit·i·cize, *v.*
  crit·i·cized,
  crit·i·ciz·ing

cri·tique, *v.*
  cri·tiqued,
  cri·tiqu·ing

crit·ter

croak

Cro·atan (N. AM.
  ISLAND)

Cro·atia
  (COUNTRY)

Cro·atian *or* Cro·at
  (FROM
  CROATIA)

cro·chet, *v.*
  cro·cheted,
  cro·chet·ing

crock·ery

croc·o·dile

cro·cus, *n. pl.*
cro·cus·es
(*occas.* cro-cus
or cro·ci)

crois·sant

cro·ny

cro·ny·ism

crook·ed

croon·er

crop, *v.* cropped,
crop·ping

crop·land

crop·per

cro·quet (GAME)

cro·quette (FOOD)

cross·bar

cross·bow

cross·breed, *v.*
cross·bred,
cross·breed·ing

cross·coun·try

cross·cur·rent

cross·cut, *v.*
cross·cut,
cross·cut·ting

cross-
ex·am·i·na·tion

cross-ex·am·ine, *v.*
cross-
ex·am·ined,
cross-
ex·am·in·ing

cross-eyed

cross·hatch

cross·ing

cross·over, *n.*

cross over, *v.*

cross·piece

cross-pol·li·nate, *v.*
cross-
pol·li·nat·ed,
cross-
pol·li·nat·ing

cross-pol·li·na·tion

cross-pur·pose

cross-ques·tion

cross-ref·er·ence

cross·road

cross·walk

cross·wind

cross·wise

crotch

crotch·et

crotch·et·i·ness

crotch·ety

crou·pi·er

crou·ton

crow·bar

crow·foot
(BOTANNICAL)
n. pl. crow·foots
or crow·feet

crow's foot
(WRINKLE), *n.*
pl. crow's feet

cru·cial

cru·ci·ble

cru·ci·fix

cru·ci·fix·ion

cru·ci·form

cru·ci·fy, *v.*
cru·ci·fied,
cru·ci·fy·ing

crude·ly

cru·di·tés (RAW
VEGETABLES),
n.

cru·di·ty
(UNREFINED
VULGAR) *n. pl.*
cru·di·ties

cru·el

cru·el·ly

cru·el·ty

cru·et

cruise, *v.* cruised,
cruis·ing

cruis·er

crul·ler

crum·ble, *v.*
crum·bled,
crum·bling

crum·my, *adj.*
crum·mi·er,
crum·mi·est

crum·pet

crum·ple, *v.*
crum·pled,
crum·pling

Cru·sade(s)
CHRISTIAN
WARS OF 11TH–
13TH C.)

crusade (ZEALOUS
ATTEMPT), *n.*

cru·sade, *v.*
cru·sad·ed,
cru·sad·ing

cru·sad·er

crus·ta·cean

crus·ta·ceous

crust·al

crusty, *adj.*
crust·i·er,
crust·i·est

crutch

crux, *n. pl.* crux·es
(*occas.* cruc·es)

cru·za·do, *n. pl.*
cru·za·dos

cru·zei·ro, *n. pl.*
cru·zei·ros

cry, *v.* cried,
cry·ing

cry·ba·by, *n. pl.*
cry·ba·bies

cryo·bi·o·log·i·cal

cryo·bi·ol·o·gist

cryo·bi·ol·o·gy

cryo·gen·ic

cryo·gen·i·cal·ly

cryo·gen·ics

cry·on·ics

cryo·sur·gery

crypt

cryp·tic

cryp·to·gram

cryp·tog·ra·pher

cryp·tog·ra·phy

crys·tal

crys·tal·line

crys·tal·li·za·tion

crys·tal·lize, *v.*
crys·tal·lized,
crys·tal·liz·ing

Cu·ba

Cu·ban

cub·by·hole

cube, *v.* cubed,
cub·ing

cu·bic

cu·bi·cal (LIKE A
CUBE)

cu·bi·cle
(COMPARTMENT)

cub·ism

cub·ist

cu·bit

cuck·old

cuck·oo, *n. pl.*
cuck·oos

cu·cum·ber

cud·dle, *v.*
cud·dled,
cud·dling

cud·gel, *v.*
cud·geled *or*
cud·gelled,
cud·gel·ing *or*
cud·gel·ling

cue, *v.* cued, cu·ing
or cue·ing

cui·sine

cul-de-sac, *n. pl.*
culs-de-sac
(*occas.* cul-de-
sacs)

cu·li·nary

cull

cul·mi·nate, *v.*
cul·mi·nat·ed,
cul·mi·nat·ing

cul·mi·na·tion

cul·pa·ble

cul·prit

cult·ist

cul·ti·vat·able

cul·ti·vate, *v.*
cul·ti·vat·ed,
cul·ti·vat·ing

cul·ti·va·tion

cul·ti·va·tor

cul·tur·al

cul·tur·al·ly

cul·ture, *v.*
cul·tured,
cul·tur·ing

cul·vert

cum·ber·some

cum·brous

cum laude

cum·mer·bund

cu·mu·la·tive

cu·mu·la·tive·ly

cu·mu·la·tive·ness

cu·mu·lo·nim·bus

cu·mu·lo·stra·tus

cu·mu·lus

cu·ne·i·form

cun·ning

cup·bear·er

cup·board

cup·cake

cup·ful, *n. pl.*
cup·fuls (*occas.*
cups·ful)

cu·pid

cu·pid·i·ty

cu·po·la

cur·able

cur·ably

cu·rate

cu·ra·tive

cu·ra·tor

curb·ing

curb·stone

cur·dle, *v.* cur·dled,
cur·dling

cure, *v.* cured,
cur·ing

cu·ré (PRIEST)

cure-all

cur·few

cu·ria

cu·rie

cu·rio, *n. pl.*
  cu·ri·os

cu·ri·os·i·ty, *n. pl.*
  cu·ri·os·i·ties

cu·ri·ous

cu·ri·ous·ly

cu·ri·um

curl·er

curl·i·cue

curly, *adj.* curl·i·er,
  curl·i·est

cur·mudg·eon

cur·rant

cur·ren·cy, *n. pl.*
  cur·ren·cies

cur·rent

cur·ric·u·lum, *n. pl.*
  cur·ric·u·la *or*
  cur·ric·u·lums

cur·ry, *n. pl.*
  cur·ries

cur·ry, *v.* cur·ried,
  cur·ry·ing

cur·ry·comb

curse, *v.* cursed
  (*occas.* curst),
  curs·ing

curs·ed (UNDER A
  CURSE), *adj.*

cur·sive

cur·so·ri·ly

cur·so·ry

cur·tail

cur·tain

Cur·tis

curt·ly

curt·sy (BOW), *n.*
  pl. curt·sies (*see
  also* courtesy)

curt·sy, *v.*
  curt·sied,
  curt·sy·ing

cur·va·ceous
  (*occas.*
  cur·va·cious)

cur·va·ture

curve, *v.* curved,
  curv·ing

curve·ball

cur·vi·lin·e·ar

cush·ion

cus·pi·dor

cus·tard

cus·to·di·al

cus·to·di·an

cus·to·dy, *n. pl.*
  cus·to·dies

cus·tom

cus·tom·ari·ly

cus·tom·ary

cus·tom-built

cus·tom·er

cus·tom·house

cus·tom·ize, *v.*
  cus·tom·ized,
  cus·tom·iz·ing

cus·tom-made

cut, *v.* cut, cut·ting

cut-and-dried

cu·ta·ne·ous

cu·ta·ne·ous·ly

cut·back, *n.*

cut back, *v.*

cute, *adj.* cuter,
  cutest

cutesy, *adj.*,
  cutsies, cut·si·est

cut glass

cu·ti·cle

cut·lass

cut·lery

cut·let

cut·off, *adj. n.*

cut off, *v.*

cut-rate

cut·ter

cut·throat

cut·ting

cut·tle·bone

cut·tle·fish

cut·up, *n.*

cut up, *v.*

cut·worm

cy·a·nide

cy·ber·nate, *v.*
  cy·ber·nat·ed,
  cy·ber·nat·ing

cy·ber·na·tion

cy·ber·net·ics

cy·borg

cy·cla·mate

cy·cla·men

cy·cle, *v.* cy·cled,
  cy·cling

cy·clic

cy·cli·cal

cy·clist

cy·clom·e·ter

cy·clone

cy·clon·ic

cyclopedia, *see* encyclopedia

cy·clo·tron

cyg·net

cyl·in·der

cyl·in·dric

cy·lin·dri·cal

cym·bal

cyn·ic

cyn·i·cal

cyn·i·cism

cy·no·sure

Cyn·thia

cy·press

Cyp·ri·ot *or* Cyp·ri·ote

Cy·prus

cyst

cys·tic

cy·to·plasm

czar (*occas.* tsar)

cza·ri·na

czar·ism

czar·ist

Czech

Czecho·slo·vak

Czecho·slo·va·kia

Czecho·slo·va·ki·an

D

dab, v. dabbed,
  dab·bing

dab·ble, v.
  dab·bled,
  dab·bling

dab·bler

dachs·hund

Da·cron ®

dac·tyl

dac·tyl·ic

dac·ty·lol·o·gy

dad·dy, n. pl.
  dad·dies

da·do, n. pl.
  da·does

daf·fo·dil

daf·fy, adj.
  daf·fi·er,
  daf·fi·est

daft (FOOLISH)
  (see also deft)

dag·ger

da·guerre·o·type

dahl·ia

Da·ho·me·an

Da·ho·mey

dai·ly, n. pl.
  dai·lies

dain·ti·ly

dain·ti·ness

dain·ty, adj.
  dain·ti·er,
  dain·ti·est

dai·qui·ri

dairy, n. pl.
  dair·ies

dairy·maid

dairy·man, n. pl.
  dairy·men

da·is

dai·sy, n. pl.
  dai·sies

dai·sy wheel, also
  daisy-wheel or
  dai·sy·wheel

Da·ko·ta, n. pl.

Da·ko·tas or
  Da·ko·ta

Dalai Lama

Dal·las

dal·li·ance

dal·ly, v. dal·lied,
  dal·ly·ing

dal·ma·tian

dam (KEEP BACK),
  v. dammed,

dam·ming (see
  also damn)

dam·age, v.
  dam·aged,
  dam·ag·ing

dam·ask

damn (CONDEMN,
  v. damned,
  damn·ing see
  also dam)

dam·na·ble

dam·na·bly

dam·na·tion

damp·en

damp·en·er

damp·er

damp·ness

dam·sel

dam·son

Da·na

dance, v. danced,
  danc·ing

danc·er

dan·de·li·on

dan·der

dan·di·fy, v.
  dan·di·fied,
  dan·di·fy·ing

88

dan·dle, *v.*
  dan·dled,
  dan·dling

dan·druff

dan·dy, *adj.*
  dan·di·er,
  dan·di·est

dan·dy, *n. pl.*
  dan·dies

dan·dy·ish

Dane

dan·ger

dan·ger·ous

dan·ger·ous·ly

dan·ger·ous·ness

dan·gle, *v.*
  dan·gled,
  dan·gling

Dan·iel

Dan·ielle

Dan·ish (FROM
  DENMARK)

dan·ish (PASTRY)

dan·seuse

Dan·ube

dap·per

dap·ple, *v.*
  dap·pled,
  dap·pling

dare, *v.* dared,
  dar·ing

dare·de·vil

dar·ing

dark·en

dark·room

dar·ling

Dar·von℠

dash·board

dash·ing

das·tard·ly

da·ta, *pl.* of datum

da·ta·bank

da·ta·base

da·ta·flow

data pro·cess

data pro·ces·sing

data pro·ces·sor

date, *v.* dat·ed,
  dat·ing

date·less

date·line

da·tive

da·tum, *n. pl.* da·ta
  (*occas.*
  da·tums)

daugh·ter

daugh·ter-in-law,
  n. pl.
  daugh·ters-in-law

daunt·less

daunt·less·ly

daunt·less·ness

dau·phin (PRINCE)
  (*see also*
  dolphin)

dav·en·port

Da·vid

da·vit

daw·dle, *v.*
  dawdled,
  daw·dling

daw·dler

day·bed

day·book

day·break

day·care

day·dream

Day-Glo℠

day·light

day·time

day-to-day

Day·ton

daze, *v.* daze,
  daz·ing

daz·zle, *v.* daz·zled,
  daz·zling

daz·zling·ly

D day

dea·con

dea·con·ess

dea·con's bench

de·ac·ti·vate, *v.*
  de·ac·ti·vat·ed,
  de·ac·ti·vat·ing

de·ac·ti·va·tion

dead·beat

dead·bolt

dead cen·ter

dead·en

dead end, *n.*

dead-end, *adj. v.*

dead·line

dead·li·ness

dead·lock

dead·ly, *adj.*
  dead·li·er,
  dead·li·est

dead·pan, *v.*
  dead·panned,
  dead·pan·ning

dead·weight

dead·wood

deaf·en

deaf·en·ing

deaf·en·ing·ly

deaf-mute

deaf·ness

deal, *v.* dealt,
  deal·ing

deal·er·ship

dean·ery, *n. pl.*
  dean·er·ies

Dear·born

dear·ly

dearth

death·bed

death·blow

death·less

death·less·ly

death·less·ness

death·ly

death·watch

de·ba·cle

de·bar, *v.*
  de·barred,
  de·bar·ring

de·bark

de·bar·ka·tion

de·base, *v.*
  de·based,
  de·bas·ing

de·bat·able

de·bate, *v.*
  de·bat·ed,
  de·bat·ing

de·bat·er

de·bauch

de·bauch·ery, *n. pl.*
  de·bauch·er·ies

de·ben·ture

de·bil·i·tate, *v.*
  de·bil·i·tat·ed,
  de·bil·i·tat·ing

de·bil·i·ta·tion

de·bil·i·ty, *n. pl.*
  de·bil·i·ties

deb·it

deb·o·nair

de·bone, *v.*
  de·boned,
  de·bon·ing

Deb·o·rah

de·brief

de·brief·ing

de·bris, *n. pl.*
  de·bris

debt·or

de·bug, *v.*
  de·bugged,
  de·bug·ging

de·bunk

de·but

deb·u·tante

de·cade

dec·a·dence

dec·a·dent

de·caf·fein·a·ted

de·cal

de·cal·co·ma·nia

dec·a·logue

de·camp

de·cant (POUR)
  (*see also*
  descant)

de·cant·er

de·cap·i·tate, *v.*
  de·cap·i·tat·ed,
  de·cap·i·tat·ing

de·cap·i·ta·tion

de·cath·lon

de·cay

de·ceased

de·ce·dent

de·ceit

de·ceit·ful

de·ceit·ful·ly

de·ceit·ful·ness

de·ceive, *v.*
  de·ceived,
  de·ceiv·ing

de·ceiv·er

de·cel·er·ate, *v.*
  de·cel·er·at·ed,
  de·cel·er·at·ing

de·cel·er·a·tion

de·cel·er·a·tor

De·cem·ber

de·cen·cy, *n. pl.*
  de·cen·cies

de·cen·ni·al

de·cen·ni·al·ly

de·cent (GOOD,
  APPROPRIATE)
  (*see also*
  descent)

de·cent·ly

de·cen·tral·iza·tion

de·cen·tral·ize, *v.*
  de·cen·tral·ized,
  de·cen·tral·iz·ing

de·cep·tion

de·cep·tive·ly

de·cep·tive·ness

de·cer·ti·fi·ca·tion

de·cer·ti·fy, *v.*
  de·cer·ti·fied,
  de·cer·ti·fy·ing

dec·i·bel

de·cide, *v.*
  de·cid·ed,
  de·cid·ing

de·cid·ing

de·cid·u·ous

de·cid·u·ous·ness

dec·i·mal

dec·i·mal·ly

dec·i·mate, *v.*
  dec·i·mat·ed,
  dec·i·mat·ing

de·ci·pher

de·ci·pher·able

de·ci·sion

de·ci·sive

de·ci·sive·ly

de·ci·sive·ness

deck·hand

de·claim

dec·la·ma·tion

de·clam·a·tory

dec·la·ra·tion

de·clar·a·tive

de·clar·a·to·ry

de·clare, *v.*
  de·clared,
  de·clar·ing

de·clar·er

de·clas·si·fy, *v.*
  de·clas·si·fied,
  de·clas·si·fy·ing

de·clen·sion

de·clin·able

dec·li·na·tion

de·cline, *v.*
  de·clined,
  de·clin·ing

de·cliv·i·ty, *n. pl.*
  de·cliv·i·ties

de·code, *v.*
  de·cod·ed,
  de·cod·ing

dé·col·le·tage

dé·col·le·té

de·col·o·ni·za·tion

de·col·o·nize, *v.*
  de·col·o·nized,
  de·col·o·niz·ing

de·com·mis·sion

de·com·pose, *v.*
  de·com·posed,
  de·com·pos·ing

de·com·po·si·tion

de·com·press

de·com·pres·sion

de·con·gest·ant

de·con·tam·i·nate,
  v.
  de·con·tam·i·nat·ed,
  de·con·tam·i·nat·ing

de·con·tam·i·na·tion

de·con·trol, *v.*
  de·con·trolled,
  de·con·trol·ling

decor *or* décor

dec·o·rate, *v.*
  dec·o·rat·ed,
  dec·o·rat·ing

dec·o·ra·tion

dec·o·ra·tive

dec·o·ra·tor

dec·o·rous

dec·o·rous·ly

dec·o·rous·ness

de·co·rum

de·cou·page *or*
  dé·cou·page

de·cou·ple, *v.*
  de·cou·pled,
  de·cou·pling

de·coy, *n. pl.*
  decoys

de·crease, *v.*
  de·creased,
  de·creas·ing

de·cree, *v.*
  de·creed,
  de·cree·ing

dec·re·ment

de·crep·it

de·crep·it·ly

de·crep·i·tude

de·cre·scen·do, *n.*
  pl. de·cre·scen·dos

de·crim·i·nal·iza·tion

de·crim·i·nal·ize, *v.*
  de·crim·i·nal·ized,
  de·crim·i·nal·iz·ing

de·cry
  (DISAPPROVE),
  v. de·cried,
  de·cry·ing (*see
  also* descry)

ded·i·cate, *v.*
  ded·i·cat·ed,
  ded·i·cat·ing

ded·i·ca·tion

ded·i·ca·to·ry

de·duce, *v.*
  de·duced,
  de·duc·ing

de·duc·ible

de·duct

de·duc·tion

de·duc·tive

de-em·pha·size, *v.*
  de-
  em·pha·sized,
  de-
  em·pha·siz·ing

deep·en

deep·ly

deep-root·ed

deep-sea, *adj.*

deep-seat·ed

deer, *n. pl.* deer (*occas.* deers)

deer·skin

de·es·ca·late, *v.* de·es·ca·lat·ed, de·es·ca·lat·ing

de·es·ca·la·tion

de·face, *v.* de·faced, de·fac·ing

de·face·ment

de fac·to

de·fal·ca·tion

de·fal·ca·tor

def·a·ma·tion

de·fam·a·to·ry

de·fame, *v.* de·famed, de·fam·ing

de·fault

de·fault·er

de·feat

de·feat·ism

de·feat·ist

def·e·cate, *v.* def·e·cat·ed, def·a·cat·ing

def·e·ca·tion

de·fect

de·fec·tion

de·fec·tive

de·fec·tive·ly

de·fec·tive·ness

de·fec·tor

de·fend

de·fen·dant

de·fend·er

de·fense, *v.* de·fensed, de·fens·ing

de·fense·less

de·fen·si·ble

de·fen·sive

de·fen·sive·ly

de·fen·sive·ness

de·fer, *v.* de·ferred, de·fer·ring

def·er·ence

def·er·en·tial

de·fer·ment

de·fer·ra·ble

de·fi·ance

de·fi·ant

de·fib·ril·late, *v.* de·fib·ril·lat·ed, de·fib·ril·lat·ing

de·fib·ril·la·tor

de·fi·cien·cy, *n. pl.* de·fi·cien·cies

de·fi·cient

def·i·cit

de·file, *v.* de·filed, de·fil·ing

de·file·ment

de·fin·able

de·fine, *v.* de·fined, de·fin·ing

de·fin·er

def·i·nite

def·i·nite·ly

def·i·nite·ness

def·i·ni·tion

de·fin·i·tive

de·fin·i·tive·ly

de·fin·i·tive·ness

de·flate, *v.* de·flat·ed, de·flat·ing

de·fla·tion

de·fla·tion·ary

de·flect

de·flec·tion

de·flec·tor

de·fog, *v.* de·fogged, de·fog·ging

de·fo·li·ant

de·fo·li·ate, *v.* de·fo·li·at·ed, de·fo·li·at·ing

de·fo·li·a·tion

de·for·es·ta·tion

de·form

de·for·ma·tion

de·for·mi·ty, *n. pl.* de·for·mi·ties

de·fraud

de·fray

de·fray·al

de·frost

deft (SKILLFUL) (*see also* daft)

deft·ly

deft·ness

de·funct

de·fuse, *v.* de·fused, de·fus·ing

de·fy (CHALLENGE) *v.* de·fied, de·fy·ing (*see also* deify)

de·gen·er·a·cy, *n.*
  pl.
  de·gen·er·a·cies

de·gen·er·ate, *v.*
  de·gen·er·at·ed,
  de·gen·er·a·ting

de·gen·er·a·tion

de·gen·er·a·tive

de·grad·able

deg·ra·da·tion

de·grade, *v.*
  de·grad·ed,
  de·grad·ing

de·gree

de·gree-day

de·hu·man·iza·tion

de·hu·man·ize, *v.*
  de·hu·man·ized,
  de·hu·man·iz·ing

de·hu·mid·i·fy, *v.*
  de·hu·mid·i·fied,
  de·hu·mid·i·fy·ing

de·hu·mid·i·fi·er

de·hy·drate, *v.*
  de·hy·drat·ed,
  de·hy·drat·ing

de·hy·dra·tion

de·ice, *v.* de·iced,
  de·ic·ing

de·ic·er

de·i·fi·ca·tion

de·i·fy (GLORIFY)
  v. de·i·fied,
  de·i·fy·ing (*see
  also* defy)

deign

de·ism

de·is·tic

de·i·ty, *n. pl.*
  de·i·ties

dé·jà vu

de·ject·ed

de·jec·tion

de ju·re

Del·a·ware

de·lay

de·le, *v.* de·led,
  de·le·ing

de·lec·ta·ble

de·lec·ta·tion

del·e·gate, *v.*
  del·e·gat·ed,
  del·e·gat·ing

del·e·ga·tion

de·lete, *v.*
  de·let·ed,
  de·let·ing

del·e·te·ri·ous

del·e·te·ri·ous·ly

del·e·te·ri·ous·ness

de·le·tion

Del·hi

deli
  (DELICATESSEN)

de·lib·er·ate, *v.*
  de·lib·er·at·ed,
  de·lib·er·at·ing

de·lib·er·ate·ly

de·lib·er·ate·ness

de·lib·er·a·tion

de·lib·er·a·tive

del·i·ca·cy, *n. pl.*
  del·i·ca·cies

del·i·cate

del·i·cate·ly

del·i·cate·ness

del·i·ca·tes·sen

de·li·cious

de·li·cious·ly

de·li·cious·ness

de·light

de·light·ed

de·light·ful·ly

de·lim·it

de·lin·e·ate, *v.*
  de·lin·e·at·ed,
  de·lin·e·at·ing

de·lin·e·a·tion

de·lin·quen·cy, *n.*
  pl.
  de·lin·quen·cies

de·lin·quent

de·lir·i·ous

de·lir·i·ous·ly

de·lir·i·ous·ness

de·lir·i·um tre·mens

de·liv·er

de·liv·er·ance

de·liv·er·er

de·liv·ery, *n. pl.*
  de·liv·er·ies

de·louse, *v.*
  de·loused,
  de·lous·ing

del·phin·i·um

del·ta

del·toid

de·lude, *v.*
  de·lud·ed,
  de·lud·ing

del·uge, *v.*
  del·uged,
  del·ug·ing

de·lu·sion

de·lu·sion·al

de·luxe (*occas.*
  delux)

delve, v. delved,
  delv·ing

de·mag·ne·tize, v.
  de·mag·ne·tized,
  de·mag·ne·tiz·ing

dem·a·gog·ic

dem·a·gogue or
  dem·a·gog

dem·a·gog·uer·y

de·mand

de·mar·cate, v.
  de·mar·cat·ed,
  de·mar·cat·ing

de·mar·ca·tion

de·marche

de·mean

de·mean·or

de·ment·ed

de·men·tia

de·merit

Dem·e·rol®

de·mesne

demi·god

demi·john

de·mil·i·tar·iza·tion

de·mil·i·ta·rize, v.
  de·mil·i·ta·rized,
  de·mil·i·ta·riz·ing

demi·monde

de·mise

demi·tasse

de·mo·bi·li·za·tion

de·mo·bi·lize, v.
  de·mo·bi·lized,
  de·mo·bi·liz·ing

de·moc·ra·cy, n. pl.
  de·moc·ra·cies

dem·o·crat

dem·o·crat·ic

dem·o·crat·i·cal·ly

de·moc·ra·ti·za·tion

de·moc·ra·tize, v.
  de·moc·ra·tized,
  de·moc·ra·tiz·ing

de·mod·u·late, v.
  de·mod·u·lat·ed,
  de·mod·u·lat·ing

de·mod·u·la·tion

de·mod·u·la·tor

de·mog·ra·pher

de·mo·graph·ic, n.
  pl.
  de·mo·graph·ics

de·mo·graph·i·cal·ly

de·mog·ra·phy

de·mol·ish

de·mol·i·tion

de·mon

de·mon·e·ti·za·tion

de·mon·e·tize, v.
  de·mon·e·tized,
  de·mon·e·tiz·ing

de·mo·ni·ac

de·mo·ni·a·cal·ly

de·mon·ic

de·mon·i·cal·ly

de·mon·ol·o·gy

de·mon·stra·ble

dem·on·strate, v.
  dem·o·strat·ed,
  dem·on·strat·ing

dem·on·stra·tion

de·mon·stra·tive

dem·on·stra·tor

de·mor·al·iza·tion

de·mor·al·ize, v.
  de·mor·al·ized,
  de·mor·al·iz·ing

de·mote, v.
  de·mot·ed,
  de·mot·ing

de·mo·tion

de·mur
  (HESITATE),
  v. de·murred,
  de·mur·ring

de·mur (PRIM)

de·mur·rage

de·mur·rer

de·mys·ti·fi·ca·tion

de·mys·ti·fy, v.
  de·mys·ti·fied,
  de·mys·ti·fy·ing

de·na·tion·al·iza·tion

de·na·tion·al·ize, v.
  de·na·tion·al·ized,
  de·na·tion·al·iz·ing

de·nat·u·ral·iza·tion

de·nat·u·ral·ize, v.
  de·nat·u·ral·ized,
  de·nat·u·ral·iz·ing

de·na·tur·ant

de·na·ture, v.
  de·na·tured,
  de·na·tur·ing

den·dro·chron·o·log·i·ca

den·dro·chro·nol·o·gy

den·dro·log·ic

den·drol·o·gist

den·drol·o·gy

den·gue

de·ni·al

de·ni·er (ONE WHO
  DENIES)

de·nier (WEIGHT)

den·i·grate, v.
  den·i·grat·ed,
  den·i·grat·ing

den·im

De·nise

den·i·zen

Den·mark

de·nom·i·nate, *v.*
  de·nom·i·nat·ed,
  de·nom·i·nat·ing

de·nom·i·na·tion

de·nom·i·na·tor

de·no·ta·tion

de·no·ta·tive

de·note, *v.*
  de·not·ed,
  de·not·ing

de·noue·ment, *or*
dé·noue·ment

de·nounce, *v.*
  de·nounced,
  de·nounc·ing

dense·ly

dense·ness

den·si·ty, *n. pl.*
  den·si·ties

den·tal

den·tal·ly

den·ti·frice

den·tin *or* den·tine

den·tist

den·tist·ry

den·ti·tion

den·ture

de·nu·da·tion

de·nude, *v.*
  de·nud·ed,
  de·nud·ing

de·nun·ci·a·tion

Den·ver

de·ny, *v.* de·nied,
  de·ny·ing

de·odor·ant

de·odor·ize, *v.*
  de·odor·ized,
  de·odor·iz·ing

de·odor·iz·er

de·ox·i·dize, *v.*
  de·ox·i·dized,
  de·ox·i·diz·ing

de·ox·i·diz·er

de·oxy·ri·bo·nu·cle·ic
  ac·id

de·part

de·part·ed, *n.*

de·part·ment

de·part·men·tal

de·part·men·tal·ize,
  v.
  de·part·men·tal·ized,
  de·part·men·tal·iz·ing

de·par·ture

de·pend

de·pend·abil·i·ty

de·pend·able

de·pen·dence
  (*occas.*
  de·pen·dance)

de·pen·den·cy, *n.*
  pl.
  de·pen·den·cies

de·pen·dent (*occas.*
  de·pen·dant)

de·per·son·al·iza·tion

de·per·son·al·ize, *v.*
  de·per·son·al·ized,
  de·per·son·al·iz·ing

de·pict

de·pic·tion

de·pil·a·to·ry, *n. pl.*
  de·pil·a·to·ries

de·plane, *v.*

de·planed,
  de·plan·ing

de·plete, *v.*
  de·plet·ed,
  de·plet·ing

de·ple·tion

de·plor·able

de·plore, *v.*
  de·plored,
  de·plor·ing

de·ploy

de·po·lar·iza·tion

de·po·lar·ize, *v.*
  de·po·lar·ized,
  de·po·lar·iz·ing

de·pop·u·late, *v.*
  de·pop·u·lat·ed,
  de·pop·u·lat·ing

de·pop·u·la·tion

de·port

de·por·ta·tion

de·por·tee

de·port·ment

de·pose, *v.*
  de·posed,
  de·pos·ing

de·pos·it

de·po·si·tion

de·pos·i·tor

de·pos·i·to·ry, *n. pl.*
  de·pos·i·to·ries

de·pot

de·pra·va·tion
  (CORRUPT) (*see*
  also deprivation)

de·prave, *v.*
  de·praved,
  de·prav·ing

de·praved

de·prav·i·ty, *n. pl.*
de·prav·i·ties

de·pre·cate, *v.*
de·pre·cat·ed,
de·pre·cat·ing

dep·re·ca·tion

dep·re·ca·to·ry

de·pre·ci·ate, *v.*
de·pre·ci·at·ed,
de·pre·ci·at·ing

de·pre·ci·a·tion

dep·re·da·tion

de·press

de·pres·sant

de·pressed, *adj.*

de·pres·sion

dep·ri·va·tion
(DOING
WITHOUT) (*see
also*
depravation)

de·prive, *v.*
de·prived,
de·priv·ing

de·pro·gram, *v.*
de·pro·grammed
or
de·pro·gramed,
de·pro·gram·ming
or
de·pro·gram·ing

depth

dep·u·ta·tion

de·pute, *v.*
de·put·ed,
de·put·ing

dep·u·tize, *v.*
dep·u·tized,
dep·u·tiz·ing

dep·u·ty, *n. pl.*
dep·u·ties

de·rail

de·rail·leur

de·range, *v.*
de·ranged,
de·rang·ing

de·range·ment

der·by, *n. pl.*
der·bies

de·reg·u·late, *v.*
de·reg·u·lat·ed,
de·reg·u·lat·ing

de·reg·u·la·tion

Der·ek

der·e·lict

der·e·lic·tion

de·ride, *v.*
de·rid·ed,
de·rid·ing

de ri·gueur

de·ri·sion

de·ri·sive

de·ri·sive·ly

de·ri·sive·ness

der·i·va·tion

de·riv·a·tive

de·rive, *v.* de·rived,
de·riv·ing

der·ma·ti·tis

der·ma·tol·o·gist

der·ma·tol·o·gy

der·mis

der·o·gate, *v.*
der·o·gat·ed,
der·o·gat·ing

der·o·ga·tion

de·rog·a·to·ri·ly

de·rog·a·to·ry

der·rick

der·ri·ere *or*
der·ri·ère

der·ring-do

der·rin·ger

der·vish

de·sal·i·nate, *v.*
de·sal·i·na·ted,
de·sal·i·nat·ing

de·sal·i·na·tion

de·sal·i·ni·za·tion

de·sal·i·nize, *v.*
de·sal·i·nized,
de·sal·i·niz·ing

de·salt

des·cant (MUSIC)
(*see also*
decant)

de·scend, *v.* (*see
also* descent)

de·scen·dant *or*
de·scen·dent

de·scent
(DOWNWARD
MOVEMENT,
LINEAGE), *n.*
(*see also* decent,
descend)

de·scrib·able

de·scribe, *v.*
de·scribed,
de·scrib·ing

de·scrip·tion

de·scrip·tive

de·scrip·tor

de·scry (SEE,
DISCOVER) *v.*
de·scried,
de·scry·ing (*see
also* decry)

des·e·crate, *v.*

des·e·crat·ed,
des·e·crat·ing

des·e·cra·tion

de·seg·re·gate, v.
de·seg·re·gat·ed,
de·seg·re·gat·ing

de·seg·re·ga·tion

de·sen·si·ti·za·tion

de·sen·si·tize, v.
de·sen·si·tized,
de·sen·si·tiz·ing

de·sen·si·tiz·er

des·ert (SANDY
REGION), n.
(see also deserts,
dessert)

de·sert
(ABANDON),
v. (see also
deserts,
dessert)

de·sert·er

de·ser·tion

de·serts
(APPROPRIATE
REWARD OR
PUNISHMENT)
(see also desert,
dessert)

de·serve, v.
de·served,
de·serv·ing

de·serv·ed·ly

de·serv·ed·ness

de·serv·ing

de·sex

des·ic·cant

des·ic·cate, v.
des·ic·cat·ed,
des·ic·cat·ing

des·ic·ca·tion

des·ic·ca·tor

de·sid·er·a·tum, n.
pl. de·sid·er·a·ta

de·sign

des·ig·nate, v.
des·ig·nat·ed,
des·ig·nat·ing

des·ig·na·tion

de·sign·er

de·sign·ing

de·sir·abil·i·ty

de·sir·able

de·sire, v. de·sired,
de·sir·ing

de·sir·ous

de·sir·ous·ly

de·sir·ous·ness

de·sist

desk·top

Des Moines

des·o·late

des·o·late·ly

des·o·late·ness

des·o·la·tion

de·spair

de·spair·ing·ly

des·patch (var. of
dis·patch)

des·per·a·do, n. pl.
des·per·a·does
or des·per·a·dos

des·per·ate
(HOPELESS)
(see also
disparate)

des·per·ate·ly

des·per·a·tion

de·spi·ca·ble

de·spi·ca·bly

de·spise, v.
de·spised,
de·spis·ing

de·spite

de·spoil

de·spo·li·a·tion

de·spoil·ment

de·spond

de·spon·den·cy, n.
pl.
de·spon·den·cies

de·spon·dent

des·pot

des·pot·ic

des·pot·i·cal·ly

des·po·tism

des·sert (SWEET
FOOD) (see also
desert, deserts)

des·sert·spoon

de·sta·bi·lize, v.
de·sta·bi·lized,
de·sta·bi·liz·ing

des·ti·na·tion

des·tine, v.
des·tined,
des·tin·ing

des·ti·ny, n. pl.
des·ti·nies

des·ti·tute

des·ti·tu·tion

de·stroy

de·stroy·er

de·struct

de·struc·ti·bil·i·ty

de·struc·ti·ble

de·struc·tion

de·struc·tive

de·struc·tive·ly
de·struc·tive·ness
de·struc·tor
de·sue·tude
des·ul·to·ry
de·tach
de·tach·able
de·tached, *adj.*
de·tach·ment
de·tail
de·tain
de·tained
de·tain·ee
de·tect
de·tect·abil·i·ty
de·tect·able
de·tec·tion
de·tec·tive
de·tec·tor
de·tent
  (MECHANICAL
  DEVICE)
dé·tente (EASING
  OF HOSTILI-
  TIES)
de·ten·tion
de·ter, *v.* de·terred,
  de·ter·ring
de·ter·gent
de·te·ri·o·rate, *v.*
  de·te·ri·o·rat·ed,
  de·te·ri·o·rat·ing
de·te·ri·o·ra·tion
de·ter·min·able
de·ter·min·ably
de·ter·mi·nant
de·ter·mi·na·tion

de·ter·mine, *v.*
  de·ter·mined,
  de·ter·min·ing
de·ter·mined·ly
de·ter·mined·ness
de·ter·min·ism
de·ter·min·ist
de·ter·rence
de·ter·rent
de·test
de·test·able
de·test·ably
de·tes·ta·tion
de·throne, *v.*
  de·throned,
  de·thron·ing
de·throne·ment
det·o·nate, *v.*
  det·o·nat·ed,
  det·o·nat·ing
det·o·na·tion
det·o·na·tor
de·tour
de·tox
de·tox·i·fi·ca·tion
de·tract
de·trac·tion
de·trac·tor
de·train
det·ri·ment
det·ri·men·tal
det·ri·men·tal·ly
de·tri·tus, *n. pl.*
  de·tri·tus
De·troit
de trop
deuce
deuc·ed

de·us ex ma·chi·na
deu·te·ri·um
Deu·ter·on·o·my
deut·sche mark
de·val·u·a·tion
de·val·ue, *v.*
  de·val·ued,
  de·val·u·ing
dev·as·tate, *v.*
  dev·as·tat·ed,
  dev·as·tat·ing
dev·as·ta·tion
de·vel·op
de·vel·op·er
de·vel·op·ment
de·vel·op·men·tal·ly
de·vi·ant
de·vi·ate, *v.*
  de·vi·at·ed,
  de·vi·at·ing
de·vi·a·tion
de·vice (THING), *n.*
  (*see also* devise)
dev·il, *v.* dev·iled
  or dev·illed,
  dev·il·ing *or*
  dev·il·ling
dev·il·ish
dev·il-may-care
dev·il·ment
dev·il·ry *or*
  dev·il·try, *n. pl.*
  dev·il·ries *or*
  dev·il·tries
devil's food cake
de·vi·ous
de·vi·ous·ly
de·vi·ous·ness
de·vis·able

de·vise (GIFT OF REAL ESTATE IN WILL), n.

de·vise (INVENT, GIVE) v. de·vised, de·vis·ing (see also device)

de·vi·see

de·vi·sor

de·vi·tal·ize, v. de·vi·tal·ized, de·vi·tal·iz·ing

de·void

de·vo·lu·tion

de·volve, v. de·volved, de·volv·ing

Dev·on

De·vo·ni·an

de·vote, v. de·vot·ed, de·vot·ing

dev·o·tee

de·vo·tion

de·vo·tion·al

de·vour

de·vour·er

de·vout

de·vout·ly

de·vout·ness

dew

dew·ber·ry, n. pl. dew·ber·ries

dew·claw

dew·drop

dew·lap

de·worm

dew point

dewy, adj. dew·i·er, dew·i·est

Dex·e·drine®

dex·ter·i·ty

dex·ter·ous or dex·trous

dex·ter·ous·ly

dex·ter·ous·ness

dex·trose

Dhaka (occas. Dacca)

dhow

di·a·be·tes

di·a·bet·ic

di·a·bol·ic

di·a·bol·i·cal

di·a·bol·i·cal·ly

di·ac·o·nate

di·a·crit·ic

dia·crit·ic·al

di·a·dem

di·aer·e·sis, n. pl. di·aer·e·ses

di·ag·nose, v. di·ag·nosed, di·ag·nos·ing

di·ag·no·sis, pl. di·ag·no·ses

di·ag·nos·tic

di·ag·nos·ti·cal·ly

di·ag·nos·ti·cian

di·ag·o·nal

di·ag·o·nal·ly

di·a·gram, v. di·a·gramed or di·a·grammed, di·a·gram·ing or di·a·gram·ming

di·a·gram·mat·ic

di·a·gram·mat·i·cal·ly

di·al, v. di·aled, or di·alled, di·al·ing or di·al·ling

di·a·lect

di·a·lec·tic

di·a·lec·ti·cal

dialogue (occas. dialog), n.

di·a·logue, v. di·a·logued, di·a·logu·ing

dial tone

di·al·y·sis, n. pl. di·al·y·ses

di·am·e·ter

di·a·met·ri·cal·ly

di·a·mond

di·a·mond·back

Di·ana

Di·ane

di·a·pa·son

di·a·per, v. di·a·pered, di·a·per·ing

di·aph·a·nous

di·aph·a·nous·ly

di·aph·a·nous·ness

di·a·phragm

di·a·rist

di·ar·rhea or di·ar·rhoea

di·ar·rhe·al

di·ar·rhet·ic

di·a·ry, n. pl. di·a·ries

di·as·po·ra

di·as·to·le

di·as·tol·ic

di·a·stroph·ic

di·a·stroph·ism

di·a·ther·my

di·a·tonic

di·a·ton·i·cal·ly

di·a·tribe

dice, *n. pl.* of die (GAMBLING CUBE)

dice, *v.* diced, dic·ing

dic·ey, *adj.* dic·i·er, dic·i·est

di·chon·dra

di·chot·o·my, *n. pl.* di·chot·o·mies

dick·er

dick·ey or dicky (*occas.* dick·ie), *pl.* dick·eys or dick·ies

di·cot·y·le·don

di·cot·y·le·don·ous

Dic·ta·phone®

dic·tate, *v.* dic·tat·ed, dic·tat·ing

dic·ta·tion

dic·ta·tor

dic·ta·to·ri·al

dic·ta·tor·ship

dic·tion

dic·tio·nary, *n. pl.* dic·tio·nar·ies

dic·tum, *n. pl.* dic·ta or dic·tums

di·dac·tic

di·dac·ti·cal·ly

di·dac·ti·cal·ly

di·dac·ti·cism

did·dle, *v.* did·dled, did·dling

di·do, *n. pl.* di·does or di·dos

die (GAMBLING CUBE), *n. pl.* dice

die (STAMPING TOOL), *n. pl.* dies

die (EXPIRE), *v.* died, dy·ing

die-hard, *adj.*

die·hard, *n.*

di·elec·tric

die·sel

di·et

di·e·tary

di·e·tet·ic

di·e·tet·ics

di·e·ti·tian or di·e·ti·cian

dif·fer

dif·fer·ence

dif·fer·ent

dif·fer·en·tial

dif·fer·en·ti·ate, *v.* dif·fer·en·ti·at·ed, dif·fer·en·ti·at·ing

dif·fer·en·ti·a·tion

dif·fer·ent·ly

dif·fi·cult

dif·fi·cul·ty

dif·fi·dence

dif·fi·dent

dif·fi·dent·ly

dif·frac·tion

dif·fuse, *v.* dif·fused, dif·fus·ing

dif·fu·sion

dig, *v.* dug, dig·ging

di·gest

di·gest·ibil·i·ty

di·gest·ible

di·ges·tion

di·ges·tive

dig·ger

dig·it

dig·i·tal

dig·i·tal·is

dig·i·tal·ly

dig·ni·fy, *v.* dig·ni·fied, dig·ni·fy·ing

dig·ni·tary, *n. pl.* dig·ni·tar·ies

dig·ni·ty, *n. pl.* dig·ni·ties

di·gress

di·gres·sion

di·gres·sive

di·gres·sive·ly

di·gres·sive·ness

Di·lan·tin®

di·lap·i·dat·ed

di·lap·i·da·tion

di·la·ta·tion

di·late, *v.* di·lat·ed, di·lat·ing

di·la·tion

dil·a·to·ry

dil·do·, *n. pl.*
dil·dos

di·lem·ma

dil·et·tante, *n. pl.*
dil·et·tantes *or*
dil·et·tan·ti

dil·i·gence

dil·i·gent

dil·i·gent·ly

dil·ly, *n. pl.* dil·lies

dil·ly·dal·ly

dil·u·ent

di·lute, *v.* di·lut·ed,
di·lut·ing

di·lu·tion

dim, *v.* dimmed,
dim·ming

di·men·sion

di·men·sion·al

di·min·ish

di·min·u·en·do

dim·i·nu·tion

di·min·u·tive

di·min·u·tive·ly

di·min·u·tive·ness

dim·i·ty

dim·ly

dim·mer

dim·out

dim·ple, *v.*
dim·pled,
dim·pling

di·nar (MONEY)
(*see also* diner)

dine, *v.* dined,
din·ing

din·er (EATER) (*see*

also dinar,
dinner)

di·nette

din·ghy (BOAT), *n.*
pl. din·ghies
(*see also* dingy)

din·gi·ness

din·go, *n. pl.*
din·goes

din·gy (DIRTY) *adj.*
din·gi·er, din·gi·est
(*see* dinghy)

din·ky, *adj.*
din·ki·er,
din·ki·est

din·ner (MEAL)
(*see also* diner)

din·ner·ware

di·no·saur

di·oc·e·san

di·o·cese

di·ode

di·o·ra·ma

di·ox·ide

di·ox·in

dip, *v.* dipped,
dip·ping

diph·the·ria

diph·thong

di·plex

di·plo·ma

di·plo·ma·cy

dip·lo·mat
(GOVERNMENTAL
REPRESENTATIVE)

dip·lo·mate
(CERTIFIED
MEDICAL
SPECIALIST)

dip·lo·mat·ic

dip·lo·mat·i·cal·ly

di·plo·ma·tist

di·pole

dip·per

dip·so·ma·ni·a

dip·so·ma·ni·ac

dip·stick

dip·ter·ous

di·rect

di·rec·tion

di·rec·tion·al

di·rec·tive

di·rect·ly

di·rect·ness

di·rec·tor

di·rec·tor·ate

di·rec·tor·ship

di·rec·to·ry, *n. pl.*
di·rec·to·ries

dire·ful

dirge

dir·ham

di·ri·gi·ble

dirndl

dirt-cheap

dirt·i·ness

dirty, *adj.* dirt·i·er,
dirt·i·est

dis·abil·i·ty, *n. pl.*
dis·abil·i·ties

dis·able, *v.*
dis·abled,
dis·abling

dis·abuse, *v.*
dis·abused,
dis·abus·ing

dis·ad·van·tage, *v.*

dis·ad·van·taged,
dis·ad·van·tag·ing

dis·ad·van·ta·geous

dis·ad·van·ta·geous·ly

dis·ad·van·ta·geous·ness

dis·af·fect

dis·af·fec·tion

dis·af·fil·i·ate, *v.*
dis·af·fil·i·at·ed,
dis·af·fil·i·at·ing

dis·a·gree

dis·a·gree·able

dis·a·gree·ably

dis·agree·ment

dis·al·low

dis·al·low·ance

dis·ap·pear

dis·ap·pear·ance

dis·ap·point

dis·ap·point·ment

dis·ap·pro·ba·tion

dis·ap·prov·al

dis·ap·prove, *v.*
dis·ap·proved,
dis·ap·prov·ing

dis·arm

dis·ar·ma·ment

dis·ar·range, *v.*
dis·ar·ranged,
dis·ar·rang·ing

dis·ar·range·ment

dis·ar·ray

dis·as·sem·ble, *v.*
dis·as·sem·bled,
dis·as·sem·bling

dis·as·so·ci·ate, *v.*
dis·as·so·ci·at·ed,
dis·as·so·ci·at·ing

di·sas·ter

di·sas·trous

di·sas·trous·ly

dis·avow

dis·avow·al

dis·band

dis·bar, *v.*
dis·barred,
dis·bar·ring

dis·bar·ment

dis·be·lief, *n.*

dis·be·lieve, *v.*
dis·be·lieved,
dis·be·liev·ing

dis·be·liev·er

dis·bur·den

dis·burse (PAY
OUT), *v.*
dis·bursed,
dis·burs·ing (*see
also* disperse)

dis·burse·ment

disc (*var. of* disk)

disc brake

dis·card

dis·cern

dis·cern·ible

dis·cern·ing

dis·cern·ing·ly

dis·cern·ment

dis·charge, *v.*
dis·charged,
dis·charg·ing

dis·charge·able

dis·ci·ple

dis·ci·pli·nar·i·an

dis·ci·plin·ary

dis·ci·pline, *v.*
dis·ci·plined,
dis·ci·plin·ing

dis·claim

dis·claim·er

dis·close, *v.*
dis·closed,
dis·clos·ing

dis·clo·sure

dis·co, *n. pl.* dis·cos

dis·cog·ra·pher

dis·cog·ra·phy, *n.
pl.*
dis·cog·ra·phies

dis·col·or

dis·col·or·a·tion

dis·com·bob·u·late,
v.
dis·com·bob·u·lat·ed,
dis·com·bob·u·lat·ing

dis·com·fit

dis·com·fi·ture

dis·com·fort

dis·com·mode, *v.*
dis·com·mod·ed,
dis·com·mod·ing

dis·com·pose, *v.*
dis·com·posed,
dis·com·pos·ing

dis·com·po·sure

dis·con·cert

dis·con·nect

dis·con·nect·ed

dis·con·nect·ed·ly

dis·con·nect·ed·ness

dis·con·so·late

dis·con·so·late·ly

dis·con·tent

dis·con·tin·u·ance

dis·con·tin·ue, *v.*
dis·con·tin·ued,
dis·con·tin·u·ing

dis·con·ti·nu·ity

dis·con·tin·u·ous

dis·con·tin·u·ous·ly

dis·co·phile

dis·cord

dis·cor·dant

dis·co·theque

dis·count

dis·count·able

dis·coun·te·nance

dis·cour·age, v.
dis·cour·aged,
dis·cour·ag·ing

dis·cour·age·ment

dis·course, v.
dis·coursed,
dis·cours·ing

dis·cour·te·ous

dis·cour·te·ous·ly

dis·cour·te·ous·ness

dis·cour·te·sy, n. pl.
dis·cour·te·sies

dis·cov·er

dis·cov·er·er

dis·cov·ery, n. pl.
dis·cov·er·ies

dis·cred·it

dis·cred·it·able

dis·creet
(CAREFUL) (see
also discrete)

dis·crep·an·cy, n.
pl. dis·crep·an·cies

dis·crete
(SEPARATE)
(see also
discreet)

dis·cre·tion

dis·cre·tion·ary

dis·crim·i·nate, v.
dis·crim·i·nat·ed,
dis·crim·i·nat·ing

dis·crim·i·nat·ing

dis·crim·i·na·tion

dis·crim·i·na·to·ry

dis·cur·sive

dis·cus (DISK), n.
pl. dis·cus·es

dis·cuss (TALK), v.

dis·cus·sant

dis·cus·sion

dis·dain

dis·dain·ful·ly

dis·ease, v.
dis·eased,
dis·eas·ing

dis·em·bark

dis·em·bar·ka·tion

dis·em·body, v.
dis·em·bod·ied,
dis·em·body·ing

dis·em·bow·el, v.
dis·em·bow·eled
or
dis·em·bow·elled,
dis·em·bow·el·ing
or
dis·em·bow·el·ling

dis·em·bow·el·ment

dis·en·chant

dis·en·cum·ber

dis·en·gage, v.
dis·en·gaged,
dis·en·gag·ing

dis·en·tan·gle, v.
dis·en·tan·gled,
dis·en·tan·gl·ing

dis·es·tab·lish

dis·es·tab·lish·ment

dis·es·teem

dis·fa·vor

dis·fig·ure, v.
dis·fig·ured,
dis·fig·ur·ing

dis·fig·ure·ment

dis·fran·chise, v.
dis·fran·chised,
dis·fran·chis·ing

dis·gorge, v.
dis·gorged,
dis·gorg·ing

dis·grace, v.
dis·graced,
dis·grac·ing

dis·grace·ful·ly

dis·grace·ful·ness

dis·grun·tle, v.
dis·grun·tled,
dis·grun·tling

dis·guise, v.
dis·guised,
dis·guis·ing

dis·gust

dis·gust·ed·ly

dis·ha·bille

dis·har·mo·ny

dish·cloth

dis·heart·en

di·shev·el, v.
di·shev·eled or
di·shev·elled,
di·shev·el·ing or
di·shev·el·ling

dis·hon·est

dis·hon·es·ty

dis·hon·or

dis·hon·or·able

dis·hon·or·ably

dish·rag

dish·wash·er

dish·wat·er

dis·il·lu·sion

dis·il·lu·sion·ment

dis·in·cli·na·tion

dis·in·cline, v.
dis·in·clined,
dis·in·clin·ing

dis·in·fect

dis·in·fec·tant

dis·in·fec·tion

dis·in·gen·u·ous

dis·in·gen·u·ous·ly

dis·in·gen·u·ous·ness

dis·in·her·it

dis·in·te·grate, v.
dis·in·te·grat·ed,
dis·in·te·grat·ing

dis·in·te·gra·tion

dis·in·ter, v.
dis·in·terred,
dis·in·ter·ring

dis·in·ter·est·ed

dis·join

dis·joint

dis·joint·ed

disk or disc

disk·ette

dis·like, v.
dis·liked,
dis·lik·ing

dis·lo·cate, v.
dis·lo·cat·ed,
dis·lo·cat·ing

dis·lo·ca·tion

dis·lodge v.
dis·lodged,
dis·lodg·ing

dis·loy·al

dis·loy·al·ty, n. pl.
dis·loy·al·ties

dis·mal

dis·mal·ly

dis·man·tle v.
dis·man·tled,
dis·man·tling

dis·may

dis·mem·ber

dis·mem·ber·ment

dis·miss

dis·miss·al

dis·mount

dis·o·be·di·ence

dis·o·be·di·ent

dis·o·bey

dis·or·der

dis·or·der·ly

dis·or·ga·ni·za·tion

dis·or·ga·nize, v.
dis·or·ga·nized,
dis·or·ga·niz·ing

dis·own

dis·par·age, v.
dis·par·aged,
dis·par·ag·ing

dis·par·age·ment

dis·par·ag·ing·ly

dis·pa·rate
(DIFFERENT)
(see also
desperate)

dis·par·i·ty, n. pl.
dis·par·i·ties

dis·pas·sion·ate

dis·pas·sion·ate·ly

dis·patch

dis·patch·er

dis·pel, v.

dis·pelled,
dis·pel·ling

dis·pens·able

dis·pen·sa·ry, n. pl.
dis·pen·sa·ries

dis·pen·sa·tion

dis·pense, v.
dis·pensed,
dis·pens·ing

dis·pens·er

dis·pers·al

dis·perse
(SCATTER), v.
dis·persed,
dis·pers·ing
(see also
disburse)

dis·per·sion

dis·pir·it

dis·place, v.
dis·placed,
dis·plac·ing

dis·place·ment

dis·play

dis·please, v.
dis·pleased,
dis·pleas·ing

dis·plea·sure

dis·port

dis·pos·able

dis·pos·al

dis·pose, v.
dis·posed,
dis·pos·ing

dis·pos·er

dis·po·si·tion

dis·pos·sess

dis·pos·sessed

dis·pos·ses·sion

dis·pro·por·tion

dis·pro·por·tion·ate

dis·pro·por·tion·ate·ly

dis·prove, *v.*
  dis·proved,
  dis·prov·ing

dis·put·able

dis·pu·tant

dis·pu·ta·tion

dis·pu·ta·tious

dis·pu·ta·tious·ly

dis·pu·ta·tious·ness

dis·pute, *v.*
  dis·put·ed,
  dis·put·ing

dis·qual·i·fi·ca·tion

dis·qual·i·fy, *v.*
  dis·qual·i·fied,
  dis·qual·i·fy·ing

dis·qui·et

dis·qui·et·ing

dis·qui·et·ing·ly

dis·qui·e·tude

dis·re·gard

dis·re·pair

dis·rep·u·ta·ble

dis·rep·u·ta·bil·i·ty

dis·rep·u·ta·bly

dis·re·pute

dis·re·spect

dis·re·spect·ful

dis·re·spect·ful·ly

dis·robe, *v.*
  dis·robed,
  dis·rob·ing

dis·rupt

dis·rup·tion

dis·rup·tive

dis·sat·is·fac·tion

dis·sat·is·fy, *v.*
  dis·sat·is·fied,
  dis·sat·is·fy·ing

dis·sect

dis·sect·ed

dis·sec·tion

dis·sem·ble, *v.*
  dis·sem·bled,
  dis·sem·bling

dis·sem·bler

dis·sem·i·nate, *v.*
  dis·sem·i·nat·ed,
  dis·sem·i·nat·ing

dis·sem·i·na·tion

dis·sen·sion

dis·sent

dis·sent·er

dis·ser·ta·tion

dis·ser·vice

dis·si·dence

dis·si·dent

dis·sim·i·lar

dis·sim·i·lar·i·ty, *n.*
pl.
  dis·sim·i·lar·i·ties

dis·sim·u·late, *v.*
  dis·sim·u·lat·ed,
  dis·sim·u·lat·ing

dis·sim·u·la·tion

dis·si·pate, *v.*
  dis·si·pat·ed,
  dis·si·pat·ing

dis·si·pa·tion

dis·so·ci·ate, *v.*
  dis·so·ci·at·ed,
  dis·so·ci·at·ing

dis·so·ci·a·tion

dis·sol·u·ble

dis·so·lute

dis·so·lute·ness

dis·so·lu·tion

dis·solve, *v.*
  dis·solved,
  dis·solv·ing

dis·so·nance

dis·so·nant

dis·suade, *v.*
  dis·suad·ed,
  dis·suad·ing

dis·sua·sion

dis·sym·me·try, *n.*
pl.
  dis·sym·me·tries

dis·taff, *n. pl.*
  dis·taffs

dis·tance, *v.*
  dis·tanced,
  dis·tanc·ing

dis·tant

dis·tant·ly

dis·taste

dis·taste·ful

dis·tem·per

dis·tend

dis·ten·sion *or*
  dis·ten·tion

dis·till (*occas.*
  dis·til), *v.*
  dis·tilled,
  dis·til·ling

dis·til·late

dis·til·la·tion

dis·till·er

dis·till·ery, *n. pl.*
  dis·till·er·ies

dis·tinct

dis·tinc·tion

dis·tinc·tive

dis·tinc·tive·ly

dis·tinc·tive·ness

dis·tin·guish

dis·tin·guish·able

dis·tin·guish·ably

dis·tort

dis·tor·tion

dis·tract

dis·trac·tion

dis·trait
   (ABSENTMINDED)

dis·traught (UPSET)

dis·tress

dis·tressed

dis·tress·ful

dis·trib·ute, *v.*
   dis·trib·ut·ed,
   dis·trib·ut·ing

dis·tri·bu·tion

dis·trib·u·tive

dis·trib·u·tor

dis·trict

Dis·trict of
   Co·lum·bia

dis·trust

dis·trust·ful

dis·trust·ful·ly

dis·trust·ful·ness

dis·turb

dis·tur·bance

dis·turbed

dis·union

dis·u·nite, *v.*
   dis·u·nit·ed,
   dis·u·nit·ing

dis·u·ni·ty

dis·use, *v.* dis·used,
   dis·u·sing

ditch, *n. pl.* ditch·es

dith·er

dit·to, *n. pl.* dit·tos

dit·ty, *n. pl.* dit·ties

di·uret·ic

di·ur·nal

di·va, *n. pl.* di·vas
   (*rarely* di·ve)

di·van

dive, *v.* dived *or*
   dove, dived,
   div·ing

div·er

di·verge, *v.*
   di·verged,
   di·verg·ing

di·ver·gence

di·ver·gent

di·vers (SEVERAL)

di·verse
   (DIFFERENT)

di·ver·si·fi·ca·tion

di·ver·si·fy, *v.*
   di·ver·si·fied,
   di·ver·si·fy·ing

di·ver·sion

di·ver·sion·ary

di·ver·si·ty, *n. pl.*
   di·ver·si·ties

di·vert

di·vest

di·vide, *v.*
   di·vid·ed,
   di·vid·ing

div·i·dend

di·vid·er

div·i·na·tion

di·vine, *v.* di·vined,
   di·vin·ing

di·vin·i·ty, *n. pl.*
   di·vin·i·ties

di·vis·ibil·i·ty

di·vis·ible

di·vi·sion

di·vi·sion·al

di·vi·sive

di·vi·sive·ly

di·vi·sive·ness

di·vi·sor

di·vorce, *v.*
   di·vorced,
   di·vorc·ing

di·vorcé, *masc.*

di·vor·cée, *fem.*

di·vot

di·vulge, *v.*
   di·vulged,
   di·vulg·ing

Dix·ie

Dix·ie·land

diz·zi·ly

diz·zi·ness

diz·zy, *adj.*
   diz·zi·er,
   diz·zi·est

Dji·bou·ti

Dnie·per

do, *v.* did, done,
   do·ing

dob·bin

Do·ber·man
   pin·scher

Do·bro℠

do·cent

doc·ile

doc·ile·ly

do·cil·i·ty

dock·age

dock·et

dock·hand

dock·work·er

dock·yard

doc·tor

doc·tor·al

doc·tor·ate

doc·tri·naire

doc·trin·al

doc·trine

doc·u·dra·ma

doc·u·ment

doc·u·men·ta·ry, *n. pl.*
  doc·u·men·ta·ries

doc·u·men·ta·tion

dod·der

dod·dery

dodge, *v.* dodged,
  dodg·ing

do·do, *n. pl.*
  do·does *or*
  do·dos

doe·skin

doff

dog, *v.* dogged,
  dog·ging

dog·cart

dog·catch·er

dog-ear, *n., v.*

dog-eared, *adj.*

dog·fight

dog·fish

dog·ged, *adj.*

dog·ger·el

dog·gie bag *or*
  dog·gy bag

dog·goned *or*
  dog·gone

dog·house

dog·leg, *v.*
  dog·legged,
  dog·leg·ging

dog·ma, *n. pl.*
  dog·mas (*occas.*
  dog·ma·ta)

dog·mat·ic

dog·mat·i·cal·ly

dog·ma·tism

dog·ma·tist

do-good·er

dog·trot

dog·wood

doi·ly, *n. pl.*
  doi·lies

do·ing

do-it-your·self

Dol·by®

dol·drums

dole·ful

dole·ful·ly

dole·ful·ness

dol·lar

dol·lop

dol·ly, *n. pl.*
  dol·lies

do·lo·mite

do·lor

do·lor·ous

do·lor·ous·ly

do·lor·ous·ness

dol·phin (ANIMAL)
  (*see also*
  dauphin)

dolt·ish

do·main

do·mes·tic

do·mes·ti·cal·ly

do·mes·ti·cate, *v.*
  do·mes·ti·cat·ed,
  do·mes·ti·cat·ing

do·mes·ti·ca·tion

do·mes·tic·i·ty

do·mi·cile, *v.*
  do·mi·ciled,
  do·mi·cil·ing

do·mi·cil·i·ary

dom·i·nance

dom·i·nant

dom·i·nate, *v.*
  dom·i·nat·ed,
  dom·i·nat·ing

dom·i·na·tion

dom·i·na·trix, *n. pl.*
  dom·i·na·trix·es

dom·i·neer

Dom·i·ni·ca

Do·min·i·can
  Re·pub·lic

do·min·ion

dom·i·no, *n. pl.*
  dom·i·noes *or*
  dom·i·nos

don, *v.* donned,
  don·ning

Don·ald

do·nate, *v.*
  do·nat·ed,
  do·nat·ing

do·na·tion

do·nee

dong

don·key, *n. pl.*
  don·keys

Don·na

don·ny·brook

do·nor

doo·dad

doo·dle, *v.*
doo·dled,
doo·dling

doo·dler

doo·hick·ey

dooms·day

door·bell

do-or-die

door·jamb

door·keep·er

door·knob

door·man, *n. pl.*
door·men

door·mat

door·plate

door·step

door-to-door

door·way

door·yard

dope, *v.* doped,
dop·ing

dop·ey or dopy,
adj. dop·i·er,
dop·i·est

dop·pel·gäng·er *or*
dop·pel·gang·er

Dop·pler

do·ra·do, *n. pl.*
do·ra·dos

dor·man·cy

dor·mant

dor·mer

dor·mi·to·ry, *n. pl.*
dor·mi·to·ries

dor·mouse, *n. pl.*
dor·mice

dor·sal

do·ry, *n. pl.* do·ries

dos·age

dos·sier

dot, *v* dot·ted,
dot·ting

dot·age

dot·ard

dote, *v.* dot·ed,
dot·ing

dot-ma·trix, *adj.*
dot ma·trix *n.*

dou·ble, *v.*
dou·bled,
dou·bling

dou·ble-bar·reled

dou·ble-blind

dou·ble-breast·ed

dou·ble-check

dou·ble-cross

dou·ble-cross·er

double date

dou·ble-deal·ing

dou·ble-deck·er

dou·ble-edged

dou·ble en·ten·dre,
n. pl. dou·ble
en·ten·dres

dou·ble·head·er

dou·ble-joint·ed

dou·ble-park

dou·ble-quick

dou·ble-space, *v.*
dou·ble-
spaced, dou·ble-
spac·ing

dou·ble·speak

doub·let

double take

dou·ble-talk

dou·ble·think

dou·bloon

dou·bly

doubt

doubt·ful

doubt·ful·ly

doubt·ful·ness

doubt·less

doubt·less·ly

doubt·less·ness

douche, *v.*
douched,
douch·ing

dough

dough·boy

dough·nut

dough·ty, *adj.*
dough·ti·er,
dough·ti·est

doughy, *adj.*
dough·i·er,
dough·i·est

Doug·las

dour

douse, *v.* doused,
dous·ing

dove·cote (*occas.*
dove·cot)

Do·ver

dove·tail

dov·ish

dow·a·ger

dowd·i·ly

dowd·i·ness

dowdy, *adj.*

dowd·i·er,
dowd·i·est

dow·el, *v.* dow·eled
or dow·elled,
dow·el·ing *or*
dow·el·ling

dow·er

down·beat

down·cast

down·draft

down·er

down·fall

down·fall·en

down·grade, *v.*
down·grad·ed,
down·grad·ing

down·heart·ed

down·heart·ed·ly

down·heart·ed·ness

down·hill

down-home

down·pour

down·range

down·right

down·size, *v.*
down·sized,
down·siz·ing

down·stage

down·stairs

down·stream

down·stroke

down·swing

down-to-earth

down·town

down·trod·den

down·turn

down·ward *or*
down·wards

down·wind

downy, *adj.*
down·i·er,
down·i·est

dow·ry, *n. pl.*
dow·ries

dox·ol·o·gy, *n. pl.*
dox·ol·o·gies

doze, *v.* dozed,
doz·ing

doz·en

doz·enth

drach·ma, *n. pl.*
drach·mas *or*
drach·mai

dra·co·ni·an

draft·ee

draft·i·ly

draft·i·ness

drafts·man, *n. pl*
drafts·men

drafts·per·son

drafty, adj.
draft·i·er,
draft·i·est

drag, *v.* dragged,
drag·ging

drag·net

drag·o·man, *n. pl.*
drag·o·mans *or*
drag·o·men

drag·on
(MYTHICAL
ANIMAL) (*see
also* dragoon)

drag·on·fly, *n. pl.*
drag·on·flies

dra·goon (*n*,
SOLDIER; *v.*,
FORCE INTO
SUBMISSION)

drain·age

drain·board

drain·pipe

dra·ma

dra·mat·ic

dra·mat·i·cal·ly

dram·a·tis
per·so·nae

dra·ma·tist

dra·ma·ti·za·tion

dra·ma·tize, *v.*
dra·ma·tized,
dra·ma·tiz·ing

dra·ma·tur·gy

drape, *v.* draped,
drap·ing

drap·er

drap·ery, *n. pl.*
drap·er·ies

dras·tic

dras·ti·cal·ly

draw, *v.* drew,
drawn, draw·ing

draw·back

draw·bridge

draw·er

draw·ing room

drawl

draw·string

dread·ful

dread·ful·ly

dread·ful·ness

dread·locks

dread·nought

dream, *v.* dreamed
or dreamt,
dream·ing

dream·boat

dream·er

dream·i·ly

dream·i·ness

dream·land

dream·like

dream·world

dreamy, *adj.*
dream·i·er,
dream·i·est

drear·i·ly

drear·i·ness

dreary, *adj.*
drear·i·er,
drear·i·est

dredge, *v.*
dredged,
dredg·ing

dredg·er

dres·sage

dress·er

dress·ing

dress·ing-down

dress·mak·er

dress·mak·ing

dressy, *adj.*
dress·i·er,
dress·i·est

drib·ble, *v.*
drib·bled,
drib·bling

drib·let

dri·er (PAINT
ADDITIVE)
(*occas.* dry·er)
(*see also* dryer)

drift·er

drift·wood

drill·er

drill·mast·er

dri·ly (*var. of*
dryly)

drink, *v.* drank,
drunk *or* drank,
drink·ing

drink·able

drip, *v.* dripped,
drip·ping

drip-dry

drip·py, *adj.*
drip·pi·er,
drip·pi·est

drive, *v.* drove,
driv·en, driv·ing

drive-in, *adj. n.*

drive in, *v.*

driv·el

driv·er

drive·way

driz·zle, *v.*
driz·zled,
driz·zling

drogue

droll·ery

drol·ly

drom·e·dary, *n. pl.*
drom·e·dar·ies

drone, *v.* droned,
dron·ing

drop, *v.* dropped,
drop·ping

drop·cloth

drop·kick

drop·let

drop·out, *n.*

drop out, *v.*

drop·per

drop·sy

dross

drought

drov·er

drowse, *v.*
drowsed,
drows·ing

drows·i·ly

drows·i·ness

drowsy, *adj.*
drows·i·er,
drows·i·est

drub, *v.* drubbed,
drub·bing

drudge, *v.*
drudged,
drudg·ing

drudg·ery

drug, *v.* drugged,
drug·ging

drug·gist

drug·store

dru·id

drum, *v.*
drummed,
drum·ming

drum·beat

drum·mer

drum·stick

drunk·ard

drunk·en·ly

drunk·en·ness

drunk·om·e·ter

dry, *adj.* dri·er,
dri·est

dry-clean

dry·er (PERSON OR
APPARATUS
THAT DRIES)
(*see also* drier)

dry·ly

dry·ness

dry·rot

du·al (TWO PARTS)
(see also duel)

du·al·ism

du·al·i·ty

du·al·ly

du·ath·lon

dub, v. dubbed,
dub·bing

du·bi·ous

du·bi·ous·ly

du·bi·ous·ness

Dub·lin

du·cal

duc·at

duch·ess

duchy, n. pl.
duch·ies

duck·bill

duck·board

duck·ling

duck·pin

duc·tile

duc·til·i·ty

duct·less

dud·geon

du·el (FIGHT) v.
dueled or
duelled, duel·ing
or duel·ling (see
also dual)

du·el·ist

du·et

duf·fel or duf·fle

duf·fel bag

duf·fer

duffle, see duffel

dug·out

du jour

duke·dom

dul·cet

dul·ci·mer

dull·ard

dull·ness (occas.
dul·ness)

dulls·ville

dul·ly (DULL
MANNER) (see
also duly)

Du·luth

du·ly (IN DUE
TIME) (see also
dully)

dumb·bell

dumb·found or
dum·found

dumb·ly

dumb·ness

dumb·struck

dumb·wait·er

dum·dum

dum·my, n. pl.
dum·mies

dump·ling

Dump·ster®

dumpy, adj.
dump·i·er,
dump·i·est

dun, v. dunned,
dun·ning

dun·der·head

dun·ga·ree

dun·geon

dung·hill

du·o·dec·i·mo, n.

pl.

du·o·dec·i·mos

du·o·de·nal

du·o·de·num, n. pl.
du·o·de·na or
du·o·de·nums

du·plex, n. pl.
du·plex·es

du·pli·cate, v.
du·pli·cat·ed,
du·pli·cat·ing

du·pli·ca·tion

du·pli·ca·tor

du·plic·i·ty, n. pl.
du·plic·i·ties

du·ra·bil·i·ty

du·ra·ble

du·ra·bly

du·rance

Du·ran·go

du·ra·tion

du·ress

dur·ing

dusk·i·ly

dusk·i·ness

dusky, adj.
dusk·i·er,
dusk·i·est

dust·bin

dust·er

dust·i·ly

Dus·tin

dust·i·ness

dust·less

dust·pan

dusty, adj.
dust·i·er,
dust·i·est

Dutch

du·te·ous

du·ti·ful

du·ti·ful·ly

du·ti·ful·ness

duty, *n. pl.* du·ties

duty-free

dwarf, *n. pl.*
dwarfs *or* dwarves

dwarf·ish

dwell, *v.* dwelt *or*
dwelled,
dwel·ling

dwin·dle, *v.*
dwin·dled,
dwin·dling

dyb·buk *n. pl.*

dyb·bu·kim
(*occas.*
dyb·buks)

dye, *v.* dyed,
dye·ing

dye·stuff

dy·nam·ic

dy·nam·i·cal·ly

dy·na·mism

dy·na·mite, *v.*
dy·na·mit·ed,
dy·na·mit·ing

dy·na·mo, *n. pl.*
dy·na·mos

dy·na·mom·e·ter

dy·nast

dy·nas·tic

dy·nas·ty, *n. pl.*
dy·nas·ties

dyne

dy·node

dys·en·tery, *n. pl.*
dys·en·ter·ies

dys·func·tion·al

dys·lex·ia

dys·pep·sia

dys·pep·ti·cal·ly

dys·pro·si·um

dys·tro·phic

dys·tro·phy, *n. pl.*
dys·tro·phies

E

ea·ger
ea·ger·ly
ea·ger·ness
ea·gle
ea·glet
ear·ache
ear·drum
ear·li·ness
ear·lobe
ear·ly, *adj.*
  ear·li·er,
  ear·li·est
ear·mark
ear·muff
ear·nest
ear·nest·ly
ear·nest·ness
earn·ings
ear·phone
ear·ring
ear·shot
ear·split·ting
earth·en
earth·en·ware
earth·i·ly
earth·i·ness

earth·ling
earth·ly
earth·quake
earth·shaking
earth·work
earth·worm
earthy, *adj.*
  earth·i·er,
  earth·i·est
ear·wax
ear·wig
ease, *v.* eased,
  eas·ing
ea·sel
ease·ment
eas·i·ly
eas·i·ness
East·er
east·er·ly, *n. pl.*
  east·er·lies
east·ern
East·ern·er
east·ern·most
east·ward
east·ward·ly
easy, *adj.* eas·i·er,
  eas·i·est

easy·go·ing
easy·go·ing·ness
eat, *v.* ate, eat·en,
  eat·ing
eat·able
eat·er
eat·er·y, *n. pl.*
  eat·er·ies
eau de cologne. *n.*
  pl. eaux de
  cologne
eaves
eaves·drop, *v.*
  eaves·dropped,
  eaves·drop·ping
eaves·drop·per
eb·o·ny, *n. pl.*
  eb·o·nies
ebul·lience
ebul·lien·cy
ebul·lient
ebul·lient·ly
ec·cen·tric
ec·cen·tri·cal·ly
ec·cen·tric·i·ty, *n.*
  pl.
  ec·cen·tric·i·ties
ec·cle·si·as·tic

ec·cle·si·as·ti·cal

ech·e·lon

echo, *n. pl.* ech·oes

echo·lo·ca·tion

éclair

éclat

eclec·tic

eclec·ti·cism

eclipse, *v.* eclipsed, eclips·ing

eclip·tic

eco·log·ic

eco·log·i·cal

eco·log·i·cal·ly

ecol·o·gist

ecol·o·gy

econ·o·met·rics

eco·nom·ic

eco·nom·i·cal

eco·nom·i·cal·ly

eco·nom·ics

econ·o·mist

econ·o·mize, *v.* econ·o·mized, econ·o·miz·ing

econ·o·my, *n. pl.* econ·o·mies

eco·sphere

eco·sys·tem

eco·tone

ec·ru

ec·sta·sy, *n. pl.* ec·sta·sies

ec·stat·ic

ec·stat·i·cal·ly

ec·to·morph

ec·to·plasm

Ec·ua·dor

Ec·ua·dor·an

Ec·ua·dor·ean *or* Ec·ua·dor·ian

ec·u·men·i·cal

ec·u·men·i·cal·ly

ec·u·me·nic·i·ty

ec·ze·ma

ec·zem·a·tous

ed·dy, *n. pl.* ed·dies

edel·weiss

ede·ma

edem·a·tous

edge, *v.* edged, edg·ing

edge·ways

edge·wise

edg·i·ly

edg·i·ness

edg·ing

edgy, *adj.* edg·i·er, edg·i·est

ed·i·bil·i·ty

ed·i·ble

ed·i·ble·ness

edict

ed·i·fi·ca·tion

ed·i·fice

ed·i·fy, *v.* ed·i·fied, ed·i·fy·ing

ed·it

edi·tion

ed·i·tor

ed·i·to·ri·al

ed·i·to·ri·al·iza·tion

ed·i·to·ri·al·ize, *v.*

ed·i·to·ri·al·ized, ed·i·to·ri·al·iz·ing

ed·i·to·ri·al·iz·er

ed·i·to·ri·al·ly

ed·i·tor·ship

Ed·mon·ton

ed·u·ca·ble

ed·u·cate, *v.* ed·u·cat·ed, ed·u·cat·ing

ed·u·ca·tion

ed·u·ca·tion·al

ed·u·ca·tion·al·ly

ed·u·ca·tion·ist

ed·u·ca·tor

educe, *v.* educed, educ·ing

educ·i·ble

educ·tion

Ed·ward

ee·rie (STRANGE) (*occas.* ee·ry), *adj.* ee·ri·er, ee·ri·est (*see also* aerie, Erie, eyrie)

ee·ri·ly

ee·ri·ness

ef·face, *v.* ef·faced, ef·fac·ing

ef·face·able

ef·face·ment.

ef·fect (RESULT), *n.* (*see also* affect)

ef·fect (BRING ABOUT), *v.* (*see also* affect)

ef·fec·tive

ef·fec·tive·ly

ef·fec·tive·ness

ef·fec·tu·al

ef·fec·tu·al·ly

ef·fec·tu·ate, *v.*
  ef·fec·tu·at·ed,
  ef·fec·tu·at·ing

ef·fem·i·na·cy

ef·fem·i·nate

ef·fer·vesce, *v.*
  ef·fer·vesced,
  ef·fer·vesc·ing

ef·fer·ves·cence

ef·fer·ves·cent

ef·fer·ves·cent·ly

ef·fete

ef·fete·ly

ef·fete·ness

ef·fi·ca·cious

ef·fi·ca·cious·ly

ef·fi·ca·cious·ness

ef·fi·ca·cy, *n. pl.*
  ef·fi·ca·cies

ef·fi·cien·cy, *n. pl.*
  ef·fi·cien·cies

ef·fi·cient

ef·fi·cient·ly

ef·fi·gy, *n. pl.*
  ef·fi·gies

ef·flo·resce, *v.*
  ef·flo·resced,
  ef·flo·resc·ing

ef·flo·res·cence

ef·flu·ence

ef·flu·ent

ef·flu·vi·um (*occas.*
  ef·flu·via), *n. pl.*
  ef·flu·via *or*
  ef·flu·vi·ums

ef·fort

ef·fort·less

ef·fort·less·ly

ef·fort·less·ness

ef·fron·tery

ef·ful·gence

ef·ful·gent

ef·fuse, *v.* ef·fused,
  ef·fus·ing

ef·fu·sion

ef·fu·sive

ef·fu·sive·ly

ef·fu·sive·ness

egal·i·tar·i·an

egal·i·tar·i·an·ism

egg·beat·er

egg·head

egg·nog

egg·plant

egg·shell

ego, *n. pl.* egos

ego·cen·tric

ego·cen·tric·i·ty, *n.*
  pl.
  ego·cen·tric·i·ties

ego·ism

ego·ist

ego·is·tic

ego·is·ti·cal

ego·is·ti·cal·ly

ego·ma·nia

ego·ma·ni·ac

ego·tism

ego·tist

ego·tis·tic

ego·tis·ti·cal

ego·tis·ti·cal·ly

egre·gious

egre·gious·ly

egre·gious·ness

egress

egret

Egypt

Egyp·tian

Egyp·tol·o·gy

ei·der

ei·der·down

ei·det·ic

eight

eigh·teen

eigh·teenth

eight·fold

eighth

eight·i·eth

eighty, *n. pl.*
  eight·ies

Ein·stein·ian
  (RELATING TO
  ALBERT
  EINSTEIN)

ein·stei·ni·um
  (ELEMENT)

either

either-or

ejac·u·late, *v.*
  ejac·u·lated,
  ejac·u·lat·ing

ejac·u·la·tion

eject

ejec·tion

ejec·tor

eke, *v.* eked,
  ek·ing

ekis·tics

elab·o·rate, *v.*

elab·o·rat·ed,
  elab·o·rat·ing

elab·o·rate·ly

elab·o·rate·ness

elab·o·ra·tion

élan (SPIRIT)

eland (ANIMAL) *n.*
  pl. eland
  (*occas.* elands)

elapse, *v.* elapsed,
  elaps·ing

elas·tic

elas·tic·i·ty

elate, *v.* elat·ed,
  elat·ing

ela·tion

el·bow

el·bow·room

el·der

el·der·ber·ry, *n. pl.*
  el·der·ber·ries

el·der·ly

el·dest

El Do·ra·do

elect·able

elec·tion

elec·tion·eer

elec·tive

elec·tor

elec·tor·al

elec·tor·ate

elec·tric

elec·tri·cal

elec·tri·cal·ly

elec·tri·cian

elec·tric·i·ty

elec·tri·fi·ca·tion

elec·tri·fy, *v.*
  elec·tri·fied,
  elec·tri·fy·ing

elec·tro·anal·y·sis

elec·tro·an·a·lyt·ic

elec·tro·car·di·o·gram

elec·tro·car·di·o·graph

elec·tro·car·di·og·ra·phy

elec·tro·chem·i·cal·ly

elec·tro·chem·is·try

elec·tro·cute, *v.*
  elec·tro·cut·ed,
  elec·tro·cut·ing

elec·tro·cu·tion

elec·trode

elec·tro·en·ceph·a·lo·
  gram

elec·tro·en·ceph·a·lo·
  graph

elec·trol·y·sis

elec·tro·lyte

elec·tro·lyt·ic

elec·tro·mag·net

elec·tro·mag·net·ic

elec·tro·mag·ne·tism

elec·trom·e·ter

elec·tro·mo·tive

elec·tron

elec·tron·ic

elec·tron·i·cal·ly

elec·tron·ics

elec·tro·plate, *v.*
  elec·tro·plat·ed,
  elec·tro·plat·ing

elec·tro·shock

elec·tro·stat·ic

elec·tro·ther·a·py

elec·tro·ther·mal

elec·tro·ther·mics

elec·tro·type

el·ee·mo·sy·nary

el·e·gance

el·e·gant

el·e·gant·ly

ele·gi·ac

ele·gi·a·cal

ele·gi·a·cal·ly

el·e·gy, *n. pl.*
  el·e·gies

el·e·ment

el·e·men·tal

el·e·men·ta·ry

el·e·phant

el·e·phan·ti·a·sis

el·e·phan·tine

el·e·vate, *v.*
  el·e·vat·ed,
  el·e·vat·ing

el·e·va·tion

el·e·va·tor

elev·en

elev·enth

elf, *n. pl.* elves

elf·in

elf·ish

elic·it (DRAW
  FORTH) (*see
  also* illicit)

elide, *v.* elid·ed,
  elid·ing

el·i·gi·bil·i·ty

el·i·gi·ble

elim·i·nate, *v.*
  elim·i·nat·ed,
  elim·i·nat·ing

elim·i·na·tion

eli·sion

elite

elit·ism

elit·ist

elix·ir

Eliz·a·beth

Eliz·a·be·than

elk, *n. pl.* elks *or* elk

el·lipse (CURVED PATH), *n. pl.* el·lip·ses

el·lip·sis (OMITTED WORD), *n. pl.* el·lip·ses

el·lip·tic

el·lip·ti·cal

el·o·cu·tion

el·o·cu·tion·ist

elon·gate, *v.* elon·gat·ed, elon·gat·ing

elon·ga·tion

elope, *v.* eloped, elop·ing

elope·ment

el·o·quence

el·o·quent

el·o·quent·ly

El Paso

El Sal·va·dor

else·where

elu·ci·date, *v.* elu·ci·dat·ed, elu·ci·dat·ing

elu·ci·da·tion

elude (EVADE), *v.* elud·ed,

elud·ing (*see also* allude)

elu·sion (ESCAPE) (*see also* allusion, illusion)

elu·sive (HARD TO PIN DOWN) (*see also* allusive, illusive)

elu·sive·ly

elu·sive·ness

elu·vi·al

elu·vi·a·tion

ely·sian

Ely·si·um

ema·ci·ate, *v.* ema·ci·at·ed, ema·ci·at·ing

ema·ci·a·tion

em·a·nate, *v.* em·a·nat·ed, em·a·nat·ing

em·a·na·tion

eman·ci·pate, *v.* eman·ci·pat·ed, eman·ci·pat·ing

eman·ci·pa·tion

eman·ci·pa·tor

emas·cu·late, *v.* emas·cu·lat·ed, emas·cu·lat·ing

emas·cu·la·tion

em·balm

em·balm·er

em·bank

em·bank·ment

em·bar·ca·dero, *n. pl.* em·bar·ca·der·os

em·bar·go, *n. pl.* em·bar·goes

em·bark

em·bar·ka·tion

em·bar·rass

em·bar·rass·ing

em·bar·rass·ing·ly

em·bar·rass·ment

em·bas·sy, *n. pl.* em·bas·sies

em·bat·tle, *v.* em·bat·tled, em·bat·tling

em·bed (*occas.* im·bed), *v.* em·bed·ded, em·bed·ding

em·bel·lish

em·bel·lish·ment

em·ber

em·bez·zle, *v.* em·bez·zled, em·bez·zling

em·bez·zle·ment

em·bez·zler

em·bit·ter

em·bla·zon

em·blem

em·blem·at·ic

em·blem·at·i·cal

em·blem·at·i·cal·ly

em·bod·i·ment

em·body, *v.* em·bod·ied, em·body·ing

em·bold·en

em·bol·ic

em·bo·lism

em·boss

em·bou·chure

em·brace, *v.*
 em·braced,
 em·brac·ing

em·brace·able

em·bra·sure

em·bro·ca·tion

em·broi·der

em·broi·dery, *n. pl.*
 em·broi·der·ies

em·broil

em·broil·ment

em·bryo, *n. pl.*
 em·bry·os

em·bry·o·log·ic

em·bry·o·log·i·cal

em·bry·ol·o·gist

em·bry·ol·o·gy

em·bry·on·ic

emend (EDIT) (*see
 also* amend)

emen·da·tion

em·er·ald

emerge, *v.*
 emerged,
 emerg·ing

emer·gence

emer·gen·cy, *n. pl.*
 emer·gen·cies

emer·gent

emer·i·ta (*fem.*
 only)

emer·i·tus (*fem. or
 masc.*), *n. pl.*
 emer·i·ti

em·ery

emet·ic

em·i·grant

em·i·grate

(LEAVE), *v.*
 em·i·grat·ed

em·i·grat·ing (*see
 also* immigrate)

em·i·gra·tion

émi·gré (*occas.*
 emi·gré)

Em·i·ly

em·i·nence

émi·nence grise, *n.
 pl.* émi·nenc·es
 gris·es

em·i·nent
 (RENOWNED)
 (*see also*
 immanent,
 imminent)

emir

em·is·sary, *n. pl.*
 em·is·sar·ies

emis·sion

emis·siv·i·ty

emit, *v.* emit·ted,
 emit·ting

emit·ter

Em·my, *pl.*
 Em·mys

emol·lient

emol·u·ment

emory, *see* emery

emote, *v.* emot·ed,
 emot·ing

emo·tion

emo·tion·al

emo·tion·al·ly

emo·tion·less

emo·tive

em·path·ic

em·pa·thy

em·pen·nage

em·per·or

em·pha·sis, *n. pl.*
 em·pha·ses

em·pha·size, *v.*
 em·pha·sized,
 em·pha·siz·ing

em·phat·ic

em·phat·i·cal·ly

em·phy·se·ma

em·pire

em·pir·i·cal

em·pir·i·cal·ly

em·pir·i·cism

em·pir·i·cist

em·place·ment

em·ploy

em·ploy·abil·i·ty

em·ploy·able

em·ploy·ee (*occas.*
 em·ploye)

em·ploy·er

em·ploy·ment

em·po·ri·um, *n. pl.*
 em·po·ri·ums *or*
 em·po·ria

em·pow·er

em·press

emp·ti·ly

emp·ti·ness

emp·ty, *adj.*
 empt·i·er,
 empt·i·est

emp·ty-hand·ed

emp·ty-head·ed

emu

em·u·late, *v.*

em·u·lat·ed,
em·u·lat·ing

em·u·la·tion

emul·si·fi·able

emul·si·fi·ca·tion

emul·si·fi·er

emul·si·fy, *v.*
emul·si·fied,
emul·si·fy·ing

emul·sion

en·able *v.*
en·abled,
en·abling

en·act

en·act·ment

enam·el, *v.*
enam·eled *or*
enam·elled,
enam·el·ing *or*
enam·el·ling

enam·el·er

enam·el·ware

en·am·or

en bloc

en·camp

en·camp·ment

en·cap·su·late, *v.*
en·cap·su·lat·ed,
en·cap·su·lat·ing

en·cap·su·la·tion

en·cap·sule, *v.*
en·cap·suled,
en·cap·sul·ing

en·case, *v.*
en·cased,
en·cas·ing

en·ceph·a·lit·ic

en·ceph·a·li·tis, *n.*
pl.
en·ceph·a·lit·i·des

en·chain

en·chant

en·chant·ed

en·chant·er

en·chant·ment

en·chant·ress

en·chi·la·da

en·ci·pher

en·cir·cle, *v.*
en·cir·cled,
en·cir·cling

en·cir·cle·ment

en·clave

en·close, *v.*
en·closed,
en·clos·ing

en·clo·sure

en·code, *v.*
en·cod·ed,
en·cod·ing

en·co·mi·um, *n. pl.*
en·co·mi·ums *or*
en·co·mia

en·com·pass

en·core, *v.*
en·cored,
en·cor·ing

en·coun·ter

en·cour·age, *v.*
en·cour·aged,
en·cour·ag·ing

en·cour·age·ment

en·croach

en·croach·ment

en·crust

en·crypt

en·cryp·tion

en·cum·ber

en·cum·brance

en·cyc·li·cal

en·cy·clo·pe·dia
(*occas.*
en·cy·clo·pae·dia)

en·cy·clo·pe·dic
(*occas.*
en·cy·clo·pae·dic)

en·cyst

en·dan·ger

en·dan·ger·ment

en·dear

en·dear·ing

en·dear·ment

en·deav·or

en·dem·ic

en·dem·i·cal·ly

end·game

end·ing

en·dive

end·less

end·less·ly

end·less·ness

end·most

en·do·crine

en·do·cri·nol·o·gy

en·do·cri·nol·o·gist

en·do·don·tics

en·do·don·tist

en·dog·a·mous

en·dog·a·my

en·do·morph

en·dor·phin

en·dorse (*occas.*
in·dorse), *v.*
en·dorsed,
en·dors·ing

en·dorse·ment

en·do·scope

en·do·scop·ic

en·dos·copy

en·dow

en·dow·ment

end·pa·per

en·dur·able

en·dur·ably

en·dur·ance

en·dure, v.
en·dured,
en·dur·ing

end·ways

end·wise

en·e·ma, n. pl.
en·e·mas or
ene·ma·ta

en·e·my, n. pl.
en·e·mies

en·er·get·ic

en·er·get·i·cal·ly

en·er·gize, v.
en·er·gized,
en·er·giz·ing

en·er·giz·er

en·er·gy, n. pl.
en·er·gies

en·er·vate, v.
en·er·vat·ed,
en·er·vat·ing

en·er·va·tion

en·fant ter·ri·ble

en·fee·ble, v.
en·fee·bled,
en·fee·bling

en·fee·ble·ment

en·fi·lade, v.
en·fi·lad·ed,
en·fi·lad·ing

en·fold

en·force, v.
en·forced,
en·forc·ing

en·force·abil·i·ty

en·force·able

en·force·ment

en·fran·chise, v.
en·fran·chised,
an·fran·chis·ing

en·fran·chise·ment

en·gage, v.
en·gaged,
en·gag·ing

en·gage·ment

en·gen·der

en·gine

en·gi·neer

en·gi·neer·ing

Eng·land

Eng·lish

en·gorge, v.
en·gorged,
en·gorg·ing

en·graft

en·grave, v.
en·graved,
en·grav·ing

en·grav·er

en·gross

en·gulf

en·hance, v.
en·hanced,
en·hanc·ing

en·hance·ment

enig·ma

enig·mat·ic

enig·mat·i·cal

enig·mat·i·cal·ly

en·jamb·ment or
en·jambe·ment

en·join

en·joy

en·joy·able

en·joy·ably

en·joy·ment

en·large, v.
en·larged,
en·larg·ing

en·large·ment

en·larg·er

en·light·en

en·light·ened

en·light·en·ment

en·list

en·list·ee

en·list·ment

en·liv·en

en masse

en·mesh

en·mi·ty, n. pl.
en·mi·ties

en·no·ble, v.
en·no·bled,
en·no·bling

en·no·ble·ment

en·nui

enor·mi·ty, n. pl.
enor·mi·ties

enor·mous

enough

Eno·vid®

en·plane, v.
en·planed,
en·plan·ing

en·quire (chiefly
Brit., var. of
inquire)

en·quiry (*chiefly
  Brit.*, *var. of*
  inquiry)

en·rage, *v.*
  en·raged,
  en·rag·ing

en·rap·ture, *v.*
  en·rap·tured,
  en·rap·tur·ing

en·rich

en·rich·ment

en·roll *or* en·rol, *v.*
  en·rolled,
  en·roll·ing

en·roll·ee

en·roll·ment

en route

en·sconce, *v.*
  en·sconced,
  en·sconc·ing

en·sem·ble

en·sheathe, *v.*
  en·sheathed,
  en·sheath·ing

en·shrine, *v.*
  en·shrined,
  en·shrin·ing

en·shroud

en·sign

en·silage, *v.*
  en·silaged,
  en·silag·ing

en·slave, *v.*
  en·slaved,
  en·slav·ing

en·slave·ment

en·snare, *v.*
  en·snared,
  en·snar·ing

en·sue, *v.*.. en·sued,
  en·su·ing

en·sure, *v.*
  en·sured,
  en·sur·ing

en·tail

en·tan·gle, *v.*
  en·tan·gled,
  en·tan·gling

en·tan·gle·ment

en·tente
  (POLITICAL
  ACTION) (*see
  also* intent)

en·ter

en·ter·i·tis

en·ter·prise

en·ter·pris·ing

en·ter·tain

en·ter·tain·er

en·ter·tain·ing

en·ter·tain·ment

en·thrall *or*
  en·thral, *v.*
  en·thralled,
  en·thrall·ing

en·throne, *v.*
  en·throned,
  en·thron·ing

en·thuse, *v.*
  en·thused,
  en·thus·ing

en·thu·si·asm

en·thu·si·ast

en·thu·si·as·tic

en·thu·si·as·ti·cal·ly

en·tice, *v.* en·ticed,
  en·tic·ing

en·tice·ment

en·tire

en·tire·ly

en·tire·ty

en·ti·tle, *v.*
  en·ti·tled,
  en·ti·tling

en·ti·tle·ment

en·ti·ty, *n. pl.*
  en·ti·ties

en·tomb

en·tomb·ment

en·to·mo·log·i·cal

en·to·mol·o·gist

en·to·mol·o·gy

en·tou·rage

en·trails

en·train

en·trance, *v.*
  en·tranced,
  en·tranc·ing

en·trant

en·trap, *v.*
  en·trapped,
  en·trap·ping

en·trap·ment

en·treat

en·treaty, *n. pl.*
  en·treat·ies

en·trée *or* en·tree

en·trench

en·trench·ment

en·tre·pre·neur

en·tro·py

en·trust

en·try, *n. pl.*
  en·tries

en·try-lev·el

en·try·way

en·twine, *v.*
  en·twined,
  en·twin·ing

enu·mer·ate, *v.*

enu·mer·at·ed,
enu·mer·at·ing

enu·mer·a·tion

enu·mer·a·tive

enu·mer·a·tor

enun·ci·ate (SPEAK
CLEARLY), v.
enun·ci·at·ed,
enun·ci·at·ing
(see also
annunciate)

enun·ci·a·tion
(CLEAR
PRONUNCIATION)
(see also
annunciation)

enun·ci·a·tor

en·ure·sis

en·vel·op (TO
WRAP), v.

en·ve·lope
(CONTAINER), n.

en·vel·op·ment

en·ven·om

en·vi·able

en·vi·ably

en·vi·ous

en·vi·ous·ly

en·vi·ous·ness

en·vi·ron·ment

en·vi·ron·men·tal

en·vi·ron·men·tal·ist

en·vi·ron·men·tal·ly

en·vi·rons

en·vis·age, v.
en·vis·aged,
en·vis·ag·ing

en·voy

en·vy, v. en·vied,
en·vy·ing

en·zy·mat·ic

en·zyme

en·zy·mic

eon or aeon

ep·au·let (occas.
ep·au·lette)

épée

epergne

ephed·rine

ephem·era, n. pl.
ephem·er·as or
ephem·er·ae

ephem·er·al

ephem·er·is, n. pl.
eph·e·mer·i·des

ephem·er·on, n. pl.
ephem·era
(occas.
ephem·er·ons)

ep·ic (POEM) (see
also epoch)

epi·cen·ter

ep·i·cure

ep·i·cu·re·an

ep·i·dem·ic

ep·i·de·mi·ol·o·gist

ep·i·de·mi·ol·o·gy

epi·der·mal

epi·der·mic

epi·der·mis

epi·glot·tis

ep·i·gram

ep·i·gram·mat·ic

ep·i·gram·mat·i·cal·ly

ep·i·graph

ep·i·graph·ic

ep·i·graph·i·cal

epig·ra·phy

ep·i·lep·sy, n. pl.
ep·i·lep·sies

ep·i·lep·tic

ep·i·logue or
ep·i·log

epi·neph·rine
(occas.
epi·neph·rin)

epiph·a·ny,
(PERCEPTION)
n. pl.
epiph·a·nies

Epiph·a·ny
(religious festival)

ep·i·phy·tot·ic

epis·co·pa·cy, n. pl.
epis·co·pa·cies

epis·co·pal

Epis·co·pa·lian

epis·co·pate

epi·si·ot·o·my, n.
pl.
epi·si·ot·o·mies

ep·i·sode

ep·i·sod·ic

ep·i·sod·i·cal

ep·i·sod·i·cal·ly

epis·te·mol·o·gy, n.
pl.
epis·te·mol·o·gies

epis·tle

epis·to·lary

ep·i·taph

ep·i·tha·la·mi·um or
ep·i·tha·la·mi·on,
n. pl.
ep·i·tha·la·mi·ums
or ep·i·tha·la·mia

ep·i·the·li·al

ep·i·the·li·um

ep·i·thet
epit·o·me
epit·o·mize, v.
  epit·o·mized,
  epit·o·miz·ing
ep·i·zo·ot·ic
ep·och (ERA) (see
  also epic)
ep·och·al
ep·ode
ep·o·nym
ep·oxy
equa·bil·i·ty
equa·ble
equa·bly
equal, v. equaled
  or equalled,
  equal·ing or
  equal·ling
equal·i·ty
equal·iza·tion
equal·ize, v.
  equal·ized,
  equal·iz·ing
equal·iz·er
equal·ly
equa·nim·i·ty
equate, v.
  equat·ed,
  equat·ing
equa·tion
equa·tor
equa·to·ri·al
Equa·to·ri·al
  Guin·ea
equer·ry, n. pl.
  equer·ries
eques·tri·an
eques·tri·enne

equi·an·gu·lar
equi·dis·tant
equi·lat·er·al
equil·i·brate, v.
  equil·i·brat·ed,
  equil·i·brat·ing
equil·i·bra·tion
equi·lib·ri·um, n.
  pl.
  equi·lib·ri·ums or
  equi·lib·ria
equine
equi·noc·tial
equi·nox
equip, v.
  equipped,
  equip·ping
eq·ui·page
equip·ment
equi·poise
eq·ui·ta·ble
eq·ui·ta·bly
eq·ui·ta·tion
eq·ui·ty, n. pl.
  eq·ui·ties
equiv·a·lence
equiv·a·lent
equiv·o·cal
equiv·o·cal·ly
equiv·o·cate, v.
  equiv·o·cat·ed,
  equiv·o·cat·ing
equiv·o·ca·tion
equiv·o·ca·tor
era
erad·i·ca·ble
erad·i·cate, v.
  erad·i·cat·ed,
  erad·i·cat·ing

erad·i·ca·tion
erad·i·ca·tor
eras·abil·i·ty
eras·able
erase, v. erased,
  eras·ing
era·sure
er·bi·um
erect
erec·tion
erect·ly
erect·ness
erec·tor
ere·long
er·go
er·go·nom·ics
er·gos·ter·ol
Er·ic
Er·ica or Er·ika
Erie (PROPER
  NAME) (see also
  eerie)
Er·in
er·mine, n. pl.
  er·mines or
  er·mine
erode, v. erod·ed,
  erod·ing
erog·e·nous
ero·sion
ero·sive
erot·ic
erot·i·ca
erot·i·cal·ly
erot·i·cism
er·ran·cy, n. pl.
  er·ran·cies
er·rand

er·rant

er·ra·ta, *pl.* of
er·ra·tum

er·rat·ic

er·rat·i·cal·ly

er·ra·tum, *n. pl.*
er·ra·ta

er·ro·ne·ous

er·ro·ne·ous·ly

er·ro·ne·ous·ness

er·ror

er·ror·less

er·satz

erst·while

er·u·dite

er·u·di·tion

erupt (BURST OUT)
(*see also* irrupt)

erup·tion

erup·tive

ery·sip·e·las

eryth·ro·my·cin

es·ca·drille

es·ca·late, *v.*
es·ca·lat·ed,
es·ca·lat·ing

es·ca·la·tion

es·ca·la·tor

es·ca·pade

es·cape, *v.*
es·caped,
es·cap·ing

es·cap·ee

es·cap·ism

es·cap·ist

es·cape·ment

es·ca·role

es·carp

es·carp·ment

es·cha·to·log·i·cal

es·cha·to·log·i·cal·ly

es·cha·tol·o·gy

es·cheat

es·chew

es·cort

es·cri·toire

es·crow

es·cu·do, *n. pl.*
es·cu·dos

es·cutch·eon

Es·ki·mo, *n. pl.*
Es·ki·mo *or*
Es·ki·mos

Es·ki·mo·an

esoph·a·ge·al

esoph·a·gus

es·o·ter·ic

es·o·ter·i·cal·ly

es·pa·drille

es·pal·ier

es·pe·cial

es·pe·cial·ly

Es·pe·ran·to

es·pi·o·nage

es·pla·nade

es·pous·al

es·pouse, *v.*
es·poused,
es·pous·ing

es·pres·so, *n. pl.*
es·pres·sos

es·prit de corps

es·py, *v.* es·pied,
es·py·ing

es·quire

es·say (*n.,*

WRITING; *v.,*
TRY) (*see also*
assay)

es·say·ist

Es·sen

es·sence

es·sen·tial

es·sen·tial·ly

es·sen·tial·ness

es·tab·lish

es·tab·lished

es·tab·lish·ment

es·tate

es·teem

es·ter

es·thete (*var. of*
aes·thete)

es·thet·ic (*var. of*
aes·thet·ic)

es·thet·ics (*var. of*
aes·thet·ics)

es·ti·ma·ble

es·ti·mate, *v.*
es·ti·mat·ed,
es·ti·mat·ing

es·ti·ma·tion

es·ti·ma·tor

es·ti·vate, *v.*
es·ti·vat·ed,
es·ti·vat·ing

es·ti·va·tion

Es·to·nia

Es·to·ni·an

es·top·, *v.*
es·topped,
es·top·ping

es·top·pel

es·trange, *v.*

es·tranged,
es·trang·ing

es·trange·ment

es·tro·gen

es·trus *or* es·trum

es·tu·ary, *n. pl.*
es·tu·ar·ies

etch

etch·er

etch·ing

eter·nal

eter·nal·ly

eter·ni·ty, *n. pl.*
eter·ni·ties

eth·ane

ether

ethe·re·al

ethe·re·al·ly

eth·i·cal

eth·i·cal·ly

eth·ics

Ethi·o·pia

Ethi·o·pi·an

eth·nic

eth·ni·cal·ly

eth·nic·i·ty

eth·no·cen·tric

eth·no·cen·tri·cal·ly

eth·no·cen·trism

eth·nog·ra·pher

eth·no·graph·ic

eth·no·graph·i·cal·ly

eth·nog·ra·phy

eth·no·log·ic

eth·no·log·i·cal·ly

eth·nol·o·gist

eth·nol·o·gy

etho·log·ical

ethol·o·gist

ethol·o·gy

ethos

eth·yl

eth·yl·ene

eti·o·log·ic

eti·ol·o·gy, *n. pl.*
eti·ol·o·gies

et·i·quette

Et·na

étude

et·y·mo·log·i·cal

et·y·mol·o·gist

et·y·mol·o·gy, *n. pl.*
et·y·mol·o·gies

et·y·mon, *n. pl.*
et·y·ma *or*
et·y·mons

eu·ca·lyp·tus, *n. pl.*
eu·ca·lyp·ti *or*
eu·ca·lyp·tu·ses

Eu·cha·rist

Eu·cha·ris·tic

eu·chre, *v.*
eu·chred,
eu·chring

eu·gen·ic

eu·gen·i·cal·ly

eu·gen·ics

eu·lo·gis·tic

eu·lo·gize, *v.*
eu·lo·gized,
eu·lo·giz·ing

eu·lo·gy, *n. pl.*
eu·lo·gies

eu·nuch

eu·phe·mism

eu·phe·mis·tic

eu·phe·mis·ti·cal·ly

eu·phon·ic

eu·pho·ni·ous

eu·pho·ni·ous·ly

eu·pho·ni·ous·ness

eu·pho·ny

eu·pho·ria

eu·phor·ic

Eu·phra·tes Riv·er

eu·phu·ism

eu·phu·is·tic

eu·phu·is·ti·cal

eu·phu·is·ti·cal·ly

Eur·asian

eu·re·ka

Eu·ro·dol·lar

Eu·rope

Eu·ro·pe·an

eu·ro·pi·um

eu·sta·chian tube

eu·tha·na·sia

eu·then·ics

evac·u·ate, *v.*
evac·u·at·ed,
evac·u·at·ing

evac·u·a·tion

evac·u·ee

evade *v.* evad·ed,
evad·ing

eval·u·ate *v.*
eval·u·at·ed,
eval·u·at·ing

eval·u·a·tion

ev·a·nesce, *v.*
ev·a·nesced,
ev·a·nesc·ing

ev·a·nes·cence

ev·a·nes·cent

evan·gel·ic
evan·gel·i·cal
evan·gel·i·cal·ism
evan·gel·i·cal·ly
evan·ge·lism
evan·ge·list
evan·ge·lis·tic
evan·ge·lis·ti·cal·ly
evan·ge·lize, *v.*
  evan·ge·lized,
  evan·ge·liz·ing
evap·o·rate, *v.*
  evap·o·rat·ed,
  evap·o·rat·ing
evap·o·ra·tion
evap·o·ra·tive
evap·o·ra·tor
evap·o·tran·spi·ra·tion
eva·sion
eva·sive
eva·sive·ly
eva·sive·ness
even·hand·ed
even·hand·ed·ly
even·hand·ed·ness
eve·ning
even·ly
even·ness
even·song
event
event·ful
even·tide
even·tu·al
even·tu·al·i·ty, *n.*
  pl.
  even·tu·al·i·ties
even·tu·al·ly

even·tu·ate, *v.*
  even·tu·at·ed,
  even·tu·at·ing
ev·er
ev·er·bloom·ing
Ev·er·est
ev·er·glade
ev·er·green
ev·er·last·ing
ev·er·more
ev·ery
ev·ery·body
ev·ery·day
ev·ery·one
ev·ery·thing
ev·ery·where
evict
evic·tion
ev·i·dence, *v.*
  ev·i·denced,
  ev·i·denc·ing
ev·i·dent
ev·i·den·tial
ev·i·den·tial·ly
ev·i·dent·ly
evil
evil·do·er
evil·ly
evil·ness
evil-mind·ed
evil-mind·ed·ly
evil-mind·ed·ness
evince, *v.* evinced,
  evinc·ing
evis·cer·ate, *v.*
  evis·cer·at·ed,
  evis·cer·at·ing
evis·cer·a·tion

evo·ca·tion
evoc·a·tive
evoke, *v.* evoked,
  evok·ing
evo·lu·tion
evo·lu·tion·ary
evo·lu·tion·ist
evolve, *v.* evolved,
  evolv·ing
ewe (FEMALE
  SHEEP) (*see
  also* yew)
ew·er
ex·ac·er·bate, *v.*
  ex·ac·er·bat·ed,
  ex·ac·er·bat·ing
ex·ac·er·ba·tion
exact
ex·ac·ta
exact·ing
exac·ti·tude
exact·ly
exact·ness
ex·ag·ger·ate, *v.*
  ex·ag·ger·at·ed,
  ex·ag·ger·at·ing
ex·ag·ger·a·tion
ex·ag·ger·a·tor
ex·alt
ex·al·ta·tion
ex·am·i·na·tion
ex·am·ine, *v.*
  ex·am·ined,
  ex·am·in·ing
ex·am·in·er
ex·am·ple
ex·as·per·ate, *v.*
  ex·as·per·at·ed,
  ex·as·per·at·ing

ex·as·per·a·tion

ex ca·the·dra

ex·ca·vate, *v.*
  ex·ca·vat·ed,
  ex·ca·vat·ing

ex·ca·va·tion

ex·ca·va·tor

ex·ceed

ex·ceed·ing·ly

ex·cel, *v.* ex·celled,
  ex·cel·ling

ex·cel·lence

ex·cel·len·cy, *n. pl.*
  ex·cel·len·cies

ex·cel·lent

ex·cel·si·or

ex·cept *or*
  ex·cept·ing

ex·cep·tion

ex·cep·tion·able

ex·cep·tion·al

ex·cep·tion·al·ly

ex·cerpt

ex·cerp·tion

ex·cess

ex·ces·sive

ex·ces·sive·ly

ex·ces·sive·ness

ex·change, *v.*
  ex·changed,
  ex·chang·ing

ex·change·able

ex·che·quer

ex·cis·able

ex·cise, *v.* ex·cised,
  ex·cis·ing

ex·ci·sion

ex·cit·abil·i·ty

ex·cit·able

ex·ci·tant

ex·ci·ta·tion

ex·cite, *v.* ex·cit·ed,
  ex·cit·ing

ex·cit·ed·ly

ex·cite·ment

ex·cit·er

ex·claim

ex·cla·ma·tion

ex·clam·a·to·ry

ex·clude, *v.*
  ex·clud·ed,
  ex·clud·ing

ex·clu·sion

ex·clu·sive

ex·clu·sive·ly

ex·clu·sive·ness

ex·clu·siv·i·ty

ex·com·mu·ni·cate,
  v.
  ex·com·mu·ni·cat·ed,
  ex·com·mu·ni·cat·ing

ex·com·mu·ni·ca·tion

ex·co·ri·ate, *v.*
  ex·co·ri·at·ed,
  ex·co·ri·at·ing

ex·co·ri·a·tion

ex·cre·ment

ex·cre·men·ti·tious

ex·cres·cence

ex·cres·cent

ex·crete, *v.*
  ex·cret·ed,
  ex·cret·ing

ex·cre·tion

ex·cre·to·ry

ex·cru·ci·at·ing

ex·cru·ci·at·ing·ly

ex·cul·pate, *v.*
  ex·cul·pat·ed,
  ex·cul·pat·ing

ex·cul·pa·tion

ex·cul·pa·to·ry

ex·cur·sion

ex·cur·sion·ist

ex·cur·sive

ex·cus·able

ex·cus·ably

ex·cuse, *v.*
  ex·cused,
  ex·cus·ing

ex·e·cra·ble

ex·e·crate, *v.*
  ex·e·crat·ed,
  ex·e·crat·ing

ex·e·cra·tion

ex·e·cute, *v.*
  ex·e·cut·ed,
  ex·e·cut·ing

ex·e·cu·tion

ex·e·cu·tion·er

ex·ec·u·tive

ex·ec·u·tor

ex·ec·u·trix, *n. pl.*
  ex·ec·u·tri·ces *or*
  ex·ec·u·trix·es

ex·e·ge·sis, *n. pl.*
  ex·e·ge·ses

ex·em·plar

ex·em·pla·ry

ex·em·pli·fi·ca·tion

ex·em·pli·fy, *v.*
  ex·em·pli·fied,
  ex·em·pli·fy·ing

ex·empt

ex·emp·tion

ex·er·cis·able

ex·er·cise (ACTIVE
USE), v.
ex·er·cised,
ex·er·cis·ing (see
also exorcise)

ex·er·cis·er

Ex·er·cy·cle℗

ex·ert

ex·er·tion

ex·e·unt

ex·ha·la·tion

ex·hale, v.
ex·haled,
ex·hal·ing

ex·haust

ex·haust·ibil·i·ty

ex·haust·ible

ex·haus·tion

ex·haus·tive

ex·haust·less

ex·hib·it

ex·hi·bi·tion

ex·hi·bi·tion·ism

ex·hi·bi·tion·ist

ex·hib·i·tor

ex·hil·a·rate, v.
ex·hil·a·rat·ed,
ex·hil·a·rat·ing

ex·hil·a·ra·tion

ex·hort

ex·hor·ta·tion

ex·hu·ma·tion

ex·hume, v.
ex·humed,
ex·hum·ing

ex·i·gen·cy, n. pl.
ex·i·gen·cies

ex·i·gent

ex·i·gu·i·ty, n. pl.
ex·i·gu·i·ties

ex·ile, v. ex·iled,
ex·il·ing

ex·ist

ex·is·tence

ex·is·tent

ex·is·ten·tial

ex·is·ten·tial·ism

ex·is·ten·tial·ist

exit

exo·crine

ex·odon·tia

ex·o·dus

ex of·fi·cio

ex·og·a·mous

ex·og·a·my, n. pl.
ex·og·a·mies

ex·og·e·nous

ex·og·e·nous·ly

ex·on·er·ate, v.
ex·on·er·at·ed,
ex·on·er·at·ing

ex·on·er·a·tion

ex·or·bi·tance

ex·or·bi·tant

ex·or·cise (DRIVE
OUT), v.
ex·or·cised,
ex·or·cis·ing
(occas.
ex·or·cize,
ex·or·cized,
ex·or·ciz·ing)
(see also
exercise)

ex·or·cism

ex·or·cist

exo·skel·e·ton

exo·sphere

ex·o·ter·ic

ex·o·ter·i·cal·ly

ex·ot·ic

ex·ot·i·cal·ly

ex·ot·i·cism

ex·pand

ex·pand·able

ex·pand·er

ex·panse

ex·pan·sion

ex·pan·sive

ex·pan·sive·ly

ex·pan·sive·ness

ex par·te

ex·pa·ti·ate, v.
ex·pa·ti·at·ed,
ex·pa·ti·at·ing

ex·pa·ti·a·tion

ex·pa·tri·ate, v.
ex·pa·tri·at·ed,
ex·pa·tri·at·ing

ex·pa·tri·a·tion

ex·pect

ex·pect·able

ex·pect·ably

ex·pec·tan·cy, n. pl.
ex·pec·tan·cies

ex·pec·tant

ex·pec·ta·tion

ex·pec·to·rant

ex·pec·to·rate, v.
ex·pec·to·rat·ed,
ex·pec·to·rat·ing

ex·pec·to·ra·tion

ex·pe·di·ence

ex·pe·di·en·cy, n.

pl.
ex·pe·di·en·cies
ex·pe·di·ent
ex·pe·dite, *v.*
  ex·pe·dit·ed,
  ex·pe·dit·ing
ex·pe·dit·er (*occas.*
  ex·pe·di·tor)
ex·pe·di·tion
ex·pe·di·tion·ary
ex·pe·di·tious
ex·pe·di·tious·ly
ex·pe·di·tious·ness
ex·pel, *v.* ex·pelled,
  ex·pel·ling
ex·pend
ex·pend·abil·i·ty
ex·pend·able
ex·pen·di·ture
ex·pense, *v.*
  ex·pensed,
  ex·spens·ing
ex·pen·sive
ex·pen·sive·ly
ex·pen·sive·ness
ex·pe·ri·ence, *v.*
  ex·pe·ri·enced,
  ex·pe·ri·enc·ing
ex·pe·ri·enced
ex·pe·ri·en·tial
ex·pe·ri·en·tial·ly
ex·per·i·ment
ex·per·i·men·tal
ex·per·i·men·tal·ly
ex·per·i·men·ta·tion
ex·per·i·ment·er
ex·pert
ex·per·tise

ex·pert·ly
ex·pert·ness
ex·pi·a·ble
ex·pi·ate, *v.*
  ex·pi·at·ed,
  ex·pi·at·ing
ex·pi·a·tion
ex·pi·a·tor
ex·pi·a·to·ry
ex·pi·ra·tion
ex·pire, *v.* ex·pired,
  ex·pir·ing
ex·plain
ex·plain·able
ex·pla·na·tion
ex·plan·a·to·ry
ex·ple·tive
ex·pli·ca·ble
ex·pli·cate, *v.*
  ex·pli·cat·ed,
  ex·pli·cat·ing
ex·pli·ca·tion
ex·pli·ca·tor
ex·pli·ca·to·ry
ex·plic·it
ex·plode, *v.*
  ex·plod·ed,
  ex·plod·ing
ex·ploit
ex·ploit·able
ex·ploi·ta·tion
ex·ploit·a·tive
ex·ploit·er
ex·plo·ra·tion
ex·plor·a·to·ry
ex·plore, *v.*
  ex·plored,
  ex·plor·ing

ex·plor·er
ex·plo·sion
ex·plo·sive
ex·plo·sive·ly
ex·plo·sive·ness
ex·po
ex·po·nent
ex·po·nen·tial
ex·po·nen·tial·ly
ex·port
ex·por·ta·tion
ex·port·er
ex·po·sé *or*
  ex·po·se, *n.*
ex·pose, *v*
  ex·posed,
  ex·pos·ing
ex·po·si·tion
ex·pos·i·tor
ex·pos·i·to·ry
ex post fac·to
ex·pos·tu·late, *v.*
  ex·pos·tu·lat·ed,
  ex·pos·tu·lat·ing
ex·pos·tu·la·tion
ex·po·sure
ex·pound
ex·press
ex·press·ible
ex·pres·sion
ex·pres·sion·ism
ex·pres·sion·is·tic
ex·pres·sive
ex·pres·sive·ly
ex·pres·sive·ness
ex·press·man, *n. pl.*
  ex·press·men

ex·press·way

ex·pro·pri·ate, v.
  ex·pro·pri·at·ed,
  ex·pro·pri·at·ing

ex·pro·pri·a·tion

ex·pul·sion

ex·punge, v.
  ex·punged,
  ex·pung·ing

ex·pur·gate, v.
  ex·pur·gat·ed,
  ex·pur·gat·ing

ex·pur·ga·tion

ex·qui·site

ex·qui·site·ly

ex·qui·site·ness

ex·san·guine

ex·tant (EXISTING),
  (see also extent)

ex·tem·po·ra·ne·ous

ex·tem·po·ra·ne·ous·ly

ex·tem·po·ra·ne·ous·
  ness

ex·tem·po·rary

ex·tem·po·re

ex·tem·po·rize, v.
  ex·tem·po·rized,
  ex·tem·po·riz·ing

ex·tend

ex·ten·sion

ex·ten·sive

ex·tent
  (MEASURE),
  (see also extant)

ex·ten·u·ate, v.
  ex·ten·u·at·ed,
  ex·ten·u·at·ing

ex·ten·u·a·tion

ex·te·ri·or

ex·ter·mi·nate, v.
  ex·ter·mi·nat·ed,
  ex·ter·mi·nat·ing

ex·ter·mi·na·tion

ex·ter·mi·na·tor

ex·tern or ex·terne

ex·ter·nal

ex·ter·nal·ly

ex·tinct

ex·tinc·tion

ex·tin·guish

ex·tin·guish·able

ex·tin·guish·er

ex·tir·pate, v.
  ex·tir·pat·ed,
  ex·tir·pat·ing

ex·tir·pa·tion

ex·tol (occas.
  ex·toll), v.
  ex·tolled,
  ex·tol·ling

ex·tol·ment

ex·tort

ex·tor·tion

ex·tor·tion·ate

ex·tor·tion·er

ex·tor·tion·ist

ex·tra

ex·tra-base hit

ex·tract

ex·tract·able

ex·trac·tion

ex·trac·tive

ex·trac·tor

ex·tra·cur·ric·u·lar

ex·tra·dit·able

ex·tra·dite, v.

ex·tra·dit·ed,
ex·tra·dit·ing

ex·tra·di·tion

ex·tra·ga·lac·tic

ex·tra·le·gal

ex·tra·le·gal·ly

ex·tra·mar·i·tal

ex·tra·mu·ral

ex·tra·ne·ous

ex·tra·ne·ous·ly

ex·tra·ne·ous·ness

ex·tra·or·di·nari·ly

ex·tra·or·di·nary

ex·trap·o·late, v.
  ex·trap·o·lat·ed,
  ex·trap·o·lat·ing

ex·trap·o·la·tion

ex·tra·sen·so·ry

ex·tra·ter·res·trial

ex·tra·ter·ri·to·ri·al

ex·tra·ter·ri·to·ri·al·i·ty

ex·trav·a·gance

ex·trav·a·gant

ex·trav·a·gant·ly

ex·trav·a·gan·za

ex·tra·ve·hic·u·lar

ex·treme

ex·treme·ly

ex·treme·ness

ex·trem·ism

ex·trem·ist

ex·trem·i·ty, n. pl.
  ex·trem·i·ties

ex·tri·cate, v.
  ex·tri·cat·ed,
  ex·tri·cat·ing

ex·tri·ca·tion

ex·trin·sic
ex·trin·si·cal·ly
ex·tro·ver·sion or
    ex·tra·ver·sion
ex·tro·vert or
    ex·tra·vert
ex·tro·vert·ed or
    ex·tra·vert·ed
ex·trude, v.
    ex·trud·ed,
    ex·trud·ing
ex·tru·sion
ex·tru·sive
ex·u·ber·ance
ex·u·ber·ant
ex·u·ber·ant·ly
ex·u·da·tion

ex·ude, v. ex·ud·ed,
    ex·ud·ing
ex·ult
ex·ul·tant
ex·ul·ta·tion
ex·urb
ex·ur·ban·ite
ex·ur·bia
eye, v. eyed,
    eye·ing or ey·ing
eye·ball
eye·brow
eye·ful
eye·glass
eye·lash

eye·let
eye·lid
eye-open·er
eye·piece
eye·sight
eye·sore
eye·spot
eye·strain
eye·tooth, n. pl.
    eye·teeth
eye·wash
eye·wit·ness
ey·rie (var. of
    aerie)
ey·rir, n. pl. au·rar

F

Fa·bi·an

Fa·bi·an·ism

fa·ble

fa·bled

fa·bric

fab·ri·cate, v.
  fab·ri·cat·ed,
  fab·ri·cat·ing

fab·ri·ca·tion

fab·ri·ca·tor

fab·u·list

fab·u·lous

fab·u·lous·ly

fab·u·lous·ness

fa·cade (occas.
  fa·çade)

face, v. faced,
  fac·ing

face·down

face-lift

face-off

fac·et

fac·et·ed or
  fac·et·ted

fa·ce·ti·ae

fa·ce·tious

fa·ce·tious·ly

fa·ce·tious·ness

face-to-face

fa·cial

fa·cile

fa·cil·i·tate, v.
  fa·cil·i·tat·ed,
  fa·cil·i·tat·ing

fa·cil·i·ty, n. pl.
  fa·cil·i·ties

fac·ing

fac·sim·i·le

fac·tion

fac·tion·al·ism

fac·tion·al·ly

fac·tious

fac·tious·ly

fac·tious·ness

fac·ti·tious

fac·ti·tious·ly

fac·ti·tious·ness

fac·toid

fac·tor

fac·tor·able

fac·to·ri·al

fac·to·ry, n. pl.
  fac·to·ries

fac·to·tum

fac·tu·al

fac·tu·al·ly

fac·ul·ty, n. pl.
  fac·ul·ties

fad·dish

fad·dish·ly

fad·dish·ness

fad·dist

fade, v. fad·ed,
  fad·ing

fade-in, n.

fade in, v.

fade-out, n.

fade out, v.

fag, v. fagged,
  fag·ging

fag·got (MALE
  HOMOSEXUAL)

fag·ot (BUNDLE OF
  STICKS)

fag·ot·ing or
  fag·got·ing

Fahr·en·heit

fail·ing

faille

fail-safe

fail·ure

132

faint

faint·heart·ed

faint·heart·ed·ly

faint·heart·ed·ness

faint·ly

faint·ness

fair·ground

fair·ing

fair·ly

fair-mind·ed

fair-mind·ed·ly

fair-mind·ed·ness

fair·ness

fair·spok·en

fair trade, n.

fair-trade, v. fair-
    trad·ed, fair-
    trad·ing

fair·way

fair-weath·er

fairy, n, pl. fair·ies

fairy·land

fait ac·com·pli, n.
    pl. faits
    ac·com·plis

faith·ful

faith·ful·ly

faith·ful·ness

faith·less

faith·less·ly

faith·less·ness

fak·er

fa·kir

fal·con

fal·con·er

fal·con·ry

Falk·land Is·lands

fall, v. fell, fall·en,
    fall·ing

fal·la·cious

fal·la·cious·ly

fal·la·cious·ness

fal·la·cy, n. pl.
    fal·la·cies

fal·li·bil·i·ty

fal·li·ble

fal·li·bly

fall·ing-out, n. pl.
    fall·ings-out or
    fall·ing-outs

fal·lo·pi·an tube

fall·out, n.

fall out, v.

fal·low

false·hood

false·ly

false·ness

fal·set·to, n. pl.
    fal·set·tos

fal·si·fi·ca·tion

fal·si·fi·er

fal·si·fy, v.
    fal·si·fied,
    fal·si·fy·ing

fal·si·ty, n. pl.
    fal·si·ties

fal·ter

fal·ter·ing·ly

fa·mil·ial

fa·mil·iar

fa·mil·iar·i·ty, n. pl.
    fa·mil·iar·i·ties

fa·mil·iar·iza·tion

fa·mil·iar·ize, v.
    fa·mil·iar·ized,
    fa·mil·iar·iz·ing

fam·i·ly, n. pl.
    fam·i·lies

fam·ine

fam·ish

fam·ished

fa·mous

fa·mous·ly

fa·mous·ness

fan, v. fanned,
    fan·ning

fa·nat·ic

fa·nat·i·cal

fa·nat·i·cal·ly

fa·nat·i·cism

fan·ci·er

fan·ci·ful

fan·ci·ful·ly

fan·ci·ful·ness

fan·ci·ly

fan·cy, adj.
    fan·ci·er,
    fan·ci·est

fan·cy-free

fan·cy·work

fan·dan·go, n. pl.
    fan·dan·gos

fan·fare

fang

fanged

fan-jet

fan mail

fan·ny, n. pl.
    fan·nies

fan·tab·u·lous

fan·tail

fan·ta·sia

fan·tas·tic

fan·tas·ti·cal

fan·tas·ti·cal·ly

fan·ta·sy, *n. pl.*
  fan·ta·sies

far·ad

far·a·day

far·away

far·ceur

far·ci·cal

far·ci·cal·ly

fare-thee-well

fare·well

far·fetched

far-flung

Far·go

fa·ri·na

far·i·na·ceous

far·kle·ber·ry, *n. pl.*
  far·kle·ber·ries

farm·er

farm·hand

farm·house

farm·ing

farm·land

farm·stead

farm·yard

fa·ro

far-off

far-out

far·ra·go, *n. pl.*
  far·ra·goes

far-reach·ing

far·ri·er

far·row

far·see·ing

Far·si

far·sight·ed

far·sight·ed·ly

far·sight·ed·ness

far·ther (GREATER
  DISTANCE)
  (*see also* further)

far·thest

far·thing

fas·cia, *n pl.*
  fas·ci·ae *or*
  fas·ci·as

fas·ci·cle

fas·ci·nate, *v.*
  fas·ci·nat·ed,
  fas·ci·nat·ing

fas·ci·na·tion

fas·cism

fas·cist

fas·cis·tic

fash·ion

fash·ion·able

fash·ion·ably

fast·back

fast·ball

fast break, *n.*

fast-break, *v.*

fas·ten

fas·ten·er

fas·ten·ing

fast-food

fas·tid·i·ous

fas·tid·i·ous·ly

fas·tid·i·ous·ness

fast·ness

fast-talk

fa·tal

fa·tal·ism

fa·tal·ist

fa·tal·is·tic

fa·tal·is·ti·cal·ly

fa·tal·i·ty, *n. pl.*
  fa·tal·i·ties

fa·tal·ly

fa·ta mor·ga·na

fat·back

fat·ed

fate·ful

fate·ful·ly

fate·ful·ness

fat·head

fa·ther

fa·ther·hood

fa·ther-in-law, *n.*
  pl. fa·thers-in-
  law

fa·ther·land

fa·ther·less

fa·ther·li·ness

fa·ther·ly

fath·om

fath·om·able

Fa·thom·e·ter℠

fath·om·less

fa·tigue, *v.*
  fa·tigued,
  fa·tigu·ing

fat·ten

fa·tu·i·ty, *n. pl.*
  fa·tu·i·ties

fat·u·ous

fat·u·ous·ly

fat·u·ous·ness

fau·cet

fault·find·er

fault·find·ing

fault·i·ly

fault·i·ness

fault·less

fault·less·ly

fault·less·ness

faulty, *adj.*
fault·i·er,
fault·i·est

faun (MYTHICAL
CREATURE)
(*see also* fawn)

fau·na, *n. pl.*
fau·nas (*occas.*
fau·nae)

faux pas, *n. pl.*
faux pas

fa·vor

fa·vor·able

fa·vor·able·ness

fa·vor·ably

fa·vored

fa·vor·ite

fa·vor·it·ism

fawn (*n.*, YOUNG
DEER; *v.*,
BOOTLICK) (*see
also* faun)

faze

fe·al·ty, *n. pl.*
fe·al·ties

fearful

fear·ful·ly

fear·ful·ness

fear·less

fear·less·ly

fear·less·ness

fear·some

fear·some·ly

fear·some·ness

fea·si·bil·i·ty

fea·si·ble

fea·si·bly

feat

feath·er, *v.*
feath·ered,
feath·er·ing

feath·er·bed, *v.*
feath·er·bed·ded,
feath·er·bed·ding

feath·ered

feath·er·edge

feath·er·weight

feath·ery

fea·ture, *v.*
fea·tured,
fea·tur·ing

fea·ture-length

fea·ture·less

fe·brile

Feb·ru·ary, *n. pl.*
Feb·ru·ar·ies

fe·cal

fe·ces

feck·less

feck·less·ly

feck·less·ness

fe·cund

fec·un·date

fec·un·da·tion

fe·cun·di·ty

fed·er·al

fed·er·al·ism

fed·er·al·ist

fed·er·al·iza·tion

fed·er·a·lize, *v.*
fed·er·a·lized,
fed·er·a·liz·ing

fed·er·ate, *v.*
fed·er·at·ed,
fed·er·at·ing

fed·er·a·tion

fed·er·a·tive

fe·do·ra

fee·ble, *adj.*
fee·bler,
fee·blest

fee·ble-mind·ed

fee·ble-mind·ed·ly

fee·ble-mind·ed·ness

fee·ble·ness

fee·bly

feed, *v.* fed,
feed·ing

feed·back, *n.*

feed back, *v.*

feed·er

feed·lot

feed·stock

feel, *v.* felt,
feel·ing

feel·er

feel·ing·ly

feel·ing·ness

feign

feint

Fe·li·cia

fe·lic·i·ta·tion

fe·lic·i·tous

fe·lic·i·tous·ly

fe·lic·i·tous·ness

fe·lic·i·ty, *n. pl.*
fe·lic·i·ties

fe·line

fel·lah, *pl.* fel·la·hin
or fel·la·heen

fel·late, *v.*
fel·lat·ed,
fel·lat·ing

fel·la·tio

fel·low

fel·low·ship

fel·on

fe·lo·ni·ous

fe·lo·ni·ous·ly

fe·lo·ni·ous·ness

fel·o·ny, *n. pl.*
fel·o·nies

fe·male

fem·i·nine

fem·i·nin·i·ty

fem·i·nism

fem·i·nist

fe·mur, *n. pl.*
fe·murs *or*
fem·o·ra

fen, *n. pl.* fen
(MONEY) *or*
fens (MARSHES)

fenc·er

fenc·ing

fend·er

fen·es·tra·tion

fen·nel

fer·ment

fer·men·ta·tion

fer·mi·um

fe·ro·cious

fe·ro·cious·ly

fe·ro·cious·ness

fe·roc·i·ty, *n. pl.*
fe·roc·i·ties

fer·ret

fer·ric

Fer·ris wheel

fer·rous

fer·rule (METAL
RING) (*see also*
ferule)

fer·ry, *n. pl.*
fer·ries

fer·ry, *v.* fer·ried,
fer·ry·ing

fer·ry·boat

fer·tile

fer·til·i·ty

fer·til·iza·tion

fer·til·ize, *v.*
fer·til·ized,
fer·til·iz·ing

fer·til·iz·er

fer·ule (FLAT
STICK) (*see also*
ferrule)

fer·ven·cy

fer·vent

fer·vent·ly

fer·vid

fer·vid·ness

fer·vor

fes·cue

fes·tal

fes·ter

fes·ti·val

fes·tive

fes·tive·ly

fes·tive·ness

fes·tiv·i·ty, *n. pl.*
fes·tiv·i·ties

fes·toon

fe·ta

fe·tal (*occas.*
foe·tal)

fetch

fetch·ing

fete *or* fête, *v.*
fet·ed, *or* fêt·ed,
fet·ing *or* fêt·ing

fet·id

fe·tish (*rarely*
fe·tich), *n. pl.*
fe·tish·es

fe·tish·ism

fe·tish·ist

fet·lock

fet·ter

fet·tle

fet·tuc·cine *or*
fet·tu·cine

fe·tus (*occas.*
foe·tus), *n. pl.*
fe·tus·es

feu·dal

feu·dal·ism

feu·dal·is·tic

feu·da·to·ry

fe·ver

fe·ver·ish

fe·ver·ish·ly

fe·ver·ish·ness

fez, *n. pl.* fez·zes
(*occas.* fez·es)

fi·an·cé (*masc.*)

fi·an·cée (*fem.*)

fi·as·co, *n. pl.*
fi·as·coes

fi·at

fib, *v.* fibbed,
fib·bing

fib·ber

fi·ber *or* fi·bre

fi·ber·board (*occas.* fi·bre·board)

Fi·ber·glas℗

fi·ber·glass

fi·bril·late, *v.* fi·bril·lat·ed, fi·bril·lat·ing

fi·bril·la·tion

fi·brin

fi·broid

fi·bro·sis

fi·brous

fib·u·la, *n. pl.* fib·u·lae *or* fib·u·las

fib·u·lar

fiche

fick·le

fick·le·ness

fic·tion

fic·tion·al

fic·tion·al·ize, *v.* fic·tion·al·ized, fic·tion·al·iz·ing

fic·tion·al·ly

fic·ti·tious

fic·ti·tious·ly

fic·ti·tious·ness

fid·dle, *v.* fid·dled, fid·dling

fid·dle-dee-dee

fid·dle-fad·dle

fid·dler

fid·dle·stick *or* fid·dle·sticks

fi·del·i·ty, *n. pl.* fi·del·i·ties

fid·get

fid·gety

fi·du·cia·ry, *n. pl.* fi·du·cia·ries

field·er

field·piece

field-test

fiend·ish

fiend·ish·ly

fiend·ish·ness

fierce·ly

fierce·ness

fi·ery, *adj.* fi·er·i·er, fi·er·i·est

fi·es·ta

fife

fif·teen

fif·teenth

fifth

fif·ti·eth

fif·ty, *n. pl.* fif·ties

fif·ty-fif·ty

fight, *v.* fought, fight·ing

fight·er

fig·ment

fig·u·ra·tion

fig·u·ra·tive

fig·u·ra·tive·ly

fig·u·ra·tive·ness

fig·ure, *v.* fig·ured, fig·ur·ing

fig·ure·head

fig·u·rine

Fi·ji

Fi·ji·an

fil·a·ment

fil·a·men·tous

fil·bert

filch

file, *v.* filed, fil·ing

fi·let (LACE) (*see also* fillet)

fi·let mi·gnon, *n. pl.* fi·lets mi·gnons

fil·ial

fil·i·bus·ter

fil·i·bus·ter·er

fil·i·gree

fil·ing (SORTING) (*see also* filling)

Fil·i·pi·no, *n. pl.* Fil·i·pi·nos

fill·er (SOMETHING THAT FILLS), *n. pl.* fillers

fil·ler (MONEY), *n. pl.* fil·lers *or* fil·ler

fil·let (*occas.* fi·let) (SLICE) (*see also* filet)

fill·ing (STUFFING) (*see also* filing)

fil·lip

fil·ly, *n. pl.* fil·lies

film·dom

film·maker

film·mak·ing

film·strip

filmy, *adj.* film·i·er, film·i·est

fils, *n. pl.* fils

fil·ter

fil·ter·able

filth·i·ly

filth·i·ness

filthy, *adj.*
  filth·i·er,
  filth·i·est

fil·trate, *v.*
  fil·trat·ed,
  fil·trat·ing

fil·tra·tion

fi·na·gle, *v.*
  fi·na·gled,
  fi·na·gling

fi·na·gler

fi·nal

fi·na·le

fi·nal·ist

fi·nal·i·ty

fi·nal·ize, *v.*
  fi·nal·ized,
  fi·nal·iz·ing

fi·nal·ly

fi·nance, *v.*
  fi·nanced,
  fi·nanc·ing

fi·nan·cial

fi·nan·cial·ly

fi·nan·cier

find, *v.* found,
  find·ing

find·er

fin de siè·cle

find·ing

fine·ly

fine·ness

fin·er·y, *n. pl.*
  fin·er·ies

fine·spun

fi·nesse, *v.*

fi·nessed,
fi·ness·ing

fin·ger, *v.*
  fin·gered,
  fin·ger·ing

fin·ger·board

fin·ger·ling

fin·ger·nail

fin·ger·post

fin·ger·print

fin·ger·tip

fin·i·al

fin·i·cal

fin·i·cal·ly

fin·ick·i·ness

fin·ick·ing

fin·icky

fi·nis

fin·ish

fin·ished

fin·ish·er

fi·nite

fi·nite·ly

fi·nite·ness

Fin·land

Finn

fin·nan had·die

Finn·ish

fiord (*var. of* fjord)

fir

fire·arm

fire·ball

fire·base

fire·boat

fire·box

fire·brand

fire·break

fire·brick

fire·bug

fire chief

fire·crack·er

fire·damp

fire-eat·er

fire·fly

fire·house

fire·light

fire·man, *n. pl.*
  fire·men

fire·place

fire·plug

fire·pow·er

fire·proof

fire·side

fire·stone

fire·trap

fire·wa·ter

fire·wood

fire·works

fir·ing

fir·ma·ment

firm·ly

firm·ness

firm·ware

first·born

first·fruits

first·hand

first·ly

first-rate

first sergeant

first-string

firth

fis·cal

fis·cal·ly

fish, *n. pl.* fish *or*
  fish·es

fish-and-chips

fish·bowl

fish·er

fish·er·man, *n. pl.*
  fish·er·men

fish·ery, *n. pl.*
  fish·er·ies

fish·hook

fish·ing

fish·mong·er

fish·tail

fish·wife, *n. pl.*
  fish·wives

fishy, *adj.* fish·i·er,
  fish·i·est

fis·sion

fis·sion·able

fis·sure, *v.*
  fis·sured,
  fis·sur·ing

fist·i·cuffs

fis·tu·la, *n. pl.*
  fis·tu·las *or*
  fis·tu·lae

fis·tu·lous

fit, *adj.* fit·ter,
  fit·test

fit, *v.* fit·ted *or* fit,
  fit·ted, fit·ting

fit·ful

fit·ful·ly

fit·ful·ness

fit·ly

fit·ness

fit·ter

fit·ting

five·fold

fix·ate, *v.* fix·at·ed,
  fix·at·ing

fix·a·tion

fix·a·tive

fix·ed·ly

fix·ed·ness

fix·i·ty

fix·ture

fiz·zle, *v.* fiz·zled,
  fiz·zling

fjord *or* fiord

flab·ber·gast

flab·bi·ly

flab·bi·ness

flab·by, *adj.*
  flab·bi·er,
  flab·bi·est

flac·cid

fla·con

flag, *v.* flagged,
  flag·ging

fla·gel·lant

flag·el·late, *v.*
  flag·el·lat·ed,
  flag·el·lat·ing

flag·el·la·tion

fla·gel·lum, *n. pl.*
  fla·gel·la (*occas.*
  fla·gel·lums)

fla·geo·let

flag·ging

flag·on

flag·pole

fla·gran·cy

fla·grant

fla·gran·te de·lic·to

flag·grant·ly

flag·ship

flag·staff

flag·stone

flag·wav·ing

flair (ABILITY) (*see
  also* flare)

flak·i·ness

flaky, *adj.* flak·i·er,
  flak·i·est

flam·bé

flam·beau, *n. pl.*
  flam·beaux *or*
  flam·beaus

flam·boy·ance

flam·boy·an·cy

flam·boy·ant

flam·boy·ant·ly

flame, *v.* flamed,
  flam·ing

fla·men·co, *n. pl.*
  fla·men·cos

flame·out

flame·proof

flame·throw·er

flam·ing

fla·min·go, *n. pl.*
  fla·min·gos
  (*occas.*
  fla·min·goes)

flam·ma·bil·i·ty

flam·ma·ble

flange, *v.* flanged,
  flang·ing

flank·er

flan·nel

flan·nel·ette

flan·nel-mouthed

flap, *v.* flapped,
  flap·ping

flap·jack

flap·per

flap·py

flare (BRIGHT LIGHT), n. (see also flair)

flare (ERUPT, SPREAD OUT), v. flared, flar·ing

flare-up

flar·ing

flash·back

flash·bulb

flash·cube

flash·er

flash-for·ward

flash·gun

flash·i·ly

flash·i·ness

flash·ing

flash·light

flashy, adj. flash·i·er, flash·i·est

flask

flat (MUSIC) v. flat·ted, flat·ting (see also flatten)

flat·bed

flat·boat

flat·car

flat-foot·ed

flat·iron

flat·ly

flat·ness

flat·ten (MAKE FLAT), v. flat·tened, flat·ten·ing

flat·ter

flat·ter·er

flat·tery, n. pl. flat·ter·ies

flat·top

flat·u·lence

flat·u·lent

flat·u·lent·ly

fla·tus

flat·ware

flat·work

flat·worm

flaunt

flau·tist (var. of flu·tist)

fla·vor

fla·vored

fla·vor·ful

fla·vor·ing

fla·vor·less

fla·vor·some

flaw

flaw·less

flaw·less·ly

flaw·less·ness

flax·en

flea·bag

flea·bite

flea-bit·ten

fledg·ling

flee, v. fled, flee·ing

fleecy, adj. fleec·i·er, fleec·i·est

fleet·ing

fleet·ing·ly

fleet·ing·ness

fleet·ly

fleet·ness

Flem·ish

flesh·i·ness

flesh·ly

flesh·pot

fleshy, adj. flesh·i·er, flesh·i·est

fleur-de-lis or fleur-de-lys, n. pl. fleurs-de-lis or fleur-de-lis or fleurs-de-lys or fleur-de-lys

flex·i·bil·i·ty

flex·i·ble

flex·i·bly

flex·or

flex·time (occas. flex·i·time)

flex·ure

flib·ber·ti·gib·bet

flick·er

fli·er (occas. fly·er)

flight·i·ly

flight·i·ness

flight·less

flight-test

flighty, adj. flight·i·er, flight·i·est

flim·flam, v. flim·flammed, flim·flam·ming

flim·si·ly

flim·si·ness

flim·sy, adj.

flim·si·er,
flim·si·est

fling, *v.* flung,
fling·ing

flint

flint·i·ly

flint·i·ness

flint·lock

flinty, *adj.*
flint·i·er,
flint·i·est

flip, *v.* flipped,
flip·ping

flip-flop, *v.* flip-
flopped, flip-
flop·ping

flip·pan·cy, *n. pl.*
flip·pan·cies

flip·pant

flip·per

flir·ta·tion

flir·ta·tious

flir·ta·tious·ly

flir·ta·tious·ness

flit, *v.* flit·ted,
flit·ting

flit·ter

fliv·ver

float·a·tion (*var. of*
flotation)

float·er

float·ing

flock·ing

floe

flog, *v.* flogged,
flog·ging

flog·ger

flood·gate

flood·light

flood·plain

flood·wa·ter

flood·way

floor·board

floor·ing

floor-length

floor·walk·er

floo·zy *or* floo·zie,
n. pl. floo·zies

flop, *v.* flopped,
flop·ping

flop·py, *adj.*
flop·pi·er,
flop·pi·est

flo·ra, *n. pl.* flo·ras
(*occas.* flo·rae)

flo·res·cence
(BLOOMING)
(*see also*
fluorescence)

flo·res·cent (*see
also*
fluorescent)

flo·ri·cul·ture

flor·id

Flor·i·da

Flor·i·dan

Flo·rid·i·an

flo·rin

flo·rist

flossy, *adj.*
floss·i·er,
floss·i·est

flo·ta·tion

flo·til·la

flot·sam

flounce, *v.*
flounced,
flounc·ing

floun·der

flour·ish

flout

flow

flow·chart

flow·er

flow·ered

flow·er·i·ness

flow·er·pot

flow·ery

flu (ILLNESS) (*see
also* flue)

flub, *v.* flubbed,
flub·bing

fluc·tu·ate, *v.*
fluc·tu·at·ed,
fluc·tu·at·ing

fluc·tu·a·tion

flue (CHIMNEY)
(*see also* flu)

flu·en·cy

flu·ent

flu·ent·ly

fluff·i·ly

fluff·i·ness

fluffy, *adj.*
fluff·i·er,
fluff·i·est

flü·gel·horn *or*
flue·gel·horn

flu·id

flu·id·i·ty

flum·mox

flun·ky, *n. pl.*
flun·kies

flu·o·resce, *v.*
flu·o·resced,
flu·o·resc·ing

flu·o·res·cence

(LIGHT) (*see also* florescence)

flu·o·res·cent (*see also* florescent)

flu·o·ri·date, *v.* flu·o·ri·dat·ed, flu·o·ri·dat·ing

flu·o·ri·da·tion

flu·o·ride

flu·o·ri·nate, *v.* flu·o·ri·nat·ed, flu·o·ri·nat·ing

flu·o·ri·nation

flu·o·rine

flu·o·ro·car·bon

flu·o·ro·scope, *v.* flu·o·ro·scoped, flu·o·ro·scop·ing

flu·o·ros·copy

flur·ry, *n. pl.* flur·ries

flur·ry, *v.* flur·ried, flur·ry·ing

flus·ter

flut·ed

flut·ing

flut·ist (*occas.* flau·tist)

flut·ter

flut·tery

fly (INSECT), *n. pl.* flies

fly (MOVE IN AIR), *v.* flew, flown, fly·ing

fly (HIT A FLYBALL), *v.* flied, fly·ing

fly·able

fly·blown

fly·by

fly-by-night

fly·catch·er

fly·er (*var. of* flier)

fly-fish·ing

fly·leaf, *n. pl.* fly·leaves

fly·over, *n.*

fly over, *v.*

fly·pa·per

fly·speck

fly·weight

fly·wheel

foam·i·ly

foam·i·ness

foamy, *adj.* foam·i·er, foam·i·est

fob, *v.* fobbed, fob·bing

fo·cal

fo·cal·ly

fo·cal·iza·tion

fo·cal·ize, *v.* fo·cal·ized, fo·ca·liz·ing

fo·cus, *n. pl.* fo·ci (*occas.* fo·cus·es)

fo·cus, *v.* fo·cused *or* fo·cussed, fo·cus·ing *or* fo·cus·sing

fod·der

foe

foe·tal (*var. of* fetal)

foe·tus (*var. of* fetus)

fog, *v.* fogged, fog·ging

fog·bound

fog·gi·ly

fog·gi·ness

fog·gy, *adj.* fog·gi·er, fog·gi·est

fog·horn

fo·gy (*occas.* fo·gey), *n. pl.* fo·gies (*occas.* fo·geys)

foi·ble

fold·away

fold·er

fol·de·rol

fold·out

fo·liage

fo·li·ate, *v.* fo·li·at·ed, fo·li·at·ing

fo·li·at·ed

fo·li·a·tion

fo·lio, *n. pl.* fo·li·os

folk, *n. pl.* folk *or* folks

folk·lore

folk·lor·ist

folksy, *adj.* folk·si·er, folk·si·est

folk·way

fol·li·cle

fol·low

fol·low·er

fol·low·ing

fol·low-through

fol·low-up, *adj., n.*

follow up, v.

fol·ly, n. pl. fol·lies

fo·ment

fo·men·ta·tion

fon·dant

fon·dle, v.
fon·dled,
fon·dling

fond·ly

fond·ness

fon·due (occas.
fon·du)

food·stuff

fool·har·di·ly

fool·har·di·ness

fool·har·dy

fool·ish

fool·ish·ly

fool·ish·ness

fool·proof

fool·scap (PAPER)

fool's cap
(JESTER'S CAP)

foot, n. pl. feet

foot·age

foot·ball

foot·board

foot·bridge

foot·can·dle

foot·ed

foot·fall

foot·hill

foot·hold

foot·ing

foot·lights

foot·lock·er

foot·loose

foot·man, n. pl.
foot·men

foot·mark

foot·note, v.
foot·not·ed,
foot·not·ing

foot·pad

foot·path

foot·pound

foot·print

foot·race

foot·rest

foot·sore

foot·step

foot·stool

foot·wear

foot·work

fop·pery, n. pl.
fop·per·ies

fop·pish

for·age, v.
for·aged,
for·ag·ing

for·ag·er

for·ay

for·bear
(CONTROL,
ABSTAIN), v.
for·bore,
for·borne,
for·bear·ing

for·bear·ance

for·bear·er (ONE
WHO
FORBEARS)
(see also
forebear)

for·bid (PROHIBIT),
v. for·bade or
for·bad,

for·bid·den,
for·bid·ding (see
also forebode)

force·ful

force·ful·ly

force·ful·ness

for·ceps, n. pl.
for·ceps

forc·ible

forc·ible·ness

forc·ibly

fore·arm

fore·bear
(ANCESTOR)
or fore·bear·ers
(see also
forbear,
forbearer)

fore·bode (WARN),
v. fore·bod·ed,
fore·bod·ing

fore·cast, v.
fore·cast or
fore·cast·ed,
fore·cast·ing

fore·cast·er

fore·cas·tle

fore·close, v.
fore·closed,
fore·clos·ing

fore·clo·sure

fore·deck

fore·doom

fore·fa·ther

fore·fin·ger

fore·foot

fore·front

fore·go (GO
BEFORE), v.
fore·went,

fore·gone,
fore·go·ing (see
also forgo)

fore·ground

fore·hand

fore·hand·ed

fore·hand·ed·ly

fore·hand·ed·ness

fore·head

for·eign

for·eign·er

fore·know·ledge

fore·lady, n. pl.
fore·lad·ies

fore·leg

fore·limb

fore·lock

fore·man, n. pl.
fore·men

fore·mast

fore·most

fore·name

fore·named

fore·noon

fo·ren·sic

fo·ren·si·cal·ly

fore·or·dain

fore·or·di·na·tion

fore·paw

fore·play

fore·quar·ter

fore·run·ner

fore·sad·dle

fore·said

fore·sail

fore·see, v.
fore·saw,

fore·seen,
fore·see·ing

fore·see·able

fore·shad·ow

fore·sheet

fore·shore

fore·short·en

fore·sight

fore·sight·ed·ly

fore·sight·ed·ness

fore·skin

for·est

fore·stall

for·es·ta·tion

for·est·ed

for·est·er

for·est·ry

fore·taste

fore·tell, v.
fore·told,
fore·tell·ing

fore·thought

fore·to·ken

fore·top

for·ev·er

for·ev·er·more

fore·warn

fore·wom·an, n. pl.
fore·wom·en

fore·word
(PREFACE)
(see also
forward)

for·feit

for·fei·ture

for·gath·er

forge, v. forged,
forg·ing

forg·er

forg·ery, n. pl.
forg·er·ies

for·get, v. for·got,
for·got·ten or
for·got,
for·get·ting

for·get·ful

for·get-me-not

for·get·ta·ble

for·giv·able

for·give, v.
for·gave,
for·giv·en,
for·giv·ing

for·give·ness

for·go (DO
WITHOUT), v.
for·went,
for·gone,
for·go·ing (see
also forego)

fo·rint, n. pl.
fo·rints (occas.
fo·rint)

forked

fork·lift

for·lorn

for·mal

form·al·de·hyde

For·ma·lin®

for·mal·ism

for·mal·i·ty, n. pl.
for·mal·i·ties

for·mal·iza·tion

for·mal·ize, v.
for·mal·ized,
for·mal·iz·ing

for·mal·ly (IN A
FORMAL

MANNER) (*see
also* formerly)

for·mat, *v.*
  for·mat·ted,
  for·mat·ting

for·ma·tion

for·ma·tive

for·mer

for·mer·ly
  (EARLIER) (*see
  also* formally)

form·fit·ting

For·mi·ca®

for·mi·da·ble

for·mi·da·bly

form·less

For·mo·sa

For·mo·san

for·mu·la, *n. pl.*
  for·mu·las *or*
  for·mu·lae

for·mu·late, *v.*
  for·mu·lat·ed,
  for·mu·lat·ing

for·mu·la·tion

for·mu·la·tor

for·ni·cate, *v.*
  for·ni·cat·ed,
  for·ni·cat·ing

for·ni·ca·tion

for·ni·ca·tor

for·sake, *v.*
  for·sook,
  for·sak·en,
  for·sak·ing

for·sooth

for·swear, *v.*
  for·swore,
  for·sworn,
  for·swear·ing

for·syth·ia

fort

forte (SKILL)

for·te (LOUDLY)

forth·com·ing

forth·right

forth·right·ly

forth·right·ness

forth·with

for·ti·eth

for·ti·fi·ca·tion

for·ti·fi·er

for·ti·fy, *v.*
  for·ti·fied,
  for·ti·fy·ing

for·tis·si·mo, *n. pl.*
  for·tis·si·mos *or*
  for·tis·si·mi

for·ti·tude

fort·night·ly

for·tress

for·tu·itous

for·tu·itous·ly

for·tu·itous·ness

for·tu·ity

for·tu·nate

for·tu·nate·ly

for·tune

for·tune·tell·er

for·tune·tell·ing

Fort Wayne

Fort Worth

for·ty, *n. pl.*
  for·ties

for·ty-five

for·ty-nin·er

fo·rum, *n. pl.*

fo·rums (*occas.*
  fo·ra)

for·ward (BOLD,
  TOWARD THE
  FRONT) (*see also*
  foreword)

for·ward·er

for·ward·ing

fos·sil

fos·sil·ize, *v.*
  fos·sil·ized,
  fos·sil·iz·ing

fos·ter

foul (DIRTY) (*see
  also* fowl)

fou·lard

foul·ly

foul·mouthed

foul·ness

foun·da·tion

foun·der
  (STUMBLE), *v.*

found·er (ONE
  WHO
  ESTABLISHES),
  n.

found·ling

found·ry, *n. pl.*
  found·ries

foun·tain

foun·tain·head

four-by-four

four-flush·er

four·fold

four-foot·ed

four-hand·ed

four-in-hand

four-post·er

four·score

four·some

four·square

four·teen

four·teenth

fourth

four-wheel·er

fowl (BIRD) (see also foul)

fox, n. pl. fox·es (occas. fox)

fox·glove

fox·hole

fox·hound

fox·i·ly

fox·i·ness

fox-trot

foxy, adj. fox·i·er, fox·i·est

foy·er

fra·cas, n. pl. fra·cas·es

frac·tion

frac·tion·al

frac·tion·al·ize, v. frac·tion·al·ized, frac·tion·al·iz·ing

frac·tion·al·ly

frac·tious

frac·tious·ly

frac·tious·ness

frac·ture·, v. frac·tured, frac·tur·ing

frag·ile

fra·gil·i·ty

frag·ment

frag·ment·al

frag·men·tal·ly

frag·men·tary

frag·men·ta·tion

fra·grance

fra·grant

fra·grant·ly

frail·ty, n. pl. frail·ties

frame, v. framed, fram·ing

fram·er

frame-up

frame·work

franc

France

fran·chise, v. fran·chised, fran·chis·ing

fran·chi·see

fran·chis·er

fran·ci·um

Fran·co·phile

fran·gi·bil·i·ty

fran·gi·ble

fran·gi·pani (occas. fran·gi·pan·ni), n. pl. fran·gi·pani or fran·gi·panis

frank

Fran·ken·stein

Frank·fort (KENTUCKY)

Frank·furt (GERMANY)

frank·furt·er or frank·fort·er or frank·furt or frank·fort

frank·in·cense

frank·ly

frank·ness

fran·tic

fran·ti·cal·ly

frap·pé or frappe

fra·ter·nal

fra·ter·nal·ly

fra·ter·ni·ty, n. pl. fra·ter·ni·ties

frat·er·ni·za·tion

frat·er·nize, v. frat·er·nized, frat·er·niz·ing

frat·ri·cid·al

frat·ri·cide

fraud·u·lence

fraud·u·lent

fraud·u·lent·ly

fraught

fraz·zle, v. fraz·zled. fraz·zling

freak·ish

freak·ish·ly

freak·ish·ness

freck·le

free base, n.

free-base, v.

free·bie or free·bee

free·boot·er

free·born

freed·man, n. pl. freed·men

free·dom

freed·wom·an, n. pl. freed·wom·en

free-fall

free-for-all

free-form

free·hand

free·hold

free lance, *n.* free-lance, *adj.*, *v.*

freer·load·er

free·ly

free·man, *n. pl.* free·men

Free·ma·son

free·stand·ing

free·stone

free·style

free·think·er

free·way

free·wheel

free·wom·an, *n. pl.* free·wom·en

freeze, *v.* froze, fro·zen, freez·ing

freeze-dry, *v.* freeze-dried, freeze-dry·ing

freez·er

freight·age

freight·er

French

French Gui·a·na

French Gui·a·nese

French·man, *n. pl.* French·men

French Poly·ne·sia

French Poly·ne·sian

French·wom·an, *n. pl.* French·wom·en

fre·net·ic

fre·net·i·cal·ly

fren·zied

fren·zy

Fre·on™

fre·quen·cy, *n. pl.* fre·quen·cies

fre·quent

fres·co, *n. pl.* fres·coes

fresh·en

fresh·et

fresh·ly

fresh·man, *n. pl.* fresh·men

fresh·ness

fresh·wa·ter

Fres·no

fret, *v.* fret·ted, fret·ting

fret·ful

fret·ful·ly

fret·ful·ness

fret·work

Freud·i·an

fri·a·ble

fri·ar (MONK)

fri·ary, *n. pl.* fri·ar·ies

fric·as·see, *v.* fric·as·seed, fric·as·see·ing

fric·tion

fric·tion·al·ly

Fri·day

friend·less

friend·li·ness

friend·ly, *adj.* friend·li·er, friend·li·est

friend·ship

fri·er (*var. of* fry·er) (*see also* friar)

frieze

frig·ate

fright·en

fright·ful

fright·ful·ly

fright·ful·ness

frig·id

Frig·id·aire™

fri·gid·i·ty

fri·gid·ly

fri·gid·ness

frilly, *adj.* frill·i·er, frill·i·est

Fris·bee ™

frisk·i·ly

frisk·i·ness

frisky, *adj.* frisk·i·er, frisk·i·est

fri·ta·ta

frit·ter

fri·vol·i·ty, *n. pl.* fri·vol·i·ties

friv·o·lous

friv·o·lous·ly

friv·o·lous·ness

frizz·i·ly

frizz·i·ness

friz·zle, *v.* friz·zled, friz·zling

friz·zy, *adj.* friz·zi·er, friz·zi·est

frog·man, *n. pl.*
frog·men

frol·ic, *v.*
frol·icked,
frol·ick·ing

frol·ic·some

front·age

fron·tal

fron·tier

fron·tiers·man, *n. pl.*
fron·tiers·men

fron·tis·piece

front-page

frost·belt

frost·bite

frost·bit·ten

frost·ed

frost·i·ly

frost·i·ness

frost·ing

frosty, *adj.*
frost·i·er,
frost·i·est

froth·i·ly

froth·i·ness

frothy, *adj.*
froth·i·er,
froth·i·est

frou·frou

fro·ward

frown

frow·zy, *adj.*
frow·zi·er,
frow·zi·est

_ro·zen

fruc·ti·fi·ca·tion

fruc·ti·fy, *v.*

fruc·ti·fied,
fruc·ti·fy·ing

fruc·tose

fruc·tu·ous

fru·gal

fru·gal·i·ty, *n. pl.*
fru·gal·i·ties

fru·gal·ly

fruit

fruit·cake

fruit·ful·ly

fruit·ful·ness

fru·ition

fruit·less

fruit·less·ly

fruit·less·ness

fruity, *adj.*
fruit·i·er,
fruit·i·est

frump·ish

frumpy, *adj.*
frump·i·er,
frump·i·est

frus·trate, *v.*
frus·trat·ed,
frus·trat·ing

frus·tra·tion

fry, *v.* fried, fry·ing

fry·er *or* fri·er

fuch·sia

fud·dle, *v.*
fud·dled,
fud·dling

fud·dy-dud·dy

fudge, *v.* fudged,
fudg·ing

fu·el, *v.* fu·eled *or*
fu·elled,

fu·el·ing *or*
fu·el·ling

fu·gi·tive

fugue

füh·rer *or* fueh·rer

ful·crum, *n. pl.*
ful·crums *or*
ful·cra

ful·fill *or* ful·fil, *v.*
ful·filled,
ful·fill·ing

ful·fill·ment

full·back

full-blood·ed

full-blown

full-bod·ied

full·er

full-fash·ioned

full-fledged

full-length

full-scale

full time, *n.*

full-time, *adj.*

ful·ly

ful·mi·nate, *v.*
ful·mi·nat·ed,
ful·mi·nat·ing

ful·mi·na·tion

ful·mi·na·tor

ful·some

ful·some·ly

ful·some·ness

fu·ma·role

fum·ble, *v.*
fum·bled,
fum·bling

fu·mi·gant

fu·mi·gate, *v.*

fu·mi·gat·ed,
fu·mi·gat·ing

fu·mi·ga·tion

fu·mi·ga·tor

func·tion

func·tion·al

func·tion·al·ism

func·tion·al·ly

func·tion·ary, *n. pl.*
func·tion·ar·ies

func·tion·less

fun·da·men·tal

fun·da·men·tal·ism

fun·da·men·tal·ist

fun·da·men·tal·ly

fund-rais·ing

fu·ner·al

fu·ner·ary

fu·ne·re·al

fun·gi·cid·al

fun·gi·cide

fun·go, *n. pl.*
fun·goes

fun·gus, *n. pl.*
fun·gi (*occas.*
fun·gus·es)

fu·nic·u·lar

funky, *adj.*
funk·i·er,
funk·i·est

fun·nel, *v.*
fun·neled
(*occas.*
fun·nelled),
fun·nel·ing
(*occas.*
fun·nel·ling)

fun·ni·ly

fun·ni·ness

fun·ny, *adj.*
fun·ni·er,
fun·ni·est

fur

fur·be·low

fur·bish

fu·ri·ous

fu·ri·ous·ly

fu·ri·ous·ness

furl

fur·long

fur·lough

fur·nace

fur·nish

fur·nished

fur·nish·ings

fur·ni·ture

fu·ror

fur·ri·er

fur·row

fur·ry (HAVING
FUR), *adj.*
fur·ri·er, fur·ri·est
(*see also* fury)

fur·ther
(ADDITIONAL)
(*see also* farther)

fur·ther·ance

fur·ther·more

fur·ther·most

fur·thest

fur·tive

fur·tive·ly

fur·tive·ness

fu·ry (ANGER), *n.*
pl. fu·ries (*see
also* furry)

fu·se·lage

fus·ibil·i·ty

fus·ible

fus·il·lade

fu·si·lier *or*
fu·sil·eer

fu·sion

fuss·bud·get

fuss·i·ly

fuss·i·ness

fussy, *adj.* fuss·i·er,
fuss·i·est

fus·tian

fus·ti·ly

fus·ti·ness

fus·ty, *adj.* fus·ti·er,
fus·ti·est

fu·tile

fu·til·i·ty

fu·ton

fu·ture

fu·tur·ism

fu·tur·ist

fu·tur·is·tic

fu·tu·ri·ty

fu·tur·ol·o·gy

fuzz·i·ly

fuzz·i·ness

fuzzy, *adj.*
fuzz·i·er,
fuzz·i·est

G

gab, *v.* gabbed,
  gab·bing
gab·ar·dine
  (FABRIC) (*see
  also* gaberdine)
gab·ble, *v.*
  gab·bled,
  gab·bling
gab·by, *adj.*
  gab·bi·er,
  gab·bi·est
gab·er·dine
  (GARMENT)
  (*see also*
  gabardine)
gab·fest
ga·ble
ga·bled
Ga·bon
Gab·o·nese
gad·about
gad·fly, *n. pl.*
  gad·flies
gad·get
gad·get·ry
gad·o·lin·i·um
Gael·ic
gaff (HOOK)

gaffe (BLUNDER)
gaf·fer
gag, *v.* gagged,
  gag·ging
gage (PLEDGE)
  (*var. of* gauge)
gag·gle
gag·man, *n. pl.*
  gag·men
gag·ster
gai·ety, *n. pl.*
  gai·eties
gai·ly
gain·er
gain·ful·ly
gain·ful·ness
gain·say, *v.*
  gain·said,
  gain·say·ing,
  gain·says
gain·sayer
gait
gai·ter
ga·la
ga·lac·tic
Ga·lá·pa·gos
  Is·lands

gal·axy, *n. pl.*
  gal·ax·ies
gal·lant
gal·lant·ly
gal·lant·ry, *n. pl.*
  gal·lant·ries
gall·blad·der
gal·le·on
gal·le·ria
gal·le·ried
gal·lery, *n. pl.*
  gal·ler·ies
gal·ley, *n. pl.*
  gal·leys
Gal·lic
gall·ing
gall·ing·ly
gal·li·um
gal·li·vant
gal·lon
gal·lop (FAST
  PACE) (*see also*
  galop)
gal·lop·er
gal·lop·ing
gal·lows, *n. pl.*
  gal·lows *or*
  gal·lows·es

gall·stone

ga·loot

ga·lop (LIVELY
  DANCE) (see
  also gallop)

ga·lore

ga·losh

gal·van·ic

gal·va·nism

gal·va·ni·za·tion

gal·va·nize, v.
  gal·va·nized,
  gal·va·niz·ing

gal·va·nom·e·ter

Gam·bia

Gam·bi·an

gam·bit

gam·ble (WAGER)
  v. gam·bled,
  gam·bling (see
  also gambol)

gam·bler

gam·bol (FROLIC)
  v. gam·boled or
  gam·bolled,
  gam·bol·ing or
  gam·bol·ling
  (see also
  gamble)

gam·brel

game, v. gamed,
  gam·ing

game·cock

game·keep·er

game·ly

games·man·ship

game·ster

ga·mete

gam·i·ly

gam·in

gam·i·ness

gam·ma glob·u·lin

gam·ut

gamy or gam·ey,
  adj. gam·i·er,
  gam·i·est

gan·der

gan·dy danc·er

gang·bust·er

gang·land

gan·gling

gan·gli·on, n. pl.
  gang·lia or
  gang·li·ons

gang·plank

gan·grene

gan·gre·nous

gang·ster

gang·ster·ism

gang·way

gan·net, n. pl.
  gan·nets (occas.
  gan·net)

gant·let (var. of
  gauntlet)

gan·try, n. pl.
  gan·tries

gap, v. gapped,
  gap·ping

gape, v. gaped,
  gap·ing

gar

ga·rage, v.
  ga·raged,
  ga·rag·ing

ga·rage·man, n. pl.
  ga·rage·men

gar·bage

gar·ban·zo, n. pl.
  gar·ban·zos

gar·ble, v. gar·bled,
  gar·bling

garçon

gar·den

gar·den·er

gar·de·nia

gar·gan·tuan

gar·gle, v. gar·gled,
  gar·gling

gar·goyle

gar·ish

gar·land

gar·lic

gar·licky

gar·ment

gar·ner

gar·net

gar·nish

gar·nish·ee

gar·nish·ment

gar·ni·ture

gar·ret

gar·ri·son

gar·rote or
  gar·rotte, v.
  gar·rot·ed or
  gar·rott·ed,
  gar·rot·ing or
  gar·rott·ing

gar·ru·li·ty

gar·ru·lous

gar·ru·lous·ly

gar·ru·lous·ness

gar·ter

Gary

gas, *n. pl.* gas·es
(*occas.* gas·ses)

gas, *v.* gassed,
gas·sing

gas·eous

gas·i·fi·ca·tion

gas·i·fy, *v.* gas·i·fied,
gas·i·fy·ing

gas·ket

gas·light

gas·o·hol

gas·o·line (*occas.*
gas·o·lene)

gas·ser

gas·si·ness

gas·sy, *adj.*
gas·si·er,
gas·si·est

gas·tric

gas·tri·tis

gas·tro·en·ter·ol·o·gist

gas·tro·en·ter·ol·o·gy

gas·tro·in·tes·ti·nal

gas·tro·nom·ic

gas·tro·nom·i·cal

gas·tro·nom·i·cal·ly

gas·tron·o·my

gas·works

gate

gate-crash·er

gate·post

gate·way

gath·er

gath·er·er

gauche

gau·che·rie

gau·cho, *n. pl.*
gau·chos

gaud·i·ly

gaud·i·ness

gaudy, *adj.*
gaud·i·er,
gaud·i·est

gauge (MEASURE),
v. gauged,
gaug·ing (*see
also* gage)

gaunt

gaunt·let (*occas.*
gant·let)

gaunt·ness

gauze

gauzy, *adj.*
gauz·i·er,
gauz·i·est

ga·vage

gav·el, *v.* gav·eled
or gav·elled,
gav·el·ing *or*
gav·el·ling

ga·votte

gawk·ish

gawk·ish·ly

gawk·ish·ness

gawky, *adj.*
gawk·i·er,
gawk·i·est

gaze, *v.* gazed,
gaz·ing

ga·ze·bo, *n. pl.*
ga·ze·bos

ga·zelle, *n. pl.*
ga·zelles (*occas.*
ga·zelle)

gaz·er

ga·zette

gaz·et·teer

gaz·pa·cho, *n. pl.*
gaz·pa·chos

gear·box

gear·ing

gear·shift

geck·o, *n. pl.*
geck·os *or*
geck·oes

gee·zer

ge·fil·te fish

gei·sha, *n. pl.*
gei·sha *or*
gei·shas

gel, *v.* gelled,
gel·ling

gel·a·tin (*occas.*
gel·a·tine)

ge·la·ti·ni·za·tion

ge·la·ti·nize, *v.*
ge·la·ti·nized,
ge·la·ti·niz·ing

ge·lat·i·nous

ge·lat·i·nous·ly

ge·lat·i·nous·ness

geld, *v.* geld·ed, *or*
gelt, geld·ing

geld·ing

gel·id

ge·lid·i·ty

gel·ig·nite

gem·i·nate
(DOUBLE), *v.*
gem·i·nat·ed,
gem·i·nat·ing
(*see also*
germinate)

gem·i·na·tion

Gem·i·ni

gem·ol·o·gist *or*
gem·mol·o·gist

gem·ol·o·gy *or*
  gem·mol·o·gy

gem·stone

gen·darme

gen·dar·mer·ie *or*
  gen·dar·mery,
  n. pl.
  gen·dar·mer·ies

gen·der

gen·der-spe·cif·ic,
  adj.

ge·ne·a·log·i·cal

ge·ne·a·log·i·cal·ly

ge·ne·al·o·gist

ge·ne·al·o·gy, *n. pl.*
  ge·ne·al·o·gies

gen·er·al

gen·er·a·lis·si·mo,
  n. pl.
  gen·er·a·lis·si·mos

gen·er·al·ist

gen·er·al·i·ty, *n. pl.*
  gen·er·al·i·ties

gen·er·al·iza·tion

gen·er·al·ize, *v.*
  gen·er·al·ized,
  gen·er·al·iz·ing

gen·er·al·ly

gen·er·al·ship

gen·er·ate, *v.*
  gen·er·at·ed,
  gen·er·at·ing

gen·er·a·tion

gen·er·a·tive

gen·er·a·tor

ge·ner·ic

ge·ner·i·cal·ly

gen·er·os·i·ty, *n. pl.*
  gen·er·os·i·ties

gen·er·ous

gen·er·ous·ly

gen·er·ous·ness

gen·e·sis, *n. pl.*
  gen·e·ses

gene-splic·ing

ge·net·ic

ge·net·i·cal·ly

ge·net·ics

ge·nial

ge·nial·i·ty

ge·nial·ly

gen·ic

ge·nie, *n. pl.* genies
  (*occas.* ge·nii)

gen·i·tal

gen·i·ta·lia

gen·i·tals

gen·i·tive

gen·i·to·uri·nary

ge·nius, *n. pl.*
  ge·nius·es

geno·cid·al

geno·cide

genre

gens, *n. pl.* gen·tes

gen·teel

gen·tian

gen·tile

gen·til·i·ty

gen·tle, *adj.*
  gen·tler,
  gen·tlest

gen·tle, *v.* gen·tled,
  gen·tling

gen·tle·folk

gen·tle·man, *n. pl.*
  gen·tle·men

gen·tle·man·ly

gen·tle·wom·an, *n.*
  pl. gen·tle·wom·en

gen·tly

gen·tri·fi·ca·tion

gen·tri·fy, *v.*
  gen·tri·fied,
  gen·tri·fy·ing

gen·try, *n. pl.*
  gen·tries

gen·u·flect

gen·u·flec·tion

gen·u·ine

gen·u·ine·ly

gen·u·ine·ness

ge·nus, *n. pl.*
  gen·era

geo·cen·tric

geo·cen·tri·cal·ly

geo·chem·i·cal

geo·chem·i·cal·ly

geo·chem·is·try

geo·chro·no·log·i·cal

geo·chro·nol·o·gy

geo·de·sic

ge·od·e·sy

geo·det·ic

geo·det·i·cal·ly

geo·graph·ic

geo·graph·i·cal

geo·graph·i·cal·ly

ge·og·ra·phy, *n. pl.*
  ge·og·ra·phies

geo·log·ic

geo·log·i·cal

geo·log·i·cal·ly

ge·ol·o·gist

ge·ol·o·gy, *n. pl.*
ge·ol·o·gies

geo·mag·net·ic

geo·mag·ne·tism

geo·met·ric

geo·met·ri·cal

geo·met·ri·cal·ly

geo·me·tri·cian

ge·om·e·try, *n. pl.*
ge·om·e·tries

geo·phys·i·cal

geo·phys·i·cist

geo·phys·ics

geo·po·lit·i·cal

geo·po·lit·i·cal·ly

geo·pol·i·ti·cian

geo·pol·i·tics

George

Geor·gia

Geor·gian

geo·sta·tion·ary

geo·ther·mal

ge·ra·ni·um

ger·bil (*occas.*
ger·bille)

ge·ri·at·ric

ger·i·a·tri·cian

Ger·man

ger·mane

Ger·man·ic

ger·ma·ni·um

Ger·ma·ny

ger·mi·cid·al

ger·mi·cide

ger·mi·nal

ger·mi·nate (TO
SPROUT), *v.*

ger·mi·nat·ed,
ger·mi·nat·ing
(*see also*
geminate)

ger·mi·na·tion

ger·on·tol·o·gist

ger·on·tol·o·gy

ger·ry·man·der

ger·und

ge·stalt, *n. pl.*
ge·stalt·en *or*
ge·stalts

ge·sta·po, *n. pl.*
ges·ta·pos

ges·tate, *v.*
ges·tat·ed,
ges·tat·ing

ges·ta·tion

ges·tic·u·late, *v.*
ges·tic·u·lat·ed,
ges·tic·u·lat·ing

ges·tic·u·la·tion

ges·ture, *v*
ges·tured,
ges·tur·ing

ge·sund·heit

get, *v.* got, got *or*
got·ten, get·ting

get·away

gew·gaw

gey·ser

Gha·na

Gha·na·ian *or*
Gha·nian

ghast·li·ness

ghast·ly, *adj.*
ghast·li·er,
ghast·li·est

gher·kin

ghet·to, *n. pl.*

ghet·tos *or*
ghet·toes

ghet·to·iza·tion

ghet·to·ize, *v.*
ghet·to·ized,
ghet·to·iz·ing

ghost·li·ness

ghost·ly, *adj.*
ghost·li·er,
ghost·li·est

ghost·write, *v.*
ghost·wrote,
ghost·written,
ghost·writ·ing

ghost·writ·er

ghoul·ish

ghoul·ish·ly

ghoul·ish·ness

gi·ant

gi·ant·ess

gi·ant·ism

gi·ar·di·a·sis, *n. pl.*
gi·ar·di·a·ses

gib, *v.* gib·bed,
gib·bing

gib·ber

gib·ber·ish

gib·bet

gib·bon

gib·bos·i·ty

gib·bous

gibe (TAUNT), *v.*
gibed, gib·ing
(*see also* jibe)

gib·er

gib·lets

Gi·bral·tar

Gi·bral·tar·i·an

gid·di·ly

gid·di·ness

gid·dy, *adj.*
gid·di·er,
gid·di·est

gift·ed

gig, *v.* gigged,
gig·ging

gi·ga·hertz

gi·gan·tic

gi·gan·ti·cal·ly

gi·gan·tism

gig·gle, *v.* gig·gled,
gig·gling

gig·gly, *adj.*
gig·gli·er,
gig·gli·est

gig·o·lo, *n. pl.*
gig·o·los

gild, *v.* gild·ed *or*
gilt, gild·ing

gilt

gilt-edged *or* gilt-
edge, *adj.*

gim·bal

gim·crack

gim·let

gim·mick

gim·mick·ry, *n. pl.*
gim·mick·ries

gim·micky

gimpy

gin, *v.* ginned,
gin·ning

gin·ger

gin·ger·bread

gin·ger·ly

gin·ger·snap

ging·ham

gin·gi·vi·tis

gink·go (*occas.*
ging·ko), *n. pl.*
gink·goes *or*
gink·gos

gin·seng

gi·raffe, *n. pl.*
gi·raffes *or*
gi·raffe

gird, *v.* gird·ed *or*
girt, gird·ing

gird·er

gir·dle, *v.* gir·dled,
gir·dling

girl·friend

girl·hood

girl·ish

girl·ish·ly

girl·ish·ness

girth

gismo, (*var. of*
gizmo)

gist

give, *v.* gave,
giv·en, giv·ing

give-and-take

give·away

giv·en

giz·mo *or* gis·mo,
n. pl. giz·mos *or*
gis·mos

giz·ard

gla·brous

gla·cé

gla·cial

gla·cial·ly

gla·ci·ate, *v.*
gla·ci·at·ed,
gla·ci·at·ing

gla·ci·a·tion

gla·cier

gla·ci·ol·o·gist

gla·ci·ol·o·gy

glad, *adj.* glad·der,
glad·dest

glad·den

glad·i·a·tor

glad·i·a·to·ri·al

glad·i·o·la, *var. pl.*
of glad·i·o·lus

glad·i·o·lus, *n. pl.*
glad·i·o·li *or*
glad·i·o·lus *or*
glad·i·o·lus·es

glad·ly

glad·ness

glad·some

glad·stone

glam·or·ize, *v.*
glam·or·ized,
glam·or·iz·ing

glam·or·ous (*occas.*
glam·our·ous*)

glam·or·ous·ly

glam·or·ous·ness

glam·our *or*
glam·or

glance, *v.* glanced,
glanc·ing

glanc·ing

glan·du·lar

glare, *v.* glared,
glar·ing

glar·ing

glas·nost

glass·ful

glass·i·ly

glass·ine

glass·i·ness

glass·ware

glassy, *adj.*
  glass·i·er,
  glass·i·est

glau·co·ma

gla·zier

glaze, *v.* glazed,
  glaz·ing

glaz·ing

glean·able

glean·er

glean·ings

glee·ful

glee·ful·ly

glee·ful·ness

glib, *adj.* glib·ber,
  glib·best

glib·ly

glib·ness

glide, *v.* glid·ed,
  glid·ing

glid·er

glim·mer

glimpse, *v.*
  glimpsed,
  glimps·ing

glis·sade, *v.*

glis·sad·ed,
  glis·sad·ing

glis·san·do, *n. pl.*
  glis·san·di *or*
  glis·san·dos

glis·ten

glitch

glit·ter

glit·tery

gloam·ing

gloat

glob·al

glob·al·ism

glob·al·ly

globe-trot·ter

globe-trot·ting

glob·u·lar

glob·ule

glob·u·lin

glock·en·spiel

glom, *v.* glommed,
  glom·ming

gloom·i·ly

gloom·i·ness

gloomy, *adj.*
  gloom·i·er,
  gloom·i·est

glo·ri·fi·ca·tion

glo·ri·fy, *v.*
  glo·ri·fied,
  glo·ri·fy·ing

glo·ri·ous

glo·ri·ous·ly

glo·ri·ous·ness

glo·ry, *n. pl.*
  glo·ries

glos·sa·ry, *n. pl.*

glos·sa·ries

gloss·i·ly

gloss·i·ness

glossy, *adj.*
  gloss·i·er,
  gloss·i·est

glot·tal

glot·tis, *pl.*
  glot·tis·es *or*
  glot·ti·des

glove, *v.* gloved,
  glov·ing

glow·er

glow·worm

glu·ca·gon

glu·cose

glue, *v.* glued,
  glu·ing

glu·ey, *adj.* glu·i·er,
  glu·i·est

glut, *v.* glut·ted,
  glut·ting

glu·ta·mate

glu·ten

glu·te·nous (OF
  GLUTEN)

glu·ti·nous
  (STICKY)

glut·ton

glut·ton·ous

glut·tony, *n. pl.*
  glut·ton·ies

glyc·er·in *or*
  glyc·er·ine

glyc·er·ol

gly·co·gen

G-man, *n. pl.* G-
  men

gnarled

gnarly, *adj.*
  gnarl·i·er,
  gnarl·i·est

gnash

gnat

gnaw

gneiss

gnoc·chi

gnome

gnom·ish

gnos·tic

gnos·ti·cism

gnu, *n. pl.* gnu *or* gnus

go, *v.* went, gone, going

goad

go-ahead, *adj., n.*

goal·ie

goal·keep·er

goal·post

goal·tend·ing

goat, *n. pl.* goats *or* goat

goa·tee

goat·skin

gob·ble, *v.* gob·bled, gob·bling

gob·ble·dy·gook *or* gob·ble·de·gook

gob·bler

go-between

gob·let

gob·lin

god·child, *n. pl.* god·chil·dren

god·dam *or* god·damn *or* god·damned

god·daught·er

god·dess

god·fa·ther

god·less

god·less·ness

god·like

god·li·ness

god·ly

god·mother

god·parent

god·send

god·son

God·speed

go-getter

gog·gle, *v.* gog·gled, gog·gling

gog·gles

go-go

go·ings-on

goi·ter

gold

gold·brick

gold·en

gold·en·rod

gold·field

gold·filled

gold·finch

gold·fish, *n. pl.* gold·fish *or* gold·fish·es

gold·smith

golf·er

go·nad

gon·do·la

gon·do·lier

gon·er

gon·fa·lon

gon·or·rhea

gon·or·rhe·al

gon·zo

good·bye

good-heart·ed

good-heart·ed·ly

good-heart·ed·ness

good-hu·mored

good-hu·mored·ly

good-hu·mored·ness

good-look·ing

good·ly, *adj.* good·li·er, good·li·est

good-na·tured

good-na·tured·ly

good-na·tured·ness

good·ness

good-tem·pered

good-tem·pered·ly

good-tem·pered·ness

good·will

goody *or* good·ie, *n. pl.* good·ies

goody-goody

goof·i·ly

goof·i·ness

goof-off

goofy, *adj.* goof·i·er, goof·i·est

goo·gol·plex

goose, *n. pl.* geese

goose·ber·ry, *n. pl.* goose·ber·ries

goose·flesh

goose·neck

go·pher

gore, *v.* gored, gor·ing

gorge, *v.* gorged, gorg·ing

gor·geous

gor·geous·ly

gor·geous·ness

Gor·gon·zola

go·ril·la (APE) (*see also* guerrilla)

gor·man·dize, *v.* gor·man·dized, gor·man·diz·ing

gor·man·diz·er

gory, *adj.* gor·i·er, gor·i·est

gos·hawk

gos·ling

gos·pel

gos·sa·mer

gos·sip

Goth·ic

Gou·da

gouge, *v.* gouged, goug·ing

gou·lash

gourd (PLANT)

gourde (MONEY)

gour·mand

gour·met

gout

gov·ern

gov·er·nance

gov·er·ness

gov·ern·ment

gov·ern·men·tal

gov·ern·men·tal·ly

gov·ern·men·tese

gov·er·nor

gov·er·nor gen·er·al, *n. pl.* gov·er·nors gen·er·al *or* gov·er·nor gen·er·als

grab, *v.* grabbed, grab·bing

grab·by, *adj.* grab·bi·er, grab·bi·est

grace, *v.* graced, grac·ing

grace·ful

grace·ful·ly

grace·less

grace·less·ly

grace·less·ness

gra·cious

gra·cious·ly

gra·cious·ness

grack·le

gra·da·tion

grade, *v.* grad·ed, grad·ing

grad·er

gra·di·ent

grad·u·al

grad·u·a·lism

grad·u·al·ly

grad·u·al·ness

grad·u·ate, *v.* grad·u·at·ed, grad·u·at·ing

grad·u·a·tion

graf·fi·ti, *n. pl. of* graf·fi·to

graft·er

grain·field

grainy, *adj.* grain·i·er, grain·i·est

gram

gram·mar

gram·mar·i·an

gram·mat·i·cal

gram·mat·i·cal·ly

Gra·na·da (SPAIN) (*see also* Grenada)

gra·na·ry, *n. pl.* gra·na·ries

grand·child, *n. pl.* grand·chil·dren

grand·daugh·ter

gran·dee

gran·deur

grand·fa·ther

gran·dil·o·quence

gran·dil·o·quent

gran·dil·o·quent·ly

gran·di·ose

gran·di·ose·ly

gran·di·ose·ness

gran·di·o·so

grand·ly

grand·moth·er

grand·par·ent

grand·son

grand·stand

grange

grang·er·ism

gran·ite

gran·ite·ware

gran·ny *or* gran·nie, *n. pl.* gran·nies

gra·no·la

grant·ee

grant-in-aid, *n. pl.* grants-in-aid

grant·or

grants·man·ship

gran·u·lar

gran·u·late
gran·u·la·tion
gran·ule
grape·fruit
grape·shot
grape·vine
graph·ic
graph·i·cal
graph·i·cal·ly
graph·ics
graph·ite
grap·nel
grap·pa
grap·ple, *v.*
  grap·pled,
  grap·pling
grasp·er
grass·hop·per
grass·land
grassy, *adj.*
  grass·i·er,
  grass·i·est
grate, *v.* grat·ed,
  grat·ing
grate·ful
grate·ful·ly
grate·ful·ness
grat·er
grat·i·fi·ca·tion
grat·i·fy, *v.*
  grat·i·fied,
  grat·i·fy·ing
grat·ing
gra·tis
grat·i·tude
gra·tu·itous
gra·tu·ity
gra·va·men, *n. pl.*

gra·va·mens *or*
gra·vam·i·na
grave, *adj.* grav·er,
  grav·est
grave·dig·ger
grav·el, *v.*
  grav·eled *or*
  grav·elled,
  grav·el·ing *or*
  grav·el·ling
grav·el·ly
grave·ly
grave·ness
grave·side
grave·stone
grave·yard
grav·i·tate, *v.*
  grav·i·tat·ed,
  grav·i·tat·ing
grav·i·ta·tion
grav·i·ty, *n. pl.*
  grav·i·ties
gra·vy, *n. pl.*
  gra·vies
gray
gray·beard
gray·ish
graze, *v.* grazed,
  graz·ing
grease, *v.* greased,
  greas·ing
grease·paint
grease·wood
greas·i·ly
greas·i·ness
greasy, *adj.*
  greas·i·er,
  greas·i·est
great-aunt

Great Brit·ain
great·coat
great·er
Great Falls
great·ly
great·ness
great-uncle
grebe
Gre·cian
Greece
greed·i·ly
greed·i·ness
greedy, *adj.*
  greed·i·er,
  greed·i·est
Greek
green·back
green·belt
green·ery, *n. pl.*
  green·er·ies
green·gro·cer
green·horn
green·house
green·ish
Green·land
Green·land·er
green·ness
Greens·boro
green·room
greet·er
greet·ing
gre·gar·i·ous
gre·gar·i·ous·ly
gre·gar·i·ous·ness
Greg·o·ry
grem·lin
Gre·na·da (WEST

INDIES) (*see
  also Granada)

gre·nade

gren·a·dier

gren·a·dine

grey (*var. of* gray,
  chiefly Brit.)

grey·hound

grid·dle, *v.*
  grid·dled,
  grid·dling

grid·iron

grid·lock

griev·ance

grieve, *v.* grieved,
  griev·ing

griev·ous

griev·ous·ly

griev·ous·ness

grill (TO COOK), *v.*
  (*see also* grille)

grille (METAL
  GRATING), *n.*
  (*see also* grill)

grill·work

grim, *adj.*
  grim·mer,
  grim·mest

gri·mace, *v.*
  gri·maced,
  gri·mac·ing

grim·i·ness

grim·ly

grimy, *adj.*
  grim·i·er,
  grim·i·est

grin, *v.* grinned,
  grin·ning

grind, *v.* ground,
  grind·ing

grind·er

grind·stone

grin·go, *n. pl.*
  grin·gos

grip (HOLD), *v.*
  gripped,
  grip·ping (*see
  also* gripe,
  grippe)

gripe (COMPLAIN),
  v. griped, grip·ing
  (*see also* grip,
  grippe)

grippe (ILLNESS),
  n. (*see also* grip,
  gripe)

gris-gris, *n. pl.*
  gris-gris

gris·li·ness

gris·ly, *adj.*
  gris·li·er,
  gris·li·est

grist

gris·tle

gris·tli·ness

gris·tly

grist·mill

grit *v.* grit·ted,
  grit·ting

grit·ti·ness

grit·ty, *adj.*
  grit·ti·er,
  grit·ti·est

griz·zled

griz·zly, *adj.*
  griz·zli·er
  griz·zli·est

gro·cer

gro·cery, *n. pl.*
  gro·cer·ies

grog·gi·ly

grog·gi·ness

grog·gy, *adj.*
  grog·gi·er,
  grog·gi·est

gro·gram

groin

grom·met

groove, *v.*
  grooved,
  groov·ing

groovy, *adj.*
  groov·i·er,
  groov·i·est

grope, *v.* groped,
  grop·ing

gro·schen, *n. pl.*
  gro·schen

gros·grain

gross, *n. pl.* gross

gross·ly

gross·ness

gro·szy (*occas.*
  grosz *or*
  grosze), *n. pl.*
  gro·szy

gro·tesque

gro·tesque·ly

gro·tesque·ness

gro·tes·que·rie
  (*occas.*
  gro·tes·que·ry),
  n. pl.
  gro·tes·que·ries

grot·to, *n. pl.*
  grot·toes
  (*occas.* grot·tos)

grouch·i·ly

grouch·i·ness

grouchy, *adj.*
  grouch·i·er,
  grouch·i·est

ground·er
ground·hog
ground·less
grounds·keep·er
ground·work
group·er
group·ie
group·ing
grouse, *n. pl.*
  grouse *or*
  grous·es
grouse, *v.* groused,
  grous·ing
grov·el, *v.*
  grov·eled *or*
  grov·elled,
  grov·el·ing *or*
  grov·el·ling
grov·el·er
grow, *v.* grew,
  grown, grow·ing
grow·er
growl·er
growl·ing
grown-up, *adj. n.*
growth
grub, *v.* grubbed,
  grub·bing
grub·bi·ly
grub·bi·ness
grub·by, *adj.*
  grub·bi·er,
  grub·bi·est
grub·stake
grudge, *v.*
  grudged,
  grudg·ing
grudg·ing·ly
gruel

gru·el·ing *or*
  gru·el·ling
grue·some
grue·some·ly
grue·some·ness
gruff·ly
grum·ble, *v.*
  grum·bled,
  grum·bling
grum·bler
grump·i·ly
grump·i·ness
grumpy, *adj.*
  grump·i·er,
  grump·i·est
grun·ion
Gru·yère
G-string
G-suit
gua·ca·mo·le
Gua·da·la·ja·ra
Gua·de·loupe
Gua·da·loup·ian
Guam
gua·no, *n. pl.*
  gua·nos
gua·ra·ni, *n. pl.*
  gua·ra·ni *or*
  gua·ra·nis
guar·an·tee
guar·an·tor
guar·an·ty, *n. pl.*
  guar·an·ties
guard·house
guard·ian
guard·rail
guard·room

guards·man, *n. pl.*
  guards·men
Gua·te·ma·la
Gua·te·ma·lan
gua·va
gu·ber·na·to·ri·al
guern·sey, *n. pl.*
  guern·seys
guer·ril·la *or*
  gue·ril·la
  (WARRIOR)
  (*see also*
  gorilla)
guess·ti·mate, *v.*
  guess·ti·mat·ed,
  guess·ti·mat·ing
guess·work
guest
guf·faw
Gui·a·na, French
Gui·a·nese, French
guid·able
guid·ance
guide, *v.* guid·ed,
  guid·ing
guide·book
guide·line
guide·post
gui·don
guild
guild·er
guild·hall
guile
guile·ful
guile·ful·ly
guile·less
guil·lo·tine, *v.*
  guil·lo·tined,
  guil·lo·tin·ing

guilt

guilt·i·ly

guilt·i·ness

guilt·less

guilty, *adj.*
guilt·i·er,
guilt·i·est

Guin·ea

Guin·ea-Bis·sau

Guin·ean

guise

gui·tar

gu·lag

gulch

gul·den, *n. pl.*
gul·dens *or*
gul·den

gull

gul·let

gull·ibil·i·ty

gull·ible

gull·ibly

gul·ly, *n. pl.*
gul·lies

gum, *v.* gummed,
gum·ming

gum·bo, *n. pl.*
gum·bos

gum·boil

gum·drop

gum·mi·ness

gum·my, *adj.*
gum·mi·er,
gum·mi·est

gump·tion

gum·shoe

gun, *v.* gunned,
gun·ning

gun·boat

gun·cot·ton

gun·fight

gun·fire

gung ho

Gun·ite®

gun·lock

gun·man, *n. pl.*
gun·men

gun·met·al

gun·ner

gun·nery

gun·ny·sack

gun·point

gun·pow·der

gun·run·ner

gun·ship

gun·shot

gun·shy

gun·smith

gun·wale

gup·py, *n. pl.*
gup·pies

gur·gle, *v.* gur·gled,
gur·gling

gu·ru

gush·er

gushy, *adj.*
gush·i·er,
gush·i·est

gus·set

gus·ta·to·ry

gust·i·ly

gust·i·ness

gus·to, *n. pl.*
gus·toes

gusty, *adj.*
gust·i·er,
gust·i·est

gut, *v.* gut·ted,
gut·ting

gut·less

gut·less·ness

gutsy, *adj.*
guts·i·er,
guts·i·est

gut·ta-per·cha

gut·ter

gut·ter·snipe

gut·tur·al

Guy·ana

Guy·a·nese

guy·ot

guz·zle, *v.* guz·zled,
guz·zling

gym·kha·na

gym·na·si·um, *n.*
pl. gym·na·si·ums
or gym·na·sia

gym·nast

gym·nast·ic

gym·no·sperm

gy·ne·co·log·i·cal

gy·ne·col·o·gist

gy·ne·col·o·gy

gyp, *v.* gypped,
gyp·ping

gyp·sum

Gyp·sy, *n. pl.*
Gyp·sies

gy·rate, *v.*
gy·rat·ed,
gy·rat·ing

gy·ra·tion

gy·ro·com·pass

gy·ro·scope

gy·ro·sta·bi·liz·er

H

ha·ba·ne·ra
ha·be·as cor·pus
hab·er·dash·er
hab·er·dash·ery, *n.*
  pl.
  hab·er·dash·er·ies
ha·bil·i·ment
hab·it
hab·it·abil·i·ty
hab·it·able
hab·it·ably
ha·bi·tant
hab·i·tat
hab·i·ta·tion
hab·it-form·ing
ha·bit·u·al
ha·bit·u·al·ly
ha·bit·u·ate, *v.*
  ha·bit·u·at·ed,
  ha·bit·u·at·ing
ha·bit·u·a·tion
ha·bi·tué
ha·ci·en·da
hack·er
hack·le
hack·ney
hack·neyed

hack·saw
hack·work
had·dock
Ha·des
haf·ni·um
hag·gard
hag·gard·ly
hag·gard·ness
hag·gis
hag·gle, *v.*
  hag·gled,
  hag·gling
hag·gler
ha·gi·og·ra·pher
ha·gio·graph·ic
ha·gi·og·ra·phy, *n.*
  pl.
  ha·gi·og·ra·phies
hahn·ium
hai·ku, *pl.* hai·ku
hail (*v.* GREET, *n.*
  ICE) (*see also*
  hale)
hail·stone
hail·storm
hair·breadth
hair·brush

hair·cloth
hair·cut
hair·do, *n. pl.*
  hair·dos
hair·dress·er
hair·i·ness
hair·less
hair·line
hair·piece
hair·pin
hair-rais·ing
hair·split·ter
hair·split·ting
hair·spring
hair·style
hair trigger, *n.*
hair-trig·ger, *adj.*
hairy, *adj.* hair·i·er,
  hair·i·est
Hai·ti
Hai·tian
ha·la·la, *n. pl.*
  ha·la·la *or*
  ha·la·las
ha·la·tion
hal·berd
hal·cy·on

hale (HEALTHY),
 (see also hail)

hale (HAUL), v.
 haled, hal·ing
 (see also hail)

hal·er

half, n. pl. halves

half-and-half

half-assed

half·back

half-baked

half-breed

half-caste

half-cocked

half-dol·lar

half·heart·ed

half·heart·ed·ly

half·heart·ed·ness

half hour

half-length

half-life

half-light

half-mast

half-moon

half nel·son

half-slip

half-staff

half·tone

half-track

half-truth

half·way

half-wit

half-wit·ted

half-wit·ted·ness

hal·i·but, n. pl.
 hal·i·but or
 hal·i·buts

ha·lide

Hal·i·fax

ha·lite

hal·i·to·sis

hal·le·lu·jah

hall·mark

hal·low

hal·lowed

Hal·low·een

hal·lu·ci·nate, v.
 hal·lu·ci·nat·ed,
 hal·lu·ci·nat·ing

hal·lu·ci·na·tion

hal·lu·ci·na·to·ry

hal·lu·ci·no·gen

hal·lu·ci·no·gen·ic

hall·way

ha·lo, n. pl. ha·los
 or ha·loes

halo·gen

hal·ter

hal·ting

halve, v. halved,
 halv·ing

hal·yard

ham, v. hammed,
 ham·ming

Ham·burg

ham·burg·er

ham·let

ham·mer

ham·mer·head

ham·mer·lock

ham·mer·toe

ham·mock

Ham·mond

ham·my, adj.

ham·mi·er,
 ham·mi·est

ham·per

Hamp·ton

ham·ster

ham·string

hand·bag

hand·ball

hand·bar·row

hand·bill

hand·book

hand·car

hand·clasp

hand·cuff

hand·ful, n. pl.
 hand·fuls
 (occas.
 hands·ful)

hand·gun

hand·i·cap, .v.
 hand·i·capped,
 hand·i·cap·ping

hand·i·cap·per

hand·i·craft

hand·i·crafts·man

hand·i·ly

hand·i·ness

hand·i·work

hand·ker·chief, n.
 pl.
 hand·ker·chiefs
 (occas.
 hand·ker·chieves)

hand·knit

han·dle, v.
 han·dled,
 han·dling

han·dle·bar

hand·made

hand·maid·en

hand-me-down

hand·off, *n.*

hand off, *v.*

hand·out, *n.*

hand out, *v.*

hand·pick, *v.*

hand·rail

hand·saw

hand·set

hand·shake

hand·some

hand·some·ly

hand·some·ness

hand·spike

hand·spring

hand-to-hand

hand-to-mouth

hand·wo·ven

hand-wring·ing

hand·writ·ing

hand·writ·ten

handy, *adj.*
  hand·i·er,
  hand·i·est

handy·man, *n. pl.*
  handy·men

handy·per·son

hang, *v.* hung
  (*occas.*
  hanged),
  hang·ing

han·gar
  (AIRCRAFT)
  (*see also* hanger)

hang·dog

hang·er (PERSON
  OR THING THAT

HANGS) (*see also*
  hangar)

hang·er-on, *n. pl.*
  hang·ers-on

hang·ing

hang·man, *n. pl.*
  hang·men

hang·nail

hang·out

hang·over, *n.*

hang over, *v.*

hang-up, *n.*

hang up, *v.*

han·ker

han·ky-pan·ky

Ha·noi

han·som

Ha·nuk·kah (*occas.*
  Cha·nu·kah)

hao·le

hap·haz·ard

hap·haz·ard·ly

hap·haz·ard·ness

hap·less

hap·less·ly

hap·less·ness

hap·pen

hap·pen·ing

hap·pen·stance

hap·pi·ly

hap·pi·ness

hap·py, *adj.*
  hap·pi·er,
  hap·pi·est

hap·py-go-lucky

hara·kiri

ha·rangue, *v.*

ha·rangued,
  ha·rangu·ing

ha·rangu·er

ha·rass

ha·rass·ment

Har·bin

har·bin·ger

har·bor

har·bor·age

hard-and-fast

hard·back

hard·ball

hard-bit·ten

hard·board

hard-boiled

hard·bound

hard-core, *adj.*

hard core, *n.*

hard·edge

hard·en

hard·ened

hard·hat

hard·head·ed

hard·head·ed·ly

hard·head·ed·ness

hard·heart·ed

hard·heart·ed·ly

hard·heart·ed·ness

hard·i·hood

hard·i·ly

hard·i·ness

hard-line

hard-lin·er

hard·ly

hard·ness

hard-of-hear·ing

hard-on
hard·pan
hard·scrab·ble
hard·shell
hard·ship
hard·stand
hard-sur·face
hard·tack
hard·top
hard·ware
hard·wood
hard·work·ing
hard·y, *adj.*
　hard·i·er,
　hard·i·est
hare·brained
hare·lip
hare·lipped
har·em
har·le·quin
har·lot
har·lot·ry
harm·ful
harm·ful·ly
harm·ful·ness
harm·less
harm·less·ly
harm·less·ness
har·mon·ic
har·mon·i·ca
har·mon·i·cal·ly
har·mon·ics
har·mo·ni·ous
har·mo·ni·ous·ly
har·mo·ni·ous·ness
har·mo·ni·um

har·mo·ni·za·tion
har·mo·nize, *v.*
　har·mo·nized,
　har·mo·niz·ing
har·mo·ny, *n. pl.*
　har·mo·nies
har·ness
harp·er
harp·ist
har·poon
harp·si·chord
har·py, *n. pl.*
　har·pies
har·que·bus
har·ri·dan
har·ri·er
Har·ris·burg
har·row
har·ry, *v.* har·ried,
　har·ry·ing
harsh·ly
harsh·ness
har·te·beest
Hart·ford
har·um-scar·um
har·vest
har·vest·er
has-been
hash·ish
has·sle, *v.* has·sled,
　has·sling
has·sock
haste
has·ten
has·tened
hast·i·ly
hast·i·ness

hasty, hast·i·er,
　hast·i·est
hat·box
hatch
hatch·back
hatch·ery, *n. pl.*
　hatch·er·ies
hatch·et
hatch·ing
hatch·way
hate, *v.* hat·ed,
　hat·ing
hate·ful
hate·ful·ly
hate·ful·ness
hate·mon·ger
hat·pin
hat·rack
ha·tred
hat·ter
haugh·ti·ly
haugh·ti·ness
haugh·ty, *adj.*
　haugh·ti·er,
　haugh·ti·est
haul·age
haul·er
haunch
haunt
haunt·ing·ly
haute cou·ture
haute cui·sine
hau·teur
Ha·vana
have, *v.* had,
　hav·ing
ha·ven

have-not
hav·er·sack
hav·oc
Ha·waii
Ha·wai·ian
hawk
hawk·er
hawk·ish
hawk·ish·ly
hawk·ish·ness
haw·ser
haw·thorn
hay·cock
hay·fork
hay·loft
hay·mow
hay·rack
hay·rick
hay·seed
hay·wire
haz·ard
haz·ard·ous
haz·ard·ous·ly
haz·ard·ous·ness
haze, v. hazed,
   haz·ing
ha·zel
ha·zel·nut
haz·i·ly
haz·i·ness
hazy, adj. haz·i·er,
   haz·i·est
head·ache
head·band
head·board
head·dress

head·ed
head·er
head·first
head·gear
head·hunt·er
head·i·ly
head·i·ness
head·ing
head·land
head·less
head·less·ness
head·light
head·line
head·lin·er
head·lock
head·long
head·man
   (LEADER), n.
   pl. head·men
   (see also
   headsman)
head·mast·er
head·mis·tress, n.
   pl.
   head·mis·tress·es
head·most
head·note
head-on
head·phone
head·piece
head·pin
head·quar·ters, n.
   pl.
   head·quar·ters
head·rest
head·set
head·ship
heads·man

(EXECUTIONER)
n. pl. heads·men
(see also
headman)
head·stall
head·stock
head·stone
head·strong
head·wait·er
head·wa·ter
head·way
head·word
head·work
heady, adj.
   head·i·er,
   head·i·est
heal
heal·er
health·ful
health·i·ly
health·i·ness
healthy, adj.
   health·i·er,
   health·i·est
heap
hear, v. heard,
   hear·ing
hear·er
hear·ken
hear·say
hearse
heart·ache
heart·beat
heart·break
heart·broken
heart·burn
heart·en
heart·felt

hearth

hearth·stone

heart·i·ly

heart·i·ness

heart·land

heart·less

heart·rend·ing

heart·sick

heart·sore

heart·string

heart·throb

heart-to-heart

hearty, *adj.*
heart·i·er,
heart·i·est

heat·ed·ly

heat·er

heath

hea·then, *n. pl.*
hea·thens *or*
hea·then

heath·er

heat·stroke

heave, *v.* heaved,
heav·ing

heav·en

heav·en·ly

heav·en·ward

heav·i·ly

heav·i·ness

heavy, *adj.*
heav·i·er,
heav·i·est

heavy-du·ty

heavy-hand·ed

heavy-hand·ed·ly

heavy-hand·ed·ness

heavy-heart·ed

heavy-heart·ed·ly

heavy-heart·ed·ness

heavy·set

heavy·weight

He·bra·ic

He·brew

heck·le, *v.*
heck·led,
heck·ling

heck·ler

hect·are

hec·tic

hec·ti·cal·ly

hec·tor

hedge, *v.* hedged,
hedg·ing

hedge·hog

hedge·hop

hedge·row

he·do·nism

he·do·nist

he·do·nis·tic

hee·bie-jee·bies

heed·ful

heed·ful·ly

heed·ful·ness

heed·less

heed·less·ly

heed·less·ness

heel

hefty, *adj.* heft·i·er,
heft·i·est

he·ge·mo·ny, *n. pl.*
he·ge·mo·nies

he·gi·ra

heif·er

height

height·en

hei·nous

hei·nous·ly

hei·nous·ness

heir

heir ap·par·ent, *n.*
pl. heirs
ap·par·ent

heir·ess

heir·loom

heir pre·sump·tive,
n. pl. heirs
pre·sump·tive

Hel·e·na

he·li·cal

he·li·coid

he·li·cop·ter

he·lio·cen·tric

he·lio·trope

he·li·port

he·li·um

he·lix, *n. pl.*
he·lic·es (*occas.*
hel·i·xes)

hell-bent

hell·cat

Hel·len·ic

Hel·le·nist

Hel·le·nis·tic

hell·hole

hel·lion

hell·ish

hell·ish·ly

hell·ish·ness

hel·lo, *n. pl.* hel·los

hel·lo, *v.* hel·loed,
hel·lo·ing

helm

hel·met

helms·man, n. pl.
  helms·men

help·er

help·ful

help·ful·ly

help·ful·ness

help·less

help·less·ly

help·less·ness

help·mate

hel·ter-skel·ter

hem, v. hemmed,
  hem·ming

he-man, n. pl. he-
  men

he·ma·tite

he·ma·tol·o·gist

he·ma·tol·o·gy

hemi·sphere

hemi·spher·i·cal

hem·line

hem·lock

he·mo·glo·bin

he·mo·phil·ia

he·mo·phil·i·ac

hem·or·rhage, v.
  hem·or·rhaged,
  hem·or·rhag·ing

hem·or·ragh·ic

hem·or·rhoid

hem·stitch

hence·forth

hence·for·ward

hench·man, n. pl.
  hench·men

hen·na, v.

hen·naed,
  hen·na·ing

hen·peck

Hen·ry (PERSON'S
  NAME), n. pl.
  Hen·rys

hen·ry
  (INDUCTANCE),
  n. pl. hen·rys or
  hen·ries

he·pat·ic

hep·a·ti·tis

hep·ta·gon

hep·tam·e·ter

her·ald

he·ral·dic

her·ald·ry

her·ba·ceous

her·bar·i·um

her·bi·cid·al

her·bi·cide

her·bi·vore

her·biv·o·rous

her·biv·o·rous·ly

her·biv·o·rous·ness

her·cu·le·an

herd·er

herds·man, n. pl.
  herds·men

here·abouts or
  here·about

here·af·ter

here·by

he·red·i·tar·i·ly

he·red·i·tary

he·red·i·ty, n. pl.
  he·red·i·ties

here·in

here·in·af·ter

here·of

here·on

her·e·sy, n. pl.
  her·e·sies

her·e·tic

he·ret·i·cal

here·to

here·to·fore

here·un·der

here·un·to

here·upon

here·with

her·i·tage

herky-jerky

her·maph·ro·dite

her·met·ic

her·met·i·cal

her·met·i·cal·ly

her·mit

her·mit·age

her·nia, n. pl.
  her·ni·as or
  her·ni·ae

her·ni·ate, v.
  her·ni·at·ed,
  her·ni·at·ing

he·ro, n. pl.
  he·roes

he·ro·ic

he·ro·i·cal·ly

he·ro·ics

her·o·in
  (NARCOTIC)

her·o·ine, fem.
  (HERO)

her·o·ism

her·on, n. pl.

her·ons (*occas.*
  her·on)

her·pes

her·pe·tol·o·gist

her·pe·tol·o·gy

her·ring, *n. pl.*
  her·ring *or*
  her·rings

her·ring·bone

her·self

hertz, *n. pl.* hertz

hes·i·tance

hes·i·tan·cy, *n. pl.*
  hes·i·tan·cies

hes·i·tant

hes·i·tate, *v.*
  hes·i·tat·ed,
  hes·i·tat·ing

hes·i·ta·tion

het·ero·dox

het·ero·doxy, *n. pl.*
  het·ero·dox·ies

het·ero·dyne

het·ero·ge·ne·ity

het·ero·ge·neous

het·ero·sex·u·al

het·ero·sex·u·al·i·ty

het·ero·sex·u·al·ly

heu·ris·tic

hew (CHOP) *v.*
  hewed, hewed
  or hewn, hewing
  (*see also* hue)

hexa·chlo·ro·phene

hexa·gon

hex·ag·o·nal

hexa·gram

hex·am·e·ter

hey·day

Hi·a·le·ah

hi·a·tus

hi·ba·chi, *n. pl.*
  hi·ba·chis

hi·ber·nate, *v.*
  hi·ber·nat·ed,
  hi·ber·nat·ing

hi·ber·na·tion

hi·ber·na·tor

hi·bis·cus

hic·cup (*occas.*
  hic·cough), *v.*
  hic·cuped *or*
  hic·cupped,
  hic·cup·ing *or*
  hic·cup·ping

hick·o·ry, *n. pl.*
  hick·o·ries

Hi·dal·go (MEXICO)

hi·dal·go (MONEY),
  n. pl. hi·dal·gos

hide, *v.* hid,
  hid·den, hid·ing

hide-and-seek

hide·away

hide·bound

hid·eous

hid·eous·ly

hid·eous·ness

hide·out

hie, *v.* hied, hy·ing

hi·er·ar·chi·cal

hi·er·ar·chi·cal·ly

hi·er·ar·chy, *n. pl.*
  hi·er·ar·chies

hi·ero·glyph·ic

hi·ero·glyph·i·cal

hi-fi

hig·gle·dy-
  pig·gle·dy

high·ball

high·born

high·boy

high·bred

high·brow

high·er-up

high·fa·lu·tin

high-flown

high-fly·ing

high-hand·ed

high-hand·ed·ly

high-hand·ed·ness

high-hat

high·land

high·land·er

high-lev·el

high·light

high-mind·ed

high-mind·ed·ly

high-mind·ed·ness

high·ness

high-oc·tane

high-rise

high·road

high-sound·ing

high-spir·it·ed

high-spir·it·ed·ly

high-spir·it·ed·ness

high-strung

high·tail

high-ten·sion

high-test

high-toned

high·way

high·way·man, *n.*
pl.
high·way·men

hi·jack

hi·jack·er

hike, *v.* hiked,
hik·ing

hik·er

hi·lar·i·ous

hi·lar·i·ous·ly

hi·lar·i·ous·ness

hi·lar·i·ty

hill·bil·ly, *n. pl.*
hill·bil·lies

hill·ock

hill·side

hill·top

hilly, *adj.* hill·i·er,
hill·i·est

him·self

hin·der

Hin·di

hind·most

hind·quar·ter

hin·drance

hind·sight

Hin·du·ism

Hin·du·stani
(*occas.*
Hin·do·stani)

hin·ter·land

hip·bone

hip·pie

hip·po·drome

hip·po·pot·a·mus,
n. pl.
hip·po·pot·a·mus·es·
or
hip·po·pot·a·mi

hip·ster

hire, *v.* hired,
hir·ing

hire·ling

hir·sute

hir·sut·ism

His·pan·ic

His·pan·io·la

his·ta·mine

his·to·gen

his·to·gen·e·sis

his·to·ge·net·ic

his·to·gram

his·tol·o·gist

his·tol·o·gy

his·to·ri·an

his·tor·ic

his·tor·i·cal

his·tor·i·cal·ly

his·to·ric·i·ty

his·to·ri·og·ra·pher

his·to·ri·og·ra·phy

his·to·ry, *n. pl.*
his·to·ries

his·tri·on·ic

his·tri·on·i·cal·ly

his·tri·on·ics

hit, *v.* hit, hit·ting

hitch·hike

hitch·hik·er

hith·er·to

hit-or-miss

hit·ter

hive

Hmong

hoard

(ACCUMULATE)
(*see also* horde)

hoar·frost

hoarse, *adj.*
hoars·er,
hoars·est

hoarse·ly

hoarse·ness

hoary, *adj.*
hoar·i·er,
hoar·i·est

hoax

hob·ble, *v.*
hob·bled,
hob·bling

hob·by, *n. pl.*
hob·bies

hob·by·horse

hob·by·ist

hob·gob·lin

hob·nail

hob·nob, *v.*
hob·nobbed,
hob·nob·bing

ho·bo, *n. pl.*
ho·boes (*occas.*
ho·bos)

Ho Chi Minh City

hock·ey

ho·cus-po·cus

hodge·podge

hoe, *v.* hoed,
hoe·ing

hog, *n. pl.* hogs
(*occas.* hog)

hog, *v.* hogged,
hog·ging

ho·gan

hog·gish

hog·gish·ly

hog·gish·ness

hogs·head

hog·tie, v. hog·tied, hog·ty·ing

hog·wash

hoi pol·loi

hoist

hoi·ty-toi·ty

Hok·kai·do

ho·kum

hold, v. held, hold·ing

hold·out, n.

hold out, v.

hold·over, n.

hold over, v.

hold·up, n.

hold up, v.

hol·i·day

ho·li·ness

ho·lis·tic

Hol·land

hol·lan·daise sauce

Hol·land·er

hol·low

Hol·ly (PERSON'S NAME), pl. Hol·lys

hol·ly (TREE), n. pl. hol·lies

hol·ly·hock

Hol·ly·wood

hol·mi·um

ho·lo·caust

ho·lo·gram

ho·lo·graph

ho·log·ra·phy

hol·stein

hol·ster

holy, adj. hol·i·er, hol·i·est

hom·age

hom·bre

hom·burg

home·body

home·bred

home·com·ing

home·grown

home·land

home·less

home·li·ness

home·ly, adj. home·li·er, home·li·est

home·made

home·mak·er

ho·meo·path·ic

ho·me·op·a·thy

home·own·er

hom·er

home·room

home·sick

home·spun

home·stead

home·stead·er

home·stretch

home·ward or home·wards

home·work

homey, adj. hom·i·er, hom·i·est

ho·mi·ci·dal

ho·mi·cide

hom·i·lec·tic

hom·i·lec·tics

hom·i·ly, n. pl. hom·i·lies

hom·ing

hom·i·ny

ho·mo·ge·ne·i·ty

ho·mo·ge·neous

ho·mog·e·ni·za·tion

ho·mog·e·nize, v. ho·mog·e·nized, ho·mog·e·niz·ing

ho·mog·e·nous

ho·mo·graph

ho·mol·o·gous

hom·o·nym

ho·mo·phone

ho·mo sa·pi·ens

ho·mo·sex·u·al

ho·mo·sex·u·al·i·ty

ho·mo·sex·u·al·ly

hon·cho, n. pl. hon·chos

hon·cho, v. hon·choed, hon·cho·ing

Hon·du·ran

Hon·du·ras

hone, v. honed, hon·ing

hon·est

hon·est·ly

hon·es·ty

hon·ey

hon·ey·bee

hon·ey·comb

hon·ey·dew

hon·eyed

hon·ey·moon

hon·ey·suck·le

Hong Kong

hon·kie *or* hon·ky (*occas.* hon·key), *n. pl.* hon·kies (*occas.* hon·keys)

hon·ky-tonk

Hon·o·lu·lu

hon·or

hon·or·able

hon·or·ably

hon·o·rar·i·um, *n. pl.* hon·o·rar·ia (*occas.* hon·o·rar·i·ums)

hon·or·ary

hon·or·if·ic

Hon·shu

hood·ed

hood·lum

hoo·doo, *n. pl.* hoo·doos

hood·wink

hoo·ey

hoof, *n. pl.* hooves *or* hoofs

hoo·kah

hook·er

hook·up

hook·worm

hoo·li·gan

hoo·li·gan·ism

hoop·la

hoo·te·nan·ny, *n. pl.* hoo·te·nan·nies

hop, *v.* hopped, hop·ping

hope, *v.* hoped, hop·ing

hope·ful

hope·ful·ly

hope·ful·ness

hope·less

hope·less·ly

hope·less·ness

hop·per

hop·scotch

horde (THRONG) (*see also* hoard)

hore·hound

ho·ri·zon

hor·i·zon·tal

hor·i·zon·tal·ly

hor·mon·al

hor·mone

horn·book

hor·net

horn·pipe

horn·swog·gle, *v.* horn·swog·gled, horn·swog·gling

horny, *adj.* horn·i·er, horn·i·est

hor·o·log·i·cal

ho·rol·o·gist

ho·rol·o·gy

horo·scope

hor·ren·dous

hor·ren·dous·ly

hor·ri·ble

hor·ri·bly

hor·rid

hor·rif·ic

hor·ri·fy, *v.* hor·ri·fied, hor·ri·fy·ing

hor·ror

hor·ror-struck

hors d'oeuvre, *n. pl.* hors d'oeuvres (*occas.* hors d'oeuvre)

horse, *n. pl.* hors·es (*occas.* horse)

horse·back

horse·flesh

horse·fly, *n. pl.* horse·flies

horse·hair

horse·hide

horse·laugh

horse·man, *n. pl.* horse·men

horse·play

horse·pow·er

horse·rad·ish

horse·shoe

horse·whip

horse·wom·an, *n. pl.* horse·wom·en

horsy, *adj.* hors·i·er, hors·i·est

hor·ta·tive

hor·ta·tory

hor·ti·cul·tur·al

hor·ti·cul·ture

hor·ti·cul·tur·ist

ho·san·na

hose, *n. pl.* hose *or* hos·es

ho·siery

hos·pice

hos·pi·ta·ble

hos·pi·ta·bly

hos·pi·tal

hos·pi·tal·i·ty, *n. pl.* hos·pi·tal·i·ties

hos·pi·tal·iza·tion

hos·pi·tal·ize, *v.* hos·pi·tal·ized, hos·pi·tal·iz·ing

hos·tage

hos·tel (INN) (*see also* hostile)

hos·tel·er

hos·tel·ry, *n. pl.* hos·tel·ries

host·ess

hos·tile (WARLIKE) (*see also* hostel)

hos·tile·ly

hos·til·i·ty, *n. pl.* hos·til·i·ties

hos·tler

hot, *adj.* hot·ter, hot·test

hot·bed

hot-blood·ed

hot·box

hot dog, *n.*

hot-dog, *v.* hot-dog·ged, hot-dog·ging

ho·tel

ho·tel·ier

hot·foot, *n. pl.* hot·foots

hot·head·ed

hot·head·ed·ly

hot·head·ed·ness

hot·house

hot-rod·der

hot·shot

hot-tem·pered

hot-wire, *v.* hot-wired, hot-wir·ing

hour·glass

hour·ly

house, *v.* housed, hous·ing

house·boat

house·boy

house·break, *v.* house·broke, house·bro·ken, house·break·ing

house·break·ing

house·broken

house·clean

house·coat

house·fly, *n. pl.* house·flies

house·ful, *n. pl.* house·fuls

house·hold

house·hus·band

house·keep·er

house·lights

house·man, *n. pl.* house·men

house·maid

house·moth·er

house·top

house·warm·ing

house·wife, *n. pl.* house·wives

house·work

hous·ing

Hous·ton

hov·el

hov·er

Hov·er·craft℠

how·dah

how·ev·er

how·it·zer

howl·er

how·so·ev·er

hoy·den

hua·ra·che

hub·bub

hub·cap

hu·bris

huck·le·ber·ry, *n. pl.* huck·le·ber·ries

huck·ster

hud·dle, *v.* hud·dled, hud·dling

Hud·son

hue (COLOR) (*see also* hew)

hue·vos ran·cher·os

huff·ish

huffy, *.adj.* huff·i·er, huff·i·est

hug, *v.* hugged, hug·ging

huge, *adj.* hug·er,
  hug·est

huge·ly

huge·ness

hug·ga·ble

hu·la

Hu·la-Hoop℗

hulk·ing

hul·la·ba·loo, *n. pl.*
  hul·la·ba·loos

hum, *v.* hummed,
  hum·ming

hu·man

hu·mane

hu·mane·ly

hu·mane·ness

hu·man·ism

hu·man·ist

hu·man·is·tic

hu·man·i·tar·i·an

hu·man·i·tar·i·an·ism

hu·man·i·ty, *n. pl.*
  hu·man·i·ties

hu·man·iza·tion

hu·man·ize, *v.*
  hu·man·ized,
  hu·man·iz·ing

hu·man·kind

hu·man·ly

hum·ble, *adj.*
  hum·bler,
  hum·blest

hum·ble, *v.*
  hum·bled,
  hum·bling

hum·bler

hum·bly

hum·bug

hum·ding·er

hum·drum

hu·mer·al

hu·mer·us, *n. pl.*
  hu·meri

hu·mid

hu·mid·i·fi·er

hu·mid·i·fy, *v.*
  hu·mid·i·fied,
  hu·mid·i·fy·ing

hu·mid·i·ty, *n. pl.*
  hu·mid·i·ties

hu·mi·dor

hu·mil·i·ate, *v.*
  hu·mil·i·at·ed,
  hu·mil·i·at·ing

hu·mil·i·a·tion

hu·mil·i·ty

hum·ming·bird

hum·mock

hu·mon·gous

hu·mor

hu·mor·ist

hu·mor·less

hu·mor·ous

hu·mor·ous·ly

hu·mor·ous·ness

hump·back

hu·mus

hunch·back

hun·dred

hun·dred·fold

hun·dredth

hun·dred·weight

Hun·gar·i·an

Hun·ga·ry

hun·ger

hun·gri·ly

hun·gry, *adj.*
  hun·gri·er,
  hun·gri·est

hun·ky-do·ry

hunt·er

Hun·ting·ton Beach

hunt·ress

hunts·man, *n. pl.*
  hunts·men

hur·dle (JUMP), *v.*
  hur·dled,
  hur·dling (*see
  also* hurtle)

hur·dy-gur·dy

hurl·er

hur·ly-bur·ly

Hu·ron

hur·rah

hur·ri·cane

hur·ried·ly

hur·ried·ness

hur·ry, *v.* hur·ried,
  hur·ry·ing

hurt, *v.* hurt,
  hurt·ing

hurt·ful

hur·tle (HURL), *v.*
  hur·tled,
  hur·tling (*see
  also* hurdle)

hus·band

hus·band·man, *n. pl.*
  hus·band·men

hus·band·ry

hush-hush

Hush Pup·pies℗
  (SHOES)

hush pup·py

(FOOD), *n. pl.*
hush pup·pies

husk·er

hus·ki·ly

hus·ki·ness

husk·ing

hus·ky, *adj.*
hus·ki·er,
hus·ki·est

hus·sar

hus·sy, *n. pl.*
hus·sies

hus·tings

hus·tle, *n. pl.*
hus·tled,
hus·tling

hus·tler

huz·zah *or* huz·za

hy·a·cinth

hy·brid

hy·brid·iza·tion

hy·brid·ize, *v.*
hy·brid·ized,
hy·brid·iz·ing

Hy·der·a·bad

hy·dran·gea

hy·drant

hy·drate, *v.*
hy·drat·ed,
hy·drat·ing

hy·drau·lic

hy·drau·lics

hy·dride

hy·dro, *n. pl.*
hy·dros

hy·dro·car·bon

hy·dro·chlo·ric acid

hy·dro·elec·tric

hy·dro·foil

hy·dro·gen

hy·dro·ge·nate, *v.*
hy·dro·ge·nat·ed,
hy·dro·ge·nat·ing

hy·dro·ge·na·tion

hy·drog·e·nous

hy·dro·log·ic

hy·drol·o·gist

hy·drol·o·gy

hy·drol·y·sis

hy·drom·e·ter

hy·dron·ic

hy·dro·pho·bia

hy·dro·pho·bic

hy·dro·phyte

hy·dro·plane, *v.*
hy·dro·planed,
hy·dro·plan·ing

hy·dro·pon·ics

hy·dro·stat·ic

hy·dro·ther·a·py

hy·drous

hy·drox·ide

hy·e·na

hy·giene

hy·gien·ic

hy·gien·i·cal·ly

hy·gien·ist

hy·grom·e·ter

hy·gro·scop·ic

hy·men

hy·me·ne·al

hymn

hym·nal

hym·no·dy

hym·nol·o·gy

hy·per·acid·i·ty

hy·per·ac·tive

hy·per·bar·ic

hy·per·bo·la
(CURVE)

hy·per·bo·le
(EXAGGERATION)

hy·per·bol·ic

hy·per·crit·i·cal

hy·per·crit·i·cal·ly

hy·per·gly·ce·mia
(EXCESS
SUGAR) (*see also*
hypoglycemia)

hy·per·sen·si·tive

hy·per·sen·si·tiv·i·ty

hy·per·son·ic

hy·per·ten·sion

hy·per·tro·phic

hy·per·tro·phy

hy·phen

hy·phen·ate, *v.*
hy·phen·at·ed,
hy·phen·at·ing

hy·phen·a·tion

hyp·no·sis, *n. pl.*
hyp·no·ses

hyp·not·ic

hyp·not·i·cal·ly

hyp·no·tism

hyp·no·tist

hyp·no·tize, *v.*
hyp·no·tized,
hyp·no·tiz·ing

hy·po·al·ler·gen·ic

hy·po·chon·dria

hy·po·chon·dri·ac

hy·poc·ri·sy, *n. pl.*,
hy·poc·ri·sies

hyp·o·crite

hyp·o·crit·i·cal
hyp·o·crit·i·cal·ly
hy·po·der·mic
hy·po·gly·ce·mia
  (LOW SUGAR)
  (*see also*
  hyperglycemia)
hy·pot·e·nuse
hy·poth·e·cate, *v.*
  hy·poth·e·cat·ed,
  hy·poth·e·cat·ing

hy·po·ther·mia
hy·poth·e·sis, *n. pl.*
  hy·poth·e·ses
hy·poth·e·size, *v.*
  hy·poth·e·sized,
  hy·poth·e·siz·ing
hy·po·thet·i·cal
hy·po·thet·i·cal·ly
hys·ter·ec·to·my, *n.*

pl.
  hys·ter·ec·to·mies
hys·ter·e·sis
hys·te·ria
hys·ter·ic
hys·ter·i·cal
hys·ter·i·cal·ly
hys·ter·ics

I

iam·bic

Ibe·ri·an

ibex, *n. pl.* ibex *or* ibex·es

ibid

ibi·dem

ibis, *n. pl.* ibis *or* ibis·es

ibu·pro·fen

ice, *v.* iced, ic·ing

ice·berg

ice·boat

ice·bound

ice·box

ice·break·er

ice·cap

ice-cold

ice-cream, *adj.*

ice cream, *n.*

ice·house

Ice·land

Ice·land·er

Ice·lan·dic

ice·man, *n. pl.* ice·men

ice-skate, *v.* ice-

skat·ed, ice-skat·ing

ich·thy·ol·o·gist

ich·thy·ol·o·gy

ici·cle

ic·i·ly

ic·i·ness

ic·ing

icky, *adj.* ick·i·er, ick·i·est

icon (*occas.* ikon)

icon·o·clasm

icon·o·clast

icy, *adj.* ic·i·er, ic·i·est

Ida·ho

Ida·ho·an

idea

ide·al

ide·al·ism

ide·al·ist

ide·al·is·tic

ide·al·is·ti·cal·ly

ide·al·iza·tion

ide·al·ize, *v.* ide·al·ized, ide·al·iz·ing

ide·al·ly

ide·ate, *v.* ide·at·ed, ide·at·ing

ide·a·tion

idée fixe, *n. pl.* idées fixes

idem

iden·ti·cal

iden·ti·cal·ly

iden·ti·fi·able

iden·ti·fi·ably

iden·ti·fi·ca·tion

iden·ti·fi·er

iden·ti·fy, *v.* iden·ti·fied, iden·ti·fy·ing

Iden·ti·kit®

iden·ti·ty, *n. pl.* iden·ti·ties

ideo·gram

ideo·graph

ideo·log·i·cal

ideo·log·i·cal·ly

ide·ol·o·gist

ide·ol·o·gy, *n. pl.* ide·ol·o·gies

id·i·ocy, *n. pl.*
　id·i·o·cies

id·i·om

id·i·om·at·ic

id·i·om·at·i·cal·ly

id·io·syn·cra·sy, *n.
　pl.*
　id·io·syn·cra·sies

id·io·syn·crat·ic

id·io·syn·crat·i·cal·ly

id·i·ot

id·i·ot·ic

id·i·ot·i·cal·ly

id·i·ot sa·vant, *n.
　pl.* id·i·ots
　sa·vants *or* id·i·ot
　sa·vants

idle, *adj.* idler,
　idlest

idle, *v.* idled,
　idling

idle·ness

idler

idly

idol

idol·a·ter

idol·a·trous

idol·a·try, *n. pl.*
　idol·a·tries

idol·iza·tion

idol·ize, *v.*
　idol·ized,
　idol·iz·ing

idyll

idyl·lic

if·fy

ig·loo, *n. pl.* ig·loos

ig·ne·ous

ig·nit·able

ig·nite, *v.* ig·nit·ed,
　ig·nit·ing

ig·ni·tion

ig·no·ble

ig·no·bly

ig·no·min·i·ous

ig·no·min·i·ous·ly

ig·no·min·i·ous·ness

ig·no·mi·ny, *n. pl.*
　ig·no·mi·nies

ig·no·ra·mus

ig·no·rance

ig·no·rant

ig·nore, *v.*
　ig·nored,
　ig·nor·ing

igua·na

ike·ba·na

ikon (*var. of* icon)

il·e·itis

il·e·um
　(INTESTINE), *n.
　pl.* il·ea

il·i·um (BONE), *n.
　pl.* il·ia

ill

ill-ad·vised

ill-ad·vised·ly

ill-be·ing

ill-bod·ing

ill-bred

ill-con·ceived

il·le·gal

il·le·gal·i·ty, *n. pl.*
　il·le·gal·i·ties

il·le·gal·ly

il·leg·i·bil·i·ty

il·leg·i·ble

il·leg·i·bly

il·le·git·i·ma·cy

il·le·git·i·mate

il·le·git·i·mate·ly

ill-fat·ed

ill-fa·vored

ill-got·ten

ill-hu·mored

il·lib·er·al

il·lic·it
　(UNLAWFUL)
　(*see also* elicit)

il·lim·it·able

il·lim·it·ably

Il·li·nois

Il·li·nois·an

il·lit·er·a·cy, *n. pl.*
　il·lit·er·a·cies

il·lit·er·ate

ill-man·nered

ill-na·tured

ill-na·tured·ly

ill·ness

il·log·i·cal

il·log·i·cal·i·ty

il·log·i·cal·ly

ill-pre·pared

ill-sort·ed

ill-starred

ill-tem·pered

ill-treat

il·lu·mi·nate, *v.*
　il·lu·mi·nat·ed,
　il·lu·mi·nat·ing

il·lu·mi·na·tion

il·lu·mi·na·tor

il·lu·mine, *v.*

il·lu·mined,
il·lu·min·ing

ill-us·age

ill-use, *v.* ill-used,
ill-us·ing

il·lu·sion (FALSE
BELIEF) (*see
also* allusion,
elusion)

il·lu·sion·ist

il·lu·sive (UNREAL)
(*see also*
allusive, elusive)

il·lu·so·ry

il·lus·trate, *v.*
il·lus·trat·ed,
il·lus·trat·ing

il·lus·tra·tion

il·lus·tra·tive

il·lus·tra·tor

il·lus·tri·ous

il·lus·tri·ous·ly

il·lus·tri·ous·ness

im·age

im·ag·ery, *n. pl.*
im·ag·er·ies

imag·in·able

imag·in·ably

imag·i·nary

imag·i·na·tion

imag·i·na·tive

imag·i·na·tive·ly

imag·i·na·tive·ness

imag·ine, *v.*
imag·ined,
imag·in·ing

im·ag·ism

im·ag·ist

im·bal·ance

im·be·cile

im·be·cil·ic

im·be·cil·i·ty, *n. pl.*
im·be·cil·i·ties

im·bed (*var. of*
embed)

im·bibe, *v.*
im·bibed,
im·bib·ing

im·bib·er

im·bri·cate, *v.*
im·bri·cat·ed,
im·bri·cat·ing

im·bri·ca·tion

im·bro·glio, *n. pl.*
im·bro·glios

im·brue (SOAK), *v.*
im·brued,
im·bru·ing

im·bue (INSPIRE),
v. im·bued,
im·bu·ing

im·i·ta·ble

im·i·tate, *v.*
im·i·tat·ed,
im·i·tat·ing

im·i·ta·tion

im·i·ta·tive

im·i·ta·tive·ly

im·i·ta·tive·ness

im·i·ta·tor

im·mac·u·late

im·ma·nent
(INHERENT) (*see
also* eminent,
imminent)

im·ma·te·ri·al

im·ma·te·ri·al·i·ty

im·ma·ture

im·ma·ture·ly

im·ma·ture·ness

im·ma·tu·ri·ty

im·mea·sur·able

im·mea·sur·ably

im·me·di·a·cy

im·me·di·ate

im·me·di·ate·ly

im·mense

im·mense·ly

im·mense·ness

im·men·si·ty, *n. pl.*
im·men·si·ties

im·merse, *v.*
im·mersed,
im·mers·ing

im·mer·sion

im·mi·grant

im·mi·grate
(ENTER), *v.*
im·mi·grat·ed,
im·mi·grat·ing
(*see also*
emigrate)

im·mi·gra·tion

im·mi·nence

im·mi·nent (SOON)
(*see also*
eminent,
immanent)

im·mis·ci·ble

im·mit·i·ga·ble

im·mo·bile

im·mo·bil·i·ty

im·mo·bi·li·za·tion

im·mo·bi·lize, *v.*
im·mo·bi·lized,
im·mo·bi·liz·ing

im·mod·er·a·cy

im·mod·er·ate

im·mod·er·ate·ly

im·mod·er·ate·ness

im·mod·est

im·mod·est·ly

im·mod·es·ty

im·mo·late, *v.*
  im·mo·lat·ed,
  im·mo·lat·ing

im·mo·la·tion

im·mor·al

im·mo·ral·i·ty, *n.*
  pl.
  im·mo·ral·i·ties

im·mor·al·ly

im·mor·tal

im·mor·tal·i·ty *n.*
  pl.
  im·mor·tal·i·ties

im·mor·tal·ize, *v.*
  im·mor·tal·ized,
  im·mor·tal·iz·ing

im·mor·tal·ly

im·mov·abil·i·ty

im·mov·able

im·mov·ably

im·mune

im·mu·ni·ty, *n. pl.*
  im·mu·ni·ties

im·mu·ni·za·tion

im·mu·nize, *v.*
  im·mu·nized,
  im·mu·niz·ing

im·mu·nol·o·gist

im·mu·nol·o·gy

im·mure, *v.*
  im·mured,
  im·mur·ing

im·mu·ta·bil·i·ty

im·mu·ta·ble

im·mu·ta·bly

im·pact

im·pact·ed

im·pair

im·pair·ment

im·pa·la

im·pale, *v.*
  im·paled,
  im·pal·ing

im·pal·pa·bil·i·ty

im·pal·pa·ble

im·pal·pa·bly

im·pan·el, *v.*
  im·pan·eled *or*
  im·pan·elled,
  im·pan·el·ing *or*
  im·pan·el·ling

im·part

im·par·tial

im·par·tial·i·ty

im·par·tial·ly

im·pass·able

im·pass·ably

im·passe

im·pas·sioned

im·pas·sive

im·pas·sive·ly

im·pas·sive·ness

im·pas·siv·i·ty

im·pa·tience

im·pa·tiens

im·pa·tient

im·pa·tient·ly

im·peach

im·peach·ment

im·pec·ca·bil·i·ty

im·pec·ca·ble

im·pec·ca·bly

im·pe·cu·nious

im·pe·cu·nious·ly

im·pe·cu·nious·ness

im·ped·ance

im·pede, *v.*
  im·ped·ed,
  im·ped·ing

im·ped·i·ment

im·ped·i·men·ta

im·pel, *v.*
  im·pelled,
  im·pel·ling

im·pel·ler

im·pend

im·pen·e·tra·bil·i·ty

im·pen·e·tra·ble

im·pen·e·tra·bly

im·pen·i·tent

im·per·a·tive

im·per·a·tive·ly

im·per·a·tive·ness

im·per·ceiv·able

im·per·cep·ti·bil·i·ty

im·per·cep·ti·ble

im·per·cep·ti·bly

im·per·cep·tive

im·per·cep·tive·ness

im·per·fect

im·per·fec·tion

im·per·fect·ly

im·per·fect·ness

im·per·fo·rate

im·pe·ri·al

im·per·ri·al·ism

im·pe·ri·al·ist

im·pe·ri·al·is·tic

im·pe·ri·al·is·ti·cal·ly
im·pe·ri·al·ly
im·per·il, *v.*
  im·per·iled *or*
  im·per·illed,
  im·per·il·ing *or*
  im·per·il·ling
im·pe·ri·ous
im·pe·ri·ous·ly
im·pe·ri·ous·ness
im·per·ish·abil·i·ty
im·per·ish·able
im·per·ish·ably
im·per·ma·nence
im·per·ma·nen·cy
im·per·ma·nent
im·per·me·abil·i·ty
im·per·me·able
im·per·me·ably
im·per·mis·si·bil·i·ty
im·per·mis·si·ble
im·per·son·al
im·per·son·al·i·ty
im·per·son·al·ize, *v.*
  im·per·son·al·ized,
  im·per·son·al·iz·ing
im·per·son·al·ly
im·per·son·ate, *v.*
  im·per·son·at·ed,
  im·per·son·at·ing
im·per·son·ation
im·per·son·ator
im·per·ti·nence
im·per·ti·nent
im·per·turb·abil·i·ty
im·per·turb·able
im·per·turb·ably
im·per·vi·ous

im·per·vi·ous·ly
im·per·vi·ous·ness
im·pe·ti·go
im·pet·u·os·i·ty
im·pet·u·ous
im·pet·u·ous·ly
im·pet·u·ous·ness
im·pe·tus
im·pi·ety, *n. pl.*
  im·pi·e·ties
im·pinge, *v.*
  im·pinged,
  im·ping·ing
im·pinge·ment
im·pi·ous
im·pi·ous·ly
im·pi·ous·ness
imp·ish
imp·ish·ly
imp·ish·ness
im·pla·ca·ble
im·pla·ca·bly
im·plant
im·plan·ta·tion
im·plau·si·bil·i·ty, *n. pl.*
  im·plau·si·bil·i·ties
im·plau·si·ble
im·plau·si·bly
im·ple·ment
im·ple·men·ta·tion
im·pli·cate, *v.*
  im·pli·cat·ed,
  im·pli·cat·ing
im·pli·ca·tion
im·plic·it
im·plic·it·ly
im·plic·it·ness

im·plode, *v.*
  im·plod·ed,
  im·plod·ing
im·plore, *v.*
  im·plored,
  im·plor·ing
im·plor·ing·ly
im·plo·sion
im·plo·sive
im·ply, *v.* im·plied,
  im·ply·ing
im·po·lite
im·pol·i·tic
im·pon·der·abil·i·ty
im·pon·der·able
im·pon·der·ably
im·port
im·port·able
im·por·tance
im·por·tant
im·por·ta·tion
im·port·er
im·por·tu·nate
im·por·tune, *v.*
  im·por·tuned,
  im·por·tun·ing
im·por·tu·ni·ty, *n. pl.*
  im·por·tu·ni·ties
im·pose, *v.*
  im·posed,
  im·pos·ing
im·pos·ing
im·po·si·tion
im·pos·si·bil·i·ty, *n. pl.*
  im·pos·si·bil·i·ties
im·pos·si·ble
im·pos·si·bly

im·post

im·pos·tor *or*
  im·pos·ter

im·pos·ture

im·po·tence

im·po·ten·cy, *n. pl.*
  im·po·ten·cies

im·po·tent

im·pound

im·pound·ment

im·pov·er·ish

im·pov·er·ished

im·prac·ti·ca·bil·i·ty

im·prac·ti·ca·ble

im·prac·ti·ca·bly

im·prac·ti·cal

im·prac·ti·cal·i·ty

im·pre·cate, *v.*
  im·pre·ca·ted,
  im·pre·cat·ing

im·pre·ca·tion

im·pre·cise

im·pre·cise·ly

im·pre·cise·ness

im·pre·ci·sion

im·preg·na·bil·i·ty

im·preg·na·ble

im·preg·na·bly

im·preg·nate, *v.*
  im·preg·nat·ed,
  im·preg·nat·ing

im·preg·na·tion

im·pre·sa·rio, *n. pl.*
  im·pre·sa·ri·os

im·press

im·press·ible

im·pres·sion

im·pres·sion·abil·i·ty

im·pres·sion·able

im·pres·sion·ably

im·pres·sion·ism

im·pres·sion·ist

im·pres·sion·is·tic

im·pres·sive

im·pres·sive·ly

im·pres·sive·ness

im·press·ment

im·pri·ma·tur

im·print

im·pris·on

im·pris·oned

im·pris·on·ment

im·prob·a·bil·i·ty, *n. pl.*
  im·prob·a·bil·i·ties

im·prob·a·ble

im·prob·a·bly

im·promp·tu

im·prop·er

im·prop·er·ly

im·pro·pri·ety, *n. pl.*
  im·pro·pri·e·ties

im·prov·abil·i·ty

im·prov·able

im·prove, *v.*
  im·proved,
  im·prov·ing

im·prove·ment

im·prov·i·dence

im·prov·i·dent

im·prov·i·dent·ly

im·pro·vi·sa·tion

im·pro·vise, *v.*
  im·pro·vised,
  im·pro·vis·ing

im·pro·vis·er *or*
im·pro·vis·or

im·pru·dence
  (RASH
  BEHAVIOR)
  (*see also*
  impudence)

im·pru·dent

im·pu·dence
  (DISRESPECTFUL)
  (*see also*
  imprudence)

im·pu·dent

im·pugn

im·pulse

im·pul·sion

im·pul·sive

im·pul·sive·ly

im·pul·sive·ness

im·pure

im·pu·ri·ty, *n. pl.*
  im·pu·ri·ties

im·put·abil·i·ty

im·put·able

im·pu·ta·tion

im·pute, *v.*
  im·put·ed,
  im·put·ing

in·abil·i·ty

in ab·sen·tia

in·ac·ces·si·bil·i·ty

in·ac·ces·si·ble

in·ac·ces·si·bly

in·ac·cu·ra·cy, *n. pl.*
  in·ac·cu·ra·cies

in·ac·cu·rate

in·ac·cu·rate·ly

in·ac·tion

in·ac·ti·vate, *v.*

in·ac·ti·vat·ed,
in·ac·ti·vat·ing
in·ac·ti·va·tion
in·ac·tive
in·ac·tiv·i·ty
in·ad·e·qua·cy, *n.*
pl.
  in·ad·e·qua·cies
in·ad·e·quate
in·ad·e·quate·ly
in·ad·e·quate·ness
in·ad·mis·si·bil·i·ty
in·ad·mis·si·ble
in·ad·mis·si·bly
in·ad·ver·tence
in·ad·ver·ten·cy, *n.*
pl.
  in·ad·ver·ten·cies
in·ad·ver·tent
in·ad·vis·abil·i·ty
in·ad·vis·able
in·alien·abil·i·ty
in·alien·able
in·alien·ably
in·al·ter·abil·i·ty
in·al·ter·able
in·al·ter·ably
in·amo·ra·ta
inane
in·an·i·mate
inan·i·ty, *n. pl.*
inan·i·ties
in·ap·pli·ca·bil·i·ty
in·ap·pli·ca·ble
in·ap·pli·ca·bly
in·ap·pre·cia·ble
in·ap·pre·cia·bly

in·ap·pro·pri·ate
in·ap·pro·pri·ate·ly
in·ap·pro·pri·ate·ness
in·apt (NOT
  SUITABLE) (*see*
  also inept,
  unapt)
in·ap·ti·tude
in·ar·gu·able
in·ar·gu·ably
in·ar·tic·u·late
in·ar·tic·u·late·ly
in·ar·tic·u·late·ness
in·as·much as
in·at·ten·tion
in·at·ten·tive
in·at·ten·tive·ly
in·at·ten·tive·ness
in·au·di·bil·i·ty
in·au·di·ble
in·au·di·bly
in·au·gu·ral
in·au·gu·rate, *v.*
  in·au·gu·rat·ed,
  in·au·gu·rat·ing
in·au·gu·ra·tion
in·aus·pi·cious
in·aus·pi·cious·ly
in·aus·pi·cious·ness
in·board
in·born
in·bound
in·bred
in·breed, *v.*
  in·bred,
  in·breed·ing
in·cal·cu·la·bil·i·ty
in·cal·cu·la·ble

in·cal·cu·la·bly
in·can·des·cence
in·can·des·cent
in·can·ta·tion
in·ca·pa·bil·i·ty
in·ca·pa·ble
in·ca·pac·i·tate, *v.*
  in·ca·pac·i·tat·ed,
  in·ca·pac·i·tat·ing
in·ca·pac·i·ta·tion
in·ca·pac·i·ty
in·car·cer·ate, *v.*
  in·car·cer·at·ed,
  in·car·cer·at·ing
in·car·cer·a·tion
in·car·nate
in·car·na·tion
in·caut·ious
in·caut·ious·ly
in·caut·ious·ness
in·cen·di·ary, *n. pl.*
  in·cen·di·a·ries
in·cense, *v.*
  in·censed,
  in·cens·ing
in·cen·tive
in·cep·tion
in·cep·tive
in·cer·ti·tude
in·ces·sant
in·cest
in·ces·tu·ous
in·ces·tu·ous·ly
in·ces·tu·ous·ness
in·cho·ate
in·ci·dence
in·ci·dent
in·ci·den·tal

in·ci·den·tal·ly

in·cin·er·ate, *v.*
  in·cin·er·at·ed,
  in·cin·er·at·ing

in·cin·er·a·tion

in·cin·er·a·tor

in·cip·i·en·cy

in·cip·i·ent

in·cise, *v.* in·cised,
  in·cis·ing

in·ci·sion

in·ci·sive

in·ci·sive·ly

in·ci·sive·ness

in·ci·sor

in·ci·ta·tion

in·cite, *v.* in·cit·ed,
  in·cit·ing

in·cite·ment

in·ci·vil·i·ty

in·clem·en·cy

in·clem·ent

in·clin·able

in·cli·na·tion

in·cline, *v.*
  in·clined,
  in·clin·ing

in·clin·ing

in·cli·nom·e·ter

in·clud·able *or*
  in·clud·ible

in·clude, *v.*
  in·clud·ed,
  in·clud·ing

in·clu·sion

in·clu·sive

in·clu·sive·ly

in·clu·sive·ness

in·cog·ni·to

in·cog·ni·zant

in·co·her·ence

in·co·her·ent

in·com·bus·ti·ble

in·come

in·com·ing

in·com·men·su·ra·
  bil·i·ty

in·com·men·su·ra·ble

in·com·men·su·ra·bly

in·com·men·su·rate

in·com·mode, *v.*
  in·com·mod·ed,
  in·com·mod·ing

in·com·mo·di·ous

in·com·mo·di·ous·ly

in·com·mo·di·ous·ness

in·com·mu·ni·ca·bil·i·ty

in·com·mu·ni·ca·ble

in·com·mu·ni·ca·bly

in·com·mu·ni·ca·do

in·com·mu·ni·ca·tive

in·com·mut·able

in·com·mut·ably

in·com·pa·ra·bil·i·ty

in·com·pa·ra·ble

in·com·pa·ra·bly

in·com·pat·i·bil·i·ty,
  n. pl.
  in·com·pat·i·bil·i·ties

in·com·pat·i·ble

in·com·pe·tence

in·com·pe·ten·cy

in·com·pe·tent

in·com·pe·tent·ly

in·com·plete

in·com·plete·ly

in·com·plete·ness

in·com·pre·hen·si·
  bil·i·ty

in·com·pre·hen·si·ble

in·com·pre·hen·si·bly

in·com·press·ible

in·con·ceiv·abil·i·ty

in·con·ceiv·able

in·con·ceiv·ably

in·con·clu·sive

in·con·gru·ent

in·con·gru·ity, *n.*
  pl. in·con·gru·i·ties

in·con·gru·ous

in·con·gru·ous·ly

in·con·gru·ous·ness

in·con·se·quen·tial

in·con·se·quen·tial·ly

in·con·sid·er·able

in·con·sid·er·ate

in·con·sid·er·ate·ly

in·con·sis·ten·cy, *n.*
  pl.
  in·con·sis·ten·cies

in·con·sis·tent

in·con·sol·able

in·con·sol·ably

in·con·spic·u·ous

in·con·spic·u·ous·ly

in·con·spic·u·ous·ness

in·con·stan·cy

in·con·stant

in·con·test·abil·i·ty

in·con·test·able

in·con·test·ably

in·con·ti·nence

in·con·ti·nent
in·con·trol·la·ble
in·con·tro·vert·ible
in·con·tro·vert·ibly
in·con·ve·nience, *v.*
　　in·con·ve·nienced,
　　in·con·ve·nienc·ing
in·con·ve·nient
in·con·vert·ibil·i·ty
in·con·vert·ible
in·con·vert·ibly
in·cor·po·rate, *v.*
　　in·cor·po·rat·ed,
　　in·cor·po·rat·ing
in·cor·po·rat·ed
in·cor·po·ra·tion
in·cor·po·ra·tor
in·cor·po·re·al
in·cor·po·re·al·ly
in·cor·rect
in·cor·rect·ly
in·cor·rect·ness
in·cor·ri·gi·bil·i·ty
in·cor·ri·gi·ble
in·cor·ri·gi·bly
in·cor·rupt
in·cor·rupt·ibil·i·ty
in·cor·rupt·ible
in·cor·rupt·ibly
in·crease, *v.*
　　in·creased,
　　in·creas·ing
in·creas·ing·ly
in·cred·ibil·i·ty
in·cred·i·ble
in·cred·i·bly
in·cre·du·li·ty

in·cred·u·lous
in·cred·u·lous·ly
in·cre·ment
in·cre·men·tal
in·crim·i·nate, *v.*
　　in·crim·i·nat·ed,
　　in·crim·i·nat·ing
in·crim·i·na·tion
in·crim·i·na·to·ry
in·crust (*var. of*
　　encrust)
in·crus·ta·tion
in·cu·bate, *v.*
　　in·cu·bat·ed,
　　in·cu·bat·ing
in·cu·ba·tion
in·cu·ba·tor
in·cu·bus, *n. pl.*
　　in·cu·bi *or*
　　in·cu·bus·es
in·cul·cate, *v.*
　　in·cul·cat·ed,
　　in·cul·cat·ing
in·cul·ca·tion
in·cul·pa·ble
in·cul·pate, *v.*
　　in·cul·pat·ed,
　　in·cul·pat·ing
in·cul·pa·tion
in·cul·pa·to·ry
in·cum·ben·cy, *n.
　　pl.*
　　in·cum·ben·cies
in·cum·bent
in·cu·nab·u·lum, *n.
　　pl.*
　　in·cu·nab·u·la
in·cur, *v.* in·curred,
　　in·cur·ring
in·cur·abil·i·ty

in·cur·able
in·cur·ably
in·cu·ri·ous
in·cu·ri·ous·ly
in·cu·ri·ous·ness
in·cur·sion
in·debt·ed
in·debt·ed·ness
in·de·cen·cy, *n. pl.*
　　in·de·cen·cies
in·de·cent
in·de·cent·ly
in·de·ci·pher·able
in·de·ci·sion
in·de·ci·sive
in·de·ci·sive·ly
in·de·ci·sive·ness
in·de·clin·able
in·de·co·rous
in·de·co·rous·ly
in·de·co·rous·ness
in·de·co·rum
in·deed
in·de·fa·ti·ga·bil·i·ty
in·de·fat·i·ga·ble
in·de·fat·i·ga·bly
in·de·fea·si·ble
in·de·fea·si·bly
in·de·fen·si·bil·i·ty
in·de·fen·si·ble
in·de·fen·si·bly
in·de·fin·able
in·def·i·nite
in·def·i·nite·ly
in·def·i·nite·ness
in·del·i·ble

in·del·i·bly

in·del·i·ca·cy, *n. pl.*
  in·del·i·ca·cies

in·del·i·cate

in·del·i·cate·ly

in·del·i·cate·ness

in·dem·ni·fi·ca·tion

in·dem·ni·fy, *v.*
  in·dem·ni·fied,
  in·dem·ni·fy·ing

in·dem·ni·ty, *n. pl.*
  in·dem·ni·ties

in·dent

in·dent·ta·tion

in·den·tion

in·den·ture, *v.*
  in·den·tured,
  in·den·tur·ing

in·de·pen·dence

in·de·pen·den·cy, *n.
pl.*
  in·de·pen·den·cies

in·de·pen·dent

in·de·pen·dent·ly

in-depth

in·de·scrib·abil·i·ty

in·de·scrib·able

in·de·scrib·ably

in·de·struc·ti·bil·i·ty

in·de·struc·ti·ble

in·de·struc·ti·bly

in·de·ter·min·able

in·de·ter·min·ably

in·de·ter·mi·na·cy

in·de·ter·mi·nate

in·de·ter·mi·nate·ly

in·de·ter·mi·na·tion

in·de·ter·min·ism

in·dex, *n. pl.*
  in·dex·es
  (BOOK) *or*
  in·dic·es
  (MATH)

in·dex·er

In·dia

In·di·an

In·di·ana

In·di·an·an

In·di·a·nap·o·lis

In·di·an·i·an

in·di·cate, *v.*
  in·di·cat·ed,
  in·di·cat·ing

in·di·ca·tion

in·dic·a·tive

in·dic·a·tive·ly

in·di·ca·tor

in·di·cia, *pl. of*
  in·di·ci·um

in·dict (CHARGE),
  (*see also* in·dite)

in·dict·able

in·dict·ment

in·dif·fer·ence

in·dif·fer·ent

in·dif·fer·ent·ly

in·di·gence

in·di·gene

in·dig·e·nous

in·dig·e·nous·ly

in·dig·e·nous·ness

in·di·gent

in·di·gest·ibil·i·ty

in·di·gest·ible

in·di·ges·tion

in·dig·nant

in·dig·nant·ly

in·dig·na·tion

in·dig·ni·ty, *n. pl.*
  in·dig·ni·ties

in·di·go, *n. pl.*
  in·di·gos *or*
  in·di·goes

in·di·rect

in·di·rec·tion

in·di·rect·ly

in·di·rect·ness

in·dis·cern·ible

in·dis·cern·ibly

in·dis·creet
  (LACKING
  PRUDENCE)

in·dis·crete (NOT
  SEPARATED)

in·dis·cre·tion

in·dis·crim·i·nate

in·dis·crim·i·nate·ly

in·dis·crim·i·nate·ness

in·dis·pens·abil·i·ty

in·dis·pens·able

in·dis·pens·ably

in·dis·pose, *v.*
  in·dis·posed,
  in·dis·pos·ing

in·dis·posed

in·dis·po·si·tion

in·dis·put·able

in·dis·put·ably

in·dis·sol·u·ble

in·dis·sol·u·bly

in·dis·tinct

in·dis·tin·guish·able

in·dis·tin·guish·ably

in·dite (TO WRITE),

v. in·dit·ed,
in·dit·ing (*see
also* indict)

in·di·um

in·di·vid·u·al

in·di·vid·u·al·ism

in·di·vid·u·al·ist

in·di·vid·u·al·is·tic

in·di·vid·u·al·is·tic·al·ly

in·di·vid·u·al·i·ty, *n.
pl.*
  in·di·vid·u·al·i·ties

in·di·vid·u·al·ly

in·di·vis·i·bil·i·ty

in·di·vis·i·ble

in·di·vis·i·bly

in·doc·tri·nate, *v.*
  in·doc·tri·nat·ed,
  in·doc·tri·nat·ing

in·doc·tri·na·tion

in·doc·tri·na·tor

in·do·lence

in·do·lent

in·do·lent·ly

in·dom·i·ta·bil·i·ty

in·dom·i·ta·ble

in·dom·i·ta·bly

In·do·ne·sia

In·do·ne·sian

in·door

in·doors

in·dorse (*var. of*
  endorse), *v.*
  in·dorsed,
  in·dors·ing

in·du·bi·ta·ble

in·du·bi·ta·bly

in·duce, *v.*

in·duced,
in·duc·ing

in·duce·ment

in·duct

in·duc·tance

in·duct·ee

in·duc·tion

in·duc·tive

in·duc·tive·ly

in·duc·tor

in·dulge, *v.*
  in·dulged,
  in·dulg·ing

in·dul·gence

in·dul·gent

in·dul·gent·ly

in·du·rate, *v.*
  in·du·rat·ed,
  in·du·rat·ing

in·du·ra·tion

in·dus·tri·al

in·dus·tri·al·ism

in·dus·tri·al·ist

in·dus·tri·al·iza·tion

in·dus·tri·a·lize, *v.*
  in·dus·tri·al·ized,
  in·dus·tri·al·iz·ing

in·dus·tri·al·ly

in·dus·tri·ous

in·dus·tri·ous·ly

in·dus·tri·ous·ness

in·dus·try, *n. pl.*
  in·dus·tries

ine·bri·ate, *v.*
  ine·bri·at·ed,
  ine·bri·at·ing

ine·bri·a·tion

in·ebri·ety

in·ed·i·ble

in·ed·u·ca·ble

in·ef·fa·bil·i·ty

in·ef·fa·ble

in·ef·fa·bly

in·ef·face·able

in·ef·fec·tive

in·ef·fec·tive·ly

in·ef·fec·tive·ness

in·ef·fec·tu·al

in·ef·fec·tu·al·ly

in·ef·fi·ca·cious

in·ef·fi·ca·cious·ly

in·ef·fi·ca·cious·ness

in·ef·fi·ca·cy

in·ef·fi·cien·cy, *n.
pl.*
  in·ef·fi·cien·cies

in·ef·fi·cient

in·elas·tic

in·elas·tic·i·ty

in·el·e·gance

in·el·e·gant

in·el·e·gant·ly

in·el·i·gi·bil·i·ty

in·el·i·gi·ble

in·el·o·quence

in·el·o·quent

in·eluc·ta·bil·i·ty

in·eluc·ta·ble

in·eluc·ta·bly

in·ept
  (INCOMPETENT)
  (*see also* inapt,
  unapt)

in·ep·ti·tude

in·equal·i·ty

in·eq·ui·ta·ble
in·eq·ui·ty
  (UNFAIRNESS),
  n. pl. in·eq·ui·ties
  (*see also*
  iniquity)
in·erad·i·ca·ble
in·erad·i·ca·bly
in·er·ran·cy
in·er·rant
in·ert
in·er·tia
in·er·tial
in·ert·ly
in·ert·ness
in·es·cap·able
in·es·cap·ably
in·es·sen·tial
in·es·ti·ma·ble
in·es·ti·ma·bly
in·ev·i·ta·bil·i·ty
in·ev·i·ta·ble
in·ev·i·ta·bly
in·ex·act
in·ex·ac·ti·tude
in·ex·act·ly
in·ex·act·ness
in·ex·cus·able
in·ex·cus·ably
in·ex·haust·ibil·i·ty
in·ex·haust·ible
in·ex·haust·ibly
in·ex·o·ra·ble
in·ex·o·ra·bly
in·ex·pe·di·en·cy
in·ex·pe·di·ent
in·ex·pen·sive

in·ex·pen·sive·ly
in·ex·pen·sive·ness
in·ex·pe·ri·ence
in·ex·pe·ri·enced
in·ex·pert
in·ex·pi·a·ble
in·ex·pli·ca·bil·i·ty
in·ex·pli·ca·ble
in·ex·pli·ca·bly
in·ex·pli·cit
in·ex·pli·cit·ly
in·ex·pli·cit·ness
in·ex·press·ibil·i·ty
in·ex·press·ible
in·ex·press·ibly
in·ex·pres·sive
in·ex·pres·sive·ly
in·ex·pres·sive·ness
in ex·ten·so
in·ex·tin·guish·able
in·ex·tin·guish·ably
in ex·tre·mis
in·ex·tri·ca·bil·i·ty
in·ex·tri·ca·ble
in·ex·tri·ca·bly
in·fal·li·bil·i·ty
in·fal·li·ble
in·fal·li·bly
in·fa·mous
in·fa·mous·ly
in·fa·my, *n. pl.*
  in·fa·mies
in·fan·cy, *n. pl.*
  in·fan·cies
in·fant
in·fan·ti·cide

in·fan·tile
in·fan·til·ism
in·fan·til·i·ty
in·fan·try, *n. pl.*
  in·fan·tries
in·fan·try·man, *n.*
  pl. in·fan·try·men
in·farct
in·farc·tion
in·fat·u·ate, *v.*
  in·fat·u·at·ed,
  in·fat·u·at·ing
in·fect
in·fec·tion
in·fec·tious
in·fec·tious·ly
in·fec·tious·ness
in·fec·tive
in·fec·tor
in·fe·lic·i·tous
in·fe·lic·i·tous·ly
in·fe·lic·i·ty, *n. pl.*
  in·fe·lic·i·ties
in·fer, *v.* in·ferred,
  in·fer·ring
in·fer·able
in·fer·ence
in·fer·en·tial
in·fer·en·tial·ly
in·fe·ri·or
in·fe·ri·or·i·ty
in·fer·nal
in·fer·nal·ly
in·fer·no, *n. pl.*
  in·fer·nos
in·fer·tile
in·fer·til·i·ty
in·fest

in·fes·ta·tion
in·fi·del
in·fi·del·i·ty, *n. pl.*
  in·fi·del·i·ties
in·field
in·field·er
in·fight·ing
in·fil·trate, *v.*
  in·fil·trat·ed,
  in·fil·trat·ing
in·fil·tra·tion
in·fil·tra·tor
in·fi·nite
in·fi·nite·ly
in·fi·nite·ness
in·fin·i·tes·i·mal
in·fin·i·tes·i·mal·ly
in·fin·i·tive
in·fin·i·tude
in·fin·i·ty, *n. pl.*
  in·fin·i·ties
in·firm
in·fir·ma·ry, *n. pl.*
  in·fir·ma·ries
in·fir·mi·ty, *n. pl.*
  in·fir·mi·ties
in fla·gran·te
  de·lic·to
in·flame, *v.*
  in·flamed,
  in·flam·ing
in·flam·ma·ble
in·flam·ma·tion
in·flam·ma·to·ry
in·flat·able
in·flate, *v.*
  in·flat·ed,
  in·flat·ing
in·flat·ed

in·fla·tion
in·fla·tion·ary
in·flect
in·flec·tion
in·flec·tion·al
in·flex·i·bil·i·ty
in·flex·i·ble
in·flex·i·bly
in·flict
in·flic·tion
in·flo·res·cence
in·flo·res·cent
in·flow
in·flu·ence, *v.*
  in·flu·enced,
  in·flu·enc·ing
in·flu·en·tial
in·flu·en·za
in·flux
in·fold
in·form
in·for·mal
in·for·mal·i·ty, *n.*
  pl.
  in·for·mal·i·ties
in·for·mal·ly
in·for·mant
in·for·ma·tion
in·for·ma·tive
in·for·ma·tive·ly
in·for·ma·tive·ness
in·formed
in·form·er
in·fra
in·frac·tion
in·fran·gi·bil·i·ty
in·fran·gi·ble

in·fran·gi·bly
in·fra·red
in·fra·stuc·ture
in·fre·quent
in·fre·quent·ly
in·fringe, *v.*
  in·fringed,
  in·fring·ing
in·fringe·ment
in·fu·ri·ate, *v.*
  in·fu·ri·at·ed,
  in·fu·ri·at·ing
in·fu·ri·a·tion
in·fuse, *v.* in·fused,
  in·fus·ing
in·fus·ible
in·fu·sion
in·gath·er·ing
in·ge·nious
  (CLEVER) (*see*
  also ingenuous)
in·ge·nious·ly
in·ge·nious·ness
in·ge·nue *or*
  in·gé·nue
in·ge·nu·i·ty, *n. pl.*
  in·ge·nu·i·ties
in·gen·u·ous
  (NAIVE) (*see*
  also ingenious)
in·gen·u·ous·ly
in·gen·u·ous·ness
in·gest
in·gest·ible
in·ges·tion
in·glo·ri·ous
in·glo·ri·ous·ly
in·glo·ri·ous·ness
in·got

in·grain

in·grained

in·grate

in·gra·ti·ate, *v.*
  in·gra·ti·at·ed,
  in·gra·ti·at·ing

in·gra·ti·at·ing

in·gra·ti·at·ing·ly

in·grat·i·tude

in·gre·di·ent

in·gress

in·group

in·grow·ing

in·grown

in·gui·nal

in·hab·it

in·hab·it·able

in·hab·it·an·cy, *n.*
  pl.
  in·hab·it·an·cies

in·hab·it·ant

in·hab·it·ed

in·hal·ant

in·ha·la·tion

in·ha·la·tor

in·hale, *v.* in·haled,
  in·hal·ing

in·hal·er

in·har·mo·ni·ous

in·har·mo·ni·ous·ly

in·har·mo·ni·ous·ness

in·har·mo·ny

in·her·ent

in·her·ent·ly

in·her·it

in·her·it·able

in·her·i·tance

in·her·i·tor

in·hib·it

in·hi·bi·tion

in·hib·i·tor

in·hib·i·to·ry

in·hos·pi·ta·ble

in·hos·pi·ta·bly

in-house

in·hu·man

in·hu·mane

in·hu·mane·ly

in·hu·man·i·ty, *n.*
  pl.
  in·hu·man·i·ties

in·hu·man·ly

in·hu·ma·tion

in·im·i·cal

in·im·i·cal·ly

in·im·i·ta·ble

in·im·i·ta·bly

in·iq·ui·tous

in·iq·ui·tous·ly

in·iq·ui·tous·ness

in·iq·ui·ty
  (WICKED), *n.*
  pl. in·iq·ui·ties
  (*see also*
  inequity)

ini·tial, *v.* ini·tialed
  or ini·tialled,
  ini·tial·ing *or*
  ini·tial·ling

ini·tial·ly

ini·ti·ate, *v.*
  ini·ti·at·ed,
  ini·ti·at·ing

ini·ti·a·tion

ini·tia·tive

ini·tia·tor

in·ject

in·jec·tion

in·jec·tor

in·ju·di·cious

in·ju·di·cious·ly

in·ju·di·cious·ness

in·junc·tion

in·jure, *v.* in·jured,
  in·jur·ing

in·ju·ri·ous

in·ju·ri·ous·ly

in·ju·ri·ous·ness

in·ju·ry, *n. pl.*
  in·ju·ries

in·jus·tice

ink·blot

ink·ling

ink·stand

ink·well

inky, *adj.* ink·i·er,
  ink·i·est

in·laid

in·land

in-law

in·lay, *v.* in·laid,
  in·lay·ing

in·let

in lo·co pa·ren·tis

in·mate

in me·di·as res

in me·mo·ri·am

in·most

in·nards

in·nate

in·nate·ly

in·nate·ness

in·ner

in·ner-di·rect·ed
in·ner·most
in·ner·sole
in·ning
inn·keep·er
in·no·cence
in·no·cent
in·noc·u·ous
in·noc·u·ous·ly
in·noc·u·ous·ness
in·no·vate, *v.*
  in·no·vat·ed,
  in·no·vat·ing
in·no·va·tion
in·no·va·tive
in·no·va·tor
in·nu·en·do, *n. pl.*
  in·nu·en·dos *or*
  in·nu·en·does
in·nu·mer·a·ble
in·nu·mer·a·bly
in·oc·u·late, *v.*
  in·oc·u·lat·ed,
  in·oc·u·lat·ing
in·oc·u·la·tion
in·of·fen·sive
in·of·fen·sive·ly
in·of·fen·sive·ness
in·op·er·a·ble
in·op·er·a·tive
in·op·por·tune
in·op·por·tune·ly
in·op·por·tune·ness
in·or·di·nate
in·or·di·nate·ly
in·or·gan·ic
in·or·gan·i·cal·ly

in·pa·tient
in·put, *v.* in·put·ted
  or in·put,
  in·put·ting
in·quest
in·qui·e·tude
in·quire, *v.*
  in·quired,
  in·quir·ing
in·quir·er
in·quir·ing·ly
in·qui·ry, *n. pl.*
  in·qui·ries
in·qui·si·tion
in·quis·i·tive
in·quis·i·tive·ness
in·quis·i·tor
in re
in rem
in·road
in·rush
in·sa·lu·bri·ous
in·sane
in·sane·ly
in·san·i·ty, *n. pl.*
  in·san·i·ties
in·sa·tia·bil·i·ty
in·sa·tia·ble
in·sa·tia·bly
in·sa·tiate
in·scribe, *v.*
  in·scribed,
  in·scrib·ing
in·scrip·tion
in·scru·ta·bil·i·ty
in·scru·ta·ble
in·scru·ta·bly
in·seam

in·sect
in·sec·ti·ci·dal
in·sec·ti·cide
in·se·cure
in·se·cure·ly
in·se·cu·ri·ty, *n. pl.*
  in·se·cu·ri·ties
in·sem·i·na·tion
in·sem·i·nate, *v.*
  in·sem·i·nat·ed,
  in·sem·i·nat·ing
in·sen·sate
in·sen·si·bil·i·ty, *n.*
  pl.
  in·sen·si·bil·i·ties
in·sen·si·ble
in·sen·si·bly
in·sen·si·tive
in·sen·si·tive·ly
in·sen·si·tive·ness
in·sen·si·tiv·i·ty, *n.*
  pl.
  in·sen·si·tiv·i·ties
in·sen·tience
in·sen·tient
in·sep·a·ra·bil·i·ty
in·sep·a·ra·ble
in·sep·a·ra·bly
in·sert
in·ser·tion
in-ser·vice
in·set, *v.* in·set,
  in·set·ting
in·shore
in·side
in·sid·er
in·sid·i·ous
in·sid·i·ous·ly

in·sid·i·ous·ness

in·sight

in·sig·nia *or*
  in·sig·ne, *n. pl.*
  in·sig·nia *or*
  in·sig·ni·as

in·sig·nif·i·cance

in·sig·nif·i·cant

in·sig·nif·i·cant·ly

in·sin·cere

in·sin·cere·ly

in·sin·cer·i·ty, *n. pl.*
  in·sin·cer·i·ties

in·sin·u·ate, *v.*
  in·sin·u·at·ed,
  in·sin·u·at·ing

in·sin·u·a·tion

in·sip·id

in·si·pid·i·ty, *n. pl.*
  in·si·pid·i·ties

in·sip·id·ly

in·sist

in·sis·tence

in·sis·tent

in·sis·tent·ly

in si·tu

in·so·far

in·so·late (EXPOSE
  TO THE SUN), *v.*
  in·so·lat·ed,
  in·so·lat·ing (*see
  also* insulate)

in·sole

in·so·lence

in·so·lent

in·so·lent·ly

in·sol·u·bil·i·ty

in·sol·u·ble

in·sol·u·bly

in·solv·able

in·solv·ably

in·sol·ven·cy, *n. pl.*
  in·sol·ven·cies

in·sol·vent

in·som·nia

in·som·ni·ac

in·so·much

in·sou·ci·ance

in·sou·ci·ant

in·sou·ci·ant·ly

in·spect

in·spec·tion

in·spec·tor

in·spi·ra·tion

in·spi·ra·tion·al

in·spi·ra·tion·al·ly

in·spire, *v.*
  in·spired,
  in·spir·ing

in·spir·er

in·spir·it

in·sta·bil·i·ty

in·stall (*rarely*
  instal), *v.*
  in·stalled,
  in·stall·ing

in·stal·la·tion

in·stall·ment

in·stance, *v.*
  in·stanced,
  in·stanc·ing

in·stant

in·stan·ta·neous

in·stan·ta·neous·ly

in·stan·ta·neous·ness

in·stant·ly

in sta·tu quo

in·stead

in·step

in·sti·gate, *v.*
  in·sti·gat·ed,
  in·sti·gat·ing

in·sti·ga·tion

in·sti·ga·tor

in·still (*occas.*
  in·stil), *v.*
  in·stilled,
  in·stil·ling

in·stinct

in·stinc·tive

in·stinc·tive·ly

in·stinc·tu·al

in·sti·tute, *v.*
  in·sti·tut·ed,
  in·sti·tut·ing

in·sti·tu·tion

in·sti·tu·tion·al

in·sti·tu·tion·al·ize,
  v.
  in·sti·tu·tion·al·ized,
  in·sti·tu·tion·al·iz·ing

in·sti·tu·tion·al·ly

in·struct

in·struc·tion

in·struc·tion·al

in·struc·tive

in·struc·tive·ly

in·struc·tive·ness

in·struc·tor

in·stru·ment

in·stru·men·tal

in·stru·men·tal·ist

in·stru·men·tal·i·ty,
  pl.
  in·stru·men·tal·i·ties

in·stru·men·tal·ly

in·stru·men·ta·tion
in·sub·or·di·nate
in·sub·or·di·na·tion
in·sub·stan·tial
in·sub·stan·ti·al·i·ty
in·suf·fer·able
in·suf·fer·ably
in·suf·fi·cien·cy, *n. pl.*
  in·suf·fi·cien·cies
in·suf·fi·cient
in·suf·fi·cient·ly
in·su·lant
in·su·lar
in·su·lar·i·ty
in·su·late (SET APART), *v.*
  in·su·lat·ed,
  in·su·lat·ing (*see also* insolate)
in·su·la·tion
in·su·la·tor
in·su·lin
in·sult
in·sult·ing·ly
in·su·per·a·ble
in·su·per·a·bly
in·sup·port·able
in·sup·port·ably
in·sup·press·ible
in·sup·press·ibly
in·sur·abil·i·ty
in·sur·able
in·sur·ance
in·sure, *v.* in·sured,
  in·sur·ing
in·sured
in·sur·er

in·sur·gence
in·sur·gen·cy, *n. pl.*
  in·sur·gen·cies
in·sur·gent
in·sur·mount·able
in·sur·mount·ably
in·sur·rec·tion
in·sur·rec·tion·ary,
  n. pl.
  in·sur·rec·tion·ar·ies
in·sur·rec·tion·ist
in·sus·cep·ti·bil·i·ty
in·sus·cep·ti·ble
in·sus·cep·ti·bly
in·tact
in·tact·ness
in·ta·glio, *n. pl.*
  in·ta·glios
in·take
in·tan·gi·bil·i·ty, *n. pl.*
  in·tan·gi·bil·i·ties
in·tan·gi·ble
in·tan·gi·bly
in·te·ger
in·te·gral
in·te·grate, *v.*
  in·te·grat·ed,
  in·te·grat·ing
in·te·gra·tion
in·te·gra·tion·ist
in·te·gra·tor
in·teg·ri·ty
in·teg·u·ment
in·tel·lect
in·tel·lec·tu·al
in·tel·lec·tu·al·ize, *v.*

in·tel·lec·tu·al·ized,
in·tel·lec·tu·al·iz·ing
in·tel·lec·tu·al·ly
in·tel·li·gence
in·tel·li·gent
in·tel·li·gent·ly
in·tel·li·gen·tsia
in·tel·li·gi·bil·i·ty
in·tel·li·gi·ble
in·tel·li·gi·bly
in·tem·per·ance
in·tem·per·ate
in·tem·per·ate·ly
in·tem·per·ate·ness
in·tend
in·tend·ed
in·tense
in·tense·ly
in·tense·ness
in·ten·si·fi·ca·tion
in·ten·si·fy, *v.*
  in·ten·si·fied,
  in·ten·si·fy·ing
in·ten·si·ty, *n. pl.*
  in·ten·si·ties
in·ten·sive
in·ten·sive·ly
in·ten·sive·ness
in·tent (MEANING)
  (*see also* entente)
in·ten·tion
in·ten·tion·al
in·ten·tion·al·ly
in·ter, *v.* in·terred,
  in·ter·ring
in·ter·act
in·ter·ac·tion

in·ter·ac·tive
in·ter·ac·tive·ly
in·ter·agen·cy
in·ter alia
in·ter·breed, v.
  in·ter·bred,
  in·ter·breed·ing
in·ter·cede, v.
  in·ter·ced·ed,
  in·ter·ced·ing
in·ter·cept
in·ter·cep·tion
in·ter·cep·tor
in·ter·ces·sion
in·ter·ces·sor
in·ter·ces·so·ry
in·ter·change, v.
  in·ter·changed,
  in·ter·chang·ing
in·ter·change·able
in·ter·change·ably
in·ter·col·le·giate
in·ter·com
in·ter·com·mu·
  ni·ca·tion
in·ter·con·nect
in·ter·con·nec·tion
in·ter·con·ti·nen·tal
in·ter·cos·tal
in·ter·course
in·ter·cul·tur·al
in·ter·de·nom·i·
  na·tion·al
in·ter·de·part·men·tal
in·ter·de·pen·dence
in·ter·de·pen·den·cy
in·ter·de·pen·dent
in·ter·dict

in·ter·dic·tion
in·ter·dis·ci·plin·ary
in·ter·est
in·ter·est·ed
in·ter·est·ing
in·ter·est·ing·ly
in·ter·face, v.
  in·ter·faced,
  in·ter·fac·ing
in·ter·faith
in·ter·fere, v.
  in·ter·fered,
  in·ter·fer·ing
in·ter·fer·ence
in·ter·fer·on
in·ter·fuse, v.
  in·ter·fused,
  in·ter·fus·ing
in·ter·ga·lac·tic
in·ter·gen·er·a·tion·al
in·ter·gov·ern·men·tal
in·ter·im
in·te·ri·or
in·ter·ject
in·ter·jec·tion
in·ter·lace, v.
  in·ter·laced,
  in·ter·lac·ing
in·ter·lard
in·ter·lay, v.
  in·ter·laid,
  in·ter·lay·ing
in·ter·lay·er
in·ter·leave, v.
  in·ter·leaved,
  in·ter·leav·ing
in·ter·line, v.
  in·ter·lined,
  in·ter·lin·ing

in·ter·lin·ear
in·ter·lin·ing
in·ter·link
in·ter·lock
in·ter·lo·cu·tion
in·ter·loc·u·tor
in·ter·loc·u·to·ry
in·ter·lope, v.
  in·ter·loped,
  in·ter·lop·ing
in·ter·lop·er
in·ter·lude
in·ter·lu·nar
in·ter·mar·riage
in·ter·mar·ry, v.
  in·ter·mar·ried,
  in·ter·mar·ry·ing
in·ter·me·di·ary, n.
  pl.
  in·ter·me·di·ar·ies
in·ter·me·di·ate
in·ter·ment
  (BURIAL) (see
  also internment)
in·ter·mez·zo, n. pl.
  in·ter·mez·zi or
  in·ter·mez·zos
in·ter·mi·na·ble
in·ter·mi·na·bly
in·ter·min·gle, v.
  in·ter·min·gled,
  in·ter·min·gling
in·ter·mis·sion
in·ter·mit·tent
in·ter·mit·tent·ly
in·ter·mix
in·ter·mon·tane
in·tern
in·ter·nal

in·ter·nal·iza·tion

in·ter·nal·ize, *v.*
in·ter·nal·ized,
in·ter·nal·iz·ing

in·ter·na·tion·al

in·ter·na·tion·al·
iza·tion

in·ter·na·tion·al·ize,
v. in·ter·na·tion·
al·ized, in·ter·
na·tion·al·iz·ing

in·ter·na·tion·al·ly

in·ter·ne·cine

in·tern·ee

in·tern·ist

in·tern·ment
(IMPRISONMENT)
(*see also*
interment)

in·tern·ship

in·ter·nun·cio

in·ter·of·fice

in·ter·per·son·al

in·ter·per·son·al·ly

in·ter·phone

in·ter·plan·e·tary

in·ter·play

in·ter·po·late, *v.*
in·ter·po·lat·ed,
in·ter·po·lat·ing

in·ter·po·la·tion

in·ter·pose, *v.*
in·ter·posed,
in·ter·pos·ing

in·ter·po·si·tion

in·ter·pret

in·ter·pre·ta·tion

in·ter·pret·er

in·ter·pre·tive

in·ter·pre·tive·ly

in·ter·ra·cial

in·ter·reg·num, *n.*
pl. in·ter·reg·nums
or in·ter·reg·na

in·ter·re·late, *v.*
in·ter·re·lat·ed,
in·ter·re·lat·ing

in·ter·re·la·tion

in·ter·ro·gate, *v.*
in·ter·ro·gat·ed,
in·ter·ro·gat·ing

in·ter·ro·ga·tion

in·ter·rog·a·tive

in·ter·rog·a·tor

in·ter·rog·a·to·ry, *n.*
pl.
in·ter·rog·a·to·ries

in·ter·rupt

in·ter·rupt·er

in·ter·rup·tion

in·ter·scho·las·tic

in·ter·sect

in·ter·sec·tion

in·ter·sperse, *v.*
in·ter·spersed,
in·ter·spers·ing

in·ter·sper·sion

in·ter·state

in·ter·stel·lar

in·ter·stice

in·ter·sti·tial

in·ter·tid·al

in·ter·trib·al

in·ter·twine, *v.*
in·ter·twined,
in·ter·twin·ing

in·ter·twist

in·ter·ur·ban

in·ter·val

in·ter·vene, *v.*
in·ter·vened,
in·ter·ven·ing

in·ter·ven·tion

in·ter·ven·tion·ism

in·ter·ven·tion·ist

in·ter·view

in·ter·view·ee

in·ter·view·er

in·ter·weave, *v.*
in·ter·wove
(*occas.*
in·ter·weaved),
in·ter·wo·ven
(*occas.*
in·ter·weaved),
in·ter·weav·ing

in·tes·tate

in·tes·ti·nal

in·tes·tine

in·ti·ma·cy, *n. pl.*
in·ti·ma·cies

in·ti·mate, *v.*
in·ti·mat·ed,
in·ti·mat·ing

in·ti·ma·tion

in·tim·i·date, *v.*
in·tim·i·dat·ed,
in·tim·i·dat·ing

in·tim·i·da·tion

in·to

in·tol·er·a·ble

in·tol·er·a·bly

in·tol·er·ance

in·tol·er·ant

in·tol·er·ant·ly

in·to·na·tion

in·tone, *v.*

in·toned,
in·ton·ing

in to·to

in·tox·i·cant

in·tox·i·cate, *v.*
in·tox·i·cat·ed,
in·tox·i·cat·ing

in·tox·i·ca·tion

in·tra·city

in·trac·ta·bil·i·ty

in·trac·ta·ble

in·trac·ta·bly

in·tra·mu·ral

in·tra·mu·ral·ly

in·tra·mus·cu·lar

in·tran·si·gence

in·tran·si·gent

in·tran·si·gent·ly

in·tran·si·tive

in·tran·si·tive·ly

in·tran·si·tive·ness

in·tra·state

in·tra·uter·ine

in·tra·ve·nous

in·tra·ve·nous·ly

in·trep·id

in·tre·pid·i·ty

in·trep·id·ly

in·trep·id·ness

in·tri·ca·cy, *n. pl.*
in·tri·ca·cies

in·tri·cate

in·tri·cate·ly

in·trigue, *v.*
in·trigued,
in·trigu·ing

in·trin·sic

in·trin·si·cal·ly

in·tro·duce, *v.*
in·tro·duced,
in·tro·duc·ing

in·tro·duc·tion

in·tro·duc·to·ry

in·tro·spec·tion

in·tro·spec·tive

in·tro·spec·tive·ly

in·tro·spec·tive·ness

in·tro·ver·sion

in·tro·vert

in·trude, *v.*
in·trud·ed,
in·trud·ing

in·trud·er

in·tru·sion

in·tru·sive

in·tru·sive·ly

in·tru·sive·ness

in·tu·i·tion

in·tu·i·tive

in·tu·i·tive·ly

in·tu·i·tive·ness

in·tu·mes·cence

in·tu·mes·cent

in·un·date, *v.*
in·un·dat·ed,
in·un·dat·ing

in·ure, *v.* in·ured,
in·ur·ing

in vac·uo

in·vade, *v.*
in·vad·ed,
in·vad·ing

in·vad·er

in·val·id (NULL OR
VOID)

in·va·lid (ILL)

in·val·i·date, *v.*
in·val·i·dat·ed,
in·val·i·dat·ing

in·val·i·da·tion

in·valu·able

in·valu·ably

In·var℠

in·vari·abil·i·ty

in·vari·able

in·vari·ably

in·va·sion

in·vec·tive

in·veigh

in·vei·gle, *v.*
in·vei·gled,
in·vei·gling

in·vent

in·ven·tion

in·ven·tive

in·ven·tive·ness

in·vent·or

in·ven·to·ry, *n. pl.*
in·ven·to·ries

in·verse

in·verse·ly

in·ver·sion

in·vert

in·ver·te·brate

in·vest

in·ves·ti·gate, *v.*
in·ves·ti·gat·ed,
in·ves·ti·gat·ing

in·ves·ti·ga·tion

in·ves·ti·ga·tive

in·ves·ti·ga·tor

in·ves·ti·ture

in·vest·ment

in·ves·tor
in·vet·er·ate
in·vid·i·ous
in·vid·i·ous·ly
in·vid·i·ous·ness
in·vig·o·rate, v.
   in·vig·o·rat·ed,
   in·vig·o·rat·ing
in·vig·o·ra·tion
in·vin·ci·bil·i·ty
in·vin·ci·ble
in·vin·ci·bly
in·vi·o·la·bil·i·ty
in·vi·o·la·ble
in·vi·o·la·bly
in·vi·o·late
in·vis·i·bil·i·ty
in·vis·i·ble
in·vis·i·bly
in·vi·ta·tion
in·vite, v. in·vit·ed,
   in·vit·ing
in·vit·ing
in·vo·ca·tion
in·voice, v.
   in·voiced,
   in·voic·ing
in·voke, v.
   in·voked,
   in·vok·ing
in·vol·un·tar·i·ly
in·vol·un·tary
in·vo·lute
in·vo·lu·tion
in·volve, v.
   in·volved,
   in·volv·ing
in·vul·ner·a·bil·i·ty

in·vul·ner·a·ble
in·vul·ner·a·bly
in·ward or in·wards
in·ward·ly
in·ward·ness
io·dide
io·dine
io·dize, v. io·dized,
   io·diz·ing
ion
ion·ic
ion·iza·tion
ion·ize, v. ion·ized,
   ion·iz·ing
ion·o·sphere
io·ta
Io·wa
Io·wan
ip·e·cac
ip·so fac·to
Iran
Irani
Ira·ni·an
Iraq
Iraqi
iras·ci·bil·i·ty
iras·ci·ble
iras·ci·bly
irate
irate·ly
irate·ness
ire·ful
Ire·land
ir·i·des·cence
ir·i·des·cent
irid·i·um

iris, *n. pl.* iris·es *or*
   iri·des
Irish
Irish·man, *n. pl.*
   Irish·men
Irish·wom·an, *n.*
   pl. Irish·wom·en
irk·some
iron
iron·bound
iron·clad
iron·ic
iron·i·cal
iron·i·cal·ly
iron·ware
iron·work
iron·work·er
iro·ny, *pl.* iro·nies
ir·ra·di·ate, v.
   ir·ra·di·at·ed,
   ir·ra·di·at·ing
ir·ra·di·a·tion
ir·ra·tio·nal
ir·ra·tio·nal·i·ty, *n.*
   pl.
   ir·ra·tio·nal·i·ties
ir·ra·tio·nal·ly
Ir·ra·wad·dy Riv·er
ir·re·claim·able
ir·rec·on·cil·abil·i·ty
ir·rec·on·cil·able
ir·rec·on·cil·ably
ir·re·cov·er·able
ir·re·cov·er·ably
ir·re·deem·able
ir·re·deem·ably
ir·re·duc·ible
ir·re·duc·ibly

ir·re·fut·able

ir·re·fut·ably

ir·reg·u·lar

ir·reg·u·lar·i·ty, *n.*
pl.
  ir·reg·u·lar·i·ties

ir·rel·e·vance

ir·rel·e·van·cy, *n.*
pl.
  ir·rel·e·van·cies

ir·rel·e·vant

ir·re·li·gious

ir·re·li·gious·ly

ir·re·me·di·a·ble

ir·re·me·di·a·bly

ir·re·mov·able

ir·re·mov·ably

ir·rep·a·ra·ble

ir·rep·a·ra·bly

ir·re·place·able

ir·re·place·ably

ir·re·press·ible

ir·re·press·ibly

ir·re·proach·able

ir·re·proach·ably

ir·re·sist·ible

ir·re·sist·ibly

ir·res·o·lute

ir·res·o·lute·ly

ir·res·o·lute·ness

ir·res·o·lu·tion

ir·re·solv·able

ir·re·spec·tive

ir·re·spec·tive·ly

ir·re·spon·si·bil·i·ty

ir·re·spon·si·ble

ir·re·spon·si·bly

ir·re·triev·able

ir·re·triev·ably

ir·rev·er·ence

ir·rev·er·ent

ir·rev·er·ent·ly

ir·re·vers·ible

ir·re·vers·ibly

ir·rev·o·ca·ble

ir·rev·o·ca·bly

ir·ri·gate, *v.*
  ir·ri·gat·ed,
  ir·ri·gat·ing

ir·ri·ga·tion

ir·ri·ta·bil·i·ty

ir·ri·ta·ble

ir·ri·ta·bly

ir·ri·tant

ir·ri·tate, *v.*
  ir·ri·tat·ed,
  ir·ri·tat·ing

ir·ri·ta·tion

ir·rupt (BURST
  INTO) (*see also*
  erupt)

ir·rup·tion

isin·glass

Is·lam

Is·lam·ic

is·land

isle

is·let

iso·bar

iso·gon·ic

iso·late, *v.*

iso·lat·ed,
iso·lat·ing

iso·la·tion

iso·la·tion·ism

iso·la·tion·ist

Iso·lette®

iso·mer

iso·met·ric

iso·met·ri·cal·ly

iso·met·rics

isos·ce·les

iso·therm

iso·ther·mal

iso·tope

iso·to·pic

Is·ra·el

Is·rae·li

Is·ra·el·ite

is·su·ance

is·sue, *v.* is·sued,
  is·su·ing

Is·tan·bul

isth·mi·an

isth·mus

Ital·ian

ital·ic

ital·i·cize, *v.*
  ital·i·cized,
  ital·i·ciz·ing

It·a·ly

itch

itch·i·ness

itchy, *adj.* itch·i·er,
  itch·i·est

item

item·iza·tion

item·ize, *v.*
 item·ized,
 item·iz·ing

it·er·ate, *v.*
 it·er·at·ed,
 it·er·at·ing

it·er·a·tion

itin·er·ant

itin·er·ant·ly

itin·er·ary, *pl.*
 itin·er·ar·ies

it·self

it·ty-bit·ty

ivied

ivo·ry

Ivo·ry Coast

ivy, *n. pl.* ivies

J

jab, v. jabbed,
jab·bing

jab·ber

jab·ber·er

jab·ber·wocky

ja·bot

ja·cal (HUT), n. pl.
ja·ca·les or
ja·cals

jack·al (WILD DOG)

jack·a·napes

jack·ass

jack·boot

jack·daw

jack·et

jack·ham·mer

jack-in-the-box, n.
pl. jack-in-the-
box·es or jacks-
in-the-box

jack-in-the-pul·pit,
n. pl. jack-in-the-
pul·pits or jacks-
in-the-pul·pit

jack·knife, n. pl.
jack·knives

jack·knife, v.
jack·knifed,
jack·knif·ing

jack-of-all-trades,
n. pl. jacks-of-
all-trades

jack-o'-lan·tern, n.
pl. jack-o'-
lan·terns

jack·pot

jack·rab·bit

jack·screw

Jack·son

Jack·son·ville

jack·straw

Ja·cob

jac·o·net

jac·quard

Jac·que·line

jac·que·rie

Ja·cuz·zi℠

jade, v. jad·ed,
jad·ing

jade·ite

jag, v. jagged,
jag·ging

jag·ged, adj.

jag·ged·ly

jag·ged·ness

jag·uar

jai alai

jail·bird

jail·break

jail·er or jail·or

Ja·kar·ta

Ja·lis·co

ja·lopy, n. pl.
ja·lop·ies

jal·ou·sie

jam, v. jammed,
jam·ming

Ja·mai·ca

Ja·mai·can

jam·ba·la·ya

jam·bo·ree

James

Ja·mie

jam·packed

jan·gle, v. jan·gled,
jan·gling

jan·i·tor

jan·i·tor·i·al

Jan·u·ary, n. pl.
Jan·u·ar·ies

Ja·pan

Jap·a·nese, n. pl.
Jap·a·nese

ja·pon·i·ca

jar, v. jarred,
jar·ring

jar·di·niere

Jar·ed

jar·gon

Jarls·berg® (CHEESE)

jas·mine

Ja·son

jas·per

ja·to

jaun·dice, v.
jaun·diced,
jaun·dic·ing

jaun·diced

jaun·ti·ly

jaun·ti·ness

jaun·ty, adj.
jaun·ti·er,
jaun·ti·est

Ja·va

Ja·va·nese, n. pl.
Ja·va·nese

jav·e·lin

jaw·bone, v.
jaw·boned,
jaw·bon·ing

jaw·break·er

jay·hawk·er

jay·walk

jay·walk·er

jay·walk·ing

jazz

jazz·i·ly

jazz·i·ness

jazzy, adj. jazz·i·er,
jazz·i·est

jeal·ous

jeal·ou·sy, n. pl.
jeal·ou·sies

jeans

jeer

Jef·fer·son City

Jef·frey

Je·ho·vah

je·june

jel·ly, n. pl. jel·lies

jel·ly, v. jel·lied,
jel·ly·ing

jel·ly·fish

je ne sais quoi

Jen·ni·fer

jen·ny, n. pl.
jen·nies

jeop·ar·dize, v.
jeop·ar·dized,
jeop·ar·diz·ing

jeop·ar·dy, n. pl.
jeop·ar·dies

jer·boa

jer·e·mi·ad

Jer·e·my

jerk·i·ly

jerk·in

jerk·i·ness

jerk·wa·ter

jerky (SPASMODIC,
FOOLISH), adj.
jerk·i·er,
jerk·i·est

jer·ky (MEAT), n.

jer·o·bo·am

Jer·ry (PERSON'S
NAME), n. pl.
Jerrys

Jer·ry (GERMAN

SOLDIER,
CHIEFLY BRIT.)
n. pl. Jerries

jer·ry-built

jer·sey, pl. jer·seys

Jer·sey City

Je·ru·sa·lem

Jes·se

Jes·si·ca

jes·ter

Je·su·it

Je·sus

jet, v. jet·ted,
jet·ting

je·té

jet·lin·er

jet·port

jet-pro·pelled

jet·sam

jet·ti·son

jet·ty, n. pl. jet·ties

jeu d'es·prit, n. pl.
jeux d'es·prit

jew·el, v. jew·eled,
or jew·elled,
jew·el·ing or
jew·el·ling

jew·el·er or
jew·el·ler

jew·el·ry

Jew·ish

Jew·ry, n. pl.
Jew·ries

Jew's-harp or
Jews'-harp

jib, v. jibbed,
jib·bing

jibe (AGREE,
SHIFT), v.

jibed, jib·ing (*see also* gibe)

ji·ca·ma

jif·fy, *n. pl.* jif·fies

jig, *v.* jigged, jig·ging

jig·ger

jig·gle, *v.* jig·gled, jig·gling

jig·saw

Jill

jim-dan·dy

jim·my, *v.* jim·mied, jim·my·ing

jim·son·weed

jin·gle, *v.* jin·gled, jin·gling

jin·go·ism

jin·go·is·tic

jin·go·is·ti·cal·ly

jin·rik·i·sha

jinx, *n. pl.* jinx·es

jit·ney, *n. pl.* jit·neys

jit·ter·bug, *v.* jit·ter·bugged, jit·ter·bug·ging

jit·ters

jit·tery

jiu·jit·su *or* jiu·jut·su (*var. of* ju·jit·su)

jive, *v.* jived, jiv·ing

job, *v.* jobbed, job·bing

job·ber

job·hold·er

job·less·ness

Joce·lyn

jock

jock·ette

jock·ey, *pl.* jock·eys

jock·strap

jo·cose

jo·cose·ly

jo·cose·ness

jo·cos·i·ty, *n. pl.* jo·cos·i·ties

joc·u·lar

joc·u·lar·i·ty, *n. pl.* joc·u·lar·i·ties

jo·cund

jo·cun·di·ty, *n. pl.* jo·cun·di·ties

jodh·pur

Jo·el

jog, *v.* jogged, jog·ging

jog·ger

jog·gle, *v.* jog·gled, jog·gling

Jo·han·nes·burg

John

John·ny (PERSON'S NAME), *n. pl.* John·nys

john·ny (HOSPITAL GOWN), *n. pl.* john·nies

John·ny-come-late·ly, *n. pl.* John·ny-come-late·lies *or* John·nies-come-late·ly

joie de vi·vre

join·er

join·ery

joint·ly

joist

joke, *v.* joked, jok·ing

jok·er

jol·li·ty, *n. pl.* jol·li·ties

jol·ly, *adj.* jol·li·er, jol·li·est

Jon·a·than

jon·quil

Jor·dan

Jor·da·ni·an

Jo·seph

josh·ing·ly

Josh·ua

jos·tle, *v.* jos·tled, jos·tling

jot, *v.* jot·ted, jot·ting

joule

jour·nal

jour·nal·ese

jour·nal·ism

jour·nal·ist

jour·nal·is·tic

jour·ney, *n. pl.* jour·neys

jour·ney·man, *n. pl.* jour·ney·men

jo·vial

jo·vi·al·i·ty

jo·vial·ly

jowl

joy·ful

joy·ful·ly
joy·ous
joy·ous·ly
joy·ride
joy·rid·er
joy·rid·ing
ju·bi·lant
ju·bi·lant·ly
ju·bi·la·tion
ju·bi·lee
Ju·da·ic
Ju·da·ism
judge, *v.* judged, judg·ing
judg·ment, *or* judge·ment
ju·di·ca·ture
ju·di·cial
ju·di·cial·ly
ju·di·cia·ry, *n. pl.* ju·di·cia·ries
ju·di·cious
ju·di·cious·ly
ju·di·cious·ness
ju·do
jug·ger·naut
jug·gle, *v.* jug·gled, jug·gling
jug·gler
jug·u·lar
juice, *v.* juiced, juic·ing
juic·er
juic·i·ly
juic·i·ness

juicy, *adj.* juic·i·er, juic·i·est
ju·jit·su *or* jiu·jit·su *or* jiu·jut·su
ju·jube
juke·box
ju·lep
Ju·lie
ju·li·enne
Ju·ly, *n. pl.* Ju·lies
jum·ble, *v.* jum·bled, jum·bling
jum·bo, *n. pl.* jum·bos
jum·per
jump·i·ness
jump·suit
jumpy, *adj.* jump·i·er, jump·i·est
jun·co, *n. pl.* jun·cos *or* jun·coes
junc·tion
junc·ture
June
Ju·neau
jun·gle
ju·nior
ju·ni·per
jun·ker
jun·ket
junk·ie *or* junky (ADDICT), *n. pl.* jun·kies

junky (TRASHY), *adj.* junk·i·er, junk·i·est
junk·yard
jun·ta
Ju·pi·ter
Ju·ras·sic
ju·ris·dic·tion
ju·ris·dic·tion·al
ju·ris·pru·dence
ju·ris·pru·den·tial·ly
ju·rist
ju·rist·ic
ju·ror
ju·ry, *n. pl.* ju·ries
jus·tice
jus·ti·cia·ble
jus·ti·fi·able
jus·ti·fi·ably
jus·ti·fi·ca·tion
just·ti·fy, *v.* jus·ti·fied, jus·ti·fy·ing
Jus·tin
just·ly
jut, *v.* jut·ted, jut·ting
jute
ju·ve·nile
ju·ve·nil·ia
jux·ta·pose, *v.* jux·ta·posed, jux·ta·pos·ing
jux·ta·po·si·tion

K

ka·bob (*occas.*
  ke·bab *or*
  ke·bob)
Ka·bu·ki
kaf·fee·klatsch
kai·ser
Ka·la·ha·ri
ka·lei·do·scope
ka·lei·do·scop·ic
ka·mi·ka·ze
Kam·pu·chea
Kam·pu·che·an
kan·ga·roo
Kan·san
Kan·sas
Kan·sas City, *n. pl.*
  Kan·sas Citys
ka·olin
ka·pok
ka·put (*occas.*
  ka·putt)
Ka·ra·chi
kar·a·kul
kar·at (*occas.*
  car·at) (GOLD)
  (*see also* carat,
  caret, carrot)

ka·ra·te
Ka·ren
kar·ma
karst
Kath·er·ine
Kath·leen
Ka·tie
ka·ty·did
kat·zen·jam·mer
kay·ak
kayo, *v.* kay·oed,
  kayo·ing
Ka·zakh
Ka·zakh So·vi·et
  So·cial·ist
  Re·pub·lic (*now*
  Kazakhstan)
Ka·zakh·stan
  (*formerly* Kazakh
  Soviet Socialist
  Republic)
ka·zoo, *n. pl.*
  ka·zoos
ke·bab *or* ke·bob
  (*var. of* kabob)
kedge, *v.* kedged,
  kedg·ing
keel·boat

keel·haul
keel·son
keen·ly
keen·ness
keep, *v.* kept,
  keep·ing
keep·er
keep·sake
kees·hond, *n. pl.*
  kees·hon·den
keg·ler
keis·ter *or* kees·ter
Keith
Kel·ly
kel·vin
ken·nel, *v.*
  ken·neled *or*
  ken·nelled,
  ken·nel·ing *or*
  ken·nel·ling
Ken·neth
ke·no
Ken·tuck·i·an
Ken·tucky
Ke·nya
Ke·nyan
ke·pi

ker·a·tin

ker·chief

ker·nel

ker·o·sene *or*
    ker·o·sine

ker·sey

ker·sey·mere

kes·trel

ketch·up *or* cat·sup

ke·tene

ke·tone

ket·tle

ket·tle·drum

Kev·in

key

key·board

key·board·ist

key·hole

key·note, *v.*
    key·not·ed,
    key·not·ing

key·not·er

key·stone

key·stroke

key·way

kha·ki

khe·dive

Khmer, *n. pl.*
    Khmer *or*
    Khmers

kib·ble, *v.* kib·bled,
    kib·bling

kib·butz, *n. pl.*
    kib·but·zim

kib·butz·nik

ki·bitz

kii·bitz·er

ki·bosh

kick·back, *n.*

kick back, *v.*

kick·off, *n.*

kick off, *v.*

kid, *v.* kid·ded,
    kid·ding

kid·nap, *v.*
    kid·napped *or*
    kid·naped,
    kid·nap·ping *or*
    kid·nap·ing

kid·ney, *pl.*
    kid·neys

kid·skin

kiel·ba·sa

Ki·ev

Kil·i·man·ja·ro

kill·deer, *n. pl.*
    kill·deers *or*
    kill·deer

kill·er

kill·ing

kill·joy

kiln

ki·lo, *n. pl.* ki·los

ki·lo·cy·cle

ki·lo·gram

ki·lo·hertz

ki·lo·li·ter

ki·lo·me·ter

ki·lo·volt

ki·lo·watt

ki·lo·watt-hour

kil·ter

Kim·ber·ly

ki·mo·no, *n. pl.*
    ki·mo·nos

kin·der·gar·ten

kind·heart·ed

kind·heart·ed·ly

kind·heart·ed·ness

kin·dle, *v.* kin·dled,
    kin·dling

kind·li·ness

kin·dling

kind·ly, *adj.*
    kind·li·er,
    kind·li·est

kin·dred

ki·ne·mat·ics

kin·e·scope

ki·ne·si·ol·o·gy

ki·net·ic

ki·net·ics

kin·folk *or*
    kin·folks

king·bolt

king·dom

king·fish

king·fish·er

king·ly

king·mak·er

king·pin

king-size *or* king-
    sized

kin·ka·jou

kinky, *adj.*
    kink·i·er,
    kink·i·est

Kin·sha·sa

kin·ship

kins·man, *n. pl.*
    kins·men

kins·wom·an, *n. pl.*
    kins·wom·en

ki·osk

Ki·o·wa

kip, *n. pl.* kip *or* kips

kip·per

Kir·ghiz So·vi·et So·cial·ist Re·pub·lic *or* Kir·giz·ia (*now* Kyrgyzstan)

kirsch·was·ser

kir·tle

kis·met

kiss·er

kitch·en

kitch·en·ette

kitch·en·ware

kite, *v.* kit·ed, kit·ing

kitsch

kit·ten

kitten·ish

kit·ty, *n. pl.* kit·ties

kit·ty-cor·ner *or* kit·ty-cor·nered (*var. of* cater-corner)

ki·wi, *n. pl.* ki·wis

Klax·on®

Klee·nex®

klep·to·ma·nia

klep·to·ma·ni·ac

klutz, *n. pl.* klutz·es

klut·zy, *adj.* klut·zi·er, klut·zi·est

knack·wurst

knap·sack

knave (RASCAL) (*see also* nave)

knav·ery, *n. pl.* knav·er·ies

knav·ish

knead

knee·cap

knee-deep

knee-high

knee-hole

knee-jerk

kneel, *v.* knelt *or* kneeled, kneel·ing

knell

knick·ers

knick·knack

knife, *n. pl.* knives

knife-edge

knight

knight-errant, *n. pl.* knights-errant

knight-hood

Knight Templar, *n. pl.* Knights Templars *or* Knights Templar

knit, *v.* knit *or* knit·ted, knit·ting

knit·ter

knit·wear

knob·by, *adj.* knob·bi·er, knob·bi·est

knock·about

knock·down

knock·er

knock-kneed

knock·out

knoll

knot, *v.* knot·ted, knot·ting

knot·hole

knot·ty, *adj.* knot·ti·er, knot·ti·est

know, *v.* knew, known, know·ing

know·able

know-how

know-it-all

knowl·edge

knowl·edge·able

knowl·edge·ably

Knox·ville

knuck·le, *v.* knuck·led, knuck·ling

knuck·le·ball

knuck·le·bone

knuck·le·head

knurl

ko·ala

ko·bo, *n. pl.* ko·bo

kohl·ra·bi

ko·ka·nee

kook (SCREWBALL)

kooka·bur·ra

kooky (ECCENTRIC) (*occas.* kook·ie) *adj.* kook·i·er, kook·i·est kook·i·ness

ko·peck *or* ko·pek

Ko·ran (SACRED
  BOOK)

Ko·rea

Ko·re·an

ko·ru·na, *n. pl.*
  ko·ru·ny *or*
  ko·ru·nas *or*
  ko·rum

ko·sher

kow·tow

kraal

Krak·a·tau *or*
  Krak·a·tao *or*
  Krak·a·toa

Krem·lin

krem·lin·ol·o·gist

krem·lin·ol·o·gy

krill

Kris·ten

Kris·tin

kro·na (SWEDISH
  MONEY), *n. pl.*
  kro·nor

kro·na (ICELANDIC
  MONEY), *n. pl.*
  kro·nur

kro·ne (DANISH
  AND
  NORWEGIAN
  MONEY), *n. pl.*
  kro·ner

Kru·ger·rand

kryp·ton

ku·chen

ku·do, *n. pl.* ku·dos

ku·lak

kum·quat

Kurd

Kurd·ish

ku·rus, *n. pl.*
  ku·rus

Ku·wait

Ku·waiti

kvetch

kwa·cha, *n. pl.*
  kwa·cha

kwash·i·or·kor

kyat

Kyle

Kyr·gyz

Kyr·gyz·stan
  (*formerly*
  Kirghiz Soviet
  Socialist
  Republic)

Kyu·shu

L

laa·ger (CAMP) (*see also* lager)
la·bel, *v.* la·beled *or* la·belled, la·bel·ing *or* la·bel·ling
la·bi·al
la·bile
la·bor
lab·o·ra·to·ry, *n. pl.* lab·o·ra·to·ries
la·bored
la·bor·er
la·bor-in·ten·sive
la·bo·ri·ous
la·bo·ri·ous·ly
la·bo·ri·ous·ness
la·bor-sav·ing
Lab·ra·dor
la·bur·num
lab·y·rinth
lab·y·rin·thine
lace, *v.* laced, lac·ing
lac·er·ate, *v.* lac·er·at·ed, lac·er·at·ing
lac·er·a·tion

la·ches, *n. pl.* la·ches
lach·ry·mal, *or* lac·ri·mal
lach·ry·mose
lac·ing
lack·a·dai·si·cal
lack·a·dai·si·cal·ly
lack·ey, *n. pl.* lack·eys
lack·lus·ter
la·con·ic
la·con·i·cal·ly
lac·quer
lac·quer·ware
la·crosse
lac·tate, *v.* lac·tat·ed, lac·tat·ing
lac·ta·tion
lac·te·al
lac·tic
lac·tose
la·cu·na, *n. pl.* la·cu·nae *or* la·cu·nas
lacy, *adj.* lac·i·er, lac·i·est

lad·der
lad·der-back
lad·en
lad·ing
la·dle, *v.* la·dled, la·dling
la·dy, *n. pl.* ladies
la·dy·bug
la·dy·fin·ger
lady-in-wait·ing, *n. pl.* ladies-in-wait·ing
lady·like
lady·love
lady·ship
la·e·trile
lag, *v.* lagged, lag·ging
la·ger (BEER) (*see also* laager)
lag·gard
la·gniappe
la·goon
La·gos
La·hore
laid-back
lair

209

lais·sez-faire

la·ity, *n. pl.* la·i·ties

lak·er

la·ma (MONK) (*see also* llama)

La·maze

lam·baste *or* lam·bast

lam·bent

lam·bre·quin

lamb·skin

lame (CRIPPLED), *adj.* lam·er, lam·est

la·mé (FABRIC)

lame·brain *or* lame·brained, *adj.*

lame·brain, *n.*

la·ment

la·men·ta·ble

la·men·ta·bly

lam·en·ta·tion

lam·i·na, *n. pl.* lam·i·nae *or* lam·i·nas

lam·i·nate, *v.* lam·i·nat·ed, lam·i·nat·ing

lam·i·nat·ed

lam·i·na·tion

lamp·black

lamp·light·er

lam·poon

lamp·post

lam·prey, *n. pl.* lam·preys

lamp·shade

la·nai

lance, *v.* lanced, lanc·ing

lanc·er

lan·cet

lan·dau

land·ed

land·fall

land·fill

land·form

land·hold·er

land·ing

land·la·dy, *n. pl.* land·la·dies

land·locked

land·lord

land·lub·ber

land·mark

land·mass

land·own·er

land·scape, *v.* land·scaped, land·scap·ing

land·slide

lands·man, *n. pl.* lands·men

land·ward

lan·guage

lan·guid

lan·guid·ly

lan·guid·ness

lan·guish

lan·guish·ing

lan·guish·ing·ly

lan·guor

lan·guor·ous

lan·guor·ous·ly

lan·guor·ous·ness

lank·i·ness

lanky, *adj.* lank·i·er, lank·i·est

lan·o·lin

Lan·sing

lan·tern

lan·tha·num

lan·yard

Lao, *n. pl.* Lao *or* Laos

Laos

Lao·tian

lap, *v.* lapped, lap·ping

lap·a·ro·scope

lap·a·ros·co·py, *n. pl.* lap·a·ros·co·pies

lap·board

lap·dog

la·pel

lap·i·dary, *n. pl.* lap·i·dar·ies

la·pis la·zu·li

lap·pet

lapse, *v.* lapsed, laps·ing

lap·strake

lar·board

lar·ce·nous

lar·ce·nous·ly

lar·ce·ny, *n. pl.* lar·ce·nies

lar·der

large, *adj.* larg·er, larg·est

large·ly

large-scale
lar·gess or lar·gesse
lar·ghet·to
lar·go, n. pl. lar·gos
la·ri, n. pl. la·ri or la·ris
lar·i·at
lark·spur
Lar·ry
lar·va, n. pl. lar·vae (occas. lar·vas)
lar·val
la·ryn·geal
lar·yn·gec·to·my, n. pl. lar·yn·gec·to·mies
lar·yn·gi·tis
lar·ynx, n. pl. la·ryn·ges or lar·ynx·es
la·sa·gna (occas. la·sa·gne)
las·car
las·civ·i·ous
las·civ·i·ous·ly
las·civ·i·ous·ness
lase, v. lased, las·ing
la·ser
lash·ing
Las·sen Peak
las·si·tude
las·so, n. pl. las·sos or las·soes
Las·tex™
last·ing
last·ing·ly
Las Ve·gas

lat·a·kia
latch
latch·key
latch·string
late, adj. lat·er, lat·est
late·com·er
la·teen
late·ly
la·ten·cy, n. pl. la·ten·cies
la·tent
lat·er·al
lat·er·al·ly
la·tex, n. pl. la·ti·ces or la·tex·es
lath (STRIP OF WOOD), n. pl. laths or lath
lathe (MACHINE), n.
lathe, v. lathed, lath·ing
lath·er
Lat·in
La·ti·no, n. pl. La·ti·nos
lat·i·tude
lat·i·tu·di·nal
lat·i·tu·di·nal·ly
la·trine
lat·ter
lat·ter-day
Latter-Day Saint
lat·tice
lat·tice·work
Lat·via

Lat·vi·an
laud·able
laud·ably
lau·da·num
lau·da·to·ry
laugh·able
laugh·ably
laugh·ing·ly
laugh·ing·stock
laugh·ter
launch·er
laun·der
laun·der·er
laun·dress
Laun·dro·mat™
laun·dry, n. pl. laun·dries
laun·dry·man, n. pl. laun·dry·men
laun·dry·wom·an, n. pl. laun·dry·wom·en
Lau·ra
lau·re·ate
lau·rel
Lau·ren
Lau·rence
Lau·ren·tian
la·va
la·va·bo, n. pl. la·va·boes
la·va·liere
lav·a·to·ry, n. pl. lav·a·to·ries
lav·en·der
lav·ish
lav·ish·ly

lav·ish·ness
law-abid·ing
law·break·er
law·ful
law·ful·ly
law·ful·ness
law·giv·er
law·less
law·less·ly
law·less·ness
law·mak·er
Law·rence
law·ren·ci·um
law·suit
law·yer
lax·a·tive
lax·ity
lax·ly
lax·ness
lay, v. laid, lay·ing
lay·away
lay·er
lay·ette
lay·man, n. pl.
   lay·men
lay·off, n.
lay off, v.
lay·out, n.
lay out, v.
lay·wom·an, n. pl.
   lay·wom·en
laze, v. lazed,
   laz·ing
la·zi·ly
la·zi·ness
la·zy, adj. la·zi·er,
   la·zi·est

la·zy·bones
leach (FILTER) (see
   also leech)
lead, v. led,
   lead·ing
lead·en
lead·er
lead·er·ship
lead-in, adj., n.
lead in, v.
lead·ing
lead·off, adj., n.
lead off, v.
leaf, n. pl. leaves
   (occas. leafs)
leaf·age
leaf·let
leafy, adj. leaf·i·er,
   leaf·i·est
league
leak (COME OUT)
   (see also leek)
leak·age
leak·proof
leaky, adj.
   leak·i·er,
   leak·i·est
lean, v. leaned,
   lean·ing
lean·ness
lean-to, n. pl. lean-
   tos
leap, v. leaped or
   leapt, leap·ing
leap·frog, v.
   leap·frogged,
   leap·frog·ging
learn, v. learned,
   learn·ing

learned
learn·ed·ly
learn·ed·ness
learn·er
learn·ing
lease, v. leased,
   leas·ing
lease·hold
least (LOWEST,
   SMALLEST) (see
   also lest)
least·ways
least·wise
leath·er
Leath·er·ette℡
leath·ery
leave, v. left,
   leav·ing
leav·en
leav·en·ing
leave-tak·ing
leav·ings
Leb·a·nese, n. pl.
   Leb·a·nese
Leb·a·non
lech·er
lech·er·ous
lech·er·ous·ly
lech·er·ous·ness
lech·ery, n. pl.
   lech·er·ies
lec·i·thin
lec·tern
lec·tion·ar·y, n. pl.
   lec·tion·ar·ies
lec·tor
lec·ture, v.

lec·tured,
lec·tur·ing

lec·tur·er

le·der·ho·sen

ledge

leech (WORM) (*see
also* leach)

leek (PLANT) (*see
also* leak)

leer·ing·ly

leery

lee·ward

lee·way

left-hand·ed

left-hand·ed·ly

left-hand·ed·ness

left·ist

left·over

left-wing·er

lefty, *n. pl.* lef·ties

leg, *v.* legged,
leg·ging

leg·a·cy, *n. pl.*
leg·a·cies

le·gal

le·gal·ese

le·gal·ism

le·gal·is·tic

le·gal·i·ty, *n. pl.*
le·gal·i·ties

le·gal·iza·tion

le·gal·ize, *v.*
le·gal·ized,
le·gal·iz·ing

le·gal·ly

leg·ate

leg·a·tee

le·ga·tion

le·ga·to, *n. pl.*
le·ga·tos

le·ga·tor

leg·end

leg·end·ary

leg·er·de·main

leg·ging

leg·gy, *adj.*
leg·gi·er,
leg·gi·est

leg·horn

leg·i·bil·i·ty

leg·i·ble

leg·i·bly

le·gion

le·gion·ary, *n. pl.*
le·gion·ar·ies

le·gion·naire

leg·is·late, *v.*
leg·is·lat·ed,
leg·is·lat·ing

leg·is·la·tion

leg·is·la·tive

leg·is·la·tive·ly

leg·is·la·tor

leg·is·la·ture

le·git·i·ma·cy

le·git·i·mate

le·git·i·mate·ly

le·git·i·mize, *v.*
le·git·i·mized,
le·git·i·miz·ing

leg·man, *n. pl.*
leg·men

leg·room

le·gume

le·gu·mi·nous

lei, *n. pl.* leis

lei·sure

lei·sure·li·ness

lei·sure·ly

leit·mo·tiv *or*
leit·mo·tif, *n.*
pl. leit·mo·tives
or leit·mo·tifs

lem·ming

lem·ming·like

lem·on

lem·on·ade

lem·pi·ra

le·mur

lend, *v.* lent,
lend·ing

lend·er

lend-lease

length

length·en

length·ways

length·wise

lengthy, *adj.*
length·i·er,
length·i·est

le·nien·cy, *n. pl.*
le·nien·cies

le·nient

le·nient·ly

Len·in·grad

len·i·tive

len·i·ty

lens(*occas.* lense),
n. pl. lens·es

Lent·en

len·tic·u·lar

len·til

Leo

le·o·nine

leop·ard

le·o·tard

lep·er

lep·re·chaun

lep·ro·sy

lep·rous

lep·ton, *pl.* lep·ta

les·bi·an

les·bi·an·ism

lese ma·jes·ty *or*
  lèse-ma·jesté

le·sion

Le·so·tho

les·see

less·en (MAKE
  LESS)

less·er (SMALLER)

les·son
  (INSTRUCTION)

les·sor (RENTER)

lest (FOR FEAR
  THAT) (*see also*
  least)

let, *v.* let, let·ting

let·down, *adj., n.*

let down, *v.*

le·thal

le·thal·ly

le·thar·gic

leth·ar·gy, *n. pl.*
  leth·ar·gies

let·ter

let·tered

let·ter·er

let·ter·head

let·ter·ing

let·ter-per·fect

let·ter·press

let·ter-qual·i·ty

let·tuce

let·up, *n.*

let up, *v.*

leu, *n. pl.* lei

leu·ke·mia

leu·ko·cyte (*occas.*
  leu·co·cyte)

lev, *n. pl.* le·va

lev·ee
  (EMBANKMENT)
  (*see also* levy)

lev·el, *v.* lev·eled
  or lev·elled,
  lev·el·ing *or*
  lev·el·ling

lev·el·er *or*
  lev·el·ler

lev·el·head·ed

lev·el·head·ed·ness

lev·el·ly

lev·er

le·ver·age, *v.*
  le·ver·aged,
  le·ver·ag·ing

le·vi·a·than

Le·vi's, ®

lev·i·tate, *v.*
  lev·i·tat·ed,
  lev·i·tat·ing

lev·i·ta·tion

lev·i·ty, *n. pl.*
  lev·i·ties

levy
  (ASSESSMENT),
  n. pl. lev·ies (*see
  also* levee)

levy, *v.* lev·ied,
  lev·y·ing

lewd

lewd·ly

lewd·ness

lex·i·cal

lex·i·cog·ra·pher

lex·i·co·graph·ic

lex·i·cog·ra·phy

lex·i·con, *n. pl.*
  lex·i·ca *or*
  lex·i·cons

Lex·ing·ton-
  Fay·ette

li·a·bil·i·ty, *n. pl.*
  li·a·bil·i·ties

li·a·ble
  (RESPONSIBLE)
  (*see also* libel)

li·ai·son

li·ar

li·ba·tion

li·bel (MALIGN), *v.*
  li·beled *or*
  li·belled,
  li·bel·ing *or*
  li·bel·ling (*see
  also* liable)

li·bel·er *or* li·bel·ler

li·bel·ous *or*
  li·bel·lous

lib·er·al

lib·er·al·ism

lib·er·al·i·ty, *n. pl.*
  lib·er·al·i·ties

lib·er·al·iza·tion

lib·er·al·ize, *v.*
  lib·er·al·ized,
  lib·er·al·iz·ing

lib·er·al·ly

lib·er·ate, *v.*

lib·er·at·ed,
lib·er·at·ing
lib·er·a·tion
lib·er·a·tor
Li·be·ria
Li·be·ri·an
lib·er·tar·i·an
lib·er·tar·i·an·ism
lib·er·tine
lib·er·ty, *n. pl.*
lib·er·ties
li·bid·i·nal
li·bid·i·nal·ly
li·bid·i·nous
li·bid·i·nous·ly
li·bid·i·nous·ness
li·bi·do, *n. pl.*
li·bi·dos
Li·bra
(CONSTELLATION),
n. pl. Li·bras
li·bra (COIN,
WEIGHT), *v. pl.*
li·brae
li·brar·i·an
li·brar·i·an·ship
li·brary, *n. pl.*
li·brar·ies
li·bret·tist
li·bret·to, *n. pl.*
li·bret·tos *or*
li·bret·ti
Lib·ya
Lib·y·an
li·cense, *v.*
li·censed,
li·cens·ing
(*occas.* li·cence,
li·cenced,
li·cenc·ing)

li·cens·ee
li·cen·ti·ate
li·cen·tious
li·cen·tious·ly
li·cen·tious·ness
li·chen
lic·it
lick·e·ty-split
lick·spit·tle
lic·o·rice
li·do, *n. pl.* li·dos
lie (RECLINE), *v.*
lay, lain, ly·ing
lie (DECEIVE), *v.*
lied, ly·ing
Liech·ten·stein
Liech·ten·stein·er
lied (SONG), *n. pl.*
lied·er
Lie·der·kranz
(CHEESE)℗
liege
lien
lieu
lieu·ten·an·cy, *n.*
pl. lieu·ten·an·cies
lieu·ten·ant
life, *n. pl.* lives
life·blood
life·boat
life-giv·ing
life·guard
life·less
life·like
life·line
life·long
lif·er

life·sav·er
life·sav·ing
life-size *or* life-
sized
life-style
life·time
life·work
lift·off, *adj., n.*
lift off, *v.*
lig·a·ment
lig·a·ture
light, *v.* light·ed *or*
lit, light·ing
light·en
light·er
light·face
light·fin·gered
light-foot·ed
light-hand·ed
light-head·ed
light·heart·ed
light·heart·ed·ly
light·heart·ed·ness
light·house
light·ing
light·ly
light·ning
light·proof
light-rail
light·ship
lights-out
light·weight
light-year
lig·ne·ous
lig·nite
lik·able *or* like·able

like, v. liked, lik·ing
like·li·hood
like·ly, adj. like·li·er, like·li·est
like-mind·ed
like-mind·ed·ly
like-mind·ed·ness
lik·en
like·ness
like·wise
lik·ing
li·ku·ta, n. pl. ma·ku·ta
li·lac
lil·li·pu·tian
lilt·ing·ly
lily, n. pl. lil·ies
lily-white
Li·ma
li·ma bean
limb
limb·er
limb·er·ness
lim·bo, n. pl. lim·bos
lime·ade
lime·light
lim·er·ick
lime·stone
lim·ey (ENGLISHMAN), n. pl. lim·eys (see also limy)
lim·it
lim·i·ta·tion
lim·it·ed

lim·it·less
limn
lim·ou·sine
lim·pet
lim·pid
limp·ly
limy (OF LIME), adj. lim·i·er, lim·i·est (see also limey)
lin·age (LINES) (see also lineage)
linch·pin
Lin·coln
Lin·da
lin·den
Lind·say
Lind·sey
line, v. lined, lin·ing
lin·eage (ANCESTRY) (see also linage)
lin·eal
lin·ea·ment (FEATURE) (see also liniment)
lin·ear
lin·ear·i·ty, n. pl. lin·ear·i·ties
lin·ear·ly
line·man (FOOTBALL PLAYER, LINE WORKER), n. pl. line·men (see also linesman)
lin·en
lin·er
lines·man

(REFEREE), n. pl. lines·men (see also lineman)
line·up, n.
line up, v.
ling·cod
lin·ger
lin·ger·ie
lin·go, n. pl. lin·goes
lin·gua fran·ca, n. pl. lin·gua fran·cas or lin·guae fran·cae
lin·gual
lin·gui·ne
lin·guist
lin·guis·tic
lin·guis·ti·cal
lin·guis·ti·cal·ly
lin·guis·tics
lin·i·ment (LIQUID) (see also lineament)
lin·ing
link·age
link·up
li·no·leum
Li·no·type℠
lin·seed
lin·sey-wool·sey
lin·tel
li·on
li·on·ess
li·on·heart·ed
li·on·iza·tion
li·on·ize, v.

li·on·ized,
li·on·iz·ing

lip·id

li·po·ma, *n. pl.*
li·po·mas *or*
li·po·ma·ta

lip·py, *adj.*
lip·pi·er,
lip·pi·est

lip·read·ing

lip·stick

liq·ue·fac·tion

liq·ue·fi·able

liq·ue·fier

liq·ue·fy, *v.*
liq·ue·fied,
liq·ue·fy·ing
(*occas.* liq·ui·fy,
liq·ui·fied,
liq·ui·fy·ing)

li·ques·cent

li·queur

liq·uid

liq·uid·am·bar

liq·uid·ly

liq·uid·ness

liq·ui·date, *v.*
liq·ui·dat·ed,
liq·ui·dat·ing

liq·ui·da·tion

liq·ui·da·tor

li·quid·i·ty

li·quor

li·ra, *n. pl.* li·re
(*occas.* li·ras)

Li·sa

Lis·bon

lisle

lis·some

lis·ten

lis·ten·er

list·ing

list·less

list·less·ly

list·less·ness

lit·a·ny, *n. pl.*
lit·a·nies

li·ter (*occas.* litre)

lit·er·a·cy

lit·er·al

lit·er·al·ly

lit·er·al·ness

lit·er·ari·ness

lit·er·ary

lit·er·ate

li·te·ra·ti

lit·er·a·ture

lithe

lithe·some

lith·i·um

lith·o·graph

li·thog·ra·pher

li·thog·ra·phy

Lith·u·a·nia

Lith·u·a·nian

lit·i·ga·ble

lit·i·gant

lit·i·gate, *v.*
lit·i·gat·ed,
lit·i·gat·ing

lit·i·ga·tion

lit·i·ga·tor

li·ti·gious

li·ti·gious·ly

li·ti·gious·ness

lit·mus

li·tre (*var. of* liter)

lit·ter

lit·ter·a·teur

lit·ter·bug

lit·tle, *adj.* lit·tler,
or less *or*
less·er, lit·tlest *or*
least

Lit·tle Rock

lit·to·ral

li·tur·gi·cal

li·tur·gi·cal·ly

lit·ur·gist

lit·ur·gy, *n. pl.*
lit·ur·gies

liv·abil·i·ty (*occas.*
live·abil·i·ty)

liv·able (*occas.*
live·able)

live, *v.* lived,
liv·ing

live·li·hood

live·li·ness

live·long

live·ly, *adj.*
live·li·er,
live·li·est

liv·en

liv·er

liv·er·ied

liv·er·wort

liv·er·wurst

liv·ery, *n. pl.*
liv·er·ies

liv·ery·man, n. pl.
liv·ery·men

live·stock

liv·id

liv·id·i·ty

liv·id·ness

liv·ing

Li·vo·nia

liz·ard

lla·ma (ANIMAL) (*see also* lama)

lla·no, *n. pl.* lla·nos

load (BURDEN) (*see also* lode)

load·ed

load·stone (*var. of* lode·stone)

loaf, *n. pl.* loaves

loaf·er

loamy

loan

loan·word

loath (UNWILLING)

loathe (HATE), *v.* loathed, loath·ing

loath·some

lob, *v.* lobbed, lob·bing

lo·bar

lob·by, *pl.* lob·bies

lob·by·ist

lo·be·lia

lob·lol·ly, *n. pl.* lob·lol·lies

lo·bo, *n. pl.* lo·bos

lo·bot·o·mize, *v.* lo·bot·o·mized, lo·bot·o·miz·ing

lo·bot·o·my, *n. pl.* lo·bot·o·mies

lob·ster

lo·cal

lo·cale

lo·cal·i·ty, *n. pl.* lo·cal·i·ties

lo·cal·iza·tion

lo·cal·ize, *v.* lo·cal·ized, lo·cal·iz·ing

lo·cal·ly

lo·cate, *v.* lo·cat·ed, lo·cat·ing

lo·ca·tion

lock·box

lock·er

lock·et

lock·jaw

lock·nut

lock·out

lock·smith

lock·step

lock·up

lo·co·mo·tion

lo·co·mo·tive

lo·co·mo·tor

lo·co·weed

lo·cus, *n. pl.* lo·ci

lo·cust

lo·cu·tion

lode (ORE DEPOSIT) (*see also* load)

lode·star

lode·stone

lodge, *v.* lodged, lodg·ing

lodg·er

lodg·ing

lodg·ment

loess

loft·i·ly

loft·i·ness

lofty, *adj.* loft·i·er, loft·i·est

log, *v.* logged, log·ging

lo·gan·ber·ry, *n. pl.* lo·gan·ber·ries

Lo·gan

log·a·rithm

log·a·rith·mic

log·a·rith·mi·cal·ly

log·book

loge

log·ger

log·ger·head

log·gia, *n. pl.* log·gias (*occas.* log·gie)

log·ic

log·i·cal

log·i·cal·ly

lo·gi·cian

lo·gis·ti·cal·ly

lo·gis·tics

log·jam

logo, *n. pl.* log·os

logo·gram

logo·graph

logo·type

log·roll·ing

lo·gy (*occas.* log·gy), *adj.* lo·gi·er, lo·gi·est

loin·cloth

loi·ter

loi·ter·er

lol·li·pop *or*
  lol·ly·pop

lol·ly·gag, *v.*
  lol·ly·gagged,
  lol·ly·gag·ging

Lon·don

lone

lone·li·ness

lone·ly

lone·some

lone·some·ness

long-ago, *adj.*

long ago, *n.*

Long Beach

long·boat

long·bow

long-dis·tance,
  adj., *adv.*

long distance, *n.*

lon·ge·ron

lon·gev·i·ty

long-hair *or* long-
  haired, *adj.*

long·hair, *n.*

long·hand

long·ing

long·ing·ly

lon·gi·tude

lon·gi·tu·di·nal

lon·gi·tu·di·nal·ly

long-lived

long-play·ing

long-range

long·shore·man, *n.*
  pl.
  long·shore·men

long-suf·fer·ing

long-term

long-wind·ed

long-wind·ed·ly

long-wind·ed·ness

look·er-on, *n. pl.*
  look·ers-on

look·out, *adj.*, *n.*

look out, *v.*

loo·ny (*occas.*
  loo·ney), *adj.*
  loo·ni·er,
  loo·ni·est

loony, *n. pl.*
  loon·ies

loop·hole

loose, *adj.* loos·er,
  loos·est

loose-fitt·ing

loose-joint·ed

loose-leaf

loose·ly

loos·en

loose·ness

loot·er

lop, *v.* lopped,
  lop·ping

lope, *v.* loped,
  lop·ing

lop-eared

lop·sid·ed

lo·qua·cious

lo·qua·cious·ly

lo·qua·cious·ness

lo·quac·i·ty

lo·quat

lord·ly, *adj.*
  lord·li·er,
  lord·li·est

lor·do·sis

lord·ship

lor·gnette

Lo·ri

lor·ry (WAGON), *n.*
  pl. lor·ries

lo·ry (PARROT), *n.*
  pl. lo·ries

Los An·ge·les

lose, *v.* lost, los·ing

los·er

lo·thar·io, *n. pl.*
  lo·thar·ios

lo·tion

lot·tery, *n, pl.*
  lot·ter·ies

lo·tus

lo·tus-eat·er

lo·tus·land

loud-mouthed

loud·speak·er

Lou·i·si·ana

Lou·i·si·an·an

Lou·is·ville

lounge, *v.* lounged,
  loung·ing

louse, *n. pl.* lice

lousy, *adj.*
  lous·i·er,
  lous·i·est

lout·ish

lou·ver *or* lou·vre

lov·able (*occas.*
  love·able)

love·li·ness

love·ly, *adj.*
  love·li·er,
  love·li·est

love·mak·ing

lov·er

love·sick

lov·ing

lov·ing·ly

lov·ing·ness

low, *adj.* low·er,
low·est

low·born

low·boy

low·bred

low·brow

low-down

low·er

low·er·case, *v.*
low·er·cased,
low·er·cas·ing

low·er-class, *adj.*

low·er class, *n.*

low·er·most

low·er·ing

low-key (*occas.*
low-keyed)

low·land

low-lev·el

low·li·ness

low·ly, *adj.*
low·li·er,
low·li·est

low-pres·sure

low·rid·er *or* low-
rid·er

low-rise

low-spir·it·ed

low-ten·sion

lox, *n. pl.* lox *or*
lox·es

loy·al

loy·al·ist

loy·al·ly

loy·al·ty, *n. pl.*
loy·al·ties

loz·enge

lu·au

lub·ber

Lub·bock

lu·bri·cant

lu·bri·cate, *v.*
lu·bri·cat·ed,
lu·bri·cat·ing

lu·bri·ca·tion

lu·bri·ca·tor

lu·bri·cious *or*
lu·bri·cous

lu·cent

lu·cid

lu·cid·i·ty

lu·cid·ly

lu·cid·ness

Lu·cite™

luck·i·ly

lucky, *adj.*
luck·i·er,
luck·i·est

lu·cra·tive

lu·cra·tive·ly

lu·cra·tive·ness

lu·cre

lu·cu·bra·tion

lu·di·crous

lu·di·crous·ly

lu·di·crous·ness

lug, *v.* lugged,
lug·ging

luge, *v.* luged,
lug·ing

lug·gage

lug·ger

lu·gu·bri·ous

lu·gu·bri·ous·ly

lu·gu·bri·ous·ness

lug·worm

luke·warm

lul·la·by, *n. pl.*
lul·la·bies

lul·la·by, *v.*
lul·la·bied,
lul·la·by·ing

lum·ba·go

lum·bar

lum·ber

lum·ber·ing

lum·ber·jack

lum·ber·yard

lu·men, *n. pl.*
lu·mi·na *or*
lu·mens

lu·mi·nary, *n. pl.*
lu·mi·nar·ies

lu·mi·nes·cence

lu·mi·nos·i·ty, *n. pl.*
lu·mi·nos·i·ties

lu·mi·nous

lu·mi·nous·ly

lu·mi·nous·ness

lum·mox

lum·pec·to·my, *n.
pl.*
lum·pec·to·mies

lump·i·ly

lump·i·ness

lump·ish

lumpy, *adj.*
lump·i·er,
lump·i·est

lu·na·cy, *n. pl.*
  lu·na·cies
lu·nar
lu·na·tic
lun·cheon
lun·cheon·ette
lunch·room
lunge, *v.* lunged,
  lung·ing
lung·fish
lung·wort
lunk·head
lu·pus
lure, *v.* lured,
  lur·ing
lu·rid
lu·rid·ly
lu·rid·ness
lus·cious
lus·cious·ly
lus·cious·ness
lush·ness
lus·ter (*occas.*
  lus·tre)
lus·ter·ware
lust·ful

lust·ful·ly
lust·ful·ness
lust·i·ly
lust·i·ness
lus·trous
lus·trous·ly
lus·trous·ness
lusty, *adj.* lust·i·er,
  lust·i·est
lu·te·ti·um (*occas.*
  lu·te·ci·um)
Lu·ther·an
Lu·ther·an·ism
lux, *n. pl.* lux or
  lux·es
Lux·em·bourg or
  Lux·em·burg
Lux·em·bourg·er or
  Lux·em·burg·er
lux·u·ri·ance
lux·u·ri·ant
lux·u·ri·ate, *v.*
  lux·u·ri·at·ed,
  lux·u·ri·at·ing
lux·u·ri·ous
lux·u·ri·ous·ly

lux·u·ri·ous·ness
lux·u·ry, *n. pl.*
  lux·u·ries
Lu·zon
ly·ce·um
Ly·cra℠
lye
ly·ing
ly·ing-in, *n. pl.*
  ly·ings-in or
  ly·ing-ins
lymph
lym·phat·ic
lym·pho·cyte
lynch
lynch·ing
lynx, *n. pl.* lynx or
  lynx·es
ly·on·naise
lyre
lyr·ic
lyr·i·cal
lyr·i·cal·ly
lyr·i·cism
lyr·i·cist

M

ma·ca·bre

mac·ad·am

mac·ad·am·ize, *v.*
mac·ad·am·ized,
mac·ad·am·iz·ing

Ma·cao

ma·caque

mac·a·ro·ni, *n. pl.*
mac·a·ro·nis *or*
mac·a·ro·nies

mac·a·roon

ma·caw

Mace℗

mac·er·ate, *v.*
mac·er·at·ed,
mac·er·at·ing

mac·er·a·tion

ma·chete

Ma·chi·a·vel·lian

mach·i·nate, *v.*
mach·i·nat·ed,
mach·i·nat·ing

mach·i·na·tion

ma·chine, *v.*
ma·chined,
ma·chin·ing

ma·chine-gun, *v.*
ma·chine-
gunned,

ma·chine-
gun·ning

ma·chine·like

ma·chin·ery, *n. pl.*
ma·chin·er·ies

ma·chin·ist

ma·chis·mo

ma·cho

mack·er·el, *n. pl.*
mack·er·el *or*
mack·er·els

mack·i·naw

mack·in·tosh

mac·ra·me

mac·ro, *n. pl.*
mac·ros

mac·ro·bi·ot·ics

mac·ro·cli·mate

mac·ro·cosm

mac·ro·ec·o·nom·ics

ma·cron

mac·ro·scop·ic

mac·ule

mad, *adj.* mad·der,
mad·dest

Mad·a·gas·can

Mad·a·gas·car

mad·am (FORM OF
ADDRESS), *n.*
pl. mad·ams *or*
mes·dames

ma·dame
(MARRIED
WOMAN), *n. pl.*
mes·dames *or*
ma·dames

mad·cap

mad·den

mad·den·ing

mad·den·ing·ly

mad·der

mad·ding

Ma·dei·ra

ma·de·moi·selle, *n.*
pl.
ma·de·moi·selles
or
mes·de·moi·selles

made-to-order

mad·house

Mad·i·son

mad·ly

mad·man, *n. pl.*
mad·men

mad·ness

ma·dras

Ma·drid

mad·ri·gal

mad·wom·an, *n. pl.*
  mad·wom·en

mael·strom

ma·es·to·so

mae·stro, *n. pl.*
  mae·stros *or*
  mae·stri

Ma·fia

Ma·fi·o·so, *n. pl.*
  Ma·fi·o·si

mag·a·zine

ma·gen·ta

mag·got

mag·goty

ma·gi

mag·ic

mag·i·cal

mag·i·cal·ly

ma·gi·cian

mag·is·te·ri·al

mag·is·te·ri·um

mag·is·tra·cy, *n. pl.*
  mag·is·tra·cies

ma·gis·tral

mag·is·trate

mag·ma

mag·na cum lau·de

mag·na·nim·i·ty, *n.*
  pl.
  mag·na·nim·i·ties

mag·nam·i·mous

mag·nan·i·mous·ly

mag·nan·i·mous·ness

mag·nate

mag·ne·sia

mag·ne·sium

mag·net

mag·net·ic

mag·ne·tism

mag·ne·ti·za·tion

mag·ne·tize, *v.*
  mag·ne·tized,
  mag·ne·tiz·ing

mag·ne·to, *n. pl.*
  mag·ne·tos

mag·ne·tom·e·ter

mag·ne·to·sphere

mag·ni·fi·ca·tion

mag·nif·i·cence

mag·nif·i·cent

mag·nif·i·cent·ly

mag·ni·fi·er

mag·ni·fy, *v.*
  mag·ni·fied,
  mag·ni·fy·ing

mag·nil·o·quence

mag·nil·o·quent

mag·nil·o·quent·ly

mag·ni·tude

mag·no·lia

mag·num

mag·num opus

mag·pie

ma·ha·ra·ja *or*
  ma·ha·ra·jah

ma·ha·ra·ni *or*
  ma·ha·ra·nee

ma·ha·ri·shi

ma·hat·ma

mah·jongg

ma·hog·a·ny, *n. pl.*
  ma·hog·a·nies

maid·en

maid·en·hair

maiden·head

maid·en·hood

maid·en·ly

maid-in-wait·ing,
  n. pl. maids-in-
  wait·ing

maid·ser·vant

mail·bag

mail·box

mail·er

Mail·gram®

mail·ing

mail·man, *n. pl.*
  mail·men

main

Maine

main·frame

main·land

main·ly

main·mast

main·sail

main·sheet

main·spring

main·stay

main·stream

main·tain

main·tain·able

main·te·nance

mai·son·ette

maî·tre d' *or*
  mai·tre d', *n.*
  pl. maî·tre d's *or*
  mai·tre d's

maî·tre d'hôtel, *n.*
  pl. maî·tres
  d'hôtel

maize (GRAIN) (*see
  also* maze)

ma·jes·tic

ma·jes·ti·cal·ly

ma·jes·ty, *n. pl.*
ma·jes·ties

ma·jol·i·ca (*occas.*
ma·iol·i·ca)

ma·jor

ma·jor·do·mo, *n.*
pl. ma·jor·do·mos

ma·jor·i·ty, *n. pl.*
ma·jor·i·ties

ma·jus·cule

mak·able *or*
make·able

make, *v.* made,
mak·ing

make-be·lieve,
adj., *n.*

make be·lieve, *v.*

make-do, *adj.*, *n.*

make do, *v.*

mak·er

make·shift

make·up, *n.*

make up, *v.*

ma·ko, *n. pl.*
ma·kos

mal·ad·ap·ta·tion

mal·adapt·ed

mal·ad·just·ed

mal·ad·min·is·ter

mal·ad·min·is·tra·tion

mal·adroit

mal·adroit·ly

mal·adroit·ness

mal·a·dy, *n. pl.*
mal·a·dies

ma·laise

mal·a·prop

mal·a·prop·ism

mal·ap·ro·pos

ma·lar·ia

ma·lar·i·al

mal·a·thi·on

Ma·la·wi

Ma·la·wi·an

Ma·lay·sia

Ma·lay·si·an

mal·con·tent

mal·con·tent·ed

mal·con·tent·ed·ly

mal·con·tent·ed·ness

mal de mer

mal·dis·tri·bu·tion

Mal·dives

Mal·div·i·an

male·dic·tion

male·fac·tion

male·fac·tor

ma·lef·ic

ma·lef·i·cence

ma·lef·i·cent

male·ness

ma·lev·o·lence

ma·lev·o·lent

ma·lev·o·lent·ly

mal·fea·sance

mal·for·ma·tion

mal·formed

mal·func·tion

mal·ice

ma·li·cious

ma·li·cious·ly

ma·li·cious·ness

ma·lign

ma·lig·nan·cy, *n.*
pl.
ma·lig·nan·cies

ma·lig·nant

ma·lig·ni·ty, *n. pl.*
ma·lig·ni·ties

ma·lin·ger

ma·lin·ger·er

Ma·li

Ma·li·an

mall

mal·lard, *n. pl.*
mal·lard *or*
mal·lards

mal·lea·bil·i·ty

mal·lea·ble

mal·let

mal·low

malm·sey

mal·nour·ished

mal·nu·tri·tion

mal·oc·clu·sion

mal·odor·ous

mal·odor·ous·ly

mal·odor·ous·ness

mal·prac·tice

Mal·ta

Mal·tese

Mal·thu·sian

malt·ose

mal·treat

ma·ma *or* mam·ma

mam·bo, *n. pl.*
mam·bos

mam·mal

mam·ma·li·an

mam·ma·ry
mam·mo·gram
mam·mog·ra·phy
mam·mon
mam·moth
man, *n. pl.* men
man, *v.* manned,
   man·ning
man-about-town,
   n. pl. men-
   about-town
man·a·cle, *v.*
   man·a·cled,
   man·a·cling
man·age, *v.*
   man·aged,
   man·ag·ing
man·age·abil·i·ty
man·age·able
man·age·ably
man·age·ment
man·ag·er
man·a·ge·ri·al
ma·ña·na
man-at-arms, *n. pl.*
   men-at-arms
man·a·tee
Man·ches·ter
man-child, *n. pl.*
   men-chil·dren
man·da·mus
man·da·rin
man·date, *v.*
   man·dat·ed,
   man·dat·ing
man·da·to·ry
man·di·ble
man·do·lin
man·drake

man·drel (METAL
   BAR) (*occas.*
   man·dril)
man·drill
   (BABOON)
man-eat·er
man-eat·ing
ma·nège
   (HORSEMANSHIP)
   (*occas.* ma·nege)
   (*see also* ménage)
ma·neu·ver
ma·neu·ver·abil·i·ty
ma·neu·ver·able
man·ful
man·ful·ly
man·ga·nese
mange
man·ger
man·gle, *v.*
   man·gled,
   man·gling
man·gler
man·go, *n. pl.*
   mang·oes
   (*occas.* mang·os)
man·grove
mangy, *adj.*
   mang·i·er,
   mang·i·est
man·han·dle, *v.*
   man·han·dled,
   man·han·dling
Man·hat·tan
man·hole
man·hood
man-hour
man·hunt
ma·nia

ma·ni·ac
ma·ni·a·cal
ma·ni·a·cal·ly
man·ic
man·ic-de·pres·sive
man·i·cot·ti, *n. pl.*
   man·i·cot·ti
man·i·cure, *v.*
   man·i·cured,
   man·i·cur·ing
man·i·cur·ist
man·i·fest
man·i·fes·ta·tion
man·i·fest·ly
man·i·fes·to, *n. pl.*
   man·i·fes·tos *or*
   man·i·fes·toes
man·i·fold
man·i·kin
Ma·nila
ma·nip·u·late, *v.*
   ma·nip·u·lat·ed,
   ma·nip·u·lat·ing
ma·nip·u·la·tion
ma·nip·u·la·tive
ma·nip·u·la·tive·ly
ma·nip·u·la·tive·ness
ma·nip·u·la·tor
Man·i·to·ba
man·kind
man·li·ness
man·ly, *adj.*
   man·li·er,
   man·li·est
man·made
man·na
manned
man·ne·quin

man·ner

man·nered

man·ner·ism

man·ner·li·ness

man·ner·ly

man·nish

man·nish·ly

man·nish·ness

man-of-war, *n. pl.*
men-of-war

ma·nom·e·ter

man·or

ma·no·ri·al

man·pow·er

man·qué

man·sard

man·serv·ant, *n. pl.*
men·serv·ants

man·sion

man-size *or* man-
sized

man·slaugh·ter

man·ta

man·teau

man·tel
(FIREPLACE
SHELF) (*see also*
mantle)

man·tel·piece

man·til·la

man·tis, *n. pl.*
man·tis·es *or*
man·tes

man·tle
(GARMENT)
(*see also* mantel)

man·tra

man·u·al

man·u·al·ly

man·u·fac·to·ry, *n.*
pl.
man·u·fac·to·ries

man·u·fac·tures, *v.*
man·u·fac·tured,
man·u·fac·tur·ing

man·u·fac·tur·er

man·u·mis·sion

man·u·mit, *v.*
man·u·mit·ted,
man·u·mit·ting

ma·nure

manu·script

many

many·fold

many-sid·ed

man·za·ni·ta

map, *v.* mapped,
map·ping

ma·ple

mar, *v.* marred,
mar·ring

ma·ra·ca

Mar·a·cai·bo

mar·a·schi·no

ma·ras·mus

mar·a·thon

mar·a·thon·er

ma·raud

ma·raud·er

mar·ble, *v.*
mar·bled,
mar·bling

mar·ble·ize, *v.*
mar·ble·ized,
mar·ble·iz·ing

mar·bling

mar·cel, *v.*

mar·celled,
mar·cel·ling

March

march·er

mar·chio·ness

Mar·cus

Mar·di Gras

Mar·ga·ret

mar·ga·rine

mar·ga·ri·ta

mar·gay

mar·gin

mar·gin·al

mar·gin·al·ly

mar·gin·na·lia

mar·grave

Ma·ria

ma·ri·a·chi

mar·i·gold

mar·i·jua·na *or*
mar·i·hua·na

ma·rim·ba

ma·ri·na

mar·i·nade

mar·i·nate, *v.*
mar·i·nat·ed,
mar·i·nat·ing

ma·ri·na·ra

ma·rine

mar·i·ner

mar·i·o·nette

mar·i·tal

mar·i·time

mar·jo·ram

mark

mark·down

marked

mark·ed·ly

mark·er

mar·ket

mar·ket·abil·i·ty

mar·ket·able

mar·ket·ing

mar·ket·place

mark·ing

mark·ka, *n. pl.*
mark·kaa
(*occas.*
mark·kas)

marks·man, *n. pl.*
marks·men

marks·man·ship

mark·up

mar·lin (FISH)

mar·line (ROPE)

mar·line·spike

mar·ma·lade

mar·mo·re·al

mar·mo·set

mar·mot

ma·roon

mar·quee

mar·quess *or*
mar·quis, *n. pl.*
mar·quess *or*
mar·quis·es *or*
mar·quis

mar·que·try

mar·quise, *n. pl.*
mar·quis·es

mar·qui·sette

mar·riage

mar·riage·able

mar·ried

mar·row

mar·row·bone

mar·ry, *v.*
mar·ried,
mar·ry·ing

Mars

mar·sa·la

mar·shal (OFFICER)
(*see also*
Mar·shall)

mar·shal, *v.*
mar·shaled *or*
mar·shalled,
mar·shal·ing *or*
mar·shal·ing

Mar·shall
(PERSON'S
NAME) (*see also*
marshal)

marsh·mal·low

marshy, *adj.*
marsh·i·er,
marsh·i·est

mar·su·pi·al

mar·ten (WEASEL-
LIKE
MAMMAL), *n. pl.*
mar·ten *or*
mar·tens (*see
also* martin)

mar·tial

mar·tian

mar·tin (BIRD) (*see
also* marten)

mar·ti·net

mar·tin·gale

mar·ti·ni

Mar·ti·nique

mar·tyr

mar·tyr·dom

mar·vel, *v.*
mar·veled *or*

mar·velled,
mar·vel·ing *or*
mar·vel·ling

mar·vel·ous

mar·vel·ous·ly

mar·vel·ous·ness

Marx·ism

Marx·ist

Mary

Mary·land

Mary·land·er

mar·zi·pan

mas·cara

mas·con

mas·cot

mas·cu·line

mas·cu·lin·i·ty

ma·ser

mask

mask·ing

mas·och·ism

mas·och·ist

mas·och·is·tic

ma·son

Ma·son·ic

Ma·son·ite®

ma·son·ry, *n. pl.*
ma·son·ries

mas·quer·ade, *v.*
mas·quer·ad·ed,
mas·quer·ad·ing

Mas·sa·chu·setts

mas·sa·cre, *v.*
mas·sa·cred,
mas·sa·cring

mas·sage, *v.*
mas·saged,
mas·sag·ing

mas·seur, *masc.*

mas·seuse, *fem.*

mas·sif (MOUNTAIN), *n.*

mas·sive (HUGE), *adj.*

mass-pro·duce, *v.* mass- pro·duced, mass- pro·duc·ing

mas·tec·to·my, *n. pl.* mas·tec·to·mies

mas·ter

mas·ter-at-arms, *n. pl.* mas·ters-at- arms

mas·ter·ful

mas·ter·ful·ly

mas·ter·ly

mas·ter·mind

mas·ter·piece

mas·ter·stroke

mas·ter·work

mas·tery, *n. pl.* mas·ter·ies

mast·head

mas·ti·cate, *v.* mas·ti·cat·ed, mas·ti·cat·ing

mas·ti·ca·tion

mas·tiff

mas·to·don

mas·toid

mas·tur·bate, *v.* mas·tur·bat·ed, mas·tur·bat·ing

mas·tur·ba·tion

mat, *v.* mat·ted, mat·ting

mat·a·dor

match·book

match·less

match·less·ly

match·less·ness

match·lock

match·mak·er

match·mak·ing

match·wood

mate, *v.* mat·ed, mat·ing

ma·te·ri·al (MATTER) (*see also* matériel)

ma·te·ri·al·ism

ma·te·ri·al·ist

ma·te·ri·al·is·tic

ma·te·ri·al·is·ti·cal·ly

ma·te·ri·al·iza·tion

ma·te·ri·al·ize, *v.* ma·te·ri·al·ized, ma·te·ri·al·iz·ing

ma·te·ri·al·ly

ma·té·ri·el *or* ma·te·ri·el (MILITARY EQUIPMENT) (*see also* material)

ma·ter·nal

ma·ter·nal·ly

ma·ter·ni·ty, *n. pl.* ma·ter·ni·ties

math·e·mat·i·cal

math·e·mat·i·cal·ly

math·e·ma·ti·cian

math·e·mat·ics

mat·i·nee *or* mat·i·née

mat·ins

ma·tri·arch

ma·tri·ar·chal

ma·tri·ar·chy, *n. pl.* ma·tri·ar·chies

ma·tri·cid·al

ma·tri·cide

ma·tric·u·lant

ma·tric·u·late, *v.* ma·tric·u·lat·ed, ma·tric·u·lat·ing

ma·tric·u·la·tion

ma·tri·lin·eal

ma·tri·lin·eal·ly

mat·ri·mo·nial

mat·ri·mo·nial·ly

mat·ri·mo·ny, *n. pl.* mat·ri·mo·nies

ma·trix, *n. pl.* ma·tri·ces *or* ma·tri·xes

ma·tron

ma·tron·ly

mat·ro·nym·ic

mat·ter

Mat·ter·horn

mat·ter-of-fact

mat·ter-of-fact·ly

mat·ter-of-fact·ness

Mat·thew

mat·ting

mat·tock

mat·tress

mat·u·rate, *v.* mat·u·rat·ed, mat·u·rat·ing

mat·u·ra·tion

ma·ture, *v.*
  ma·tured,
  ma·tur·ing

ma·tu·ri·ty

mat·zo *or* mat·zoh,
  n. pl. mat·zoth
  or mat·zos *or*
  mat·zohs

maud·lin

maul

maun·der

Mau·ri·ta·nia

Mau·ri·ta·nian

Mau·ri·tian

Mau·ri·ti·us

mau·so·le·um, *n.*
  pl.
  mau·so·le·ums *or*
  mau·so·lea

mauve

ma·ven

mav·er·ick

maw·kish

maw·kish·ly

maw·kish·ness

max·il·la, *n. pl.*
  max·il·lae *or*
  max·il·las

max·il·lary

max·im

max·i·mal

max·i·mal·ly

max·i·mize, *v.*
  max·i·mized,
  max·i·miz·ing

max·i·mum, *n. pl.*
  max·i·ma *or*
  max·i·mums

May

may·ap·ple

may·be

may·flow·er

may·hem

may·on·naise

may·or

may·or·al·ty, *n. pl.*
  may·or·al·ties

may·pole

maze
  (LABYRINTH)
  (*see also* maize)

ma·zur·ka

McKin·ley, Mount

mea cul·pa

mead·ow

mead·ow·lark

mea·ger

mea·ger·ly

mea·ger·ness

meal·time

mealy, *adj.*
  meal·i·er,
  meal·i·est

mealy·mouthed

mean, *v.* meant,
  mean·ing

me·an·der

mean·ing

mean·ing·ful

mean·ing·ful·ly

mean·ing·ful·ness

mean·ing·less

mean·ing·less·ly

mean·ing·less·ness

mean·ly

mean·ness

means, *n. pl.*
  means

mean·time

mean·while

mea·sles

mea·sly, *v.*
  mea·sli·er,
  mea·sli·est

mea·sur·abil·i·ty

mea·sur·able

mea·sur·ably

mea·sure, *v.*
  mea·sured,
  mea·sur·ing

mea·sure·less

mea·sure·ment

mea·sur·er

meat

meat·ball

meat·i·ness

meat·loaf

meat·pack·ing

me·atus, *n. pl.*
  me·atus·es *or*
  me·atus

meaty, *adj.*
  meat·i·er,
  meat·i·est

Mec·ca

me·chan·ic

me·chan·i·cal

me·chan·i·cal·ly

me·chan·ics

mech·a·nism

mech·a·nis·tic

mech·a·nis·ti·cal·ly

mech·a·ni·za·tion

mech·a·nize, *v.*
  mech·a·nized,
  mech·a·niz·ing
med·al
med·al·ist
me·dal·ion
med·dle, *v.*
  med·dled,
  med·dling
med·dler
med·dle·some
med·dle·some·ness
med·e·vac
me·dia
  (COMMUNICATIONS),
  pl. of medium
me·dia (VOICED
  STOP, VESSEL
  WALL), *n. pl.*
  me·di·ae
me·di·al
me·di·an
me·di·ate, *v.*
  me·di·at·ed,
  me·di·at·ing
me·di·a·tion
me·di·a·tor
med·ic
med·i·ca·ble
Med·ic·aid
med·i·cal
med·i·cal·ly
Medi·care
med·i·cate, *v.*
  med·i·cat·ed,
  med·i·cat·ing
med·i·ca·tion
me·dic·i·nal
me·dic·i·nal·ly

med·i·cine
med·i·co, *n. pl.*
  med·i·cos
me·di·eval
me·di·eval·ism
me·di·eval·ist
me·di·o·cre
me·di·oc·ri·ty, *n. pl.*
  me·di·oc·ri·ties
med·i·tate, *v.*
  med·i·tat·ed,
  med·i·tat·ing
med·i·ta·tion
med·i·ta·tive
med·i·ta·tive·ly
med·i·ta·tive·ness
Med·i·ter·ra·nean
me·di·um, *n. pl.*
  me·di·ums *or*
  me·dia
  (COMMUNICATIONS)
me·dium-sized
med·ley
me·dul·la, *n. pl.*
  me·dul·las *or*
  me·dul·lae
me·dul·la
  ob·lon·ga·ta, *n.*
  pl. me·dul·la
  ob·lon·ga·tas
  or me·dul·la
  ob·lon·ga·tae
meek·ly
meek·ness
meer·schaum
meet, *v.* met,
  meet·ing
meet·ing·house
mega·cy·cle
mega·deaths

mega·hertz
mega·lith
meg·a·lo·ma·nia
meg·a·lo·ma·ni·ac
meg·a·lo·ma·ni·a·cal
meg·a·lop·o·lis
Meg·an
mega·phone
mega·ton
mega·vi·ta·mins
mega·watt
meg·ohm
mei·o·sis
Me·kong Riv·er
mel·a·mine
mel·an·cho·lia
mel·an·cho·lic
mel·an·choly, *n. pl.*
  mel·an·chol·ies
mé·lange
Mel·a·nie
mel·a·nin
mel·a·no·ma, *n. pl.*
  mel·a·no·mas *or*
  mel·a·no·ma·ta
Mel·ba toast
Mel·bourne
me·lee (*occas.*
  mê·lée)
me·lio·rate, *v.*
  me·lio·rat·ed,
  me·lio·rat·ing
me·lio·ra·tion
me·lio·ra·tive
Me·lis·sa
mel·lif·lu·ous
mel·lif·lu·ous·ly

mel·lif·lu·ous·ness

Mel·lo·tron®

mel·low

me·lo·de·on

me·lod·ic

me·lod·i·cal·ly

me·lo·di·ous

me·lo·di·ous·ly

me·lo·di·ous·ness

melo·dra·ma

melo·dra·mat·ic

melo·dra·mat·i·cal·ly

mel·o·dy, *n. pl.*
  mel·o·dies

mel·on

melt

melt·down

mel·ton

melt·wa·ter

mem·ber

mem·ber·ship

mem·brane

mem·bra·nous

me·men·to, *n. pl.*
  me·men·tos *or*
  me·men·toes

me·men·to mo·ri,
 n. pl.
  me·men·to mo·ri

memo, *pl.* mem·os

mem·oir

mem·o·ra·bil·ia

mem·o·ra·ble

mem·o·ra·bly

mem·o·ran·dum, *n.*
 pl.
  mem·o·ran·dums

  or
  mem·o·ran·da

me·mo·ri·al

me·mo·ri·al·ize, *v.*
  me·mo·ri·al·ized,
  me·mo·ri·al·iz·ing

mem·o·ri·za·tion

mem·o·rize, *v.*
  mem·o·rized,
  mem·o·riz·ing

mem·o·ry, *n. pl.*
  mem·o·ries

Mem·phis

mem·sa·hib

men·ace, *v.*
  men·aced,
  men·ac·ing

men·ac·ing·ly

mé·nage
  (HOUSEHOLD)
  (*see also*
  manège)

me·nag·er·ie

men·ar·che

men·da·cious

men·da·cious·ly

men·da·cious·ness

men·dac·i·ty, *n. pl.*
  men·dac·i·ties

men·de·le·vi·um

men·di·cant

men·folk *or*
  men·folks

men·ha·den, *n. pl.*
  men·ha·den *or*
  men·ha·dens

me·nial

me·nial·ly

men·in·gi·tis, *n. pl.*
  men·in·git·i·des

me·nis·cus, *n. pl.*
  me·nis·ci (*occas.*
  me·nis·cus·es)

meno·paus·al

meno·pause

me·no·rah

men·ses

men·stru·al

men·stru·ate, *v.*
  men·stru·at·ed,
  men·stru·at·ing

men·stru·a·tion

men·su·ra·ble

men·su·ra·tion

men·tal

men·tal·ist

men·tal·i·ty, *n. pl.*
  men·tal·i·ties

men·tal·ly

men·thol

men·tho·lat·ed

men·tion

men·tion·able

men·tor

menu

me·phit·ic

mer·can·tile

mer·can·til·ism

mer·ce·nary, *n. pl.*
  mer·ce·nar·ies

mer·cer·ize, *v.*
  mer·cer·ized,
  mer·cer·iz·ing

mer·chan·dise, *v.*
  mer·chan·dised,
  mer·chan·dis·ing

mer·chan·dis·er

mer·chant

mer·ci·ful

mer·ci·ful·ly

mer·ci·ful·ness

mer·ci·less

mer·ci·less·ly

mer·ci·less·ness

mer·cu·ri·al

mer·cu·ri·al·ly

mer·cu·ric

Mer·cu·ro·chrome℠

mer·cu·ry

mer·cy, *n. pl.*
mer·cies

mere·ly

mer·en·gue
(DANCE) (*see also*
meringue)

mer·e·tri·cious

mer·e·tri·cious·ly

mer·e·tri·cious·ness

mer·gan·ser

merge, *v.* merged,
merg·ing

merg·er

me·rid·i·an

me·ringue
(FROSTING)
(*see also*
merengue)

me·ri·no, *n. pl.*
me·ri·nos

mer·it

mer·i·to·ri·ous

mer·i·to·ri·ous·ly

mer·i·to·ri·ous·ness

mer·maid

mer·man, *n. pl.*
mer·men

merri·ly

mer·ri·ment

mer·ry, *adj.*
merr·i·er,
merr·i·est

mer·ry-an·drew

mer·ry-go-round

mer·ry·mak·er

mer·ry·mak·ing

Mer·thi·o·late℠

me·sa

més·al·liance

mes·cal

mes·ca·line

mesh·work

mes·mer·ism

mes·mer·ize, *v.*
mes·mer·ized,
mes·mer·iz·ing

me·so·morph

me·so·mor·phic

me·son

Me·so·zo·ic

mes·quite

mes·sage, *v.*
mes·saged,
mes·sag·ing

mes·sen·ger

mes·si·ah

mes·si·an·ic

mess·i·ly

mess·i·ness

mess·mate

messy, *adj.*
mess·i·er,
mess·i·est

mes·ti·zo, *n. pl.*
mes·ti·zos

met·a·bol·ic

me·tab·o·lism

me·tab·o·lize, *v.*
me·tab·o·lized,
me·tab·o·liz·ing

met·al, *v.* met·aled,
or met·alled,
met·al·ing, *or*
met·al·ling

meta·lan·guage

meta·lin·guis·tic

meta·lin·guis·tics

me·tal·lic

met·al·lur·gi·cal

met·al·lur·gist

met·al·lur·gy

met·al·ware

met·al·work

meta·mor·phic

meta·mor·phism

meta·mor·phose, *v.*
meta·mor·phosed,
meta·mor·phos·ing

meta·mor·pho·sis

met·a·phor

met·a·phor·i·cal

met·a·phor·i·cal·ly

meta·phys·ic

meta·phys·i·cal

meta·phys·i·cal·ly

meta·phys·ics

me·tas·ta·sis, *n. pl.*
me·tas·ta·ses

meta·tar·sal

meta·tar·sus

mete

me·te·or

me·te·or·ic

me·te·or·i·cal·ly
me·te·or·ite
me·te·or·oid
me·te·o·ro·log·i·cal
me·te·o·ro·log·i·cal·ly
me·te·o·rol·o·gist
me·te·o·rol·o·gy
me·ter
meth·a·done
meth·am·phet·a·mine
meth·ane
meth·a·nol
Meth·e·drine®
meth·od
me·thod·i·cal
me·thod·i·cal·ly
Meth·od·ist
meth·od·o·log·i·cal
meth·od·o·log·i·cal·ly
meth·od·ol·o·gy
me·tic·u·lous
me·tic·u·lous·ly
me·tic·u·lous·ness
mé·tier (*occas.*
   me·tier)
me-too·ism
met·ric
met·ri·cal
met·ri·cal·ly
met·ro, *pl.* met·ros
met·ro·nome
me·trop·o·lis
met·ro·pol·i·tan
met·tle
met·tle·some
Mex·i·can

Mex·i·co
mez·za·nine
mez·zo-so·pra·no,
   n. pl. mez·zo-
   so·pra·nos
Mi·ami
mi·as·ma, *n. pl.*
   mi·as·mas *or*
   mi·as·ma·ta
mi·ca
Mi·chael
Mi·chelle
Mich·i·gan
Mich·i·ga·ni·an
Mich·i·gan·ite
Mi·cho·a·cán
mi·crobe
mi·cro·bi·ol·o·gist
mi·cro·bi·ol·o·gy
mi·cro·cir·cuit
mi·cro·cli·mate
mi·cro·com·put·er
mi·cro·copy, *n. pl.*
   mi·cro·cop·ies
mi·cro·cosm
mi·cro·ec·o·nom·ics
mi·cro·far·ad
mi·cro·fiche, *n. pl.*
   mi·cro·fich·es *or*
   mi·cro·fiche
mi·cro·film
mi·cro·form
mi·cro·groove
mi·crom·e·ter
   (INSTRUMENT)
mi·cro·me·ter
   (MICRON)
mi·cron, *n. pl.*

mi·crons (*occas.*
   mi·cra)
mi·cro·or·gan·ism
mi·cro·phone
mi·cro·print
mi·cro·probe
mi·cro·read·er
mi·cro·scope
mi·cro·scop·ic
mi·cro·scop·i·cal·ly
mi·cros·co·py
mi·cro·sec·ond
mi·cro·wave, *v.*
   mi·cro·waved,
   mi·cro·wav·ing
mic·tu·rate
mid·air
mid·day
mid·den
mid·dle
mid·dle-aged
mid·dle·brow
mid·dle·man, *n. pl.*
   mid·dle·men
mid·dle-of-the-road
mid·dle-of-the-
   road·er
mid·dle·weight
mid·dling
mid·dy (BLOUSE)
   (*see also* midi),
   n. pl. mid·dies
mid·field
mid·get
midi (SKIRT) (*see
   also* middy), *n.
   pl.* mid·is
mid·land

mid·most

mid·night

mid·point

mid·riff

mid·sec·tion

mid·ship·man, *n.*
pl.
mid·ship·men

mid·ships

mid·size

midst

mid·stream

mid·sum·mer

mid·way

mid·week

mid·wife, *n. pl.*
mid·wives

mid·wife·ry

mid·wint·er

mid·year

mien

might

might·i·ly

might·i·ness

mighty, *adj.*
might·i·er,
might·i·est

mi·gnon·ette

mi·graine

mi·grant

mi·grate, *v.*
mi·grat·ed,
mi·grat·ing

mi·gra·tion

mi·gra·to·ry

mi·ka·do, *n. pl.*
mi·ka·dos

Mi·lan

mil·dew

mild·ly

mild·ness

mile·age

mile·post

mil·er

mile·stone

mi·lieu, *n. pl.*
mi·lieus *or*
mi·lieux

mil·i·tan·cy

mil·i·tant

mil·i·tant·ly

mil·i·tant·ness

mil·i·tar·i·ly

mil·i·tar·ism

mil·i·tar·is·tic

mil·i·ta·ri·za·tion

mil·i·tar·ize, *v.*
mil·i·tar·ized,
mil·i·tar·iz·ing

mil·i·tary, *n. pl.*
mil·i·tary
(*occas.*
mil·i·tar·ies)

mil·i·tate, *v.*
mil·i·tat·ed,
mil·i·tat·ing

mi·li·tia

mi·li·tia·man, *n. pl.*
mi·li·tia·men

milk·er

milk·i·ness

milk·maid

milk·man, *n. pl.*
millk·men

milk·shake

milk·sop

milk·weed

milk·wort

milky, *adj.*
milk·i·er,
milk·i·est

mill·dam

mil·len·ni·al

mil·len·ni·um, *n.*
pl. mil·len·nia
or mil·len·ni·ums

mill·er

mil·let

mil·liard

mil·li·bar

mil·li·gram

mil·li·li·ter

mil·lime

mil·li·me·ter

mil·li·ner

mil·li·nery

mill·ing

mil·lion

mil·lion·aire

mil·lionth

mil·li·sec·ond

mill·pond

mill·race

mill·stone

mill·stream

mill·wright

mi·lo, *n. pl.* mi·los

milque·toast

Mil·wau·kee

mime, *v.* mimed,
mim·ing

mim·eo·graph

mim·er

mi·me·sis

mi·met·ic

mim·ic, *v.*
  mim·icked,
  mim·ick·ing

mim·ic·ry, *n. pl.*
  mim·ic·ries

mi·mo·sa

min·a·ret

mi·na·to·ry

mince, *v.* minced,
  minc·ing

mince·meat

minc·ing

Min·da·nao

mind·ed

mind-blow·ing

mind-bog·gling

mind-ex·pand·ing

mind·ful

mind·ful·ly

mind·ful·ness

mind·less

mind·less·ly

mind·less·ness

mind-set

mine, *v.* mined,
  min·ing

mine·lay·er

miner

min·er·al

min·er·al·iza·tion

min·er·al·ize, *v.*
  min·er·al·ized,
  min·er·al·iz·ing

min·er·al·og·i·cal

min·er·al·o·gist

min·er·al·o·gy

min·e·stro·ne

mine·sweep·er

min·gle, *v.*
  min·gled,
  min·gling

min·ia·ture

min·ia·tur·ist

min·ia·tur·iza·tion

min·ia·tur·ize, *v.*
  min·ia·tur·ized,
  min·ia·tur·iz·ing

mini·bus

mini·com·put·er

min·ié·ball

min·im

min·i·mal

min·i·mal·ism

min·i·mal·ist

min·i·mal·ly

min·i·mi·za·tion

min·i·mize, *v.*
  min·i·mized,
  min·i·miz·ing

min·i·mum, *n. pl.*
  min·i·ma *or*
  min·i·mums

min·ing

min·ion

min·is·cule

mini·se·ries, *n. pl.*
  mini·se·ries

mini·skirt

mini·state

min·is·ter

min·is·te·ri·al

min·is·trant

min·is·tra·tion

min·is·try, *n. pl.*
  min·is·tries

mini·track

min·i·ver

mink, *n. pl.* mink
  or minks

Min·ne·ap·o·lis

min·ne·sing·er

Min·ne·so·ta

Min·ne·so·tan

min·now, *n. pl.*
  min·nows
  (*occas.* min·now)

mi·nor

mi·nor·i·ty, *n. pl.*
  mi·nor·i·ties

min·strel

min·strel·sy, *n. pl.*
  min·strel·sies

min·tage

mint·er

minty, *adj.*
  mint·i·er,
  mint·i·est

min·u·end

min·u·et

mi·nus

mi·nus·cule

mi·nute, *adj.*

min·ute, *n.*

mi·nute·ly

mi·nute·man, *n. pl.*
  min·ute·men

mi·nu·tia, *n. pl.*
  mi·nu·ti·ae

minx

mir·a·cle

mi·rac·u·lous

mi·rac·u·lous·ly

mi·rac·u·lous·ness

mir·a·dor

mi·rage

mire, *v.* mired,
mir·ing

mir·ror

mirth·ful

mirth·ful·ly

mirth·ful·ness

mirth·less

mirth·less·ness

mis·ad·ven·ture

mis·align·ment

mis·al·li·ance

mis·al·lo·ca·tion

mis·an·thrope

mis·an·throp·ic

mis·an·throp·i·cal·ly

mis·ap·pli·ca·tion

mis·ap·ply, *v.*
mis·ap·plied,
mis·ap·ply·ing

mis·ap·pre·hend

mis·ap·pre·hen·sion

mis·ap·pro·pri·ate,
v.
mis·ap·pro·pri·at·ed,
mis·ap·pro·pri·at·ing

mis·ap·pro·pri·a·tion

mis·be·got·ten

mis·be·have, *v.*
mis·be·haved,
mis·be·hav·ing

mis·be·hav·ior

mis·be·lief

mis·be·liev·er

mis·brand

mis·cal·cu·late, *v.*

mis·cal·cu·lat·ed,
mis·cal·cu·lat·ing

mis·cal·cu·la·tion

mis·call

mis·car·riage

mis·car·ry, *v.*
mis·car·ried,
mis·car·ry·ing

mis·cast, *v.*
mis·cast,
mis·cast·ing

mis·ce·ge·na·tion

mis·cel·la·nea

mis·cel·la·ne·ous

mis·cel·la·ne·ous·ly

mis·cel·la·ny, *n. pl.*
mis·cel·la·nies

mis·chance

mis·chief

mis·chie·vous

mis·chie·vous·ly

mis·chie·vous·ness

mis·ci·bil·i·ty

mis·ci·ble

mis·con·ceive, *v.*
mis·con·ceived,
mis·con·ceiv·ing

mis·con·cep·tion

mis·con·duct

mis·con·struc·tion

mis·con·strue, *v.*
mis·con·strued,
mis·con·stru·ing

mis·count

mis·cre·ant

mis·cue, *v.*
mis·cued,
mis·cu·ing

mis·deal

mis·deed

mis·de·mean·or

mis·di·ag·nose, *v.*
mis·di·ag·nosed,
mis·di·ag·nos·ing

mis·di·rect

mis·di·rec·tion

mis·do·er

mis·do·ing

mise-en-scène, *n.*
pl. mise-en-
scènes

mi·ser

mis·er·a·ble

mis·er·a·bly

mi·ser·li·ness

mi·ser·ly

mis·ery, *n. pl.*
mis·er·ies

mis·es·ti·mate, *v.*
mis·es·ti·mat·ed,
mis·es·ti·mat·ing

mis·es·ti·ma·tion

mis·fea·sance

mis·file, *v.*
mis·filed,
mis·fil·ing

mis·fire, *v.*
mis·fired,
mis·fir·ing

mis·fit

mis·for·tune

mis·giv·ing

mis·gov·ern

mis·gov·ern·ment

mis·guid·ance

mis·guide, *v.*
mis·guid·ed,
mis·guid·ing

mis·guid·ed·ly

mis·guid·ed·ness

mis·han·dle, *v.*
  mis·han·dled,
  mis·han·dling

mis·hap

mish·mash

mis·in·form

mis·in·for·ma·tion

mis·in·ter·pret

mis·in·ter·pre·ta·tion

mis·judge, *v.*
  mis·judged,
  mis·judg·ing

mis·judg·ment

mis·lay, *v.* mis·laid,
  mis·lay·ing

mis·lead

mis·man·age, *v.*
  mis·man·aged,
  mis·man·ag·ing

mis·man·age·ment

mis·match

mis·mate, *v.*
  mis·mat·ed,
  mis·mat·ing

mis·name, *v.*
  mis·named,
  mis·nam·ing

mis·no·mer

mi·sog·y·nist

mis·sog·y·ny

mis·per·cep·tion

mis·place, *v.*
  mis·placed,
  mis·plac·ing

mis·play

mis·print

mis·pri·sion

mis·pro·nounce, *v.*
  mis·pro·nounced,
  mis·pro·nounc·ing

mis·pro·nun·ci·a·tion

mis·quo·ta·tion

mis·quote, *v.*
  mis·quot·ed,
  mis·quot·ing

mis·read, *v.*
  mis·read,
  mis·read·ing

mis·rep·re·sent

mis·rep·re·sen·ta·tion

mis·rule, *v.*
  mis·ruled,
  mis·rul·ing

mis·sal

mis·send, *v.*
  mis·sent,
  mis·send·ing

mis·shape, *v.*
  mis·shaped,
  mis·shap·ing

mis·shap·en

mis·shap·en·ly

mis·shap·en·ness

mis·sile

mis·sile·ry

miss·ing

mis·sion

mis·sion·ary, *n. pl.*
  mis·sion·ar·ies

mis·sion·er

Mis·sis·sip·pi

Mis·sis·sip·pi·an

mis·sive

Mis·sou·ri

Mis·sou·ri·an

mis·speak, *v.*

mis·spoke,
mis·spok·en,
mis·speak·ing

mis·spell

mis·spend

mis·state, *v.*
  mis·stat·ed,
  mis·stat·ing

mis·state·ment

mis·step

mis·tak·able

mis·take, *v.*
  mis·took,
  mis·tak·en,
  mis·tak·ing

mis·tak·en·ly

mis·ter

mist·i·ly

mis·time, *v.*
  mis·timed,
  mis·tim·ing

mist·i·ness

mis·tle·toe

mis·tral

mis·treat

mis·treat·ment

mis·tress

mis·tri·al

mis·trust

misty, *adj.*
  mist·i·er,
  mist·i·est

mis·un·der·stand

mis·us·age

mis·use, *v.*
  mis·used,
  mis·us·ing

mis·val·ue

mis·ven·ture

Mitch·ell

mite

mi·ter

mit·i·gate, *v.*
  mit·i·gat·ed,
  mit·i·gat·ing

mit·i·ga·tion

mit·i·ga·tive

mit·i·ga·tor

mi·to·sis, *n. pl.*
  mi·to·ses

mitt

mit·ten

mix·able

mix·er

mix·ol·o·gist

mix·ture

mix-up

miz·zen

miz·zen·mast

mne·mon·ic

mne·mon·ics

moat

mob, *v.* mobbed,
  mob·bing

Mo·bile

mo·bile

mo·bil·i·ty

mo·bi·li·za·tion

mo·bi·lize, *v.*
  mo·bi·lized,
  mo·bi·liz·ing

mob·oc·ra·cy

mob·ster

moc·ca·sin

mo·cha

mock·er

mock·ery, *n. pl.*
  mock·er·ies

mock-he·ro·ic

mock·ing·bird

mock-up

mod·al

mo·dal·i·ty, *n. pl.*
  mo·dal·i·ties

mod·el, *v.*
  mod·eled *or*
  mod·elled,
  mod·el·ing *or*
  mod·el·ling

mod·el·er

mo·dem

mod·er·ate, *v.*
  mod·er·at·ed,
  mod·er·at·ing

mod·er·ate·ly

mod·er·a·tion

mod·er·a·to

mod·er·a·tor

mod·ern

mod·ern·ism

mod·ern·is·tic

mo·der·ni·ty

mod·ern·iza·tion

mod·ern·ize, *v.*
  mod·ern·ized,
  mod·ern·iz·ing

mod·ern·iz·er

mod·ern·ly

mod·ern·ness

mod·est

mod·es·ty

mod·i·cum

mod·i·fi·ca·tion

mod·i·fi·er

mod·ify, *v.*
  mod·i·fied,
  mod·i·fy·ing

mod·ish

mo·diste

mod·u·lar

mod·u·late, *v.*
  mod·u·lat·ed,
  mod·u·lat·ing

mod·u·la·tion

mod·u·la·tor

mod·ule

mo·dus ope·ran·di,
  n. pl. mo·di
  ope·ran·di

mo·dus vi·ven·di, *n.
  pl.* mo·di
  vi·ven·di

mo·gul

mo·hair

Mo·ham·med (*var.
  of* Muhammad)

moi·e·ty, *n. pl.*
  moi·e·ties

moi·ré *or* moire

moist·en

moist·ly

moist·ness

mois·ture

mois·tur·ize, *v.*
  mois·tur·ized,
  mois·tur·iz·ing

mo·lar

mo·las·ses

Mol·da·vian
  So·vi·et
  So·cial·ist
  Re·pub·lic *or*
  Mol·da·via (*now*
  Moldova)

Mol·da·vian

Mol·do·va
(*formerly*
Moldavian
Soviet Socialist
Republic)

Mol·do·van

mold·board

mold·er

mold·i·ness

mold·ing

moldy, *adj.*
mold·i·er,
mold·i·est

mo·lec·u·lar

mol·e·cule

mole·hill

mole·skin

mo·lest

mo·les·ta·tion

mo·lest·er

mol·li·fi·ca·tion

mol·li·fy, *v.*
mol·li·fied,
mol·li·fy·ing

mol·lusk

mol·ly·cod·dle, *v.*
mol·ly·cod·dled,
mol·ly·cod·dling

molt

mol·ten

mol·to

mo·lyb·de·num

mo·ment

mo·men·tar·i·ly

mo·men·tary

mo·ment·ly

mo·men·tous

mo·men·tum, *n. pl.*
mo·men·ta *or*
mo·men·tums

mom·ism

Mo·na·can

Mo·na·co

mo·nad

mo·nan·drous

mo·nan·dry, *n. pl.*
mo·nan·dries

mon·arch

mo·nar·chic

mo·nar·chi·cal

mon·ar·chism

mon·ar·chist

mon·ar·chy, *n. pl.*
mon·ar·chies

mon·as·te·ri·al

mon·as·tery, *n. pl.*
mon·as·ter·ies

mo·nas·tic

mo·nas·ti·cal·ly

mo·nas·ti·cism

mon·au·ral

Mon·day

Mon·e·gasque

mon·e·tar·i·ly

mon·e·tary

mon·e·ti·za·tion

mon·e·tize, *v.*
mon·e·tized,
mon·e·tiz·ing

mon·ey, *n. pl.*
mon·eys *or*
mon·ies

mon·ey·bags

mon·eyed (*occas.*
mon·ied)

mon·ey·lend·er

mon·ey·mak·er

mon·ey·wort

mon·ger

Mon·go·lia

Mon·go·lian

mon·gol·ism

Mon·gol·oid

mon·goose, *n. pl.*
mon·goos·es
(*occas.*
mon·geese)

mon·grel

mon·grel·iza·tion

mon·grel·ize, *v.*
mon·grel·ized,
mon·grel·iz·ing

Mon·i·ca

mo·nism

mo·nist

mon·i·tor

mon·i·to·ry, *n. pl.*
mon·i·to·ries

mon·key, *n. pl.*
mon·keys

mon·key·shine

monk·ish

monks·hood

mono·chro·mat·ic

mono·chro·mat·i·cal·ly

mono·chrome

mon·o·cle

mon·oc·u·lar

mon·o·dy, *n. pl.*
mon·o·dies

mo·nog·a·mist

mo·nog·a·mous

mo·nog·a·my

mono·gram

mono·graph

mo·nog·y·ny

mono·lith

mono·logue (*occas.* mono·log)

mono·logu·ist *or* mo·no·lo·gist

mono·ma·nia

mono·ma·ni·ac

mono·ma·ni·ac·al

mono·nu·cle·o·sis

mono·pho·nic

mono·plane

mo·nop·o·list

mo·nop·o·lis·tic

mo·nop·o·lis·ti·cal·ly

mo·nop·o·li·za·tion

mo·nop·o·lize, *v.* mo·nop·o·lized, mo·nop·o·liz·ing

mo·nop·o·ly, *n. pl.* mo·nop·o·lies

mono·rail

mono·syl·lab·ic

mono·syl·lab·i·cal·ly

mono·syl·la·ble

mono·the·ism

mono·the·ist

mono·tone

mo·not·o·nous

mo·not·o·nous·ly

mo·not·o·nous·ness

mo·not·o·ny

mono·type

mon·ox·ide

mon·sie·gneur, *n.*

pl. mes·sie·gneurs

mon·sieur, *n. pl.* mes·sieurs

mon·si·gnor, *n. pl.* mon·si·gnors *or* mon·si·gno·ri

mon·soon

mon·ster

mon·strance

mon·stros·i·ty

mon·stros·i·ties

mon·strous

mon·strous·ly

mon·strous·ness

mon·tage

mon·ta·gnard

Mon·tana

Mon·tan·an

mon·tane

mon·te

Mon·te Car·lo

Mon·te·rey (CALIFORNIA)

Mon·ter·rey (MEXICO)

Mont·gom·ery

month·ly

Mont·pe·lier

Mon·tre·al

mon·u·ment

mon·u·men·tal

mon·u·men·tal·ly

mood·i·ly

mood·i·ness

moody, *adj.* mood·i·er, mood·i·est

moon·beam

moon-eyed

moon·light

moon·lit

moon·scape

moon·shine

moon·stone

moon·struck

moor·age

moor·ing

moor·land

moose, *n. pl.* moose

mop, *v.* mopped, mop·ping

mop·board

mope, *v.* moped, mop·ing

mo·ped (MOTORIZED VEHICLE)

mop·pet

mop-up, *n.*

mop up, *v.*

mo·raine

mor·al

mo·rale

mor·al·ist

mor·al·is·tic

mor·al·is·ti·cal·ly

mo·ral·i·ty, *n. pl.* mo·ral·i·ties

mor·al·iza·tion

mor·al·ize, *v.* mor·al·ized, mor·al·iz·ing

mor·al·iz·er

mor·al·ly

mo·rass

mor·a·to·ri·um, *n.*
pl.
mor·a·to·ri·ums
or mor·a·to·ria

mor·bid

mor·bid·i·ty, *n. pl.*
mor·bid·i·ties

mor·dant
(CAUSTIC)

mor·dent (MUSIC)

Mo·re·los

more·over

mo·res

mor·ga·nat·ic

mor·ga·nat·i·cal·ly

morgue

mor·i·bund

mor·i·bun·di·ty

Mor·mon

Mor·mon·ism

morn·ing (EARLY
DAY) (*see also*
mourning)

morn·ing glo·ry

Mo·roc·can

Mo·roc·co

mo·ron

mo·ron·ic

mo·ron·i·cal·ly

mo·rose

mor·pheme

mor·phe·mic

mor·phia

mor·phine

mor·pho·log·i·cal

mor·pho·log·i·cal·ly

mor·phol·o·gist

mor·phol·o·gy

mor·ris

mor·row

mor·sel

mor·ta·del·la

mor·tal

mor·tal·i·ty

mor·tal·ly

mor·tar

mor·tar·board

mort·gage, *v.*
mort·gaged,
mort·gag·ing

mort·gag·ee

mort·gag·or (*occas.*
mort·gag·er)

mor·ti·cian

mor·ti·fi·ca·tion

mor·ti·fy, *v.*
mor·ti·fied,
mor·ti·fy·ing

mor·tise, *v.*
mor·tised,
mor·tis·ing

mort·main

mor·tu·ary, *n. pl.*
mor·tu·ar·ies

mo·sa·ic

Mos·cow

mo·sey

Mos·lem (*var. of*
Muslim)

mosque

mos·qui·to, *n. pl.*
mos·qui·toes
(*occas.*
mos·qui·tos)

moss·back

moss-grown

mossy, *adj.*
moss·i·er,
moss·i·est

most·ly

mote

mo·tel

mo·tet

moth

moth·ball

moth-eat·en

moth·er

moth·er·board

moth·er·hood

moth·er·house

moth·er-in-law, *n.*
pl. moth·ers-in-
law

moth·er·land

moth·er·li·ness

moth·er·ly

moth·er-of-pearl

mo·tif

mo·tile

mo·til·i·ty

mo·tion

mo·ti·vate, *v.*
mo·ti·vat·ed,
mo·ti·vat·ing

mo·ti·va·tion

mo·tive

mo·tiv·i·ty

mot·ley

mo·to·cross

mo·tor

mo·tor·boat

mo·tor·cade

mo·tor·car

mo·tor·cy·cle, *v.*
mo·tor·cy·cled,
mo·tor·cy·cling

mo·tor·cy·clist

mo·tor·drome

mo·tor·ist

mo·tor·iza·tion

mo·tor·ize, *v.*
mo·tor·ized,
mo·tor·iz·ing

mo·tor·man, *n. pl.*
mo·tor·men

mo·tor·truck

Mo·town®

mot·tle, *v.*
mot·tled,
mot·tling

mot·to, *n. pl.*
mot·toes (*occas.*
mot·tos)

mou·lage

mound

mount·able

moun·tain

moun·tain·eer

moun·tain·ous

moun·tain·ous·ly

moun·tain·ous·ness

moun·tain·side

moun·tain·top

mounte·bank

mount·ed

mount·ing

mourn·er

mourn·ful

mourn·ful·ly

mourn·ful·ness

mourn·ing (GRIEF)

(*see also*
morning)

mouse, *n. pl.* mice

mous·er

mouse·trap

mous·sa·ka

mousse

mous·se·line

mousy, *adj.*
mous·i·er,
mous·i·est

mouth·ful

mouth·part

mouth·piece

mouth-to-mouth

mouth·wash

mouth·wa·ter·ing

mou·ton
(SHEEPSKIN)
(*see also* mutton)

mov·able *or*
move·able

mov·ably

move, *v.* moved,
mov·ing

move·ment

mov·er

mov·ie

mov·ie·go·er

mov·ing

mow, *v.* mowed,
mowed *or*
mown, mow·ing

mow·er

mox·ie

Mo·zam·bic·an

Mo·zam·bique

mu·ci·lage

mu·ci·lag·i·nous

mu·ci·lag·i·nous·ly

muck·rak·er

mu·cous, *adj.*

mu·cus, *n.*

mud·di·ly

mud·di·ness

mud·dle, *v.*
mud·dled,
mud·dling

mud·dle·head·ed

mud·dle·head·ed·ly

mud·dle·head·ed·ness

mud·dler

mud·dy, *adj.*
mud·di·er,
mud·di·est

mud·guard

mud·pack

mud·room

mud·sling·er

mu·ez·zin

muf·fin

muf·fle, *v.*
muf·fled,
muf·fling

muf·fler

muf·ti

mug, *v.* mugged,
mug·ging

mug·ger

mug·gi·ness

mug·gy, *adj.*
mug·gi·er,
mug·gi·est

mug·wump

Mu·ham·mad
(*occas.*
Mo·ham·med)

muk·luk

mu·lat·to, *n. pl.*
  mu·lat·toes *or*
  mu·lat·tos

mul·ber·ry, *n. pl.*
  mul·ber·ries

mulch

mulct

mul·ish

mul·ish·ly

mul·ish·ness

mul·lah

mul·let, *n. pl.*
  mul·let *or*
  mul·lets

mul·li·ga·taw·ny

mul·lion

mul·ti·col·ored

mul·ti·far·i·ous

mul·ti·far·i·ous·ly

mul·ti·far·i·ous·ness

mul·ti·form

mul·ti·lane

mul·ti·lat·er·al

mul·ti·lat·er·al·ly

mul·ti·lev·el

mul·ti·me·dia

mul·ti·mil·lion·aire

mul·ti·na·tion·al

mul·ti·par·tite

mul·ti·par·ty

mul·ti·ple

mul·ti·ple-choice

mul·ti·plex

mul·ti·pli·cand

mul·ti·pli·ca·tion

mul·ti·plic·i·ty

mul·ti·pli·er

mul·ti·ply, *v.*
  mul·ti·plied,
  mul·ti·ply·ing

mul·ti·pur·pose

mul·ti·tude

mul·ti·tu·di·nous

mul·ti·tu·di·nous·ly

mul·ti·tu·di·nous·ness

mul·ti·ver·si·ty, *n.
  pl.*
  mul·ti·ver·si·ties

mul·ti·vi·ta·min

mum·ble, *v.*
  mum·bled,
  mum·bling

mum·bler

mum·ble·ty-peg *or*
  mum·ble-the-
  peg

mum·bo jum·bo

mum·mer

mum·mery, *n. pl.*
  mum·mer·ies

mum·mi·fi·ca·tion

mum·mi·fy, *v.*
  mum·mi·fied,
  mum·mi·fy·ing

mum·my, *n. pl.*
  mum·mies

munch·ies

munch·kin

mun·dane

mun·dane·ly

mun·dane·ness

mu·nic·i·pal

mu·nic·i·pal·i·ty, *n.
  pl.*
  mu·nic·i·pal·i·ties

mu·nic·i·pal·ly

mu·nif·i·cence

mu·nif·i·cent

mu·nif·i·cent·ly

mu·ral

mu·ral·ist

mur·der

mur·der·er

mur·der·ess

mur·der·ous

mur·der·ous·ly

mur·der·ous·ness

murk·i·ly

murk·i·ness

murky, *adj.*
  murk·i·er,
  murk·i·est

mur·mur

mur·mur·er

mur·rain

mus·ca·dine

mus·cat

mus·ca·tel

mus·cle, *v.*
  mus·cled,
  mus·cling

mus·cle·bound

mus·cu·lar

mus·cu·lar·i·ty

mus·cu·la·ture

muse, *v.* mused,
  mus·ing

mu·sette

mu·se·um

mush·i·ly

mush·i·ness

mush·room

mushy, *adj.*
mush·i·er,
mush·i·est

mu·sic

mu·si·cal (OF
MUSIC)

mu·si·cale
(MUSICAL
ENTERTAINMENT)

mu·si·cal·ly

mu·si·cian

mu·si·cian·ship

mu·si·col·o·gist

mu·si·col·o·gy

mus·keg

mus·kel·lunge, *n.*
pl.
mus·kel·lunge

mus·ket

mus·ke·teer

mus·ket·ry

musk·i·ness

musk·mel·on

musk·rat, *n. pl.*
musk·rat *or*
musk·rats

musky, *adj.*
musk·i·er,
musk·i·est

Mus·lim (*occas.*
Mos·lem)

mus·lin

mus·sel

muss·i·ly

muss·i·ness

mussy, *adj.*
muss·i·er,
muss·i·est

mus·tache

mus·ta·chio, *n. pl.*
mus·ta·chios

mus·ta·chioed

mus·tang

mus·tard

mus·ter

must·i·ly

must·i·ness

musty, *adj.*
must·i·er,
must·i·est

mu·ta·bil·i·ty

mu·ta·ble

mu·ta·bly

mu·tant

mu·tate, *v.*
mu·tat·ed,
mu·tat·ing

mu·ta·tion

mu·ta·tis mu·tan·dis

mute, *v.* mut·ed,
mut·ing

mute·ly

mu·ti·late, *v.*
mu·ti·lat·ed,
mu·ti·lat·ing

mu·ti·la·tion

mu·ti·la·tor

mu·ti·neer

mu·ti·nous

mi·ti·nous·ly

mu·ti·nous·ness

mu·ti·ny, *n. pl.*
mu·ti·nies

mu·ti·ny, *v.*
mu·ti·nied,
mu·ti·ny·ing

mut·ter

mut·ton (MEAT)

(*see also*
mouton)

mut·ton·chops

mu·tu·al

mu·tu·al·i·ty

mu·tu·al·ly

muu·muu

muz·zle, *v.*
muz·zled,
muz·zling

muz·zle·load·er

My·an·mar

my·as·the·nia
gra·vis

my·col·o·gist

my·col·o·gy

my·co·sis, *n. pl.*
my·co·ses

my·elin

my·eli·tis

my·ia·sis

My·lar℠

my·nah *or* my·na

myo·gen·ic

my·o·pia

my·o·pic

my·o·pi·cal·ly

myr·i·ad

myr·mi·don

myrrh

myr·tle

my·self

mys·te·ri·ous

mys·te·ri·ous·ly

mys·te·ri·ous·ness

mys·tery, *n. pl.*
mys·ter·ies

mys·tic

mys·ti·cal

mys·ti·cal·ly

mys·ti·cism

mys·ti·fi·ca·tion

mys·ti·fy, *v.*

mys·ti·fied,
  mys·ti·fy·ing

mys·tique

myth

myth·i·cal

myth·i·cal·ly

myth·o·log·i·cal

myth·o·log·i·cal·ly

my·thol·o·gist

my·thol·o·gy, *n. pl.*
  my·thol·o·gies

N

nab, *v.* nabbed,
    nab·bing
na·bob
na·celle
na·cho, *n. pl.*
    na·chos
na·cre
na·dir
nag, *v.* nagged,
    nag·ging
Na·go·ya
na·iad, *n. pl.*
    na·iads *or*
    na·ia·des
nain·sook
nai·ra
na·ive *or* na·ïve,
    adj. na·iv·er,
    na·iv·est
na·ive·ly
na·ive·té (*occas.*
    na·ive·té *or*
    na·ive·te)
na·ive·ty (*occas.*
    na·ïve·ty, *chiefly*
    Brit.)
na·ked
na·ked·ly

na·ked·ness
nam·by-pam·by
name, *v.* named,
    nam·ing
name·able (*occas.*
    nam·able)
name-drop·per
name-drop·ping
name·less
name·less·ly
name·less·ness
name·ly
name·plate
name·sake
Na·mi·bia
nan·keen
nan·ny (*occas.*
    nan·nie), *n. pl.*
    nan·nies
na·no·sec·ond
nap, *v.* napped,
    nap·ping
na·palm
na·pery
naph·tha
naph·tha·lene
nap·kin

Na·ples
Na·po·leon (MAN'S
    NAME)
na·po·leon
    (PASTRY, COIN)
nap·per
nap·py, *n. pl.*
    nap·pies (*chiefly*
    Brit.)
nar·cis·sism
nar·cis·sist
nar·cis·sis·tic
nar·cis·sus, *n. pl.*
    nar·cis·si *or*
    nar·cis·sus·es *or*
    nar·cis·sus
nar·co·lep·sy
nar·co·lep·tic
nar·co·sis, *n. pl.*
    nar·co·ses
nar·cot·ic
nar·co·tize, *v.*
    nar·co·tized,
    nar·co·tiz·ing
na·res
nar·rate, *v.*
    nar·rat·ed,
    nar·rat·ing
nar·ra·tion

nar·ra·tive

nar·ra·tor

nar·row

nar·row·ly

nar·row-mind·ed

nar·row·ness

nar·whal (*occas.* nar·whale)

na·sal

na·sal·i·ty

na·sal·iza·tion

na·sal·ize, *v.* na·sal·ized, na·sal·iz·ing

na·sal·ly

na·scene

na·scent

Nash·ville

na·so·phar·ynx

nas·ti·ly

nas·ti·ness

nas·tur·tium

nas·ty, *adj.* nas·ti·er, nas·ti·est

na·tal

Nat·a·lie

na·tal·i·ty

na·tant

Na·ta·sha

na·ta·to·ri·al

na·ta·to·ri·um

Na·than

na·tion

na·tion·al

na·tion·al·ism

na·tion·al·ist

na·tion·al·is·tic

na·tion·al·is·ti·cal·ly

na·tion·al·i·ty, *n. pl.* na·tion·al·i·ties

na·tion·al·iza·tion

na·tion·al·ize, *v.* na·tion·al·ized, na·tion·al·iz·ing

na·tion·al·ly

na·tion·hood

na·tion-state

na·tion·wide

na·tive

na·tiv·ism

na·tiv·ist

na·tiv·i·ty, *n. pl.* na·tiv·i·ties

nat·ti·ly

nat·ti·ness

nat·ty, *adj.* nat·ti·er, nat·ti·est

nat·u·ral

nat·u·ral·ism

nat·u·ral·ist

nat·u·ral·is·tic

nat·u·ral·is·ti·cal·ly

nat·u·ral·iza·tion

nat·u·ral·ize, *v.* nat·u·ral·ized, nat·u·ral·iz·ing

nat·u·ral·ly

na·ture

Naug·a·hyde®

naught (NOTHING) (*occas.* nought)

naugh·ti·ly

naugh·ti·ness

naugh·ty, *adj.* naugh·ti·er, naugh·ti·est

Na·u·ru

Na·u·ru·an

nau·sea

nau·se·ate, *v.* nau·se·at·ed, nau·se·at·ing

nau·seous

nau·ti·cal

nau·ti·cal·ly

nau·ti·lus, *n. pl.* nau·ti·lus·es *or* nau·ti·li

na·val (OF A NAVY) (*see also* navel)

nave (PART OF A CHURCH) (*see also* knave)

na·vel (BELLY BUTTON) (*see also* naval)

nav·i·ga·bil·i·ty

nav·i·ga·ble

nav·i·gate, *v.* nav·i·gat·ed, nav·i·gat·ing

nav·i·ga·tion

nav·i·ga·tion·al

nav·i·ga·tor

na·vy, *n. pl.* na·vies

nay

Naz·a·reth

Na·zi

Na·zi·fi·ca·tion

Na·zism *or* Na·zi·ism

Ne·an·der·thal

Ne·a·pol·i·tan

near·by

near·ly

near·ness

near·sight·ed

near·sight·ed·ness

neat·ly

neat·ness

Ne·bras·ka

Ne·bras·kan

neb·u·la, *n. pl.*
  neb·u·las *or*
  neb·u·lae

neb·u·lar

neb·u·lous

neb·u·lous·ly

neb·u·lous·ness

nec·es·sar·i·ly

nec·es·sary

ne·ces·si·tate, *v.*
  ne·ces·si·tat·ed,
  ne·ces·si·tat·ing

ne·ces·si·tous

ne·ces·si·ty, *n. pl.*
  ne·ces·si·ties

neck·er·chief, *n. pl.*
  neck·er·chiefs
  (*occas.*
  neck·er·chieves)

neck·lace

neck·line

neck·tie

ne·crol·o·gist

ne·crol·o·gy, *n. pl.*
  ne·crol·o·gies

nec·ro·man·cer

nec·ro·man·cy

nec·rop·o·lis, *n. pl.*

ne·crop·o·lis·es
  or ne·crop·o·les
  or ne·crop·o·leis

nec·rop·sy, *n. pl.*
  nec·rop·sies

ne·cro·sis, *n. pl.*
  ne·cro·ses

nec·tar

nec·tar·ine

née *or* nee

need·ful

need·ful·ly

need·ful·ness

need·i·ness

nee·dle, *v.*
  nee·dled,
  nee·dling

nee·dle·like

nee·dle·point

nee·dler

need·less

nee·dle·work

needy, *adj.*
  need·i·er,
  need·i·est

ne'er-do-well

ne·far·i·ous

ne·far·i·ous·ly

ne·gate, *v.*
  ne·gat·ed,
  ne·gat·ing

ne·ga·tion

neg·a·tive

neg·a·tive·ly

neg·a·tive·ness

neg·a·tiv·ism

neg·a·tiv·ist

neg·a·tiv·is·tic

neg·a·tiv·i·ty

ne·glect

ne·glect·ful

neg·li·gee (*occas.*
  neg·li·gé)

neg·li·gence

neg·li·gent

neg·li·gi·bil·i·ty

neg·li·gi·ble

neg·li·gib·ly

ne·go·tia·bil·i·ty

ne·go·tia·ble

ne·go·ti·ate, *v.*
  ne·go·ti·at·ed,
  ne·go·ti·at·ing

ne·go·ti·a·tion

ne·go·ti·a·tor

ne·gri·tude

Ne·gro (RACE), *n.
  pl.* Ne·groes
  (*see also* Negros)

Ne·groid

Ne·gros
  (PHILIPPINE
  ISLAND) (*see
  also* Negro)

ne·gus

neigh

neigh·bor

neigh·bor·hood

neigh·bor·ing

neigh·bor·li·ness

neigh·bor·ly

nei·ther (NOT
  EITHER) (*see
  also* nether)

nem·a·tode

Nem·bu·tal®

nem·e·sis, *n. pl.*
  nem·e·ses
ne·moph·i·la
neo·clas·sic
neo·clas·si·cal
neo·clas·si·cism
neo·co·lo·nial
neo·co·lo·nial·ism
neo·con·ser·va·tism
neo·con·ser·va·tive
neo·dym·i·um
neo-Freud·ian
neo·lith·ic
ne·ol·o·gism
neo·my·cin
ne·on
neo·na·tal
neo·nate
neo·phyte
neo·plasm
neo·prene
Ne·pal
Nep·a·lese, *n. pl.*
  Nep·a·lese
Ne·pali, *n. pl.*
  Ne·pali (*occas.*
  Ne·pal·is)
ne·pen·the
neph·ew
ne·phri·tis, *n. pl.*
  ne·phrit·i·des
ne plus ul·tra
nep·o·tism
Nep·tune
nep·tu·ni·um
nerve·less
nerve·less·ly

nerve·less·ness
nerve·rack·ing *or*
  nerve·wrack·ing
nerv·ous
nerv·ous·ly
nerv·ous·ness
nervy, *adj.*
  nerv·i·er,
  nerv·i·est
nes·tle, *v.* nes·tled,
  nes·tling
nest·ling (YOUNG
  BIRD)
net, *v.* net·ted,
  net·ting
¬eth·er (LOWER)
  (*see also*
  neither)
Neth·er·land·er
Neth·er·lands
Neth·er·lands
  An·til·le·an
Neth·er·lands
  An·til·les
neth·er·most
neth·er·world
net·ting
net·tle, *v.* net·tled,
  net·tling
net·tle·some
net·work
net·work·ing
neu·ral
neu·ral·gia
neu·ral·gic
neur·as·the·nia
neur·as·then·ic
neu·rit·ic

neu·ri·tis, *n. pl.*
  neu·rit·i·des
neu·ro·log·i·cal
neu·rol·o·gist
neu·rol·o·gy
neu·ro·mus·cu·lar
neu·ron
neu·ro·sis, *n. pl.*
  neu·ro·ses
neu·rot·ic
neu·rot·i·cal·ly
neu·ro·trans·mit·ter
neu·ter
neu·tral
neu·tral·ism
neu·tral·i·ty
neu·tral·iza·tion
neu·tral·ize, *v.*
  neu·tral·ized,
  neu·tral·iz·ing
neu·tral·iz·er
neu·tri·no, *n. pl.*
  neu·tri·nos
neu·tron
Ne·va·da
Ne·va·dan
nev·er
nev·er·mind
nev·er·more
nev·er-nev·er land
nev·er·the·less
ne·vus, *n. pl.* ne·vi
New·ark
new·born
New Bruns·wick
New Cal·e·do·nia
New Cal·e·do·ni·an

new·com·er
new·el
new·fan·gled
new-fash·ioned
new·found
New·found·land
New·found·land·er
New Guin·ea
New Guin·e·an
New Hamp·shire
New Hamp·shir·ite
New Ha·ven
New Heb·ri·de·an
New Heb·ri·des
new·ish
New Jer·sey
New Jer·sey·an
New Jer·sey·ite
new·ly
new·ly·wed
New Mex·i·can
New Mex·i·co
new·ness
New Or·leans
news·boy
news·break
news·cast
news·cast·er
news·let·ter
news·man, *n. pl.*
  news·men
news·mon·ger
news·pap·er
news·pap·er·man,
  n. pl.
  news·pap·er·men
news·pap·er·wom·an,

n. pl.
  news·pap·er·wom·en
new·speak
news·peo·ple
news·per·son
news·print
news·reel
news·stand
news·wom·an, *n.*
  pl.
  news·wom·en
news·wor·thy
New York
New York City
New York·er
New Zea·land
New Zea·land·er
next-door, *adj.*
next door, *adv.*
nex·us, *n. pl.*
  nex·us·es *or*
  nex·us
Nez Per·cé
ngwee, *n. pl.*
  ngwee
ni·a·cin
Ni·ag·a·ra Falls
nib·ble, *v.* nib·bled,
  nib·bling
Nic·a·ra·gua
Nic·a·ra·gu·an
Nice (CITY)
nice, *adj.* nic·er,
  nic·est
nice·ly
nice·ness
nice·ty, *n. pl.*
  nice·ties

niche
Nich·o·las
nick
nick·el (*occas.*
  nick·le)
nick·el·ode·on
nick·name
Ni·cole
nic·o·tine
nic·o·tin·ic
niece
nif·ty, *adj.* nif·ti·er,
  nif·ti·est
Ni·ger
Ni·ge·ria
Ni·ge·ri·an
nig·gard·li·ness
nig·gard·ly
nig·gling
night·cap
night·clothes
night·club
night·dress
night·fall
night·gown
night·hawk
night·ie *or* nighty,
  n. pl. night·ies
night·in·gale
night·light
night·long
night·ly
night·mare
night·mar·ish
night rid·er
night·shade
night·shirt

night·stick

night·time

night·walk·er

ni·hil·ism

ni·hil·ist

ni·hil·is·tic

Nile Riv·er

nim·ble, *adj.*
nim·bler,
nim·blest

nim·bly

nim·bo·stra·tus

nim·bus, *n. pl.*
nim·bi *or*
nim·bus·es

nim·rod

nin·com·poop

nine·pins

nine·teen

nine·teenth

nine·ti·eth

nine·ty, *n. pl.*
nine·ties

nin·ja, *n. pl.* nin·ja
or nin·jas

nin·ny, *n. pl.*
nin·nies

ni·non

ninth

ni·o·bi·um

nip, *v.* nipped,
nip·ping

nip·per

nip·ple

nip·py, *adj.*
nip·pi·er,
nip·pi·est

nip-up

nir·va·na

ni·sei, *n. pl.* ni·sei
(*occas.* ni·seis)

ni·ter

nit·pick

nit·pick·ing

ni·trate, *v.*
ni·trat·ed,
ni·trat·ing

ni·tra·tion

ni·tric

ni·tro·gen

ni·trog·e·nous

ni·tro·glyc·er·in *or*
ni·tro·glyc·er·ine

ni·tro·sa·mine
(*occas.*
ni·tro·so·mine)

ni·trous

nit·ty-grit·ty

nit·wit

no, *n. pl.* noes *or*
nos

no-ac·count

no·bel·i·um

no·bil·i·ty, *n. pl.*
no·bil·i·ties

no·ble, *adj.*
no·bler, no·blest

no·ble·man, *n. pl.*
no·ble·men

no·blesse oblige

no·ble·wom·an, *n.
pl.*
no·ble·wom·en

no·bly

no·body, *n. pl.*
no·bod·ies

noc·tur·nal

noc·tur·nal·ly

noc·turne

noc·u·ous

nod, *v.* nod·ded,
nod·ding

nod·al

node

nod·u·lar

nod·ule

no·el

no-fault, *adj.*

no-frills, *adj.*

nog·gin

no-go, *adj.*

no-good, *adj.*

noise·less

noise·less·ly

noise·mak·er

nois·i·ly

nois·i·ness

noi·some

noi·some·ly

noi·some·ness

noisy, *adj.*
nois·i·er,
nois·i·est

no-knock, *adj.*

no·li me tan·ge·re

nol·le pro·se·qui

no-load, *adj.*

no·lo con·ten·de·re

no·mad

no·mad·ic

no-man's-land

nom de guerre, *n.
pl.* noms de
guerre

nom de plume, *n.*
  pl. noms de
  plume
no·men·cla·ture
No·mex®
nom·i·nal
nom·i·nal·ly
nom·i·nate, *v.*
  nom·i·nat·ed,
  nom·i·nat·ing
nom·i·na·tion
nom·i·na·tive
nom·i·na·tor
nom·i·nee
no·na·ge·nar·i·an
non·aligned
non·align·ment
non-Arab
non·book
non·can·di·date
nonce
non·cha·lance
non·cha·lant
non-Chris·tian
non·com
non·com·ba·tant
non·com·mis·sioned
  of·fi·cer
non·com·mit·tal
non·com·pli·ance
non com·pos
  men·tis
non·con·duc·tor
non·con·form·ist
non·con·for·mi·ty
non·co·op·er·a·tion
non·de·script

non·en·ti·ty, *pl.*
  non·en·ti·ties
non·es·sen·tial
none·such
none·the·less
non·fic·tion
non-In·di·an
non·in·ter·ven·tion
non-Jew·ish
non·met·al
non·me·tal·lic
no-no, *pl.* no-no's
  or no-nos
no-non·sense, *adj.*
non·pa·reil
non·par·ti·san
non·plus, *v.*
  non·plussed
  (*occas.*
  non·plused),
  non·plus·sing
  (*occas.*
  non·plus·ing)
non·prof·it
non·res·i·dent
non·re·sis·tance
non·re·stric·tive
non-Rus·sian
non·sched·uled
non·sense
non·sen·si·cal
non·sen·si·cal·ly
non se·qui·tur
non·skid
non·stand·ard
non·stop
non·sup·port
non trop·po

non·union
non·vi·o·lence
non·vi·o·lent
noo·dle, *v.*
  noo·dled,
  noo·dling
noon·day
noon·time
no-par *or* no-par-
  val·ue
Nor·dic
Nor·folk
nor·mal
nor·mal·cy
nor·mal·i·ty
nor·mal·iza·tion
nor·mal·ize, *v.*
  nor·mal·ized,
  nor·mal·iz·ing
nor·mal·ly
Nor·man
nor·ma·tive
north·bound
North Car·o·li·na
North Car·o·li·ni·an
North Da·ko·ta
North Da·ko·tan
north·east
north·east·er·ly
north·east·ern
north·er·ly, *n. pl.*
  north·er·lies
north·ern
North·ern·er
north·ern·most
North Ko·rea
North Ko·re·an

north-north-east

north-north-west

north-ward

north-ward-ly

north-west

north-west-er-ly

north-west-ern

Nor-way

Nor-we-gian

nose-band

nose-bleed

nose-gay

nose-piece

no-show

nos-i-ly

nos-i-ness

nos-tal-gia

nos-tal-gic

nos-tal-gi-cal-ly

nos-tril

nos-trum

nosy *or* nos-ey, *adj.*
nos-i-er,
nos-i-est

no-ta be-ne

no-ta-bil-i-ty, *pl.*
no-ta-bil-i-ties

no-ta-ble

no-ta-bly

no-tar-i-al

no-ta-ri-za-tion

no-ta-rize, *v.*
no-ta-rized,
no-ta-riz-ing

no-ta-ry, *n. pl.*
no-ta-ries

no-ta-ry pub-lic, *n.
pl.* no-ta-ries

pub-lic *or*
no-ta-ry pub-lics

no-ta-tion

no-ta-tion-al

notch

notch-back

note, *v.* not-ed,
not-ing

note-book

note-case

not-ed

note-wor-thi-ly

note-wor-thi-ness

note-wor-thy

noth-ing

noth-ing-ness

no-tice, *v.* no-ticed,
no-tic-ing

no-tice-able

no-tice-ably

no-ti-fi-ca-tion

no-ti-fi-er

no-ti-fy, *v.*
no-ti-fied,
no-ti-fy-ing

no-tion

no-tion-al

no-to-chord

no-to-ri-e-ty, *n. pl.*
no-to-ri-e-ties

no-to-ri-ous

no-to-ri-ous-ly

no-to-ri-ous-ness

no-trump

not-with-stand-ing

nou-gat

nought (*var. of*
naught)

nour-ish

nour-ish-ing

nour-ish-ment

nou-veau riche, *n.
pl.* nou-veaux
riches

nou-velle cui-sine

no-va, *n. pl.* no-vas
or no-vae

No-va Sco-tia

nov-el

nov-el-ette

nov-el-ist

nov-el-iza-tion

nov-el-ize *v.*
nov-el-ized,
nov-el-iz-ing

no-vel-la, *n. pl.*
no-vel-las *or*
no-vel-le

nov-el-ty, *n. pl.*
nov-el-ties

No-vem-ber

no-ve-na

nov-ice

no-vi-tiate

No-vo-cain®

no-vo-caine
(CHEMICAL)

now-a-days

no-way *or* no-ways

no-where

no-wise

nox-ious

nox-ious-ly

nox-ious-ness

noz-zle

nth

nu·ance
nub·ble
nub·bly
nu·bile
nu·cle·ar
nu·cle·ate, *v.*
   nu·cle·at·ed,
   nu·cle·at·ing
nu·cle·ic acid
nu·cle·on
nu·cle·on·ics
nu·cle·us, *n. pl.*
   ne·clei *or*
   nu·cle·us·es
nu·clide
nude
nudge, *v.* nudged,
   nudg·ing
nud·ism
nud·ist
nu·di·ty, *pl.*
   nu·di·ties
Nue·vo Le·ón
nu·ga·to·ry
nug·get
nui·sance
nul·li·fi·ca·tion
nul·li·fi·er
nul·li·fy, *v.*
   nul·li·fied,
   nul·li·fy·ing
nul·li·ty, *n. pl.*
   nul·li·ties

numb
num·ber
num·ber·less
num·bly
numb·ness
numb·skull (*var. of*
   num·skull)
nu·mer·able
nu·mer·al
nu·mer·ate, *v.*
   nu·mer·at·ed,
   nu·mer·at·ing
nu·mer·a·tion
nu·mer·a·tor
nu·mer·ic
nu·mer·i·cal
nu·mer·i·cal·ly
nu·mer·ol·o·gy
nu·mer·ous
nu·mer·ous·ly
nu·mer·ous·ness
nu·mis·mat·ic
nu·mis·mat·ics
nu·mis·ma·tist
num·skull (*occas.*
   numb·skull)
nun·ci·a·ture
nun·cio, *n. pl.*
   nun·ci·os
nun·nery
nup·tial

nurse, *v.* nursed.
   nurs·ing
nurse·maid
nurs·ery, *n. pl.*
   nurs·er·ies
nurs·ery·man, *n.*
   pl. nurs·ery·men
nur·ture, *v.*
   nur·tured,
   nur·tur·ing
nut·crack·er
nut·hatch
nut·meg
nut·pick
nu·tria
nu·tri·ent
nu·tri·ment
nu·tri·tion
nu·tri·tious
nu·tri·tious·ly
nu·tri·tious·ness
nu·tri·tive
nut·shell
nut·ty, *adj.*
   nut·ti·er,
   nut·ti·est
nuz·zle, *v.*
   nuz·zled,
   nuz·zling
ny·lon
nym·pho·ma·nia
nym·pho·ma·ni·ac

O

oaf·ish
oaf·ish·ly
oaf·ish·ness
oak, *n. pl.* oaks *or* oak
oak·en
Oak·land
oa·kum
oar
oar·lock
oars·man, *n. pl.* oars·men
oars·man·ship
oa·sis, *n. pl.* oa·ses
oat·cake
oat·en
oath, *n. pl.* oaths
oat·meal
Oa·xa·ca
ob·bli·ga·to, *n. pl.* ob·bli·ga·tos (*occas.* ob·bli·ga·ti)
ob·du·ra·cy
ob·du·rate
ob·du·rate·ly
ob·du·rate·ness

obe·di·ence
obe·di·ent
obe·di·ent·ly
obei·sance
obei·sant
obe·lisk
obese
obe·si·ty
obey
ob·fus·cate, *v.* ob·fus·cat·ed, ob·fus·cat·ing
ob·fus·ca·tion
ob·fus·ca·to·ry
obi
obit
obi·ter dic·tum, *n. pl.* obi·ter dic·ta
obit·u·ary, *n. pl.* obit·u·ar·ies
ob·ject
ob·jec·ti·fy, *v.* ob·jec·ti·fied, ob·jec·ti·fy·ing
ob·jec·tion
ob·jec·tion·able
ob·jec·tion·ably

ob·jec·tive
ob·jec·tive·ly
ob·jec·tive·ness
ob·jec·tiv·i·ty
ob·jec·tor
ob·jet d'art, *n. pl.* ob·jets d'art
ob·jur·gate, *v.* ob·jur·gat·ed, ob·jur·gat·ing
ob·jur·ga·tion
ob·last
ob·late
ob·la·tion
ob·li·gate, *v.* ob·li·gat·ed, ob·li·gat·ing
ob·li·ga·tion
oblig·a·to·ry
oblige, *v.* obliged, oblig·ing
oblig·ing
oblig·ing·ly
oblig·ing·ness
oblique
oblique·ly
oblique·ness

obliq·ui·ty, *n. pl.*
  obliq·ui·ties

oblit·er·ate, *v.*
  oblit·er·at·ed,
  oblit·er·at·ing

oblit·er·a·tion

obliv·i·on

obliv·i·ous

obliv·i·ous·ly

obliv·i·ous·ness

ob·long

ob·lo·quy, *n. pl.*
  ob·lo·quies

ob·nox·ious

ob·nox·ious·ly

ob·nox·ious·ness

oboe

obo·ist

ob·scene

ob·scene·ly

ob·scen·i·ty, *n. pl.*
  ob·scen·i·ties

ob·scu·ran·tism

ob·scu·ran·tist

ob·scure, *v.*
  ob·scured,
  ob·scur·ing

ob·scure·ly

ob·scure·ness

ob·scu·ri·ty, *n. pl.*
  ob·scu·ri·ties

ob·se·quies, *pl. of*
  ob·se·quy

ob·se·qui·ous

ob·se·qui·ous·ly

ob·se·qui·ous·ness

ob·se·quy, *n. pl.*
  ob·se·quies

ob·serv·able

ob·serv·ably

ob·serv·ance

ob·ser·vant

ob·ser·va·tion

ob·serva·to·ry, *n.*
  pl.
  ob·ser·va·to·ries

ob·serve, *v.*
  ob·served,
  ob·serv·ing

ob·serv·er

ob·sess

ob·ses·sion

ob·ses·sive

ob·ses·sive·ly

ob·ses·sive·ness

ob·sid·i·an

ob·so·lesce, *v.*
  ob·so·lesced,
  ob·so·lesc·ing

ob·so·les·cence

ob·so·les·cent

ob·so·lete, *v.*
  ob·so·let·ed,
  ob·so·let·ing

ob·sta·cle

ob·stet·ric

ob·stet·ri·cal

ob·ste·tri·cian

ob·stet·rics

ob·sti·na·cy, *n. pl.*
  ob·sti·na·cies

ob·sti·nate

ob·sti·nate·ly

ob·sti·nate·ness

ob·strep·er·ous

ob·strep·er·ous·ly

ob·strep·er·ous·ness

ob·struct

ob·struc·tion

ob·struc·tion·ism

ob·struc·tion·ist

ob·struc·tive

ob·struc·tor

ob·tain

ob·tain·able

ob·trude, *v.*
  ob·trud·ed,
  ob·trud·ing

ob·tru·sion

ob·tru·sive

ob·tru·sive·ly

ob·tru·sive·ness

ob·tuse, *adj.*
  ob·tus·er,
  ob·tus·est

ob·tuse·ly

ob·tuse·ness

ob·verse

ob·verse·ly

ob·vi·ate, *v.*
  ob·vi·at·ed,
  ob·vi·at·ing

ob·vi·a·tion

ob·vi·ous

ob·vi·ous·ly

ob·vi·ous·ness

oc·a·ri·na

oc·ca·sion

oc·ca·sion·al

oc·ca·sion·al·ly

Oc·ci·dent

oc·ci·den·tal

oc·clude, *v.*

oc·clud·ed,
oc·clud·ing
oc·clu·sion
oc·clu·sive
oc·cult
oc·cul·ta·tion
oc·cult·ism
oc·cu·pan·cy, *n. pl.*
oc·cu·pan·cies
oc·cu·pant
oc·cu·pa·tion
oc·cu·pa·tion·al
oc·cu·pa·tion·al·ly
oc·cu·pi·er
oc·cu·py, *v.*
oc·cu·pied,
oc·cu·py·ing
oc·cur, *v.*
oc·curred,
oc·cur·ring
oc·cur·rence
ocean
ocean·ar·i·um
ocean·go·ing
oce·an·ic
ocean·og·ra·pher
ocean·og·ra·phic
ocean·og·ra·phy
ocean·ol·o·gist
ocean·ol·o·gy
oce·lot
ocher *or* ochre
o'clock
oco·ti·llo, *n. pl.*
oco·ti·llos
oc·ta·gon
oc·tag·o·nal
oc·tag·o·nal·ly

oc·tane
oc·tave
oc·ta·vo, *n. pl.*
oc·ta·vos
oc·tet
Oc·to·ber
oc·to·ge·nar·i·an
oc·to·pod
oc·to·pus, *n. pl.*
oc·to·pus·es *or*
oc·to·pi
oc·to·roon
oc·u·lar
oc·u·list
oda·lisque
odd·ball
odd·i·ty, *n. pl.*
odd·i·ties
odd·ly
odd·ment
odds-on
odi·ous
odi·ous·ly
odi·ous·ness
odi·um
odom·e·ter
odor
odor·ant
odor·if·er·ous
odor·if·er·ous·ly
odor·less
odor·ous
odor·ous·ly
odor·ous·ness
od·ys·sey
oe·di·pal
Oe·di·pus

of·fal
off·beat
off-cen·ter
off-col·or
of·fend
of·fend·er
of·fense (*occas.*
of·fence, *Brit.*)
of·fen·sive
of·fen·sive·ly
of·fen·sive·ness
of·fer
of·fer·ing
of·fer·to·ry, *n. pl.*
of·fer·to·ries
off·hand
off·hand·ed
off·hand·ed·ly
off·hand·ed·ness
of·fice
of·fice·hold·er
of·fi·cer
of·fi·cial
of·fi·cial·dom
of·fi·cial·ese
of·fi·cial·ly
of·fi·ci·ant
of·fi·ci·ary
of·fi·ci·ate, *v.*
of·fi·ci·at·ed,
of·fi·ci·at·ing
of·fi·ci·a·tion
of·fi·cious
of·fi·cious·ly
of·fi·cious·ness
off·ing
off·ish

off-lim·its
off-line
off-load
off-peak
off-price
off·print
off-put·ting
off·ramp
off-road
off-sea·son
off·set, v. off·set, off·set·ting
off·shoot
off·shore
off·side
off·spring, n. pl. off·spring (occas. off·springs)
off·stage
off-the-cuff
off-the-rec·ord
off-the-shelf
off-the-wall
off·track
off-white
of·ten
of·ten·times or oft·times
ogle, v. ogled, ogling
ogre
ogre·ish
Ohio
Ohi·o·an
ohm
ohm·me·ter

oil·can
oil·cloth
oil·er
oil·i·ly
oil·i·ness
oil·seed
oil·skin
oil·stone
oily, adj. oil·i·er, oil·i·est
oint·ment
OK or okay, v. OK'd or okayed, OK'·ing or okay·ing
okey·doke or okey·do·key
Okla·ho·ma
Okla·ho·ma City
Okla·ho·man
okra
old, adj. old·er or eld·er, old·est or eld·est
olden
old-fash·ioned
old·ie, n. pl. ol·dies
old·ish
old-line
old·ster
old-tim·er
Old World, n.
old-world, adj.
ole·ag·i·nous
ole·ag·i·nous·ly
ole·ag·i·nous·ness
ole·an·der

ole·fin
oleo (OLEOMARGARINE), n. pl. ole·os (see also olio)
oleo·mar·ga·rine
ol·fac·tion
ol·fac·to·ry
oli·garch
oli·gar·chy, n. pl. oli·gar·chies
oli·gop·o·ly, n. pl. oli·gop·o·lies
olio (MISCELLANY) n. pl. oli·os (see also oleo)
ol·ive
Olym·pia
olym·pi·ad
Olym·pi·an
Olym·pic
Olym·pus
Oma·ha
Oman
Omani
om·buds·man, n. pl. om·buds·men
ome·ga
om·elet or om·elette
omen
om·i·nous
om·i·nous·ly
om·i·nous·ness
omis·si·ble
omis·sion
omit, v. omit·ted, omit·ting

om·ni·bus, *n. pl.*
  om·ni·bus·es

om·ni·di·rec·tion·al

om·nip·o·tence

om·nip·o·tent

om·nip·o·tent·ly

om·ni·pres·ence

om·ni·pres·ent

om·ni·range

om·ni·science

om·ni·scient

om·niv·o·rous

om·niv·o·rous·ly

om·niv·o·rous·ness

onan·ism

once-over

on·co·log·i·cal

on·col·o·gist

on·col·o·gy

on·com·ing

one-di·men·sion·al

one-lin·er

one·ness

one-on-one

oner·ous

oner·ous·ly

oner·ous·ness

one·self

one-shot

one-sid·ed

one-sid·ed·ly

one-sid·ed·ness

one·time

one-to-one

one-track

one-up·man·ship

(*occas.* one-
ups·man·ship)

one-way

on·go·ing

on·ion

on·ion·skin

on-line

on·look·er

on·ly

on·o·mato·poe·ia

on·o·mato·peo·ic *or*
  on·o·mato·po·et·ic

on·o·mato·poe·i·cal·ly
  or on·o·mato·po·
  et·i·cal·ly

on·rush

on·set

on·shore

on·side

on-site

on·slaught

On·tar·io

on-the-job

on·to

onus

on·ward

on·yx

oo·dles

oo·long

ooze, *v.* oozed,
  ooz·ing

oozy, *adj.* ooz·i·er,
  ooz·i·est

opac·i·ty, *n. pl.*
  opac·i·ties

opal

opal·es·cence

opal·es·cent

opaque

opaque·ly

opaque·ness

open-air

open-and-shut

open-end

open-end·ed

open·er

open-eyed

open·hand·ed

open·hand·ed·ly

open·hand·ed·ness

open-hearth

open·ing

open-mind·ed

open-mind·ed·ly

open-mind·ed·ness

open·mouthed

open·mouth·ed·ly

open·mouth·ed·ness

open·ness

open·work

op·era

op·er·a·ble

op·er·a·bly

op·era·go·er

op·er·ant

op·er·ate, *v.*
  op·er·at·ed,
  op·er·at·ing

op·er·at·ic

op·er·at·i·cal·ly

op·er·a·tion

op·er·a·tion·al

op·er·a·tive

op·er·a·tive·ly

op·er·a·tive·ness

op·er·a·tor

op·er·et·ta

oph·thal·mic

oph·thal·mol·o·gist

oph·thal·mol·o·gy

opi·ate

opine, v. opined,
opin·ing

opin·ion

opin·ion·at·ed

opi·um

opos·sum, n. pl.
opos·sums
(occas.
opos·sum)

op·po·nent

op·por·tune

op·por·tune·ly

op·por·tune·ness

op·por·tun·ism

op·por·tun·ist

op·por·tu·nis·tic

op·por·tu·ni·ty, n.
pl.
op·por·tu·ni·ties

op·pos·able

op·pose, v.
op·posed,
op·pos·ing

op·po·site
(REVERSE SIDE
OF, ANTITHESIS)
(see also
apposite)

op·po·si·tion
(AGAINST)
(see also
apposition)

op·press

op·pres·sion

op·pres·sive

op·pres·sive·ly

op·pres·sive·ness

op·pres·sor

op·pro·bri·ous

op·pro·bri·ous·ly

op·pro·bri·ous·ness

op·pro·bri·um

op·tic

op·ti·cal

op·ti·cal·ly

op·ti·cian

op·tics

op·ti·mal

op·ti·mal·ly

op·ti·mism

op·ti·mist

op·ti·mis·tic

op·ti·mis·ti·cal·ly

op·ti·mize, v.
op·ti·mized,
op·ti·miz·ing

op·ti·mum, n. pl.
op·ti·ma (occas.
op·ti·mums)

op·tion

op·tion·al

op·tion·al·ly

op·to·met·ric

op·tom·e·trist

op·tom·e·try

op·u·lence

op·u·lent

opus, n. pl. op·era
(occas. opus·es)

or·a·cle

orac·u·lar

oral

oral·ly

or·ange

or·ange·ade

orang·utan

or·angy or
or·ang·ey

orate, v. orat·ed,
orat·ing

ora·tion

or·a·tor

or·a·tor·i·cal

or·a·tor·i·cal·ly

or·a·to·rio, n. pl.
or·a·to·ri·os

or·a·to·ry, n. pl.
or·a·to·ries

or·bic·u·lar

or·bit

or·bit·al

or·chard

or·chard·ist

or·ches·tra

or·ches·tral

or·ches·trate, v.
or·ches·trat·ed,
or·ches·trat·ing

or·ches·tra·tion

or·chid

or·dain

or·dain·ment

or·deal

or·der

or·dered

or·der·li·ness

or·der·ly n. pl.
or·der·lies

or·di·nal

or·di·nance (LAW)
(*see also*
ordnance)

or·di·nar·i·ly

or·di·nary, *n. pl.*
or·di·nar·ies

or·di·nate

or·di·na·tion

ord·nance
(MILITARY
WEAPONS) (*see
also* ordinance)

Or·do·vi·cian

or·dure

ore (MINERAL), *n.
pl.* ores

ore
(SCANDINAVIAN
MONEY), *n. pl.*
ore

oreg·a·no

Or·e·gon

Or·e·go·ni·an

or·gan

or·gan·dy (*occas.*
or·gan·die), *n.
pl.* or·gan·dies

or·gan-grind·er

or·gan·ic

or·gan·i·cal·ly

or·gan·ism

or·gan·ist

or·gan·iz·able

or·ga·ni·za·tion

or·ga·ni·za·tion·al

or·gan·ize, *v.*
or·gan·nized,
or·ga·niz·ing

or·ga·niz·er

or·gan·za

or·gasm

or·gi·as·tic

or·gi·as·ti·cal·ly

or·gu·lous

or·gy, *n. pl.* or·gies

ori·el

ori·ent, *v.*
Orient, *n.*

ori·en·tal (OF THE
ORIENT
GENERALLY)

Ori·en·tal
(PERSON)

ori·en·tate, *v.*
ori·en·tat·ed,
ori·en·tat·ing

ori·en·ta·tion

ori·en·teer·ing

or·i·fice

ori·flamme

ori·ga·mi

or·i·gin

orig·i·nal

orig·i·nal·i·ty

orig·i·nal·ly

orig·i·nate, *v.*
orig·i·nat·ed,
orig·i·nat·ing

orig·i·na·tion

orig·i·na·tor

Ori·no·co Riv·er

ori·ole

ori·son

Or·lon℠

or·mo·lu

or·na·ment

or·na·men·tal

or·na·men·tal·ly

or·na·men·ta·tion

or·nate

or·nate·ly

or·nate·ness

or·ner·i·ness

or·nery

or·ni·thol·o·gist

or·ni·thol·o·gy

orog·e·ny, *n. pl.*
orog·e·nies

oro·tund

oro·tund·i·ty

or·phan

or·phan·age

or·ris

orth·odon·tia

orth·odon·tics

orth·odon·tist

or·tho·dox, *n. pl.*
or·tho·dox
(*occas.*
or·tho·dox·es)

or·tho·doxy, *n. pl.*
or·tho·dox·ies

or·tho·graph·ic

or·tho·graph·i·cal

or·thog·ra·phy, *n.
pl.*
or·thog·ra·phies

or·tho·ker·a·tol·o·gy

or·tho·pe·dic
(*occas.*
or·tho·pae·dic)

or·tho·pe·dics
(*occas.*
or·tho·pae·dics)

or·thot·ic

or·thot·ics

os·cil·late, *v.*
  os·cil·lat·ed,
  os·cil·lat·ing

os·cil·la·tion

os·cil·la·tor

os·cil·la·to·ry

os·cil·lo·scope

os·cu·late, *v.*
  os·cu·lat·ed,
  os·cu·lat·ing

os·cu·la·tion

osier

os·mi·um

os·mo·sis

os·mot·ic

os·prey, *n. pl.*
  os·preys

os·si·fi·ca·tion

os·si·fy, *v.*
  os·si·fied,
  os·si·fy·ing

os·su·ary, *n. pl.*
  os·su·ar·ies

os·ten·si·ble

os·ten·si·bly

os·ten·ta·tion

os·ten·ta·tious

os·ten·ta·tious·ly

os·ten·ta·tious·ness

os·teo·ar·thri·tis

os·teo·path

os·teo·path·ic

os·te·op·a·thy

os·teo·po·ro·sis, *n. pl.*
  os·teo·po·ro·ses

os·to·my, *n. pl.*
  os·to·mies

os·tra·cism

os·tra·cize, *v.*
  os·tra·cized,
  os·tra·ciz·ing

os·trich, *n. pl.*
  os·trich·es *or*
  os·trich

oth·er

oth·er·wise

oth·er·world·ly

oti·ose

Ot·ta·wa

ot·ter, *n. pl.* ot·ters
  (*occas.* ot·ter)

ot·to·man (CHAIR)

Ot·to·man Em·pire

ought (SHOULD)
  (*see also* aught)

Oui·ja® (BOARD)

our·selves

oust·er

out·age

out-and-out

out·bid

out·board

out·bound

out·break

out·build·ing

out·burst

out·cast

out·class

out·come

out·crop, *v.*
  out·cropped,
  out·crop·ping

out·cry, *n. pl.*
  out·cries

out·dat·ed

out·dis·tance, *v.*
  out·dis·tanced,
  out·dis·tanc·ing

out·do, *v.* out·did,
  out·done,
  out·do·ing,
  out·does

out·door (*occas.*
  out·doors), *adj.*

out·doors, *adv., n.*

out·draw, *v.*
  out·drew,
  out·drawn,
  out·draw·ing

out·er

out·er·most

out·er space

out·field

out·field·er

out·fight, *v.*
  out·fought,
  out·fight·ing

out·fit, *v.*
  out·fit·ted,
  out·fit·ting

out·fit·ter

out·flank

out·flow

out·fox

out·gen·er·al

out·go, *n. pl.*
  out·goes

out·go·ing

out·grow, *v.*
  out·grew,
  out·grown,
  out·grow·ing

out·growth

out·guess

out·house

out·ing

out·land·ish

out·land·ish·ly

out·land·ish·ness

out·last

out·law

out·law·ry, *n. pl.*
  out·law·ries

out·lay, *v.* out·laid,
  out·lay·ing

out·let

out·li·er

out·line, *v.*
  out·lined,
  out·lin·ing

out·live, *v.*
  out·lived,
  out·liv·ing

out·look

out·ly·ing

out·man, *v.*
  out·manned,
  out·man·ning

out·ma·neu·ver

out·match

out·mod·ed

out·most

out·num·ber

out-of-bounds

out-of-date

out-of-door *or* out-
  of-doors, *adj.*

out-of-doors, *n.*

out-of-the-way

out·pace

out·pa·tient

out·place·ment

out·play

out·point

out·post

out·pour

out·put

out·rage, *v.*
  out·raged,
  out·rag·ing

out·ra·geous

out·ra·geous·ly

out·ra·geous·ness

out·rank

ou·tré

out·reach

out·ride, *v.*
  out·rode,
  out·rid·den,
  out·rid·ing

out·rid·er

out·rig·ger

out·right

out·run, *v.* out·ran,
  out·run,
  out·run·ning

out·sell, *v.*
  out·sold,
  out·sell·ing

out·set

out·shine, *v.*
  out·shone *or*
  out·shined,
  out·shin·ing

out·side

out·sid·er

out·sit, *v.* out·sat,
  out·sit·ting

out·size (*occas.*
  out·sized), *adj.*

out·size, *n.*

out·skirts

out·smart

out·source, *v.*
  out·sourced,
  out·sourc·ing

out·spo·ken

out·spo·ken·ly

out·spo·ken·ness

out·spread, *v.*
  out·spread,
  out·spread·ing

out·stand·ing

out·sta·tion

out·stay

out·stretch

out·strip, *v.*
  out·stripped,
  out·strip·ping

out·think, *v.*
  out·thought,
  out·think·ing

out·ward

out·ward-bound

out·ward·ly

out·wear, *v.*
  out·wore,
  out·worn,
  out·wear·ing

out·weigh

out·wit, *v.*
  out·wit·ted,
  out·wit·ting

out·work

out·worn

oval

oval·ly

ovar·i·an

ova·ry, *n. pl.*
  ova·ries

ova·tion

ov·en

ov·en·bird

ov·en·proof

over·abun·dance

over·abun·dant

over·acheiv·er

over·act

over·ac·tive

over·age

over·all

over·arch·ing

over·arm

over·awe, v.
    over·awed,
    over·aw·ing

over·bal·ance

over·bear·ing

over·bid, v.
    over·bid,
    over·bid·ding

over·blown

over·board

over·build

over·bur·den

over·call

over·cap·i·tal·iza·tion

over·cap·i·tal·ize, v.
    over·cap·i·tal·ized,
    over·cap·i·tal·iz·ing

over·cast

over·charge, v.
    over·charged,
    over·charg·ing

over·cloud

over·coat

over·come, v.
    over·came,
    over·come,
    over·com·ing

over·com·pen·sate,
    v.
    over·com·pen·sat·ed,
    over·com·pen·sat·ing

over·con·fi·dence

over·con·fi·dent

over·con·fi·dent·ly

over·crowd

over·do, v.
    over·did,
    over·done,
    over·do·ing

over·dose, v.
    over·dosed,
    over·dos·ing

over·draft

over·draw, v.
    over·drew,
    over·drawn,
    over·draw·ing

over·dress

over·drive

over·due

over·em·pha·size,
    v.
    over·em·pha·sized,
    over·em·pha·siz·ing

over·es·ti·mate, v.
    over·es·ti·mat·ed,
    over·es·ti·mat·ing

over·ex·pose, v.
    over·ex·posed,
    over·ex·pos·ing

over·ex·po·sure

over·ex·tend

over·flight

over·flow

over·fly, v.
    over·flew,
    over·flown,
    over·fly·ing

over·grow, v.
    over·grew,
    over·grown,
    over·grow·ing

over·hand

over·hang, v.
    over·hung,
    over·hang·ing

over·haul

over·head

over·hear, v.
    over·heard,
    over·hear·ing

over·heat

over·in·dulge, v.
    over·in·dulged,
    over·in·dulg·ing

over·in·dul·gence

over·in·dul·gent

over·joy

over·kill

over·land

over·lap, v.
    over·lapped,
    over·lap·ping

over·lay, v.
    over·laid,
    over·ly·ing

over·leap, v.
    over·leaped or
    over·leapt,
    over·leap·ing

over·lie, v.
    over·lay,
    over·lain,
    over·ly·ing

over·load

over·long

over·look

over·lord

over·ly

over·match

over·much

over·night

over·pass

over·pay, *v.*
over·paid,
over·pay·ing

over·play

over·pow·er

over·price, *v.*
over·priced,
over·pric·ing

over·print

over·pro·tect

over·pro·tec·tive

over·qual·i·fied

over·rate, *v.*
over·rat·ed,
over·rat·ing

over·reach

over·ride, *v.*
over·rode,
over·rid·den,
over·rid·ing

over·ripe

over·rule, *v.*
over·ruled,
over·rul·ing

over·run, *v.*
over·ran,
over·run,
over·run·ning

over·seas

over·see, *v.*
over·saw,
over·seen,
over·see·ing

over·seer

over·sell, *v.*
over·sold,
over·sell·ing

over·sen·si·tive

over·sen·si·tive·ness

over·sen·si·tiv·i·ty

over·set, *v.*
over·set,
over·set·ting

over·sexed

over·shad·ow

over·shoe

over·shoot, *v.*
over·shot,
over·shoot·ing

over·sight

over·sim·pli·fi·ca·tion

over·sim·pli·fy, *v.*
over·sim·pli·fied,
over·sim·pli·fy·ing

over·size *or*
over·sized

over·sleep, *v.*
over·slept,
over·sleep·ing

over·spend, *v.*
over·spent,
over·spend·ing

over·spread

over·state, *v.*
over·stat·ed,
over·stat·ing

over·state·ment

over·stay

over·step, *v.*
over·stepped,
over·step·ping

over·strung

over·stuff

over·sub·scribe, *v.*
over·sub·scribed,
over·sub·scrib·ing

over·sup·ply, *v.*

over·sup·plied,
over·sup·ply·ing

overt

over·take, *v.*
over·took,
over·tak·en,
over·tak·ing

over·tax

over-the-count·er

over-the-hill

over·throw, *v.*
over·threw,
over·thrown,
over·throw·ing

over·time

over·tone

over·train

over·trick

over·trump

over·ture

over·turn

over·use, *v.*
over·used,
over·us·ing

over·ween·ing

over·weigh

over·weight

over·whelm

over·wind, *v.*
over·wound,
(*occas.*
over·wind·ed),
over·wind·ing

over·work

over·write, *v.*
over·wrote,
over·writ·ten,
over·writ·ing

over·wrought

ovip·a·rous

ovoid *or* ovoi·dal

ovu·late, *v.*
  ovu·lat·ed,
  ovu·lat·ing

ovu·la·tion

ovu·la·tory

ovule

ovum, *n. pl.* ova

owe, *v.* owed,
  ow·ing

owl·ish

owl·ish·ly

owl·ish·ness

own·er

own·er·ship

ox, *n. pl.* ox·en

ox·blood

ox·bow

ox·ford

ox·i·dant

ox·i·da·tion

ox·ide

ox·i·dize, *v.*
  ox·i·dized,
  ox·i·diz·ing

oxy·acet·y·lene

ox·y·gen

ox·y·gen·ate, *v.*
  ox·y·gen·at·ed,
  ox·y·gen·at·ing

ox·y·gen·a·tion

oxy·moron, *n. pl.*
  oxy·mo·ra

oys·ter

Oz·a·lid℠

ozone

P

pa·an·ga

Pab·lum®

pab·u·lum

pace, *v.* paced,
pac·ing

pace·mak·er

pac·er

pa·chin·ko

pa·chu·co, *n. pl.*
pa·chu·cos

pachy·derm

pach·ys·an·dra

pa·cif·ic

pac·i·fi·ca·tion

Pa·cif·ic Ocean

pac·i·fi·er

pac·i·fism

pac·i·fist

pac·i·fy, *v.*
pac·i·fied,
pac·i·fy·ing

pack·age, *v.*
pack·aged,
pack·ag·ing

pack·ag·er

pack·er

pack·et

pack·ing

pack·ing·house

pack·sack

pack·sad·dle

pack·thread

pact

pad, *v.* pad·ded,
pad·ding

pad·dle, *v.*
pad·dled,
pad·dling

pad·dle·ball

pad·dock

pad·dy (*rarely*
padi), *n. pl.*
pad·dies (*rarely*
padis)

pad·lock

pa·dre

pa·dro·ne, *n. pl.*
pa·dro·nes *or*
pa·dro·ni

pae·an (SONG) (*see
also* peon)

pa·gan

pa·gan·ism

page, *v.* paged,
pag·ing

pag·eant

pag·eant·ry

page·boy

pag·i·nate, *v.*
pag·i·nat·ed,
pag·i·nat·ing

pag·i·na·tion

pa·go·da

Pa·go Pa·go

pail

pail·ful, *n. pl.*
pail·fuls

pain

pain·ful

pain·ful·ly

pain·ful·ness

pain·kill·er

pain·less

pain·less·ly

pain·less·ness

pains·tak·ing

pains·tak·ing·ly

paint·brush

paint·er

paint·ing

pair

pai·sa, *n. pl.* pai·sa
  or pai·se

pais·ley

pa·ja·mas

Pa·ki·stan

Pa·ki·stani

pal·ace

pal·a·din

pa·lan·quin

pal·at·abil·i·ty

pal·at·able

pal·at·ably

pal·a·tal

pal·a·tal·iza·tion

pal·a·tal·ize, *v.*
  pal·a·tal·ized,
  pal·a·tal·iz·ing

pal·ate (ROOF OF
  THE MOUTH)
  (*see also* palette,
  pallet)

pa·la·tial

pal·a·tine

pa·la·ver

pale, *v.* paled,
  pal·ing

pale·face

pa·le·og·ra·pher

pa·le·og·ra·phy

Pa·leo·lith·ic

pa·le·on·tol·o·gist

pa·le·on·tol·o·gy

Pa·leo·zo·ic

Pal·es·tine

Pal·es·tin·ian

pal·ette (PAINTER'S
  BOARD) (*see*

  also palate,
  pallet)

pal·i·mo·ny

pa·limp·sest

pal·in·drome

pal·i·sade

pall, *v.* palled,
  pall·ing

pal·la·di·um, *pl.*
  pal·la·dia *or*
  pal·la·di·um

pall·bear·er

pal·let (LOW
  PLATFORM)
  (*see also* palate,
  palette)

pal·li·ate, *v.*
  pa·li·at·ed,
  pal·li·at·ing

pal·lia·tive

pal·lid

pal·lid·ly

pal·lid·ness

pal·lor

pal·mate (*occas.*
  pal·mat·ed)

pal·met·to, *pl.*
  pal·met·tos *or*
  pal·met·toes

palm·is·try

pal·o·mi·no, *n. pl.*
  pal·o·mi·nos

pa·loo·ka

pal·pa·ble

pal·pa·bly

pal·pate, *v.*
  pal·pat·ed,
  pal·pat·ing

pal·pi·tate, *v.*

pal·pi·tat·ed,
  pal·pi·tat·ing

pal·pi·ta·tion

pal·sied

pal·sy, *n. pl.*
  pal·sies

pal·sy, *v.* pal·sied,
  pal·sy·ing

pal·sy-wal·sy

pal·tri·ness

pal·try, *adj.*
  pal·tri·er,
  pal·tri·est

Pam·e·la

pam·pas, *n. pl* of
  pam·pa

pam·per

pam·phlet

pam·phle·teer

pan, *v.* panned,
  pan·ning

pan·a·cea

pa·nache

Pan·a·ma

Pan·a·ma·ni·an

Pan-Amer·i·can

Pan-Amer·i·can·ism

pan·a·tela

pan·cake, *v.*
  pan·caked,
  pan·cak·ing

pan·chro·mat·ic

pan·cre·as

pan·cre·at·ic

pan·da

pan·dem·ic

pan·do·mo·ni·um

pan·der

pan·der·er

pan·dow·dy, *n. pl.*
  pan·dow·dies

pane

pan·e·gy·ric

pan·e·gy·rist

pan·el, *v.* pan·eled
  or pan·elled,
  pan·el·ing *or*
  pan·el·ling

pan·el·ist

pan·fish

pan·han·dle, *v.*
  pan·han·dled,
  pan·han·dling

pan·ic, *v.*
  pan·icked,
  pan·ick·ing

pan·icky

pan·i·cle

pan·ic-strick·en

pan·jan·drum, *n.*
  pl.
  pan·jan·drums
  (*occas.*
  pan·jan·dra)

pan·nier (*occas.*
  pan·ier)

pan·o·plied

pan·o·ply, *n. pl.*
  pan·o·plies

pan·o·ra·ma

pan·o·ram·ic

pan·pipe

pan·sy, *n. pl.*
  pan·sies

pan·ta·loons

pant·dress

pan·the·ism

pan·the·ist

pan·the·is·tic

pan·the·on

pan·ther, *n. pl.*
  pan·thers
  (*occas.* pan·ther)

pan·ties, *n. pl. of*
  pan·tie *of* panty

pan·to·mime, *v.*
  pan·to·mimed,
  pan·to·mim·ing

pan·to·mim·ic

pan·try, *n. pl.*
  pan·tries

pant·suit

panty (*var. of*
  pantie)

panty hose

panty·waist

pan·zer

pa·pa·cy, *n. pl.*
  pa·pa·cies

pa·pal

pa·pa·raz·zo, *n. pl.*
  pa·pa·raz·zi

pa·paw

pa·pa·ya

pa·per

pa·per·back

pa·per·boy

pa·per·girl

pa·per·hang·er

pa·per·weight

pa·pery

pa·pier-mâ·ché

pa·pil·la, *n. pl.*
  pa·pil·lae

pap·il·lary

pap·il·lo·ma, *n. pl.*

pap·il·lo·mas *or*
  pap·il·lo·ma·ta

pa·pil·lon

pa·pil·lote

pa·pist

pa·poose

pa·pri·ka

Pa·pua

Pap·u·an

pap·ule

pa·py·rus, *n. pl.*
  pa·py·rus·es *or*
  pa·py·ri

pa·ra, *n. pl.* pa·ras
  or pa·ra

par·a·ble

pa·rab·o·la

par·a·bol·ic

para·chute, *v.*
  para·chut·ed,
  para·chut·ing

para·chut·ist

pa·rade, *v.*
  pa·rad·ed,
  pa·rad·ing

par·a·digm

par·a·dise

par·a·di·sa·ic *or*
  par·a·di·sa·ic,
  var of
  paradisiacal

par·a·di·si·a·cal·ly

par·a·dox

par·a·dox·i·cal

par·a·dox·i·cal·ly

par·af·fin

par·a·gon

para·graph

Par·a·guay

Par·a·guay·an
para·keet
para·le·gal
par·al·lax
par·al·lel
par·al·lel·ism
par·al·lel·o·gram
pa·ral·y·sis, *n. pl.*
  pa·ral·y·ses
par·a·lyt·ic
par·a·ly·za·tion
par·a·lyze, *v.*
  par·a·lyzed,
  par·a·lyz·ing
par·a·me·cium, *n.*
  pl.
  par·a·me·cia
  (*occas.*
  par·a·me·ciums)
para·med·ic
para·med·ic·al
pa·ram·e·ter
para·mil·i·tary
par·a·mount
par·a·mount·cy
par·amour
para·noia
para·noi·ac
para·noid
par·a·pet
par·a·pher·na·lia
para·phrase, *v.*
  para·phrased,
  para·phras·ing
para·ple·gia
para·ple·gic
para·pro·fes·sion·al
para·psy·chol·o·gy

para·quat
para·site
para·sit·ic
par·a·sit·i·cal
par·a·sit·i·cal·ly
par·a·sit·ism
par·a·si·tol·o·gist
par·a·si·tol·o·gy
para·sol
para·thy·roid
para·troop·er
para·troops
para·ty·phoid
par·boil
par·cel, *v.*
  par·celed *or*
  par·celled,
  par·cel·ing *or*
  par·cel·ling
Par·chee·si℠
parch·ment
par·don
par·don·able
par·don·ably
pare, *v.* pared,
  par·ing
par·e·gor·ic
par·ent
par·ent·age
pa·ren·tal
pa·ren·the·sis, *n.*
  pl. pa·ren·the·ses
pa·ren·the·size, *v.*
  pa·ren·the·sized,
  pa·ren·the·siz·ing
par·en·thet·ic
par·en·thet·i·cal
par·en·thet·i·cal·ly

par·ent·hood
par·ent·ing
pa·re·sis, *n. pl.*
  pa·re·ses
par ex·cel·lence
par·fait
pa·ri·ah
pa·ri·etal
pari-mu·tu·el
par·ing
pa·ri pas·su
Par·is
par·ish
pa·rish·io·ner
Pa·ri·sian
par·i·ty, *n. pl.*
  par·i·ties
par·ka
park·way
par·lance
par·lay (*n.*, BET;
  v., INCREASE)
par·ley (TALK), *n.*
  pl. par·leys
par·lia·ment
par·lia·men·tar·i·an
par·lia·men·ta·ry
par·lor
par·lor·maid
Par·me·san
par·mi·gia·na
pa·ro·chi·al
pa·ro·chi·al·ism
pa·ro·chi·al·ly
par·o·dist
par·o·dy, *n. pl.*
  par·o·dies

pa·rol (WORD OF MOUTH)

pa·role (RELEASE FROM PRISON)

pa·rol·ee

par·ox·ysm

par·ox·ys·mal

par·quet, *v.* par·queted, par·quet·ing

par·que·try

par·ri·cide

par·rot

par·ry, *n. pl.* par·ries

par·ry, *v.* par·ried, par·ry·ing

parse, *v.* parsed, pars·ing

par·sec

par·si·mo·ni·ous

par·si·mo·ni·ous·ly

par·si·mo·ni·ous·ness

par·si·mo·ny

pars·ley

pars·nip

par·son

par·son·age

par·take, *v.* par·took, par·tak·en, par·tak·ing

par·tak·er

part·ed

par·terre

par·the·no·gen·e·sis

Par·the·non

par·tial

par·tial·i·ty

par·tial·ly

par·tic·i·pant

par·tic·i·pate, *v.* par·tic·i·pat·ed, par·tic·i·pat·ing

par·tic·i·pa·tion

par·tic·i·pa·tor

par·tic·i·pa·to·ry

par·ti·cip·i·al

par·ti·cip·i·al·ly

par·ti·ci·ple

par·ti·cle

par·ti·cle·board

par·ti-col·or *or* par·ti-col·ored

par·tic·u·lar

par·tic·u·lar·i·ty, *n. pl.* par·tic·u·lar·i·ties

par·tic·u·lar·iza·tion

par·tic·u·lar·ize, *v.* par·tic·u·lar·ized, par·tic·u·lar·iz·ing

par·tic·u·lar·ly

par·tic·u·late

part·ing

par·ti·san

par·ti·san·ship

par·tite

par·ti·tion

par·ti·tive

par·ti·tive·ly

part·ly

part·ner

part·ner·ship

par·tridge, *n. pl.*

par·tridge, *or* par·tridg·es

part-time, *adj., adv.*

par·tu·ri·ent

par·tu·ri·tion

part·way

par·ty, *n. pl.* par·ties

par·ve·nu

par·vo·vi·rus

pa·sha

pasque·flow·er

pass, *v.* passed, pass·ing

pass·able

pass·ably

pas·sage

pas·sage·way

pass·book

pas·sé

pas·sel

pas·sen·ger

passe-par·tout

pass·er

pass·er-by, *n. pl.* pass·ers·by

pas·ser·ine

pass-fail

pas·si·ble

pas·sim

pass·ing

pas·sion·ate

pas·sion·ate·ly

pas·sion·less

pas·sive

pas·sive·ly

pas·sive·ness
pas·siv·i·ty
pass·key
Pass·over
pass·port
pass·word
pas·ta
paste, v. past·ed,
  past·ing
paste·board
pas·tel
pas·tern
paste-up, n.
paste up, v.
pas·teur·iza·tion
pas·teur·ize, v.
  pas·teur·ized,
  pas·teur·iz·ing
pas·teur·iz·er
pas·tiche
past·ies, n. pl.
  (NIPPLE
  COVERINGS) (see
  also pasty)
pas·tille (occas
  pas·til)
pas·time
past·i·ness
pas·tor
pas·to·ral (RURAL
  LIFE)
pas·to·rale
  (MUSICAL
  COMPOSITION)
pas·tor·ate
pas·tra·mi (occas.
  pas·tromi)
past·ry, n. pl.
  past·ries

pas·tur·age
pas·ture, v.
  pas·tured,
  pas·tur·ing
pas·ty (LIKE
  PASTE), adj.
  past·i·er,
  past·i·est (see
  also pasties)
pas·ty (MEAT PIE),
  n. pl. pas·ties
  (see also pasties)
pat, v. pat·ted,
  pat·ting
patch
patch·board
patch·work
pâté de foie gras
pa·tel·la, n. pl.
  pa·tel·lae or
  pa·tel·las
pat·en (PLATE) (see
  also patten,
  platen)
pa·ten·cy
pat·ent (EVIDENT)
pat·ent (RIGHT TO
  AN INVENTION)
pat·ent·able
pat·en·tee
pat·ent leath·er
pa·tent·ly
pat·ent of·fice
pa·ter·fa·mil·i·as, n.
  pl.
  pa·ters·fa·mil·i·as
pa·ter·nal
pa·ter·nal·ism
pa·ter·nal·is·tic
pa·ter·nal·is·ti·cal·ly

pa·ter·nal·ly
pa·ter·ni·ty
Pat·er·son
pa·thet·ic
pa·thet·i·cal·ly
path·find·er
patho·gen
patho·gen·ic
patho·ge·nic·i·ty
patho·log·i·cal
patho·log·i·cal·ly
pa·thol·o·gist
pa·thol·o·gy, n. pl.
  pa·thol·o·gies
pa·thos
path·way
pa·tience
pa·tient
pa·tient·ly
pa·ti·na, n. pl.
  pa·ti·nas or
  pa·ti·nae
pa·tio, n. pl.
  pa·ti·os
pa·tois, n. pl.
  pa·tois
pa·tri·arch
pa·tri·ar·chal
pa·tri·arch·ate
pa·tri·ar·chy, n. pl.
  pa·tri·ar·chies
Pa·tri·cia
pa·tri·cian
pa·ri·cid·al
pat·ri·cide
Pat·rick
pa·ri·lin·eal

pat·ri·mo·ni·al

pat·ri·mo·ny, *n. pl.*
  pat·ri·mo·nies

pa·tri·ot

pa·tri·ot·ic

pa·tri·ot·i·cal·ly

pa·tri·o·tism

pa·tris·tic

pa·trol, *v.*
  pa·trolled,
  pa·trol·ling

pa·trol·man, *n. pl.*
  pa·trol·men

pa·tron

pa·tron·age

pa·tron·ess

pa·tron·ize, *v.*
  pa·tron·ized,
  pa·tron·iz·ing

pat·ro·nym·ic

pa·troon

pat·sy, *n. pl.*
  pat·sies

pat·ten (SANDAL)
  (*see also* paten,
  platen)

pat·ter

pat·tern

pat·ty, *n. pl.*
  pat·ties

pat·ty cake

patty shell

pau·ci·ty

Paul

paunch·i·ness

paunchy, *adj.*
  paunch·i·er,
  paunch·i·est

pau·per

pau·per·ize, *v.*
  pau·per·ized,
  pau·per·iz·ing

pause, *v.* paused,
  paus·ing

pa·vane

pave, *v.* paved,
  pav·ing

pave·ment

pa·vil·ion

pav·ing

pawl

pawn·brok·er

pawn·shop

pay, *v.* paid (*occas.*
  payed), pay·ing

pay·able

pay·check

pay·day

pay·ee

pay·er

pay·load

pay·mas·ter

pay·ment

pay·off

pay·ola

pay·roll

pea, *n. pl.* peas
  (*occas.* pease)

peace·able

peace·ably

peace·ful

peace·ful·ly

peace·ful·ness

peace·mak·er

peace·nik

peace·time

peach

peachy, *adj.*
  peach·i·er,
  peach·i·est

pea·cock

pea·fowl

pea·hen

peak

peal (RING) (*see
  also* peel)

pea·nut

pearl

pearly, *adj.*
  pearl·i·er,
  pearl·i·est

pear-shaped

peas·ant

peas·ant·ry

pea·shoot·er

peb·ble, *v.*
  peb·bled,
  peb·bling

peb·bly, *adj.*
  peb·bli·er,
  peb·bli·est

pe·can

pec·ca·dil·lo, *n. pl.*
  pec·ca·dil·loes
  or pec·ca·dil·los

pec·ca·ry, *n. pl.*
  pec·ca·ries

peck·er

peck·ing

pec·tate

pec·tin

pec·to·ral

pec·u·late, *v.*
  pec·u·lat·ed,
  pec·u·lat·ing

pec·u·la·tion

pe·cu·liar

pe·cu·liar·i·ty, *n. pl.*
  pe·cu·liar·i·ties

pe·cu·liar·ly

pe·cu·ni·ary

ped·a·gog·ic

ped·a·gog·i·cal

ped·a·gog·i·cal·ly

ped·a·gogue (*occas.*
  ped·a·gog)

ped·a·go·gy

ped·al, *v.* ped·aled
  (*occas.*
  ped·alled)
  ped·al·ing
  (*occas.*
  ped·al·ling)

ped·ant

pe·dan·tic

pe·dan·ti·cal·ly

ped·ant·ry, *n. pl.*
  ped·ant·ries

ped·dle, *v.*
  ped·dled,
  ped·dling

ped·dler (*occas.*
  ped·lar)

ped·er·ast

ped·er·as·ty

ped·es·tal

pe·des·tri·an

pe·di·at·ric

pe·di·a·tri·cian

pe·di·at·rics

pedi·cab

ped·i·cure

ped·i·gree

ped·i·greed

ped·i·ment

pe·dol·o·gist

pe·dol·o·gy

pe·dom·e·ter

pe·do·phile

pe·do·phil·ia

pe·dun·cle

peek·a·boo

peel (*n.*, RIND; *v.*,
  REMOVE) (*see
  also* peal)

peel·ing

peen

peep·hole

peer (*n.*, EQUAL;
  v. LOOK) (*see
  also* pier)

peer·age

peer·less

peer·less·ly

peer·less·ness

peeve, *v.* peeved,
  peev·ing

peev·ish

peev·ish·ly

peev·ish·ness

pee·wee

peg, *v.* pegged,
  peg·ging

Peg·board℠

pei·gnoir

pe·jo·ra·tive

pe·jo·ra·tive·ly

Pe·king·ese *or*
  Pe·kin·ese, *n.
  pl.* Pe·king·ese *or*
  Pe·kin·ese

pe·koe

pel·age

pe·lag·ic

pel·i·can

pel·la·gra

pel·let

pell-mell

pel·lu·cid

pel·lu·cid·i·ty

pel·lu·cid·ly

pel·vic

pel·vis, *n. pl.*
  pel·vis·es (*rarely*
  pel·ves)

pem·mi·can (*occas.*
  pem·i·can)

pen, *v.* penned,
  pen·ning

pe·nal

pe·nal·iza·tion

pe·nal·ize, *v.*
  pe·nal·ized,
  pe·nal·iz·ing

pen·al·ty, *n. pl*
  pen·al·ties

pen·ance

pen·chant

pen·cil, *v.* pen·ciled
  or pen·cilled,
  pen·cil·ing *or*
  pen·cil·ling

pen·dant (*occas.*
  pen·dent) (ITEM
  THAT HANGS),
  n.

pen·dent *or*
  pen·dant
  (JUTTING
  OVER,
  PENDING), *adj.*

pend·ing

pen·drag·on
pen·du·lous
pen·du·lous·ly
pen·du·lous·ness
pen·du·lum
pe·ne·plain (*occas.*
  pe·ne·plane)
pen·e·tra·bil·i·ty
pen·e·tra·ble
pen·e·tra·bly
pen·e·trate, *v.*
  pen·e·trat·ed,
  pen·e·trat·ing
pen·e·trat·ing
pen·e·tra·tion
pen·e·tra·tive
pen·e·tra·tive·ly
pen·e·tra·tive·ness
pen·guin
pen·hold·er
pen·i·cil·lin
pen·in·su·la
pen·in·su·lar
pe·nis, *n. pl.* pe·nes
  or pe·ni·ses
pen·i·tence
pen·i·tent
pen·i·ten·tial
pen·i·ten·tial·ly
pen·i·ten·tia·ry, *n.*
  pl.
  pen·i·ten·tia·ries
pen·knife, *n. pl.*
  pen·knives
pen·man·ship
pen·nant
pen·ni, *n. pl.*
  pen·nia (*occas.*

pen·ni *or*
  pen·nis)
pen·ni·less
pen·ni·less·ness
pen·non
Penn·syl·va·nia
Penn·syl·va·nian
pen·ny, *n. pl.*
  pen·nies *or*
  pence
pen·ny-pinch·er
pen·ny-pinch·ing
pen·ny·roy·al
pen·ny·weight
pen·ny-wise
pen·ny·wort
pe·no·log·i·cal
pe·nol·o·gist
pe·nol·o·gy
pen·sion
pen·sion·er
pen·sive
pen·sive·ly
pen·sive·ness
pen·ta·cle
pen·ta·gon
pen·tag·o·nal
pen·tam·e·ter
pen·ta·ton·ic
Pen·te·cost
Pen·te·cos·tal
pent·house
pen·tom·ic
pe·nu·che
pen·ul·ti·mate
pen·ul·ti·mate·ly
pen·um·bra, *n. pl.*

pen·um·brae *or*
  pen·um·bras
pe·nu·ri·ous
pe·nu·ri·ous·ly
pe·nu·ri·ous·ness
pen·u·ry
pe·on (LABORER),
  n. pl pe·ons *or*
  pe·o·nes (*see also*
  paean)
pe·on·age
pe·o·ny, *n. pl.*
  pe·o·nies
peo·ple, *n. pl.*
  peo·ple *or*
  peo·ples
Pe·o·ria
pep, *v.* pepped,
  pep·ping
pep·lum
pep·per
pep·per·box
pep·per·corn
pep·per·mint
pep·per·o·ni
pep·pery
pep·pi·ness
pep·py, *adj.*
  pep·pi·er,
  pep·pi·est
pep·sin
pep·tic
pep·tone
per·ad·ven·ture
per·am·bu·late, *v.*
  per·ambu·lat·ed,
  per·am·bu·lat·ing
per·am·bu·la·tion
per·am·bu·la·tor

per an·num
per·cale
per cap·i·ta
per·ceiv·able
per·ceiv·ably
per·ceive, *v.*
  per·ceived,
  per·ceiv·ing
per·cent, *n. pl.*
  per·cent *or*
  per·cents
per·cent·age
per·cen·tile
per·cept
per·cep·ti·bil·i·ty
per·cep·ti·ble
per·cep·ti·bly
per·cep·tion
per·cep·tive
per·cep·tive·ly
per·cep·tive·ness
per·cep·tiv·i·ty
per·cep·tu·al
per·cep·tu·al·ly
perch (FISH), *n. pl.*
  perch *or*
  perch·es
per·chance
per·cip·i·ence
per·cip·i·ent
oer·co·late, *v.*
  per·co·lat·ed,
  per·co·lat·ing
per·co·la·tion
per·co·la·tor
per·cus·sion
per·cus·sion·ist
per·cus·sive

per·cus·sive·ly
per·cus·sive·ness
per di·em
per·di·tion
per·du·ra·bil·i·ty
per·du·ra·ble
per·du·ra·bly
per·e·gri·na·tion
pe·remp·to·ri·ly
pe·remp·tor·i·ness
pe·remp·to·ry
pe·ren·ni·al
pe·ren·ni·al·ly
per·es·troi·ka
per·fect
per·fec·ta
per·fect·ibil·i·ty
per·fect·ible
per·fec·tion
per·fec·tion·ism
per·fec·tion·ist
per·fect·ly
per·fec·to, *n. pl.*
  per·fec·tos
per·fid·i·ous
per·fid·i·ous·ly
per·fid·i·ous·ness
per·fi·dy, *n. pl.*
  per·fi·dies
per·fo·rate, *v.*
  per·fo·rat·ed,
  per·fo·rat·ing
per·fo·ra·tion
per·fo·ra·tor
per·force
per·form
per·form·able

per·for·mance
per·form·er
per·fume, *v.*
  per·fumed,
  per·fum·ing
per·fum·ery, *n. pl.*
  per·fum·er·ies
per·func·to·ri·ly
per·func·to·ri·ness
per·func·to·ry
per·go·la
per·haps
peri·car·di·um
peri·cyn·thi·on
peri·gee
peri·he·li·on
per·il, *v.* per·iled
  (*occas.*
  per·illed),
  per·il·ing
  (*occas.*
  per·il·ling)
per·il·ous
per·il·ous·ly
per·il·ous·ness
peri·lune
pe·rim·e·ter
pe·ri·od
pe·ri·od·ic
pe·ri·od·i·cal
per·ri·od·i·cal·ly
pe·ri·od·ic·i·ty, *n.*
  pl.
  pe·ri·od·ic·i·ties
peri·odon·tal
peri·odon·tics
peri·odon·tist
peri·pa·tet·ic

peri·pa·tet·i·cal·ly

pe·riph·er·al

pe·riph·er·al·ly

pe·riph·er·y, *n. pl.*
  pe·riph·er·ies

pe·riph·ra·sis, *n. pl.*
  pe·riph·ra·ses

peri·phras·tic

pe·rique

peri·scope

peri·scop·ic

per·ish

per·ish·abil·i·ty

per·ish·able

peri·stal·sis

peri·stal·tic

peri·style

peri·to·ne·um, *n.*
  pl.
  peri·to·ne·ums *or*
  peri·to·nea

peri·to·ni·tis

peri·wig

per·i·win·kle

per·jure, *v.*
  per·jured,
  per·jur·ing

per·jur·er

per·ju·ri·ous

per·ju·ry, *n. pl.*
  per·ju·ries

perk·i·ly

perk·i·ness

perky, *adj.*
  perk·i·er,
  perk·i·est

per·ma·frost

Perm·al·loy℠

per·ma·nence

per·ma·nen·cy

per·ma·nent

per·ma·nent·ly

per·ma·nent·ness

per·man·ga·nate

per·me·abil·i·ty

per·me·able

per·me·ably

per·me·ance

per·me·ate, *v.*
  per·me·at·ed,
  per·me·at·ing

per·me·ation

Perm·ian

per·mis·si·bil·i·ty

per·mis·si·ble

per·mis·si·bly

per·mis·sion

per·mis·sive

per·mis·sive·ly

per·mis·sive·ness

per·mit, *v.*
  per·mit·ted,
  per·mit·ting

per·mu·ta·tion

per·mute, *v.*
  per·mut·ed,
  per·mut·ing

per·ni·cious

per·ni·cious·ly

per·ni·cious·ness

per·orate, *v.*
  per·orat·ed,
  per·orat·ing

per·ora·tion

per·ox·ide

per·pen·dic·u·lar

per·pen·dic·u·lar·i·ty

per·pen·dic·u·lar·ly

per·pe·trate, *v.*
  per·pe·trat·ed,
  per·pe·trat·ing

per·pe·tra·tion

per·pe·tra·tor

per·pet·u·al

per·pet·u·al·ly

per·pet·u·ate, *v.*
  per·pet·u·at·ed,
  per·pet·u·at·ing

per·pet·u·a·tion

per·pet·u·a·tor

per·pe·tu·ity, *n. pl.*
  per·pe·tu·i·ties

per·plex

per·plexed

per·plexed·ly

per·plex·i·ty, *n. pl.*
  per·plex·i·ties

per·qui·site
  (PRIVILEGE)
  (*see also*
  prerequisite)

per se

per·se·cute, *v.*
  per·se·cut·ed,
  per·se·cut·ing

per·se·cu·tion

per·se·cu·tor

per·se·ver·ance

per·se·vere, *v.*
  per·se·vered,
  per·se·ver·ing

Per·sia

Per·sian

per·si·flage

per·sim·mon

per·sist
per·sis·tence
per·sis·ten·cy
per·sis·tent
per·sis·tent·ly
per·snick·e·ty
per·son
per·so·na, *n. pl.*
  per·so·nae
  (DRAMA) *or*
  per·so·nas
  (PSYCHOLOGY)
per·son·able
per·son·age
per·son·al
per·son·al·i·ty
  (BEHAVIOR), *n.
  pl.*
  per·son·al·i·ties
  (*see also*
  personalty)
per·son·al·ize, *v.*
  per·son·al·ized,
  per·son·al·iz·ing
per·son·al·ly
per·son·al·ty
  (PROPERTY), *n.
  pl.* per·son·al·ties
  (*see also*
  personality)
per·so·na non
  gra·ta
per·son·i·fi·ca·tion
per·son·i·fy, *v.*
  per·son·i·fied,
  per·son·i·fy·ing
per·son·nel
per·son-to-per·son
per·spec·tive
per·spec·tive·ly

per·spi·ca·cious
per·spi·ca·cious·ly
per·spi·ca·cious·ness
per·spi·cac·i·ty
per·spi·cu·i·ty
per·spic·u·ous
per·spic·u·ous·ly
per·spic·u·ous·ness
per·spi·ra·tion
per·spi·ra·to·ry
per·spire, *v.*
  per·spired,
  per·spir·ing
per·suad·able
per·suade, *v.*
  per·suad·ed,
  per·suad·ing
per·sua·si·ble
per·sua·sion
per·sua·sive
per·sua·sive·ly
per·sua·sive·ness
per·tain
per·ti·na·cious
per·ti·na·cious·ly
per·ti·na·cious·ness
per·ti·nac·i·ty
per·ti·nence
per·ti·nen·cy
per·ti·nent
per·ti·nent·ly
pert·ly
pert·ness
per·turb
per·tur·ba·tion
per·tus·sis
Pe·ru

pe·rus·al
pe·ruse, *v.*
  pe·rused,
  pe·rus·ing
Pe·ru·vi·an
per·vade, *v.*
  per·vad·ed,
  per·vad·ing
per·va·sive
per·verse
per·verse·ly
per·verse·ness
per·ver·sion
per·ver·si·ty, *n. pl.*
  per·ver·si·ties
per·ver·sive
per·vert
per·vi·ous
per·vi·ous·ness
pe·se·ta
pe·se·wa
pes·ky, *adj.*
  pes·ki·er,
  pes·ki·est
pe·so, *n. pl.* pe·sos
pes·si·mism
pes·si·mist
pes·si·mis·tic
pes·si·mis·ti·cal·ly
pes·ter
pest·hole
pes·ti·ci·dal
pes·ti·cide
pes·tif·er·ous
pes·tif·er·ous·ly
pes·tif·er·ous·ness
pes·ti·lence
pes·ti·lent

pes·ti·len·tial

pes·tle, *v.* pes·tled,
 pes·tling

pes·to, *n. pl.*
 pes·tos

pet, *v.* pet·ted,
 pet·ting

pet·al

pe·tard

pet·cock

pe·ter

pet·i·ole

pet·it

pe·tite

pe·tit four, *n. pl.*
 pe·tits fours *or*
 pe·tit fours

pe·ti·tion

pe·ti·tion·er

pet·it point

pet·rel

pet·ri·fac·tion

pet·ri·fy, *v.*
 pet·ri·fied,
 pet·ri·fy·ing

pet·ro·chem·i·cal

pet·ro·dol·lars

pe·trog·ra·phy

pet·rol

pet·ro·la·tum

pe·tro·leum

pet·ro·log·ic

pe·trol·o·gist

pe·trol·o·gy

pet·ti·coat

pet·ti·fog, *v.*
 pet·ti·fogged,
 pet·ti·fog·ging

pet·ti·fog·ger

pet·ti·ly

pet·ti·ness

pet·tish

pet·ty, *adj.*
 pet·ti·er,
 pet·ti·est

pet·u·lance

pet·u·lant

pe·tu·nia

pew·ter

pey·o·te

pfen·nig, *n. pl.*
 pfen·nig (*occas.*
 pfen·nigs)

pha·eton

phago·cyte

pha·lanx, *n. pl.*
 pha·lanx·es *or*
 pha·lan·ges

phal·a·rope, *n. pl.*
 phal·a·ropes
 (*occas.*
 phal·a·rope)

phal·lic

phal·lus, *n. pl.*
 phal·li *or*
 phal·lus·es

phan·tasm

phan·tas·ma·go·ria

phan·tas·ma·go·ric

phan·tom

pha·raoh

phar·i·sa·ic

phar·i·sa·i·cal

phar·i·sa·i·cal·ly

Phar·i·see

phar·ma·ceu·ti·cal

phar·ma·ceu·tics

phar·ma·cist

phar·ma·cog·no·sy

phar·ma·co·log·i·cal

phar·ma·co·log·i·cal·ly

phar·ma·col·o·gist

phar·ma·col·o·gy

phar·ma·co·poe·ia
 (*occas.*
 phar·ma·co·pe·ia)

phar·ma·cy, *n. pl.*
 phar·ma·cies

pha·ryn·geal

phar·ynx, *n. pl.*
 phar·yn·ges *or*
 phar·ynx·es

phase, *v.* phased,
 phas·ing

phase·out

pheas·ant, *n. pl.*
 pheas·ant *or*
 pheas·ants

phe·no·bar·bi·tal

phe·nol

phe·no·lic

phe·nom·e·nal

phe·nom·e·non, *n.
 pl.*
 phe·nom·e·na *or*
 phe·nom·e·nons

phi·al

Phil·a·del·phia

phi·lan·der

phi·lan·der·er

phil·an·throp·ic

phi·lan·thro·pist

phi·lan·thro·py, *n.
 pl.*
 phi·lan·thro·pies

phil·a·tel·ic

phi·lat·e·list

phi·lat·e·ly

phil·har·mon·ic

Phil·ip

phi·lip·pic

Phil·ip·pine

Phil·ip·pines

Phi·lis·tine

Phil·lip

phil·o·den·dron, *n.*
pl.
　phil·o·den·drons
　or
　phil·o·den·dra

phil·o·log·i·cal

phi·lol·o·gist

phi·lol·o·gy

phi·los·o·pher

philo·soph·ic

philo·soph·i·cal

philo·soph·i·cal·ly

phi·los·o·phize, *v.*
　phi·los·o·phized,
　phi·los·o·phiz·ing

phi·los·o·phy, *n. pl.*
　phi·los·o·phies

phil·ter (*occas.*
　phil·tre)

phle·bi·tis

phlegm

phleg·mat·ic

phleg·mat·i·cal·ly

phlox, *n. pl.* phlox
　or phlox·es

pho·bia

pho·bic

Phoe·nix

phone, *v.* phoned,
　phon·ing

pho·neme

pho·ne·mic

pho·ne·mi·cal·ly

pho·ne·mics

pho·net·ic

pho·net·i·cal·ly

pho·ne·ti·cian

pho·net·ics

phon·ic

pho·ni·cal·ly

phon·ics

pho·ni·ly

pho·ni·ness

pho·no·graph

pho·no·graph·ic

pho·no·log·i·cal

pho·no·log·i·cal·ly

pho·nol·o·gist

pho·nol·o·gy

pho·ny (*occas.*
　pho·ney), *adj.*
　phon·i·er,
　phon·i·est

phos·gene

phos·phate

phos·phat·ic

phos·pho·res·cence

phos·pho·res·cent

phos·phor·ic

phos·pho·rus

pho·to, *n. pl.*
　pho·tos

pho·to·cell

pho·to·chro·mic

pho·to·com·po·si·tion

pho·to·cop·y, *v.*
　pho·to·cop·ied,
　pho·to·copy·ing

pho·to·elec·tric

pho·to·elec·tron

pho·to·emis·sive

pho·to·en·grave, *v.*
　pho·to·en·graved,
　pho·to·engrav·ing

pho·to·en·grav·ing

pho·to·flash

pho·to·flood

pho·to·gen·ic

pho·to·graph

pho·tog·ra·pher

pho·to·graph·ic

pho·to·graph·i·cal·ly

pho·tog·ra·phy

pho·to·gra·vure

pho·to·lith·o·graph

pho·to·li·thog·ra·phy

pho·to·map, *v.*
　pho·to·mapped,
　pho·to·map·ping

pho·tom·e·ter

pho·to·met·ric

pho·tom·e·try

pho·to·mi·cro·graph

pho·to·mu·ral

pho·ton

pho·to·off·set

pho·to·sen·si·tive

pho·to·sen·si·tiv·i·ty

pho·to·sen·si·ti·za·tion

pho·to·syn·the·sis

pho·to·vol·ta·ic

phrase, *v.* phrased,
　phras·ing

phra·se·ol·o·gy, *n.*
pl.
  phra·se·ol·o·gies

phras·ing

phre·nol·o·gist

phre·nol·o·gy

phy·lac·ter·y, *n. pl.*
  phy·lac·ter·ies

phyl·lox·e·ra

phy·log·e·ny, *n. pl.*
  phy·log·e·nies

phy·lum, *n. pl.*
  phy·la

phys·ic

phys·i·cal

phys·i·cal·ly

phy·si·cian

phys·i·cist

phys·ics

phys·i·og·no·my

phys·i·o·graph·ic

phys·i·og·ra·phy

phys·i·o·log·i·cal

phys·i·o·log·i·cal·ly

phys·i·ol·o·gist

phys·i·ol·o·gy

phys·io·ther·a·pist

phys·io·ther·a·py

phy·sique

phy·to·gen·ic

pi, *n. pl.* pis
  (MATHEMATICAL)
  or pies
  (JUMBLED
  TYPE)

pi (*occas.* pie) (TO
  JUMBLE
  TYPE), *v.* pied,

pi·ing, *or*
  pie·ing

pia ma·ter

pi·a·nis·si·mo, *n. pl.*
  pi·a·nis·si·mi *or*
  pi·a·nis·si·mos

pi·an·ist

pi·ano, *n. pl.*
  pi·anos

pi·ano·forte

pi·as·ter (*occas.*
  pi·as·tre)

pi·az·za

pi·ca

pic·a·dor

pic·a·resque

pic·a·ro, *n. pl.*
  pic·a·ros

pic·a·yune

pic·a·yun·ish

pic·ca·lil·li

pic·co·lo, *n. pl.*
  pic·co·los

pice, *n. pl.* pice

pick·ax

pick·er·el

pick·et

pick·ings

pick·le, *v.* pick·led,
  pick·ling

pick-me-up

pick·pock·et

pick·up

picky, *adj.*
  pick·i·er,
  pick·i·est

pic·nic, *v.*
  pic·nicked,
  pic·nick·ing

pic·nick·er

pi·co·sec·ond

pi·cot

pic·to·graph

pic·to·ri·al

pic·to·ri·al·ly

pic·ture, *v.*
  pic·tured,
  pic·tur·ing

pic·tur·esque

pic·tur·esque·ly

pic·tur·esque·ness

pid·dle, *v.* pid·dled,
  pid·dling

pid·dling

pid·gin
  (LANGUAGE)
  (*see also* piggin)

pie

pie·bald

piece, *v.* pieced,
  piec·ing

pièce de
  ré·sis·tance

piece·meal

piece·work

piece·work·er

pied-à-terre

pied·mont

pier (STRUCTURE)
  (*see also* peer)

pierce, *v.* pierced,
  pierc·ing

Pierre (CAPITAL
  OF SOUTH
  DAKOTA)

Pi·erre (MAN'S
  NAME)

pi·e·tism

pi·e·tis·tic

pi·ety, *n. pl.*
pi·e·ties

pi·ezo·elec·tric

pig

pi·geon

pi·geon·hole, *v.*
pi·geon·holed,
pi·geon·hol·ing

pi·geon-toed

pig·gin (PAIL) (*see
also* pidgin)

pig·gish

pig·gish·ly

pig·gish·ness

pig·gy, *adj.*
pig·gi·er,
pig·gi·est

pig·gy, *n. pl.*
pig·gies

pig·gy·back

pig·head·ed

pig·head·ed·ly

pig·head·ed·ness

pig·ment

pig·men·ta·tion

pig·pen

pig·skin

pig·sty

pig·tail

pike, *n. pl.* pike *or*
pikes

pik·er

Pikes Peak

pi·las·ter

pil·chard

pile, *v.* piled,
pil·ing

pile·up, *n.*

pile up, *v.*

pil·fer

pil·fer·age

pil·fer·er

pil·grim

pil·grim·age

pil·ing

pil·lage, *v.*
pil·laged,
pil·lag·ing

pil·lar

pill·box

pil·lion

pil·lo·ry, *n. pl.*
pil·lo·ries

pil·low

pil·low·case

pil·lowy

pi·lot

pi·lot·age

pi·lot·house

pi·lot·less

pil·sner (*occas.*
pil·sen·er)

pi·mien·to, *n. pl.*
pi·mien·tos

pim·per·nel

pim·ple, *adj.*
pim·pli·er,
pim·pli·est

pim·pled

pim·ply

pin, *v.* pinned,
pin·ning

pi·ña co·la·da

pin·a·fore

pi·ña·ta *or* pi·na·ta

pin·ball

pince-nez, *n. pl.*
pince-nez

pin·cers

pinch·cock

pinch-hit, *v.* pinch-
hit, pinch-hit·ting

pinch-hit·ter

pin·cush·ion

pine, *v.* pined,
pin·ing

pine·ap·ple

pine·wood

pin·feath·er

pin·fish

Ping-Pong®

pin·head

pin·hole

pin·ion

pink·eye

pin·kie *or* pin·ky,
n. pl. pin·kies

pin·nace

pin·na·cle

pin·nate

pi·noch·le

pi·ñon *or* pin·yon,
n. pl. pi·ñons *or*
pin·yons *or*
pi·ño·nes

pinot noir

pin·point

pin·prick

pin·set·ter

pin·stripe

pin·striped

pin·to, *n. pl.*

pin·tos *or* pin·toes

pint-size *or* pint-sized

pin·up

pin·wale

pin·wheel

pin·work

pin·worm

pi·o·neer

pi·o·neer·ing

pi·ous

pi·ous·ly

pi·ous·ness

pipe, *v.* piped, pip·ing

pipe·ful, *n. pl.* pipe·fuls

pipe·line

pip·er

pipe·stem

pi·pette *or* pi·pet

pip·ing

pip·pin

pip-squeak

pi·quan·cy

pi·quant

pi·qué *or* pi·que (FABRIC)

pique (RESENTMENT)

pique (PROVOKE, AROUSE), *v.* piqued, piqu·ing

pi·quet (CARD GAME)

pi·ra·cy, *n. pl.* pi·ra·cies

pi·ra·nha

pi·rate, *v.* pi·rat·ed, pi·rat·ing

pi·rat·i·cal

pi·rat·i·cal·ly

pi·rogue

pir·ou·ette, *v.* pir·ou·et·ted, pir·ou·et·ting

pis·ca·to·ri·al

Pis·ces

pis·tach·io, *n. pl.* pis·ta·chi·os

pis·til

pis·til·late

pis·tol

pis·tol-whip, *v.* pis·tol-whipped, pis·tol-whip·ping

pis·ton

pit, *v.* pit·ted, pit·ting

pit-a-pat

pitch

pitch-black

pitch·blende

pitch-dark

pitch·er

pitch·fork

pitch·man, *n. pl.* pitch·men

pitch·out

pit·e·ous

pit·e·ous·ly

pit·e·ous·ness

pit·fall

pith·e·can·thro·pine

pith·e·can·thro·poid

pith·i·ly

pith·i·ness

pithy, *adj.* pith·i·er, pith·i·est

piti·able

piti·ably

piti·ful

piti·ful·ly

piti·ful·ness

piti·less

piti·less·ly

piti·less·ness

pit·man (PERSON), *n. pl.* pit·men

pit·man (STEERING ARM), *n. pl.* pit·mans

pi·ton

pit·tance

pit·ted

pit·ter-pat·ter

Pitts·burg (CALIFORNIA, KANSAS)

Pitts·burgh (PENNSYLVANIA)

pi·tu·itary, *n. pl.* pi·tu·itar·ies

pity, *n. pl.* pit·ies

pity, *v.* pit·ied, pity·ing

pity·ing

piv·ot

piv·ot·al

pix·ie *or* pixy, *n. pl.* pix·ies

pix·ie·ish

pix·i·lat·ed or
  pix·il·lat·ed

piz·za

piz·zazz or pi·zazz

piz·ze·ria

piz·zi·ca·to, n. pl.
  piz·zi·ca·ti

pla·ca·bil·i·ty

pla·ca·ble

pla·ca·bly

plac·ard

pla·cate, v.
  pla·cat·ed,
  pla·cat·ing

place, v. placed,
  plac·ing

pla·ce·bo, n. pl.
  pla·ce·bos

place·ment

pla·cen·ta, n. pl.
  pla·cen·tas or
  pla·cen·tae

pla·cen·tal

plac·er

plac·id

pla·cid·i·ty

plac·id·ly

plac·id·ness

plack·et

pla·gia·rism

pla·gia·rist

pla·gia·rize, v.
  pla·gia·rized,
  pla·gia·riz·ing

plague, v. plagued,
  plagu·ing

plaid

plain

plain·clothes·man

n. pl.
  plain·clothes·men

plain·ly

plain·ness

plain·spo·ken

plaint

plain·tiff

plain·tive

plain·tive·ly

plain·tive·ness

plait

plan, v. planned,
  plan·ning

plane, v. planed,
  plan·ing

plan·et

plan·e·tar·i·um, n.
  pl.
  plan·e·tar·i·ums
  or plan·e·tar·ia

plan·e·tary

plan·e·tes·i·mal

plan·e·toid

plan·gen·cy

plan·gent

pla·ni·sphere

plank·ing

plank·ton

plan·tain

plan·tar (SOLE OF
  FOOT) (see also
  planter)

plan·ta·tion

plant·er (ONE WHO
  PLANTS) (see
  also plantar)

plaque

plas·ma

plas·ter

plas·ter·board

plas·tered

plas·ter·er

plas·ter·ing

plas·tic

plast·ti·cal·ly

plas·tic·i·ty

plas·ti·cize, v.
  plas·ti·cized,
  plas·ti·ciz·ing

plat, v. plat·ted,
  plat·ting

plate, v. plat·ed,
  plat·ing

pla·teau, n. pl.
  pla·teaus or
  pla·teaux

plate·ful, n. pl.
  plate·fuls

plate·let

plat·en (ROLLER)
  (see also paten,
  patten)

plat·form

plat·ing

plat·i·num

plat·i·tude

plat·i·tu·di·nous

plat·i·tu·di·nous·ly

pla·ton·ic

pla·ton·i·cal·ly

pla·toon

plat·ter

platy·pus, n. pl.
  platy·pus·es or
  platy·pi

plau·dit

plau·si·bil·i·ty

plau·si·ble
plau·si·bly
pla·ya
play·able
play·act
play·back
play·bill
play·book
play·boy
play-by-play
play·er
play·ful
play·ful·ly
play·ful·ness
play·go·er
play·ground
play·house
play·ing
play·land
play·mate
play·off
play·pen
play·room
play·suit
play·thing
play·time
play·wear
play·wright
pla·za
plea
plea-bar·gain, v.
plead, v. plead·ed
  or pled,
  plead·ing
plead·er
pleas·ant

pleas·ant·ly
pleas·ant·ness
pleas·ant·ry, n. pl.
  pleas·ant·ries
please, v. pleased,
  pleas·ing
pleas·ing
pleas·ing·ly
pleas·ing·ness
plea·sur·able
plea·sur·ably
plea·sure, v.
  plea·sured,
  plea·sur·ing
ple·be·ian
pleb·i·scite
plec·trum, n. pl.
  plec·tra or
  plec·trums
pledge, v. pledged,
  pledg·ing
ple·na·ry
pleni·po·ten·tia·ry
plen·i·tude
plen·te·ous
plen·te·ous·ly
plen·te·ous·ness
plen·ti·ful
plen·ti·ful·ly
plen·ti·ful·ness
plen·ti·tude
plen·ty, n. pl.
  plen·ties
ple·num, n. pl.
  ple·nums or
  ple·na
pleo·nasm
pleth·o·ra

pleu·ri·sy
Plex·i·glas®
plex·us
pli·abil·i·ty
pli·able
pli·ably
pli·an·cy
pli·ant
pli·ant·ly
pli·ant·ness
pli·ers
plight
plinth
plis·sé or plis·se
plod, v. plod·ded,
  plod·ding
plod·der
plop, v. plopped,
  plop·ping
plot, v. plot·ted,
  plot·ting
plot·less
plot·less·ness
plot·ter
plov·er, n. pl.
  plov·er or
  plov·ers
plow
plow·boy
plow·share
pluck·i·ly
pluck·i·ness
plucky, adj.
  pluck·i·er,
  pluck·i·est
plug, v. plugged,
  plug·ging

plug-ug·ly, *n. pl.*
plug-ug·lies

plum (FRUIT) (*see also* plumb)

plum·age

plumb (LEAD WEIGHT) (*see also* plum)

plumb·er

plumb·ing

plume, *v.* plumed,
plum·ing

plum·met

plump·ish

plump·ness

plun·der

plun·der·er

plunge, *v.* plunged,
plung·ing

plung·er

plu·per·fect

plu·ral

plu·ral·ism

plu·ral·is·tic

plu·ral·i·ty, *n. pl.*
plu·ral·i·ties

plu·ral·iza·tion

plu·ral·ize, *v.*
plu·ral·ized,
plu·ral·iz·ing

plus, *n. pl.* plus·es
(*occas.* plus·ses)

plush·ly

plushy, *adj.*
plush·i·er,
plush·i·est

Plu·to

plu·toc·ra·cy, *n. pl.*
plu·toc·ra·cies

plu·to·crat

plu·to·crat·ic

plu·to·crat·i·cal·ly

plu·to·ni·um

plu·vi·al

ply, *v.* plied,
ply·ing

ply·wood

pneu·mat·ic

pneu·mo·nia

poach·er

po·chard

pock·et

pock·et·book

pock·et·ful, *n. pl.*
pock·et·fuls

pock·et·knife, *n. pl.*
pock·et·knives

pock·et-size (*occas.*
pock·et-sized)

pock·mark

pock·marked

po·co·sin

po·di·a·trist

po·di·a·try

po·di·um, *n. pl.*
po·di·ums *or*
po·dia

po·em

po·esy (POETRY) *n. pl.* po·es·ies (*see also* posy)

po·et

po·et·ess

po·et·ic

po·et·i·cal

po·et·i·cal·ly

po·et·ry

po·grom

poi·gnan·cy

poi·gnant

poi·gnant·ly

poin·ci·ana

poin·set·tia

point-blank

point·ed

point·ed·ly

point·ed·ness

point·er

poin·til·lism

poin·til·list

point·less

point·less·ly

point·less·ness

poise, *v.* poised,
pois·ing

poi·son

poi·son·ous

poi·son·ous·ly

poi·son·ous·ness

poke, *v.* poked,
pok·ing

pok·er

pok·ey (JAIL), *n. pl.* pok·eys *or* pok·ies

poky (SLOW), *adj.*
pok·i·er,
pok·i·est

Po·land

po·lar

Po·lar·is

po·lar·i·ty, *n. pl.*
po·lar·i·ties

po·lar·i·za·tion

po·lar·ize, v.
  po·lar·ized,
  po·lar·iz·ing

Po·lar·oid®

pol·der

pole (STAFF) (see also poll)

pole·ax, v.
  pole·axed,
  pole·ax·ing

pole·cat, n. pl.
  pole·cats or
  pole·cat

po·lem·ic

po·lem·i·cal

po·lem·i·cal·ly

po·lem·i·cist

po·lem·ics

po·len·ta

pole·star

po·lice, v. po·liced,
  po·lic·ing

po·lice·man, n. pl.
  po·lice·men

po·lice·wom·an, n.
  pl. po·lice·wom·en

pol·i·cy, n. pl.
  pol·i·cies

pol·i·cy·hold·er

po·lio

po·lio·my·eli·tis

Pol·ish

pol·ish

pol·ished

po·lit·bu·ro

po·lite

po·lite·ly

po·lite·ness

po·li·tesse

pol·i·tic, v.
  pol·i·ticked,
  pol·i·tick·ing

po·lit·i·cal

po·lit·i·cal·ly

pol·i·ti·cian

po·lit·i·cize, v.
  po·lit·i·cized,
  po·lit·i·ciz·ing

po·lit·i·co, n. pl.
  po·lit·i·cos
  (occas.
  po·lit·i·coes)

pol·i·tics

pol·i·ty

pol·ka

poll (SURVEY) (see also pole)

pol·len

pol·li·nate, v.
  pol·li·nat·ed,
  pol·li·nat·ing

pol·li·na·tion

pol·li·na·tor

pol·li·nize, v.
  pol·li·nized,
  pol·li·niz·ing

pol·li·wog or
  pol·ly·wog

poll·ster

pol·lut·ant

pol·lute, v.
  pol·lut·ed,
  pol·lut·ting

pol·lut·er

pol·lu·tion

po·lo

po·lo·naise

po·lo·ni·um

pol·ter·geist

pol·troon

poly·an·drous

poly·an·dry

poly·cen·tric

poly·chro·mat·ic

poly·clin·ic

poly·es·ter

poly·eth·yl·ene

po·lyg·a·mist

po·lyg·a·mous

po·lyg·amy

poly·glot

poly·gon

po·lyg·o·nal

poly·graph

po·lyg·y·nous

po·lyg·y·ny

poly·mer

poly·mer·ic

po·ly·mer·iza·tion

Poly·ne·sia

Poly·ne·sian

poly·no·mi·al

pol·yp

poly·phon·ic

poly·phon·ous

po·lyph·o·ny

poly·pro·pyl·ene

poly·sty·rene

poly·syl·lab·ic

poly·syl·la·ble

poly·tech·nic

poly·the·ism

poly·the·is·tic

poly·un·sat·u·rat·ed

poly·ure·thane

po·made, v.
  po·mad·ed,
  po·mad·ing

pome·gran·ate

pom·mel, v.
  pom·meled, or
  pom·melled,
  pom·mel·ing or
  pom·mel·ling

pom·pa·dour

pom·pa·no, n. pl.
  pom·pa·no or
  pom·pa·nos

pom·pom

pom·pon

pom·pos·i·ty, n. pl.
  pom·pos·i·ties

pom·pous

pom·pous·ly

pom·pous·ness

pon·cho, n. pl.
  pon·chos

pon·der

pon·der·able

pon·der·o·sa

pon·der·ous

pon·der·ous·ly

pon·der·ous·ness

pon·gee

pon·iard

Pont·char·train

pon·tiff

pon·tif·i·cal

pon·tif·i·cal·ly

pon·tif·i·cate, v.
  pon·tif·i·cat·ed,
  pon·tif·i·cat·ing

pon·toon

po·ny, n. pl.
  po·nies

po·ny·tail

poo·dle

pooh-pooh

pool·room

poor·house

poor·ly

pop, v. popped,
  pop·ping

pop·corn

pop·ery

pop-eyed

pop·gun

pop·in·jay

pop·ish

pop·lar

pop·lin

Po·po·ca·té·petl

pop-off, n.

pop off, v.

pop·over

pop·py, n. pl.
  pop·pies

pop·py·cock

Pop·si·cle®

pop·u·lace
  (MASSES) (see
  also populous)

pop·u·lar

pop·u·lar·i·ty

pop·u·lar·iza·tion

pop·u·lar·ize, v.
  pop·u·lar·ized,
  pop·u·lar·iz·ing

pop·u·lar·iz·er

pop·u·lar·ly

pop·u·late, v.

pop·u·lat·ed,
  pop·u·lat·ing

pop·u·la·tion

pop·u·lous
  (POPULATION
  DENSITY) (see
  also populace)

pop·u·lous·ly

pop·u·lous·ness

pop-up

por·ce·lain

por·ce·lain·ize, v.
  por·ce·lain·ized,
  por·ce·lain·iz·ing

por·cine

por·cu·pine

pore (PONDER), v.
  pored, por·ing
  (see also pour)

pork·er

porky, adj.
  pork·i·er,
  pork·i·est

por·nog·ra·pher

por·no·graph·ic

por·nog·ra·phy

po·ros·i·ty, n. pl.
  po·ros·i·ties

po·rous

po·rous·ly

po·rous·ness

por·phy·ry, n. pl.
  por·phy·ries

por·poise

por·ridge

por·rin·ger

por·ta·bil·i·ty

por·ta·ble
por·ta·bly
por·tage, *v.*
  por·taged,
  por·tag·ing
por·tal
por·tal-to-por·tal
port·cul·lis
por·tend
por·tent
por·ten·tous
por·ten·tous·ly
por·ten·tous·ness
por·ter
por·ter·house
port·fo·lio, *n. pl.*
  port·fo·lios
port·hole
por·ti·co, *n. pl.*
  por·ti·coes *or*
  por·ti·cos
por·tiere
por·tion
Port·land
port·li·ness
port·ly, *adj.*
  port·li·er,
  port·li·est
port·man·teau, *n.*
pl.
  port·man·teaus
  or
  port·man·teaux
Pôr·to Aleg·re
por·trait
por·trait·ist
por·trai·ture
por·tray
por·tray·al

Por·tu·gal
Por·tu·guese, *n. pl.*
  Por·tu·guese
pose, *v.* posed,
  pos·ing
pos·er
po·seur
pos·it
po·si·tion
pos·i·tive
pos·i·tive·ly
pos·i·tiv·ism
pos·i·tron
pos·se
pos·se co·mi·ta·tus
pos·sess
pos·sessed
pos·ses·sion
pos·ses·sive
pos·ses·sive·ly
pos·ses·sive·ness
pos·ses·sor
pos·si·bil·i·ty
pos·si·ble
pos·si·bly
pos·sum
post·age
post·al
post·box
post·card
post·clas·si·cal
post·con·so·nan·tal
post·date, *v.*
  post·dat·ed,
  post·dat·ing
post·di·lu·vi·an
post·doc·tor·al

post·doc·tor·ate
post·er
pos·te·ri·or
pos·ter·i·ty
post·grad·u·ate
post·haste
post·hole
post·hu·mous
post·hu·mous·ly
post·hu·mous·ness
post·hyp·not·ic
pos·til·ion *or*
  pos·til·lion
Post·im·pres·sion·ism
post·in·dus·tri·al
post·lude
post·man, *n. pl.*
  post·men
post·mark
post·mas·ter
post me·ri·di·em
post·mis·tress
post·mod·ern
post·mor·tem
post·na·sal
post·na·tal
post of·fice
post·op·er·a·tive
post·op·er·a·tive·ly
post·paid
post·par·tum
post·pone, *v.*
  post·poned,
  post·pon·ing
post·pone·ment
post·script
pos·tu·lant

pos·tu·late, *v.*
  pos·tu·lat·ed,
  pos·tu·lat·ing
pos·tu·la·tion
pos·tu·la·tor
pos·ture, *v.*
  pos·tured,
  pos·tur·ing
post·war
po·sy (FLOWER) *n.*
  pl. po·sies, (*see*
  also poesy)
pot, *v.* pot·ted,
  pot·ting
po·ta·bil·i·ty
po·ta·ble
po·tage
pot·ash
po·tas·si·um
po·ta·tion
po·ta·to, *n. pl.*
  po·ta·toes
pot·bel·lied
pot·bel·ly, *n. pl.*
  pot·bel·lies
pot·boil·er
po·ten·cy, *n. pl.*
  po·ten·cies
po·tent
po·ten·tate
po·ten·tial
po·ten·ti·al·i·ty, *n.*
  pl.
  po·ten·ti·al·i·ties
po·ten·tial·ly
po·ten·ti·om·e·ter
pot·ful, *n. pl.*
  pot·fuls
pot·head

poth·er
pot·herb
pot·hole
pot·hook
po·tion
pot·latch
pot·luck
pot·pie
pot·pour·ri
pot·sherd
pot·shot
pot·tage
pot·ter
pot·tery, *n. pl.*
  pot·ter·ies
pouched
poul·tice
poul·try
poul·try·man, *n. pl.*
  poul·try·men
pounce, *v.*
  pounced,
  pounc·ing
pound
pound·age
pound·cake
pound-fool·ish
pour (FLOW) (*see*
  also pore)
pout
pov·er·ty
pov·er·ty-strick·en
pow·der
pow·dery
pow·er
pow·er·boat
pow·er·ful

pow·er·ful·ly
pow·er·house
pow·er·less
pow·wow
pox
prac·ti·ca·bil·i·ty
prac·ti·ca·ble
prac·ti·ca·bly
prac·ti·cal
prac·ti·cal·i·ty, *n.*
  pl.
  prac·ti·cal·i·ties
prac·ti·cal·ly
prac·tice, *v.*
  prac·ticed,
  prac·tic·ing
prac·ticed
prac·tic·er
prac·ti·tion·er
prae·to·ri·an
prag·mat·ic
prag·mat·i·cal
prag·mat·i·cal·ly
prag·ma·tism
prag·ma·tist
prai·rie
praise, *v.* praised,
  prais·ing
praise·wor·thi·ly
praise·wor·thi·ness
praise·wor·thy
pra·line
prance, *v.* pranced,
  pranc·ing
pranc·er
prank·ster
pra·se·o·dym·i·um

prat·fall
pra·tique
prat·tle, *v.*
  prat·tled,
  prat·tling
prawn
pray
prayer (REQUEST)
pray·er (ONE WHO
  PRAYS)
prayer·ful
prayer·ful·ly
prayer·ful·ness
preach·er
preach·ment
pre·ad·o·les·cence
pre·ad·o·les·cent
pre·am·ble
pre·am·pli·fi·er
pre·ar·range, *v.*
  pre·ar·ranged,
  pre·ar·rang·ing
pre·ar·range·ment
pre·as·signed
pre·can·cel, *v.*
  pre·can·celed *or*
  pre·can·celled,
  pre·can·cel·ing
  or
  pre·can·cel·ling
pre·can·cel·la·tion
pre·car·i·ous
pre·car·i·ous·ly
pre·car·i·ous·ness
pre·cau·tion
pre·cau·tion·ary
pre·cede, *v.*
  pre·ced·ed,
  pre·ced·ing

pre·ce·dence
pre·ce·dent
  (PRIOR)
prec·e·dent
  (EXAMPLE)
pre·ced·ing
pre·cept
pre·cep·tor
pre·cess
pre·ces·sion
pre·cinct
pre·ci·os·i·ty, *n. pl.*
  pre·ci·os·i·ties
pre·cious
pre·cious·ly
pre·cious·ness
prec·i·pice
pre·cip·i·tan·cy, *n.*
  pl.
  pre·cip·i·tan·cies
pre·cip·i·tate, *v.*
  pre·cip·i·tat·ed,
  pre·cip·i·tat·ing
pre·cip·i·tate·ly
pre·cip·i·ta·tion
pre·cip·i·tous
pre·cip·i·tous·ly
pre·cip·i·tous·ness
pré·cis
  (SUMMARY), *n.*
  pl. pré·cis
pre·cise
  (ACCURATE)
pre·cise·ly
pre·cise·ness
pre·ci·sion
pre·clude, *v.*
  pre·clud·ed,
  pre·clud·ing

pre·clu·sive
pre·co·cious
pre·co·cious·ly
pre·co·cious·ness
pre·coc·i·ty
pre-Co·lum·bi·an
pre·con·ceive, *v.*
  pre·con·ceived,
  pre·con·ceiv·ing
pre·con·cep·tion
pre·con·di·tion
pre·cook
pre·cur·sor
pre·da·ceous *or*
  pre·da·cious
pre·dac·i·ty
pre·date, *v.*
  pre·dat·ed,
  pre·dat·ing
pred·a·tor
pred·a·to·ri·ly
pred·a·to·ry
pre·de·cease, *v.*
  pre·de·ceased,
  pre·de·ceas·ing
pre·de·ces·sor
pre·des·ig·nate, *v.*
  pre·des·ig·nat·ed,
  pre·des·ig·nat·ing
pre·des·ig·na·tion
pre·des·ti·na·tion
pre·des·tine, *v.*
  pre·des·tined,
  pre·des·tin·ing
pre·de·ter·mine, *v.*
  pre·de·ter·mined,
  pre·de·ter·min·ing
pred·i·ca·ble
pre·dic·a·ment

pred·i·cate *v.*
  pred·i·cat·ed,
  pred·i·cat·ing

pred·i·ca·tion

pre·dict

pre·dict·abil·i·ty

pre·dict·able

pre·dict·ably

pre·dic·tion

pre·di·gest

pre·di·ges·tion

pre·di·lec·tion

pre·dis·pose, *v.*
  pre·dis·posed,
  pre·dis·pos·ing

pre·dis·po·si·tion

pred·ni·sone

pre·dom·i·nance

pre·dom·i·nant

pre·dom·i·nant·ly

pre·dom·i·nate, *v.*
  pre·dom·i·nat·ed,
  pre·dom·i·nat·ing

pre·em·i·nence

pre·em·i·nent

pre·em·i·nent·ly

pre·empt

pre·emp·tion

pre·emp·tive

pre·emp·tor

pre·ex·ist

pre·ex·is·tence

pre·ex·is·tent

pre·fab

pre·fab·ri·cate, *v.*
  pre·fab·ri·cat·ed,
  pre·fab·ri·cat·ing

pre·fab·ri·ca·tion

pref·ace, *v.*
  pref·aced,
  pref·ac·ing

pref·a·to·ry

pre·fect

pre·fec·ture

pre·fer, *v.*
  pre·ferred,
  pre·fer·ring

pref·er·abil·i·ty

pref·er·able

pref·er·ably

perf·er·ence

pref·er·en·tial

pre·fer·ment

pre·fig·u·ra·tion

pre·fig·u·ra·tive

pre·fig·ure, *v.*
  pre·fig·ured,
  pre·fig·ur·ing

pre·fix

pre·flight

pre·form

pre·front·al

preg·nan·cy, *n. pl.*
  preg·nan·cies

preg·nant

pre·heat

pre·hen·sile

pre·his·tor·ic

pre·his·tor·i·cal

pre·his·tor·i·cal·ly

pre·his·to·ry

pre·ig·ni·tion

pre·judge, *v.*
  pre·judged,
  pre·judg·ing

prej·u·dice, *v.*

prej·u·diced,
  prej·u·dic·ing

prej·u·di·cial

prel·a·cy, *n. pl.*
  prel·a·cies

prel·ate

pre·lim·i·nary, *n.
pl.*
  pre·lim·i·nar·ies

pre·lude

pre·mar·i·tal

pre·ma·ture

pre·ma·ture·ly

pre·ma·ture·ness

pre·med

pre·med·i·cal

pre·med·i·tate, *v.*
  pre·med·i·tat·ed,
  pre·med·i·tat·ing

pre·med·i·ta·tion

pre·mier (CHIEF)

pre·miere (FIRST
PERFORMANCE)

prem·ise

pre·mi·um

pre·mix

pre·mo·ni·tion

pre·mon·i·to·ry

pre·na·tal

pre·nup·tial

pre·oc·cu·pa·tion

pre·oc·cu·pied

pre·oc·cu·py, *v.*
  pre·oc·cu·pied,
  pre·oc·cu·py·ing

pre·op·er·a·tive

pre·op·er·a·tive·ly

pre·or·dain

prep, *v.* prepped,
  prep·ping
prep·a·ra·tion
pre·pa·ra·to·ry
pre·pare, *v.*
  pre·pared,
  pre·par·ing
pre·pared·ness
pre·pay, *v.*
  pre·paid,
  pre·pay·ing
pre·pon·der·ance
pre·pon·der·ant
pre·pon·der·ant·ly
prep·o·si·tion
prep·o·si·tion·al
pre·pos·sess
pre·pos·ses·sing
pre·pos·ses·sion
pre·pos·ter·ous
pre·pos·ter·ous·ly
pre·pos·ter·ous·ness
prep·py *or*
  prep·pie, *n. pl.*
  prep·pies
pre·puce
pre·re·cord
pre·re·cord·ed
pre·req·ui·site
  (REQUIRED
  BEFOREHAND)
  (*see also*
  perquisite)
pre·rog·a·tive
pres·age, *n.*
pre·sage, *v.*
  pre·saged,
  pre·sag·ing
pres·by·ter

Pres·by·te·ri·an
pres·by·tery
pre·school
pre·science
pre·scient
pre·scient·ly
pre·scribe, *v.*
  pre·scribed,
  pre·scrib·ing
pre·scrip·tion
pre·scrip·tive
pre·scrip·tive·ly
pre·sell
pres·ence
pres·ent, *n.*
pre·sent, *v.*
pre·sent·abil·i·ty
pre·sent·able
pre·sent·ably
pre·sen·ta·tion
pres·ent-day
pre·sen·ti·ment
pres·ent·ly
pre·serv·able
pres·er·va·tion
pres·er·va·tion·ist
pre·ser·va·tive
pre·serve, *v.*
  pre·served,
  pre·serv·ing
pre·serv·er
pre·set
pre·shrunk
pre·side, *v.*
  pre·sid·ed,
  pre·sid·ing
pres·i·den·cy, *n. pl.*
  pres·i·den·cies

pres·i·dent
pres·i·dent-elect, *n.*
  pl. pres·i·dents-
  elect
pres·i·den·tial
pre·si·dio, *n. pl.*
  pre·si·di·os
pre·sid·i·um, *n. pl.*
  pre·sid·ia *or*
  pre·sid·i·ums
pre·sig·ni·fy, *v.*
  pre·sig·ni·fied,
  pre·sig·ni·fy·ing
pre·soak
press·board
press·er
press·ing
press·man, *n. pl.*
  press·men
press·room
press·run
pres·sure, *v.*
  pres·sured,
  pres·sur·ing
pres·sur·iza·tion
pres·sur·ize, *v.*
  pres·sur·ized,
  pres·sur·iz·ing
press·work
pres·ti·dig·i·ta·tion
pres·ti·dig·i·ta·tor
pres·tige
pres·ti·gious
pres·ti·gious·ly
pres·ti·gious·ness
pres·tis·si·mo, *n. pl.*
  pres·tis·si·mos
pres·to, *n. pl.*
  pres·tos

pre·stress
pre·sum·able
pre·sum·ably
pre·sume, *v.*
    pre·sumed,
    pre·sum·ing
pre·sump·tion
pre·sump·tive
pre·sump·tive·ly
pre·sump·tu·ous
pre·sump·tu·ous·ly
pre·sump·tu·ous·ness
pre·sup·pose, *v.*
    pre·sup·posed,
    pre·sup·pos·ing
pre·sup·po·si·tion
pre·teen
pre·tend
pre·tend·er
pre·tense
pre·ten·sion
pre·ten·tious
pre·ten·tious·ly
pre·ten·tious·ness
pret·er·it *or*
    pret·er·ite
pre·ter·nat·u·ral
pre·ter·nat·u·ral·ly
pre·test
pre·text
pre·tri·al
pret·ti·fy, *v.*
    pret·ti·fied,
    pret·ti·fy·ing
pret·ti·ly
pret·ti·ness
pret·ty, *adj.*

pret·ti·er,
    pret·ti·est
pret·zel
pre·vail
pre·vail·ing
prev·a·lence
prev·a·lent
prev·a·lent·ly
pre·var·i·cate, *v.*
    pre·var·i·cat·ed,
    pre·var·i·cat·ing
pre·var·i·ca·tion
pre·var·i·ca·tor
pre·vent
pre·vent·abil·i·ty
pre·vent·able
pre·ven·ta·tive
pre·ven·tion
pre·ven·tive
pre·ven·tive·ly
pre·ven·tive·ness
pre·view
pre·vi·ous
pre·vi·ous·ly
pre·vi·ous·ness
pre·vi·sion
pre·war
prey
price, *v.* priced,
    pric·ing
price·less
prick·le, *v.*
    prick·led,
    prick·ling
prick·li·ness
prick·ly
pride·ful

pride·ful·ly
pride·ful·ness
prie-dieu, *n. pl.*
    prie-dieux
priest·ess
priest·hood
priest·li·ness
priest·ly
prig·gish
prim, *adj.*
    prim·mer,
    prim·mest
pri·ma bal·le·ri·na
pri·ma·cy, *n. pl.*
    pri·ma·cies
pri·ma don·na
pri·ma fa·cie
pri·mal
pri·mar·i·ly
pri·ma·ry, *n. pl.*
    pri·ma·ries
pri·mate
pri·ma·tol·o·gist
pri·ma·tol·o·gy
prime, *v.* primed,
    prim·ing
prim·er
pri·me·val
prim·i·tive
prim·i·tive·ly
prim·i·tive·ness
pri·mo·gen·i·tor
pri·mo·gen·i·ture
pri·mor·dial
prim·rose
prince·ly
prin·cess

prin·ci·pal (CHIEF)
(see also
principle)

prin·ci·pal·i·ty, n.
pl.
prin·ci·pal·i·ties

prin·ci·pal·ly

prin·ci·ple (RULE)
(see also
principal)

prin·ci·pled

print·able

print·er

print·ing

print·out

pri·or

pri·or·ess

pri·or·i·tize, v.
pri·or·i·tized,
pri·or·i·tiz·ing

pri·or·i·ty, n. pl.
pri·or·i·ties

pri·o·ry, n. pl.
pri·o·ries

prism

pris·mat·ic

pris·on

pris·on·er

pris·si·ness

pris·sy, adj.
pris·si·er,
pris·si·est

pris·tine

pris·tine·ly

pri·va·cy, n. pl.
pri·va·cies

pri·vate

pri·va·teer

pri·vate·ly

pri·va·tion

pri·vat·iza·tion

pri·vat·ize, v.
pri·vat·ized,
pri·vat·iz·ing

priv·et

priv·i·lege

priv·i·leged

privy, n. pl.
priv·ies

prize·fight

prize·fight·er

prize·fight·ing

prize·win·ner

prob·a·bil·i·ty, n.
pl.
prob·a·bil·i·ties

prob·a·ble

prob·a·bly

pro·bate, v.
pro·bat·ed,
pro·bat·ing

pro·ba·tion

pro·ba·tion·ary

pro·ba·tion·er

pro·ba·tive

pro·ba·to·ry

probe, v. probed,
prob·ing

pro·bi·ty

prob·lem

prob·lem·at·ic

prob·lem·at·i·cal

prob·lem·at·i·cal·ly

pro bo·no

pro·bos·cis, n. pl.
pro·bos·cis·es
(occas.
pro·bos·ci·des)

pro·ca·the·dral

pro·ce·dur·al

pro·ce·dur·al·ly

pro·ce·dure

pro·ceed

pro·ceed·ing

pro·ceeds

pro·cess

pro·ces·sion

pro·ces·sion·al

pro·ces·sor

pro·claim

proc·la·ma·tion

pro·cliv·i·ty, n. pl.
pro·cliv·i·ties

pro·con·sul

pro·cras·ti·nate, v.
pro·cras·ti·nat·ed,
pro·cras·ti·nat·ing

pro·cras·ti·na·tion

pro·cras·ti·na·tor

pro·cre·ant

pro·cre·ate, v.
pro·cre·at·ed,
pro·cre·at·ing

pro·cre·a·tion

pro·cre·a·tive

pro·cre·a·tor

pro·crus·te·an

proc·tol·o·gist

proc·tol·o·gy

proc·tor

proc·to·ri·al

pro·cur·able

proc·u·ra·tor

pro·cure, v.
pro·cured,
pro·cur·ing

pro·cure·ment

pro·cur·er

prod, *v.* prod·ded, prod·ding

prod·i·gal

prod·i·gal·i·ty

prod·i·gal·ly

pro·di·gious

pro·di·gious·ly

pro·di·gious·ness

prod·i·gy, *n. pl.* prod·i·gies

pro·duce, *v.* pro·duced, pro·duc·ing

pro·duc·er

prod·uct

pro·duc·tion

pro·duc·tive

pro·duc·tive·ly

pro·duc·tive·ness

pro·duc·tiv·i·ty

pro·fa·na·tion

pro·fa·na·to·ry

pro·fane, *v.* pro·faned, pro·fan·ing

pro·fane·ly

pro·fane·ness

pro·fan·i·ty, *n. pl.* pro·fan·i·ties

pro·fess

pro·fessed

pro·fessed·ly

pro·fes·sion

pro·fes·sion·al

pro·fes·sion·al·ism

pro·fes·sion·al·ly

pro·fes·sor

pro·fes·so·ri·al

pro·fes·sor·ship

prof·fer

pro·fi·cien·cy, *n. pl.* pro·fi·cien·cies

pro·fi·cient

pro·fi·cient·ly

pro·file, *v.* pro·filed, pro·fil·ing

prof·it

prof·it·abil·i·ty

prof·it·able

prof·it·ably

prof·i·teer

prof·li·ga·cy

prof·li·gate

pro for·ma

pro·found

pro·found·ly

pro·found·ness

pro·fun·di·ty, *n. pl.* pro·fun·di·ties

pro·fuse

pro·fuse·ly

pro·fuse·ness

pro·fu·sion

pro·gen·i·tor

prog·e·ny, *n. pl.* prog·e·nies

pro·ges·ter·one

prog·na·thous

prog·no·sis, *n. pl.* prog·no·ses

prog·nos·tic

prog·nos·ti·cate, *v.*

prog·nos·ti·cat·ed, prog·nos·ti·cat·ing

prog·nos·ti·ca·tion

prog·nos·ti·ca·tor

pro·gram (*occas.* pro·gramme), *v.* pro·grammed *or* pro·gramed, pro·gram·ming *or* pro·gram·ing

pro·gram·ma·ble

pro·gram·mat·ic

pro·gram·mer

prog·ress, *n.*

pro·gress, *v.*

pro·gres·sion

pro·gres·sive

pro·gres·sive·ly

pro·gres·sive·ness

pro·hib·it

pro·hi·bi·tion

pro·hi·bi·tion·ist

pro·hib·i·tive

pro·hib·i·tive·ly

pro·hib·i·tive·ness

pro·hib·i·to·ry

proj·ect, *n.*

pro·ject, *v.*

pro·ject·able

pro·jec·tile

pro·jec·tion

pro·jec·tion·ist

pro·jec·tive

pro·jec·tive·ly

pro·jec·tor

pro·lapse, *v.* pro·lapsed, pro·laps·ing

pro·le·gom·e·non,
n. pl.
  pro·le·gom·e·na

pro·le·tar·i·an

pro·le·tar·i·an·iza·tion

pro·le·tar·i·an·ize,
v.
  pro·le·tar·i·an·ized,
  pro·le·tar·i·an·iz·ing

pro·le·tar·i·at

pro·lif·er·ate, v.
  pro·lif·er·at·ed,
  pro·lif·er·at·ing

pro·lif·er·a·tion

pro·lif·ic

pro·lif·i·cal·ly

pro·lix

pro·lix·i·ty

pro·loc·u·tor

pro·logue (occas.
  pro·log)

pro·long

pro·lon·gate, v.
  pro·lon·gated,
  pro·lon·gat·ing

pro·lon·ga·tion

prom·e·nade, v.
  prom·e·nad·ed,
  prom·e·nad·ing

pro·me·thi·um

prom·i·nence

prom·i·nent

prom·i·nent·ly

pro·mis·cu·ity, n.
pl.
  pro·mis·cu·i·ties

pro·mis·cu·ous

pro·mis·cu·ous·ly

pro·mis·cu·ous·ness

prom·ise, v.
  prom·ised,
  prom·is·ing

prom·is·ing

prom·is·so·ry

prom·on·to·ry, n.
pl.
  prom·on·to·ries

pro·mote, v.
  pro·mot·ed,
  pro·mot·ing

pro·mot·er

pro·mo·tion

pro·mo·tion·al

prompt·book

prompt·er

promp·ti·tude

prompt·ly

prompt·ness

pro·mul·gate, v.
  pro·mul·gat·ed,
  pro·mul·gat·ing

pro·mul·ga·tion

prone·ness

prong·horn, n. pl.
  prong·horn
  (occas.
  prong·horns)

pro·noun

pro·nounce, v.
  pro·nounced,
  pro·nounc·ing

pro·nounce·abil·i·ty

pro·nounce·able

pro·nounced

pro·nounce·ment

pron·to

pro·nun·ci·a·men·to,
n. pl.
  pro·nun·ci·a·men·tos

or
  pro·nun·ci·a·men·toes

pro·nun·ci·a·tion

proof·read

proof·read·er

prop, v. propped,
  prop·ping

pro·pa·gan·da

pro·pa·gan·dist

pro·pa·gan·dize, v.
  pro·pa·gan·dized,
  pro·pa·gan·diz·ing

prop·a·gate, v.
  prop·a·gat·ed,
  prop·a·gat·ing

prop·a·ga·tion

pro·pane

pro·pel, v.
  pro·pelled,
  pro·pel·ling

pro·pel·lant

pro·pel·ler

pro·pen·si·ty, n. pl.
  pro·pen·si·ties

prop·er

prop·er·tied

prop·er·ty, n. pl.
  prop·er·ties

proph·e·cy (occas.
  proph·e·sy)
  (PREDICTION),
  n. pl.
  proph·e·cies
  (occas.
  proph·e·sies) (see
  also prophesy)

proph·e·sy (TO
  PREDICT), v.
  proph·e·sied,
  proph·e·sy·ing

(*see also*
prophecy)

proph·et

proph·et·ess

pro·phet·ic

pro·phet·i·cal

pro·phet·i·cal·ly

pro·phy·lac·tic

pro·phy·lax·is, *n.*
  pl. pro·phy·lax·es

pro·pin·qui·ty

pro·pi·ti·ate, *v.*
  pro·pi·ti·at·ed,
  pro·pi·ti·at·ing

pro·pi·ti·a·tion

pro·pi·tia·to·ry

pro·pi·tious

pro·pi·tious·ly

pro·pi·tious·ness

prop·jet

prop·man, *n. pl.*
  prop·men

pro·po·nent

pro·por·tion

pro·por·tion·able

pro·por·tion·ably

pro·por·tion·al

pro·por·tion·al·ly

pro·por·tion·ate

pro·por·tion·ate·ly

pro·pos·al

pro·pose, *v.*
  pro·posed,
  pro·pos·ing

pro·pos·er

prop·o·si·tion

pro·pound

pro·pri·e·tary, *n.*
  pl. pro·pri·e·tar·ies

pro·pri·e·tor

pro·pri·e·tress

pro·pri·e·ty, *n. pl.*
  pro·pri·e·ties

pro·pul·sion

pro·pul·sive

pro ra·ta

pro·rate, *v.*
  pro·rat·ed,
  pro·rat·ing

pro·ro·ga·tion

pro·rogue, *v.*
  pro·rogued,
  pro·rogu·ing

pro·sa·ic

pro·sa·i·cal·ly

pro·sce·ni·um

pro·sciut·to, *n. pl.*
  pro·sciut·ti *or*
  pro·sciut·tos

pro·scribe, *v.*
  pro·scribed,
  pro·scrib·ing

pro·scrib·er

pro·scrip·tion

pro·scrip·tive

pro·scrip·tive·ly

pros·e·cut·able

pros·e·cute, *v.*
  pros·e·cut·ed,
  pros·e·cut·ing

pros·e·cu·tion

pros·e·cu·tor

pros·e·lyte, *v.*
  pros·e·lyt·ed,
  pros·e·lyt·ing

pros·e·ly·tism

pros·e·ly·tize, *v.*
  pros·e·ly·tized,
  pros·e·ly·tiz·ing

pro·sem·i·nar

pros·o·dy, *n. pl.*
  pros·o·dies

pros·pect

pro·spec·tive

pro·spec·tive·ly

pros·pec·tor

pro·spec·tus

pros·per

pros·per·i·ty, *n. pl.*
  pros·per·i·ties

pros·per·ous

pros·per·ous·ly

pros·per·ous·ness

pros·tate (GLAND)
  (*see also*
  prostrate)

pros·the·sis, *n. pl.*
  pros·the·ses

pros·thet·ic

pros·ti·tute, *v.*
  pros·ti·tut·ed,
  pros·ti·tut·ing

pros·ti·tu·tion

pros·trate (LYING
  FACEDOWN), *v.*
  pros·trat·ed,
  pros·trat·ing
  (*see also*
  prostate)

pros·tra·tion

prosy, *adj.*
  pros·i·er,
  pros·i·est

pro·tac·tin·i·um

pro·tag·o·nist

pro·te·an

pro·tect

pro·tec·tion

pro·tec·tion·ism

pro·tec·tion·ist

pro·tec·tive

pro·tec·tive·ly

pro·tec·tive·ness

pro·tec·tor

pro·tec·tor·ate

pro·tec·tress

pro·té·gé (*masc.*)

pro·té·gée (*fem.*)

pro·tein

pro tem

pro tem·po·re

Pro·tero·zo·ic

pro·test

Prot·es·tant

Prot·es·tant·ism

pro·tes·ta·tion

pro·tho·rax

pro·to·col

pro·to·his·to·ry

pro·ton

pro·to·plasm

pro·to·type

pro·to·typ·i·cal

pro·to·zo·an, *n. pl.*
pro·to·zoa

pro·tract

pro·trac·tion

pro·trac·tor

pro·trude, *v.*
pro·trud·ed,
pro·trud·ing

pro·tru·sion

pro·tru·sive

pro·tru·sive·ly

pro·tu·ber·ance

pro·tu·ber·ant

proud·ly

prov·able

prov·ably

prove, *v.* proved,
proved *or*
prov·en, prov·ing

prov·e·nance

prov·en·der

pro·ve·nience

prov·erb

pro·ver·bi·al

pro·ver·bi·al·ly

pro·vide, *v.*
pro·vid·ed,
pro·vid·ing

prov·i·dence

prov·i·dent

prov·i·den·tial

prov·i·den·tial·ly

prov·i·dent·ly

pro·vid·er

pro·vid·ing

prov·ince

pro·vin·cial

pro·vin·cial·ism

pro·vin·cial·ly

pro·vi·sion

pro·vi·sion·al

pro·vi·sion·al·ly

pro·vi·so, *n. pl.*
pro·vi·sos *or*
pro·vi·soes

pro·vi·so·ry

prov·o·ca·tion

pro·voc·a·tive

pro·voc·a·tive·ly

pro·voc·a·tive·ness

pro·voke, *v.*
pro·voked,
pro·vok·ing

pro·vok·ing

pro·vost

pro·vost mar·shal

prow·ess

prowl

prowl·er

prox·i·mal

prox·i·mal·ly

prox·i·mate

prox·im·i·ty

prox·i·mo

proxy, *n. pl.*
prox·ies

pru·dence

pru·dent

pru·den·tial

pru·dent·ly

prud·ery

prud·ish

prud·ish·ly

prud·ish·ness

prune, *v.* pruned,
prun·ing

pru·nel·la

pru·ri·ence

pru·ri·ent

pru·ri·ent·ly

pry, *n. pl.* pries

pry, *v.* pried,
pry·ing

psalm

psalm·book

psalm·ist

psalm·o·dy

Psal·ter

psal·tery (*occas.* psal·try), *n. pl.* psal·ter·ies (*occas.* psal·tries)

pseu·do

pseu·do·nym

pseu·don·y·mous

pseu·don·y·mous·ly

pseu·do·sci·en·tif·ic

psit·ta·co·sis

pso·ri·a·sis

psych, *v.* psyched, psych·ing

psyche

psy·che·del·ia

psy·che·del·ic

psy·che·del·i·cal·ly

psy·chi·at·ric

psy·chi·at·ri·cal·ly

psy·chi·a·trist

psy·chi·a·try

psy·chic

psy·chi·cal

psy·chi·cal·ly

psy·cho, *n. pl.* psy·chos

psy·cho·anal·y·sis

psy·cho·an·a·lyst

psy·cho·an·a·lyt·ic

psy·cho·an·a·lyt·i·cal·ly

psy·cho·an·a·lyze, *v.* psy·cho·an·a·lyzed, psy·cho·an·a·lyz·ing

psy·cho·bab·ble

psy·cho·bi·og·ra·phy

psy·cho·bi·o·log·i·cal

psy·cho·bi·ol·o·gy

psy·cho·chem·i·cal

psy·cho·dra·ma

psy·cho·dy·nam·ic

psy·cho·dy·nam·i·cal·ly

psy·cho·dy·nam·ics

psy·cho·gen·e·sis

psy·cho·ge·net·ic

psy·cho·his·to·ry

psy·cho·log·i·cal

psy·cho·log·i·cal·ly

psy·chol·o·gist

psy·chol·o·gy, *n. pl.* psy·chol·o·gies

psy·cho·met·ric

psy·cho·met·ri·cal·ly

psy·cho·met·rics

psy·cho·mo·tor

psy·cho·neu·ro·sis, *n. pl.* psy·cho·neu·ro·ses

psy·cho·neu·rot·ic

psy·cho·path

psy·cho·path·ic

psy·cho·path·i·cal·ly

psy·cho·path·o·log·i·cal

psy·cho·phar·ma·ceu·ti·cal

psy·cho·sis, *n. pl.* psy·cho·ses

psy·cho·so·mat·ic

psy·cho·so·mat·i·cal·ly

psy·cho·ther·a·pist

psy·chot·ic

psy·chot·i·cal·ly

ptar·mi·gan, *n. pl.* ptar·mi·gan *or* ptar·mi·gans

ptero·dac·tyl

pto·maine

pu·ber·ty

pu·bes·cence

pu·bes·cent

pu·bic, *n. pl.* pubes

pub·lic

pub·li·ca·tion

pub·li·cist

pub·lic·i·ty

pub·li·cize, *v.* pub·li·cized, pub·li·ciz·ing

pub·lic·ly

pub·lic-spir·it·ed

pub·lic-spir·it·ed·ness

pub·lish

pub·lish·able

pub·lish·er

puck·er

puck·ish

puck·ish·ly

puck·ish·ness

pud·ding

pud·dle, *v.* pud·dled, pud·dling

pu·den·dum, *n. pl.* pu·den·da

pudg·i·ness

pudgy, *adj.*

pudg·i·er,
pudg·i·est

Pueb·la

Pueb·lo (INDIANS, CITY)

pueb·lo (ADOBE HOUSE), *n. pl.* pueb·los

pu·re·ile

pu·er·il·i·ty

pu·er·per·al

Puer·to Ri·can

Puer·to Ri·co

puff·ball

puff·ery

puf·fin

puffy, *adj.* puff·i·er, puff·i·est

pu·gi·lism

pu·gi·list

pu·gi·lis·tic

pug·na·cious

pug·na·cious·ly

pug·na·cious·ness

pug·nac·i·ty

pu·is·sance

pu·is·sant

puke, *v.* puked, puk·ing

puk·ka

pul, *n. pl.* puls *or* pul

pul·chri·tude

pul·chri·tu·di·nous

pull·back

pul·let

pul·ley, *n. pl.* pul·leys

pull·out

pull·over

pul·mo·nary

pul·mo·tor

pulp·i·ness

pul·pit

pulp·wood

pulpy, *adj.* pulp·i·er, pulp·i·est

pul·sar

pul·sate, *v.* pul·sat·ed, pul·sat·ing

pul·sa·tion

pul·sa·tor

pulse, *v.* pulsed, puls·ing

pul·ver·i·za·tion

pul·ver·ize, *v.* pul·ver·ized, pul·ver·iz·ing

pu·ma, *n. pl.* pu·mas *or* pu·ma

pum·ice

pum·mel, *v.* pum·meled (*occas.* pum·melled), pum·mel·ing (*occas.* pum·mel·ling)

pum·per·nick·el

pump·kin

pun, *v.* punned, pun·ning

punch·board

punch-drunk

pun·cheon

punch·er

punc·til·io, *n. pl.* punc·til·i·os

punc·til·i·ous

punc·til·i·ous·ly

punc·til·i·ous·ness

punc·tu·al

punc·tu·al·i·ty

punc·tu·al·ly

punc·tu·ate, *v.* punc·tu·at·ed, punc·tu·at·ing

punc·tu·a·tion

punc·ture, *v.* punc·tured, punc·tur·ing

pun·dit

pun·gen·cy

pun·gent

pun·gent·ly

pu·ni·ly

pu·ni·ness

pun·ish

pun·ish·able

pun·ish·ment

pu·ni·tive

pu·ni·tive·ly

pu·ni·tive·ness

pun·ster

punt·er

pu·ny, *adj.* pu·ni·er, pu·ni·est

pu·pa, *n. pl.* pu·pae *or* pu·pas

pu·pil

pup·pet

pup·pe·teer

pup·pe·try

pup·py, *n. pl.*
  pup·pies

pur·blind

pur·chas·able

pur·chase, *v.*
  pur·chased,
  pur·chas·ing

pur·chas·er

pur·dah

pure·bred

pu·ree, *v.* pu·reed,
  pu·ree·ing

pure·ly

pur·ga·tion

pur·ga·tive

pur·ga·to·ry, *n. pl.*
  pur·ga·to·ries

purge, *v.* purged,
  purg·ing

pu·ri·fi·ca·tion

pu·ri·fi·ca·to·ry

pu·ri·fi·er

pu·ri·fy, *v.*
  pu·ri·fied,
  pu·ri·fy·ing

Pu·rim

pur·ism

pur·ist

pu·ri·tan

pu·ri·tan·i·cal

pu·ri·tan·i·cal·ly

pu·ri·ty

purl

pur·lieu

pur·loin

pur·ple, *v.*
  pur·pled,
  pur·pling

pur·plish

pur·port

pur·pose, *v.*
  pur·posed,
  pur·pos·ing

pur·pose·ful

pur·pose·ful·ly

pur·pose·ful·ness

pur·pose·less

pur·pose·less·ness

pur·pose·ly

purse, *v.* pursed,
  purs·ing

purs·er

purs·lane

pur·su·ance

pur·su·ant

pur·sue, *v.*
  pur·sued,
  pur·su·ing

pur·su·er

pur·suit

pu·ru·lence

pu·ru·lent

pur·vey

pur·vey·ance

pur·vey·or

pur·view

Pu·san

push·cart

push·er

push·over

push·pin

pushy, *adj.*

push·i·er,
  push·i·est

pu·sil·la·nim·i·ty

pu·sil·lan·i·mous

pu·sil·lan·i·mous·ly

pussy, *n. pl.*
  puss·ies

pussy·foot

pus·tu·lant

pus·tule

put (PLACE), *v.*
  put, put·ting
  (*see also* putt)

pu·ta·tive

put·down, *n.*

put down, *v.*

put-on, *adj., n.*

put on, *v.*

put·out, *n.*

put out, *v.*

pu·tre·fac·tion

pu·tre·fy, *v.*
  pu·tre·fied,
  pu·tre·fy·ing

pu·tres·cence

pu·tres·cent

pu·trid

putsch

putt (GOLF
  STROKE), *v.*
  putt·ed, putt·ing
  (*see also* put)

put·tee

put·ter (ONE WHO
  PUTS)

putt·er (GOLF
  CLUB)

put·ty, *v.* put·tied,
  put·ty·ing

puz·zle, *v.*
  puz·zled,
  puz·zling

puz·zle·ment

puz·zler

pya

pyg·my, *pl.*
  pyg·mies

py·lon

py·lo·rus, *n. pl.*
  py·lo·ri

py·or·rhea

pyr·a·mid

pyr·a·mi·dal

pyre

py·re·thrum

Py·rex®

py·rite, *n. pl.*
  py·rites

py·rol·y·sis

py·ro·ma·nia

py·ro·ma·ni·ac

py·rom·e·ter

py·ro·tech·nics

py·rox·y·lin

pyr·rhic

py·thon

Q

Qa·tar
Qa·tari
Qi·a·na™
qin·tar
Quaa·lude™
quack·ery
quack·ish
quack·ish·ly
quad
quad·ran·gle
qua·dran·gu·lar
quad·rant
quad·ra·phon·ic
qua·drat·ic
qua·drat·ics
quad·ra·ture
qua·dren·ni·al
qua·dren·ni·al·ly
qua·dren·ni·um, n.
  pl.
  qua·dren·ni·ums
  or qua·dren·nia
quad·ri·ceps
quad·ri·lat·er·al
quad·ri·lat·er·al·ly
qua·drille

qua·dril·lion
quad·ri·par·tite
quad·ri·phony
quad·ri·ple·gic
qua·droon
quad·ru·ped
qua·dru·ple, v.
  qua·dru·pled,
  qua·dru·pling
qua·drup·let
qua·dru·pli·cate, v.
  qua·dru·pli·cat·ed,
  qua·dru·pli·cat·ing
quaff
quag·mire
qua·hog (occas.
  qua·haug)
quail, n. pl. quail
  or quails
quaint·ly
quaint·ness
quake, v. quaked,
  quak·ing
Quak·er
qual·i·fi·ca·tion
qual·i·fied
qual·i·fi·er
qual·i·fy, v.

qual·i·fied,
  qual·i·fy·ing
qual·i·ta·tive
qual·i·ty, n. pl.
  qual·i·ties
qualm
quan·da·ry, n. pl.
  quan·da·ries
quan·ti·fi·able
quan·ti·fi·ca·tion
quan·ti·fi·er
quan·ti·fy, v.
  quan·ti·fied,
  quan·ti·fy·ing
quan·ti·ta·tive
quan·ti·ta·tive·ly
quan·ti·ta·tive·ness
quan·ti·ty, n. pl.
  quan·ti·ties
quan·tum, n. pl.
  quan·ta
quar·an·tin·able
quar·an·tine, v.
  quar·an·tined,
  quar·an·tin·ing
quark
quar·rel, v.
  quar·reled or
  quar·relled,

quar·rel·ing *or*
quar·rel·ling

quar·rel·some

quar·ry, *n. pl.*
quar·ries

quart

quar·ter

quar·ter·back

quar·ter·deck

quar·tered

quar·ter·final

quar·ter·ly

quar·ter·mas·ter

quar·ter·saw

quar·tet (*occas.*
quar·tette)

quar·tile

quar·to, *n. pl.*
quar·tos

quartz

quartz·ite

qua·sar

quash

qua·si

qua·si-ju·di·cial

qua·ter·na·ry, *n. pl.*
qua·ter·na·ries

qua·train

qua·ver

qua·ver·ing

qua·ver·ing·ly

quay

queas·i·ly

queas·i·ness

quea·sy (*occas.*
quea·zy), *adj.*
quea·si·er,
quea·si·est

Que·bec *or*
Qué·bec

Que·be·cois *or*
Qué·be·cois, *n.*
pl. Que·be·cois
or Qué·be·cois

que·bra·cho, *n. pl.*
que·bra·chos

queen·like

queer·ly

quell

quench·able

Que·ré·ta·ro

quer·u·lous

quer·u·lous·ly

quer·u·lous·ness

que·ry, *n. pl.*
que·ries

que·sa·dil·la

quest

ques·tion

ques·tion·able

ques·tion·ably

ques·tion·naire

quet·zal, *n. pl.*
quet·zals, *or*
quet·za·les

queue, *v.* queued,
queu·ing

quib·ble, *v.*
quib·bled,
quib·bling

quick·en

quick-freeze, *v.*
quick-froze,
quick-froz·en,
quick-freez·ing

quick·ie

quick·lime

quick·ly

quick·ness

quick·sand

quick·sil·ver

quick·step

quick-tem·pered

quick-wit·ted

quick-wit·ted·ly

quick-wit·ted·ness

quid, *n. pl.* quid
(*occas.* quids)

quid·nunc

quid pro quo

qui·es·cence

qui·es·cent

qui·et·ly

qui·et·ness

qui·e·tude

qui·e·tus

quill·wort

quilt·ing

quince

qui·nie·la *or*
qui·nel·la

qui·nine

quin·quen·ni·al

quin·quen·ni·al·ly

quin·sy

quin·tal

Quin·ta·na Roo

quin·tes·sence

quint·es·sen·tial

quin·tet (*occas.*
quin·tette)

quin·til·lion

quin·tu·ple, *v.*

quin·tu·pled,
quin·tu·pling
quin·tup·let
quin·tu·pli·cate, *v.*
quin·tu·pli·cat·ed,
quin·tu·pli·cat·ing
quip, *v.* quipped,
quip·ping
quire
quirk
quirk·i·ly
quirk·i·ness
quirky, *adj.*
quirk·i·er,
quirk·i·est
quirt

quis·ling
quit, *v.* quit (*occas.*
quit·ted),
quit·ting
quit·claim
quite
quit·tance
quit·ter
quiv·er
quix·ot·ic
quix·ot·i·cal·ly
quiz, *n. pl.* quiz·zes
quiz, *v.* quizzed,
quiz·zing

quiz·mas·ter
quiz·zi·cal
quiz·zi·cal·ly
quoit
quon·dam
Quon·set℠
quo·rum
quo·ta
quot·able
quo·ta·tion
quote, *v.* quot·ed,
quot·ing
quo·tid·i·an
quo·tient

R

rab·bet (GROOVE)
  (*see also* rabbit)
rab·bi
rab·bin·ate
rab·bin·ic
rab·bin·i·cal
rab·bit (ANIMAL),
  n. pl. rab·bit *or*
  rab·bits (*see also*
  rabbet)
rab·ble, *v.*
  rab·bled,
  rab·bling
rab·ble-rous·er
rab·ble-rous·ing
ra·bid
ra·bies
rac·coon, *n. pl.*
  rac·coon *or*
  rac·coons
race, *v.* raced,
  rac·ing
race·course
race·horse
ra·ceme
rac·er
race·track
race·way

Ra·chel
ra·chis, *n. pl.*
  ra·chis·es *or*
  ra·chi·des
ra·cial
ra·cial·ism
ra·cial·ly
rac·i·ly
rac·i·ness
rac·ing
rac·ism
rac·ist
rack·et
rack·e·teer
rack·e·teer·ing
ra·con·teur
rac·quet·ball
racy, *adj.* rac·i·er,
  rac·i·est
ra·dar
ra·dar·scope
ra·di·al
ra·di·al·ly
ra·di·ance
ra·di·an·cy
ra·di·ant
ra·di·ant·ly

ra·di·ate, *v.*
  ra·di·at·ed,
  ra·di·at·ing
ra·di·a·tion
ra·di·a·tor
rad·i·cal
rad·i·cal·ism
rad·i·cal·ly
ra·dic·chio, *n. pl.*
  ra·dic·chios
ra·dio, *n. pl.*
  ra·di·os
ra·dio, *v.* ra·di·oed,
  ra·di·o·ing
ra·dio·ac·tive
ra·dio·ac·tive·ly
ra·dio·ac·tiv·i·ty
ra·dio·car·bon
ra·dio·gen·ic
ra·dio·gram
ra·dio·graph
ra·di·og·ra·phy
ra·dio·iso·tope
ra·di·ol·o·gist
ra·di·ol·o·gy
ra·di·om·e·ter

ra·di·o·pho·to, *n. pl.*
　ra·di·o·pho·tos

ra·di·os·co·py

ra·di·o·sonde

ra·di·o·tel·e·graph

ra·di·o·te·leg·ra·phy

ra·di·o·tele·phone

ra·di·o·ther·a·pist

ra·di·o·ther·a·py

rad·ish

ra·di·um

ra·di·us, *n. pl.*
　ra·dii *or*
　ra·di·us·es

ra·dix, *n. pl.*
　ra·di·ces *or*
　ra·dix·es

ra·dome

ra·don

raf·fia

raf·fish

raf·fish·ly

raf·fish·ness

raf·fle, *v.* raf·fled,
　raf·fling

raf·ter

rag·a·muf·fin

rag·bag

rage, *v.* raged,
　rag·ing

rag·ged

rag·ged·ly

rag·ged·ness

rag·gedy

rag·ing

rag·lan

ra·gout

rag·pick·er

rag·time

rag·top

rag·weed

rail·head

rail·ing

rail·lery

rail·road

rail·road·ing

rail-split·ter

rail·way

rai·ment

rain

rain·bow

rain·coat

rain·drop

rain·fall

Rai·nier, Mount

rain·less

rain·mak·ing

rain·proof

rain·storm

rain·wa·ter

rain·wear

rainy, *adj.* rain·i·er,
　rain·i·est

raise, *v.*, raised,
　rais·ing

rai·sin

rai·son d'être

ra·ja *or* ra·jah

rake, *v.* raked,
　rak·ing

rak·ish

rak·ish·ly

rak·ish·ness

Ra·leigh

ral·len·tan·do

ral·ly, *n. pl.* ral·lies

ral·ly, *v.* ral·lied,
　ral·ly·ing

ral·ly·ist

ram, *v.* rammed,
　ram·ming

ram·ble, *v.*
　ram·bled,
　ram·bling

ram·bler

ram·bunc·tious

ram·bunc·tious·ly

ram·bunc·tious·ness

ram·e·kin *or*
　ram·e·quin

ra·mie

ram·i·fi·ca·tion

ram·i·fy, *v.*
　ram·i·fied,
　ram·i·fy·ing

ram·jet

ram·page, *v.*
　ram·paged,
　ram·pag·ing

ram·pa·geous

ram·pa·geous·ly

ram·pa·geous·ness

ram·pan·cy

ram·pant

ram·pant·ly

ram·part

ram·rod

ram·shack·le

ranch·er

ran·che·ro, *n. pl.*
　ran·che·ros

ran·cho, *n. pl.*
　ran·chos

ran·cid

ran·cid·i·ty

ran·cid·ly

ran·cid·ness

ran·cor

ran·cor·ous

ran·cor·ous·ly

rand (SOUTH
AFRICAN
CURRENCY), n.
pl. rand

ran·dom

ran·dom-ac·cess

ran·dom·iza·tion

ran·dom·ize, pl.
ran·dom·ized,
ran·dom·iz·ing

ran·dom·ly

ran·dom·ness

ran·dy

range, v. ranged,
rang·ing

rang·er

rang·i·ness

Ran·goon (now
Yangon)

rangy, adj.
rang·i·er,
rang·i·est

ra·ni or ra·nee

rank·ing

ran·kle, v.
ran·kled,
ran·kling

ran·sack

ran·som

rant·er

rap, v. rapped,
rap·ping

ra·pa·cious

ra·pa·cious·ly

ra·pa·cious·ness

ra·pac·i·ty

rape, v. raped,
rap·ing

rape·seed

rap·id

rap·id-fire

ra·pid·i·ty

rap·id·ly

rap·id·ness

ra·pi·er

rap·ine

rap·ist

rap·pen, n. pl.
rap·pen

rap·per

rap·port

rap·proche·ment

rap·scal·lion

rapt

rapt·ly

rapt·ness

rap·ture

rap·tur·ous

rap·tur·ous·ly

rap·tur·ous·ness

ra·ra avis, n. pl.
ra·ra avis·es or
ra·rae aves

rare, adj. rar·er,
rar·est

rare·bit

rar·efac·tion

rar·efy (occas.
rar·ify), v.
rar·e·fied,
rar·e·fy·ing

rare·ly

rar·i·ty, n. pl.
rar·i·ties

ras·cal

ras·cal·i·ty, n. pl.
ras·cal·i·ties

ras·cal·ly

rash·er

rash·ly

rash·ness

rasp·ber·ry, n. pl.
rasp·ber·ries

raspy, adj.
rasp·i·er,
rasp·i·est

rat, v. rat·ted,
rat·ting

ratch·et

rate, v. rat·ed,
rat·ing

rate·pay·er

rath·er

raths·kel·ler

rat·i·fi·ca·tion

rat·i·fy, v. rat·i·fied,
rat·i·fy·ing

ra·ti·né or ra·tine

rat·ing

ra·tio, n. pl. ra·tios

ra·ti·o·ci·nate, v.
ra·ti·o·ci·nat·ed,
ra·ti·o·ci·nat·ing

ra·ti·o·ci·na·tion

ra·tion

ra·tio·nal

ra·tio·nale

ra·tio·nal·ism

ra·tio·nal·ist

ra·tio·nal·is·tic

ra·tio·nal·i·ty, *n. pl.*
  ra·tio·nal·i·ties

ra·tio·nal·iza·tion

ra·tio·nal·ize, *v.*
  ra·tio·nal·ized,
  ra·tio·nal·iz·ing

ra·tio·nal·ly

rat·line

rat·tan

rat·teen

rat·tle, *v.* rat·tled,
  rat·tling

rat·tle·brain

rat·tle·brained

rat·tler

rat·tle·snake

rat·tle·trap

rat·tling

rat·trap

rat·ty, *adj.* rat·ti·er,
  rat·ti·est

rau·cous

rau·cous·ly

rau·cous·ness

raun·chi·ness

raun·chy, *adj.*
  raun·chi·er,
  raun·chi·est

rau·wol·fia

rav·age, *v.*
  rav·aged,
  rav·ag·ing

rav·ag·er

rave, *v.* raved,
  rav·ing

rav·el, *v.* rav·eled
  or rav·elled,

rav·el·ing *or*
  rav·el·ling

ra·ven

rav·en·ous

rav·en·ous·ly

rav·en·ous·ness

ra·vine

rav·i·oli, *n. pl.*
  rav·i·oli *or*
  rav·i·olis

rav·ish

rav·ish·ing

rav·ish·ing·ly

raw·boned

raw·hide

ra·win·sonde

Ray·mond

ray·on

raze

ra·zor

ra·zor·backed *or*
  ra·zor·back

ra·zor·bill

raz·zle-daz·zle

razz·ma·tazz

reach·able

re·act

re·ac·tion

re·ac·tion·ary, *n.*
  pl. re·ac·tion·ar·ies

re·ac·ti·vate, *v.*
  re·ac·ti·vat·ed,
  re·ac·ti·vat·ing

re·ac·ti·va·tion

re·ac·tive

re·ac·tive·ly

re·ac·tive·ness

re·ac·tiv·i·ty

re·ac·tor

read·abil·i·ty

read·able

read·ably

read·er

read·i·ly

read·i·ness

read·ing

read·out

ready, *adj.*
  read·i·er,
  read·i·est

ready-made

ready-to-wear

re·agent

re·al

re·al·ism

re·al·ist

re·al·is·tic

re·al·is·ti·cal·ly

re·al·i·ty (REAL), *n.*
  pl. re·al·i·ties
  (*see also* realty)

re·al·iz·able

re·al·iza·tion

re·al·ize, *v.*
  re·al·ized,
  re·al·iz·ing

re·al-life

re·al·ly

realm

re·al·po·li·tik

re·al-time

re·al·tor

re·al·ty (REAL
  ESTATE) (*see
  also* reality)

ream·er

reap·er

re·ap·pear

re·ap·praise, *v.*
re·ap·praised,
re·ap·prais·ing

re·arm

re·ar·ma·ment

rear·most

re·ar·range, *v.*
re·ar·ranged,
re·ar·rang·ing

rear·ward (*occas.*
rear·wards)

rea·son

rea·son·abil·i·ty

rea·son·able

rea·son·ably

rea·son·ing

re·as·sur·ance

re·as·sure, *v.*
re·as·sured,
re·as·sur·ing

re·bate, *v.*
re·bat·ed,
re·bat·ing

Re·bec·ca

reb·el, *n.*

re·bel, *v.* re·belled,
re·bel·ling

re·bel·lion

re·bel·lious

re·bel·lious·ly

re·bel·lious·ness

re·birth

re·born

re·bound

re·broad·cast

re·buff

re·build, *v.* re·built,
re·build·ing

re·buke, *v.* re·buked,
re·buk·ing

re·bus

re·but, *v.* re·but·ted,
re·but·ting

re·but·tal

re·cal·ci·trance

re·cal·ci·trant

re·cal·ci·trant·ly

re·cal·cu·late, *v.*
re·cal·cu·lat·ed,
re·cal·cu·lat·ing

re·cal·cu·la·tion

re·call

re·call·able

re·cant

re·can·ta·tion

re·cap, *v.*
re·capped,
re·cap·ping

re·ca·pit·u·late, *v.*
re·ca·pit·u·lat·ed,
re·ca·pit·u·lat·ing

re·ca·pit·u·la·tion

re·cap·pa·ble

re·cap·ture, *v.*
re·cap·tured,
re·cap·tur·ing

re·cast

re·cede, *v.*
re·ced·ed,
re·ced·ing

re·ceipt

re·ceiv·able

re·ceive, *v.*
re·ceived,
re·ceiv·ing

re·ceiv·er

re·ceiv·er·ship

re·cen·cy

re·cen·sion

re·cent

re·cent·ly

re·cep·ta·cle

re·cep·tion

re·cep·tion·ist

re·cep·tive

re·cep·tive·ly

re·cep·tive·ness

re·cep·tiv·i·ty

re·cep·tor

re·cess

re·ces·sion

re·ces·sion·al

re·ces·sive

re·ces·sive·ly

re·ces·sive·ness

re·charge, *v.*
re·charged,
re·charg·ing

re·cher·ché

re·cid·i·vism

re·cid·i·vist

rec·i·pe

re·cip·i·ent

re·cip·ro·cal

re·cip·ro·cal·ly

re·cip·ro·cate, *v.*
re·cip·ro·cat·ed,
re·cip·ro·cat·ing

re·cip·ro·ca·tion

rec·i·proc·i·ty, *n. pl.*
rec·i·proc·i·ties

re·ci·sion

re·cit·al

rec·i·ta·tion

rec·i·ta·tive

re·cite, *v.* re·cit·ed,
re·cit·ing

reck·less

reck·less·ly

reck·less·ness

reck·on

reck·on·ing

re·claim

re·claim·able

rec·la·ma·tion

re·cline, *v.*
re·clined,
re·clin·ing

re·clin·er

re·cluse

re·clu·sive

rec·og·ni·tion

rec·og·niz·abil·i·ty

rec·og·niz·able

rec·og·niz·ably

re·cog·ni·zance

rec·og·nize, *v.*
rec·og·nized,
rec·og·niz·ing

re·coil

re·coil·less

rec·ol·lect

rec·ol·lec·tion

re·com·bi·nant

re·com·bi·na·tion

rec·om·mend

rec·om·mend·able

rec·om·men·da·tion

re·com·mit, *v.*
re·com·mit·ted,
re·com·mit·ting

re·com·mit·tal

rec·om·pense, *v.*
rec·om·pensed,
rec·om·pens·ing

rec·on·cil·abil·i·ty

rec·on·cil·able

rec·on·cile, *v.*
rec·on·ciled,
rec·on·cil·ing

rec·on·cil·i·a·tion

re·con·dite

re·con·di·tion

re·con·firm

re·con·fir·ma·tion

re·con·nais·sance

re·con·noi·ter

re·con·sid·er

re·con·sid·er·a·tion

re·con·sti·tute, *v.*
re·con·sti·tut·ed,
re·con·sti·tut·ing

re·con·struct

re·con·struc·tion

re·con·ver·sion

re·con·vert

rec·ord, *n.*

re·cord, *v.*

re·cord·er

re·cord·ing

re·cord·ist

re·count

re·coup

re·course

re·cov·er (GET
BACK)

re-cov·er (COVER
AGAIN)

re·cov·er·able

re·cov·ery

rec·re·ant

rec·re·ate (TO
REFRESH), *v.*
rec·re·at·ed,
rec·re·at·ing

re-cre·ate (TO
CREATE
ANEW), *v.* re-
cre·at·ed, re-
cre·at·ing

rec·re·a·tion (PLAY)

re-cre·a·tion
(RENEWAL)

rec·re·a·tion·al

re·crim·i·nate, *v.*
re·crim·i·nat·ed,
re·crim·i·nat·ing

re·crim·i·na·tion

re·crim·i·na·to·ry

re·cru·des·cence

re·cru·des·cent

re·cruit

rec·tal

rect·an·gle

rect·an·gu·lar

rec·ti·fi·able

rec·ti·fi·ca·tion

rec·ti·fi·er

rec·ti·fy, *v.*
rec·ti·fied,
rec·ti·fy·ing

rec·ti·lin·ear

rec·ti·tude

rec·to, *n. pl.* rec·tos

rec·tor

rec·to·ry, *n. pl.*
rec·to·ries

rec·tum, *n. pl.*

rec·tums *or* rec·ta

re·cum·ben·cy

re·cum·bent

re·cu·per·ate, *v.* re·cu·per·at·ed, re·cu·per·at·ing

re·cu·per·a·tion

re·cu·per·a·tive

re·cur, *v.* re·curred, re·cur·ring

re·cur·rence

re·cur·rent

re·cur·rent·ly

re·cy·cle, *v.* re·cy·cled, re·cy·cling

red, *adj.* red·der, red·dest

re·dact

re·dac·tion

re·dac·tor

red-blood·ed

red·cap

red-car·pet

red·coat

red·den

red·dish

red·dish·ness

re·dec·o·rate, *v.* re·dec·o·rat·ed, re·dec·o·rat·ing

re·dec·o·ra·tion

re·deem

re·deem·able

re·deem·er

re·demp·tion

re·demp·tive

re·demp·to·ry

re·de·ploy

re·de·ploy·ment

re·de·sign

re·de·vel·op

re·de·vel·op·ment

red-eye, *adj.*

red-hand·ed

red·head

red-hot

re·di·rect

re·di·rec·tion

re·dis·tri·bute, *v.* re·dis·tri·but·ed, re·dis·tri·but·ing

re·dis·tri·bu·tion

re·dis·trict

red-let·ter

red·neck

red·o·lence

red·o·lent

re·dou·ble, *v.* re·dou·bled, re·dou·bling

re·doubt

re·doubt·able

re·doubt·ably

re·dound

red·out

red-pen·cil, *v.* red-pen·ciled *or* red-pen·cilled, red-pen·cil·ing *or* red-pen·cil·ling

re·dress

red·skin

red·top

re·duce, *v.* re·duced, re·duc·ing

re·duc·ible

re·duc·tion

re·dun·dan·cy, *n. pl.* re·dun·dan·cies

re·dun·dant

re·dun·dant·ly

re·du·pli·cate, *v.* re·du·pli·cat·ed, re·du·pli·cat·ing

re·du·pli·ca·tion

red·wood

re·echo, *v.* re·echoed, re·ech·o·ing

re·ed·u·cate, *v.* re·ed·u·cat·ed, re·ed·u·cat·ing

re·ed·u·ca·tion

reedy, *adj.* reed·i·er, reed·i·est

reef·er

reek

reel

re·elect

reel-to-reel

re·em·ploy

re·en·act

re·en·try, *n. pl.* re·en·tries

re·ex·am·i·na·tion

re·ex·am·ine, *v.* re·ex·am·ined, re·ex·am·in·ing

re·fash·ion

re·fec·tion

re·fec·to·ry, *n. pl.*
re·fec·to·ries

re·fer, *v.* re·ferred,
re·fer·ring

ref·er·able

ref·er·ee

ref·er·ence

ref·er·en·dum, *n.
pl.* ref·er·en·da
or ref·er·en·dums

ref·er·ent

ref·er·en·tial

re·fer·ral

re·fill

re·fill·able

re·fi·nance, *v.*
re·fi·nanced,
re·fi·nanc·ing

re·fine, *v.* re·fined,
re·fin·ing

re·fined

re·fine·ment

re·fin·er

re·fin·ery, *n. pl.*
re·fin·er·ies

re·fin·ish

re·fit, *v.* re·fit·ted,
re·fit·ting

re·flect

re·flec·tion

re·flec·tive

re·flec·tive·ly

re·flec·tive·ness

re·flec·tiv·i·ty

re·flec·tor

re·flex

re·flex·ive

re·flex·ive·ly

re·flex·ive·ness

re·for·est

re·for·es·ta·tion

re-form (IMPROVE)

re-form (FORM
AGAIN)

ref·or·ma·tion

re·for·ma·to·ry, *n.
pl.*
re·for·ma·to·ries

re·form·er

re·fract

re·frac·tion

re·frac·tive

re·frac·tive·ly

re·frac·tive·ness

re·frac·tor

re·frac·to·ry, *n. pl.*
re·frac·to·ries

re·frain

re·fran·gi·ble

re·fresh

re·fresh·er

re·fresh·ing

re·fresh·ing·ly

re·fresh·ment

re·frig·er·ant

re·frig·er·ate, *v.*
re·frig·er·at·ed,
re·frig·er·at·ing

re·frig·er·a·tion

re·frig·er·a·tor

re·fu·el, *v.*
re·fu·eled *or*
re·fu·elled,
re·fu·el·ing *or*
re·fu·el·ling

ref·uge

ref·u·gee

re·ful·gence

re·ful·gent

re·fund

re·fund·able

re·fur·bish

re·fus·al

ref·use, *n.*

re·fuse, *v.* re·fused,
re·fus·ing

re·fuse·nik

re·fut·able

re·fut·ably

ref·u·ta·tion

re·fute, *v.* re·fut·ed,
re·fut·ing

re·gain

re·gal (ROYAL)

re·gale
(ENTERTAIN),
v. re·galed,
re·gal·ing

re·ga·lia

re·gal·ly

re·gard

re·gard·ing

re·gard·less

re·gard·less·ly

re·gard·less·ness

re·gat·ta

re·gen·cy, *n. pl.*
re·gen·cies

re·gen·er·a·cy

re·gen·er·ate, *v.*
re·gen·er·at·ed,
re·gen·er·at·ing

re·gen·er·a·tion

re·gen·er·a·tive

re·gen·er·a·tor

re·gent

reg·gae

reg·i·cide

re·gime (*occas.*
  ré·gime)

reg·i·men

reg·i·ment

reg·i·men·tal

reg·i·men·ta·tion

Re·gi·na

re·gion

re·gion·al

re·gion·al·ism

re·gion·al·ly

reg·is·ter

reg·is·tered

reg·is·trant

reg·is·trar

reg·is·tra·tion

reg·is·try, *n. pl.*
  reg·is·tries

re·gress

re·gres·sion

re·gres·sive

re·gres·sive·ly

re·gres·sive·ness

re·gret, *v.*
  re·gret·ted,
  re·gret·ting

re·gret·ful

re·gret·ful·ly

re·gret·ful·ness

re·gret·ta·ble

re·gret·ta·bly

re·group

reg·u·lar

reg·u·lar·i·ty

reg·u·lar·ize, *v.*
  reg·u·lar·ized,
  reg·u·lar·iz·ing

reg·u·lar·ly

reg·u·late, *v.*
  reg·u·lat·ed,
  reg·u·lat·ing

reg·u·la·tion

reg·u·la·tor

reg·u·la·to·ry

re·gur·gi·tate, *v.*
  re·gur·gi·tat·ed,
  re·gur·gi·tat·ing

re·gur·gi·ta·tion

re·ha·bil·i·tate, *v.*
  re·ha·bil·i·tat·ed,
  re·ha·bil·i·tat·ing

re·ha·bil·i·ta·tion

re·ha·bil·i·ta·tive

re·hash

re·hear·ing

re·hears·al

re·hearse, *v.*
  re·hearsed,
  re·hears·ing

re·heat

re·hy·drate, *v.*
  re·hy·drat·ed,
  re·hy·drat·ing

re·hy·dra·tion

reichs·mark, *n. pl.*
  reichs·marks
  (*occas.*
  reichs·mark)

reign

re·im·burs·able

re·im·burse, *v.*
  re·im·bursed,
  re·im·burs·ing

re·im·burse·ment

rein

re·in·car·nate, *v.*
  re·in·car·nat·ed,
  re·in·car·nat·ing

re·in·car·na·tion

rein·deer

re·in·fect

re·in·fec·tion

re·in·force, *v.*
  re·in·forced,
  re·in·forc·ing

re·in·force·ment

re·in·state, *v.*
  re·in·stat·ed,
  re·in·stat·ing

re·in·state·ment

re·in·sur·ance

re·in·sure, *v.*
  re·in·sured,
  re·in·sur·ing

re·in·ter·pret

re·in·ter·pre·ta·tion

re·is·sue, *v.*
  re·is·sued,
  re·is·su·ing

re·it·er·ate, *v.*
  re·it·er·at·ed,
  re·it·er·at·ing

re·it·er·a·tion

re·ject

re·jec·tion

re·joice, *v.*
  re·joiced,
  re·joic·ing

re·join

re·join·der

re·ju·ve·nate, *v.*
  re·ju·ve·nat·ed,
  re·ju·ve·nat·ing

re·ju·ve·na·tion

re·lapse, *v.*
  re·lapsed,
  re·laps·ing

re·lat·able

re·late, *v.* re·lat·ed,
  re·lat·ing

re·lat·ed

re·la·tion

re·la·tion·ship

rel·a·tive

rel·a·tive·ly

rel·a·tiv·ism

rel·a·tiv·is·tic

rel·a·tiv·i·ty

re·lax

re·lax·ant

re·lax·a·tion

re·lay (CONVEY A
  MESSAGE), *v.*
  relayed,
  relay·ing

re·lay (LAY
  AGAIN), *v.* re·
  laid, re·lain, re·
  lay·ing

re·lease, *v.*
  re·leased,
  re·leas·ing

rel·e·gate, *v.*
  rel·e·gat·ed,
  rel·e·gat·ing

rel·e·ga·tion

re·lent

re·lent·less

re·lent·less·ly

re·lent·less·ness

rel·e·vance

rel·e·van·cy

rel·e·vant

rel·e·vant·ly

re·li·abil·i·ty

re·li·able

re·li·ably

re·li·ance

re·li·ant

rel·ic

re·lief

re·liev·able

re·lieve, *v.*
  re·lieved,
  re·liev·ing

re·liev·er

re·li·gion

re·li·gi·os·i·ty

re·li·gious

re·li·gious·ly

re·li·gious·ness

re·line, *v.* re·lined,
  re·lin·ing

re·lin·quish

re·lin·quish·ment

rel·i·quary, *n. pl.*
  rel·i·quar·ies

rel·ish

re·lo·cate, *v.*
  re·lo·cat·ed,
  re·lo·cat·ing

re·luc·tance

re·luc·tant

re·ly, *v.* re·lied,
  re·ly·ing

re·main

re·main·der

re·mains

re·make, *v.*

re·made,
  re·mak·ing

re·mand

re·mark

re·mark·able

re·mark·ably

re·me·di·a·ble

re·me·di·al

re·me·di·al·ly

rem·e·dy, *n. pl.*
  rem·e·dies

re·mem·ber

re·mem·brance

re·mind

rem·i·nisce, *v.*
  rem·i·nisced,
  rem·i·nisc·ing

rem·i·nis·cence

rem·i·nis·cent

re·miss

re·mis·si·ble

re·mis·sion

re·mit, *v.*
  re·mit·ted,
  re·mit·ting

re·mit·tal

re·mit·tance

rem·nant

re·mod·el, *v.*
  re·mod·eled *or*
  re·mod·elled,
  re·mod·el·ing *or*
  re·mod·el·ling

re·mon·strance

re·mon·strant

re·mon·strate, *v.*
  re·mon·strat·ed,
  re·mon·strat·ing

re·mon·stra·tion

re·mon·stra·tive

re·mon·stra·tive·ly

re·mon·stra·tor

re·morse

re·morse·ful

re·morse·ful·ly

re·morse·ful·ness

re·morse·less

re·morse·less·ly

re·morse·less·ness

re·mote, *adj.*
re·mot·er,
re·mot·est

re·mote·ly

re·mote·ness

re·mount

re·mov·abil·i·ty

re·mov·able (*occas.*
re·move·able)

re·mov·al

re·move, *v.*
re·moved,
re·mov·ing

re·mu·da

re·mu·ner·ate, *v.*
re·mu·ner·at·ed,
re·mu·ner·at·ing

re·mu·ner·a·tion

re·mu·ner·a·tive

re·mu·ner·a·tive·ly

re·mu·ner·a·tive·ness

re·mu·ner·a·tor

re·nais·sance

re·nal

re·nas·cence

re·nas·cent

rend, *v.* rent,
rend·ing

ren·der

ren·der·ing

ren·dez·vous, *n. pl.*
ren·dez·vous

ren·dez·vous, *v.*
ren·dez·voused,
ren·dez·vous·ing

ren·di·tion

ren·e·gade

re·nege, *v.*
re·neged,
re·neg·ing

re·ne·go·ti·ate, *v.*
re·ne·go·ti·at·ed,
re·ne·go·ti·at·ing

re·new

re·new·able

re·new·al

ren·net

ren·nin

re·nom·i·nate, *v.*
re·nom·i·nat·ed,
re·nom·i·nat·ing

re·nounce, *v.*
re·nounced,
re·nounc·ing

ren·o·vate, *v.*
ren·o·vat·ed,
ren·o·vat·ing

ren·o·va·tion

ren·o·va·tor

re·nown

re·nowned

rent·al

rent·er

re·num·ber

re·nun·ci·a·tion

re·oc·cur·rence

re·open

re·or·der

re·or·ga·ni·za·tion

re·or·ga·nize, *v.*
re·or·ga·nized,
re·or·ga·niz·ing

re·pack·age, *v.*
re·pack·aged,
re·pack·ag·ing

re·pair

re·pair·able

re·pair·man, *n. pl.*
re·pair·men

rep·a·ra·ble

rep·a·ra·tion

re·par·a·tive

rep·ar·tee

re·past

re·pa·tri·ate, *v.*
re·pa·tri·at·ed,
re·pa·tri·at·ing

re·pa·tri·a·tion

re·pay, *v.* re·paid,
re·pay·ing

re·pay·able

re·pay·ment

re·peal

re·peat

re·peat·ed

re·peat·ed·ly

re·peat·er

re·pel, *v.* re·pelled,
re·pel·ling

re·pel·lent

re·pent

re·pen·tance

re·pen·tant

re·per·cus·sion

rep·er·toire

rep·er·tory, *n. pl.*
  rep·er·to·ries

rep·e·ti·tion

rep·e·ti·tious

rep·e·ti·tious·ly

rep·e·ti·tious·ness

re·pet·i·tive

re·pet·i·tive·ly

re·pet·i·tive·ness

re·phrase, *v.*
  re·phrased,
  re·phras·ing

re·place, *v.*
  re·placed,
  re·plac·ing

re·place·able

re·place·ment

re·plen·ish

re·plen·ish·ment

re·plete

re·plete·ness

re·ple·tion

re·plev·in

rep·li·ca

rep·li·cate, *v.*
  rep·li·cat·ed,
  rep·li·cat·ing

rep·li·ca·tion

re·ply, *v.* re·plied,
  re·ply·ing

re·port

re·port·able

re·port·age

re·port·ed·ly

re·port·er

rep·or·to·ri·al

re·pose, *v.*

re·posed,
  re·pos·ing

re·pos·i·to·ry, *n. pl.*
  re·pos·i·to·ries

re·pos·sess

re·pos·ses·sion

rep·re·hend

rep·re·hen·si·ble

rep·re·hen·si·bly

rep·re·hen·sion

rep·re·sent

rep·re·sen·ta·tion

rep·re·sen·ta·tive

rep·re·sen·ta·tive·ly

rep·re·sen·ta·tive·ness

re·press

re·pres·sion

re·pres·sive

re·pres·sive·ly

re·pres·sive·ness

re·prieve, *v.*
  re·prieved,
  re·priev·ing

rep·ri·mand

re·print

re·pri·sal

re·prise, *v.*
  re·prised,
  re·pris·ing

re·pro, *n. pl.*
  re·pros

re·proach

re·proach·able

re·proach·ful

re·proach·ful·ly

rep·ro·bate

rep·ro·ba·tion

re·pro·duce, *v.*

re·pro·duced,
  re·pro·duc·ing

re·pro·duc·ibil·i·ty

re·pro·duc·ible

re·pro·duc·tion

re·pro·duc·tive

re·pro·duc·tive·ly

re·proof

re·prove, *v.*
  re·proved,
  re·prov·ing

re·prov·ing·ly

rep·tile

rep·til·i·an

re·pub·lic

re·pub·li·can

re·pub·li·can·ism

re·pub·li·ca·tion

Re·pub·lic of South
  Af·ri·ca

re·pub·lish

re·pu·di·ate, *v.*
  re·pu·di·at·ed,
  re·pu·di·at·ing

re·pu·di·a·tion

re·pug·nance

re·pug·nant

re·pug·nant·ly

re·pulse, *v.*
  re·pulsed,
  re·puls·ing

re·pul·sion

re·pul·sive

re·pul·sive·ly

re·pul·sive·ness

rep·u·ta·bil·i·ty

rep·u·ta·ble

rep·u·ta·bly

rep·u·ta·tion

re·pute, *v.*
  re·put·ed,
  re·put·ing

re·put·ed

re·put·ed·ly

re·quest

re·qui·em

re·quire, *v.*
  re·quired,
  re·quir·ing

re·quire·ment

req·ui·site

req·ui·si·tion

re·quit·al

re·quite, *v.*
  re·quit·ed,
  re·quit·ing

rere·dos

re·route, *v.*
  re·rout·ed,
  re·rout·ing

re·run, *v.* re·ran,
  re·run,
  re·run·ning

re·sal·able

re·sale

re·scind

re·scis·sion

re·script

res·cue, *v.*
  res·cued,
  res·cu·ing

res·cu·er

re·search

re·search·er

re·sec·tion

re·sem·blance

re·sem·ble, *v.*

re·sem·bled,
  re·sem·bling

re·sent

re·sent·ful

re·sent·ful·ly

re·sent·ful·ness

re·sent·ment

re·ser·pine

res·er·va·tion

re·serve, *v.*
  re·served,
  re·serv·ing

re·served

re·serv·ed·ly

re·serv·ed·ness

re·serv·ist

res·er·voir

res ges·tae

re·shape, v.
  re·shaped,
  re·shap·ing

re·ship, *v.*
  re·shipped,
  re·ship·ping

re·shuf·fle, *v.*
  re·shuf·fled,
  re·shuf·fling

re·side, *v.* re·sid·ed,
  re·sid·ing

res·i·dence

res·i·den·cy, *n. pl.*
  res·i·den·cies

res·i·dent

res·i·den·tial

res·i·den·tial·ly

re·sid·u·al

re·sid·u·al·ly

re·sid·u·ary

res·i·due

re·sid·u·um, *n. pl.*
  re·sid·ua

re·sign

res·ig·na·tion

re·sign·ed·ly

re·sign·ed·ness

re·sil·ience

re·sil·ien·cy

re·sil·ient

res·in

res·in·ate (TO
  TREAT WITH
  RESIN), *v.*
  res·in·at·ed,
  res·in·at·ing (*see
  also* resonate)

res·in·ous

re·sist

re·sis·tance

re·sis·tant

re·sist·er (ONE
  WHO RESISTS)
  (*see also*
  resistor)

re·sist·ible

re·sist·ive

re·sist·ive·ly

re·sist·ive·ness

re·sis·tor
  (ELECTRICAL
  RESISTANCE)
  (*see also*
  resister)

res·o·lute

res·o·lute·ly

res·o·lute·ness

res·o·lu·tion

re·solv·able

re·solve, *v.*

re·solved,
re·solv·ing
res·o·nance
res·o·nant
res·o·nate (ECHO),
v. res·o·nat·ed,
res·o·nat·ing
(see also
resinate)
res·o·na·tor
re·sorb
re·sorp·tion
re·sort
re·sound
re·sound·ing
re·source
re·source·ful
re·source·ful·ly
re·source·ful·ness
re·spect
re·spect·abil·i·ty
re·spect·able
re·spect·ably
re·spect·ful
re·spect·ful·ly
re·spect·ful·ness
re·spect·ing
re·spec·tive
re·spec·tive·ly
re·spec·tive·ness
res·pi·ra·tion
res·pi·ra·tor
res·pi·ra·to·ry
re·spire, v.
re·spired,
re·spir·ing
re·spite
re·splen·dence

re·splen·dent
re·splen·dent·ly
re·spond
re·spon·dent
re·sponse
re·spon·si·bil·i·ty, n.
pl.
re·spon·si·bil·i·ties
re·spon·si·ble
re·spon·si·bly
re·spon·sive
re·spon·sive·ly
re·spon·sive·ness
re·start
re·state, v.
re·stat·ed,
re·stat·ing
res·tau·rant
res·tau·ra·teur or
res·tau·ran·teur
rest·ful
rest·ful·ly
rest·ful·ness
rest·ing
res·ti·tu·tion
res·tive
res·tive·ly
res·tive·ness
rest·less
rest·less·ly
rest·less·ness
re·stor·able
res·to·ra·tion
re·stor·a·tive
re·store, v.
re·stored,
re·stor·ing
re·strain

re·strain·able
re·strained
re·straint
re·strict
re·stric·tion
re·stric·tive
re·stric·tive·ly
re·stric·tive·ness
re·sult
re·sul·tant
ré·su·mé or
re·su·mé or
re·su·me
(SUMMARY)
re·sume (START
AGAIN)
re·sump·tion
re·su·pi·nate
re·sur·face, v.
re·sur·faced,
re·sur·fac·ing
re·sur·gence
re·sur·gent
res·ur·rect
res·ur·rec·tion
re·sus·ci·tate, v.
re·sus·ci·tat·ed,
re·sus·ci·tat·ing
re·sus·ci·ta·tion
re·sus·ci·ta·tor
ret, v. ret·ted,
ret·ting
re·tail
re·tail·er
re·tain
re·tain·er
re·take, v. re·took,
re·tak·en,
re·tak·ing

re·tal·i·ate, v.
  re·tal·i·at·ed,
  re·tal·i·at·ing

re·tal·i·a·tion

re·tal·ia·to·ry

re·tard

re·tar·da·tion

re·tard·ed

retch

re·tell, v. re·told,
  re·tel·ling

re·ten·tion

re·ten·tive

re·ten·tive·ly

re·ten·tive·ness

re·ten·tiv·i·ty

re·test

re·think, v.
  re·thought,
  re·think·ing

ret·i·cence

ret·i·cent

ret·i·cent·ly

ret·i·cle

re·tic·u·lar

re·tic·u·late, v.
  re·tic·u·lat·ed,
  re·tic·u·lat·ing

ret·i·cule

ret·i·na, n. pl.
  ret·i·nas or
  ret·i·nae

Ret·in-A ®

ret·i·ni·tis
  pig·men·to·sa

ret·i·nue

re·tire, v. re·tired,
  re·tir·ing

re·tir·ee

re·tire·ment

re·tir·ing

re·took

re·tool

re·tort

re·touch

re·trace, v.
  re·traced,
  re·trac·ing

re·tract

re·tract·able

re·trac·tile

re·trac·tion

re·trac·tor

re·tread

re·treat

re·trench

re·trench·ment

re·tri·al

re·tri·bu·tion

re·trib·u·tive

re·trib·u·tive·ly

re·trib·u·to·ry

re·triev·able

re·triev·al

re·trieve, v.
  re·trieved,
  re·triev·ing

re·triev·er

ret·ro·ac·tive

ret·ro·ac·tive·ly

ret·ro·ac·tiv·i·ty

ret·ro·cede, v.
  ret·ro·ced·ed,
  ret·ro·ced·ing

ret·ro·ces·sion

ret·ro·fire, v.

ret·ro·fired,
ret·ro·fir·ing

ret·ro·fit, v.
  ret·ro·fit·ted,
  ret·ro·fit·ting

ret·ro·grade, v.
  ret·ro·grad·ed,
  ret·ro·grad·ing

ret·ro·gress

ret·ro·gres·sion

ret·ro-rock·et

ret·ro·spect

ret·ro·spec·tion

ret·ro·spec·tive

ret·ro·spec·tive·ly

Ret·ro·vir ®

ret·ro·vi·rus

ret·si·na

re·turn

re·turn·able

re·turn·ee

re·uni·fi·ca·tion

re·uni·fy, v.
  re·uni·fied,
  re·uni·fy·ing

re·union

re·unite, v.
  re·unit·ed,
  re·unit·ing

re·us·abil·i·ty

re·us·able

re·use, v. re·used,
  re·us·ing

rev, v. revved,
  rev·ving

re·val·u·ate, v.
  re·val·u·at·ed,
  re·val·u·at·ing

re·val·u·a·tion

re·val·ue, v.
re·val·ued,
re·val·u·ing

re·vamp

re·vanche

re·vanch·ist

re·veal

rev·eil·le

rev·el, v. rev·eled
or rev·elled,
rev·el·ing or
rev·el·ling

rev·e·la·tion

rev·el·er or
rev·el·ler

rev·el·ry, n. pl.
rev·el·ries

re·venge, v.
re·venged,
re·veng·ing

re·venge·ful

re·venge·ful·ly

re·venge·ful·ness

re·veng·er

rev·e·nue

rev·e·nu·er

re·ver·ber·ate, v.
re·ver·ber·at·ed,
re·ver·ber·at·ing

re·ver·ber·a·tion

re·vere, v.
re·vered,
re·ver·ing

rev·er·ence

rev·er·end

rev·er·ent

rev·er·en·tial

rev·er·en·tial·ly

rev·er·ent·ly

rev·er·ie

re·vers (LAPEL)
(see also
reverse)

re·ver·sal

re·verse
(OPPOSITE), v.
re·versed,
re·vers·ing (see
also revers)

re·vers·ibil·i·ty

re·vers·ible

re·vers·ibly

re·ver·sion

re·ver·sion·ary

re·vert

re·vert·ible

re·view
(EVALUATION)
(see also revue)

re·view·er

re·vile, v. re·viled,
re·vil·ing

re·vil·er

re·vis·able

re·vise, v. re·vised,
re·vis·ing

re·vis·er or re·vis·or

re·vi·sion

re·vi·sion·ism

re·vi·sion·ist

re·vi·so·ry

re·vi·tal·iza·tion

re·vi·tal·ize, v.
re·vi·tal·ized,
re·vi·tal·iz·ing

re·viv·al

re·viv·al·ist

re·vive, v. re·vived,
re·viv·ing

re·viv·i·fy, v.
re·viv·i·fied,
re·viv·i·fy·ing

re·vo·ca·ble

re·vo·ca·tion

re·voke, v.
re·voked,
re·vok·ing

re·volt

re·volt·ing

rev·o·lu·tion

rev·o·lu·tion·ary, n.
pl.
rev·o·lu·tion·ar·ies

rev·o·lu·tion·ist

rev·o·lu·tion·ize, v.
rev·o·lu·tion·ized,
rev·o·lu·tion·iz·ing

re·volv·able

re·volve, v.
re·volved,
re·volv·ing

re·volv·er

re·volv·ing

re·vue (MUSICAL
SHOW) (see also
review)

re·vul·sion

re·wake

re·wak·en

re·ward

re·ward·ing

re·wind, v.
re·wound,
re·wind·ing

re·work

re·write, v.
re·wrote,

re·writ·ten,
re·writ·ing

re·zone, *v.*
re·zoned,
re·zon·ing

rhap·sod·ic

rhap·sod·i·cal

rhap·sod·i·cal·ly

rhap·so·dize, *v.*
rhap·so·dized,
rhap·so·diz·ing

rhap·so·dy, *n. pl.*
rhap·so·dies

rhe·ni·um

rheo·stat

rhe·sus mon·key, *n.
pl.* rhe·sus
mon·keys

rhet·o·ric

rhe·tor·i·cal

rhe·tor·i·cal·ly

rhet·o·ri·cian

rheu·mat·ic

rheu·mat·i·cal·ly

rheu·ma·tism

rheu·ma·toid

rheumy, *adj.*
rheum·i·er,
rheum·i·est

rhine·stone

rhi·noc·er·os, *n. pl.*
rhi·noc·er·os·es
or rhi·noc·er·os

rhi·zome

Rhode Is·land

Rhode Is·land·er

rho·di·um

rho·do·den·dron

rhom·boid

rhom·boid·al

rhom·bus, *n. pl.*
rhom·bus·es *or*
rhom·bi

rhu·barb

rhyme, *v.* rhymed,
rhym·ing

rhy·o·lite

rhythm

rhythm·ic

rhythm·i·cal

rhythm·i·cal·ly

ri·al

ri·al·to, *n. pl.*
ri·al·tos

ri·a·ta

rib, *v.* ribbed,
rib·bing

rib·ald

rib·ald·ry

rib·bon

ri·bo·fla·vin

ri·bo·nu·cle·ic acid

Rich·ard

rich·es

rich·ly

Rich·mond

rich·ness

rick·et·i·ness

rick·ets

rick·ett·sia, *n. pl.*
rick·ett·si·as *or*
rick·ett·si·ae

rick·ety

rick·ey

rick·rack

rick·sha *or*
rick·shaw

ric·o·chet, *v.*
ric·o·cheted *or*
ric·o·chet·ted,
ric·o·chet·ing *or*
ric·o·chet·ting

ri·cot·ta

ric·tus

rid, *v.* rid (*occas.*
rid·ded),
rid·ding

rid·able *or*
ride·able

rid·dance

rid·dle, *v.* rid·dled,
rid·dling

ride, *v.* rode,
rid·den, rid·ing

rid·er

rid·er·less

ride·share

ridge, *v.* ridged,
ridg·ing

ridge·pole

rid·i·cule, *v.*
rid·i·culed,
rid·i·cul·ing

ri·dic·u·lous

ri·dic·u·lous·ly

ri·dic·u·lous·ness

rid·ing

ri·el

riff

rif·fle, *v.* rif·fled,
rif·fling

riff·raff

ri·fle, *v.* ri·fled,
ri·fling

ri·fle·man, *n. pl.*
ri·fle·men

ri·fling

rig, v. rigged
  rig·ging

rig·a·ma·role (var.
  of rig·ma·role)

rig·a·to·ni

rig·ger

rig·ging

right

right-an·gled or
  right-an·gle

righ·teous

righ·teous·ly

righ·teous·ness

right·ful

right·ful·ly

right·ful·ness

right-hand

right-hand·ed

right-hand·ed·ly

right-hand·ed·ness

right·ist

right·ly

right-of-way, n. pl.
  rights-of-way
  (occas. right-of-
  ways)

right-on

right-to-die

right-to-life

right-to-lif·er

right-to-work

right·wing·er

rig·id

ri·gid·i·ty

ri·gid·ness

rig·ma·role

rig·or

rig·or mor·tis

rig·or·ous

rig·or·ous·ly

rig·or·ous·ness

rile, v. riled, ril·ing

rim, v. rimmed,
  rim·ming

rim·fire

rim·rock

rin·der·pest

ring (SOUND A
  BELL), v. rang,
  rung, ring·ing

ring (SURROUND),
  v. ringed,
  ring·ing

ring·er

ring·lead·er

ring·let

ring·mas·ter

ring-necked
  pheas·ant

ring·side

ring·toss

ring·worm

rink

rinky-dink

rinse, v. rinsed,
  rins·ing

Rio de Ja·nei·ro

Rio Gran·de

riot

riot·er

ri·ot·ous

ri·ot·ous·ly

ri·ot·ous·ness

rip, v. ripped,
  rip·ping

ri·par·i·an

ripe·ly

rip·en

ripe·ness

rip-off, n.

rip off, v.

ri·poste

rip·per

rip·ple, v. rip·pled,
  rip·pling

rip·rap, v.
  rip·rapped,
  rip·rap·ping

rip-roar·ing

rip·saw

rip-snort·er

rip·stop

rip·tide

rise, v. rose, risen,
  ris·ing

ris·er

ris·i·bil·i·ty, n. pl.
  ris·i·bil·i·ties

ris·i·ble

risk·i·ness

risky, adj. risk·i·er,
  risk·i·est

ri·sot·to, n. pl.
  ri·sot·tos

ris·qué

ri·tar·dan·do, n. pl.
  ri·tar·dan·dos

rite

rit·u·al

rit·u·al·ism

rit·u·al·is·tic

rit·u·al·is·ti·cal·ly

rit·u·al·ly

ritzy, *adj.* ritz·i·er, ritz·i·est

ri·val, *v.* ri·valed, *or* ri·valled, ri·val·ing *or* ri·val·ling

ri·val·ry, *n. pl.* ri·val·ries

riv·er

riv·er·bed

riv·er·boat

riv·er·side

riv·et

riv·et·er

riv·u·let

ri·yal

roach

road·abil·i·ty

road·bed

road·block

road·house

road·run·ner

road·show

road·side

road·ster

road·way

road·work

roam·er

roan

roar·ing

roast·er

rob, *v.* robbed, rob·bing

rob·ber

rob·bery, *n. pl.* rob·ber·ies

Rob·ert

rob·in

ro·bot

ro·bot·ics

ro·bust

ro·bust·ly

ro·bust·ness

Roch·es·ter

rock·bound

rock·er

rock·et

rock·et·ry

rock·fish

Rock·ford

rock·hound

rock-ribbed

rocky, *adj.* rock·i·er, rock·i·est

ro·co·co

ro·dent

ro·deo, *n. pl.* ro·deos

roe·buck, *n. pl.* roe·buck *or* roe·bucks

roent·gen

ro·ga·tion

Rog·er

rogue

rogu·ery, *n. pl.* ro·guer·ies

rogu·ish

rogu·ish·ly

rogu·ish·ness

roil

rois·ter

rois·ter·er

role (*occas.* rôle)

(PART) (*see also* roll)

Rolf·ing®

roll (BREAD, LIST, MOVEMENT) (*see also* role)

roll·back

roll·er

roll·er-skate, *v.* roll·er-skat·ed, roll·er-skat·ing

rol·lick

ro·ly-po·ly

ro·maine

Ro·man

ro·man à clef, *n. pl.* ro·mans à clef

Ro·man Ca·tho·lic

ro·mance, *v.* ro·manced, ro·manc·ing

Ro·ma·nia *or* Ru·ma·nia

Ro·ma·ni·an *or* Ru·ma·ni·an

ro·man·tic

ro·man·ti·cal·ly

ro·man·ti·cism

ro·man·ti·cist

ro·man·ti·ci·za·tion

ro·man·ti·cize, *v.* ro·man·ti·cized, ro·man·ti·ciz·ing

Rome

romper

Ron·ald

ron·do, *n. pl.* ron·dos

roof, *n. pl.* roofs

roof·ing

roof·top

rook·ery, *n. pl.*
rook·er·ies

rook·ie

room·er

room·ette

room·ful, *n. pl.*
room·fuls

room·i·ness

room·mate

roomy, *adj.*
room·i·er,
room·i·est

roost·er

root

root·er

root·less

root·less·ly

root·less·ness

root·let

root·stock

rope, *v.* roped,
rop·ing

rop·er

rope·way

Roque·fort
(CHEESE)®

ro·sa·ry, *n. pl.*
ro·sa·ries

ro·se·ate

rose-col·ored

rose·mary

ro·se·o·la

ro·sette

rose·wood

Rosh Ha·sha·nah

ros·i·ly

ros·in

ros·i·ness

ros·i·nous

ros·ter

ros·trum, *n. pl.*
ros·trums *or*
ros·tra

rosy, *adj.* ros·i·er,
ros·i·est

rot, *v.* rot·ted,
rot·ting

ro·ta·ry, *n. pl.*
ro·ta·ries

ro·tat·able

ro·tate, *v.* ro·tat·ed,
ro·tat·ing

ro·ta·tion

ro·ta·tor

ro·ti·fer

ro·tis·ser·ie

ro·to·gra·vure

ro·tor

ro·to·til·ler

rot·ten

rot·ten·ly

rot·ten·ness

rot·ten·stone

ro·tund

ro·tun·da

ro·tun·di·ty

roué

rouge, *v.* rouged,
roug·ing

rough

rough·age

rough-and-ready

rough-and-tum·ble

rough·cast

rough-dry, *v.*
rough-dried,
rough-dry·ing

rough·en

rough-hew, *v.*
rough-hewed,
rough-hewn,
rough-hew·ing

rough·house, *v.*
rough·housed,
rough·hous·ing

rough·ish

rough·neck

rough·shod

rou·lade

rou·lette

round·about

round·ed

roun·de·lay

round·er

round·house.

round·ish

round·ly

round-shoul·dered

round-the-clock

round·up

round·worm

rouse, *v.* roused,
rous·ing

rous·ing

roust·about

rout (RETREAT)

route (ROAD), *v.*
rout·ed,
rout·ing

route·man, *n. pl.*
route·men

rou·tine

rou·tine·ly

rove, v. roved, rov·ing

row

row·boat

row·di·ly

row·di·ness

row·dy, adj. row·di·er, row·di·est

row·dy, n. pl. row·dies

row·dy·ish

row·dy·ism

row·el, v. row·eled or row·elled, row·el·ing or row·el·ling

roy·al

roy·al·ist

roy·al·ly

roy·al·ty, n. pl. roy·al·ties

rub, v. rubbed, rub·bing

ru·ba·to, n. pl. ru·ba·tos

rub·ber

rub·ber·ize, v. rub·ber·ized, rub·ber·iz·ing

rub·ber·neck

rub·ber-stamp, adj. v.

rub·ber stamp, n.

rub·bery

rub·bing

rub·bish

rub·ble (DEBRIS) (see also ruble)

rub·down

ru·bel·la

ru·be·o·la

ru·bid·i·um

ru·ble (CURRENCY) (see also rubble)

ru·bric

ru·by, n. pl. ru·bies

ruck·sack

ruck·us

rud·der

rud·der·less

rud·di·ness

rud·dy, adj. rud·di·er, rud·di·est

rude, adj. rud·er, rud·est

rude·ly

rude·ness

ru·di·ment

ru·di·men·ta·ri·ly

ru·di·men·ta·ri·ness

ru·di·men·ta·ry

rue, v. rued, ru·ing

rue·ful

rue·ful·ly

rue·ful·ness

ruff

ruf·fi·an

ruf·fle, v. ruf·fled, ruf·fling

rug·ged

rug·ged·ly

rug·ged·ness

ru·in

ru·in·a·tion

ru·in·ous

ru·in·ous·ly

ru·in·ous·ness

rule, v. ruled, rul·ing

rul·er

rul·ing

rum·ba

rum·ble, v. rum·bled, rum·bling

ru·mi·nant

ru·mi·nate, v. ru·mi·nat·ed, ru·mi·nat·ing

ru·mi·na·tion

rum·mage, v. rum·maged, rum·mag·ing

rum·my, n. pl. rum·mies

rum·my, adj. rum·mi·er, rum·mi·est

ru·mor

ru·mor·mon·ger

rum·ple, v. rum·pled, rum·pling

rum·pus

rum·run·ner

rum·run·ning

run, v. ran, run, run·ning

run·about

run·around

run·away

run·down
(BASEBALL
PLAY,
SUMMARY)

run·down
(DILAPIDATED)

rung

run-in

run·ner

run·ner-up, *n. pl.*
run·ners-up

run·ning

run·ny, *adj.*
run·ni·er,
run·ni·est

run·off

run-of-the-mill

run-on

runt, *adj.* runt·i·er,
runt·i·est

runt·i·ness

run·way

ru·pee

ru·pi·ah, *n. pl.*

ru·pi·ah *or*
ru·pi·ahs

rup·ture, *v.*
rup·tured,
rup·tur·ing

ru·ral

rush·er

rus·set

Rus·sia (*formerly*
Russian Soviet
Socialist
Republic)

Rus·sian

Rus·sian So·vi·et
So·cial·ist
Re·pub·lic (*now*
Russia)

rust-col·ored

rus·tic

rus·ti·cal·ly.

rus·ti·cate, *v.*
rus·ti·cat·ed,
rus·ti·cat·ing

rus·ti·ca·tion

rust·i·ly

rust·i·ness

rus·tle, *v.* rus·tled,
rus·tling

rus·tler

rust·proof

rusty, *adj.* rust·i·er,
rust·i·est

rut, *v.* rut·ted,
rut·ting

ru·ta·ba·ga

ru·the·ni·um

ruth·er·for·di·um

ruth·less

ruth·less·ly

ruth·less·ness

rut·ty, *adj.* rut·ti·er,
rut·ti·est

Rwan·da

Rwan·dan

Ry·an

rye

rye·grass

S

Sab·bath

sab·bat·ic

sab·bat·i·cal

sa·ber *or* sa·bre

sa·ber-toothed

sa·bin

sa·ble, *n. pl.* sa·bles

sa·ble·fish

sa·bot

sab·o·tage, *v.*
   sab·o·taged,
   sab·o·tag·ing

sab·o·teur

sac

sac·cha·rin, *n.*

sac·cha·rine, *adj.*

sac·er·do·tal

sac·er·do·tal·ism

sac·er·do·tal·ly

sa·chem

sa·chet

sack

sack·cloth

sack·ful, *n. pl.*
   sack·fuls

sack·ing

sac·ra·ment

sac·ra·men·tal

sac·ra·men·tal·ly

Sac·ra·men·to

sa·cred

sac·ri·fice, *v.*
   sac·ri·ficed,
   sac·ri·fic·ing

sac·ri·fi·cial

sac·ri·fi·cial·ly

sac·ri·lege

sac·ri·le·gious

sac·ri·le·gious·ly

sac·ri·le·gious·ness

sac·ris·tan

sac·ris·ty, *n. pl.*
   sac·ris·ties

sa·cro·il·i·ac

sac·ro·sanct

sa·crum, *n. pl.*
   sa·cra

sad, *adj.* sad·der,
   sad·dest

sad·den

sad·dle, *v.*
   sad·dled,
   sad·dling

sad·dle·bag

sad·dle·bow

sad·dle·cloth

sad·dlery, *n. pl.*
   sad·dler·ies

sad·iron

sa·dism

sa·dist

sa·dis·tic

sa·dis·ti·cal·ly

sad·ly

sad·ness

sad·o·mas·och·ism

sad·o·mas·och·ist

sad·o·mas·och·is·tic

sa·fa·ri

safe, *adj.* saf·er,
   saf·est

safe-con·duct

safe·crack·er

safe·crack·ing

safe-de·pos·it box

safe·guard

safe·keep·ing

safe·light

safe·ly

safe·ty, *n. pl.*
   safe·ties

saf·flow·er

saf·fron

sag, *v.* sagged,
sag·ging

sa·ga

sa·ga·cious

sa·ga·cious·ly

sa·ga·cious·ness

sa·gac·i·ty, *n. pl.*
sa·gac·i·ties

sage, *adj.* sag·er,
sag·est

sage·brush

sage·ly

Sag·it·tar·i·an

Sag·it·tar·i·us

sa·go, *n. pl.* sa·gos

sa·gua·ro

Sa·ha·ra

sa·hib

sail·boat

sail·cloth

sail·er (BOAT) (*see
also* sailor)

sail·fish

sail·ing

sail·or (PERSON
WHO SAILS)
(*see also* sailer)

sail·plane, *v.*
sail·planed,
sail·plan·ing

saint·ed

Saint Hel·ens,
Mount

saint·hood

saint·li·ness

Saint Lou·is

saint·ly

Saint Paul

Saint Pe·ters·burg

Saint Val·en·tine's
Day

sake (PURPOSE)

sa·ke *or* sa·ki (RICE
WINE)

Sa·kha·lin

sa·laam

sal·abil·i·ty

sal·able *or* sale·able

sa·la·cious

sa·la·cious·ly

sa·la·cious·ness

sal·ad

sal·a·man·der

sa·la·mi

sal·a·ried

sal·a·ry, *n. pl.*
sal·a·ries

Sa·lem

sal·era·tus

sales·clerk

sales·girl

sales·lady, *n. pl.*
sales·lad·ies

sales·man, *n. pl.*
sales·men

sales·man·ship

sales·people

sales·per·son

sales·room

sales·wom·an, *n.
pl.*
sales·wom·en

sa·lience

sa·lient

Sa·li·na (KANSAS)

Sa·li·nas
(CALIFORNIA)

sa·line

sa·lin·i·ty

sa·li·va

sal·i·vary

sal·i·vate, *v.*
sal·i·vat·ed,
sal·i·vat·ing

sal·i·va·tion

sal·low

Sal·ly (PERSON'S
NAME), *n. pl.*
Sal·lys

sal·ly (RUSHING
FORTH), *n. pl.*
sal·lies

sal·ly, *v.* sal·lied,
sal·ly·ing

sal·ma·gun·di

salm·on, *n. pl.*
salm·on (*occas.*
sal·mons)

sal·mo·nel·la, *n. pl.*
sal·mo·nel·lae *or*
sal·mo·nel·las *or*
sal·mo·nel·la

sa·lon

sa·loon

sa·loon·keep·er

sal·sa

salt-and-pep·per

salt·box

salt·cel·lar

salt·er

salt·i·ly

sal·tine

salt·i·ness

Salt Lake City

Sal·ton Sea

salt·pe·ter

salt·shak·er

salt·wa·ter

salt·wort

salty, *adj.* salt·i·er,
salt·i·est

sa·lu·bri·ous

sa·lu·bri·ous·ly

sa·lu·bri·ous·ness

sal·u·tary

sal·u·ta·tion

sa·lu·ta·to·ri·an

sa·lu·ta·to·ry, *n. pl.*
sa·lu·ta·to·ries

sa·lute, *v.* sa·lut·ed,
sa·lut·ing

salv·able

Sal·va·dor·an

Sal·va·dor·ean *or*
Sal·va·dor·ian

sal·vage, *v.*
sal·vaged,
sal·vag·ing

sal·vage·able

sal·va·tion

salve, *v.* salved,
salv·ing

sal·ver

sal·vo, *n. pl.* sal·vos
or sal·voes

Sal·ween

Sa·man·tha

sa·ma·ra

sa·mar·i·tan

sa·mar·i·um

sam·ba

same·ness

sam·i·sen

Sa·moa

Sa·mo·an

sam·o·var

sam·pan

sam·ple, *v.*
sam·pled,
sam·pling

sam·pler

sam·pling

sam·u·rai, *n. pl.*
sam·u·rai

San An·to·nio

san·a·ta·ri·um, *n.
pl.*
san·a·ta·ri·ums *or*
san·a·ta·ria

san·a·to·ri·um, *n.
pl.*
san·a·to·ri·ums *or*
san·a·to·ria

San Ber·nar·di·no

sanc·ti·fi·ca·tion

sanc·ti·fy, *v.*
sanc·ti·fied,
sanc·ti·fy·ing

sanc·ti·mo·nious

sanc·ti·mo·nious·ly

sanc·ti·mo·nious·ness

sanc·ti·mo·ny

sanc·tion

sanc·ti·ty, *n. pl.*
sanc·ti·ties

sanc·tu·ary, *n. pl.*
sanc·tu·ar·ies

sanc·tum, *n. pl.*
sanc·tums
(*oecas.* sanc·ta)

sanc·tum
sanc·to·rum

san·dal

san·daled

san·dal·wood

san·da·rac

sand·bag, *v.*
sand·bagged,
sand·bag·ging

sand·bank

sand·bar

sand·blast

sand·box

sand·er

sand·hog

San Di·ego

sand·i·ness

sand·lot

sand·man

sand·pa·per

sand·pip·er

San·dra

sand·soap

sand·stone

sand·storm

sand·wich

sandy, *adj.*
sand·i·er,
sand·i·est

sane, *adj.* san·er,
san·est

sane·ly

San·for·ized℠

San Fran·cis·co

sang·froid

san·gria

san·gui·nary

san·guine

san·guine·ly

san·guine·ness

san·i·tar·i·an

san·i·tar·i·ly

san·i·tar·i·um, *n. pl.*
san·i·tar·i·ums
or san·i·tar·i·a

san·i·tary

san·i·ta·tion

san·i·tize, *v.*
san·i·tized,
san·i·tiz·ing

san·i·to·ri·um, *n. pl.*
san·i·to·ri·ums
or san·i·to·ria

san·i·ty

San Jo·se

San Juan

San Lu·is Po·to·sí

San·mar·i·nese, *n.
pl.*
San·mar·i·nese

San Ma·ri·no

sans cu·lotte

san·sei, *n. pl.*
san·sei (*occas.*
san·seis)

San·skrit

sans ser·if *or*
san·ser·if

San·ta Ana

San·ta Claus

San·ta Fe

San·ti·a·go

São Pau·lo

São To·mé

sap, *v.* sapped,
sap·ping

sa·pi·ens

sap·ling

sap·per

sap·phire

sap·py, *adj.*
sap·pi·er,
sap·pi·est

sap·suck·er

sap·wood

sar·a·band *or*
sar·a·bande

Sa·rah

sa·ran

sar·casm

sar·cas·tic

sar·cas·ti·cal·ly

sar·co·ma, *n. pl.*
sar·co·mas *or*
sar·co·ma·ta

sar·coph·a·gus, *n.
pl.*
sar·coph·a·gi
(*occas.*
sar·coph·a·gus·es)

sar·dine, *n. pl.*
sar·dines
(*occas.* sar·dine)

sar·don·ic

sar·don·i·cal·ly

Sar·gas·so Sea

sa·ri (*occas.* sa·ree)

sa·rong

sar·sa·pa·ril·la

sar·to·ri·al

sa·shay

Sas·katch·e·wan

Sas·ka·toon

sas·quatch

sas·sa·fras

sassy, *adj.* sass·i·er,
sass·i·est

Sa·tan

sa·tang, *n. pl.*
sa·tang *or* sa·tangs

sa·tan·ic

sa·tan·i·cal·ly

sa·tan·ism

satch·el

sate, *v.* sat·ed,
sat·ing

sa·teen

sat·el·lite

sa·tia·ble

sa·tiate, *adj.*

sa·ti·ate, *v.*
sa·ti·at·ed,
sa·ti·at·ing

sa·ti·ety

sat·in

sat·in·wood

sat·iny

sat·ire

sa·tir·ic

sa·tir·i·cal

sa·tir·i·cal·ly

sat·i·rist

sat·i·rize, *v.*
sat·i·rized,
sat·i·riz·ing

sat·is·fac·tion

sat·is·fac·to·ri·ly

sat·is·fac·to·ri·ness

sat·is·fac·to·ry

sat·is·fi·able

sat·is·fy, *v.*
sat·is·fied,
sat·is·fy·ing

sa·trap

sat·u·rant

sat·u·rate, v.
sat·u·rat·ed,
sat·u·rat·ing

sat·u·rat·ed

sat·u·ra·tion

Sat·ur·day

Sat·urn

sat·ur·nine

sa·tyr

sa·ty·ri·a·sis

sauce, v. sauced,
sauc·ing

sauce·pan

sau·cer

sauc·i·ly

sauc·i·ness

saucy, adj.
sauc·i·er,
sauc·i·est

Sau·di

Sau·di Ara·bia

Sau·di Ara·bi·an

sau·er·bra·ten

sau·er·kraut

sau·na

saun·ter

sau·sage

sau·té, v. sau·téed
or sau·téd,
sau·té·ing

sau·terne

sau·vi·gnon blanc

sav·able or
save·able

sav·age, v.

sav·aged,
sav·ag·ing

sav·age·ly

sav·age·ness

sav·age·ry, n. pl.
sav·age·ries

sa·van·na (occas.
sa·van·nah)
(TREELESS
PLAIN)

Sa·van·nah (CITY,
RIVER)

sa·vant

save, v. saved,
sav·ing

sav·er (ONE WHO
SAVES) (see
also savor)

sav·ing

sav·ior or sav·iour

sa·voir faire

sa·vor (occas.
sa·vour)
(TASTE) (see also
saver)

sa·vor·i·ly

sa·vor·i·ness

sa·vo·ry (occas.
sa·vou·ry)

saw, v. sawed,
sawed or sawn,
saw·ing

saw·dust

sawed-off

saw·horse

saw·mill

saw·tooth or saw-
toothed

saw·yer

sax·o·phone

sax·o·phon·ist

say, v. said,
say·ing, says

say·able

say·ing

sa·yo·na·ra

say-so

scab, v. scabbed,
scab·bing

scab·bard

scab·by, adj.
scab·bi·er,
scab·bi·est

sca·bies, n. pl.
sca·bies

scab·rous

scab·rous·ly

scab·rous·ness

scaf·fold

scaf·fold·ing

scal·able

scal·age

scal·a·wag

scald·ing

scale, v. scaled,
scal·ing

scale-down

scale·less

scale-up

scal·i·ness

scal·lion

scal·lop

sca·lop·pi·ne or
scal·lo·pi·ni

scal·pel

scalp·er

scaly, adj. scal·i·er,
scal·i·est

scamp·er

scam·pi, *n. pl.*
scam·pi

scan, *v.* scanned,
scan·ning

scan·dal

scan·dal·ize, *v.*
scan·dal·ized,
scan·dal·iz·ing

scan·dal·mon·ger

scan·dal·ous

scan·dal·ous·ly

scan·dal·ous·ness

Scan·di·na·vi·an

scan·di·um

scan·ner

scan·sion

scant·i·ly

scant·i·ness

scant·ling

scant·ly

scant·ness

scanty, *adj.*
scant·i·er,
scant·i·est

scape·goat

scape·grace

scap·u·la, *n. pl.*
scap·u·lae *or*
scap·u·las

scap·u·lar

scar, *v.* scarred,
scar·ring

scar·ab

scarce, *adj.*
scarc·er,
scarc·est

scarce·ly

scarce·ness

scar·ci·ty, *n. pl.*
scar·ci·ties

scare, *v.* scared,
scar·ing

scare·crow

scaredy-cat

scarf, *n. pl.* scarves
or scarfs

scar·i·fi·ca·tion

scar·i·fy, *v.*
scar·i·fied,
scar·i·fy·ing

scar·let

scary, *adj.* scar·i·er,
scar·i·est

scat, *v.* scat·ted,
scat·ting

scathe, *v.* scathed,
scath·ing

scath·ing

scath·ing·ly

scat·o·log·i·cal

sca·tol·o·gy

scat·ter

scat·ter·brain, *n.*

scat·ter·brained,
adj.

scat·ter·ing

scat·ter·shot

scav·enge, *v.*
scav·enged,
scav·eng·ing

scav·en·ger

sce·nar·io, *n. pl.*
sce·nar·i·os

sce·nar·ist

scene

scen·ery, *n. pl.*
scen·er·ies

sce·nic

sce·ni·cal

sce·ni·cal·ly

scent

scep·ter

sched·ule, *v.*
sched·uled,
sched·ul·ing

sche·ma, *n. pl.*
sche·ma·ta (*occas.*
sche·mas)

sche·mat·ic

sche·mat·i·cal·ly

scheme, *v.*
schemed,
schem·ing

schem·er

schem·ing

scher·zan·do, *n. pl.*
scher·zan·dos

scher·zo, *n. pl.*
scher·zos *or*
scher·zi

schil·ling

schism

schis·mat·ic

schis·mat·i·cal

schis·to·some

schis·to·so·mi·a·sis,
n. pl.
schis·to·so·mi·a·ses

schizo

schiz·oid

schizo·phre·nia

schizo·phren·ic

schle·miel

schlepp *or* schlep

schlock (*occas.*
schlocky)

schmaltz (*occas.* schmalz)

schmaltzy

schmooze *or* shmooze, *v.* schmoozed, schmooz·ing

schmuck

schnapps, *n. pl.* schnapps

schnau·zer

schnit·zel

schnook

schnor·rer

schnoz·zle

schol·ar

schol·ar·ly

schol·ar·ship

scho·las·tic

scho·las·ti·cal·ly

scho·las·ti·cism

school·bag

school·boy

school·child, *n. pl.* school·chil·dren

school·girl

school·house

school·ing

school·marm *or* school·ma'am

school·marm·ish

school·mas·ter

school·mate

school·room

school·teach·er

school·work

schoo·ner

schoo·ner-rigged

schot·tische

schwa

sci·at·ic

sci·at·i·ca

sci·ence

sci·en·tif·ic

sci·en·tif·i·cal·ly

sci·en·tist

sci·en·tol·o·gy

scim·i·tar

scin·til·la

scin·til·late, *v.* scin·til·lat·ed, scin·til·lat·ing

scin·til·lat·ing

scin·til·la·tion

sci·on

scis·sors, *sing. or pl.*

scle·ro·sis, *n. pl.* scle·ro·ses

scle·rot·ic

scoff·er

scoff·law

scold·ing

scone

scoop·ful, *n. pl.* scoop·fuls

scoot·er

scor·bu·tic

scorch·er

scorch·ing

score, *n. pl.* scores *or* score

score, *v.* scored, scor·ing

score·board

score·card

score·keep·er

score·less

scor·er

scorn·er

scorn·ful

scorn·ful·ly

scorn·ful·ness

Scor·pio

scor·pi·on

Scor·pi·us

Scot

Scotch (OF SCOTLAND)

scotch (STIFLE)

scot·free

Scot·land

Scott

Scot·tish

scoun·drel

scoun·drel·ly

scour

scourge, *v.* scourged, scourg·ing

scout·ing

scout·mas·ter

scowl

Scrab·ble℗

scrab·ble, *v.* scrab·bled, scrab·bling

scrag·gly, *adj.* scrag·gli·er, scrag·gli·est

scrag·gy, *adj.* scrag·gi·er, scrag·gi·est

scram, *v.*

scrammed,
scram·ming

scram·ble, *v.*
scram·bled,
scram·bling

Scran·ton

scrap, *v.* scrapped,
scrap·ping

scrap·book

scrape, *v.* scraped,
scrap·ing

scrap·er

scrap·heap

scrap·per

scrap·pi·ly

scrap·pi·ness

scrap·ple

scrap·py, *adj.*
scrap·pi·er,
scrap·pi·est

scratch

scratch·i·ness

scratchy, *adj.*
scratch·i·er,
scratch·i·est

scrawl

scraw·ni·ness

scraw·ny, *adj.*
scraw·ni·er,
scraw·ni·est

scream·er

scream·ing

screech

screed

screen·able

screen·ing

screen·play

screen·writ·er

screw·ball

screw·driv·er

screw·worm

screwy, *adj.*
screw·i·er,
screw·i·est

scrib·al

scrib·ble, *v.*
scrib·bled,
scrib·bling

scrib·bler

scrim·mage, *v*
scrim·maged,
scrim·mag·ing

scrim·mag·er

scrimp

scrim·shaw

scrip
(CERTIFICATE)

script (WRITING)

scrip·tur·al

scrip·tur·al·ly

scrip·ture

script·writ·er

scriv·en·er

scrof·u·la

scroll·work

scro·tum, *n. pl.*
scro·ta *or*
scro·tums

scrounge, *v.*
scrounged,
scroung·ing

scroung·er

scroung·ing

scroungy, *adj.*
scroung·i·er,
scroung·i·est

scrub, *v.* scrubbed,
scrub·bing

scrub·by, *adj.*
scrub·bi·er,
scrub·bi·est

scruffy, *adj.*
scruff·i·er,
scruff·i·est

scrump·tious

scrump·tious·ly

scrump·tious·ness

scru·ple, *v.*
scru·pled,
scru·pling

scru·pu·lous

scru·pu·lous·ly

scru·pu·lous·ness

scru·ta·ble

scru·ti·nize, *v.*
scru·ti·nized,
scru·ti·niz·ing

scru·ti·ny, *n. pl.*
scru·ti·nies

scu·ba

scud, *v.* scud·ded,
scud·ding

scuf·fle, *v.*
scuf·fled,
scuf·fling

scull (OAR) (*see
also* skull)

scul·lery, *n. pl.*
scul·ler·ies

scul·lion

scul·pin, *n. pl.*
scul·pins (*occas.*
scul·pin)

sculp·tor

sculp·tur·al

sculp·tur·al·ly

sculp·ture, *v.*

sculp·tured,
sculp·tur·ing

scum·my, *adj.*
  scum·mi·er,
  scum·mi·est

scup·per

scup·per·nong

scur·ril·i·ty, *n. pl.*
  scur·ril·i·ties

scur·ri·lous

scur·ri·lous·ly

scur·ri·lous·ness

scur·ry, *v.*
  scur·ried,
  scur·ry·ing

scur·vy

scutch·eon

scut·tle, *v.*
  scut·tled,
  scut·tling

scut·tle·butt

scuz·zy, *adj.*
  scuz·zi·er,
  scuz·zi·est

scythe

sea·bag

sea·bed

sea·bird

sea·board

sea·borne

sea·coast

sea·cock

sea·far·er

sea·far·ing

sea·food

sea·go·ing

seal, *n. pl.* seals
  (DEVICES),
  seals (*occas.*

seal)
(ANIMALS)

sea-lane

seal·ant

seal·skin

sea·man, *n. pl.*
  sea·men

sea·man·like

sea·man·ship

seam·less

seam·less·ly

seam·less·ness

seam·stress

seamy, *adj.*
  seam·i·er,
  seam·i·est

Sean

sé·ance

sea·plane

sea·port

sear

search·er

search·ing

search·ing·ly

search·light

sea·scape

sea·shell

sea·shell

sea·shore

sea·sick

sea·sick·ness

sea·side

sea·son

sea·son·able

sea·son·able·ness

sea·son·ably

sea·son·al

sea·son·al·ly

sea·son·ing

seat·ing

seat-of-the-pants

Se·at·tle

sea·wall

sea·ward (*occas.*
  sea·wards)

sea·wa·ter

sea·way

sea·weed

sea·wor·thi·ness

sea·wor·thy

se·ba·ceous

se·cant

se·cede, *v.*
  se·ced·ed,
  se·ced·ing

se·ces·sion

se·ces·sion·ist

se·clude, *v.*
  se·clud·ed,
  se·clud·ing

se·clud·ed

se·clud·ed·ly

se·clud·ed·ness

se·clu·sion

se·clu·sive

se·clu·sive·ly

se·clu·sive·ness

Sec·o·nal®

sec·ond

sec·ond·ari·ly

sec·ond·ary, *n. pl.*
  sec·ond·ar·ies

sec·ond-best

sec·ond-class

sec·ond-guess
sec·ond·hand
sec·ond·ly
sec·ond-rate
sec·ond-string
sec·ond-string·er
se·cre·cy, *n. pl.*
  se·cre·cies
se·cret
sec·re·tar·i·al
sec·re·tar·i·at
sec·re·tary, *n. pl.*
  sec·re·tar·ies
sec·re·tary-
  gen·er·al, *n. pl.*
  sec·re·tar·ies-
  gen·er·al
sec·re·tary-
  trea·sur·er, *n.*
  pl. sec·re·tar·ies-
  trea·sur·er
se·crete, *v.*
  se·cret·ed,
  se·cret·ing
se·cre·tion
se·cre·tive
se·cre·tive·ly
se·cre·tive·ness
se·cret·ly
se·cre·to·ry
sect
sec·tar·i·an
sec·tar·i·an·ism
sec·tion
sec·tion·al
sec·tion·al·ism
sec·tion·al·ly
sec·tor

sec·u·lar
sec·u·lar·ism
sec·u·lar·iza·tion
sec·u·lar·ize, *v.*
  sec·u·lar·ized,
  sec·u·lar·iz·ing
se·cure, *v.*
  se·cured,
  se·cur·ing
se·cure·ly
se·cure·ness
se·cu·ri·ty, *n. pl.*
  se·cu·ri·ties
se·dan
se·date, *v.*
  se·dat·ed,
  se·dat·ing
se·date·ly
se·date·ness
se·da·tion
sed·a·tive
sed·en·tary
Se·der
sed·i·ment
sed·i·men·ta·ry
sed·i·men·ta·tion
se·di·tion
se·di·tious
se·di·tious·ly
se·di·tious·ness
se·duce, *v.*
  se·duced,
  se·duc·ing
se·duc·er
se·duc·tion
se·duc·tive
se·duc·tive·ly
se·duc·tive·ness

se·duc·tress
se·du·li·ty
sed·u·lous
sed·u·lous·ly
sed·u·lous·ness
see, *v.* saw, seen,
  see·ing
see·able
seed, *n pl.* seed *or*
  seeds
seed·bed
seed·ed
seed·i·ly
seed·i·ness
seed·ling
seed·time
seedy, *adj.*
  seed·i·er,
  seed·i·est
seek, *v.* sought,
  seek·ing
seek·er
seem·ing
seem·ing·ly
seem·li·ness
seem·ly
seep·age
seer
seer·suck·er
see·saw
seethe, *v.* seethed,
  seeth·ing
seeth·ing
see-through
seg·ment
seg·men·tal
seg·men·tal·ly

seg·men·tary
seg·men·ta·tion
seg·re·gate, v.
  seg·re·gat·ed,
  seg·re·gat·ing
seg·re·gat·ed
seg·re·ga·tion
seg·re·ga·tion·ist
se·gue, v. se·gued,
  se·gue·ing
sei·gneur
sei·gneur·i·al
sei·gneury, n. pl.
  sei·gneur·ies
seine, v. seined,
  sein·ing
seis·mic
seis·mi·cal·ly
seis·mo·graph
seis·mog·ra·pher
seis·mo·graph·ic
seis·mog·ra·phy
seis·mol·o·gist
seis·mol·o·gy
seize, v. seized,
  seiz·ing
sei·zure
sel·dom
sel·dom·ly
se·lect
se·lect·ed
se·lect·ee
se·lec·tion
se·lec·tive
se·lec·tive·ly
se·lec·tive·ness
se·lec·tiv·i·ty

se·lect·man, n. pl.
  se·lect·men
se·lec·tor
se·le·ni·um
self, n. pl. selves
self-ab·ne·ga·tion
self-abuse
self-ac·cu·sa·tion
self-act·ing
self-ad·dressed
self-ad·just·ing
self-ag·gran·dize·
  ment
self-anal·y·sis
self-ap·point·ed
self-as·sert·ing
self-as·sur·ance
self-as·sured
self-cen·tered
self-cen·tered·ly
self-cen·tered·ness
self-clean·ing
self-com·mand
self-con·fi·dence
self-con·fi·dent
self-con·fi·dent·ly
self-con·scious
self-con·scious·ly
self-con·scious·ness
self-con·tained
self-con·trol
self-con·trolled
self-crit·i·cism
self-de·feat·ing
self-de·fense
self-de·ter·mi·
  na·tion

self-dis·ci·pline
self-doubt
self-ed·u·cat·ed
self-ef·fac·ing
self-em·ployed
self-es·teem
self-ev·i·dent
self-ex·plan·a·to·ry
self-ex·pres·sion
self-gov·erned
self-gov·ern·ing
self-im·age
self-im·por·tance
self-im·posed
self-im·prove·ment
self-in·crim·i·na·
  tion
self-in·dul·gence
self-in·flict·ed
self-in·ter·est
self·ish
self·ish·ly
self·ish·ness
self·less
self-liq·ui·dat·ing
self-load·ing
self-lock·ing
self-made
self-mail·ing
self-op·er·at·ing
self-per·pet·u·a·ting
self-pity
self-pity·ing
self-por·trait
self-pos·sessed
self-pres·er·va·tion

self-pro·claimed
self-pro·pelled
self-pro·tec·tion
self-reg·u·lat·ing
self-re·li·ance
self-re·spect
self-right·teous
self-right·teous·ly
self-right·teous·ness
self-ris·ing
self-rule
self-sac·ri·fice
self-same
self-sat·is·fac·tion
self-sat·is·fied
self-seal·ing
self-seek·ing
self-ser·vice
self-start·ing
self-styled
self-suf·fi·cien·cy
self-suf·fi·cient
self-sus·tain·ing
self-taught
self-wind·ing
self-worth
sell, *v.* sold,
  sell·ing
sell·er
sell-off
sell·out
selt·zer
sel·vage *or*
  sel·vedge
se·man·tic
se·man·ti·cal

se·man·ti·cist
se·man·tics
sem·a·phore, *v.*
  sem·a·phored,
  sem·a·phor·ing
sem·blance
se·men
se·mes·ter
semi·an·nu·al
semi·an·nu·al·ly
semi·ar·id
semi·au·to·mat·ic
semi·cir·cle
semi·cir·cu·lar
semi·clas·si·cal
semi·co·lon
semi·con·duc·tor
semi·con·scious
semi·con·scious·ness
semi·fi·nal
semi·fi·nal·ist
semi·flu·id
semi·for·mal
semi·lu·nar
semi·month·ly
sem·i·nal
sem·i·nar
sem·i·nar·i·an
sem·i·nary, *n. pl.*
  sem·i·nar·ies
semi·of·fi·cial
semi·of·fi·cial·ly
se·mi·ot·ic *or*
  se·mi·ot·ics, *n. pl.*
  se·mi·ot·ics
semi·per·me·able
semi·pre·cious

semi·pri·vate
semi·pro
semi·pro·fes·sion·al
semi·pub·lic
semi·rig·id
semi·skilled
semi·soft
semi·sol·id
semi·sweet
Sem·ite
Se·mit·ic
semi·trail·er
semi·trop·i·cal
semi·week·ly
semi·year·ly
sem·o·lina
sem·per fi·de·lis
sem·per pa·ra·tus
sen, *n. pl.* sen
sen·ate
sen·a·tor
sen·a·to·ri·al
send, *v.* sent,
  send·ing
send-off
se·ne, *n. pl.* se·ne
Sen·e·gal
Sen·e·ga·lese, *n pl.*
  Sen·e·ga·lese
se·nes·cence
sen·gi, *n. pl.* sen·gi
se·nile
se·nil·i·ty
se·nior
se·nior·i·ty, *n. pl.*
  se·nior·i·ties

sen·i·ti, *n. pl.*
  sen·i·ti

sen·na

sen·sa·tion

sen·sa·tion·al

sen·sa·tion·al·ism

sen·sa·tion·al·ize, *v.*
  sen·sa·tion·al·ized,
  sen·sa·tion·al·iz·ing

sen·sa·tion·al·ly

sense, *v.* sensed,
  sens·ing

sense·less

sense·less·ly

sense·less·ness

sen·si·bil·i·ty, *n. pl.*
  sen·si·bil·i·ties

sen·si·ble

sen·si·bly

sen·si·tive

sen·si·tive·ly

sen·si·tive·ness

sen·si·tiv·i·ty, *n. pl.*
  sen·si·tiv·i·ties

sen·si·ti·za·tion

sen·si·tize, *v.*
  sen·si·tized,
  sen·si·tiz·ing

sen·sor
  (DETECTION
  DEVICE) (*see
  also* censor)

sen·so·ri·mo·tor

sen·so·ry

sen·su·al

sen·su·al·i·ty

sen·su·al·ly

sen·su·ous

sen·su·ous·ly

sen·su·ous·ness

sen·tence, *v.*
  sen·tenced,
  sen·tenc·ing

sen·ten·tious

sen·ten·tious·ly

sen·ten·tious·ness

sen·ti·, *n. pl.* sen·ti

sen·tience

sen·tient

sen·tient·ly

sen·ti·ment

sen·ti·men·tal

sen·ti·men·tal·i·ty

sen·ti·men·tal·ize,
  v.
  sen·ti·men·tal·ized,
  sen·ti·men·tal·iz·ing

sen·ti·men·tal·ly

sen·ti·mo, *n. pl.*
  sen·ti·mos

sen·ti·nel

sen·try, *n. pl.*
  sen·tries

Seoul

se·pal

sep·a·ra·bil·i·ty

sep·a·ra·ble

sep·a·ra·bly

sep·a·rate, *v.*
  sep·a·rat·ed,
  sep·a·rat·ing

sep·a·rate·ly

sep·a·ra·tion

sep·a·ra·tist

sep·a·ra·tive

sep·a·ra·tor

se·pia

sep·sis, *n. pl.*
  sep·ses

Sep·tem·ber

sep·tic

sep·ti·ce·mia

sep·tu·a·ge·nar·i·an

sep·tum, *n. pl.*
  sep·ta

sep·ul·cher *or*
  sep·ul·chre

se·pul·chral

se·quel

se·quence, *v.*
  se·quenced,
  se·quenc·ing

se·quen·tial

se·quen·tial·ly

se·ques·ter

se·ques·tered

se·ques·trate, *v.*
  se·ques·trat·ed,
  se·ques·trat·ing

se·ques·tra·tion

se·quin

se·quoia

se·ra·glio, *n. pl.*
  se·ra·glios

se·ra·pe

ser·aph *n. pl.*
  ser·a·phim *or*
  ser·aphs

se·raph·ic

ser·a·phim

Ser·bia

Ser·bo-Cro·atian

ser·e·nade, *v.*
  ser·e·nad·ed,
  ser·e·nad·ing

ser·en·dip·i·tous

ser·en·dip·i·tous·ly

ser·en·dip·i·ty

se·rene

se·rene·ly

se·rene·ness

se·ren·i·ty, *n. pl.*
  se·ren·i·ties

serf (PEASANT)
  (*see also* surf)

serf·dom

serge (CLOTH) (*see
  also* surge)

ser·geant

ser·geant ma·jor, *n.
  pl.* ser·geants
  ma·jor *or*
  sergeant
  ma·jors

se·ri·al

se·ri·al·iza·tion

se·ri·al·ize, *v.*
  se·ri·al·ized,
  se·ri·al·iz·ing

se·ri·al·ly

se·ries, *n. pl.*
  se·ries

ser·if

seri·graph

se·ri·ous

se·ri·ous·ly

se·ri·ous·ness

ser·mon

ser·mon·ette

ser·pent

ser·pen·tine

ser·rate, *v.*
  ser·rat·ed,
  ser·rat·ing

ser·ra·tion

se·rum, *n. pl.*
  se·rums *or* se·ra

ser·vant

serve, *v.* served,
  serv·ing

serv·er

ser·vice, *v.*
  ser·viced,
  ser·vic·ing

ser·vice·abil·i·ty

ser·vice·able

ser·vice·ably

ser·vice·man, *n. pl.*
  ser·vice·men

ser·vile

ser·vil·i·ty

serv·ing

ser·vi·tor

ser·vi·tude

ser·vo, *n. pl.*
  ser·vos

ser·vo·mech·a·nism

ser·vo·mo·tor

ses·a·me

ses·qui·cen·ten·ni·al

ses·qui·pe·da·lian

ses·sion (MEETING)
  (*see also*
  cession)

set, *v.* set, set·ting

set·back

set·screw

set·tee

set·ter

set·ting

set·tle, *v.* set·tled,
  set·tling

set·tle·ment

set·tler

set-to, *n. pl.* set-tos

set to, *v.*

set·up, *n.*

set up, *v.*

sev·en

sev·en·fold

sev·en·teen

sev·enth

sev·en·ti·eth

sev·en·ty, *n. pl.*
  sev·en·ties

sev·er

sev·er·abil·i·ty

sev·er·able

sev·er·al

sev·er·al·ly

sev·er·ance

se·vere, *adj.*
  se·ver·er,
  se·ver·est

se·vere·ly

se·vere·ness

se·ver·i·ty, *n. pl.*
  se·ver·i·ties

sew (STITCH), *v.*
  sewed, sewn *or*
  sewed, sew·ing
  (*see also* sow)

sew·age

sew·er

sew·er·age

sex·a·ge·nar·i·an

sex·i·ly

sex·i·ness

sex·ism

sex·ist

sex·less

sex·less·ly

sex·less·ness

sex-linked

sex·ol·o·gist

sex·ol·o·gy

sex·ploi·ta·tion

sex·pot

sex·tant

sex·tet

sex·to·dec·i·mo, *n. pl.*
sex·to·dec·i·mos

sex·ton

sex·tu·ple

sex·tu·plet

sex·u·al

sex·u·al·i·ty

sex·u·al·ly

sexy, *adj.* sex·i·er,
sex·i·est

Sey·chelles

Sey·chel·lois

sfor·zan·do, *n. pl.*
sfor·zan·dos *or*
sfor·zan·di

shab·bi·ly

shab·bi·ness

shab·by, *adj.*
shab·bi·er,
shab·bi·est

shack·le, *v.*
shack·led,
shack·ling

shad, *n. pl.* shad

shade, *v.* shad·ed,
shad·ing

shad·i·ly

shad·i·ness

shad·ing

shad·ow

shad·ow·box

shad·owy

shady, *adj.*
shad·i·er,
shad·i·est

shaft·ing

shag, *v.* shagged,
shag·ging

shag·gi·ly

shag·gi·ness

shag·gy, *v.*
shag·gi·er,
shag·gi·est

shak·able *or*
shake·able

shake, *v.* shook,
shak·en,
shak·ing

shake·down

shake·out

shak·er

Shake·spear·ean *or*
Shake·spear·ian
(*occas.*
Shake·sper·ean
or
Shake·sper·ian)

shake-up, *n.*

shake up, *v.*

shak·i·ly

shak·i·ness

sha·ko, *n. pl.*
sha·kos *or*
sha·koes

shaky, *adj.*
shak·i·er,
shak·i·est

shale

shall

shal·lot

shal·low

shal·low·ness

sham, *v.* shammed,
sham·ming

sha·man

sha·man·ism

sham·ble, *v.*
sham·bled,
sham·bling

sham·bles

shame, *v.* shamed,
sham·ing

shame·faced

shame·faced·ly

shame·faced·ness

shame·ful

shame·ful·ly

shame·ful·ness

shame·less

shame·less·ly

shame·less·ness

sham·poo, *n. pl.*
sham·poos

sham·rock

sha·mus

Shang·hai

shang·hai, *v.*
shang·haied,
shang·hai·ing

shank

Shan·non

shan·ty (HUT), *n.*
pl. shan·ties (*see*
also chantey)

shan·ty·town

shape, *v.* shaped,
    shap·ing
shape·less
shape·less·ly
shape·less·ness
shape·li·ness
shape·ly, *adj.*
    shape·li·er,
    shape·li·est
share, *v.* shared,
    shar·ing
share·crop·per
share·hold·er
shark·skin
Shar·on
sharp·en
sharp·en·er
sharp-eyed
sharp·ly
sharp·ness
sharp·shoot·er
sharp-tongued
Shas·ta, Mount
shat·ter
shat·ter·proof
shave, *v.* shaved,
    shaved *or* shaven,
    shav·ing
shawl
sheaf, *n. pl.*
    sheaves
shear (TO CUT), *v.*
    sheared,
    sheared *or*
    shorn, shear·ing
    (*see also* sheer)
sheath, *n.*
sheathe (*occas.*
    sheath), *v.*

sheathed,
    sheath·ing
sheathed
sheath·ing
she·bang
shed, *v.* shed,
    shed·ding
sheen
sheep, *n. pl.* sheep
sheep-dip
sheep·fold
sheep·her·der
sheep·ish
sheep·ish·ly
sheep·ish·ness
sheep·skin
sheer (THIN,
    ABRUPT
    CHANGE) (*see
    also* shear)
sheet·ing
sheikh *or* sheik
shek·el
shelf, *n. pl.* shelves
shel·lac, *v.*
    shel·lacked,
    shel·lack·ing
shell·fish
shell·proof
shell·work
shel·ter
shel·ter·belt
shel·ty *or* shel·tie,
    n. pl. shel·ties
shelv·ing
she·nan·i·gan
Shen·yang
shep·herd

shep·herd·ess
sher·bet *or*
    sher·bert
sher·iff
sher·ry, *n. pl.*
    sher·ries
shi·at·su (*occas.*
    shi·at·zu)
shib·bo·leth
shield
shift·i·ly
shift·i·ness
shift·less
shift·less·ly
shift·less·ness
shifty, *adj.*
    shift·i·er,
    shift·i·est
Shih Tzu, *n. pl.*
    Shih Tzus *or*
    Shih Tzu
Shi·ite
shi·lingi, *n. pl.*
    shi·lingi
shil·le·lagh (*occas.*
    shil·la·lah)
shil·ling
shil·ly-shal·ly, *v.*
    shil·ly-
    shal·lied, shil·ly-
    shal·ly·ing
shim, *v.* shimmed,
    shim·ming
shim·mer
shim·mery
shim·my, *n. pl.*
    shim·mies
shim·my, *v.*
    shim·mied,
    shim·my·ing

shin, v. shinned,
  shin·ning
shin·bone
shin·dig
shine, v. shone or
  shined, shin·ing
shin·er
shin·gle, v.
  shin·gled,
  shin·gling
shin·gles
shin·guard
shin·i·ness
shin·ing
shin·splints
Shin·to
Shin·to·ism
shiny, adj.
  shin·i·er,
  shin·i·est
ship, v. shipped,
  ship·ping
ship·board
ship·build·er
ship·build·ing
ship·mate
ship·ment
ship·per
ship·ping
ship·shape
ship·worm
ship·wreck
ship·wright
ship·yard
shirk·er
shirr
shirr·ing
shirt·ing

shirt·mak·er
shirt·sleeve (occas.
  shirt·sleeves or
  shirt·sleeved),
  adj.
shirt·sleeve, n.
shirt·tail
shirt·waist
shish ke·bab
shit, v. shit or shat,
  shit·ting
shiv·a·ree
shiv·er
shoal
shoat
shock·er
shock·ing
shock·proof
shod·di·ly
shod·di·ness
shod·dy, adj.
  shod·di·er,
  shod·di·est
shoe, v. shod or
  shoed, shoe·ing
shoe·horn
shoe·lace
shoe·mak·er
shoe·shine
shoe·string
sho·gun
shoo·fly
shoo-in
shoot, v. shot,
  shoot·ing
shoot-'em-up
shoot·er
shoot-out

shop, v. shopped,
  shop·ping
shop·girl
shop·keep·er
shop·lift·er
shop·per
shop·talk
shop·worn
sho·ran
shore·bird
shor·ing
short·age
short·bread
short·cake
short·change, v.
  short·changed,
  short·chang·ing
short cir·cuit, n.
short-cir·cuit, v.
short·com·ing
short·cut
short·en
short·en·ing
short·fall
short·hand
short·hand·ed
short·hand·ed·ness
short·horn
short·lived
short·ly
short·ness
short·sight·ed
short·sight·ed·ly
short·sight·ed·ness
short·stop
short·tem·pered
short-term

short·wave

short-wind·ed

shot·gun

should

shoul·der

shout

shove, *v.* shoved,
shov·ing

shov·el, *v.*
shov·eled *or*
shov·elled,
shov·el·ing *or*
shov·el·ling

shov·el·ful, *n. pl.*
shov·el·fuls
(*occas.*
shov·els·ful)

show, *v.* showed,
shown *or*
showed,
show·ing

show·boat

show·case, *v.*
show·cased,
show·cas·ing

show·down

show·er

show·ery

show·i·ly

show·i·ness

show·man, *n. pl.*
show·men

show·man·ship

show·piece

show·place

show·room

show·stop·per

showy, *adj.*
show·i·er,
show·i·est

shrap·nel

shred, *v.*
shred·ded,
shred·ding

shred·der

Shreve·port

shrew

shrewd

shrewd·ly

shrewd·ness

shrew·ish

shrew·ish·ly

shrew·ish·ness

shriek

shrift

shrike

shrill·ness

shril·ly

shrimp, *n. pl.*
shrimps *or*
shrimp

shrine

shrink, *v.* shrank
(*occas.* shrunk),
shrunk *or*
shrunk·en,
shrink·ing

shrink·able

shrink·age

shrink-wrap, *v.*
shrink-wrapped,
shrink-wrap·ping

shrive, *v.* shrived
or shrove,
shriv·en *or*
shrived,
shriv·ing

shriv·el, *v.*
shriv·eled *or*
shriv·elled,

shriv·el·ing *or*
shriv·el·ling

shroud

shrub·bery

shrug, *v.* shrugged,
shrug·ging

shtick (*occas.*
shtik)

shuck

shud·der

shuf·fle, *v.*
shuf·fled,
shuf·fling

shuf·fle·board

shun, *v.* shunned,
shun·ning

shun·pik·er

shunt

shut, *v.* shut,
shut·ting

shut·down

shut-eye

shut-in, *adj., n.*

shut in, *v.*

shut·off, *n.*

shut off, *v.*

shut·out, *n.*

shut out, *v.*

shut·ter

shut·ter·bug

shut·tle, *v.*
shut·tled,
shut·tling

shut·tle·cock

shy, *adj.* shi·er *or*
shy·er, shi·est *or*
shy·est

shy, *v.* shied,
shy·ing

shy·ly

shy·ness

shy·ster

Si·a·mese, *n. pl.*
  Si·a·mese

sib·i·lant

sib·ling

sic, *v.* sicced *or*
  sicked, sic·cing
  or sick·ing

Si·cil·i·an

Sic·i·ly

sick·bed

sick call

sick·en

sick·en·ing

sick·ish

sick·ish·ly

sick·ish·ness

sick·le

sick·li·ness

sick·ly, *adj.*
  sick·li·er,
  sick·li·est

sick·ness

sick-out

sick·room

side, *v.* sid·ed,
  sid·ing

side·arm

side·band

side·bar

side·board

side·burns

side·car

side·glance

side·kick

side·light

side·line, *v.*
  side·lined,
  side·lin·ing

side·long

side·man, *n. pl.*
  side·men

side·piece

si·de·re·al

side·sad·dle

side·show

side·slip, *v.*
  side·slipped,
  side·slip·ping

side·split·ting

side·step, *v.*
  side·stepped,
  side·step·ping

side·stroke

side·swipe, *v.*
  side·swiped,
  side·swip·ing

side·track

side·walk

side·wall

side·ways

sid·ing

si·dle, *v.* si·dled,
  si·dling

siege

si·en·na

Si·er·ra Le·one

Si·er·ra Le·o·ne·an

Si·er·ra Ma·dre

Si·er·ra Ne·vada

si·es·ta

sieve, *v.* sieved,
  siev·ing

sift·er

sigh

sight

sight·ed

sight·less

sight·less·ly

sight·less·ness

sight·ly

sight-read

sigh·see·ing

sight·seer

sig·moid·o·scope

sig·moid·os·co·py

sign

sign·age

sig·nal, *v.* sig·naled
  or sig·nalled,
  sig·nal·ing *or*
  sig·nal·ling

sig·nal·ize, *v.*
  sig·nal·ized,
  sig·nal·iz·ing

sig·nal·ly

sig·na·to·ry, *n. pl.*
  sig·na·to·ries

sig·na·ture

sign·board

sign·er

sig·net

sig·nif·i·cance

sig·nif·i·cant

sign·nif·i·cant·ly

sig·ni·fi·ca·tion

sig·ni·fy, *v.*
  sig·ni·fied,
  sig·ni·fy·ing

sign·post

si·lage

si·lence, *v.*

si·lenced,
si·lenc·ing

si·lenc·er

si·lent

sil·hou·ette, *v.*
sil·hou·ett·ed,
sil·hou·ett·ing

sil·i·ca

sil·i·cate

sil·i·con
(CHEMICAL
ELEMENT)

sil·i·cone
(CHEMICAL
COMPOUND)

sil·i·co·sis

silk·en

silk·i·ly

silk·i·ness

silk-screen

silk·weed

silk·worm

silky, *adj.* silk·i·er,
silk·i·est

sil·li·ness

sil·ly, *adj.* sil·li·er,
sil·li·est

si·lo, *n. pl.* si·los

Si·lu·ri·an

sil·ver

sil·ver·fish

sil·ver·smith

sil·ver-tongued

sil·ver·ware

sil·very

sil·vi·cul·ture

sim·i·an

sim·i·lar

sim·i·lar·i·ty, *n. pl.*
sim·i·lar·i·ties

sim·i·lar·ly

sim·i·le

si·mil·i·tude

sim·mer

si·mo·ny

sim·per

sim·ple, *adj.*
sim·pler,
sim·plest

sim·ple-mind·ed

sim·ple-mind·ed·ly

sim·ple-mind·ed·ness

sim·ple·ton

sim·plex, *n. pl.*
sim·plex·es *or*
sim·pli·ces

sim·plic·i·ty

sim·pli·fi·ca·tion

sim·pli·fi·er

sim·pli·fy, *v.*
sim·pli·fied,
sim·pli·fy·ing

sim·plis·tic

sim·plis·ti·cal·ly

sim·ply

sim·u·late, *v.*
sim·u·lat·ed,
sim·u·lat·ing

sim·u·la·tion

sim·u·la·tor

si·mul·cast

si·mul·ta·neous

si·mul·ta·neous·ly

si·mul·ta·neous·ness

sin, *v.* sinned,
sin·ning

sin·cere, *adj.*
sin·cer·er,
sin·cer·est

sin·cere·ly

sin·cere·ness

sin·cer·i·ty, *n. pl.*
sin·cer·i·ties

sine

si·ne·cure

si·ne die

si·ne qua non

sin·ew

sin·ewy

sin·ful

sin·ful·ly

sin·ful·ness

sing, *v.* sang *or*
sung, sung,
sing·ing

sing-along

Sin·ga·pore

Sin·ga·po·re·an

singe, *v.* singed,
singe·ing

sing·er

sin·gle, *v.* sin·gled,
sin·gling

sin·gle-ac·tion

sin·gle-breast·ed

sin·gle-foot

sin·gle-hand·ed

sin·gle-hand·ed·ly

sin·gle-
hand·ed·ness

sin·gle-mind·ed

sin·gle-mind·ed·ly

sin·gle-
mind·ed·ness

sin·gle-space, v.
  sin·gle-spaced,
  sin·gle-spac·ing

sin·gle·ton

sin·gle-track

sin·gly

sing·song

sin·gu·lar

sin·gu·lar·i·ty, n. pl.
  sin·gu·lar·i·ties

sin·is·ter

sink, v. sank or
  sunk, sunk,
  sink·ing

sink·able

sink·age

sink·er

sink·hole

sin·less

sin·less·ly

sin·less·ness

sin·ner

sin·u·os·i·ty, n. pl.
  sin·u·os·i·ties

sin·u·ous

sin·u·ous·ly

sin·u·ous·ness

si·nus

si·nus·itis

sip, v. sipped,
  sip·ping

si·phon

sire, v. sired,
  sir·ing

si·ren

sir·loin

si·roc·co, n. pl.
  si·roc·cos

si·sal

sis·si·fied

sis·sy, n. pl. sis·sies

sis·ter

sis·ter·hood

sis·ter-in-law, n. pl.
  sis·ters-in-law

sis·ter·ly

sit, v. sat, sit·ting

si·tar

sit·com

sit-down, adj., n.

sit down, v.

site, v. sit·ed,
  sit·ing

sit-in, n.

sit in, v.

sit·ter

sit·ting

sit·u·ate, v.
  sit·u·at·ed,
  sit·u·at·ing

sit·u·at·ed

sit·u·a·tion

sitz bath

sitz·mark

six·fold

six-gun

six-pack

six·pence

six·pen·ny

six-shoot·er

six·teen

six·teenth

sixth

six·ti·eth

six·ty, n. pl. six·ties

siz·able, or
  size·able

siz·ably

size, v. sized,
  siz·ing

siz·ing

siz·zle, v. siz·zled,
  siz·zling

skate, v. skat·ed,
  skat·ing

skate·board

skat·er

skeet

skein

skel·e·tal

skel·e·tal·ly

skel·e·ton

skep·tic

skep·ti·cal

skep·ti·cal·ly

skep·ti·cism

sketch·book

sketch·i·ly

sketch·i·ness

sketchy, adj.
  sketch·i·er,
  sketch·i·est

skew·er

ski, n. pl. skis
  (occas. ski)

ski, v. skied,
  ski·ing

skid, v. skid·ded,
  skid·ding

ski·er

skiff

ski·ing

skilled

skil·let

skill·ful *or* skil·ful

skill·ful·ly

skill·ful·ness

skim, *v.* skimmed,
  skim·ming

skim·mer

skimp·i·ly

skimp·i·ness

skimpy, *adj.*
  skimp·i·er,
  skimp·i·est

skin, *v.* skinned,
  skin·ning

skin-deep

skin·flint

skin·ful

skin·head

skin·less

skin·ni·ness

skin·ny, *adj.*
  skin·ni·er,
  skin·ni·est

skin·ny-dip, *v.*
  skin·ny-
  dipped, skin·ny-
  dip·ping

skin·tight

skip, *v.* skipped,
  skip·ping

skip·jack, *n. pl.*
  skip·jacks *or*
  skip·jack

ski·plane

skip·per

skir·mish

skir·mish·er

skirt

skit

skit·ter

skit·tish

skit·tish·ly

skit·tish·ness

skiv·vies

ski·wear

skoal

skul·dug·gery *or*
  skull·dug·gery

skulk·er

skull (HEAD) (*see
  also* scull)

skull·cap

skunk, *n. pl.*
  skunks (*occas.*
  skunk)

sky, *n. pl.* skies

sky, *v.* skied,
  sky·ing

sky·borne

sky·cap

sky·dive, *v.*
  sky·dived,
  sky·div·ing

sky-high

sky·jack

sky·jack·er

Sky·lab

sky·lark

sky·light

sky·line

sky·lounge

sky·rock·et

sky·scrap·er

sky·ward

sky·way

sky·writ·ing

slack·en

slack·er

slack·ly

slack·ness

slake, *v.* slaked,
  slak·ing

sla·lom

slam, *v.* slammed,
  slam·ming

slam-bang

slam dunk, *n.*

slam-dunk, *v.*

slam·mer

slan·der

slan·der·ous

slan·der·ous·ly

slan·der·ous·ness

slang·i·ness

slangy

slant·ing

slant·ing·ly

slant·ways

slant·wise

slap, *v.* slapped,
  slap·ping

slap·dash

slap·hap·py

slap·stick

slash-and-burn

slash·ing

slat, *v.* slat·ted,
  slat·ting

slate, *v.* slat·ed,
  slat·ing

slat·tern

slat·tern·li·ness

slat·tern·ly

slaugh·ter

slaugh·ter·house

slave, *v.* slaved, slav·ing

slave·hold·er

slav·er

slav·ery

slav·ish

slav·ish·ly

slav·ish·ness

slay, *v.* slew, slain, slay·ing

slay·er

sleaze

slea·zi·ly

slea·zi·ness

slea·zy, *adj.* slea·zi·er, slea·zi·est

sled, *v.* sled·ded, sled·ding

sled·ding, *n.*

sledge, *v.* sledged, sledg·ing

sledge·ham·mer

sleek·ly

sleek·ness

sleep, *v.* slept, sleep·ing

sleep·er

sleep·i·ly

sleep·i·ness

sleep·less

sleep·less·ly

sleep·less·ness

sleep·walk

sleep·walk·ing

sleep·wear

sleepy, *adj.*

sleep·i·er, sleep·i·est

sleepy·head

sleet

sleeve, *v.* sleeved, sleev·ing

sleeve·less

sleigh

sleight (DEXTERITY) (*see also* slight)

slen·der

slen·der·ize, *v.* slen·der·ized, slen·der·iz·ing

sleuth

slew (LARGE AMOUNT) (*see also* slough, slue)

slice, *v.* sliced, slic·ing

slic·er

slick·er

slick·ly

slick·ness

slide, *v.* slid, slid·ing

slid·er

slight (SLENDER) (*see also* sleight)

slight·ly

slim, *adj.* slim·mer, slim·mest

slim, *v.* slimmed, slim·ming

slim·i·ly

slim·i·ness

slim·ness

slimy, *adj.* slim·i·er, slim·i·est

sling, *v.* slung, sling·ing

sling·shot

slink, *v.* slunk slink·ing

slink·i·ly

slink·i·ness

slinky, *adj.* slink·i·er, slink·i·est

slip, *v.* slipped, slip·ping

slip·case

slip·cov·er

slip·knot

slip-on, *n.*

slip on, *v.*

slip·over

slip·page

slip·per

slip·peri·ness

slip·pery, *adj.* slip·peri·er, slip·peri·est

slip·shod

slip·stream

slip·up, *n.*

slip up, *v.*

slit, *v.* slit, slit·ting

slith·er

slith·ery

sliv·er

sliv·o·vitz

slob·ber

sloe

sloe-eyed

slog, v. slogged, slog·ging

slo·gan

slo·gan·eer

slo·gan·ize, v. slo·gan·ized, slo·gan·iz·ing

sloop

sloop-rigged

slop, v. slopped, slop·ping

slope, v. sloped, slop·ing

slop·pi·ly

slop·pi·ness

slop·py, adj. slop·pi·er, slop·pi·est

slop·work

slosh

slot, v. slot·ted, slot·ting

sloth·ful

sloth·ful·ly

sloth·ful·ness

slouch·er

slouchy, adj. slouch·i·er, slouch·i·est

slough (WATERWAY), n. (see also slew, slue)

slough or sluff (DISPOSE OF), v. (see also slew, slue)

Slo·ven·ia

slov·en·li·ness

slov·en·ly

slow

slow·down

slow-mo·tion

slow·poke

slow-wit·ted

slow-wit·ted·ly

slow-wit·ted·ness

sludge

$ludgy, adj. sludg·i·er, sludg·i·est

slue (SWING AROUND), v. slued, slu·ing (see also slew, slough)

slug, v. slugged, slug·ging

slug·abed

slug·fest

slug·gard

slug·ger

slug·gish

slug·gish·ly

slug·gish·ness

sluice, v. sluiced, sluic·ing

sluice·way

slum, v. slummed, slum·ming

slum·ber

slum·ber·ous or slum·brous

slum·gul·lion

slum·lord

slump

slur, v. slurred, slur·ring

slurp

slur·ry, n. pl. slur·ries

slush·i·ness

slushy, adj. slush·i·er, slush·i·est

slut·tish

slut·tish·ly

slut·tish·ness

sly, adj. sli·er (occas. sly·er), sli·est (occas. sly·est)

sly·ly

sly·ness

small·ish

small-mind·ed

small-mind·ed·ly

small-mind·ed·ness

small·pox

small-scale

small-time

small-town

smart·ly

smart·ness

smash·ing

smash·ing·ly

smash·up

smat·ter·ing

smeary

smell, v. smelled or smelt, smell·ing

smelly, adj. smell·i·er, smell·i·est

smelt, n. pl. smelts or smelt

smelt·er

smid·gen (*occas.* smid·geon *or* smid·gin)

smile, *v.* smiled, smil·ing

smil·ing·ly

smirk.

smite, *v.* smote, smit·ten *or* smote, smit·ing

smith·er·eens

smithy, *n. pl.* smith·ies

smit·ten

smock·ing

smog·gy, *adj.* smog·gi·er, smog·gi·est

smok·able *or* smoke·able

smoke, *v.* smoked, smok·ing

smoke-filled

smoke·less

smoke·stack

smok·i·ly

smok·i·ness

smoky (*occas.* smok·ey), *adj.* smok·i·er, smok·i·est

smol·der *or* smoul·der

smooch

smooth·bore

smooth·en

smooth·ly

smooth·ness

smooth-tongued

smoothy *or* smooth·ie, *n. pl.* smooth·ies

smor·gas·bord

smoth·er

smudge, *v.* smudged, smudg·ing

smudg·i·ly

smudg·i·ness

smudgy

smug·gle, *v.* smug·gled, smug·gling

smug·gler

smug·ly

smut·ti·ly

smut·ti·ness

smut·ty, *adj.* smut·ti·er, smut·ti·est

sna·fu, *v.* sna·fued, sna·fu·ing

snag, *v.* snagged, snag·ging

snag·gle·tooth, *n. pl.* snag·gle·teeth

snail-paced

snake, *v.* snaked, snak·ing

snake·bite

snake·like

snake·skin

snak·i·ly

snaky (*occas.* snak·ey)

snap, *v.* snapped, snap·ping

snap·back

snap-brim

snap·drag·on

snap·per

snap·pish

snap·pish·ly

snap·pish·ness

snap·py, *adj.* snap·pi·er, snap·pi·est

snap·shot

snare, *v.* snared, snar·ing

snar·er

snatch

snaz·zy, *adj.* snaz·zi·er, snaz·zi·est

sneak, *v.* sneaked *or* snuck, sneak·ing

sneak·er

sneak·i·ly

sneak·i·ness

sneak·ing

sneaky, *adj.* sneak·i·er, sneak·i·est

sneeze, *v.* sneezed, sneez·ing

snick·er

snide

snide·ly

snide·ness

snif·fle, *v.* snif·fled, snif·fling

snif·ter

snig·ger

snip, v. snipped,
  snip·ping

snipe, n. pl. snipes
  or snipe

snipe, v. sniped,
  snip·ing

snip·er·scope

snip·pet

snip·py, adj.
  snip·pi·er,
  snip·pi·est

snit

snitch

sniv·el, v. sniv·eled
  or sniv·elled,
  sniv·el·ing or
  sniv·el·ling

snob·bery, n. pl.
  snob·ber·ies

snob·bish

snob·bish·ly

snob·bish·ness

Sno-Cat®

snood

snook, n. pl. snook
  or snooks

snook·er

snoop·er

snoop·er·scope

snoopy, adj.
  snoop·i·er,
  snoop·i·est

snooty, adj.
  snoot·i·er,
  snoot·i·est

snooze, v.
  snoozed,
  snooz·ing

snore, v. snored,
  snor·ing

snor·kel, v.
  snor·keled,
  snor·kel·ing

snort

snot

snot·ty, adj.
  snot·ti·er,
  snot·ti·est

snout

snow·ball

snow·bank

snow·ber·ry, n. pl.
  snow·ber·ries

snow-blind or
  snow-blind·ed

snow·bound

snow·cap

snow·drift

snow·drop

snow·fall

snow·flake

snow·man, n. pl.
  snow·men

snow·mo·bile, v.
  snow·mo·biled,
  snow·mo·bil·ing

snow·pack

snow·plow

snow·shoe, v.
  snow·shoed,
  snow·shoe·ing

snow·storm

snow·suit

snow-white

snowy, adj.
  snow·i·er,
  snow·i·est

snub, v. snubbed,
  snub·bing

snub-nosed

snuff·er

snuf·fle, v.
  snuf·fled,
  snuf·fling

snug, adj. snug·ger,
  snug·gest

snug, v. snugged,
  snug·ging

snug·gle, v.
  snug·gled,
  snug·gling

snug·ly

snug·ness

soak·age

so-and-so, n. pl.
  so-and-sos or
  so-and-so's

soap·ber·ry, n. pl.
  soap·ber·ries

soap·box

soap·stone

soap·suds

soapy, adj.
  soap·i·er,
  soap·i·est

soar (FLY) (see also
  sore)

sob, v. sobbed,
  sob·bing

so·ber

so·bri·ety

so·bri·quet

so-called

soc·cer

so·cia·bil·i·ty, n. pl.
  so·cia·bil·i·ties

so·cia·ble

so·cia·bly

so·cial

so·cial·ism

so·cial·ist

so·cial·is·tic

so·cial·ite

so·cial·iza·tion

so·cial·ize, v.
  so·cial·ized,
  so·cial·iz·ing

so·cial·ly

so·ci·e·tal

so·ci·e·tal·ly

so·ci·e·ty, n. pl.
  so·ci·et·ies

so·cio·bi·ol·o·gist

so·cio·bi·ol·o·gy

so·cio·eco·nom·ic

so·cio·lin·guis·tic

so·cio·lin·guis·tics

so·cio·log·i·cal

so·cio·log·i·cal·ly

so·ci·ol·o·gist

so·ci·ol·o·gy

so·ci·om·e·try

so·cio·po·lit·i·cal

so·cio·re·li·gious

sock, n. pl. socks
  or sox

sock·et

sock·eye

sod, v. sod·ded,
  sod·ding

so·da

so·dal·i·ty, n. pl.
  so·dal·i·ties

sod·bust·er

sod·den

sod·den·ly

sod·den·ness

so·di·um

sod·om·ize, v.
  sod·om·ized,
  sod·om·iz·ing

sod·omy

so·ev·er

so·fa

sof·fit

soft·ball

soft-boiled

soft·bound

soft·en

soft·en·er

soft·heart·ed

soft·heart·ed·ly

soft·heart·ed·ness

soft-ped·al, v. soft-
  ped·aled or
  soft-ped·alled,
  soft-ped·al·ing
  or soft-
  ped·al·ling

soft-shell or soft-
  shelled

soft·soap

soft-spoken

soft·ware

soft·wood

softy, n. pl. soft·ies

sog·gi·ly

sog·gi·ness

sog·gy, adj.
  sog·gi·er,
  sog·gi·est

soig·né (masc.) or
  soig·née (fem.)

soil·borne

soi·ree or soi·rée

so·journ

so·journ·er

sol, n. pl. so·les

so·lace

so·lar

so·lar·i·um, n. pl.
  so·lar·ia (occas.
  so·lar·i·ums)

so·lar plex·us

sol·der

sol·dier

sole

so·le·cism

sole·ly

sol·emn

so·lem·ni·fy, v.
  so·lem·ni·fied,
  so·lem·ni·fy·ing

so·lem·ni·ty, n. pl.
  so·lem·ni·ties

sol·em·ni·za·tion

sol·em·nize, v.
  sol·em·nized,
  sol·em·niz·ing

sol·emn·ly

sol·emn·ness

so·le·noid

so·le·noid·al

sole·plate

sol-fa, v. sol-faed,
  sol-fa·ing

sol·fège

sol·feg·gio, n. pl.
  sol·feg·gios or
  sol·feg·gi

so·lic·it

so·lic·i·ta·tion

so·lic·i·tor

so·lic·i·tor gen·er·al,
  n. pl.
  so·lic·i·tors
  gen·er·al

so·lic·i·tous

so·lic·i·tous·ly

so·lic·i·tous·ness

so·lic·i·tude

sol·id

sol·i·dar·i·ty

so·lid·i·fi·ca·tion

so·lid·i·fy, *v.*
  so·lid·i·fied,
  so·lid·i·fy·ing

so·lid·i·ty, *n. pl.*
  so·lid·i·ties

sol·id-state

sol·i·dus, *n. pl.*
  sol·i·di

so·lil·o·quize, *v.*
  so·lil·o·quized,
  so·lil·o·quiz·ing

so·lil·o·quy, *n. pl.*
  so·lil·o·quies

so·lip·sism

sol·i·taire

sol·i·tar·i·ly

sol·i·tar·i·ness

sol·i·tary, *n. pl.*
  sol·i·tar·ies

sol·i·tude

so·lo, *n. pl.* so·los

so·lo, *v.* so·loed,
  so·lo·ing

so·lo·ist

so·lon

sol·stice

sol·u·bil·i·ty

so·lu·ble

so·lu·tion

solv·abil·i·ty

solv·able

solve, *v.* solved,
  solv·ing

sol·ven·cy

sol·vent

so·ma, *n. pl.*
  so·ma·ta *or*
  so·mas

So·ma·li, *n. pl.*
  So·ma·li *or*
  So·ma·lis

So·ma·lia

So·ma·lian

so·mat·ic

so·ma·tol·o·gy

som·ber *or* som·bre

som·ber·ly

som·ber·ness

som·bre·ro, *n. pl.*
  som·bre·ros

some·body, *n. pl.*
  some·bod·ies

some·day

some·how

some·one

some·place

som·er·sault

some·thing

some·time

some·times

some·what

some·where

som·me·lier

som·nam·bu·late, *v.*

som·nam·bu·lat·ed,
som·nam·bu·lat·ing

som·nam·bu·lism

som·nam·bu·list

som·no·lence

som·no·lent

som·no·lent·ly

so·nar

so·na·ta

son·a·ti·na

sonde

song·bird

song·book

song·fest

song·ster

song·stress

song·writ·er

son·ic

son-in-law, *n. pl.*
  sons-in-law

son·net

son·net·eer

son·o·gram

So·no·ra

so·nor·i·ty, *n. pl.*
  so·nor·i·ties

so·no·rous

so·no·rous·ly

so·no·rous·ness

soon·er

soothe, *v.* soothed,
  sooth·ing

sooth·er

sooth·ing·ly

sooth·ing·ness

sooth·say·er

soot·i·ly

soot·i·ness

sooty, adj.
  soot·i·er,
  soot·i·est

sop, v. sopped,
  sop·ping

soph·ism

soph·ist

so·phis·tic

so·phis·ti·cal

so·phis·ti·cate, v.
  so·phis·ti·cat·ed,
  so·phis·ti·cat·ing

so·phis·ti·cat·ed

so·phis·ti·ca·tion

soph·ist·ry, n. pl.
  soph·ist·ries

soph·o·more

soph·o·mor·ic

so·po·rif·er·ous

so·po·rif·ic

so·pra·no, n. pl.
  so·pra·nos

sor·bent

sor·bet

sor·bic acid

sor·cer·er

sor·cer·ess (WITCH)

sor·cer·ous (OF
  SORCERY)

sor·cery, n. pl.
  sor·cer·ies

sor·did

sor·did·ly

sor·did·ness

sore, adj. sor·er,
  sor·est

sore (TENDER,

ANGRY) (see also
  soar)

sore·head

sore·ly

sore·ness

sor·ghum

so·ror·i·ty, n. pl.
  so·ror·i·ties

sor·rel

sor·ri·ly

sor·ri·ness

sor·row

sor·row·ful

sor·row·ful·ly

sor·row·ful·ness

sor·ry, adj.
  sor·ri·er,
  sor·ri·est

sor·tie

so-so

sos·te·nu·to, n. pl.
  sos·te·nu·tos or
  sos·te·nu·ti

sot·to vo·ce

sou

sou·brette

souf·flé

soul

soul·ful

soul·ful·ly

soul·ful·ness

soul-search·ing

sound·board

sound·ing

sound·ly

sound·proof

soup·çon

soupy, adj.
  soup·i·er,
  soup·i·est

source, v. sourced,
  sourc·ing

source·book

sour·dough

sour·ish

sour·ly

sour·ness

sou·sa·phone

souse, v. soused,
  sous·ing

sou·tane

South Af·ri·ca

South Af·ri·can

South Amer·i·ca

South Amer·i·can

South·amp·ton

South Bend

south·bound

South Car·o·li·na

South Car·o·li·ni·an

South Da·ko·ta

South Da·ko·tan

south·east

south·east·er·ly

south·east·ern

south·east·ward

south·er·ly

south·ern

South·ern·er

south·ern·most

South Ko·rea

South Ko·re·an

south·paw

south-south·east

south-south-west

south·ward

south·ward·ly

south·west

south·west·er·ly

south·west·ern

south·west·ward

sou·ve·nir

sov·er·eign

sov·er·eign·ty, *n. pl.*
    sov·er·eign·ties

so·vi·et

sow (PLANT SEED),
    v. sowed, sown *or*
    sowed, sow·ing
    (*see also* sew)

sow·er

soy·bean (*occas.*
    soya bean)

space, *v.* spaced,
    spac·ing

space·craft, *n. pl.*
    space·craft

spaced-out

space·flight

space·man, *n. pl.*
    space·men

space·port

space·ship

space·suit

space-time

space walk

spac·ey (*occas.*
    spacy), *adj.*
    spac·i·er,
    spac·i·est

spac·ing

spa·cious

spa·cious·ly

spa·cious·ness

Spack·le®

spack·le, *v.*
    spack·led,
    spack·ling

spack·led

spade, *v.* spad·ed,
    spad·ing

spade·ful

spade·work

spa·ghet·ti

Spain

span, *v.* spanned,
    span·ning

span·dex

span·drel

span·gle, *v.*
    span·gled,
    span·gling

Span·iard

span·iel

Span·ish

spank·ing

span·ner

spar, *v.* sparred,
    spar·ring

spare, *v.* spared,
    spar·ing

spare·ribs

spar·ing·ly

spar·kle, *v.*
    spar·kled,
    spar·kling

spark·ler

spar·row

sparse·ly

sparse·ness

spasm

spas·mod·ic

spas·mod·i·cal·ly

spas·tic

spas·ti·cal·ly

spat, *v.* spat·ted,
    spat·ting

spate

spa·tial

spa·tial·ly

spat·ter

spat·u·la

spav·in

spav·ined

spawn

spay

speak, *v.* spoke,
    spok·en,
    speak·ing

speak·easy, *n. pl.*
    speak·eas·ies

speak·er

speak·er·phone

spear·fish

spear·head

spear·mint

spear·wort

spe·cial

spe·cial·ist

spe·cial·iza·tion

spec·cial·ize, *v.*
    spe·cial·ized,
    spe·cial·iz·ing

spe·cial·ly

spe·cial·ty, *n. pl.*
    spe·cial·ties

spe·cie (MONEY)

spe·cies (KIND), *n.*
    pl. spe·cies
spec·i·fi·able
spe·cif·ic
spe·cif·i·cal·ly
spec·i·fi·ca·tion
spec·i·fic·i·ty
spec·i·fi·er
spec·i·fy, *v.*
    spec·i·fied,
    spec·i·fy·ing
spec·i·men
spe·cious
spe·cious·ly
spe·cious·ness
speck·le, *v.*
    speck·led,
    speck·ling
spec·ta·cle
spec·ta·cled
spec·tac·u·lar
spec·tac·u·lar·ly
spec·ta·tor
spec·ter
spec·tral
spec·trom·e·ter
spec·tro·scope
spec·tro·scop·ic
spec·tro·scop·i·cal·ly
spec·tros·co·pist
spec·tros·co·py
spec·trum, *n. pl.*
    spec·tra or
    spec·trums
spec·u·late, *v.*
    spec·u·lat·ed,
    spec·u·lat·ing
spec·u·la·tion

spec·u·la·tive
spec·u·la·tive·ly
spec·u·la·tor
spec·u·lum, *n. pl.*
    spec·u·la or
    spec·u·lums
speech·less
speech·less·ly
speech·less·ness
speed, *v.* sped or
    speed·ed,
    speed·ing
speed·ball
speed·boat
speed·er
speed·i·ly
speed·i·ness
speed·om·e·ter
speed·up, *n,*
speed up, *v.*
speed·way
speed·well
speedy, *adj.*
    speed·i·er,
    speed·i·est
spe·le·ol·o·gist
spe·le·ol·o·gy
spell, *v.* spelled,
    spell·ing
spell·bind, *v.*
    spell·bound,
    spell·bind·ing
spell·bind·er
spell·er
spe·lunk·er
spe·lunk·ing
spend, *v.* spent,
    spend·ing

spend·able
spend·thrift
sperm, *n. pl.*
    sperm or
    sperms
sper·ma·ce·ti
sper·ma·to·zo·an, *n.*
    pl.
    sper·ma·to·zoa
sperm·i·cide
spew
sphag·num
sphere
spher·ic
spher·i·cal
spher·i·cal·ly
spher·oid
sphinc·ter
sphinx, *n. pl.*
    sphinx·es or
    sphin·ges
sphyg·mo·ma·nom·e·ter
spice, *v.* spiced,
    spic·ing
spic·i·ly
spic·i·ness
spick-and-span or
    spic-and-span
spicy, *adj.* spic·i·er,
    spic·i·est
spi·der
spi·der·wort
spi·dery
spiel
spiffy, *adj.*
    spiff·i·er,
    spiff·i·est
spig·ot

spike, v. spiked,
  spik·ing

spill, v. spilled
  (*occas.* spilt),
  spill·ing

spill·age

spill·way

spin, v. spun,
  spin·ning

spi·na bi·fi·da

spin·ach

spi·nal

spi·nal·ly

spin·dle, v.
  spin·dled,
  spin·dling

spin·dling

spin·dly

spin·drift

spine·less

spine·less·ly

spine·less·ness

spin·et

spin·na·ker

spin·ner

spin-off, n.

spin off, v.

spin·ster

spin·ster·hood

spin·ster·ish

spiny, adj.
  spin·i·er,
  spin·i·est

spi·ral, v. spi·raled
  or spi·ralled,
  spi·ral·ing *or*
  spi·ral·ling

spi·ral·ly

spir·it

spir·it·ed

spir·it·ed·ly

spir·it·ed·ness

spir·it·less

spir·it·less·ly

spir·it·less·ness

spir·i·tu·al

spir·i·tu·al·ism

spir·i·tu·al·ist

spir·i·tu·al·i·ty, n.
  pl.
  spir·i·tu·al·i·ties

spir·i·tu·al·ly

spir·i·tu·al·ness

spir·i·tu·ous

spir·i·tu·ous·i·ty

spi·ro·chete (*occas.*
  spi·ro·chaete)

spit (IMPALE), v.
  spit·ted,
  spit·ting

spit
  (EXPECTORATE),
  v. spit *or* spat,
  spit·ting

spit·ball

spite·ful

spite·ful·ly

spite·ful·ness

spit·fire

spit·tle

spit·toon

splash·board

splash·down

splat·ter

splay·foot, n. pl.
  splay·feet

spleen·ful

spleen·wort

splen·did

splen·did·ly

splen·did·ness

splen·dor

sple·net·ic

splen·ic

splice, v. spliced,
  splic·ing

splic·er

spline

splin·ter

splin·tery

split, v. split,
  split·ting

split-lev·el

split-up, n.

split up, v.

splotch

splurge, v.
  splurged,
  splurg·ing

splut·ter

Spode™

spoil, v. spoiled *or*
  spoilt, spoil·ing

spoil·able

spoil·age

spoil·er

spoil·sport

Spo·kane

spo·ken

spoke·shave

spokes·man, n. pl.
  spokes·men

spokes·per·son

spokes·wom·an, n.

pl.
spokes·wom·en

spo·li·ate, *v.*
spo·li·at·ed,
spo·li·at·ing

spo·li·a·tion

sponge, *v.*
sponged,
spong·ing

spong·er

spong·i·ness

spongy, *adj.*
spong·i·er,
spong·i·est

spon·son

spon·sor

spon·sor·ship

spon·ta·ne·ity

spon·ta·ne·ous

spon·ta·ne·ous·ly

spon·ta·ne·ous·ness

spooky, *adj.*
spook·i·er,
spook·i·est

spool

spoo·ner·ism

spoon·feed, *v.*
spoon·fed,
spoon·feed·ing

spoon·ful, *n. pl.*
spoon·fuls (*occas.*
spoons·ful)

spoor (TRAIL), *n.*
pl. spoor *or*
spoors (*see also*
spore)

spo·rad·ic

spo·rad·i·cal·ly

spore
(REPRODUCTIVE

BODY) (*see also*
spoor)

sport·i·ly

sport·i·ness

sport·ing

sport·ive

sports·cast

sports·cast·er

sports·man, *n. pl.*
sports·men

sports·man·ship

sports·wear

sports·wom·an, *n.*
pl.
sports·wom·en

sports·writ·er

sporty, *adj.*
sport·i·er,
sport·i·est

spot, *v.* spot·ted,
spot·ting

spot-check

spot·less

spot·less·ly

spot·less·ness

spot·light, *v.*
spot·light·ed *or*
spot·lit,
spot·light·ing

spot·ter

spot·ti·ly

spot·ti·ness

spot·ty, *adj.*
spot·ti·er,
spot·ti·est

spous·al

sprawl

spray·er

spread, *v.* spread,
spread·ing

spread eagle, *n.*

spread-ea·gle, *adj.*

spread-ea·gle, *v.*
spread-ea·gled,
spread-ea·gling

spread·er

spread·sheet

spree

sprig

spright·li·ness

spright·ly, *adj.*
spright·li·er,
spright·li·est

spring, *v.* sprang *or*
sprung, sprung,
spring·ing

spring·board

spring·bok, *n. pl.*
spring·bok *or*
spring·boks

spring-clean·ing

spring·er

Spring·field

spring·house

spring·i·ly

spring·i·ness

spring·time

springy, *adj.*
spring·i·er,
spring·i·est

sprin·kle, *v.*
sprin·kled,
sprin·kling

sprin·kler

sprin·kling

sprint·er

spritz·er

sprock·et

spruce, v. spruced,
spruc·ing

spry, adj. spri·er or
spry·er, spri·est
or spry·est

spry·ly

spry·ness

spu·mo·ni

spunk·i·ly

spunk·i·ness

spunky, adj.
spunk·i·er,
spunk·i·est

spur, v. spurred,
spur·ring

spu·ri·ous

spu·ri·ous·ly

spu·ri·ous·ness

sput·nik

sput·ter

spu·tum, n. pl.
spu·ta

spy, v. spied,
spy·ing

spy·glass

squab, n. pl.
squabs or squab

squab·ble, v.
squab·bled,
squab·bling

squad·ron

squal·id

squal·id·ly

squal·id·ness

squall

squa·lor

squan·der

square, adj.

squar·er,
squar·est

square, v. squared,
squar·ing

square·ly

square·ness

square-rigged

square-rig·ger

square-shoul·dered

squash, n. pl.
squash·es or
squash

squash·i·ly

squash·i·ness

squashy, adj.
squash·i·er,
squash·i·est

squat, adj.
squat·ter,
squat·test

squat, v. squat·ted,
squat·ting

squat·ter

squaw

squawk

squeak·er

squeaky

squeaky-clean

squeal·er

squea·mish

squea·mish·ly

squea·mish·ness

squee·gee, v.
squee·geed,
squee·gee·ing

squeeze, v.
squeezed,
squeez·ing

squeez·er

squelch

squib, v. squibbed,
squib·bing

squid, n. pl. squid
or squids

squig·gle, v.
squig·gled,
squig·gling

squint·eyed

squint·ing

squirmy

squir·rel, n pl.
squir·rels
(occas. squir·rel)

squir·rel, v.
squir·reled or
squir·relled,
squir·rel·ing or
squir·rel·ling

squir·rel·ly

squish·i·ness

squishy, adj.
squish·i·er,
squish·i·est

Sri Lan·ka

Sri Lan·kan

stab, v. stabbed,
stab·bing

sta·bile

sta·bil·i·ty, n. pl.
sta·bil·i·ties

sta·bi·li·za·tion

sta·bi·lize, v.
sta·bi·lized,
sta·bi·liz·ing

sta·bi·liz·er

sta·ble, v. sta·bled,
sta·bling

stac·ca·to

Sta·cey

Sta·cy

sta·di·um, n. pl.
sta·dia or
sta·di·ums

staff, n. pl. staffs
(GROUPS OF
WORKERS),
staffs or staves
(STICKS,
MUSICAL
SCORES)

stag

stage, v. staged,
stag·ing

stage·coach

stage·craft

stage·hand

stage-man·age, v.
stage-
man·aged, stage-
man·ag·ing

stage man·ag·er

stage·struck

stag·fla·tion

stag·ger

stag·ger·ing

stag·i·ly

stag·i·ness

stag·ing

stag·nan·cy

stag·nant

stag·nant·ly

stag·nate, v.
stag·nat·ed,
stag·nat·ing

stag·na·tion

stagy or stag·ey,
adj. stag·i·er,
stag·i·est

staid

staid·ly

staid·ness

stain·able

stain·less

stair·case

stair·way

stair·well

stake (BET, POST),
v. staked,
stak·ing (see also
steak)

stake·hold·er

stake·out

sta·lac·tite

sta·lag·mite

stale, adj. stal·er,
stal·est

stale·ly

stale·mate

stale·ness

stalk·ing-horse

stal·lion

stal·wart

stal·wart·ly

stal·wart·ness

sta·men, n. pl.
sta·mens (occas.
sta·mi·na)

stam·i·na

stam·mer

stam·mer·er

stam·pede, v.
stam·ped·ed,
stam·ped·ing

stamp·er

stance

stanch

stan·chion

stand, v. stood,
stand·ing

stand-alone

stan·dard

stan·dard-bear·er

stan·dard·iza·tion

stan·dard·ize, v.
stan·dard·ized,
stan·dard·iz·ing

stand·by, n. pl.
stand·bys

stand·ee

stand-in

stand·ing

stand·off

stand·off·ish

stand·off·ish·ly

stand·off·ish·ness

stand·out

stand·pat

stand·pipe

stand·point

stand·still

stand-up, adj.

stand up, v.

stan·za

staph·y·lo·coc·cus,
n. pl.
staph·y·lo·coc·ci

sta·ple, v. sta·pled,
sta·pling

sta·pler

star, v. starred,
star·ring

star·board

star-cham·ber

starch·i·ly

starch·i·ness

starchy, *adj.*
  starch·i·er,
  starch·i·est

star-crossed

star·dom

star·dust

stare, *v.* stared,
  star·ing

sta·re de·ci·sis

star·fish

star·gaze, *v.*
  star·gazed,
  star·gaz·ing

star·gaz·er

stark·ly

stark·ness

star·less

star·let

star·light

star·like

star·ling

star·lit

star·ry, *adj.*
  star·ri·er,
  star·ri·est

star·ry-eyed

star-span·gled

start·er

star·tle, *v.* star·tled,
  star·tling

star·tling

star·va·tion

starve, *v.* starved,
  starv·ing

starve·ling

sta·sis, *n. pl.* sta·ses

stat·able *or*
  state·able

state, *v.* stat·ed,
  stat·ing

state·craft

state·hood

state·house

state·less

state·li·ness

state·ly, *adj.*
  state·li·er,
  state·li·est

state·ment

state·room

state·side

states·man, *n. pl.*
  states·men

states' rights

stat·ic

stat·i·cal·ly

stat·icky

sta·tion

sta·tion·ary (NOT
  MOVING) (*see
  also* stationery)

sta·tion·er

sta·tion·ery
  (WRITING PAPER)
  (*see also*
  stationary)

sta·tion·mas·ter

stat·ism

sta·tis·tic

sta·tis·ti·cal

sta·tis·ti·cal·ly

stat·is·ti·cian

sta·tis·tics

sta·tor

stat·u·ary, *n. pl.*
  stat·u·ar·ies

stat·ue

stat·u·esque

stat·u·esque·ly

stat·u·esque·ness

stat·u·ette

stat·ure

sta·tus, *n. pl.*
  sta·tus·es

sta·tus quo

stat·ute

stat·u·to·ry

staunch

stave, *v.* staved *or*
  stove, stav·ing

stay, *v.* stayed
  (*occas.* staid),
  stay·ing

stay-at-home

stead·fast

stead·fast·ly

stead·fast·ness

stead·i·ly

stead·i·ness

steady, *adj.*
  stead·i·er,
  stead·i·est

steak (MEAT) (*see
  also* stake)

steak·house

steal, *v.* stole,
  stol·en, steal·ing

stealth·i·ly

stealth·i·ness

stealthy, *adj.*
  stealth·i·er,
  stealth·i·est

steam·boat

steam·er

steam·fit·ter

steam·i·ly

steam·i·ness

steam·roll·er, n.

steam·roll·er (occas. steam·roll), v.

steam·ship

steamy, adj. steam·i·er, steam·i·est

steel

steel·head, n. pl. steel·head or steel·heads

steel·i·ness

steel·work

steely, adj. steel·i·er, steel·i·est

steel·yard

stee·ple

stee·ple·chase

stee·ple·jack

steep·ly

steep·ness

steer·able

steer·age

steer·er

steers·man, n. pl. steers·men

stein

stel·lar

stem, v. stemmed, stem·ming

stem·less

stem·ware

sten·cil, v. sten·ciled or

sten·cilled, stenp·cil·ing or sten·cil·ling

ste·nog·ra·pher

sten·o·graph·ic

sten·o·graph·i·cal·ly

ste·nog·ra·phy

steno·type, v. steno·typed, steno·typ·ing

steno·typ·ist

sten·to·ri·an

step, v. stepped, step·ping

step·broth·er

step-by-step

step·child, n. pl. step-chil·dren

step·daugh·ter

step-down, n.

step down, v.

step·fa·ther

Ste·pha·nie

step-in, adj. n.

step in, v.

step·lad·der

step·moth·er

step·par·ent

steppe

step·ping-stone

step·sis·ter

step·son

step-up, n.

step up, v.

ster·eo, n. pl. ste·re·os

ste·reo·phon·ic

ste·reo·scope

ste·reo·scop·ic

ste·re·os·co·py

ste·reo·type, v. ste·reo·typed, ste·reo·typ·ing

ste·reo·typ·i·cal

ster·ile

ste·ril·i·ty

ster·il·iza·tion

ster·il·ize, v. ster·il·ized, ster·il·iz·ing

ster·il·iz·er

ster·ling

stern·ly

stern·ness

ster·num, n. pl. ster·nums or ster·na

ster·oid

ster·to·rous

ster·to·rous·ly

ster·to·rous·ness

stet. v. stet·ted, stet·ting

stetho·scope

Stet·son™

ste·ve·dore, v. ste·ve·dored, ste·ve·dor·ing

Ste·ven

stew·ard

stew·ard·ess

stew·ard·ship

stewed

stick, v. stuck, stick·ing

stick·ball

stick·er

stick·i·ly

stick·i·ness

stick-in-the-mud

stick·ler

stick·pin

stick-to-it·ive·ness

sticky, *adj.*
stick·i·er,
stick·i·est

stiff-arm

stiffed

stiff·en

stiff·ly

stiff-necked

stiff·ness

sti·fle, *v.* sti·fled,
sti·fling

stig·ma, *n. pl.*
stig·ma·ta *or*
stig·mas

stig·mat·ic

stig·ma·tism

stig·ma·tize, *v.*
stig·ma·tized,
stig·ma·tiz·ing

stile (FENCE) (*see
also* style)

sti·let·to, *n. pl.*
sti·let·tos *or*
sti·let·toes

still·birth

still·born

stilt·ed

stilt·ed·ly

stilt·ed·ness

stim·u·lant

stim·u·late, *v.*

stim·u·lat·ed,
stim·u·lat·ing

stim·u·la·tion

stim·u·la·tive

stim·u·la·tor

stim·u·lus, *n. pl.*
stim·u·li

sting, *v.* stung,
sting·ing

sting·er

stin·gi·ly

stin·gi·ness

sting·ray

stin·gy, *adj.*
stin·gi·er,
stin·gi·est

stink, *v.* stank *or*
stunk, stunk,
stink·ing

stink·wood

sti·pend

stip·ple, *v.*
stip·pled,
stip·pling

stip·u·late, *v.*
stip·u·lat·ed,
stip·u·lat·ing

stip·u·la·tion

stip·u·la·tor

stir, *v.* stirred,
stir·ring

stir-cra·zy

stir-fry, *v.* stir-
fried, stir-fry·ing

stir·ring

stir·rup

stitch

stitch·ery, *n. pl.*
stitch·er·ies

stoa

stoat, *n. pl.* stoat
(*occas.* stoats)

sto·chas·tic

stock·ade, *v.*
stock·ad·ed,
stock·ad·ing

stock·breed·er

stock·bro·ker

stock·hold·er

stock·i·ly

stock·i·ness

stock·i·nette *or*
stock·i·net

stock·ing

stock-in-trade

stock·man, *n. pl.*
stock·men

stock·pile, *v.*
stock·piled,
stock·pil·ing

stock·pot

stock·room

Stock·ton

stocky, *adj.*
stock·i·er,
stock·i·est

stock·yard

stodg·i·ly

stodg·i·ness

stodgy, *adj.*
stodg·i·er,
stodg·i·est

sto·gie *or* sto·gy, *n.
pl.* sto·gies

sto·ic

sto·i·cal

sto·i·cal·ly

sto·i·cism

stoke, v. stoked,
  stok·ing

stoke·hole

stok·er

stol·id

sto·lid·i·ty

sto·lid·ly

stol·id·ness

stom·ach

stom·ach·ache

stone, v. stoned,
  ston·ing

stone-blind

stone·cut·ter

stone·cut·ting

stone-deaf

stone·ma·son

stone·wall

stone·ware

stone·work

ston·i·ly

ston·i·ness

stony (occas.
  ston·ey), adj.
  ston·i·er,
  ston·i·est

stop, v. stopped,
  stop·ping

stop·cock

stop·gap

stop·light

stop·over

stop·page

stop·per

stop·watch

stor·able

stor·age

store, v. stored,
  stor·ing

store·house

store·keep·er

store·room

store·wide

sto·ried

stork

storm·bound

storm·i·ly

storm·i·ness

storm·proof

stormy, adj.
  storm·i·er,
  storm·i·est

sto·ry, n. pl.
  sto·ries

sto·ry·board

sto·ry·book

sto·ry·tell·er

sto·tin·ka, n. pl.
  sto·tin·ki

stout·heart·ed

stout·heart·ed·ly

stout·heart·ed·ness

stout·ly

stout·ness

stove·pipe

stow·age

stow·away

stra·bis·mus

strad·dle, v.
  strad·dled,
  strad·dling

strafe, v. strafed,
  straf·ing

strag·gle, v.

strag·gled,
  strag·gling

strag·gler

strag·gly, adj.
  strag·gli·er,
  strag·gli·est

straight

straight-arm

straight·away

straight·edge

straight·en (MAKE
  STRAIGHT) (see
  also straiten)

straight-faced

straight-faced·ly

straight·for·ward

straight·ness

strain·er

strait

strait·en
  (RESTRICT) (see
  also straighten)

strait·jack·et or
  straight·jack·et

strait·laced or
  straight·laced

strand·ed

strange, adj.
  strang·er,
  strang·est

strange·ly

strange·ness

strang·er

stran·gle, v.
  stran·gled,
  stran·gling

stran·gle·hold

stran·gler

stran·gu·late, v.

stran·gu·lat·ed,
stran·gu·lat·ing

stran·gu·la·tion

strap, *v.* strapped,
strap·ping

strap·hang·er

strap·less

strap·ping

strat·a·gem

stra·te·gic

stra·te·gi·cal·ly

strat·e·gist

strat·e·gy, *n. pl.*
strat·e·gies

strat·i·fi·ca·tion

strat·i·fy, *v.*
strat·i·fied,
strat·i·fy·ing

stra·tig·ra·phy

stra·to·cu·mu·lus

strato·sphere

strato·sphere·ic

stra·tum, *n. pl.*
stra·ta

stra·tus, *n. pl.*
stra·ti

straw·ber·ry, *n. pl.*
straw·ber·ries

straw·flow·er

straw·worm

streak·i·ness

streaky, *adj.*
streak·i·er,
streak·i·est

stream·er

stream·let

stream·line, *v.*
stream·lined,
stream·lin·ing

stream·lined

street·car

street·walk·er

street·wise

strength·en

stren·u·ous

stren·u·ous·ly

stren·u·ous·ness

strep·to·coc·cus, *n.
pl.*
strep·to·coc·ci

strep·to·my·cin

stressed

stress·ful

stretch·abil·i·ty

stretch·able

stretch·er

stretch·er-bear·er

streu·sel

strew, *v.* strewed,
strewed *or*
strewn, strew·ing

stri·ate, *v.*
stri·at·ed,
stri·at·ing

stri·a·tion

strick·en

strict·ly

strict·ness

stric·ture

stride, *v.* strode,
strid·den,
strid·ing

stri·den·cy

stri·dent

strife

strike, *v.* struck,
struck (*occas.*

strick·en),
strik·ing

strike-bound

strike·break·er

strike·out

strike·over

strik·er

strik·ing

string, *v.* strung,
string·ing

strin·gen·cy, *n. pl.*
strin·gen·cies

strin·gent

strin·gent·ly

strin·gent·ness

string·er

string·i·ness

stringy, *adj.*
string·i·er,
string·i·est

strip, *v.* stripped
(*occas.* stript),
strip·ping

strip-crop·ping

strip·er (STRIPED
BASS, ONE WHO
WEARS STRIPES)
(*see also*
stripper)

strip·ling

strip·per (ONE
WHO STRIPS)
(*see also* striper)

strip·tease

strive, *v.* strove
(*occas.* strived),
striv·en *or*
strived, striv·ing

strobe

stro·bo·scope

stro·bo·scop·ic

stro·ga·noff

stroke, *v.* stroked, strok·ing

stroll·er

strong, *adj.* strong·er, strong·est

strong-arm

strong·box

strong·hold

strong·ly

strong·man, *n. pl.* strong·men

strong-mind·ed

strong-mind·ed·ly

strong-mind·ed·ness

stron·tium

strop, *v.* stropped, strop·ping

stro·phe

stro·phic

struc·tur·al

struc·tur·al·ly

struc·ture, *v.* struc·tured, struc·tur·ing

stru·del

strug·gle, *v.* strug·gled, strug·gling

strum, *v.* strummed, strum·ming

strum·pet

strut, *v.* strut·ted, strut·ting

strych·nine

stub, *v.* stubbed, stub·bing

stub·ble

stub·bly

stub·born

stub·born·ly

stub·born·ness

stub·by

stuc·co, *n. pl.* stuc·cos *or* stuc·coes

stuck-up, *adj.*

stud, *v.* stud·ded, stud·ding

stud·book

stud·ding

stu·dent

stud·horse

stud·ied

stu·dio, *n. pl.* stu·dios

stu·di·ous

stu·di·ous·ly

stu·di·ous·ness

study, *n. pl.* stud·ies

study, *v.* stud·ied, stud·y·ing

stuff·i·ly

stuff·i·ness

stuff·ing

stuffy, *adj.* stuff·i·er, stuff·i·est

stul·ti·fi·ca·tion

stul·ti·fy, *v.* stul·ti·fied, stul·ti·fy·ing

stum·ble, *v.* stum·bled, stum·bling

stum·ble·bum

stun, *v.* stunned, stun·ning

stunt·man, *n. pl.* stunt·men

stu·pe·fac·tion

stu·pe·fy, *v.* stu·pe·fied, stu·pe·fy·ing

stu·pen·dous

stu·pen·dous·ly

stu·pen·dous·ness

stu·pid

stu·pid·i·ty

stu·pid·ly

stu·pid·ness

stu·por

stur·di·ly

stur·dy, *adj.* stur·di·er, stur·di·est

stur·geon

stut·ter

stut·ter·er

sty (PIG PEN), *n. pl.* sties (*occas.* styes)

sty *or* stye (EYELID SWELLING), *n. pl.* sties *or* styes

style (DISTINCTIVE MANNER) (*see also* stile)

style·book

styl·ish

styl·ish·ly
styl·ish·ness
styl·ist
sty·lis·tic
sty·lis·ti·cal·ly
sty·lis·tics
styl·i·za·tion
styl·ize, v. styl·ized,
  styl·iz·ing
sty·lus, n. pl. sty·li
  (occas.
  sty·lus·es)
sty·mie, v.
  sty·mied,
  sty·mie·ing
styp·tic
sty·rene
Sty·ro·foam®
su·able
sua·sion
sua·sive
sua·sive·ly
sua·sive·ness
suave·ly
suave·ness
sua·vi·ty
sub, v. subbed,
  sub·bing
sub·agen·cy, n. pl.
  sub·agen·cies
sub·al·tern
sub·arc·tic
sub·ar·ea
sub·as·sem·bly, n.
  pl.
  sub·as·sem·blies
sub·atom·ic
sub·av·er·age

sub·base·ment
sub·bing
sub·class
sub·com·mit·tee
sub·con·scious
sub·con·scious·ly
sub·con·scious·ness
sub·con·ti·nent
sub·con·tract
sub·con·trac·tor
sub·cul·ture
sub·cu·ta·ne·ous
sub·cu·ta·ne·ous·ly
sub·di·vide, v.
  sub·di·vid·ed,
  sub·di·vid·ing
sub·di·vi·sion
sub·due, v.
  sub·dued,
  sub·du·ing
sub·en·try
sub·fam·i·ly
sub·floor
sub·freez·ing
sub·group
sub·gum
sub·head or
  sub·head·ing
sub·hu·man
sub·ject
sub·jec·tion
sub·jec·tive
sub·jec·tive·ly
sub·jec·tive·ness
sub·jec·tiv·i·ty
sub·join
sub ju·di·ce

sub·ju·gate, v.
  sub·ju·gat·ed,
  sub·ju·gat·ing
sub·ju·ga·tion
sub·junc·tive
sub·lease, v.
  sub·leased,
  sub·leas·ing
sub·let, v. sub·let,
  sub·let·ting
sub·li·mate, v.
  sub·li·mat·ed,
  sub·li·mat·ing
sub·li·ma·tion
sub·lime
sub·lime·ly
sub·lime·ness
sub·lim·i·nal
sub·lim·i·nal·ly
sub·lim·i·ty, n. pl.
  sub·lim·i·ties
sub·lu·nar
sub·lu·na·ry
sub·mar·gin·al
sub·mar·gin·al·ly
sub·ma·rine, v.
  sub·ma·rined,
  sub·ma·rin·ing
sub·ma·ri·ner
sub·merge, v.
  sub·merged,
  sub·merg·ing
sub·mer·gence
sub·mers·ible
sub·mer·sion
sub·min·ia·ture
sub·mis·sion
sub·mis·sive
sub·mis·sive·ly

sub·mis·sive·ness

sub·mit, *v.*
  sub·mit·ted,
  sub·mit·ting

sub·nor·mal

sub·nor·mal·i·ty

sub·nor·mal·ly

sub·or·bit·al

sub·or·der

sub·or·di·nate, *v.*
  sub·or·di·nat·ed,
  sub·or·di·nat·ing

sub·or·di·na·tion

sub·orn

sub·or·na·tion

sub·plot

sub·poe·na, *v.*
  sub·poe·naed,
  sub·poe·na·ing

sub·re·gion

sub·ro·gate, *v.*
  sub·ro·gat·ed,
  sub·ro·gat·ing

sub ro·sa, *adv.*

sub·ro·sa, *adj.*

sub·scribe, *v.*
  sub·scribed,
  sub·scrib·ing

sub·scrib·er

sub·script

sub·scrip·tion

sub·sec·tion

sub·se·quent

sub·se·quent·ly

sub·se·quent·ness

sub·ser·vi·ence

sub·ser·vi·ent

sub·ser·vi·ent·ly

sub·side, *v.*
  sub·sid·ed,
  sub·sid·ing

sub·si·dence

sub·sid·i·ary, *n. pl.*
  sub·sid·i·ar·ies

sub·si·di·za·tion

sub·si·dize, *v.*
  sub·si·dized,
  sub·si·diz·ing

sub·si·dy, *n. pl.*
  sub·si·dies

sub·sist

sub·sis·tence

sub·soil

sub·son·ic

sub·spe·cies

sub·stance

sub·stan·dard

sub·stan·tial

sub·stan·tial·ly

sub·stan·ti·ate, *v.*
  sub·stan·ti·at·ed,
  sub·stan·ti·at·ing

sub·stan·ti·a·tion

sub·stan·tive

sub·stan·tive·ly

sub·stan·tive·ness

sub·sta·tion

sub·sti·tut·able

sub·sti·tute, *v.*
  sub·sti·tut·ed,
  sub·sti·tut·ing

sub·sti·tu·tion

sub·stra·tum, *n. pl.*
  sub·stra·ta

sub·struc·ture

sub·sume, *v.*

sub·sumed,
  sub·sum·ing

sub·sur·face

sub·sys·tem

sub·teen

sub·ter·fuge

sub·ter·ra·nean

sub·ti·tle, *v.*
  sub·ti·tled,
  sub·ti·tling

sub·tle, *adj.*
  sub·tler,
  sub·tlest

sub·tle·ness

sub·tle·ty

sub·tly

sub·to·tal, *v.*
  sub·to·taled *or*
  sub·to·talled,
  sub·to·tal·ing *or*
  sub·to·tal·ling

sub·tract

sub·trac·tion

sub·tra·hend

sub·trop·i·cal

sub·urb

sub·ur·ban

sub·ur·ban·ite

sub·ur·bia

sub·vene, *v.*
  sub·vened,
  sub·ven·ing

sub·ven·tion

sub·ver·sion

sub·ver·sive

sub·ver·sive·ly

sub·ver·sive·ness

sub·vert

sub·way

suc·ceed
suc·cess
suc·cess·ful
suc·cess·ful·ly
suc·cess·ful·ness
suc·ces·sion
suc·ces·sive
suc·ces·sive·ly
suc·ces·sive·ness
suc·ces·sor
suc·cinct
suc·cinct·ly
suc·cinct·ness
suc·cor
suc·co·tash
suc·cu·lence
suc·cu·lent
suc·cumb
suck·er
suck·le, *v.* suck·led,
  suck·ling
suck·ling
su·cre
su·crose
suc·tion
Su·dan
Su·da·nese, *n. pl.*
  Su·da·nese
sud·den
sud·den·ly
sud·den·ness
su·do·rif·ic
sudsy, *adj.*
  suds·i·er,
  suds·i·est
sue, *v.* sued, su·ing
suede *or* suède

su·et
suf·fer
suf·fer·able
suf·fer·ably
suf·fer·ance
suf·fer·ing
suf·fice, *v.*
  suf·ficed,
  suf·fic·ing
suf·fi·cien·cy
suf·fi·cient
suf·fi·cient·ly
suf·fix
suf·fo·cate, *v.*
  suf·fo·cat·ed,
  suf·fo·cat·ing
suf·fo·ca·tion
suf·fra·gan
suf·frage
suf·frag·ette
suf·frag·ist
suf·fuse, *v.*
  suf·fused,
  suf·fus·ing
suf·fu·sion
sug·ar
sug·ar·cane
sug·ar·coat
sug·ar·less
sug·ar·plum
sug·ary
sug·gest
sug·gest·ibil·i·ty
sug·gest·ible
sug·ges·tion
sug·ges·tive
sug·ges·tive·ly

sug·ges·tive·ness
sui·ci·dal
sui·ci·dal·ly
sui·cide
sui ge·ner·is
sui ju·ris
suit
suit·abil·i·ty
suit·able
suit·ably
suit·case
suite (*see also*
  sweet)
suit·ing
suit·or
su·ki·ya·ki
sul·fa
sul·fate
sul·fide
sul·fur *or* sul·phur
sul·fu·ric
sul·fu·rous
sul·fu·rous·ly
sul·fu·rous·ness
sulk·i·ly
sulk·i·ness
sulky, *n. pl.*
  sul·kies
sul·len
sul·len·ly
sul·len·ness
sul·ly, *v.* sul·lied,
  sul·ly·ing
sul·tan
sul·ta·na
sul·tan·ate
sul·tri·ness

sul·try, *adj.*
sul·tri·er,
sul·tri·est

sum, *v.* summed,
sum·ming

su·mac *or* su·mach

Su·ma·tra

Su·ma·tran

sum·ma cum laude

sum·mar·i·ly

sum·ma·rize, *v.*
sum·ma·rized,
sum·ma·riz·ing

sum·ma·ry (BRIEF
FORM) (*see also*
summery)

sum·ma·tion

sum·mer

sum·mer·house

sum·mer·time

sum·mery (LIKE
SUMMER) (*see
also* summary)

sum·mit

sum·mon

sum·mons, *n. pl.*
sum·mons·es

su·mo

sump·tu·ous

sump·tu·ous·ly

sump·tu·ous·ness

sun, *v.* sunned,
sun·ning

sun·baked

sun·bathe, *v.*
sun·bathed,
sun·bath·ing

sun·beam

sun·belt

sun·bon·net

sun·burn, *v.*
sun·burned *or*
sun·burnt,
sun·burn·ing

sun·burst

sun·cured

sun·dae

Sun·day

sun·der

sun·di·al

sun·down

sun·dry, *n. pl.*
sun·dries

sun·fish

sun·flow·er

sun·glass·es

sunk·en

sun·lamp

sun·light

sun·lit

sun·ni·ly

sun·ni·ness

Sun·nite

sun·ny, *adj.*
sun·ni·er,
sun·ni·est

sun·rise

sun·roof

sun·screen

sun·set

sun·shade

sun·shine

sun·spot

sun·stroke

sun·suit

sun·tan

sun·up

sup, *v.* supped,
sup·ping

su·per

su·per·abun·dance

su·per·abun·dant

su·per·abun·dant·ly

su·per·an·nu·ate, *v.*
su·per·an·nu·at·ed,
su·per·an·nu·at·ing

su·per·an·nu·at·ed

su·perb

su·perb·ly

su·perb·ness

su·per·car·go, *n. pl.*
su·per·car·goes
or su·per·car·gos

su·per·charge, *v.*
su·per·charged,
su·per·charg·ing

su·per·charg·er

su·per·cil·ious

su·per·cil·ious·ly

su·per·cil·ious·ness

su·per·con·duc·tiv·i·ty

su·per·con·duc·tor

su·per·ego, *n. pl.*
su·per·egos

su·per·fi·cial

su·per·fi·ci·al·i·ty

su·per·fi·cial·ly

su·per·flu·ity

su·per·flu·ous

su·per·flu·ous·ly

su·per·flu·ous·ness

su·per·high·way

su·per·hu·man

su·per·hu·man·ly

su·per·hu·man·ness

su·per·im·pose, *v.*
  su·per·im·posed,
  su·per·im·pos·ing

su·per·in·tend

su·per·in·ten·dence

su·per·in·ten·den·cy,
  n. pl.
  su·per·in·ten·den·cies

su·per·in·ten·dent

Su·pe·ri·or, Lake

su·pe·ri·or·i·ty

su·per·la·tive

su·per·la·tive·ly

su·per·la·tive·ness

su·per·man, *n. pl.*
  su·per·men

su·per·mar·ket

su·per·nal

su·per·nal·ly

su·per·nat·u·ral

su·per·nat·u·ral·ly

su·per·no·va

su·per·nu·mer·ary,
  n. pl.
  su·per·nu·mer·ar·ies

su·per·pow·er

su·per·scribe, *v.*
  su·per·scribed,
  su·per·scrib·ing

su·per·script

su·per·scrip·tion

su·per·sede, *v.*
  su·per·sed·ed,
  su·per·sed·ing

su·per·sed·ence

su·per·se·dure

su·per·sen·si·tive

su·per·sen·si·tiv·i·ty

su·per·son·ic

su·per·son·i·cal·ly

su·per·star

su·per·sti·tion

su·per·sti·tious

su·per·sti·tious·ly

su·per·sti·tious·ness

su·per·struc·ture

su·per·tan·ker

su·per·vene, *v.*
  su·per·vened,
  su·per·ven·ing

su·per·ven·tion

su·per·vise, *v.*
  su·per·vised,
  su·per·vis·ing

su·per·vi·sion

su·per·vi·sor

su·per·vi·so·ry

su·pine

su·pine·ly

su·pine·ness

sup·per

sup·plant

sup·ple

sup·ple·ment

sup·ple·men·tal

sup·ple·men·ta·ry

sup·pli·ant *or*
  sup·pli·cant

sup·pli·cate, *v.*
  sup·pli·cat·ed,
  sup·pli·cat·ing

sup·pli·ca·tion

sup·pli·er

sup·ply, *n. pl.*
  sup·plies

sup·ply, *v.*

sup·pli·er,
  sup·ply·ing

sup·ply-side

sup·ply-sid·er

sup·port

sup·port·able

sup·port·er

sup·port·ing

sup·port·ive

sup·pose, *v.*
  sup·posed,
  sup·pos·ing

sup·pos·ed·ly

sup·po·si·tion

sup·pos·i·to·ry, *n.*
  pl.
  sup·pos·i·to·ries

sup·press

sup·pres·sant

sup·press·ible

sup·pres·sion

sup·pres·sor

sup·pu·rate, *v.*
  sup·pu·rat·ed,
  sup·pu·rat·ing

sup·pu·ra·tion

su·pra

su·prem·a·cist

su·prem·a·cy, *n. pl.*
  su·prem·a·cies

su·preme

su·preme·ly

su·preme·ness

sur·cease, *v.*
  sur·ceased,
  sur·ceas·ing

sur·charge, *v.*
  sur·charged,
  sur·charg·ing

sur·cin·gle

sure, *adj.* sur·er,
  sur·est

sure·fire

sure·foot·ed

sure·foot·ed·ly

sure·foot·ed·ness

sure·ly

sure·ness

sure·ty, *n. pl.*
  sure·ties

surf (WAVES) (*see
  also* serf)

sur·face, *v.*
  sur·faced,
  sur·fac·ing

sur·face-to-air

surf·board

surf·boat

sur·feit

surf·er

surf·ing

surge
  (MOVEMENT), *v.*
  surged, surg·ing
  (*see also* serge)

sur·geon

sur·gery, *n. pl.*
  sur·ger·ies

sur·gi·cal

sur·gi·cal·ly

Su·ri·name

Su·ri·nam·er

sur·li·ness

sur·ly, *adj.* sur·li·er,
  sur·li·est

sur·mise, *v.*
  sur·mised,
  sur·mis·ing

sur·mount

sur·mount·able

sur·name, *v.*
  sur·named,
  sur·nam·ing

sur·pass

sur·pass·ing·ly

sur·plice
  (ECCLESIASTICAL
  VESTMENT)

sur·plus (EXTRA)

sur·prise, *v.*
  sur·prised,
  sur·pris·ing

sur·pris·ing

sur·re·al·ism

sur·re·al·ist

sur·re·al·is·ti·cal·ly

sur·ren·der

sur·rep·ti·tious

sur·rep·ti·tious·ly

sur·rep·ti·tious·ness

sur·rey, *n. pl.*
  sur·reys

sur·ro·gate

sur·round

sur·round·ings

sur·tax

sur·veil·lance

sur·vey

sur·vey·ing

sur·vey·or

sur·viv·al

sur·viv·al·ist

sur·vive, *v.*
  sur·vived,
  sur·viv·ing

sur·vi·vor

sur·vi·vor·ship

Su·san

sus·cep·ti·bil·i·ty, *n.
  pl.*
  sus·cep·ti·bil·i·ties

sus·cep·ti·ble

sus·cep·ti·bly

su·shi

sus·pect

sus·pend

sus·pend·ers

sus·pense

sus·pense·ful

sus·pen·sion

sus·pen·sive

sus·pen·so·ry

sus·pi·cion

sus·pi·cious

sus·pi·cious·ly

sus·pi·cious·ness

sus·tain

sus·tain·able

sus·te·nance

sut·ler

su·tra

sut·tee

su·ture, *v.* su·tured,
  su·tur·ing

su·zer·ain

su·zer·ain·ty

svelte

swab, *v.* swabbed,
  swab·bing

swad·dle, *v.*
  swad·dled,
  swad·dling

swad·dling

swag·ger

swag·man, *n. pl.*
swag·men

Swa·hi·li

swale

swal·low

swal·low·tail, *n.*

swal·low-tailed,
adj.

swamp·i·ness

swamp·land

swampy, *adj.*
swamp·i·er,
swamp·i·est

swan, *n. pl.* swan
or swans

swank, *adj.*
swank·er *or,*
swank·est

swank·i·ly

swank·i·ness

swanky, *adj.*
swank·i·er,
swank·i·est

swans·down

swap, *v.* swapped,
swap·ping

swarm

swarth·i·ly

swarth·i·ness

swar·thy, *adj.*
swar·thi·er,
swar·thi·est

swash·buck·ler

swash·buck·ling

swas·ti·ka

swat, *v.* swat·ted,
swat·ting

swatch

swath (TRACK)

swathe (WRAP), *v.*
swathed,
swath·ing

sway·back

Swa·zi, *pl.* Swa·zi
or Swa·zis

Swa·zi·land

swear, *v.* swore,
sworn,
swear·ing

swear·word

sweat, *v.* sweat *or*
sweated,
sweat·ing

sweat·band

sweat·box

sweat·er

sweat·i·ly

sweat·i·ness

sweat·shop

sweaty, *adj.*
sweat·i·er,
sweat·i·est

Swede

Swe·den

Swe·dish

sweep, *v.* swept,
sweep·ing

sweep·back

sweep·er

sweep·stakes
(*occas.* sweep-
stake), *n. pl.*
sweep·stakes

sweet (CANDY)
(*see also* suite)

sweet·bread

sweet·bri·er

sweet·en

sweet·heart

sweet·meat

sweet·sop

sweet talk, *n.*

sweet-talk, *v.*

swell, *v.* swelled,
swelled, *or*
swol·len,
swell·ing

swel·ter

swel·ter·ing

swept-back

swerve, *v.*
swerved,
swerv·ing

swift·ly

swift·ness

swig, *v.* swigged,
swig·ging

swill

swim, *v.* swam,
swum,
swim·ming

swim·mer

swim·suit

swim·wear

swin·dle, *v.*
swin·dled,
swin·dling

swin·dler

swine, *n. pl.* swine

swing, *v.* swung,
swing·ing

swing·er

swin·ish

swipe, *v.* swiped,
swip·ing

swirl

swishy, *adj.*
swish·i·er,
swish·i·est

Swiss, *n. pl.* Swiss

switch

switch·back

switch·board

switch-hit, *v.*
switch-hit,
switch-hit·ting
switch-hit·ter

switch·man, *n. pl.*
switch·men

switch·yard

Swit·zer·land

swiv·el, *v.*
swiv·eled *or*
swiv·elled,
swiv·el·ing *or*
swiv·el·ling

sword·fish

sword·play

swords·man, *n. pl.*
swords·men

sword·tail

Syb·a·rite

syb·a·rit·ic

syc·a·more

syc·o·phant

syc·o·phan·tic

Syd·ney

syl·lab·ic

syl·lab·i·ca·tion

syl·lab·i·fi·ca·tion

syl·lab·i·fy, *v.*
syl·lab·i·fied,
syl·lab·i·fy·ing

syl·la·ble

syl·la·bus, *n. pl.*

syl·la·bi *or*
syl·la·bus·es

syl·lo·gism

syl·lo·gis·tic

syl·lo·gis·ti·cal·ly

sylph

syl·van

sym·bi·o·sis, *n. pl.*
sym·bi·o·ses

sym·bi·ot·ic

sym·bol

sym·bol·ic

sym·bol·i·cal

sym·bol·i·cal·ly

sym·bol·ism

sym·bol·iza·tion

sym·bol·ize, *v.*
sym·bol·ized,
sym·bol·iz·ing

sym·met·ric

sym·met·ri·cal

sym·met·ri·cal·ly

sym·me·try, *n. pl.*
sym·me·tries

sym·pa·thet·ic

sym·pa·thet·i·cal·ly

sym·pa·thize, *v.*
sym·pa·thized,
sym·pa·thiz·ing

sym·pa·thiz·er

sym·pa·thy, *n. pl.*
sym·pa·thies

sym·phon·ic

sym·phon·i·cal·ly

sym·pho·ni·ous

sym·pho·ni·ous·ly

sym·pho·ny, *n. pl.*
sym·pho·nies

sym·po·sium, *n. pl.*
sym·po·sia *or*
sym·po·siums

symp·tom

symp·tom·at·ic

syn·a·gogue *or.*
syn·a·gog

syn·apse

sync (*occas.*
synch), *v.*
synced (*occas.*
synched),
sync·ing (*occas.*
synch·ing)

syn·chro

syn·chro·mesh

syn·chron·ic

syn·chro·nic·i·ty

syn·chro·nism

syn·chro·ni·za·tion

syn·chro·nize, *v.*
syn·chro·nized,
syn·chro·niz·ing

syn·chro·nous

syn·chro·nous·ly

syn·chro·nous·ness

syn·chro·ton

syn·co·pate, *v.*
syn·co·pat·ed,
syn·co·pat·ing

syn·co·pa·tion

syn·co·pe

syn·cret·ic

syn·cre·tism

syn·di·cal·ism

syn·di·cate, *v.*
syn·di·cat·ed,
syn·di·cat·ing

syn·di·ca·tion

syn·drome

syn·ec·do·che

syn·ecol·o·gy

syn·er·gism

syn·er·gist

syn·er·gis·ti·cal·ly

syn·er·gy

syn·fu·el

syn·od

syn·od·ic

syn·od·i·cal

syn·o·nym

syn·on·y·mous

syn·on·y·mous·ly

syn·on·y·my, *n. pl.*
  syn·on·y·mies

syn·op·sis, *n. pl.*
  syn·op·ses

syn·op·size, *v.*
  syn·op·sized,
  syn·op·siz·ing

syn·op·tic

syn·op·ti·cal

syn·tac·tic

syn·tac·ti·cal

syn·tac·ti·cal·ly

syn·tax

syn·the·sis, *n. pl.*
  syn·the·ses

syn·the·size, *v.*
  syn·the·sized,
  syn·the·siz·ing

syn·thet·ic

syn·thet·i·cal

syn·thet·i·cal·ly

syph·i·lis

syph·i·lit·ic

Syr·a·cuse

Sy·rette℠

Syr·ia

Syr·i·an

sy·ringe

syr·up

syr·upy

sys·tal·tic

sys·tem

sys·tem·at·ic

sys·tem·at·i·cal

sys·tem·at·i·cal·ly

sys·tem·ati·za·tion

sys·tem·a·tize, *v.*
  sys·tem·a·tized,
  sys·tem·a·tiz·ing

sys·tem·ic

sys·tem·iza·tion

sys·tem·ize, *v.*
  sys·tem·ized,
  sys·tem·iz·ing

sys·tole

sys·tol·ic

syz·y·gy, *n. pl.*
  syz·y·gies

Sze·chuan *or*
  Sze·chwan

T

tab, *v.* tabbed,
tab·bing

Ta·bas·co® (SAUCE)

Ta·bas·co (MEXICAN STATE)

tab·by, *n. pl.* tab·bies

tab·er·na·cle

ta·ble

tab·leau, *n. pl.* tab·leaux (*occas.* tab·leaus)

ta·ble·cloth

ta·ble d'hôte, *n. pl.* ta·bles d'hôte

ta·ble-hop, *v.* ta·ble-hopped, ta·ble-hop·ping

ta·ble·land

ta·ble·spoon, *n. pl.* ta·ble·spoons

ta·ble·spoon·ful, *n. pl.* ta·ble·spoon·fuls (*occas.* ta·ble·spoons·fuls)

tab·let

ta·ble·top

ta·ble·ware

tab·loid

ta·boo (*occas.* ta·bu), *n. pl.* ta·boos (*occas.* ta·bus)

ta·bor (*occas.* ta·bour)

tab·o·ret *or* tab·ou·ret

tab·u·lar

tab·u·late, *v.* tab·u·lat·ed, tab·u·lat·ing

tab·u·la·tion

tab·u·la·tor

ta·chom·e·ter

tachy·car·dia

tac·it

tac·it·ly

tac·it·ness

tac·i·turn

tac·i·tur·ni·ty

tacki·ly

tacki·ness

tack·le, *v.* tack·led, tack·ling

tacky, *adj.* tack·i·er, tack·i·est

ta·co, *n. pl.* ta·cos

Ta·co·ma

tact·ful

tact·ful·ly

tact·ful·ness

tac·tic

tac·ti·cal

tac·ti·cal·ly

tac·ti·cian

tac·tics

tac·tile

tact·less

tact·less·ly

tact·less·ness

tad·pole

Ta·dzhik So·vi·et So·cial·ist Re·pub·lic *or* Ta·dzhik·i·stan (*now* Tajikstan)

Tae·gu

tae kwon do

taf·fe·ta

taff·rail

taf·fy

tag, *v.* tagged, tag·ging

Tag·a·log, *n. pl.* Tag·a·log *or* Tag·a·logs

Ta·hi·ti

Ta·hi·ti·an

tai chi

tai·ga

tail·board

tail·coat

tail·gate, *v.* tail·gat·ed, tail·gat·ing

tail·less

tail·light

tail·like

tai·lor

tai·lor-made

tail·piece

tail·pipe

tail·race

tail·spin

Tai·pei

Tai·wan

Tai·wan·ese, *n. pl.* Tai·wan·ese

Tai·wa·ni·an

Ta·jik

Ta·jik·stan (*formerly* Tadzhik Soviet Socialist Republic)

ta·ka, *n. pl.* ta·ka

take, *v.* took, tak·en, tak·ing

take·off

take·out

take-over

tak·er

tak·ing

ta·la, *n. pl.* ta·la

tal·cum pow·der

tale·bear·er

tal·ent

tal·ent·ed

tal·is·man, *n. pl.* tal·is·mans

talk·a·thon

talk·a·tive

talk·a·tive·ly

talk·a·tive·ness

talk·er

talk·ing-to

talky, *adj.* talk·i·er, talk·i·est

Tal·la·has·see

tall·ish

tal·low

tal·ly, *n. pl.* tal·lies

tal·ly, *v.* tal·lied, tal·ly·ing

tal·ly·ho, *n. pl.* tal·ly·hos

tal·ly·man, *n. pl.* tal·ly·men

Tal·mud

tal·mu·dic

tal·on

ta·lus, *n. pl.* ta·lus·es (SLOPES) *or* ta·li (ANKLES)

tam·able *or* tame·able

ta·ma·le

Ta·ma·ra

tam·a·rack

tam·a·rind

tam·a·risk

Ta·mau·li·pas

tam·ba·la, *n. pl.* tam·ba·la *or* tam·ba·las

tam·bour

tam·bou·rine

tame, *adj.* tam·er, tam·est

tame, *v.* tamed, tam·ing

tame·ly

tame·ness

tam·er

tam-o'-shan·ter

Tam·pa

tam·per

tam·pon

tan, *v.* tanned, tan·ning

tan·a·ger

tan·bark

tan·dem

Tan·gan·yi·ka

Tan·gan·yi·kan

tan·ge·lo, *n. pl.* tan·ge·los

tan·gent

tan·gen·tial

tan·gen·tial·ly

tan·ger·ine

tan·gi·bil·i·ty

tan·gi·ble

tan·gi·bly

tan·gle, *v.* tan·gled,
  tan·gling

tan·go, *n. pl.*
  tan·gos

tangy, *adj.*
  tang·i·er,
  tang·i·est

tank·age

tan·kard

tank·er

tan·ner

tan·nery, *n. pl.*
  tan·ner·ies

tan·nic

tan·nin

tan·ning

tan·ta·lize, *v.*
  tan·ta·lized,
  tan·ta·liz·ing

tan·ta·lum

tan·ta·mount

tan·trum

Tan·za·nia

Tan·za·ni·an

tap, *v.* tapped,
  tap·ping

tape, *v.* taped,
  tap·ing

ta·per

tape-re·cord

tap·es·tried

tap·es·try, *n. pl.*
  tap·es·tries

tape·worm

tap·house

tap·i·o·ca

ta·pir, *n. pl.* ta·pir
  or ta·pirs

tap·pet

tap·room

tap·root

tar, *v.* tarred,
  tar·ring

Ta·ra

tar·an·tel·la

ta·ran·tu·la

tar·di·ly

tar·di·ness

tar·dy, *adj.*
  tard·i·er,
  tard·i·est

tare, *v.* tared,
  tar·ing

tar·get

tar·iff

tar·nish

tar·nished

ta·ro (PLANT), *n.*
  pl. ta·ros

tar·ot (CARDS)

tar·pau·lin

tar·pon, *n. pl.*
  tar·pon *or*
  tar·pons

tar·ra·gon

tar·ry, *v.* tar·ried,
  tar·ry·ing

tar·tan

tar·tar

tar·tar·ic acid

tart·ly

tart·ness

Tash·kent

task·mas·ter

Tas·ma·nia

Tas·ma·ni·an

tas·sel, *v.* tas·seled
  or tas·selled,
  tas·sel·ing *or*
  tas·sel·ling

taste, *v.* tast·ed,
  tast·ing

taste·ful

taste·ful·ly

taste·ful·ness

taste·less

taste·less·ly

taste·less·ness

tast·er

tast·i·ly

tast·i·ness

tasty, *adj.* tast·i·er,
  tast·i·est

tat, *v.* tat·ted,
  tat·ting

tat·ter

tat·ter·de·ma·lion

tat·tered

tat·ter·sall

tat·ting

tat·tle, *v.* tat·tled,
  tat·tling

tat·tle·tale

tat·too, *n. pl.*
  tat·toos

tat·too, *v.*
  tat·tooed,
  tat·too·ing

taught

taunt·er

taunt·ing·ly

taupe

Tau·rus

taut

taut·ly

taut·ness

tau·to·log·i·cal

tau·to·log·i·cal·ly

tau·tol·o·gy, *n. pl.* tau·tol·o·gies

tav·ern

taw·dri·ly

taw·dri·ness

taw·dry, *adj.* taw·dri·er, taw·dri·est

taw·ny, *adj.* taw·ni·er, taw·ni·est

tax·abil·i·ty

tax·able

tax·a·tion

tax-ex·empt

tax-free

taxi, *n. pl.* tax·is (*occas.* tax·ies)

taxi, *v.* tax·ied, taxi·ing *or* taxy·ing, tax·is *or* tax·ies

taxi·cab

taxi·der·mist

taxi·der·my

taxi·me·ter

tax·ing

taxi·way

tax·o·nom·ic

tax·on·o·my, *n. pl.* tax·on·o·mies

tax·pay·er

T-bar

T-bill

T-bone

T cell

tea

teach, *v.* taught, teach·ing

teach·abil·i·ty

teach·able

teach·er

teach-in

tea·cup

tea·cup·ful, *n. pl.* tea·cup·fuls

tea·house

tea·ket·tle

teak·wood

teal, *n. pl.* teal *or* teals

team

team·mate

team·ster

team·work

tea·pot

tear, *v.* tore, torn, tear·ing

tear·drop

tear·ful

tear·ful·ly

tear·ful·ness

tear-jerk·er

tear·less

tear·less·ly

tear·less·ness

tea·room

tear·stained

teary, *adj.* tear·i·er, tear·i·est

tease, *v.* teased, teas·ing

tea·sel (*occas.* tea·zel *or* tea·zle)

teas·er

tea·spoon

tea·spoon·ful, *n. pl.* tea·spoon·fuls (*occas.* tea·spoons·ful)

teat

tea·time

tech·ne·ti·um

tech·nic

tech·ni·cal

tech·ni·cal·i·ty, *n. pl.* tech·ni·cal·i·ties

tech·ni·cal·ly

tech·ni·cian

Tech·ni·col·or®

tech·nique

tech·noc·ra·cy, *n. pl.* tech·noc·ra·cies

tech·no·crat

tech·no·lo·gic

tech·no·log·i·cal

tech·no·log·i·cal·ly

tech·nol·o·gist

tech·nol·o·gy, *n. pl.* tech·nol·o·gies

tec·ton·ic

tec·ton·ics

ted·dy, *n. pl.* ted·dies

te·dious

te·dious·ly

te·dious·ness

te·di·um

tee, v. teed, tee·ing

teem

teen·age or
  teen·aged

teen·ag·er

tee·ny, adj.
  tee·ni·er,
  tee·ni·est

teeny·bop·per

tee·ny-wee·ny

tee·pee (var. of
  tepee)

tee·ter

tee·ter-tot·ter

teethe, v. teethed,
  teeth·ing

tee·to·tal·er or
  tee·to·tal·ler

tee·to·tal·ism

Tef·lon®

Teh·ran (occas.
  Te·he·ran)

tek·tite

Tel Aviv

tele·cast, v.
  tele·cast (occas.
  tele·cast·ed),
  tele·cast·ing

tele·cast·er

tele·com·mu·ni·ca·tion

tele·com·mute, v.
  tele·com·mut·ed,
  tele·com·mut·ing

tele·con·fer·ence, v.
  tele·con·fer·enced,
  tele·con·fer·enc·ing

tele·course

tele·film

tele·gen·ic

tele·gram

tele·graph

te·leg·raph·er

tele·graph·ic

tele·graph·i·cal·ly

te·leg·ra·phy

tele·ki·ne·sis

tele·ki·ne·tic

tele·mar·ket

tele·me·ter

te·lem·e·try

te·le·o·log·ic

te·le·o·log·i·cal

te·le·ol·o·gy

tele·path·ic

tele·path·i·cal·ly

te·lep·a·thy

tele·phone, v.
  tele·phoned,
  tele·phon·ing

tele·phon·ic

tele·phon·i·cal·ly

te·le·pho·ny

tele·pho·to

tele·pho·tog·ra·phy

tele·play

tele·print·er

Tele·Promp·Ter®

tele·ran

tele·scope, v.
  tele·scoped,
  tele·scop·ing

tele·scop·ic

tel·e·sis, n. pl.
  tel·e·ses

tele·thon

tele·type·writ·er

tele·view·er

tele·vise, v.
  tele·vised,
  tele·vis·ing

tele·vi·sion

tel·ex

tell, v. told, tell·ing

tell·er

tell·tale

tel·lu·ri·um

tem·blor

te·mer·i·ty, n. pl.
  te·mer·i·ties

tem·per

tem·pera

tem·per·a·ment

tem·per·a·men·tal

tem·per·a·men·tal·ly

tem·per·ance

tem·per·ate

tem·per·ate·ly

tem·per·ate·ness

tem·per·a·ture

tem·pered

tem·pest

tem·pes·tu·ous

tem·pes·tu·ous·ly

tem·pes·tu·ous·ness

tem·plate

tem·ple

tem·po, n. pl.
  tem·pi or
  tem·pos

tem·po·ral

tem·po·rar·i·ly

tem·po·rar·i·ness
tem·po·rary
tem·po·ri·za·tion
tem·po·rize, v.
  tem·po·rized,
  tem·po·riz·ing
temp·ta·tion
tempt·er
tempt·ress
ten·a·bil·i·ty
ten·a·ble
te·na·cious
te·na·cious·ly
te·na·cious·ness
te·nac·i·ty
ten·an·cy, n. pl.
  ten·an·cies
ten·ant
ten·ant·less
ten·ant·ry
ten·den·cy, n.. pl.
  ten·den·cies
ten·den·tious
  (occas.
  ten·den·cious)
ten·den·tious·ly
ten·den·tious·ness
ten·der (SOFT,
  OFFER)
tend·er (ONE WHO
  TENDS)
ten·der·foot, n. pl.
  ten·der·feet
  (occas.
  ten·der·foots)
ten·der·heart·ed
ten·der·heart·ed·ly
ten·der·heart·ed·ness
ten·der·ize, v.

ten·der·ized,
  ten·der·iz·ing
ten·der·loin
ten·der·ly
ten·der·ness
ten·di·ni·tis or
  ten·don·i·tis
ten·don
ten·dril
ten·e·brous
ten·e·ment
ten·et
ten·fold
Ten·nes·see
Ten·nes·see·an
ten·nis
ten·on
ten·or
ten·pin
tense, adj. tens·er,
  tens·est
tense, v. tensed,
  tens·ing
tense·ly
tense·ness
ten·sile
ten·sion
ten·si·ty
ten·sor
ten·ta·cle
ten·ta·cled
ten·ta·tive·ly
ten·ta·tive·ness
ten·ter
ten·ter·hook
tenth
tenth-rate

te·nu·i·ty
ten·u·ous
ten·u·ous·ly
ten·u·ous·ness
ten·ure
ten·ured
te·pee
tep·id
tep·id·ly
tep·id·ness
te·qui·la
ter·bi·um
ter·cen·te·na·ry
te·rete
ter·i·ya·ki
ter·ma·gant
ter·mi·na·ble
ter·mi·na·bly
ter·mi·nal
ter·mi·nal·ly
ter·mi·nate, v.
  ter·mi·nat·ed,
  ter·mi·nat·ing
ter·mi·na·tion
ter·mi·na·tor
ter·mi·nol·o·gy, n.
  pl.
  ter·mi·nol·o·gies
ter·mi·nus, n. pl.
  ter·mi·ni or
  ter·mi·nus·es
ter·mite
ter·na·ry
terp·sich·o·re·an
ter·race, v.
  ter·raced,
  ter·rac·ing
ter·ra-cot·ta

ter·ra fir·ma

ter·rain

ter·ra in·cog·ni·ta,
n. pl. ter·rae
in·cog·ni·tae

Ter·ra·my·cin®

ter·ra·pin

ter·rar·i·um, n. pl.
ter·rar·ia or
ter·rar·i·ums

ter·raz·zo

ter·res·tri·al

ter·ri·ble

ter·ri·ble·ness

ter·ri·bly

ter·ri·er

ter·rif·ic

ter·rif·i·cal·ly

ter·ri·fy, v.
ter·ri·fied,
ter·ri·fy·ing

ter·ri·fy·ing

ter·ri·to·ri·al

ter·ri·to·ri·al·i·ty

ter·ri·to·ry, n. pl.
ter·ri·to·ries

ter·ror

ter·ror·ism

ter·ror·ist

ter·ror·iza·tion

ter·ror·ize, v.
ter·ror·ized,
ter·ror·iz·ing

Ter·ry (PERSON'S
NAME), n. pl.
Ter·rys

ter·ry (FABRIC), n.
pl. ter·ries

terse, adj. ters·er,
ters·est

terse·ly

terse·ness

ter·tia·ry

tes·sel·late, v.
tes·sel·lat·ed,
tes·sel·lat·ing

tes·sel·lat·ed

tes·sel·la·tion

tes·ta·ment

tes·ta·men·ta·ry

tes·tate

tes·ta·tor

tes·ta·trix

tes·ti·cle

tes·ti·cu·lar

tes·ti·fi·er

tes·ti·fy, v.
tes·ti·fied,
tes·ti·fy·ing

tes·ti·ly

tes·ti·mo·ni·al

tes·ti·mo·ny, n. pl.
tes·ti·mo·nies

tes·ti·ness

tes·tos·ter·one

test-tube, adj.

test tube, n.

tes·ty, adj. tes·ti·er,
tes·ti·est

tet·a·nus

tête-à-tête

teth·er

teth·er·ball

tet·ra·cy·cline

tet·ra·eth·yl

tet·ra·he·dron, n.

pl.
tet·ra·he·drons or
tet·ra·he·dra

te·tral·o·gy, n. pl.
te·tral·o·gies

te·tram·e·ter

Teu·ton·ic

Tex·an

Tex·as

text·book

tex·tile

tex·tu·al

tex·tu·al·ly

tex·tur·al

tex·ture, v.
tex·tured,
tex·tur·ing

Thai, n. pl. Thai or
Thais

Thai·land

tha·lid·o·mide

thal·li·um

Thames River

than·a·top·sis

thank·ful

thank·ful·ly

thank·ful·ness

thank·less

thank·less·ly

thank·less·ness

thanks·giv·ing

that

thatch

thaw

the·ater or the·atre

the·ater·go·er or
the·atre·go·er

the·ater-in-the-round

the·at·ri·cal

the·at·rics

theft

the·ism

the·ist

the·is·tic

the·mat·ic

the·mat·i·cal·ly

theme, *v.* themed, them·ing

them·selves

thence·forth

thence·for·ward

the·oc·ra·cy, *n. pl.* the·oc·ra·cies

theo·crat·ic

theo·crat·i·cal

the·od·o·lite

theo·lo·gian

theo·log·ic

theo·log·i·cal

the·ol·o·gy, *n. pl.* the·ol·o·gies

the·o·rem

the·o·ret·ic

the·o·ret·i·cal

the·o·ret·i·cal·ly

the·o·re·ti·cian

the·o·rize, *v.* the·o·rized, the·o·riz·ing

the·o·ry, *n. pl.* the·o·ries

theo·soph·ic

theo·soph·ic·al

theo·soph·ic·al·ly

the·os·o·phist

the·os·o·phy

ther·a·peu·tic

ther·a·peu·ti·cal·ly

ther·a·peu·tics

ther·a·pist

ther·a·py, *n. pl.* ther·a·pies

there·abouts *or* there·about

there·af·ter

there·at

there·by

there·for (IN RETURN FOR)

there·fore (FOR THAT REASON)

there·from

there·in

there·of

there·on

The·re·sa

there·to

there·up·on

there·with

ther·mal

ther·mic

therm·ion

therm·is·tor

ther·mo·cou·ple

ther·mo·dy·nam·ic

ther·mo·dy·nam·i·cal·ly

ther·mo·dy·nam·ics

ther·mo·form

ther·mom·e·ter

ther·mo·nu·cle·ar

ther·mo·plas·tic

ther·mos

ther·mo·sphere

ther·mo·stat

ther·mo·stat·i·cal·ly

the·sau·rus, *n. pl.* the·sau·ri *or* the·sau·ruses

the·sis, *n. pl.* the·ses

thes·pi·an

thi·a·mine (*occas.* thi·a·min)

thick·en

thick·et

thick·ish

thick·head·ed

thick·head·ed·ness

thick·ly

thick·ness

thick·set

thick-skinned

thick-wit·ted

thief, *n. pl.* thieves

thieve, *v.* thieved, thiev·ing

thiev·ery, *n. pl.* thiev·er·ies

thigh·bone

thim·ble

thim·ble·ful, *n. pl.* thim·ble·fuls

thin, *adj.* thin·ner, thin·nest

thin, *v.* thinned, thin·ning

thing·am·a·bob

thing·am·a·jig *or* thing·um·a·jig

thing-in-it·self, *n.*
pl. things-in-
them·selves

think, *v.* thought,
think·ing

think·able

think·er

thin·ly

thin·ner

thin·ness

thin-skinned

third-class, *adj.*

third class, *n.*

third-rate

thirst·i·ly

thirst·i·ness

thirsty, *adj.*
thirst·i·er,
thirst·i·est

thir·teen

thir·teenth

thir·ti·eth

thir·ty, *n. pl.*
thir·ties

this

this·tle

this·tle·down

thi·ther

thi·ther·ward
(*occas.*
thi·ther·wards)

thole

Thom·as

thong

tho·rac·ic

tho·rax, *n. pl.*
tho·rax·es *or*
tho·ra·ces

tho·ri·um

thorny, *adj.*
thorn·i·er,
thorn·i·est

thor·ough

thor·ough·bred

thor·ough·fare

thor·ough·go·ing

thor·ough·ly

thor·ough·ness

though

thought

thought·ful

thought·ful·ly

thought·ful·ness

thought·less

thought·less·ly

thought·less·ness

thou·sand, *n. pl.*
thou·sands *or*
thou·sand

thou·sandth

thrall·dom *or*
thral·dom

thrash·er

thread·bare

thread·i·ness

thready, *adj.*
thread·i·er,
thread·i·est

threat·en

threat·en·ing·ly

three-deck·er

three-
di·men·sion·al

three·fold

three-hand·ed

three-legged

three-phase

three-piece

three-quar·ter

three·score

three·some

three-way

thren·o·dy, *n. pl.*
thren·o·dies

thresh·er

thresh·old

thrice

thrift·i·ly

thrift·i·ness

thrift·less

thrifty, *adj.*
thrift·i·er,
thrift·i·est

thril·ler

thrive, *v.* throve *or*
thrived, thriv·en
(*occas.* thrived),
thriv·ing

throat·i·ly

throat·i·ness

throat·latch

throaty, *adj.*
throat·i·er,
throat·i·est

throb, *v.* throbbed,
throb·bing

throe

throm·bo·sis, *n. pl.*
throm·bo·ses

throne, *v.* throned,
thron·ing

throng

throt·tle, *v.*
throt·tled,
throt·tling

through

through·out

through·way (*var. of* thru·way)

throw, *v.* threw, thrown, throw·ing

throw·away

throw·back

thrum, *v.* thrummed, thrum·ming

thrust, *v.* thrust, thrust·ing

thrust·er

thru·way

thud, *v.* thud·ded, thud·ding

thu·li·um

thumb·hole

thumb·nail

thrumb·print

thumb·screw

thumb·tack

thump

thun·der

thun·der·bird

thun·der·bolt

thun·der·clap

thun·der·cloud

thun·der·head

thun·der·ing·ly

thun·der·ous

thun·der·ous·ly

thun·der·show·er

thun·der·storm

thun·der·struck

Thurs·day

thwack

thwart

thyme

thy·mus

thy·ra·tron

thy·ris·tor

thy·roid

thy·roid·al

ti·ara

tib·ia, *n. pl.* tib·i·ae (*occas.* tib·i·as)

tic (MUSCULAR CONTRACTION)

tick (INSECT, TAPPING SOUND)

tick·er

tick·et

tick·ing

tick·le, *v.* tick·led, tick·ling

tick·ler

tick·lish

tick·lish·ly

tick·lish·ness

tick·tack·toe (*occas.* tic·tac·toe)

tid·al

tid·bit

tid·dle·dy·winks *or* tid·dly·winks

tide·land

tide·mark

tide·wa·ter

tide·way

ti·di·ly

ti·di·ness

tid·ing

ti·dy, *adj.* ti·di·er, ti·di·est

tie, *v.* tied, ty·ing *or* tie·ing

tie·back

tie·break·er

tie-dye, *v.* tie-dyed, tie-dye·ing

tie-in, *n.*

tie in, *v.* tied-in, ty·ing-in *or* tie·ing-in

tie·pin

tier

tie-up, *n.*

tie up, *v.* tied-up, ty·ing-up *or* tie·ing-up

Tif·fa·ny (PERSON'S NAME), *n. pl.* Tif·fa·nys

tif·fa·ny (CLOTH), *n. pl.* tif·fa·nies

ti·ger, *n. pl.* ti·gers (*occas.* ti·ger)

ti·ger·eye *or* ti·ger's·eye

ti·ger·ish

tight·en

tight·fist·ed

tight-lipped

tight·ly

tight-mouthed

tight·ness

tight·rope

tights

tight·wad

ti·glon

ti·gress

Ti·jua·na
tile, *v.* tiled, til·ing
till·able
till·age
till·er
tilt-top
tim·bal (DRUM)
tim·bale (FOOD)
tim·ber
tim·bered
tim·ber·land
tim·ber·line
tim·bre
tim·brel
time, *v.* timed, tim·ing
time·card
time-con·sum·ing
time-hon·ored
time·keep·er
time-lapse
time·less
time·less·ly
time·less·ness
time·li·ness
time·ly, *adj.* time·li·er, time·li·est
time-out
time·piece
tim·er
time·sav·er
time·sav·ing
time·serv·er
time-shar·ing
time·ta·ble
time-test·ed

time·worn
tim·id
ti·mid·i·ty
tim·id·ly
tim·id·ness
tim·ing
Ti·mor
tim·o·rous
tim·o·rous·ly
tim·o·rous·ness
Tim·o·thy
tim·pa·ni
tim·pa·nist
tin, *v.* tinned, tin·ning
tinc·ture, *v.* tinc·tured, tinc·tur·ing
tin·der
tin·der·box
tin·foil
tinge, *v.* tinged, tinge·ing *or* ting·ing
tin·gle, *v.* tin·gled, tin·gling
tin·horn
ti·ni·ly
ti·ni·ness
tin·ker
tin·ker·er
Tin·ker·toy®
tin·kle, *v.* tin·kled, tin·kling
tinned
tin·ni·ly
tin·ni·ness
tin·ny, *adj.*

tin·ni·er, tin·ni·est
tin·plate, *v.* tin·plat·ed, tin·plat·ing
tin·sel, *v.* tin·seled *or* tin·selled, tin·sel·ing *or* tin·sel·ling
tin·smith
tint·ing
tin·tin·nab·u·la·tion
tin·type
tin·ware
tin·work
ti·ny, *adj.* ti·ni·er, ti·ni·est
tip, *v.* tipped, tip·ping
ti·pi (*var. of* tepee)
tip-off
tip·pet
tip·ple, *v.* tip·pled, tip·pling
tip·pler
tip·si·ly
tip·si·ness
tip·ster
tip·sy, *adj.* tip·si·er, tip·si·est
tip·toe, *v.* tip·toed, tip·toe·ing
tip-top
ti·rade
tire, *v.* tired, tir·ing
tired
tired·ly
tired·ness
tire·less

tire·less·ly

tire·less·ness

tire·some

tire·some·ly

tire·some·ness

tis·sue

ti·tan

ti·tan·ic

ti·ta·ni·um

tithe, v. tithed,
   tith·ing

tith·ing

ti·tian

tit·il·late, v.
   tit·il·lat·ed,
   tit·il·lat·ing

tit·il·la·tion

ti·tle, v. ti·tled,
   ti·tling

ti·tled

ti·tle·hold·er

tit·list

tit·mouse, n. pl.
   tit·mice

ti·tra·tion

tit·ter

tit·u·lar

tiz·zy, n. pl. tiz·zies

Tlax·ca·la

T-man, n. pl. T-
   men

toad·stool

toady, n. pl.
   toad·ies

toady, v. toad·ied,
   toad·y·ing

to-and-fro

toast·er

toast·mas·ter

toast·mis·tress

toasty, adj.
   toast·i·er,
   toast·i·est

to·bac·co, n. pl.
   to·bac·cos

to·bac·co·nist

To·ba·go

to·bog·gan

toc·ca·ta

toc·sin

to·day

tod·dle, v.
   tod·dled,
   tod·dling

tod·dler

tod·dy, n. pl.
   tod·dies

to-do, n. pl. to-dos

toe, v. toed,
   toe·ing

toe·cap

toe-dance, v. toe-
   danced, toe-
   danc·ing

toe·hold

toe-in

toe·less

toe·nail

toe·piece

tof·fee or tof·fy

tog, v. togged,
   tog·ging

to·ga

to·geth·er

to·geth·er·ness

tog·gle, v. tog·gled,
   tog·gling

To·go

To·go·land

To·go·lese, n. pl.
   To·go·lese

toi·let

toi·let·ry, n. pl.
   toi·let·ries

toil·some

toil·some·ly

toil·some·ness

toil·worn

to·ken

to·ken·ism

To·kyo

To·le·do

tol·er·a·ble

tol·er·a·bly

tol·er·ance

tol·er·ant

tol·er·ant·ly

tol·er·ate, v.
   tol·er·at·ed,
   tol·er·at·ing

tol·er·a·tion

toll

toll·booth

toll·gate

toll·house

toll·man, n. pl.
   toll·men

tol·u·ene

tom·a·hawk

to·ma·to, n. pl.
   to·ma·toes

tom·boy

tom·boy·ish

tom·boy·ish·ly

tom·boy·ish·ness

tomb·stone

tom·cat

tome

tom·fool·ery, *n. pl.*
  tom·fool·er·ies

Tom·my (BRITISH
  SOLDIER), *n.*
  pl. Tom·mies

Tom·my (PERSON'S
  NAME), *pl.*
  Tom·mys

tom·my·rot

to·mor·row

tom-tom

ton, *n. pl.* tons
  (*occas.* ton)

ton·al

to·nal·i·ty, *n. pl.*
  to·nal·i·ties

tone, *v.* toned,
  ton·ing

tone·arm

tone-deaf

tone-deaf·ness

tone·less

tone·less·ly

tone·less·ness

Ton·ga

Ton·gan

tongs

tongue, *v.*
  tongued,
  tongu·ing

tongue-lash

tongue-tie, *v.*
  tongue-tied,
  tongue-ty·ing

ton·ic

to·night

ton·nage

ton·neau

to·nom·e·ter

ton·sil

ton·sil·lec·to·my, *n.*
  pl.
  ton·sil·lec·to·mies

ton·sil·li·tis

ton·so·ri·al

ton·sure

ton·tine

tony, *adj.* ton·i·er,
  ton·i·est

tool·box

tool·head

tool·ing

tool·mak·er

tool·room

tool·shed

tooth, *n. pl.* teeth

tooth·ache

tooth·brush

tooth·less

tooth·paste

tooth·pick

tooth·some

tooth·some·ly

tooth·some·ness

tooth·wort

toothy, *adj.*
  tooth·i·er,
  tooth·i·est

toot·sy (*occas.*
  toot·sie), *n. pl.*
  toot·sies

top, *v.* topped,
  top·ping

to·paz

top·coat

top-draw·er

top-dress·ing

to·pee *or* to·pi

To·pe·ka

top·er

top·gal·lant

top-heavy

top·ic

top·i·cal

top·i·cal·i·ty

top·i·cal·ly

top·knot

top·less

top-lev·el

top·mast

top·most

top-notch

to·pog·ra·pher

top·o·graph·ic

top·o·graph·i·cal

top·o·graph·i·cal·ly

to·pog·ra·phy, *n.*
  pl.
  to·pog·ra·phies

to·po·log·i·cal

to·po·log·i·cal·ly.

to·pol·o·gist

to·pol·o·gy, *n. pl.*
  to·pol·o·gies

to·pos, *n. pl.* to·poi

top·ping

top·ple, *v.*
  top·pled,
  top·pling

top·sail

top se·cret

top·side

top·soil

top·stitch

top·sy-tur·vy

toque

To·rah

torch·bear·er

torch·light

to·re·ador

tor·ment

tor·ment·ing·ly

tor·men·tor (*occas.* tor·men·ter)

tor·na·do, *n. pl.* tor·na·does *or* tor·na·dos

To·ron·to

tor·pe·do, *n. pl.* tor·pe·does

tor·pe·do, *v.* tor·pe·doed, tor·pe·do·ing

tor·pid

tor·pid·i·ty

tor·por

torque, *v.* torqued, torqu·ing

tor·rent

tor·ren·tial

tor·ren·tial·ly

tor·rid

tor·rid·ly

tor·rid·ness

tor·sion

tor·sion·al

tor·so, *n. pl.* tor·sos *or* tor·si

tort

torte, *n. pl.* tor·ten *or* tortes

tor·til·la

tor·toise

tor·toise·shell

tor·to·ni

tor·tu·ous (TWISTING) (*see also* torturous)

tor·tu·ous·ly

tor·tu·ous·ness

tor·ture, *v.* tortured, tor·tur·ing

tor·tur·er

tor·tur·ous (PAINFUL) (*see also* tortuous)

tor·tur·ous·ly

toss-up

tos·ta·da (*occas.* tos·ta·do)

tot, *v.* tot·ted, tot·ting

to·tal, *v.* to·taled *or* to·talled, to·tal·ing *or* to·tal·ling

to·tal·i·tar·i·an

to·tal·i·tar·i·an·ism

to·tal·i·ty, *n. pl.* to·tal·i·ties

to·tal·i·za·tor (RACETRACK COMPUTER)

to·tal·iz·er (ANYTHING THAT COMPUTES TOTALS)

to·tal·ly

tote, *v.* tot·ed, tot·ing

to·tem

tot·ter

tou·can

touch·able

touch-and-go

touch·back

touch·down

tou·ché

touch·i·ly

touch·i·ness

touch·ing

touch·ing·ly

touch·mark

touch·stone

touch-type, *v.* touch-typed, touch-typ·ing

touch-typ·ist

touchy, *adj.* touch·i·er, touch·i·est

tough·en

tough·ly

tough-mind·ed

tough-mind·ed·ness

tough·ness

tou·pee

tour de force, *n. pl.* tours de force

tour·ism

tour·ist

tour·ma·line

tour·na·ment

tour·ney, *n. pl.* tour·neys

tour·ni·quet

tou·sle, v. tou·sled, tou·sling

tow·age

to·ward or to·wards

tow·boat

tow·el, v. tow·eled or tow·elled, tow·el·ing or tow·el·ling

tow·er

tow·er·ing

tow·er·ing·ly

tow·head

tow·head·ed

tow·line

towns·folk

town·ship

towns·man, n. pl. towns·men

towns·peo·ple

tow·path

tow·rope

tox·e·mia

tox·ic

tox·i·cant

tox·ic·i·ty

tox·i·co·log·ic

tox·i·co·log·i·cal·ly

tox·i·col·o·gist

tox·i·col·o·gy

tox·in

tox·in-an·ti·tox·in

toy·shop

trace, v. traced, trac·ing

trace·able

trac·er

trac·ery, n. pl. trac·er·ies

tra·chea, n. pl. tra·che·ae or tra·che·as

tra·che·ot·o·my, n. pl. tra·che·ot·o·mies

tra·cho·ma

trac·ing

track

track·age

track-and-field

track·lay·er

track·less

track·walk·er

tract

trac·ta·bil·i·ty

trac·ta·ble

trac·ta·bly

trac·tion

trac·tor

trade-in, n.

trade in, v.

trade·mark

trade-off, n.

trade off, v.

trad·er

trades·man, n. pl. trades·men

trades·people

trades·wom·an, n. pl. trades·wom·en

tra·di·tion

tra·di·tion·al

tra·di·tion·al·ism

tra·di·tion·al·ist

tra·di·tion·al·ly

tra·duce, v. tra·duced, tra·duc·ing

tra·duc·er

traf·fic, v. traf·ficked, traf·fick·ing

traf·fick·er

tra·ge·di·an

tra·ge·di·enne

trag·e·dy, n. pl. trag·e·dies

trag·ic

trag·i·cal

trag·i·cal·ly

tragi·com·e·dy, n. pl. tragi·com·e·dies

tragi·com·ic

tragi·com·i·cal

trail·blaz·er

trail·blaz·ing

trail·er

train·able

train·ee

train·er

train·ing

train·load

train·man, n. pl. train·men

train·mas·ter

traipse, v. traipsed, traips·ing

trait

trai·tor

trai·tor·ous

trai·tor·ous·ly

trai·tress *or*
  trait·or·ess

tra·jec·to·ry, *n. pl.*
  tra·jec·to·ries

tram·mel, *v.*
  tram·meled *or*
  tram·mel·led,
  tram·mel·ing *or*
  tram·mel·ling

tram·ple, *v.*
  tram·pled,
  tram·pling

tram·po·line

tram·way

tran·quil

tran·quil·ize (*occas.*
  tran·quil·lize),
  v. tran·quil·ized
  (*occas.*
  tran·quil·lized),
  tran·quil·iz·ing
  (*occas.*
  tran·quil·liz·ing)

tran·quil·iz·er
  (*occas.*
  tran·quil·liz·er)

tran·quil·li·ty *or*
  tran·quil·i·ty

tran·quil·ly

tran·quil·ness

trans·act

trans·ac·tion

trans·ac·tion·al

trans·ac·tor

trans·at·lan·tic

trans·ceiv·er

tran·scend

tran·scen·dence

tran·scen·dent

tran·scen·den·tal

tran·scen·den·tal·ism

trans·con·ti·nen·tal

tran·scribe, *v.*
  tran·scribed,
  tran·scrib·ing

tran·script

tran·scrip·tion

trans·duc·er

tran·sect

tran·sec·tion

tran·sept

trans·fer, *v.*
  trans·ferred,
  trans·fer·ring

trans·fer·able

trans·fer·al

trans·fer·ence

trans·fig·u·ra·tion

trans·fig·ure, *v.*
  trans·fig·ured,
  trans·fig·ur·ing

trans·fix

trans·fix·ion

trans·form

trans·form·able

trans·for·ma·tion

trans·for·ma·tion·al

trans·form·er

trans·fuse, *v.*
  trans·fused,
  trans·fus·ing

trans·fus·ible

trans·fu·sion

trans·gress

trans·gres·sion

trans·gres·sor

tran·sience

tran·sient

tran·sis·tor

tran·sis·tor·ize, *v.*
  tran·sis·tor·ized,
  tran·sis·tor·iz·ing

tran·sit

tran·si·tion

tran·si·tion·al

tran·si·tion·al·ly

tran·si·tive

tran·si·tive·ly

tran·si·tive·ness

tran·si·to·ri·ly

tran·si·to·ri·ness

tran·si·to·ry

trans·lat·abil·i·ty

trans·lat·able

trans·late, *v.*
  trans·lat·ed,
  trans·lat·ing

trans·la·tion

trans·la·tor

trans·lit·er·ate, *v.*
  trans·lit·er·at·ed,
  trans·lit·er·at·ing

trans·lit·er·a·tion

trans·lu·cence

trans·lu·cent

trans·lu·cent·ly

trans·ma·rine

trans·mi·grate, *v.*
  trans·mi·grat·ed,
  trans·mi·grat·ing

trans·mi·gra·tion

trans·mi·gra·to·ry

trans·mis·si·bil·i·ty

trans·mis·si·ble

trans·mis·sion

trans·mit, *v.*
  trans·mit·ted,
  trans·mit·ting

trans·mit·ta·ble

trans·mit·tal

trans·mit·tance

trans·mit·ter

trans·mog·ri·fi·ca·tion

trans·mog·ri·fy, *v.*
  trans·mog·ri·fied,
  trans·mog·ri·fy·ing

trans·mut·able

trans·mu·ta·tion

trans·mute, *v.*
  trans·mut·ed,
  trans·mut·ing

trans·na·tion·al

trans·oce·an·ic

tran·som

tran·son·ic (*occas.*
  trans·son·ic)

trans·pa·cif·ic

trans·par·en·cy, *n.*
  pl.
  trans·par·en·cies

trans·par·ent

tran·spi·ra·tion

tran·spire, *v.*
  tran·spired,
  tran·spir·ing

trans·plant

trans·plant·able

trans·po·lar

tran·spon·der

trans·port

trans·por·ta·tion

trans·port·er

trans·pos·able

trans·pose, *v.*

trans·posed,
  trans·pos·ing

trans·po·si·tion

trans·sex·u·al

trans·ship, *v.*
  trans·shipped,
  trans·ship·ping

trans·ship·ment

tran·sub·stan·ti·a·tion

trans·val·u·a·tion

trans·val·ue, *v.*
  trans·val·ued,
  trans·val·u·ing

trans·ver·sal

trans·verse

trans·verse·ly

trans·ves·tism

trans·ves·tite

trap, *v.* trapped,
  trap·ping

trap·door

tra·peze

tra·pe·zi·um, *n. pl.*
  tra·pe·zi·ums *or*
  tra·pe·zia

trap·e·zoid

trap·e·zoid·al

trap·per

trap·pings

trap·shoot·ing

tra·pun·to, *n. pl.*
  tra·pun·tos

trash·i·ness

trashy, *adj.*
  trash·i·er,
  trash·i·est

trau·ma, *n. pl.*
  trau·ma·ta *or*
  trau·mas

trau·mat·ic

trau·mat·i·cal·ly

trau·ma·tize, *v.*
  trau·ma·tized,
  trau·ma·tiz·ing

tra·vail

trav·el, *v.* trav·eled
  or trav·el·led,
  trav·el·ing *or*
  trav·el·ling

trav·el·er *or*
  trav·el·ler

trav·el·ogue *or*
  trav·el·og

tra·vers·able

tra·verse, *v.*
  tra·versed,
  tra·vers·ing

trav·er·tine

trav·es·ty, *n. pl.*
  trav·es·ties

Trav·is

trawl·er

tray (FLAT
  RECEPTACLE)
  (*see also* trey)

treach·er·ous

treach·er·ous·ly

treach·er·ous·ness

treach·ery, *n. pl.*
  treach·er·ies

trea·cle

tread, *v.* trod
  (*occas.*
  tread·ed),
  trod·den *or*
  trod, tread·ing

trea·dle, *v.*
  trea·dled,
  trea·dling

tread·mill

trea·son

trea·son·able

trea·son·ous

trea·son·ous·ly

trea·son·ous·ness

trea·sur·able

trea·sure, *v.*
trea·sured,
trea·sur·ing

trea·sur·er

trea·sury, *n. pl.*
trea·sur·ies

treat·abil·i·ty

treat·able

trea·tise

treat·ment

trea·ty, *n. pl.*
trea·ties

tre·ble, *v.* tre·bled,
tre·bling

tree, *v.* treed,
tree·ing

tree·house

tree·less

tree·nail (*occas.*
tre·nail)

tree·top

tre·foil

treil·lage

trek, *v.* trekked,
trek·king

trel·lis

trel·lis·work

trem·ble, *v.*
trem·bled,
trem·bling

trem·bling·ly

trem·bly

tre·men·dous

tre·men·dous·ly

tre·men·dous·ness

trem·o·lo, *n. pl.*
trem·o·los

trem·or

trem·u·lous

trem·u·lous·ly

trem·u·lous·ness

tren·chant

tren·cher

tren·cher·man, *n.
pl.*
tren·cher·men

trend·i·ly

trend·i·ness

trend·set·ter

trendy, *adj.*
trend·i·er,
trend·i·est

Tren·ton

tre·pan, *v.*
tre·panned,
tre·pan·ning

trep·i·da·tion

tres·pass

tres·pass·er

tres·tle

tres·tle·work

trey (THREE
SPOTS) (*see also*
tray)

tri·able

tri·ad

tri·age

tri·al

tri·an·gle

tri·an·gu·lar

tri·an·gu·late, *v.*
tri·an·gu·lat·ed,
tri·an·gu·lat·ing

tri·an·gu·la·tion

Tri·as·sic

tri·ath·lete

tri·ath·lon

tri·ax·i·al

trib·al

trib·al·ism

trib·al·ly

tribes·man, *n. pl.*
tribes·men

trib·u·la·tion

tri·bu·nal

trib·une

trib·u·tary, *n. pl.*
trib·u·tar·ies

trib·ute

tri·cam·er·al

trice, *v.* triced,
tric·ing

tri·cen·ten·ni·al

tri·ceps, *n. pl.*
tri·ceps·es
(*occas.* tri·ceps)

tri·chi·na, *n. pl.*
tri·chi·nae
(*occas.*
tri·chi·nas)

trich·i·no·sis

tri·chot·o·mous

tri·chot·o·my

tri·chro·mat·ic

trick·ery, *n. pl.*
trick·er·ies

trick·i·ly

trick·i·ness

trick·le, *v.*

trick·led,
trick·ling

trick·le-down

trick·ster

tricky, *adj.*
trick·i·er,
trick·i·est

tri·col·or

tri·cor·nered

tri·cot

tri·cus·pid

tri·cy·cle

tri·dent

tri·di·men·sion·al

tri·en·ni·al

tri·en·ni·um

tri·er

tri·fec·ta

tri·fle, *v.* tri·fled,
tri·fling

tri·fler

tri·fling

tri·fo·cal

tri·fur·cate

trig·ger

tri·glyc·er·ide

trig·o·no·met·ric

trig·o·no·met·ri·cal

trig·o·nom·e·try, *n.*
pl.
trig·o·nom·e·tries

tri·lat·er·al

tri·lin·gual

tril·lion

tril·lionth

tril·o·gy, *n. pl.*
tril·o·gies

trim, *v.* trimmed,
trim·ming

tri·ma·ran

tri·mes·ter

trim·e·ter

trim·mer

tri·month·ly

Trin·i·dad

Trin·i·da·di·an

trin·i·ty, *n. pl.*
trin·i·ties

trin·ket

tri·no·mi·al

trio, *n. pl.* tri·os

tri·ode

trip, *v.* tripped,
trip·ping

tri·par·tite

trip-ham·mer

triph·thong

tri·ple, *v.* tri·pled,
tri·pling

tri·ple-space, *v.*
tri·ple-spaced,
tri·ple-spac·ing

trip·let

tri·plex

trip·li·cate, *v.*
trip·li·cat·ed,
trip·li·cat·ing

tri·ply

tri·pod

trip·tych

trip·wire

tri·reme

tri·sect

trite, *adj.* trit·er,
trit·est

trite·ly

trite·ness

trit·u·rate, *v.*
trit·u·rat·ed,
trit·u·rat·ing

tri·umph

tri·um·phal

tri·um·phant

tri·um·phant·ly

tri·um·vir, *n. pl.*
tri·um·virs *or*
tri·um·vi·ri

tri·um·vi·rate

triv·et

triv·ia

triv·i·al

triv·i·al·i·ty, *n. pl.*
triv·i·al·i·ties

triv·i·al·ize, *v.*
triv·i·al·ized,
triv·i·al·iz·ing

triv·i·al·ly

tri·week·ly, *n. pl.*
tri·week·lies

tro·cha·ic

tro·che (LOZENGE)

tro·chee (POETIC
METER)

trof·fer

trog·lo·dyte

troi·ka

troll

trol·ley, *n. pl.*
trol·leys

trol·lop

trom·bone

trom·bon·ist

troop (SOLDIERS)

(*see also*
troupe)

troop·er

troop·ship

tro·phy, *n. pl.*
tro·phies

trop·ic

trop·i·cal

tro·pism

tro·po·pause

tro·po·sphere

trot, *v.* trot·ted,
trot·ting

trot·line

trot·ter

trou·ba·dor

trou·ble, *v.*
trou·bled,
trou·bling

trou·ble·mak·er

trou·ble·shoot·er

trou·ble·some

trou·ble·some·ly

trou·ble·some·ness

trou·blous

trou·blous·ly

trou·blous·ness

trough

trounce, *v.*
trounced,
trounc·ing

troupe (ACTORS),
v. trouped,
troup·ing (*see
also* troop)

troup·er

trou·sers

trous·seau, *n. pl.*

trous·seaux *or*
trous·seaus

trout, *n. pl.* trout
(*occas.* trouts)

tro·ver

trow·el, *v.*
trow·eled *or*
trow·el·led,
trow·el·ing *or*
trow·el·ling

tru·an·cy, *n. pl.*
tru·an·cies

tru·ant

truce

truck·age

truck·er

truck·ing

truck·le, *v.*
truck·led,
truck·ling

truck·line

truck·load

truc·u·lence

truc·u·lent

truc·u·lent·ly

trudge, *v.* trudged,
trudg·ing

true, *adj.* tru·er,
tru·est

true, *v.* trued,
tru·ing (*occas.*
tru·ing)

true-blue

true·heart·ed

true·heart·ed·ness

true-life

true·love

true·ness

truf·fle

tru·ism

tru·is·tic

tru·ly

trumped-up

trum·pery, *n. pl.*
trump·er·ies

trum·pet

trum·pet·er

trun·cate, *v.*
trun·cat·ed,
trun·cat·ing

trun·ca·tion

trun·cheon

trun·dle, *v.*
trun·dled,
trun·dling

truss

truss·ing

trust·bust·er

trust·ee
(OVERSEER)
(*see also* trusty)

trust·ee·ship

trust·ful

trust·ful·ly

trust·ful·ness

trust·i·ness

trust·ing

trust·ing·ly

trust·wor·thi·ly

trust·wor·thi·ness

trust·wor·thy

trusty (CONVICT)
(*see also*
trustee)

truth·ful

truth·ful·ly

truth·ful·ness

try, v. tried, try·ing

try·out

tryst

tsar (*var. of.* czar)

tsa·ri·na (*var. of.* czarina)

tset·se fly

T-shirt

tsu·na·mi

tub, v. tubbed, tub·bing

tu·ba

tub·by, *adj.* tub·bi·er, tub·bi·est

tube, v. tubed, tub·ing

tube·less

tu·ber

tu·ber·cle

tu·ber·cu·lar

tu·ber·cu·lated (*occas.* tu·ber·cu·late)

tu·ber·cu·lin

tu·ber·cu·lo·sis

tu·ber·cu·lous

tube·rose

tu·ber·ous

tub·ing

tu·bu·lar

tu·bule

tuck·er

Tuc·son

Tues·day

tu·fa

tuft

tuft·ed

tug, v. tugged, tug·ging

tug·boat

tug-of-war, *n. pl.* tugs-of-war

tu·ition

tu·la·re·mia

tu·lip

tulle

Tul·sa

tum·ble, v. tum·bled, tum·bling

tum·ble·down

tum·bler

tum·ble·weed

tum·bril (*occas.* tum·brel)

tu·mes·cence

tu·mes·cent

tu·mid

tu·mid·i·ty

tum·my, *n. pl.* tum·mies

tu·mor

tu·mor·ous

tu·mult

tu·mul·tu·ous

tu·mul·tu·ous·ly

tu·mul·tu·ous·ness

tu·na, *n. pl.* tu·na *or* tu·nas

tun·able

tun·dra

tune, v. tuned, tun·ing

tune·ful

tune·ful·ly

tune·ful·ness

tune·less

tune·less·ly

tune·less·ness

tun·er

tune·smith

tune-up, *n.*

tune up, v.

tung·sten

tu·nic

Tu·ni·sia

Tu·ni·sian

tun·nel, v. tun·nel·ed *or* tun·nel·led, tun·nel·ing *or* tun·nel·ling

tun·ny, *n. pl.* tun·nies *or* tun·ny

tu·pe·lo, *n. pl.* tu·pe·los

tuque

tur·ban

tur·bid

tur·bid·i·ty

tur·bine

tur·bo, *n. pl.* tur·bos

tur·bo-charge, v. tur·bo-charged, tur·bo-charg·ing

tur·bo-charg·er

tur·bo·fan

tur·bo·jet

tur·bo·prop

tur·bo·su·per·charg·er

tur·bot, *n. pl.*

tur·bot (*occas.* tur·bots)

tur·bu·lence

tur·bu·lent

tur·bu·lent·ly

tu·reen

turf, *n. pl.* turfs *or* turves

tur·gid

tur·gid·i·ty

Tur·key

tur·key, *n. pl.* tur·keys

Turk·ish

Turk·men

Turk·men So·vi·et So·cial·ist Re·pub·lic (*now* Turkmenistan)

Turk·men·i·stan (*formerly* Turkmen Soviet Socialist Republic)

tur·mer·ic

tur·moil

turn·about

turn·around

turn·buck·le

turn·coat

turn·down

turn·er

turn-in, *n.*

turn in, *v.*

turn·ing

tur·nip

turn·key, *n. pl.* turn·keys

turn·off, *n.*

turn off, *v.*

turn-on, *n.*

turn on, *v.*

turn·out, *n.*

turn out, *v.*

turn·over, *adj. n.*

turn over, *v.*

turn·pike

turn·spit

turn·stile

turn·ta·ble

tur·pen·tine, *v.* tur·pen·tined, tur·pen·tin·ing

tur·pi·tude

tur·quoise (*occas.* tur·quois)

tur·ret

tur·ret·ed

tur·tle, *n. pl.* tur·tles (*occas.* tur·tle)

tur·tle·back *or* tur·tle-backed

tur·tle·dove

tur·tle·neck

tusk·er

tus·sle, *v.* tus·sled, tus·sling

tus·sock

tut, *v.* tut·ted, tut·ting

tu·te·lage

tu·te·lary, *n. pl.* tu·te·lar·ies

tu·tor

tu·to·ri·al

tut·ti-frut·ti

tu·tu

Tu·va·lu

tux·e·do, *n. pl.* tux·e·dos *or* tux·e·does

twain

twang

tweak

tweed·i·ness

tweedy, *adj.* tweed·i·er, tweed·i·est

tweet·er

tweeze, *v.* tweezed, tweez·ing

tweez·ers

twelfth

twelve

twelve·fold

twelve·month

twen·ti·eth

twen·ty, *n. pl.* twen·ties

twice-told

twid·dle, *v.* twid·dled, twid·dling

twig·gy, *adj.* twig·gi·er, twig·gi·est

twi·light

twi·lit

twill

twin, *v.* twinned, twin·ning

twinge

twin·kle, *v.*

twin·kled,
twin·kling

twin·kler

twin·kling

twirl·er

twist·er

twit, *v.* twit·ted,
twit·ting

twitch

twit·ter

two-bit

two-by-four

two-cycle

two-di·men·sion·al

two-faced

two-fisted

two·fold

two-hand·ed

two-leg·ged

two-phase

two-ply

two-sid·ed

two·some

two-step

two-time, *v.* two-
timed, two-
tim·ing

two-way

ty·coon

tyke

Ty·ler

tym·pan·ic

tym·pa·num, *n. pl.*
tym·pa·na
(*occas.*
tym·pa·nums)

type, *v.* typed,
typ·ing

type·bar

type·cast, *v.*
type·cast,
type·cast·ing

type·face

type·found·ry, *n.*
pl.
type·found·ries

type·script

type·set, *v.*
type·set,
type·set·ting

type·set·ter

type·write, *v.*
type·wrote,
type·writ·ten,
type·writ·ing

type·writ·er

ty·phoid

ty·phoon

ty·phus

typ·i·cal

typ·i·cal·ly

typ·i·fy, *v.*
typ·i·fied,
typ·i·fy·ing

typ·ist

ty·po, *n. pl.* ty·pos

ty·pog·ra·pher

ty·po·graph·ic

ty·po·graph·i·cal

ty·po·graph·i·cal·ly

ty·pog·ra·phy

ty·po·log·i·cal

ty·po·log·i·cal·ly

ty·pol·o·gy

ty·ran·ni·cal

ty·ran·ni·cal·ly

tyr·an·nize, *v.*
tyr·an·nized,
tyr·an·niz·ing

tyr·an·niz·er

tyr·an·nous

tyr·an·nous·ly

tyr·an·ny, *n. pl.*
tyr·an·nies

ty·rant

ty·ro, *n. pl.* ty·ros

tzar (*var. of* czar)

tza·ri·na (*var. of*
czarina)

U

Uban·gi

uibiq·ui·tous

ubiq·ui·tous·ly

ubiq·ui·tous·ness

ubiq·ui·ty

U-boat

ud·der

Ugan·da

Ugan·dan

ug·li·ness

ug·ly, *adj.* ug·li·er,
ug·li·est

ukase

Ukraine (*formerly*
Ukrainian Soviet
Socialist
Republic)

Ukrai·ni·an

Ukrai·ni·an So·vi·et
So·cial·ist
Re·pub·lic (*now*
Ukraine)

uku·le·le (*occas.*
uke·le·le)

Ulan Ba·tor

ul·cer

ul·cer·ate, *v.*

ul·cer·at·ed,
ul·cer·at·ing

ul·cer·a·tion

ul·cer·a·tive

ul·cer·ous

ul·cer·ous·ly

ul·lage

ul·na

Ul·ster (IRELAND,
NEW YORK)

ul·ster (COAT)

ul·te·ri·or

ul·ti·mate

ul·ti·mate·ly

ul·ti·ma·tum, *n. pl.*
ul·ti·ma·tums *or*
ul·ti·ma·ta

ul·ti·mo

ul·tra

ul·tra·cen·tri·fuge,
v.
ul·tra·cen·tri·fuged,
ul·tra·cen·tri·fug·ing

ul·tra·con·ser·va·tive

ul·tra·high
fre·quen·cy

ul·tra·ism

ul·tra·light

ul·tra·ma·rine

ul·tra·mi·cro

ul·tra·mi·cro·scope

ul·tra·min·ia·ture

ul·tra·mod·ern

ul·tra·mon·tane

ul·tra·mun·dane

ul·tra·na·tion·al

ul·tra·na·tion·al·ism

ul·tra·pure

ul·tra·short

ul·tra·son·ic

ul·tra·sound

ul·tra·vi·o·let

ul·tra vi·res

ul·u·late

ul·u·la·tion

um·bel

um·bel·late

um·ber

um·bil·i·cal

um·bil·i·cus, *n. pl.*
um·bil·i·ci *or*
um·bil·i·cus·es

um·bra, *n. pl.*
um·bras *or*
um·brae

um·brage
um·bra·geous
um·bra·geous·ly
um·bra·geous·ness
um·brel·la
umi·ak
um·laut
um·pire, *v.*
  um·pired,
  um·pir·ing
ump·teen
ump·teenth
un·abashed
un·abashed·ly
un·abat·ed
un·able
un·abridged
un·ac·cept·abil·i·ty
un·ac·cept·able
un·ac·cept·ably
un·ac·com·pa·nied
un·ac·count·abil·i·ty
un·ac·count·able
un·ac·count·ably
un·ac·count·ed-for
un·ac·cus·tomed
un·ac·cus·tomed·ly
un·ac·quaint·ed
un·adorned
un·adul·ter·at·ed
un·adul·ter·at·ed·ly
un·af·fect·ed
un·af·fect·ed·ly
un·af·fect·ed·ness
un·af·fil·i·at·ed
un·afraid

un·aligined
un·al·loyed
un·al·ter·able
un·al·ter·ably
un-Amer·i·can
una·nim·i·ty
unan·i·mous
unan·i·mous·ly
un·an·nounced
un·an·swer·able
un·an·swer·ably
un·ap·peal·ing
un·ap·pe·tiz·ing
un·ap·pe·tiz·ing·ly
un·apt (NOT
  SUITABLE) (*see
  also* inapt, inept)
un·apt·ly
un·apt·ness
un·ar·gu·able
un·armed
un·ar·tis·tic
un·ashamed
un·asham·ed·ly
un·asked
un·as·sail·abil·i·ty
un·as·sail·able
un·as·sail·ably
un·as·sist·ed
un·as·sum·ing
un·at·tached
un·at·trac·tive
un·au·tho·rized
un·avail·ing
un·avail·ing·ly
un·avoid·able

un·avoid·ably
un·aware, *adj.*
un·awares, *adv.*
un·bal·ance, *v.*
  un·bal·anced,
  un·bal·anc·ing
un·bar, *v.*
  un·barred,
  un·bar·ring
un·bear·able
un·bear·ably
un·beat·able
un·beat·en
un·be·com·ing
un·be·com·ing·ly
un·be·com·ing·ness
un·be·fit·ting
un·be·knownst
  (*occas.*
  un·be·known)
un·be·lief
un·be·liev·able
un·be·liev·ably
un·be·liev·er
un·be·liev·ing
un·be·liev·ing·ly
un·bend, *v.*
  un·bent,
  un·bend·ing
un·bi·ased
un·bid·den (*occas.*
  un·bid)
un·bind, *v.*
  un·bound,
  un·bind·ing
un·blem·ished
un·blush·ing
un·blush·ing·ly
un·bolt

un·born
un·bound·ed
un·bowed
un·braid
un·break·able
un·bri·dled
un·bro·ken
un·buck·le, *v.*
  un·buck·led,
  un·buck·ling
un·bur·den
un·busi·ness·like
un·but·ton
un·cage, *v.*
  un·caged,
  un·cag·ing
un·called-for
un·can·ni·ly
un·can·ny
un·cap, *v.*
  un·capped,
  un·cap·ping
un·car·ing
un·ceas·ing
un·ceas·ing·ly
un·cen·sored
un·cer·e·mo·ni·ous
un·cer·e·mo·ni·ous·ly
un·cer·e·mo·ni·ous·ness
un·cer·tain
un·cer·tain·ly
un·cer·tain·ness
un·cer·tain·ty, *n.*
  pl. un·cer·tain·ties
un·chain
un·change·able
un·change·ably
un·char·ac·ter·is·tic

un·char·ac·ter·is·ti·cal·ly
un·char·i·ta·ble
un·char·i·ta·ble·ness
un·char·i·ta·bly
un·chart·ed
un·chiv·al·rous
un·chiv·al·rous·ly
un·chris·tian
un·cial
un·civ·il
un·civ·i·lized
un·claimed
un·clamp
un·clasp
un·clas·si·fied
un·cle
un·clean
un·clean·li·ness
un·clear
un·clench
Un·cle Sam
Un·cle Tom
un·cloak
un·clothe, *v.*
  un·clothed *or*
  un·clad,
  un·cloth·ing
un·clut·tered
un·coil
un·col·lect·ible
un·com·fort·able
un·com·fort·able·ness
un·com·fort·ably
un·com·mit·ted
un·com·mon
un·com·mon·ly
un·com·mon·ness

un·com·mu·ni·ca·tive
un·com·mu·ni·ca·tive·ly
un·com·mu·ni·ca·tive·ne
un·com·pen·sat·ed
un·com·pli·cat·ed
un·com·pli·men·ta·ry
un·com·pre·hend·ing
un·com·pre·hend·ing·ly
un·com·pro·mis·ing
un·com·pro·mis·ing·ly
un·con·cerned
un·con·cerned·ly
un·con·cerned·ness
un·con·di·tion·al
un·con·di·tion·al·ly
un·con·for·mi·ty
un·con·quer·able
un·con·quer·ably
un·con·quered
un·con·scio·na·ble
un·con·scio·na·bly
un·con·scious
un·con·scious·ly
un·con·scious·ness
un·con·sti·tu·tion·al
un·con·sti·tu·tion·al·i·ty
un·con·sti·tu·tion·al·ly
un·con·trol·la·ble
un·con·trol·la·bly
un·con·ven·tion·al
un·con·ven·tion·al·i·ty
un·con·ven·tion·al·ly
un·con·vinc·ing
un·con·vinc·ing·ly
un·cooked
un·co·op·er·a·tive

un·co·or·di·nat·ed
un·cork
un·cor·rob·o·rat·ed
un·count·ed
un·cou·ple, v.
  un·cou·pled,
  un·cou·pling
un·couth
un·couth·ly
un·couth·ness
un·cov·er
un·crate, v.
  un·crat·ed,
  un·crat·ing
un·crit·i·cal
un·crit·i·cal·ly
un·cross
unc·tion
unc·tu·ous
unc·tu·ous·ly
unc·tu·ous·ness
un·curl
un·cut
un·dam·aged
un·daunt·ed
un·daunt·ed·ly
un·de·cid·ed
un·de·cid·ed·ly
un·de·cid·ed·ness
un·de·fined
un·dem·o·crat·ic
un·dem·o·crat·i·cal·ly
un·de·mon·stra·tive
un·de·mon·stra·tive·ly
un·de·mon·stra·tive·ness
un·de·ni·able
un·de·ni·ably

un·der
un·der·achiev·er
un·der·act
un·der·age
un·der·arm
un·der·bel·ly
un·der·bid, v.
  un·der·bid,
  un·der·bid·ding
un·der·brush
un·der·cap·i·tal·iza·tion
un·der·cap·i·tal·iize, v.
  un·der·cap·i·tal·ized,
  un·der·cap·i·tal·iz·ing
un·der·car·riage
un·der·charge, v.
  un·der·charged,
  un·der·charg·ing
un·der·class·man, pl.
  un·der·class·men
un·der·clothes
un·der·cloth·ing
un·der·coat
un·der·coat·ing
un·der·cov·er
un·der·cur·rent
un·der·cut, v.
  un·der·cut,
  un·der·cut·ting
un·der·de·vel·oped
un·der·dog
un·der·done
un·der·es·ti·mate, v.
  un·der·es·ti·mat·ed,
  un·der·es·ti·mat·ing
un·der·es·ti·ma·tion

un·der·ex·pose, v.
  un·der·ex·posed,
  un·der·ex·pos·ing
un·der·ex·po·sure
un·der·feed, v.
  un·der·fed,
  un·der·feed·ing
un·der·foot
un·der·gar·ment
un·der·go, v.
  un·der·went,
  un·der·gone,
  un·der·go·ing
un·der·grad·u·ate
un·der·ground
un·der·growth
un·der·hand
un·der·hand·ed
un·der·hand·ed·ly
un·der·hand·ed·ness
un·der·hung
un·der·in·sured
un·der·lay, v.
  un·der·laid,
  un·der·lay·ing
un·der·lie, v.
  un·der·lay,
  un·der·lain,
  un·der·ly·ing
un·der·line
un·der·ling
un·der·lip
un·der·ly·ing
un·der·mine, v.
  un·der·mined,
  un·der·min·ing
un·der·most
un·der·neath
un·der·nour·ished

un·der·nour·ish·ment

un·der·paid

un·der·pants

un·der·pass

un·der·pay, *v.*
  un·der·paid,
  un·der·pay·ing

un·der·pin·ning

un·der·play

un·der·priv·i·leged

un·der·pro·duc·tion

un·der·rate, *v.*
  un·der·rat·ed,
  un·der·rat·ing

un·der·score, *v.*
  un·der·scored,
  un·der·scor·ing

un·der·sea *or*
  un·der·seas,
  adv.

un·der·sea, *adj.*

un·der·sec·re·tary,
  n. pl.
  un·der·sec·re·tar·ies

un·der·sell, *v.*
  un·der·sold,
  un·der·sell·ing

un·der·sexed

un·der·shirt

un·der·shoot, *v.*
  un·der·shot,
  un·der·shoot·ing

un·der·shorts

un·der·side

un·der·signed, *n.*
  pl.
  un·der·signed

un·der·sized (*occas.*
  un·der·size)

un·der·skirt

un·der·slung

un·der·stand, *v.*
  un·der·stood,
  un·der·stand·ing

un·der·stand·abil·i·ty

un·der·stand·able

un·der·stand·ably

un·der·stand·ing

un·der·state, *v.*
  un·der·stat·ed,
  un·der·stat·ing

un·der·state·ment

un·der·stood

un·der·study, *n. pl.*
  un·der·stud·ies

un·der·take, *v.*
  un·der·took,
  un·der·tak·en,
  un·der·tak·ing

un·der·tak·er

un·der·tak·ing

un·der-the-count·er

un·der·tone

un·der·tow

un·der·val·u·a·tion

un·der·val·ue, *v.*
  un·der·val·ued,
  un·der·val·u·ing

un·der·wa·ter

un·der·way

un·der·wear

un·der·world

un·der·write, *v.*
  un·der·wrote,
  un·der·writ·ten,
  un·der·writ·ing

un·der·writ·er

un·de·served

un·de·sir·able

un·de·sir·ably

un·de·tect·ed

un·de·ter·mined

un·de·vi·at·ing

un·dies

un·dip·lo·mat·ic

un·dip·lo·mat·i·cal·ly

un·dis·ci·plined

un·dis·cour·aged

un·do, *v.* un·did,
  un·done,
  un·do·ing

un·doc·u·ment·ed

un·do·mes·ti·cat·ed

un·doubt·ed

un·doubt·ed·ly

un·draped

un·dress

un·due

un·du·lant

un·du·late, *v.*
  un·du·lat·ed,
  un·du·lat·ing

un·du·la·tion

un·du·ly

un·dy·ing

un·earned

un·earth

un·eas·i·ly

un·eas·i·ness

un·easy

un·ed·it·ed

un·ed·u·ca·ble

un·ed·u·cat·ed

un·em·ploy·able

un·em·ployed

un·em·ploy·ment

un·end·ing

un·equal

un·equaled *or*
　un·equalled

un·equal·ly

un·equip·ped

un·equiv·o·cal

un·equiv·o·cal·ly

un·err·ing

un·err·ing·ly

un·es·sen·tial

un·eth·i·cal

un·even

un·even·ly

un·even·ness

un·event·ful

un·ex·cep·tion·able

un·ex·cep·tion·ably

un·ex·pect·ed

un·ex·pect·ed·ly

un·ex·pect·ed·ness

un·ex·plored

un·fail·ing

un·fail·ing·ly

un·fair

un·fair·ly

un·fair·ness

un·faith·ful

un·faith·ful·ly

un·faith·ful·ness

un·fa·mil·iar

un·fa·mil·iar·i·ty

un·fas·ten

un·fa·vor·able

un·fa·vor·ably

un·feel·ing

un·feel·ing·ly

un·fet·ter

un·fit

un·fit·ness

un·flap·pa·bil·i·ty

un·flap·pa·ble

un·flinch·ing

un·flinch·ing·ly

un·fo·cused (*occas.*
　un·fo·cussed)

un·fold

un·for·get·ta·ble

un·for·get·ta·bly

un·for·giv·ing

un·formed

un·for·tu·nate

un·for·tu·nate·ly

un·found·ed

un·freeze, *v.*
　un·froze,
　un·froz·en,
　un·freez·ing

un·friend·li·ness

un·friend·ly

un·frock

un·fruit·ful

un·furl

un·gain·li·ness

un·gain·ly

un·gen·er·ous

un·gen·er·ous·ly

un·glue, *v.*
　un·glued,
　un·glu·ing

un·god·ly

un·gov·ern·able

un·grace·ful

un·grace·ful·ly

un·gra·cious

un·gra·cious·ly

un·gra·cious·ness

un·gram·mat·i·cal

un·gram·mat·i·cal·ly

un·grate·ful

un·grate·ful·ly

un·grate·ful·ness

un·guard·ed

un·guard·ed·ly

un·guard·ed·ness

un·guent

un·gu·late

un·hand

un·hap·pi·ly

un·hap·pi·ness

un·hap·py, *adj.*
　un·hap·pi·er,
　un·hap·pi·est

un·harmed

un·healthy

un·heard-of

un·hes·i·tat·ing

un·hes·i·tat·ing·ly

un·hinge, *v.*
　un·hinged,
　un·hing·ing

un·hitch

un·hook

un·horse, *v.*
　un·horsed,
　un·hors·ing

un·hur·ried

uni·cam·er·al

uni·cel·lu·lar

uni·corn

uni·cy·cle
uni·di·rec·tion·al
uni·fi·ca·tion
uni·form
uni·for·mi·ty
uni·form·ly
uni·fy, *v.* uni·fied,
  uni·fy·ing
uni·lat·er·al
uni·lat·er·al·ly
un·imag·in·able
un·imag·in·ably
un·imag·i·na·tive
un·im·peach·able
un·im·peach·ably
un·im·por·tance
un·im·por·tant
un·im·pres·sive
un·in·cor·po·rat·ed
un·in·hib·it·ed
un·in·sur·able
un·in·sured
un·in·tel·li·gent
un·in·tel·li·gi·ble
un·in·tel·li·gi·bly
un·in·ten·tion·al
un·in·ten·tion·al·ly
un·in·ter·rup·ted
un·in·vit·ed
union
union·ism
union·iza·tion
union·ize, *v.*
  union·ized,
  union·iz·ing
Union of So·vi·et
  So·cial·ist

Re·pub·lics
  (nonexistent
  after Jan. 1,
  1992; *see*
  Commonwealth
  of Independent
  States)
unique
unique·ly
unique·ness
uni·sex
uni·son
unit
Uni·tar·i·an
Uni·tar·i·an·ism
uni·tary
unite, *v.* unit·ed,
  unit·ing
unit·ed
Unit·ed Ar·ab
  Emir·ates
Unit·ed King·dom
  of Great Brit·ain
  and Nor·thern
  Ire·land
Unit·ed Na·tions
Unit·ed States of
  Amer·i·ca
uni·ty, *n. pl.*
  uni·ties
uni·ver·sal
uni·ver·sal·i·ty
uni·ver·sal·ly
uni·verse
uni·ver·si·ty, *n. pl.*
  uni·ver·si·ties
un·just
un·jus·ti·fied
un·kempt

un·kind
un·know·ing
un·known
un·lace, *v.*
  un·laced,
  un·lac·ing
un·latch
un·law·ful
un·law·ful·ly
un·law·ful·ness
un·lead·ed
un·learn
un·learned
un·leash
un·less
un·let·tered
un·like
un·like·li·hood
un·like·li·ness
un·like·ly
un·lim·ber
un·lim·it·ed
un·list·ed
un·load
un·lock
un·looked-for
un·loose
un·loos·en
un·luck·i·ly
un·luck·i·ness
un·lucky, *adj.*
  un·luck·i·er,
  un·luck·i·est
un·make, *v.*
  un·made,
  un·mak·ing
un·man·age·able

un·man·ly
un·man·ner·ly
un·mar·ried
un·mask
un·men·tion·able
un·mer·ci·ful
un·mer·ci·ful·ly
un·mind·ful
un·mind·ful·ly
un·mis·tak·able
un·mis·tak·ably
un·mit·i·gat·ed
un·muf·fle, *v.*
  un·muf·fled,
  un·muf·fling
un·muz·zle, *v.*
  un·muz·zled,
  un·muz·zling
un·nat·u·ral
un·nat·u·ral·ly
un·nat·u·ral·ness
un·nec·es·sar·i·ly
un·nec·es·sary
un·nerve, *v.*
  un·nerved,
  un·nerv·ing
un·num·bered
un·ob·tru·sive
un·ob·tru·sive·ly
un·ob·tru·sive·ness
un·oc·cu·pied
un·or·ga·nized
un·or·tho·dox
un·pack
un·par·al·leled
un·par·don·able
un·paved

un·pin, *v.*
  un·pinned,
  un·pin·ning
un·pleas·ant
un·pleas·ant·ness
un·plug, *v.*
  un·plugged,
  un·plug·ging
un·plumbed
un·pop·u·lar
un·pop·u·lar·i·ty
un·prec·e·dent·ed
un·prec·e·dent·ed·ly
un·pre·dict·abil·i·ty
un·pre·dict·able
un·prej·u·diced
un·pre·pos·ses·sing
un·pre·sent·able
un·pre·ten·tious
un·pre·ten·tious·ly
un·pre·ten·tious·ness
un·prin·ci·pled
un·print·able
un·prof·it·able
un·prof·it·ably
un·prom·is·ing
un·pro·nounced
un·pro·tect·ed
un·proved
un·prov·en
un·pro·voked
un·qual·i·fied
un·ques·tion·able
un·ques·tion·ably
un·ques·tion·ing
un·quote
un·rav·el, *v.*

un·rav·eled *or*
un·rav·elled,
un·rav·el·ing *or*
un·rav·el·ling
un·read
un·read·able
un·read·iness
un·ready
un·re·al
un·re·al·is·tic
un·re·al·is·ti·cal·ly
un·re·al·i·ty
un·rea·son·able
un·rea·son·ably
un·rea·son·ing
un·rec·og·niz·able
un·rec·og·nized
un·re·con·struct·ed
un·reel
un·re·gen·er·ate
un·reg·is·tered
un·reg·u·lat·ed
un·re·hearsed
un·re·lent·ing
un·re·mem·bered
un·re·quit·ed
un·re·served
un·re·serv·ed·ly
un·re·served·ness
un·re·solved
un·res·pon·sive
un·rest
un·re·strained
un·re·ward·ing
un·righ·teous
un·righ·teous·ly
un·righ·teous·ness

un·ripe
un·ripe·ness
un·ri·valed *or*
  un·ri·valled
un·roll
un·ro·man·tic
un·ro·man·ti·cal·ly
un·ruf·fled
un·rul·i·ness
un·ruly, *adj.*
  un·rul·i·er,
  un·rul·i·est
un·sad·dle, *v.*
  un·sad·dled,
  un·sad·dling
un·sanc·tioned
un·san·i·tary
un·sat·is·fac·to·ri·ly
un·sat·is·fac·to·ry
un·sat·u·rat·ed
un·sa·vor·i·ness
un·sa·vory
un·scathed
un·schol·ar·ly
un·schooled
un·sci·en·tif·ic
un·sci·en·tif·i·cal·ly
un·scram·ble, *v.*
  un·scram·bled,
  un·scram·bling
un·screw
un·scru·pu·lous
un·scru·pu·lous·ly
un·scru·pu·lous·ness
un·seal
un·sea·son·able
un·sea·son·able·ness
un·sea·son·ably

un·seat
un·seem·li·ness
un·seem·ly
un·seen
un·seg·re·gat·ed
un·self·ish
un·self·ish·ly
un·self·ish·ness
un·set·tle, *v.*
  un·set·tled,
  un·set·tling
un·set·tled
un·shack·le, *v.*
  un·shack·led,
  un·shack·ling
un·shak·en
un·shaved
un·shav·en
un·sheathe, *v.*
  un·sheathed, *v.*
  un·sheath·ing
un·sight·li·ness
un·sight·ly
un·skilled
un·skill·ful
un·skill·ful·ly
un·skill·ful·ness
un·sling, *v.*
  un·slung,
  un·sling·ing
un·snap, *v.*
  un·snapped,
  un·snap·ping
un·snarl
un·so·phis·ti·cat·ed
un·sought
un·sound
un·spar·ing

un·spar·ing·ly
un·speak·able
un·speak·ably
un·sports·man·like
un·sta·ble
un·states·man·like
un·stead·i·ly
un·stead·i·ness
un·steady
un·ster·i·lized
un·stop, *v.*
  un·stopped,
  un·stop·ping
un·strap, *v.*
  un·strapped,
  un·strap·ping
un·stressed
un·string, *v.*
  un·strung,
  un·string·ing
un·stud·ied
un·suc·cess·ful
un·suc·cess·ful·ly
un·suit·abil·i·ty
un·suit·able
un·suit·ably
un·sung
un·su·per·vised
un·sup·port·able
un·sup·port·ed
un·sure
un·sur·passed
un·sweet·ened
un·swerv·ing
un·swerv·ing·ly
un·swol·len
un·tam·able

un·tamed

un·tan·gle, v.
  un·tan·gled,
  un·tan·gling

un·taught

un·ten·able

un·tend·ed

un·think·able

un·think·ing

un·thought

un·thought-of

un·ti·dy, adj.
  un·tid·i·er,
  un·tid·i·est

un·tie, v. un·tied,
  un·ty·ing or
  un·tie·ing

un·til

un·time·li·ness

un·time·ly

un·ti·tled

un·to

un·told

un·touch·abil·i·ty

un·touch·able

un·to·ward

un·trace·able

un·trav·eled or
  un·trav·elled

un·tried

un·true

un·trust·ful

un·trust·wor·thy

un·truth

un·truth·ful

un·truth·ful·ly

un·truth·ful·ness

un·tu·tored

un·twist

un·us·able

un·used

un·usu·al

un·usu·al·ly

un·ut·ter·able

un·ut·ter·ably

un·var·nished

un·veil

un·voiced

un·war·rant·able

un·war·i·ly

un·warned

un·wary

un·washed

un·wa·ver·ing

un·well

un·whole·some

un·whole·some·ly

un·whole·some·ness

un·wield·i·ly

un·wield·i·ness

un·wieldy

un·will·ing

un·will·ing·ly

un·will·ing·ness

un·wind, v.
  un·wound,
  un·wind·ing

un·wise

un·wise·ly

un·wit·ting

un·wit·ting·ly

un·work·able

un·world·li·ness

un·world·ly

un·wor·thi·ly

un·wor·thi·ness

un·wor·thy, adj.
  un·wor·thi·er,
  un·wor·thi·est

un·wrap, v.
  un·wrapped,
  un·wrap·ping

un·written

un·yield·ing

un·yield·ing·ly

un·yoke, v.
  un·yoked,
  un·yok·ing

un·zip, v.
  un·zipped,
  un·zip·ping

up-and-com·ing

up-and-down, adj.

up and down, adv.

up·beat

up·braid

up·bring·ing

up·com·ing

up-coun·try

up·date, v.
  up·dat·ed,
  up·dat·ing

up·draft

up·end

up·grade, v.
  up·grad·ed,
  up·grad·ing

up·heav·al

up·hill

up·hold, v.
  up·held,
  up·hold·ing

up·hol·ster

up·hol·ster·er

up·hol·stery, *n. pl.*
  up·hol·ster·ies

up·keep

up·land

up·lift

up·most

up·on

up·per

up·per·case, *v.*
  up·per·cased,
  up·per·cas·ing

up·per-class *adj.*

up·per class, *n.*

up·per·class·man,
  n. pl.
  up·per·class·men

up·per·cut, *v.*
  up·per·cut,
  up·per·cut·ting

up·per·most

Up·per Vol·ta

Up·per, Vol·tan

up·pish

up·pish·ly

up·pish·ness

up·pi·ty

up·right

up·right·ly

up·right·ness

up·ris·ing

up·roar

up·roar·i·ous

up·roar·i·ous·ly

up·roar·i·ous·ness

up·root

up·scale

up·set, *v.* up·set,
  up·set·ting

up·shot

up·side down

up·side-down cake

up·stage, *v.*
  up·staged,
  up·stag·ing

up·stairs

up·stand·ing

up·start

up·state

up·stream

up·stroke

up·surge, *v.*
  up·surged,
  up·surg·ing

up·swept

up·swing

up·take

up·tem·po

up·thrust

up·tight

up-to-date

up·town

up·trend

up·turn

up·turned

up·ward, *or*
  up·wards

up·wind

Ural

ura·ni·um

Ura·nus

ur·ban (CITY)

ur·bane (REFINED)

ur·ban·ism

ur·ban·ite

ur·ban·i·ty, *n. pl.*
  ur·ban·i·ties

ur·ban·iza·tion

ur·ban·ize, *v.*
  ur·ban·ized,
  ur·ban·iz·ing

ur·ban·ol·o·gist

ur·ban·ol·o·gy

ur·chin

Ur·du

urea

ure·mia

ure·ter

ure·thane *or*
  ure·than

ure·thra, *n. pl.*
  ure·thras *or*
  ure·thrae

urge, *v.* urged,
  urg·ing

ur·gen·cy, *n. pl.*
  ur·gen·cies

ur·gent

ur·gent·ly

uric

uri·nal

uri·nal·y·sis, *n. pl.*
  uri·nal·y·ses

uri·nary

uri·nate, *v.*
  uri·nat·ed,
  uri·nat·ing

uri·na·tion

urine

urn

uro·log·ic

uro·log·i·cal

urol·o·gist

urol·o·gy

ur·sine

Ur·u·guay

Uru·guay·an

us·abil·i·ty

us·able (*occas.* use·able)

us·age

use, *v.* used, us·ing

use·ful

use·ful·ly

use·ful·ness

use·less

use·less·ly

use·less·ness

us·er

ush·er

ush·er·ette

usu·al

usu·al·ly

usu·fruct

usu·rer

usu·ri·ous

usu·ri·ous·ly

usu·ri·ous·ness

usurp

usur·pa·tion

usur·per

usu·ry, *n. pl.* usu·ries

Utah

Utah·an

uten·sil

uter·ine

uter·us, *n. pl.* uteri (*occas.* uter·us·es)

utile

util·i·tar·i·an

util·i·tar·i·an·sm

util·i·ty, *n. pl.* util·i·ties

uti·liz·able

uti·li·za·tion

uti·lize, *v.* uti·lized, uti·liz·ing

ut·most

uto·pia

uto·pi·an

uto·pi·an·ism

ut·ter

ut·ter·ance

ut·ter·most

U-turn

uvu·la, *n. pl.* uvu·las *or* uvu·lae

ux·o·ri·ous

ux·o·ri·ous·ly

ux·o·ri·ous·ness

Uz·bek

Uz·bek So·vi·et So·cial·ist Re·pub·lic (*now* Uz·bek·i·stan)

Uz·bek·i·stan (*formerly* Uzbek Soviet Socialist Republic)

V

va·can·cy, *n. pl.*
va·can·cies

va·cant

va·cate, *v.* va·cat·ed

va·ca·tion

va·ca·tion·er

vac·ci·nate, *v.*
vac·ci·nat·ed,
vac·ci·nat·ing

vac·ci·na·tion

vac·cine

vac·il·late, *v.*
vac·il·lat·ed,
vac·il·lat·ing

vac·il·la·tion

vac·il·la·tor

va·cu·i·ty, *n. pl.*
va·cu·i·ties

vac·u·ole

vac·u·ous

vac·u·ous·ly

vac·u·ous·ness

vac·u·um, *n. pl.*
vac·u·ums *or*
vac·ua

vac·u·um-packed

va·de me·cum *n.*

pl. va·de
me·cums

vag·a·bond

vag·a·bond·age

va·ga·ry, *n. pl.*
va·ga·ries

va·gi·na, *n. pl.*
va·gi·nae *or*
va·gi·nas

va·gi·nal

vag·i·nis·mus

va·gran·cy, *n. pl.*
va·gran·cies

va·grant

vague, *adj.*
va·guer,
va·guest

vague·ly

vague·ness

vain (FUTILE,
CONCEITED)
(*see also* vane,
vein)

vain·glo·ri·ous

vain·glo·ri·ous·ly

vain·glo·ri·ous·ness

vain·glory

va·lance

(DRAPERY) (*see
also* valence)

vale

val·e·dic·tion

val·e·dic·to·ri·an

val·e·dic·to·ry, *n.
pl.*
val·e·dic·to·ries

va·lence
(CHEMISTRY)
(*see also*
valance)

val·en·tine

Va·le·rie

va·let

val·e·tu·di·nar·i·an

Val·hal·la

val·iant

val·id

val·i·date, *v.*
val·i·dat·ed,
val·i·dat·ing

val·i·da·tion

va·lid·i·ty

va·lise

Val·i·um℠

val·ley, *n. pl.*
val·leys

val·or

val·o·ri·za·tion

val·o·rize, v.
val·o·rized,
val·o·riz·ing

val·or·ous

val·or·ous·ly

valu·able

valu·ably

val·u·a·tion

val·ue, v. val·ued,
val·u·ing

val·ued

val·ue·less

va·lu·ta

valve, v. valved,
valv·ing

val·vu·lar

va·moose, v.
va·moosed,
va·moos·ing

vam·pire

va·na·di·um

Van·cou·ver

van·dal

van·dal·ism

van·dal·ize, v.
van·dal·ized,
van·dal·iz·ing

vane (WIND
INDICATOR)
(see also vain,
vein)

Va·nes·sa

van·guard

va·nil·la

van·ish

van·i·ty, n. pl.
van·i·ties

van·quish

van·tage

Van·u·atu

va·pid

va·pid·i·ty, n. pl.
va·pid·i·ties

va·por

va·por·iza·tion

va·por·ize, v.
va·por·ized,
va·por·iz·ing

va·por·iz·er

va·por·ous

va·por·ous·ly

va·por·ous·ness

va·que·ro, n. pl.
va·que·ros

vari·abil·i·ty

vari·able

vari·ably

vari·ance

vari·ant

vari·a·tion

vari·col·ored

var·i·cose

var·i·cos·i·ty

var·ied

var·ie·gate, v.
var·ie·gat·ed,
var·ie·gat·ing

var·ie·ga·tion

va·ri·etal

va·ri·ety, n. pl.
va·ri·et·ies

vari·o·rum

var·i·ous

var·i·ous·ly

var·mint

var·nish

var·si·ty, n. pl.
var·si·ties

vary, v. var·ied,
vary·ing

vas·cu·lar

vas def·er·ens, n.
pl. va·sa
def·er·en·tia

va·sec·to·my, n. pl.
va·sec·to·mies

Vas·e·line℠

vaso·mo·tor

vas·sal

vas·sal·age

vast·ness

vat-dyed

Vat·i·can City

vaude·ville

vaude·vil·lian

vault·ed

vault·ing

vaunt

veal

vec·tor

Ve·dan·ta

veer

Ve·ga

ve·gan

veg·e·ta·ble

veg·e·tal

veg·e·tar·i·an

veg·e·tar·i·an·ism

veg·e·tate, v.
veg·e·tat·ed,
veg·e·tat·ing

veg·e·ta·tion

veg·e·ta·tive

veg·e·ta·tive·ly

veg·e·ta·tive·ness

ve·he·mence

ve·he·ment

ve·he·ment·ly

ve·hi·cle

ve·hic·u·lar

V-6

veil

veil·ing

vein (BLOOD VESSEL, QUALITY) (see also vain, vane)

Vel·cro™

veld or veldt

vel·lum (STRONG PAPER) (see also velum)

ve·loc·i·pede

ve·loc·i·ty, n. pl. ve·loc·i·ties

ve·lo·drome

ve·lour or ve·lours, n. pl. ve·lours

ve·lum (MEMBRANOUS COVERING), n. pl. ve·la (see also vellum)

vel·vet

vel·ve·teen

vel·vety

ve·nal (BRIBABLE, CORRUPTIBLE) (see also venial)

ve·nal·i·ty, n. pl. ve·nal·i·ties

ve·nal·ly

vend·ee

ven·det·ta

vend·ible or vend·able

ven·dor

ve·neer

ven·er·a·ble

ven·er·a·ble·ness

ven·er·a·bly

ven·er·ate, v. ven·er·at·ed, ven·er·at·ing

ven·er·a·tion

ve·ne·re·al

ven·ery

ve·ne·tian blind

Ven·e·zu·e·la

Ven·e·zu·e·lan

ven·geance

venge·ful

venge·ful·ly

venge·ful·ness

ve·nial (PARDONABLE) (see also venal)

ve·ni·re

ve·ni·re·man, n. pl. ve·ni·re·men

ven·i·son

ven·om

ven·om·ous

ven·om·ous·ly

ven·om·ous·ness

ve·nous

ve·nous·ly

ven·ti·late, v. ven·ti·lat·ed, ven·ti·lat·ing

ven·ti·la·tion

ven·ti·la·tor

ven·tral

ven·tral·ly

ven·tri·cle

ven·tril·o·quism

ven·tril·o·quist

ven·ture, v. ven·tured, ven·tur·ing

ven·ture·some

ven·ture·some·ly

ven·ture·some·ness

ven·tu·ri

ven·tur·ous

ven·tur·ous·ly

ven·tur·ous·ness

ven·ue

Ve·nus

Ve·nus's-fly·trap (occas. Ve·nus fly·trap)

ve·ra·cious (HONEST) (see also voracious)

ve·ra·cious·ly

ve·ra·cious·ness

ve·rac·i·ty, n. pl. ve·rac·i·ties

Ve·ra·cruz

ve·ran·da or ve·ran·dah

ver·bal

ver·bal·iza·tion

ver·bal·ize, v. ver·bal·ized, ver·bal·iz·ing

ver·bal·ly

ver·ba·tim

ver·be·na

ver·bi·age

ver·bose

ver·bose·ly

ver·bose·ness

ver·bos·i·ty

ver·bo·ten

ver·dant

ver·dict

ver·di·gris

ver·dure

verge, v. verged,
    verg·ing

ver·i·fi·able

ver·i·fi·ably

ver·i·fi·ca·tion

ver·i·fi·er

ver·i·fy, v.
    ver·i·fied,
    ver·i·fy·ing

ver·i·ly

veri·si·mil·i·tude

ver·i·ta·ble

ver·i·ta·bly

ver·i·ty, n. pl.
    ver·i·ties

ver·meil

ver·mi·cel·li

ver·mi·form

ver·mi·fuge

ver·mil·ion (occas.
    ver·mil·lion)

ver·min, n. pl.
    ver·min

Ver·mont

Ver·mont·er

ver·mouth

ver·nac·u·lar

ver·nal

ver·nier

Ve·ron·i·ca
    (PERSON'S
    NAME)

ve·ron·i·ca (PLANT,
    CLOTH)

ver·sa·tile

ver·sa·til·i·ty

verse, v. versed,
    vers·ing

ver·si·cle

ver·si·fi·ca·tion

ver·si·fy, v.
    ver·si·fied,
    ver·si·fy·ing

ver·sion

ver·so n. pl. ver·sos

ver·sus

ver·te·bra, n. pl.
    ver·te·bras or
    ver·te·brae

ver·te·bral

ver·te·brate

ver·tex, n. pl.
    ver·ti·ces
    (occas.
    ver·tex·es)

ver·ti·cal

ver·ti·cal·ly

ver·ti·cil·late

ver·tig·i·nous

ver·tig·i·nous·ly

ver·ti·go, n. pl.
    ver·ti·goes or
    ver·ti·gos

ver·vain

verve

very

ves·i·cant

ves·i·cle

ve·sic·u·lar

ves·per

ves·pers

ves·sel

ves·tal

vest·ed

ves·ti·bule

ves·tige

ves·ti·gial

ves·ti·gial·ly

vest·ing

vest·ment

vest-pock·et

ves·try, n. pl.
    ves·tries

ves·try·man, n. pl.
    ves·try·men

ves·ture

Ve·su·vi·us, Mount

vetch

vet·er·an

vet·er·i·nar·i·an

vet·er·i·nary, pl.
    vet·er·i·nar·ies

ve·to, n. pl. ve·toes

ve·to, v. ve·toed,
    ve·to·ing

ve·to·er

vex, v. vexed
    (occas. vext),
    vex·ing

vex·a·tion

vex·a·tious

vex·a·tious·ly
vi·a·bil·i·ty
vi·a·ble
vi·a·bly
via·duct
vi·al (SMALL
    BOTTLE) (see
    also vile, viol)
vi·and
vi·at·i·cum, n. pl.
    vi·at·i·cums or
    vi·at·i·ca
vibes
vi·bran·cy
vi·brant
vi·brant·ly
vi·bra·phone
vi·brate, v.
    vi·brat·ed,
    vi·brat·ing
vi·bra·tion
vi·bra·to, n. pl.
    vi·bra·tos
vi·bra·tor
vi·bra·to·ry
vi·bur·num
vic·ar
vic·ar·age
vic·ar-gen·er·al, n.
    pl. vic·ars-
    gen·er·al
vi·car·i·al
vi·car·i·ate
vi·car·i·ous
vi·car·i·ous·ly
vi·car·i·ous·ness
vice (CHARACTER
    FLAW, IN

PLACE OF) (see
    also vise)
vice ad·mi·ral
vice-chan·cel·lor
vice-con·sul
vice pres·i·den·cy,
    n. pl. vice
    pres·i·den·cies
vice pres·i·dent
vice pres·i·den·tial
vic-re·gent
vice·roy
vice squad
vice ver·sa
vi·chys·soise
vi·cin·i·ty, n. pl.
    vi·cin·i·ties
vi·cious
vi·cious·ly
vi·cious·ness
vi·cis·si·tude
vic·tim
vic·tim·iza·tion
vic·tim·ize, v.
    vic·tim·ized,
    vic·tim·iz·ing
vic·tim·i·zer
vic·tim·less
vic·tor
Vic·to·ria
Vic·to·ri·an
Vic·to·ri·ana
vic·to·ri·ous
vic·to·ri·ous·ly
vic·to·ri·ous·ness
vic·to·ry, n. pl.
    vic·to·ries
vict·ual, v.

vict·ualed or
    vict·ualled,
    vict·ual·ing or
    vict·ual·ling
vic·cu·ña or vi·cu·na
vi·de
vid·eo
vid·eo·cas·sette
vid·eo·disc or
    vid·eo·disk
vid·eo game
vid·eo·tape, v.
    vid·eo·taped,
    vid·eo·tap·ing
vie, v. vied, vy·ing
Vi·en·na
Vi·en·nese, n. pl.
    Vi·en·nese
Viet·cong, n. pl.
    Viet·cong
Viet·minh, n. pl.
    Viet·minh
Viet·nam
Viet·nam·ese, n.
    pl. Viet·nam·ese
view·er
view·point
vig·il
vig·i·lance
vig·i·lant
vig·i·lan·te
vig·i·lan·tism
vig·i·lant·ly
vi·gnette
vig·or
vig·o·rish
vi·go·ro·so
vig·or·ous

vig·or·ous·ly

vig·or·ous·ness

Vi·king

vile (DISGUSTING)
(see also vial,
viol)

vile·ly

vile·ness

vil·i·fi·ca·tion

vil·i·fi·er

vil·i·fy, v. vil·i·fied,
vil·i·fy·ing

vil·la

vil·lage

vil·lag·er

vil·lain

vil·lain·ous

vil·lain·ous·ly

vil·lainy, n. pl.
vil·lain·ies

vil·lous (COVERED
WITH VILLI)

vil·lus (HAIRLIKE),
n. pl. vil·li

vin·ai·grette

vin·ci·ble

vin·di·ca·ble

vin·di·cate, v.
vin·di·cat·ed,
vin·di·cat·ing

vin·di·ca·tion

vin·di·ca·tor

vin·di·ca·to·ry

vin·dic·tive

vin·dic·tive·ly

vin·dic·tive·ness

vin·e·gar

vin·e·gary

vin·ery, n. pl.
vin·er·ies

vine·yard

vi·ni·cul·ture

vi·ni·cul·tur·ist

vi·nous

vin·tage

vint·ner

vi·nyl

vi·ol (MUSICAL
INSTRUMENT)
(see also vial,
vile)

vi·o·la

vi·o·la·ble

vi·o·late, v.
vi·o·lat·ed,
vi·o·lat·ing

vi·o·la·tion

vi·o·la·tor

vi·o·lence

vi·o·lent

vi·o·lent·ly

vi·o·let

vi·o·lin

vi·o·lin·ist

vi·o·list

vi·o·lon·cel·list

vi·o·lon·cel·lo, n.
pl.
vi·o·lon·cel·los

vi·per

vi·per·ous

vi·per·ous·ly

vi·ra·go, n. pl.
vi·ra·goes or
vi·ra·gos

vi·ral

vir·eo, n. pl.
vir·e·os

vir·ga

vir·gin

vir·gin·al

vir·gin·al·ly

Vir·gin·ia

Vir·gin·ian

Vir·gin Is·lands

vir·gin·i·ty, n. pl.
vir·gin·i·ties

Vir·go

vir·gule

vir·ile

vi·ril·i·ty

vi·rol·o·gist

vi·rol·o·gy

vir·tu (OF ART) (see
also virtue)

vir·tu·al

vir·tu·al·ly

vir·tue
(GOODNESS)
(see also virtu)

vir·tu·os·i·ty, n. pl.
vir·tu·os·i·ties

vir·tu·o·so, n. pl.
vir·tu·o·sos or
vir·tu·o·si

vir·tu·ous

vir·tu·ous·ly

vir·tu·ous·ness

vir·u·lence

vir·u·len·cy

vir·u·lent

vir·u·lent·ly

vi·rus

vi·sa, *v.* vi·saed,
  vi·sa·ing

vis·age

vis-à-vis, *n. pl.* vis-
  à-vis

vis·cera, *n. pl. of*
  vis·cus

vis·cer·al

vis·cer·al·ly

vis·cid

vis·cid·i·ty

vis·cose

vis·cos·i·ty, *n. pl.*
  vis·cos·i·ties

vis·count

vis·count·ess

vis·cous (COHESIVE
  FLUID) (*see also*
  viscus)

vis·cous·ly

vis·cous·ness

vis·cus (BODY
  ORGANS), *n. pl.*
  vis·cera (*see also*
  viscous)

vise (CLAMP) (*see
  also* vice)

vis·i·bil·i·ty, *n. pl.*
  vis·i·bil·i·ties

vis·i·ble

vis·i·bly

vi·sion

vi·sion·ary, *n. pl.*
  vi·sion·ar·ies

vis·it

vis·i·ta·tion

vis·it·ing

vis·i·tor

vi·sor

vis·ta

vi·su·al

vi·su·al·iza·tion

vi·su·al·ize, *v.*
  vi·su·al·ized,
  vi·su·al·iz·ing

vi·su·al·iz·er

vi·su·al·ly

vi·ta, *n. pl.* vi·tae

vi·tal

vi·tal·i·ty, *n. pl.*
  vi·tal·i·ties

vi·tal·iza·tion

vi·tal·ize, *v.*
  vi·tal·ized,
  vi·tal·iz·ing

vi·tal·ly

vi·tals

vi·ta·min

vi·ti·ate, *v.*
  vi·ti·at·ed,
  vi·ti·at·ing

vi·ti·a·tion

vi·ti·a·tor

vi·ti·cul·ture

vi·ti·cul·tur·ist

vit·re·ous

vit·re·ous·ness

vit·ri·fi·ca·tion

vit·ri·fyy, *v.*
  vit·ri·fied,
  vit·ri·fy·ing

vit·ri·ol

vit·ri·ol·ic

vit·tles

vi·tu·per·ate, *v.*
  vi·tu·per·at·ed,
  vi·tu·per·at·ing

vi·tu·per·a·tion

vi·tu·per·a·tive

vi·tu·per·a·tive·ly

vi·va

vi·va·ce

vi·va·cious

vi·va·cious·ly

vi·va·cious·ness

vi·vac·i·ty, *n. pl.*
  vi·vac·i·ties

vi·var·i·um, *n. pl.*
  vi·var·ia *or*
  vi·var·i·ums

vi·va vo·ce

Viv·i·an

viv·id

viv·id·ly

viv·id·ness

viv·i·fi·ca·tion

viv·i·fi·er

viv·i·fy, *v.*
  viv·i·fied,
  viv·i·fy·ing

vi·vip·a·rous

vi·vip·a·rous·ly

vi·vip·a·rous·ness

vivi·sect

vivi·sec·tion

vivi·sec·tion·ist

vix·en

viz·ard

vi·zier

vo·ca·ble

vo·cab·u·lary, *n. pl.*
  vo·cab·u·lar·ies

vo·cal

vo·cal·ic

vo·cal·ist

vo·cal·iza·tion

vo·cal·ize, v.
  vo·cal·ized,
  vo·cal·iz·ing

vo·cal·ly

vo·ca·tion

vo·ca·tion·al

voc·a·tive

voc·a·tive·ly

vo·cif·er·ate, v.
  vo·cif·er·at·ed,
  vo·cif·er·at·ing

vo·cif·er·ous

vo·cif·er·ous·ly

vo·cif·er·ous·ness

vod·ka

vogue

vogu·ish

voice, v. voiced,
  voic·ing

voiced

voice·less

voice·less·ly

voice·less·ness

voice-over

voice·print

void·able

void·er

voi·là (occas.
  voi·la)

voile

voir dire

vol·a·tile

vol·a·til·i·ty

vol·ca·nic

vol·ca·nism

vol·ca·no, n. pl.

vol·ca·noes or
  vol·ca·nos

vol·ca·no·log·ic

vol·ca·no·log·i·cal

vol·can·ol·o·gist

vol·ca·nol·o·gy

Vol·ga Riv·er

vo·li·tion

vol·ley, n. pl.
  vol·leys

vol·ley·ball

volt·age

vol·ta·ic

vol·ta·me·ter

volt·am·me·ter

volt-am·pere

volte-face

volt·me·ter

vol·u·bil·i·ty

vol·u·ble

vol·u·ble·ness

vol·u·bly

vol·ume

vol·u·met·ric

vo·lu·mi·nous

vo·lu·mi·nous·ly

vo·lu·mi·nous·ness

vol·un·ta·ri·ly

vol·un·ta·rism
  (occas.
  vol·un·teer·ism)

vol·un·tary

vol·un·teer

vol·un·teer·ism
  (var. of
  vol·un·ta·rism)

vo·lup·tu·ary, n. pl.
  vo·lup·tu·ar·ies

vo·lup·tu·ous

vo·lup·tu·ous·ly

vo·lup·tu·ous·ness

vo·lute

vom·it

vom·i·to·ry, pl.
  vom·i·to·ries

vom·i·tus

voo·doo, n. pl.
  voo·doos

voo·doo·ism

vo·ra·cious
  (INSATIABLE)
  (see also
  veracious)

vo·ra·cious·ly

vo·ra·cious·ness

vo·rac·i·ty

vor·la·ge

vor·tex, n. pl.
  vor·ti·ces
  (occas.
  vor·tex·es)

vor·ti·cal

vo·ta·ry, n. pl.
  vo·ta·ries

vote, v. vot·ed,
  vot·ing

vot·er

vo·tive

vouch·er

vouch·safe, v.
  vouch·safed,
  vouch·saf·ing

vow·el

vox po·pu·li

voy·age, v.
  voy·aged,
  voy·ag·ing

voy·ag·er
(TRAVELER)

vo·ya·geur
(CANADIAN
WILDERNESS
TRAVELER)

voy·eur

voy·eur·ism

voy·eur·is·tic

vul·ca·ni·za·tion

vul·can·ize, *v.*

vul·can·ized,
vul·can·iz·ing

vul·can·iz·er

vul·gar

vul·gar·i·an

vul·gar·ism

vul·gar·i·ty, *n. pl.*
vul·gar·i·ties

vul·gar·iza·tion

vul·gar·ize, *v.*

vul·gar·ized,
vul·gar·iz·ing

vul·gar·iz·er

vul·ner·a·bil·i·ty

vul·ner·a·ble

vul·ner·a·bly

vul·ture

vul·tur·ous

vul·va, *n. pl.*
vul·vae

W

wacky, *adj.*
wack·i·er,
wack·i·est

wad, *v.* wad·ded,
wad·ding

wad·ding

wad·dle, *v.*
wad·dled,
wad·dling

wade, *v.* wad·ed,
wad·ing

wad·er

wa·di

wa·fer

waf·fle, *v.* waf·fled,
waf·fling

wa·fle-stomp·er

waft

wag, *v.* wagged,
wag·ging

wage, *v.* waged,
wag·ing

wa·ger

wa·ger·er

wag·gish

wag·gish·ly

wag·gle, *v.*

wag·gled,
wag·gling

wag·gly

wag·on

wag·on·ette

wa·gon-lit, *n. pl.*
wa·gons-lits *or*
wa·gon-lits

wag·on·load

wa·hi·ne

waif

wail (CRY) (*see
also* wale,
whale)

wain·scot, *v.*
wain·scot·ed *or*
wain·scot·ted,
wain·scot·ing *or*
wain·scot·ting

wain·wright

waist (MIDDLE)
(*see also* waste)

waist·band

waist·coat

waist·line

wait·er

wait·ing

wait·ress

waive (GIVE UP),
v. waived,
waiv·ing (*see also*
wave)

waiv·er

wake, *v.* woke
(*occas.* waked),
wok·en (*occas.*
waked),
wak·ing

wake·ful

wake·ful·ly

wake·ful·ness

wak·en

wale (PLANK,
RIDGE,
TEXTURE), *v.*
waled, wal·ing
(*see also* wail,
whale)

Wales

walk·about

walk·away

walk·er

walk·ie-talk·ie

walk-in

walk·ing

walk-on

walk·out

walk·over

walk-up

walk·way

wal·la·by, *n. pl.*
wal·la·bies
(*occas.* wal·la·by)

wall·board

wal·let

wall·eye

wall·flow·er

wal·lop

wal·lop·ing

wal·low

wall·pa·per

wall-to-wall

wal·nut

wal·rus, *n. pl.*
wal·rus *or*
wal·rus·es

waltz

wam·pum

wan, *adj.* wan·ner,
wan·nest

wan·der

wan·der·lust

wane, *v.* waned,
wan·ing

wan·gle, *v.*
wan·gled,
wan·gling

wan·i·gan *or*
wan·ni·gan

wan·na-be

want·ing

wan·ton

wan·ton·ly

wan·ton·ness

wa·pi·ti, *n. pl.*

wa·pi·ti *or*
wa·pi·tis

war, *v.* warred,
war·ring

war·ble, *v.*
war·bled,
war·bling

war·bler

war·bon·net

war·den

ward·er

ward·robe

ward·room

ware·house, *v.*
ware·housed,
ware·hous·ing

war·fare

war-game, *v.* war-
gamed, war-
gam·ing

war·head

war-horse

wari·ly

wari·ness

war·like

war·lock

war·lord

warm, *adj.*
warm·er,
warm·est

warm-blood·ed

warm-
blood·ed·ness

warmed-over

warm·heart·ed

warm·heart·ed·ly

warm·heart·ed·ness

war·mon·ger

warmth

warm-up

warn·ing

warp

war·path

war·plane

war·rant·able

war·ran·tor (*occas.*
war·ran·ter)

war·ran·ty, *n. pl.*
war·ran·ties

war·ren

war·rior

War·saw

war·ship

war·time

wary, *adj.* war·i·er,
war·i·est

wash·able

wash-and-wear

wash·ba·sin

wash·board

wash·bowl

wash·cloth

washed-out

washed-up

wash·er

wash·er·wom·an, *n.
pl.*
wash·er·wom·en

wash·house

wash·ing

Wash·ing·ton

Wash·ing·to·ni·an

wash·out

wash·room

wash·stand

wash·tub

wasp·ish

wasp·ish·ly

wasp·ish·ness

was·sail

wast·age

waste (RUIN), *v.*
  wast·ed wast·ing
  (*see also* waist)

waste·bas·ket

wast·ed

waste·ful

waste·ful·ly

waste·ful·ness

waste·land

waste·pa·per

wast·rel

watch·band

watch·case

watch·dog

watch·ful

watch·ful·ly

watch·ful·ness

watch·mak·er

watch·mak·ing

watch·man, *n. pl.*
  watch·men

watch·tow·er

watch·word

wa·ter

wa·ter·borne

wa·ter·col·or

wa·ter-cool, *v.*

wa·ter-cooled, *adj.*

wa·ter·course

wa·ter·craft, *pl.*
  wa·ter·craft

wa·ter·cress

wa·tered

wa·ter·fall

wa·ter·fowl, *n. pl.*
  wa·ter·fowl

wa·ter·front

wa·ter·i·ness

wa·ter·leaf, *n. pl.*
  wa·ter·leafs

wa·ter·less

wa·ter·lily, *n. pl.*
  wa·ter·lil·ies

wa·ter·line

wa·ter·logged

wa·ter·loo, *n. pl.*
  wa·ter·loos

wa·ter·mark

wa·ter·mel·on

wa·ter·pow·er

wa·ter·proof

wa·ter-re·pel·lent

wa·ter-res·is·tant

wa·ter·scape

wa·ter·shed

wa·ter-ski, *v.*
  wa·ter-skied,
  wa·ter-ski·ing

wa·ter-ski·er

wa·ter·ski·ing, *n.*

wa·ter·soak

wa·ter-sol·u·ble

wa·ter·spout

wa·ter·tight

wa·ter·way

wa·ter·wheel

wa·ter·works

wa·ter·worn

wa·tery

watt·age

watt-hour

watt·me·ter

wave (SWAY, SEA
  SWELL), *v.*
  waved, wav·ing
  (*see also* waive)

wave·guide

wave·length

wave·let

wa·ver

wav·i·ly

wav·i·ness

wavy, *adj.* wav·i·er,
  wav·i·est

wax, *v.* waxed,
  waxed, wax·ing

wax·en

wax·i·ness

wax·ing

wax·work

waxy, *adj.* wax·i·er,
  wax·i·est

way

way·bill

way·far·er

way·far·ing

way·lay, *v.*
  way·laid,
  way·lay·ing

way-out

way·side

way·ward

way·ward·ly

way·ward·ness

weak·en

weak·heart·ed

weak-kneed

weak·ling

weak·ly

weak·mind·ed

weak·ness

weal (WELL-BEING, WELT) (*see also* wheal, wheel)

wealth·i·ly

wealth·i·ness

wealthy, *adj.* wealth·i·er, wealth·i·est

wean

weap·on

weap·on·eer

weap·on·less

weap·on·ry

wear, *v.* wore, worn, wear·ing

wear·able

wear·er

wea·ri·ly

wea·ri·ness

wea·ri·some

wea·ry, *adj.* wea·ri·er, wea·ri·est

wea·sel, *n. pl.* wea·sels *or* wea·sel

weath·er

weath·er·abil·i·ty

weath·er-beat·en

weath·er·board

weath·er-bound

weath·er·cock

weath·ered

weath·er·glass

weath·er·ing

weath·er·man, *n. pl.* weath·er·men

weath·er·proof

weath·er·strip, *v.* weath·er·stripped, weath·er·strip·ping

weath·er-wise

weath·er·worn

weave, *v.* wove *or* weaved, wov·en *or* weaved, weav·ing

weav·er

web, *v.* webbed, web·bing

web-foot·ed

wed, *v.* wed·ded (*occas.* wed), wed·ding

wedge, *v.* wedged, wedg·ing

wedge·like

wedg·ies

Wedg·wood®

wed·lock

Wednes·day

weed·er

weedy, *adj.* weed·i·er, weed·i·est

week·day

week·end

week·ly, *n. pl.* week·lies

weep, *v.* wept, weep·ing

weep·er

weepy, *adj.* weep·i·er, weep·i·est

wee·vil

weigh

weight·i·ly

weight·i·ness

weight·less

weighty, *adj.* weight·i·er, weight·i·est

weir

weird

weird·ly

weird·ness

weir·do, *n. pl.* weir·dos

welch *or* welsh (RENEGE) (*see also* Welsh)

wel·come, *v.* wel·comed, wel·com·ing

weld·er

wel·fare

wel·far·ism

well-ad·vised

well-ap·point·ed

well-be·ing

well-be·loved

well-born

well-bred

well-con·di·tioned

well-de·fined

well-dis·posed

well-done

well-fa·vored

well-fixed

well-found·ed
well-groomed
well-ground·ed
well-han·dled
well·head
well-heeled
well-knit
well-known
well-mean·ing
well-nigh
well-off
well-or·dered
well-read
well-set
well-spo·ken
well·spring
well-thought-of
well-timed
well-to-do
well-turned
well-wish·er
well-worn
Welsh (OF WALES)
  (see also welch)
wel·ter
wel·ter·weight
welt·schmerz
wench·er
were·wolf, n. pl.
  were·wolves
wes·kit
west·bound
west·er·ly, n. pl.
  west·er·lies
west·ern
West·ern·er
west·ern·iza·tion

west·ern·ize, v.
  west·ern·ized,
  west·ern·iz·ing
West·ern Sa·moa
West·ern Sa·mo·an
West Vir·gin·ia
West Vir·gin·ian
west·ward
west·ward·ly
wet (MOIST), adj.
  wet·ter, wet·test
  (see also whet)
wet, v. wet or
  wet·ted,
  wet·ting
wet·back
wet·land
wet·ness
wet·tish
whale (BIG FISH)
  (see also wail,
  wale)
whale·back
whale·boat
whale·bone
whal·er
wharf, n. pl.
  wharves (occas.
  wharfs)
wharf·age
wharf·in·ger
what·ev·er
what·not
what·so·ev·er
wheal (SKIN WELT)
  (see also weal,
  wheel)
wheat
whee·dle, v.

whee·dled,
  whee·dling
wheel (DISK) (see
  also weal,
  wheal)
wheel·bar·row
wheel·base
wheel·chair
wheel·er
wheel·er-deal·er
wheel·horse
wheel·house
wheel·ie
wheel·wright
wheeze, v.
  wheezed,
  wheez·ing
wheez·i·ly
wheez·i·ness
wheezy, adj.
  wheez·i·er,
  wheez·i·est
whelp
whence
when·ev·er
when·so·ev·er
where·abouts
where·as
where·at
where·by
where·fore
where·from
where·in
where·of
where·on
where·so·ev·er
where·to
where·up·on

wher·ev·er

where·with

where·with·al

wher·ry, *n. pl.*
wher·ries

whet (SHARPEN),
v. whet·ted,
whet·ting (*see
also* wet)

wheth·er

whet·stone

whey

which·ev·er

which·so·ev·er

whiff

while, *v.* whiled,
whil·ing

whim

whim·per

whim·per·ing·ly

whim·si·cal

whim·si·cal·i·ty, *n.
pl.*
whim·si·cal·i·ties

whim·si·cal·ly

whim·sy *or*
whim·sey, *n. pl.*
whim·sies *or*
whim·seys

whine, *v.* whined,
whin·ing

whin·er

whin·ny, *adj.*
whin·ni·er,
whin·ni·est

whin·ny, *n. pl.*
whin·nies

whin·ny, *v.*
whin·nied,
whin·ny·ing

whip, *v.* whipped,
whip·ping

whip·cord

whip·lash

whip·per·snap·per

whip·pet

whip·poor·will

whip·saw

whip·stitch

whip·stock

whip·worm

whir, *v.* whirred,
whir·ring

whirl

whirl·i·gig

whirl·pool

whirl·wind

whirly·bird

whisk

whisk·er

whis·key *or*
whis·ky, *n. pl.*
whis·keys *or*
whis·kies

whis·per

whis·per·ing

whis·per·ing·ly

whis·tle, *v.*
whis·tled,
whis·tling

whis·tle-blow·er

whis·tler

whis·tle-stop

whis·tling

whit

white, *adj.* whit·er
whit·est

white·bait

white·cap

white-col·lar

white-faced

white·fish

white·fly, *n. pl.*
white·flies

white-haired

white·head

white-hot

white-liv·ered

whit·en·er

white·ness

whit·en·ing

white·out

white·wall

white·wash

whitey

whith·er (WHERE)
(*see also*
wither)

whit·ish

Whit·ney, Mount

whit·tle, *v.*
whit·tled,
whit·tling

whiz *or* whizz, *n.
pl.* whiz·zes

whiz *or* whizz, *v.*
whizzed,
whiz·zing

whiz·zer

who·dun·it (*occas.*
who·dun·nit)

who·ev·er

whole·heart·ed

whole·heart·ed·ly

whole·heart·ed·ness

whole-hog

whole·ness

whole·sale, *v.*
  whole·saled,
  whole·sal·ing

whole·sal·er

whole·some

whole·some·ly

whole·some·ness

whole-wheat

whol·ly

whom·ev·er

whom·so·ev·er

whoop-de-do *or*
  whoop-de-doo

whoop·ee

whoop·la

whop·per

whop·ping

whore, *v.* whored,
  whor·ing

whore·house

whore·mon·ger

whorl

who's (*contraction
  for* who is, who
  has)

whose (*possessive*)

who·so·ev·er

why, *n. pl.* whys

Wich·i·ta

wick·ed

wick·ed·ly

wick·ed·ness

wick·er

wick·er·work

wick·et

wick·i·up

wide, *adj.* wid·er,
  wid·est

wide-an·gle

wide-awake

wide-eyed

wide-mouthed

wid·en

wide-screen

wide·spread

wid·get

wid·ish

wid·ow

wid·ow·er

wid·ow·hood

width

width·wise

wield

wie·ner

Wie·ner schnit·zel

wife, *n. pl.* wives

wife·less

wife·li·ness

wife·ly, *adj.*
  wife·li·er,
  wife·li·est

wig·an

wi·geon *or*
  wid·geon, *n. pl.*
  wi·geon *or*
  wi·geons *or*
  wid·geon *or*
  wid·geons

wig·gle, *v.*
  wig·gled,
  wig·gling

wig·gly, *adj.*
  wig·gli·er,
  wig·gli·est

wig·let

wig·mak·er

wig·wag, *v.*
  wig·wagged,
  wig·wag·ging

wig·wam

wild·cat

wild·cat, *v.*
  wild·cat·ted,
  wild·cat·ting

wild·cat·ter

wil·de·beest

wil·der·ness

wild-eyed

wild·fire

wild·fowl

wild·ing

wild·life

wild·wood

wile

wil·i·ly

wil·i·ness

will·ful *or* wil·ful

will·ful·ly

will·ful·ness

Wil·liam

wil·lies

will·ing

will·ing·ly

will·ing·ness

wil·li·waw

will-o'-the-wisp

wil·low

wil·lowy

will·pow·er

wil·ly-nil·ly

Wil·ming·ton

wilt

wily, *adj.* wil·i·er,
  wil·i·est

wimp·ish

wim·ple

wimpy

win, *v.* won,
  win·ning

wince, *v.* winced,
  winc·ing

winch

wind, *v.* wound
  (*occas.*
  wind·ed),
  wind·ing

wind·age

wind·bag

wind·blown

wind·break

Wind·break·er℠

wind·burn

wind·ed

wind·er

wind·fall

wind·i·ly

wind·i·ness

wind·ing-sheet

wind·jam·mer

wind·lass (WINCH)

wind·less
  (WITHOUT
  WIND)

wind·mill

win·dow

win·dow·pane

win·dow-shop, *v.*
  win·dow-
  shopped,
  win·dow-
  shop·ping

win·dow-shop·per

win·dow·sill

wind·pipe

wind·proof

wind·row

wind·shield

wind·sock

Wind·sor

wind·storm

wind·swept

wind·up

wind·ward

wind-wing

windy, *adj.*
  wind·i·er,
  wind·i·est

wine

wine·glass

wine·grow·er

wine·press

win·ery, *n. pl.*
  win·er·ies

wine·shop

wine·skin

wing·back

wing·ding

wing-foot·ed

wing·span

wing·spread

wing·tip

win·na·ble

win·ner

win·ning

Win·ni·peg

win·now

wino, *n. pl.* win·os

win·some

Win·ston-Sa·lem

win·ter

win·ter·green

win·ter·iza·tion

win·ter·ize, *v.*
  win·ter·ized,
  win·ter·iz·ing

win·ter·kill

win·ter·time

win·try (*occas.*
  win·tery), *adj.*
  win·tri·er,
  win·tri·est

wip·er

wir·able

wire, *v.* wired,
  wir·ing

wire-hair, *n.*

wire-haired, *adj.*

wire·less

wire-pull·er

wir·er

wire·tap, *v.*
  wire·tapped,
  wire·tap·ping

wire·work

wire·worm

wir·i·ness

wir·ing

wiry, *adj.* wir·i·er,
  wir·i·est

Wis·con·sin

Wis·con·sin·ite

wis·dom

wise, *adj.* wis·er,
  wis·est

wise·acre

wise·ass

wise·crack

wise guy

wise·ly

wish·bone

wish·ful

wish·ful·ly

wish·ful·ness

wishy-wash·i·ly

wishy-wash·i·ness

wishy-washy

wispy, *adj.*
  wisp·i·er,
  wisp·i·est

wis·te·ria *or*
  wis·tar·ia

wist·ful

wist·ful·ly

wist·ful·ness

wit

witch·craft

witch·er·y, *n. pl.*
  witch·er·ies

witch·hunt

witch·ing

with·al

with·draw, *v.*
  with·drew,
  with·drawn,
  with·draw·ing

with·draw·al

with·drawn

with·er (DRY UP
  (*see also*
  whither)

with·ers

with·hold, *v.*
  with·held,
  with·hold·ing

with·in

with·out

with·stand, *v.*
  with·stood,
  with·stand·ing

wit·less

wit·less·ly

wit·less·ness

wit·ness

wit·ti·cism

wit·ti·ly

wit·ti·ness

wit·ty, *adj.*
  wit·ti·er,
  wit·ti·est

wiz·ard

wiz·ard·ry, *n. pl.*
  wiz·ard·ries

wiz·en

wob·ble, *v.*
  wob·bled,
  wob·bling

wob·bly, *adj.*
  wob·bli·er,
  wob·bli·est

woe·be·gone

woe·ful

woe·ful·ly

woe·ful·ness

wok

wolf, *n. pl.* wolves
  (*occas.* wolf)

wolf·hound

wol·ver·ine

wom·an, *n. pl.*
  wom·en

wom·an·hood

wom·an·ish

wom·an·ize, *v.*

wom·an·ized,
  wom·an·iz·ing

wom·an·iz·er

wom·an·kind

wom·an·li·ness

wom·an·ly

womb

wom·bat

wom·en·folk
  (*occas.*
  wom·en·folks)

won (CURRENCY),
  n. pl. won

won·der

won·der·ful

won·der·ful·ly

won·der·land

won·der·ment

won·der-work·er

won·drous

won·drous·ly

won·drous·ness

wont (HABIT)

won't (*contraction
  of* will not)

won ton

woo, *v.* wooed,
  woo·ing

wood·bin

wood·bine

wood-carv·er

wood·chuck

wood·craft

wood·cut

wood·cut·ter

wood·ed

wood·en

wood·en·head

wood·en·head·ed

wood·en·ly

wood·en·ness

wood·en·ware

wood·land

wood·peck·er

wood·pile

wood·shed

woods·man, *n. pl.*
woods·men

woodsy, *adj.*
woods·i·er,
woods·i·est

wood·wind

wood·work

woody, *adj.*
wood·i·er,
wood·i·est

woof·er

wool·en *or*
wool·len

wool·gath·er·ing

wool·li·ness

wool·ly (*occas.*
wooly), *adj.*
wool·li·er,
wool·li·est

wool·ly (*occas.*
wool·ie), *or*
wooly, *n. pl.*
wool·lies

wool·ly-head·ed

wool·pack

woo·zi·ly

woo·zi·ness

woo·zy, *adj.*
woo·zi·er,
woo·zi·est

Worces·ter

Worces·ter·shire
sauce

word·age

word·book

word·i·ly

word·i·ness

word·ing

word·less

word·less·ly

word·less·ness

word·mon·ger

word-of-mouth

word·play

wordy, *adj.*
word·i·er,
word·i·est

work, *v.* worked *or*
wrought (TO
FASHION),
work·ing

work·abil·i·ty

work·able

work·a·day

work·a·hol·ic

work·bas·ket

work·bench

work·book

work·day

work·er

work·fare

work·horse

work·house

work·ing·man, *n.*
pl.
work·ing·men

work·ing·wom·an,

n. pl.
work·ing·wom·en

work·man, *n. pl.*
work·men

work·man·like

work·man·ship

work·out

work·room

work·shop

work·ta·ble

work·week

world-beat·er

world-class

world·li·ness

world·ly, *adj.*
world·li·er,
world·li·est

world·ly-wise

world-shak·ing

world·view

world-wea·ri·ness

world-weary

world·wide

worm-eat·en

worm·hole

worm·wood

wormy, *adj.*
worm·i·er,
worm·i·est

worn-out

wor·ri·er

wor·ri·ment

wor·ri·some

wor·ry, *n. pl.*
wor·ries

wor·ry, *v.* wor·ried,
wor·ry·ing

wor·ry·wart

worse

wors·en

wor·ship, *v.*
  wor·shiped *or*
  wor·shipped,
  wor·ship·ing *or*
  wor·ship·ping

wor·ship·er *or*
  wor·ship·per

wor·ship·ful

wor·ship·ful·ly

wor·ship·ful·ness

worst

worst-case

wor·sted

wor·thi·ly

wor·thi·ness

worth·less

worth·less·ly

worth·less·ness

worth·while

wor·thy, *adj.*
  wor·thi·er,
  wor·thi·est

would-be

wound

wound·wort

wrack

wraith

wran·gle, *v.*
  wran·gled,
  wran·gling

wran·gler

wrap, *v.* wrapped,
  wrap·ping

wrap·around

wrap·per

wrap·ping

wrap-up

wrath·ful

wrath·ful·ly

wrath·ful·ness

wreak

wreath, *n. pl.*
  wreaths

wreathe, *v.*
  wreathed,
  wreath·ing

wreck·age

wreck·er

wreck·ing

wren

wrench

wrest

wres·tle, *v.*
  wres·tled,
  wres·tling

wres·tler

wres·tling

wretch

wretch·ed

wretch·ed·ly

wretch·ed·ness

wrig·gle, *v.*
  wrig·gled,
  wrig·gling

wrig·gler

wrig·gly, *adj.*
  wrig·gli·er,
  wrig·gli·est

wring, *v.* wrung,
  wring·ing

wring·er

wrin·kle, *v.*
  wrin·kled,
  wrin·kling

wrin·kly, *adj.*

wrin·kli·er,
wrin·kli·est

wrist·band

wrist·let

wrist·lock

wrist·watch

writ

write, *v.* wrote,
  writ·ten (*occas.*
  writ), writ·ing

write-down

write-in

write-off

writ·er

write-up

writhe, *v.* writhed,
  writh·ing

wrong·do·er

wrong·do·ing

wrong·ful

wrong·ful·ly

wrong·ful·ness

wrong·head·ed

wrong·head·ed·ly

wrong·head·ed·ness

wrong·ly

wrought

wrung

wry, *adj.* wry·er,
  wry·est

wry·ly

Wu·han

Wy·o·ming

Wy·o·ming·ite

X

x-ax·is *n. pl.* x-
   ax·es
xe·bec
xe·non
xe·no·phobe
xe·no·pho·bia
xe·no·pho·bic
xe·ric

xe·ro·graph·ic
xe·rog·ra·phy
xe·roph·i·lous
xe·roph·thal·mia
xe·ro·phyte
Xe·rox®
Xmas

x-ra·di·a·tion
X-rat·ed
X-ray, *adj.*
X ray, *n.*
X-ray, *v.*
xy·lo·phone
xy·lo·phon·ist

Y

yacht

yacht·ing

yachts·man, *n. pl.*
  yachts·men

yachts·man·ship

yachts·wom·an, *n.*
  pl.
  yachts·wom·en

ya·gi

ya·hoo, *n. pl.*
  ya·hoos

Yah·weh (*occas.*
  Yah·veh)

yak (OX) *n. pl.*
  yaks (*occas.*
  yak)

yak (*occas.* yack)
  (TALK), *v.*
  yakked (*occas.*
  yacked),
  yak·king (*occas.*
  yack·ing)

yam·mer

Yan·gon (*formerly*
  Rangoon)

Yang·tze

Yan·kee

yap, *v.* yapped,
  yap·ping

yard·age

yard·arm

yard·bird

yard·man, *n. pl.*
  yard·men

yard·mast·er

yard·stick

yar·mul·ke (*occas.*
  yar·mel·ke)

yarn-dye

yar·row

yawl

yawn

yaws

y-ax·is, *n. pl.* y-
  ax·es

yea

yeah

year·book

year-end

year·ling

year·long

year·ly

yearn

yearn·ing

year-round

yea·say·er

yeasty, *adj.*
  yeast·i·er,
  yeast·i·est

yel·low

yel·low-dog

yel·low·ish

yel·low·ness

yelp

Ye·men

Ye·me·ni

Ye·men·ite

yen (CURRENCY),
  n. pl. yen

yen (LONGING), *n.*
  pl. yens

yen, *v.* yenned,
  yen·ning

yeo·man, *n. pl.*
  yeo·men

ye·shi·va *or*
  ye·shi·vah, *pl.*
  ye·shi·vas *or*
  ye·shi·voth

yes-man, *n. pl.*
  yes-men

yes·ter·day

yes·ter·year

ye·ti

yew (TREE) (*see also* ewe)

Yid·dish

yield

yield·ing

yo·del, *v.* yo·deled *or* yo·delled, yo·del·ing *or* yo·del·ling

yo·del·er

yo·ga

yo·gi (*occas.* yo·gin)

yo·gurt

yoke (COUPLE), *n. pl.* yokes (*see also* yolk)

yoke, *v.* yoked, yok·ing

yo·kel

Yo·ko·ha·ma

yolk (YELLOW OF AN EGG) (*see also* yoke)

Yom Kip·pur

yon·der

Yon·kers

Yo·sem·i·te

young, *adj.* youn·ger, youn·gest

young·ber·ry, *n. pl.* young·ber·ries

young·ish

young·ster

Youngs·town

your·self

your·selves

youth, *n. pl.* youths

youth·ful

youth·ful·ly

youth·ful·ness

yowl

yo-yo, *n. pl.* yo-yos

yt·ter·bi·um

yt·tri·um

yu·an, *n. pl.* yu·an

Yu·ca·tán

yuc·ca

yucky, *adj.* yuck·i·er, yuck·i·est

Yu·go·slav

Yu·go·sla·via *or* Ju·go·sla·via

Yu·go·sla·vi·an

Yu·go·sla·vic

Yu·kon

yule·tide

yum·my, *adj.* yum·mi·er, yum·mi·est

yup·pie

Z

za-ba-glio-ne

Za-ca-te-cas

Zach-a-ry

Za-ire *or* Za-ïre

Za-ir-i-an *or*
  Za-ïr-i-an

Zam-bezi *or*
  Zam-besi

Zam-bia

Zam-bi-an

za-ni-ly

za-ni-ness

zany, *adj.* zan-i-er,
  zan-i-est

Zan-zi-bar

zap, *v.* zapped,
  zap-ping

zar-zue-la

z-ax-is, *n. pl.* z-
  ax-es

zeal

zeal-ot

zeal-ous

zeal-ous-ly

zeal-ous-ness

ze-bra, *n. pl.*

ze-bras (*occas.*
  ze-bra)

ze-bra-wood

ze-bu

zeit-geist

Zen

ze-nith

ze-o-lite

zeph-yr

zep-pe-lin

ze-ro, *n. pl.* ze-ros
  (*occas.* ze-roes)

ze-ro-base, *or*
  ze-ro-based,
  adj.

ze-ro-sum, *adj.*

ze-ro-ze-ro, *adj.*

zest-ful

zest-ful-ly

zest-ful-ness

zesty, *adj.* zest-i-er,
  zest-i-est

zeug-ma

zig, *v.* zigged,
  zig-ging

zig-zag, *v.*
  zig-zagged,
  zig-zag-ging

zilch

zil-lion

Zim-bab-we

Zim-bab-we-an

zinc, *v.* zinced *or*
  zincked,
  zinc-ing, *or*
  zinck-ing

zin-fan-del

zing

zing-er

zingy, *adj.*
  zing-i-er,
  zing-i-est

zin-nia

Zi-on

Zi-on-ism

Zi-on-ist

Zi-on-ist-ic

zip, *v.* zipped,
  zip-ping

ZIP code

zip-per

zip-py, *adj.*
  zip-pi-er,
  zip-pi-est

zir-con

zir-con-i-um

zith·er

zlo·ty

zo·di·ac

zo·di·a·cal

zom·bie (*occas.* zom·bi)

zon·al

zon·al·ly

zone, *v.* zoned, zon·ing

zonked

zoo, *n. pl.* zoos

zoo·keep·er

zoo·log·i·cal

zo·ol·o·gist

zo·ol·o·gy

zoom

zoo·no·sis, *n. pl.* zoo·no·ses

Zo·ro·as·tri·an

Zo·ro·as·tri·an·ism

Zou·ave

zow·ie

zoy·sia

zuc·chet·to, *n. pl.* zuc·chet·tos

zuc·chi·ni, *n. pl.* zuc·chi·ni *or* zuc·chi·nis

Zu·lu

zwie·back

zy·deco

zy·mur·gy

Appendixes

The following appendixes will help the reader to become familiar with the basic rules of spelling, word division, capitalization, abbreviations, writing numbers, and other important style elements. They are not intended to constitute a complete guide to the styling of written English. Readers are advised to consult a thorough style manual for matters in addition to spelling. Appendix 8 can be used as a quick reference for chemical elements and symbols, state abbreviations, and metric conversion.

Definitions

The following definitions apply to terms used in the appendixes.

CLAUSE. A group of words that contains a verb.
CLOSE (SOLID) COMPOUND. Two or more words that were originally separate words but are now spelled as one word. Examples of close compounds are *fainthearted*, *manhandle*, and *stonecutter*.

COMPOUND WORD. A word made up of two or more words.

HYPHENATED COMPOUND. A combination of words joined with a hyphen or hyphens. Examples of hyphenated compounds are *forget-me-not*, *hee-haw*, *off-hours*, and *right-of-way*.

OPEN (SPACED) COMPOUND. A combination of words that makes up a single concept but is spelled as separate words. Examples of open compounds are *blood pressure*, *fellow citizen*, and *real estate*.

PHRASE. A group of words that does not contain a verb.

Appendix 1
The Formation of Plurals

1.1 Plurals—General

1.1.1 The basic rule. An English noun generally becomes a plural by adding *s*:

book *becomes* books
committee *becomes* committees
glance *becomes* glances
menu *becomes* menus
quota *becomes* quotas
taxi *becomes* taxis

Exception: Plurals of animals may not end with *s*: *mink* in the singular may be *mink* or *minks* in the plural.

1.1.2 Noun ending in *ch, sh, s, x, or z.* When the singular form of a noun ends in *ch, sh, s, x,* or *z,* the plural is usually formed by adding *es* to the singular:

bush *becomes* bushes
business *becomes* businesses
razz *becomes* razzes
tax *becomes* taxes
waltz *becomes* waltzes
witch *becomes* witches

Exception: Among the exceptions is *quiz*, which adds *zes* to become *quizzes*.

1.1.3 Noun ending in y. A noun ending with *y* preceded by a *consonant* is pluralized by changing the *y* to *i* and adding *es*:

city *becomes* cities
policy *becomes* policies

A noun ending with *y* preceded by a *vowel* is pluralized by adding *s* to the singular. Examples include:

attorney *becomes* attorneys
donkey *becomes* donkeys
monkey *becomes* monkeys
turkey *becomes* turkeys

Exceptions: Among the exceptions are *colloquy*, which becomes *colloquies*; *obloquy*, which becomes *obloquies*; and *soliloquy*, which becomes *soliloquies*.

1.1.4 Noun ending in f, fe, or ff. Most singular nouns that end in *f, fe*, or *ff* become plural by adding *s*:

belief becomes *beliefs*
safe *becomes* safes
sheriff *becomes* sheriffs

Some nouns in this group become plural by changing the ending to *ves*:

half *becomes* halves
knife *becomes* knives
leaf *becomes* leaves
life *becomes* lives
shelf *becomes* shelves
wife *becomes* wives
wolf *becomes* wolves

Other nouns in this group have two plural forms:

dwarf *can be* dwarfs *or* dwarves

scarf *can be* scarfs *or* scarves

1.1.5 Noun ending in *o*. Nouns ending in *o* sometimes have *s* added and sometimes *es*. Spanish words and terms from music generally add only *s*. However, no set pattern exists, and your best recourse is to consult a dictionary.

1.1.6 Noun the same in singular and plural. Some nouns are the same in singular and plural:

chassis
clothes
corps
gross
headquarters
means
measles
mumps
series
species

1.1.7 Changes to internal spelling. Some nouns become plural by changing the internal spelling:

goose *becomes* geese
man *becomes* men
mouse *becomes* mice
woman *becomes* women

In addition, *foot* usually becomes *feet*, as in "He is six feet tall." However, the singular *foot* serves as a plural in expressions such as "six-foot tape measure."

1.1.8 Words not completely anglicized. Words not yet completely adapted to English usage may have both an English plural and a plural in the original language. As examples, *appendix* has an English plural of *appendixes* and a Latin-derived plural of *appendices; bureau* has an English plural of *bureaus* and a French-derived plural of *bureaux*; but *hypothesis* is pluralized only in its Greek-derived form as *hypotheses*.

A dictionary provides guidance in the pluralization of foreign words.

1.2 Plurals of Abbreviations

1.2.1 Single word. A single word is abbreviated by shortening the word and ending it with a period: *building* becomes *bldg.* The plural is formed by adding *s* before the period:

bldg. *becomes* bldgs.
no. *becomes* nos.
vol. *becomes* vols.
Dr. *becomes* Drs.

1.2.2 Phrase. When a phrase is formed into abbreviation, the abbreviation can be either punctuated or unpunctuated.

A *punctuated* abbreviation of a pharse or compound expression can be pluralized by adding *s* or *'s* after the last period:

	M.B.A.s	M.D.s	Ph.D.s
or	M.B.A.'s	M.D.'s	Ph.D.'s

If the abbreviation is *unpunctuated* and written in all capital letters, the apostrophe is usually not necessary:

CEOs	CPUs	ICBMs	IOUs
IQs	PTAs	VIPs	YMCAs

However, readability can be improved in some instances by using the *'s*:

SOS's, *not* SOSs

1.2.3 Single letter. An abbreviation formed by a single letter is often pluralized by repeating the letter:

p. *becomes* pp. (pages)
1. *becomes* 11. (lines)

1.2.4 Internal word plurals. When an internal word of an abbreviated phrase is a plural, a small *s* is occasionally added to the end of the shortened form. An apostrophe is sometimes used before the *s*. Thus "runs batted in" may be written as *RBI* or *RBIs* or even *RBI's*.

Strictly speaking, it doesn't make much sense to say or write *RBIs*, for that literally stands for "runs batted ins"; "runs" makes sense, but what about "ins"? However, ballplayers use "RBIs," and many writers do the same so that their writing will sound natural.

Whether to use an apostrophe with the plural of an abbreviation defies logic. In current use are expressions such as *snag* (*s*ensitive *n*ew *a*ge *g*uy, pluralized without an apostrophe as *snags*) and *rpm's* (*r*evolutions *p*er *m*inute, pluralized with an apostrophe).

Usually the apostrophe isn't necessary, and its presence may contribute to confusion. That is, the apostrophe may allow the shortened form to be interpreted as a contraction, a possessive, or a plural.

1.3 Plurals of Compound Terms

With compound terms, pluralize the significant word. That is the predominant style, even though dictionaries show occasional spelling variants.

1.3.1 Significant word first.

adjutants general
aides-de-camp
ambassadors at large
attorneys at law
attorneys general
autos-da-fe
bases on balls
billets-doux
bills of fare
brothers-in-law
chargés d'affaires
commanders in chief
comptrollers general
counsels general
coups d'état

courts-martial
crepes suzette
daughters-in-law
editors in chief
governors general
grants-in-aid
heirs apparent
heirs at law
inspectors general
knights-errant
ladies-in-waiting
men-of-war
ministers-designate
mothers-in-law
notaries public
pilots-in-command
postmasters general
powers of attorney
presidents-elect
prisoners of war
revolutions per minute
rights-of-way
secretaries general
sergeants at arms
sergeants major
surgeons general
vicars-general

1.3.2 Significant word in the middle.

assistant attorneys general
assistant chiefs of staff
assistant comptrollers general
assistant surgeons general
deputy chiefs of staff

1.3.3 Significant word last.

assistant attorneys
assistant commissioners
assistant secretaries
brigadier generals
deputy sheriffs

general counsels
judge advocates
judge advocate generals
lieutenant colonels
major generals
provost marshals
provost marshal generals
trade unions
vice chairmen

1.3.4 Words of equal significance.

coats of arms
masters at arms
men employees
secretaries-treasurers
women writers

1.3.5 -ful or -fuls? A compound noun written as a single word and ending with *ful* forms the plural by adding *s* at the end: "five *bucketfuls* of earth." The meaning is that there was enough earth to fill one bucket five times.

However, if there are five separate buckets each filled with earth, the correct form is expressed in two words: "five *buckets full* of earth."

1.4 Plurals of Letters and Words

1.4.1 Letters. The plural of a lowercase letter is usually formed by the addition of *'s*:

p's and q's   cross your t's
a's and *i*'s (rather than *as* and *is*)

An uppercase letter is frequently pluralized by the addition of *s* alone:

a report card with all Fs
the three Rs

1.4.2 Words. A word referred to as a word is usually

italicized, and plurals of italicized terms are treated according to these rules: (1) The singular form is italicized;
(2) the added *e* or *es* is not:

> They bought eight *Chronicle*s and five *Times*es.
> He used too many *and*s in his writing.

1.5 Plurals of Units of Measurement

The table below shows the singular, spelled-out plural,
and abbreviated plural forms of common units of measurement. Note that abbreviations of units of measurement are the same in the singular and the plural:

SINGULAR	SPELLED-OUT PLURAL	ABBREVIATION
barrel	barrels	bbl.
degree	degrees	deg.
foot	feet	ft.
gallon	gallons	gal.
inch	inches	in.
kilogram	kilograms	kg.
kilometer	kilometers	km.
mile	miles	mi.
milliliter	milliliters	ml.
minute	minutes	min.
ounce	ounces	oz.
second	seconds	sec.

Exception: Speakers and writers of English commonly
use the singular form in plural expressions such as these:

> six-pound, five-ounce baby girl
> eight-quart capacity.
> forty-yard pass

Note: Units of measurement are sometimes abbreviated
without periods: *lb.* or *lb* for pound, as an example.

1.6 Plurals of Numbers

1.6.1 Numbers written as words. Numbers written as words are pluralized by adding *s* or *es*:

ones	twos	threes	sixes
thirds	sixths	twenty-fives	

For a spelled-out number ending in *y*, change the *y* to *i* and add *es*: *twenties*.

1.6.2 Numbers written as numerals. Numerals are pluralized by adding *s* without the apostrophe:

1960s	Boeing 707s
mid-$40,000s	the W-4s

1.7 Plurals of Proper Names

1.7.1 First names. To form the plural of a first name, add *s* or *es*, but do not otherwise change the spelling:

Mary *becomes* Marys (including Bloody Marys, Typhoid Marys)
Marie *becomes* Maries
Waldo *becomes* Waldos
Douglas *becomes* Douglases
Gladys *becomes* Gladyses
Beatrix *becomes* Beatrixes
Fritz *becomes* Fritzes

1.7.2 Last names. Many last names are pluralized simply by adding *s*:

Scott *becomes* Scotts
Romero *becomes* Romeros

When a last name ends with an *s, x, ch, sh,* or *z* sound, add *es* to form the plural:

Stevens *becomes* Stevenses
Hastings *becomes* Hastingses
Church *becomes* Churches
Wish *becomes* Wishes
Maddox *becomes* Maddoxes
Katz *becomes* Katzes
Velasquez *becomes* Velasquezes

Do not add *es* if it makes the name awkward to pro-
nounce or read: "*McDonald's* restaurants," not "*Mc-
Donald'ses* restaurants."

Do not change the spelling of a last name. Simply add
s or *es*:

McCarthys, *not* McCarthies
Wolfs, *not* Wolves
Martinos, *not* Martinoes
Goodmans, *not* Goodmen

Last names ending in *Jr.* or *Sr.* or with a numeral like
III can be pluralized in either of these ways:

ORDINARY USAGE	FORMAL USAGE
the William Strunk, Jrs.	the William Strunks, Jr.
the Nelson Rockefeller IIIs	the Nelson Rockefellers III

1.7.3 Other proper names. To form the plurals of other
proper names, add *s* or *es* but do not change the original
spelling:

Mercury *becomes* Mercurys
February *becomes* Februarys
Nissan 300-ZX *becomes* Nissan 300-ZXes

But Allegheny Mountains *becomes* the Alleghenies
Rocky Mountains *becomes* the Rockies
Ptolemy *becomes* Ptolemies
Sicily *becomes* The Two Sicilies

Appendix 2
The Formation of Possessives

2.1 Possession—General

You show possession in most instances by adding an apostrophe to a noun or by adding an apostrophe and an *s*. Often the choice is determined not by some rigid grammatical rule but by whether a word sounds right with one, two, or even three *s*'s tacked onto the end of it.

You can also show possession by using a personal pronoun such as *his* or *ours*.

2.2 To Show Singular Possession

2.2.1 Singular noun not ending in s. The possessive form of a singular noun not ending in *s* is formed by adding an apostrophe and an *s*:

The ruckus started when he stepped on the dog's tail.
They ordered the chef's special.
It is the city's most comprehensive record shop.
Coke is made according to the company's secret formula.
Why is she wearing a man's hat?

2.2.2 Singular noun ending with an s or an s sound. Here advice on style varies. One school of thought says that the possessive form of a singular noun ending in *s* or an *s* sound should be formed by adding the apostrophe and the *s*. The other school says that you can get by with adding only the apostrophe.

According to the first school of thought, you would write "The proprietess's rules proved to be a bother." According to the second, you would write "The proprietess' rules proved to be a bother."

Either way is acceptable and is a matter of personal preference.

baroness's jewels	*or*	baroness' jewels
Berlioz's opera	*or*	Berlioz' opera
Butz's policies	*or*	Butz' policies
Charles's tonsils	*or*	Charles' tonsils
cutlass's crew	*or*	cutlass' crew
fox's lair	*or*	fox' lair
Mays's home run	*or*	Mays' home run

Tradition has left us with an apostrophe but no added *s* in these constructions:

in Jesus' name   Moses' laws

2.3 To Show Plural Possession

2.3.1 Plural noun not ending in s. Some plural nouns do not end in s. When writing with those nouns, add an apostrophe and an s:

The children's toys were scattered all over the floor.
Men's and women's shoes are on sale today.
They gratefully accepted the alumni's contributions.

2.3.2 Plural noun ending in s. In many cases, a singular noun becomes plural by adding an s, thereby forming a plural noun. The plural noun then becomes a plural possessive by placing an apostrophe after the s:

They formed a patients' rights committee.
Management contended that the players' money demands were excessive.
Do not place a dollar value on our infants' lives.
Arguments over states' rights are old stuff.
They could not keep up with the Joneses' life-style.

2.4 Possessive Forms of Nouns Ending in an *eez* Sound

To avoid awkward-sounding endings, an apostrophe without the s is used to form the possessive of a word ending with an *eez* sound:

Hercules' labors are the subject of a great story.
Xerxes' troops put down revolts in Egypt and Babylonia.
The aborigines' traditions are going the way of the people.

2.5 Possessive Forms of Nouns the Same in Singular and Plural

When forming the possessive of a noun that is spelled the same whether singular or plural, add an apostrophe and an *s* to a noun not ending in *s*, but add only an apostrophe to a noun ending in *s*. This style applies whether singular or plural is meant:

The corps' location was treated as a secret.
As neophyte hunters, they quickly lost the three deer's tracks.

2.6 Possessive Forms of Nouns Plural in Form, Singular in Meaning

To show possession with a noun that is plural in form but singular in meaning, add the apostrophe only:

General Motors' profits were an item of discussion.
He wanted to emphasize mathematics' rigidity.

The sound of that last example can be improved by re-writing it to read:

He wanted to emphasize the rigidity of mathematics.

2.7 Double Possessives

A double possessive is an expression such as "I am a friend of Raoul's." In a double possessive, the word *of* is used in its possessive function, and some form of possessive noun is used:

This is a cat of my nephew's.

This wonderful land of ours.
Sonia is a friend of mine.

2.8 Possession by Inanimate Objects

Granted, an inanimate object such as a table doesn't own anything, but it's still acceptable to write:

The table's leg was broken.
The factory's whistle was silent.
Blueberry compote is tonight's dessert.

2.9 Possessive Forms of Compound Nouns

When using a compound noun, add an apostrophe and an *s* to the noun nearest the item possessed:

The attorney general's opinion became a matter of record.

That was an example of a singular possession by a compound noun. If you were to convert *attorney general* (singular) to a plural form of *attorney general*, you would still add an apostrophe and an *s*:

The attorneys general's opinions became a matter of record.

Similarly:

The brothers-in-law's books did not balance.

2.10 Alternative and Joint Possession

Alternative possession occurs when each noun individually possesses something. Joint possession occurs when the nouns together possess something.

2.10.1 Alternative possession. When constructing an alternative possession, show possession on each element:

These same problems arose during Nixon's and Reagan's administrations.

Mr. Gonzalez's and Mr. Koya's children made up half of the Little League team.

2.10.2 Joint possession. When constructing a joint possession, show possession on the last element of the series:

Jones and McCoughlin's department store had its annual sale early.

When Green and Bronowski's theory is applied, the results are different.

Or When the Green-Bronowski theory is applied, the results are different.

2.11 Apostrophes with Holidays, Names, and Titles

2.11.1 Holidays. Use of the apostrophe with popular holidays is as shown here:

April Fools' Day	Mother's Day
Father's Day	New Year's Day

2.11.2 Names and titles. Use of the apostrophe with names and titles varies. For instance, we have Hudson Bay but Hudson's Bay Company, Harpers Ferry but Martha's Vineyard, Columbia University Teachers College but Young Men's Christian Association, and *Publishers Weekly* but *Ladies' Home Journal*.

If in doubt, check with the originator of the term or consult a current reference work.

2.12 Apostrophes and Descriptive Terms

Apostrophes are seldom used with terms that are more descriptive than possessive:

Before you can receive a permit, you must take a test on citizens band radio rules.
They attended a House of Representatives session.

2.13 Apostrophes with Traditional Expressions

For perhaps no reason other than tradition, an apostrophe without the *s* is used with *appearance' sake, conscience' sake, goodness' sake*, and *righteousness' sake*.

"For goodness' sake," she lamented, "what have you done now?"

If you wrote the expression without the word *sake*, the apostrophe-*s* combination would be correct:

My conscience's voice told me I had done wrong.

An apostrophe is used with popular expressions such as these:

I am at my wit's end.
Our house is but a stone's throw from where you live.
You get your money's worth at that restaurant.

2.14 Possessives and Italics

When writing an italicized term, the possessive ending should not be placed in italics:

Esquire's 50th anniversary issue was a big one.

The Publicity Handbook's suggestions on news releases should be followed.

Of course, a possessive in the title is italicized along with the rest of the title:

Barron's is a valuable source of information.

2.15 Possessive Pronouns

2.15.1 Use of the apostrophe. Use an apostrophe when forming the possessive of pronouns such as shown here:

They relied on someone else's plans.
It is anyone's guess.
They borrowed each other's notes.
Others' plans have failed.

2.15.2 Apostrophe not used. An apostrophe is not used when forming the possessive of *mine, our, ours, your, yours, his, hers, its, their, theirs,* or *whose*:

It is our house.
This house is ours.
The car is theirs.
Whose sweater is that?

In addition:
• Do not write *it's* ("it is") for the possessive *its*.
• Do not write *there* ("place") or *they're* ("they are") for the possessive *their*.
• Do not write *who's* ("who is") for the possessive *whose*.
• Do not write *you're* ("you are") for the possessive *your*.

Appendix 3
The Joining of Words

3.1 Hyphens—General

This appendix gives a few guidelines regarding the use of hyphens to join words. For situations not covered by the guidelines, always use hyphens to aid readers and to prevent ambiguity. Each of the examples below could be misread if not for the use of hyphens:

Specifications called for 10-foot-long rods.
He is an old-clothes dealer.
I'll be wearing a light-blue hat.
Meals consisted of canned baby-food.
I bought a little-used car.

3.2 Compound Words That Are Typically Hyphenated

3.2.1 *In-laws* and *great*-relatives. Hyphenate all *in-laws* and all *great*-relatives:

Have you met my mother-in-law?
These three ladies are sisters-in-law.
This picture was taken with our great-great-grand-father.

*Grand*relatives are joined directly, without hyphens:

Our grandfather took the picture.

3.2.2 Colloquial descriptions. Informal speech has given rise to a number of colloquial descriptions that are hyphenated wherever they appear. Among these are:

He's a know-it-all and a stick-in-the-mud.
They have the know-how to get the job done.

Others include *Alice-sit-by-the-fire*, *Johnny-on-the-spot*, *light-o'-my-life*, and *stay-at-home*.

3.2.3 Compounds with letters. Use a hyphen when joining a capital letter to a word in instances such as these:

H-bomb	S-iron	U-boat
I-beam	T-square	V-necked

3.2.4 Ad hoc compounds. Writers sometimes form ad hoc compounds, compounds meant to serve an immediate and temporary purpose.

The remark was attributed to Richard Billings, a Las Vegas-lawyer-turned-desert developer.
He is an isolationist-traditionalist.

3.3 Hyphens with Prefixes

Most prefixes are joined directly to their base words without the use of hyphens. Following are the typical uses in which hyphens are standard.

3.3.1 Prefixes to words beginning with capital letters.
A hyphen joins a prefix to a word that begins with a
capital letter:

No one was in the mood to attend the un-American
rallies of the 1930s.
Explorers unearthed numerous pre-Columbian artifacts.

In this same category are words such as *anti-Arab*, *pro-
British*, *post-World War II*, and *pre-McCarthy era*.

3.3.2 Prefixes of *all*, *ex*, *quasi*, or *self*. When *all*, *ex*,
quasi, or *self* is used as a prefix, a hyphen usually follows.

The proposal called for an all-encompassing solution.
He called his ex-wife.

Quasi is joined to its base word with a hyphen:

With the filing of one document, the charity became a
quasi-corporation.
It was a quasi-academic argument.

With only a few exceptions, *self* prefixes are hyphenated:

Few boys in a toy store could show the self-restraint
that he did.
To rephrase the cliché, she is a self-made woman.

Exceptions: Dictionaries current at the writing of this
book show *selfhood*, *selfless*, and *selfsame* without
hyphens.

3.3.3 Duplicated prefixes. A hyphen is used to join
duplicated prefixes:

Let me re-redirect your attention to yesterday's
testimony.
The sub-subcommittee began its work yesterday.

3.3.4 Awkward or misleading prefixes. Hyphens help
to keep matters straight in sentences such as these:

When her tax refund came, she decided to re-cover the sofa (not "recover," as in "get back again").

Measurements showed that the particles were un-ionized (not "unionized").

Take time this weekend to re-create your special kinship with your family (not "recreate").

Similarly, hyphens are valuable in words such as *co-op* (not *coop*), *pre-position* (a verb having to do with "before" and not the noun *preposition*, referring to words), *re-sort* ("sort again"), and *re-treat* ("treat again," not "withdraw from battle").

Cross-reference: See also Section 3.7.3, "*Vice* as prefix."

3.4 Hyphens That Join Adjectives before a Noun

3.4.1 Hyphenated adjectives—the general rule. Use a hyphen between words, or between abbreviations and words, that form an adjective immediately before a noun. Use no hyphen if the adjective appears elsewhere in the sentence:

This is a large-scale project.
But: The project is large scale.

You will have to get involved in the decision-making process.
But: He is a skilled decision maker.

The shale is purged by a fossil-fuel-fired steam generator.
But: The shale is purged by a steam generator fired by fossil fuels.

The contractor tied in the roof-to-wall connection.
But: The contractor tied in the connection from roof to wall.

Officials could do nothing about the situation on U.S.-owned property.

But: Officials could do nothing about the situation on property that was owned by the U.S.

"United 201, you are cleared for a straight-in approach."
But: "Roger, tower. We will land straight in."

We are looking for five health-conscious, success-oriented people.
But: We are looking for five people who are health conscious and success oriented.

He despised get-it-done, make-it-happen thinking.
But: He despised thinking that said get it done, make it happen.

3.4.2 *Long-lived* and *short-lived*. *Long-lived* and *short-lived* are hyphenated wherever they appear:

It was a short-lived prophecy.
The prophecy was short-lived.
They say yogurt eaters are long-lived.

3.4.3 *Well-known* and similar compounds. Hyphens are used with adjectives that begin with *best, better, ill, lesser, little,* or *well.*

She is a well-known performer.
They formulated an ill-advised policy.

Exception: Hyphens are not used when the adjective follows the noun modified.

She is very well known
The policy is ill advised.

3.4.4 Adjectives of color. Adjectives that describe color are hyphenated.

The iron-gray ship slowly sailed into view.
To save money they settled for black-and-white printing.

Exception: No need exists to hyphenate *black and white* in this next example because the colors apply to many tiles:

The floor was covered with black and white tiles.

However:

The tiles were laid in a black-and-white pattern.

3.4.5 Compound adjectives before a noun. Compound adjectives—two or more words per adjective—are hyphenated as shown here. The idea is to join the main elements, not every word:

The biggest establishment in town is the Circus-owned 600-room Edgewater Hotel.
Water flowed today for the first time through the Folsom Lake-East Side diversion project.
An old book dealt with the Herbert Hoover-Department of Agriculture program.

3.4.6 Compound numerical adjectives before a noun. When using a number to form a compound numerical adjective before a noun, join the parts of the adjective with a hyphen:

Employees like the four-day work week.
Congress approved a five-cent-per-bottle tax.
The captain announced a 10-minute delay.

3.5 Unnecessary Hyphens

3.5.1 Adverbs ending in *ly*. Hyphens are not used with adverbs that end in ly:

It is a *wholly owned* subsidiary.
The signal came from a *rapidly approaching* ship.
For his age, he is an *unusually well-preserved* specimen.

3.5.2 When clarity is not a problem. When an expression is easy to read and meaning is clear, hyphens are not necessary. In the examples below, the italicized words do not need hyphens:

New Testament language is not as poetic as *Old Testament* language.

The wealthy live in *Lake Shore Drive* mansions.

County officials approved the *child welfare* plan.

Bids were taken on a new *word processing* system.

He attended *speech correction* class.

Her *social security pension* check came on the third of the month.

Because of the festivities, they took a *longer than usual* lunch period.

In the *not too distant* future we will be finished.

3.5.3 Foreign phrases. Do not use hyphens in phrases adapted from a foreign language:

He was convicted on *prima facie* evidence.

His statement was based on *a priori* analysis.

3.5.4 Phrases in quotation marks. Do not use a hyphen if a compound term is in quotation marks:

Our town adopted a "prior use" ordinance years ago.

3.6 The Suspensive Hyphen

When two or more words in a hyphenated compound have the same basic element and this element is mentioned in the last term only, a suspensive hyphen is used:

Old colleges are noted for their moss- and ivy-covered walls.

Before opening an account, he checked the long- and short-term interest rates.

They bought 8-, 10-, and 16-foot boards.

3.7 Hyphens with Titles

3.7.1 Double titles. Use a hyphen with double titles such as these:

He retired from his post as secretary-treasurer.
In an economy move, the organization created the post of treasurer-manager.
Pete Rose served as player-manager.

3.7.2 Single titles. Do not use a hyphen in titles such as the following:

William Henry Seward served as secretary of state.
Frederick Lord North was prime minister of England.

3.7.3 *Vice* as prefix. Titles with *vice* in them may be written without hyphens:

Vice President Andrew Johnson followed Lincoln.
The vice commander was promoted last week.

3.7.4 Suffixes to titles. A hyphen is used when *elect* or *designate* is suffixed to a title:

President-elect Wong called the meeting to order.
As ambassador-designate he was very careful with his remarks.

But do not use hyphens if the name of the office is two or more words:

The vice president elect seemed to have kept on campaigning even though the elections were over.

3.8 Hyphens for Visual Effect

To avoid awkward-looking terms, hyphens should be used with words like *Inverness-shire, bell-like, gull-like,* and *hull-less.*

Although we have grown used to seeing *cooperate* or *coordinate* without a hyphen after *co, semi-independent* and *semi-indirect* are easier to follow if hyphens are used, perhaps because the *ii* would be a visual burden.

Similarly, many readers will handle *non-native* easier than *nonnative,* and *co-worker* will be more pleasing to the eye (and the mind) than *coworker.*

Appendix 4
Word Division

4.1 Word Division—General

It is sometimes necessary to divide a word at the end of a line and to carry over part of the word to the next line. The division point is shown in dictionaries with a symbol such as a raised dot (·). In text, the division is shown with a hyphen (-) at the end of the line.

Therefore, a dictionary entry for *fas·ci·na·tion* allows divisions that

END ON ONE LINE AS	AND CONTINUE ON THE NEXT LINE AS
fas-	cination
fasci-	nation
fascina-	tion

Under ideal conditions, word division is accomplished so that the page looks neat and so that the reader is neither confused nor distracted. Unfortunately, ideal conditions do not always exist, especially when setting type on a narrow page or column.

A line can occasionally be rewritten *without changing the meaning* to make the line longer or shorter and thereby do away with the need for a hyphen at the end of the line. When the line cannot be rewritten, any confusion or distraction caused by an end-of-line word break is usually momentary, and context helps make the meaning clear.

For best results, careful word dividers should follow as closely as possible the guidelines given in this appendix. The guidelines are based on factors common to word division: pronunciation and appearance. Principal references are the entries in *Webster's Ninth New Collegiate Dictionary* (Merriam-Webster, 1990) and articles on word division in *Webster's Third New International Dictionary* (Merriam-Webster, 1976) and the *Chicago Manual of Style* (University of Chicago Press, 1982).

4.1.1 Short words. Avoid dividing short words, words of five or fewer letters. Words such as *basal, duty,* and *oleo* should not be broken at the end of a line even if a dictionary shows a break point.

4.1.2 One-syllable words. Do not divide a one-syllable word no matter how long. A word such as *through* or *straight* is pronounced as one syllable and has no logical division point.

4.1.3 One-letter divisions. A single letter at the end of a line does not give the reader much of a clue as to what follows on the next line. In addition, ending a line with a hyphen instead of a single letter is ridiculous, for if there is room for the hyphen, there is room for a solitary letter.

Consequently, a one-letter division should be avoided if at all possible:

again, *not* a-gain
mighty, *not* might-y

In addition, a one-letter division should not be made immediately before or after a hyphen:

voice-over, *not* voice-o-ver
mini-camera, *not* min-i-camera

Exception: In narrow page- or column-widths, it is permissible to break an expression like *Grade-A milk* at either side of the *A*.

Try to avoid making a one-letter division of the suffixes *-able, -ible, -ably,* and *-ibly.* In many uses, these suffixes stand as words in their own right. That is, *considerable* should be divided as *consider-able.* If divided as *considera-ble,* the resulting *considera-* at the end of a line looks awkward.

4.1.4 Contractions. Do not divide contractions such as *hadn't* or *doesn't.*

4.1.5 Adjoining consonants. Where two adjoining consonants separate the syllables, divide between the consonants:

mis-sion
con-fuse
con-version *or* conver-sion.

Where three or more adjoining consonants separate the syllables, place at least one consonant with its preceding vowel and divide the way the syllables are pronounced:

claus-trophobia, *not* claust-rophobia
mis-creant, *not* misc-reant

Exception: Do not break up a root word: *miss-ing,* not *mis-sing.* (See also Section 4.2.6, "*-ing* Suffixes.")
Exception: Do not keep any combination of letters together that results in an awkward break: *Father* is divided as *fa-ther,* not *fat-her.*

4.1.6 Adjoining vowels. Where adjoining vowels are pronounced separately, division should occur between the vowels:

cre-ation *is better than* crea-tion
re-adjust *is better than* read-just

4.1.7 Different usages—different divisions. Where different usages of a word exist, the word should be divided according to the pronunciations that are part of the usages:

proj-ect (*noun*) *or* pro-ject (*verb*)
microm-eter (*an instrument*) *or* micro-meter (*a unit of measurement*)

4.1.8 Suggestive divisions. A division should suggest the rest of the word and the word's pronunciation:

criti-cism, *not* crit-icism
offi-cial, *not* off-icial
posi-tion, *not* pos-ition
divi-sion, *not* div-ision

4.1.9 Consecutive lines. Try to avoid dividing words at the ends of more than two consecutive lines.

4.1.10 Paragraph breaks. Try to avoid dividing the last word of a paragraph. If you must divide it, carry over at least four letters to the following line.

4.1.11 Page breaks. Try to avoid dividing the last word on a right-hand page.

4.1.12 Embarrassing breaks. Avoid embarrassing word breaks:

thera-pist, *not* the-rapist
amass, *not* am-ass
fric-as-see, *not* fric-ass-ee

4.2. Division of Prefixes and Suffixes

Division of prefixes and suffixes is accomplished according to these guidelines.

4.2.1 Short prefixes. Divide after a short prefix:

non-taxable

post-partum
pre-arranged
un-grammatical

4.2.2 Long or multisyllabic prefixes. Try not to divide
a long or multisyllabic prefix:

anti-depressant *is better than* an-tidepressant
multi-vitamin *is better than* mul-tivitamin
semi-trailer, *not* sem-itrailer

4.2.3 Suffixes—general. When the root word does *not*
end with an *e*, the suffix is set off from the end of the
word by using a hyphen:

moist *becomes* moist-en, moist-er, moist-est

When the root word ends with an *e*, the *e* is usually
dropped, and the suffix is set off from word by using a
hyphen:

take *becomes* tak-en
white *becomes* whit-er, whit-est, whit-ish

Exceptions: *White* becomes *white-ness*. In addition, pronunciation sometimes dictates divisions where the hyphen is placed before the suffix: *cho-sen*, not *chos-en;*
fro-zen, not *froz-en*.

4.2.4 Suffixes with one-syllable sounds. A one-syllable
sound in these suffixes is rarely divided. *-ceous, -cial,
-cion, -cious, -geous, -gion, -gious, -sial, -sion, -tial,
-tion, -tious.*

4.2.5 -ed suffixes. A pronounced *-ed* suffix is separated
from its root word: *stat-ed*.
When the last syllable contains a silent *e*, that syllable
should not be separated from the word:

aimed, *not* aim-ed
plugged, *not* plug-ged
stig-matized *or* stigma-tized, *not* stigmatiz-ed.

4.2.6 -*ing* suffixes. When the final consonant is doubled to form an -*ing* suffix, divide between the doubled consonants:

grin-ning, *not* grinn-ing

Single or double consonants that are part of the root word are usually not carried over:

forc-ing, *not* for-cing
grill-ing, *not* gril-ling

When the root word ends in *e*, the *e* is dropped:

state *becomes* stat-ing
file *becomes* fil-ing

When the root word ends in *le*, the *e* is dropped. The *l* and sometimes one or more of the preceding consonants are carried over with the -*ing*:

chuckle *becomes* chuck-ling
twinkle *becomes* twin-kling

4.2.7 -*le* endings. When the word ends in an *le* syllable that sounds like a vowel, carry over one or more of the letters that come before the *le*:

star-tle, *not* start-le
prin-ciples *or* princi-ples, *not* princip-les

4.3 Division of Compound Words

4.3.1 Solid compounds. A solid compound word is made up of two or more words not joined by a hyphen or hyphens. *Crabgrass* is a solid compound, as is *outreach*.
A solid compound should be divided between the elements of the compound:

sales-woman *is better than* saleswom-an

news-paper (*1st choice*) *or* newspa-per (*2d choice*), *but not* new-spaper

4.3.2 Hyphenated compounds. A hyphenated compound is two or more words joined by a hyphen or hyphens. *Self-centered* is a hyphenated compound.

A hyphenated compound should be divided at the hyphen; the idea is to avoid two hyphens close together:

self-satisfied (*1st choice*) *or* self-satis-fied (*2d choice*) *or* self-sat-isfied (*3d choice*)
self-centeredness (*1st choice*) *or* self-centered-ness (*2d choice*) *or* self-cen-teredness (*3d choice*)

A break at the hyphen is especially disconcerting in short compounds such as *Mason-Dixon* or with a word like *master-at-arms* that already has two hyphens.

4.4 Division of Personal Names

Every effort should be made to place on one line a person's name and any identifying titles or abbreviations. If that is not possible, the name should be broken after a middle initial. The breaks shown below are listed in descending order of acceptability.

Rev. William A. Medlich, Jr. (all on one line)
Rev. William A.- Medlich, Jr.
Rev. William A. Med- lich, Jr.
Rev. William- A. Medlich, Jr.
Rev. Wil- liam A. Medlich, Jr.
Rev. William A. Medlich, - Jr.

Although it is permissible to separate *Jr.*, numerical suffixes as in *Richard III* should not be separated from the name.

When initials are used in place of given names, break the name after the second or last initial:

T. A.- Johnson, *not* T.- A. Johnson.

4.5 Division of Abbreviations, Numerals, Dates, Headings, and Titles

4.5.1 Abbreviations. Do not divide short abbreviations such as *B.C.*, *M.A.*, *YWCA*. A long abbreviation may be divided as a word is: *YUP-PIES*.

4.5.2 Numerals. Try to avoid dividing closely connected numerals and their abbreviations: *$10,000* or 55 MPH. A long string of numerals may be divided at a comma, and the comma should be retained on the first line: (*1,300,-000*).

4.5.3 Dates. When writing dates, do not divide the month and the day. The year may be carried over to the next line.

4.5.4 Headings and titles. Do not divide words in headings and titles. Similarly, do not separate references such as *5(a)* or *4.3* from the matter to which the references pertain.

Appendix 5
The Writing of Numbers

5.1 Numerals or Words—General

Whether to write numbers as numerals or spelled out as words has been the subject of two general rules for quite some time. One rule says to spell out whole numbers from one through nine (or ten, according to some authorities). The other rule says to spell out whole numbers for one through ninety-nine (or one hundred, according to some authorities).

These are the ways that numbers would be written according to the Rule of 9 or the Rule of 99:

RULE OF 9	RULE OF 99
man of 52	man of fifty-two
76th birthday	seventy-sixth birthday
son six years old	son six years old
50 million degrees Fahrenheit	fifty million degrees Fahrenheit
size 10 dress	size ten dress
\$0.87 or 87 cents	eighty-seven cents
10th Amendment	Tenth Amendment
19th century	nineteenth century
Gay '90s	Gay Nineties
$13 \times 10_6$ or 13 million	thirteen million

5.2 The Writing of Numbers and Numerals

5.2.1 Spelled-out numbers: how to write. The simplest form of a spelled-out number is single word such as *ten*, *fifty*, or *ninety*. When you start combining numbers into compound words, follow these rules.

Use a hyphen to connect a word ending in *y* to another word:

A twenty-first birthday is a big event.
She turned twenty-one today.

Do not use a hyphen, or any other punctuation, between other separate words that are part of one number:

Our company celebrated its one hundred and twenty-first birthday this year.
This year our company celebrated birthday number one hundred twenty-one.
When you add it all up, it comes to one thousand one hundred fifty-five.

5.2.2 Cardinal numbers versus ordinal numbers. A cardinal number is a number such as eight, 55, or 101. An ordinal number is a number such as eighth, 55th, or 101st.

When using numerals for the ordinal numbers second and third, write 2d and 3d, not 2nd and 3rd (no *n*, no *r*).

5.2.3 Matters of consistency. Treat like subjects alike. That is, if you must use numerals for one of the numbers pertaining to a subject, then use numerals for all references to that subject:

For every five questionnaires mailed, three were returned, and the results will be announced in 6 to 18 months.

A sample of 750 essays was selected from the top quarter and the bottom half for each of nine topics assigned;

683 essays were written on the first four topics, but only 67 on the last five.

In addition, this list of *don'ts* applies to the use of numbers.
• Don't use numerals at the start of a sentence or a heading. Either write out the number or recast the sentence:

Nineteen ninety-two is a presidential election year.
In 1992 the nation will elect a president.

• Don't mix cardinal and ordinal numbers to mean the same thing. Do not write, "Rankings were first, third, eight, and nine." Instead write:

Rankings were first, third, eighth, and ninth.

• Don't mix complete numbers with abbreviations of numbers. Instead of writing "1920s and '30s," write:

We need a popular history book of the 1920s and 1930s.
Or We need a popular history book of the '20s and '30s.
Or We need a popular history book of the twenties and thirties.

5.2.4 Clarity and combinations of numbers. When several numbers appear before a noun, confusing appearances can be avoided by using words for some and numerals for others.

The order is for three 12-foot ladders.
Begin by ripping two ¾-inch boards.

Sometimes the solution is to rewrite the sentence. Either of the following is acceptable, but the second version's consistent use of numerals makes it easier to grasp:

In the first group of twelve hundred, 300 were symptom-free.
Or In the first group, 300 of the 1,200 patients were symptom-free.

In any event, quick comprehension is not gained by writing: "In the first group of 1,200, 300 were symptom-free."

5.2.5 Compound numerical adjectives before a noun. When using a number to form a compound numerical adjective before a noun, join the parts of the adjective with a hyphen:

Employees like the four-day work week.
Congress approved a five-cent-per-bottle tax.
The captain announced a 10-minute delay.

5.2.6 Plurals of numerals. To form the plural of a numeral, add *s* alone:

He is a man in his 40s.
She participated in the revolutions of the 1930s.

5.2.7 Plurals of spelled-out numbers. The plurals of spelled-out numbers are written like the plurals of other nouns:

They came in twos and threes.
We were all sixes and sevens.

For a spelled-out number ending in *y*, change the *y* to *i* and add *es*: *twenty* becomes *twenties*.

5.2.8 Suffixes of *fold*, *some*, *score*, or *square*. When you suffix *fold*, *some*, *score*, or *square* to a number, follow these rules for use of the hyphen: (1) Use a hyphen if the compound is formed with a numeral and a word, but (2) do not use a hyphen if the compound is spelled out; instead write the term as a close compound:

Production increased 20-fold over a two-year period.
I stand foursquare behind you.
"They're quite a twosome, aren't they?"

5.2.9 *Odd* as a suffix. When you add *odd* as a suffix to a number, use a hyphen whether the term is spelled out or written with numerals:

The manuscript consisted of 420-odd pages.

Critics raved about the play, which ran for sixteen-hundred-odd performances.

He spoke for fifty-odd minutes.

5.2.10 Abbreviations and symbols with numbers. When an abbreviation or a symbol is used with a number, the quantity is written as a numeral and not spelled out. Punctuation is as follows: (1) When the expression forms a compound adjective before a noun, a hyphen joins the terms in the adjective; (2) otherwise, a space is placed between a numeral and the abbreviation but not between the numeral and the symbol.

reading of 6.3 V	a 16-mm film
output of 45 MW	capacity of 24 sq. ft.
9′ x 11′	27° to 33°
8 cm	limit of 55 MPH
6-mg dose	

Abbreviations of units of measure are the same in singular and plural:

Trap dimensions are 1 m by 13 m.

5.2.11 Numbers in formal documents. In formal documents such as proclamations, numbers are spelled out:

In the year nineteen hundred and forty-one we set upon a dangerous mission.

The Eighty-second Congress now stands adjourned.

Be it hereby proclaimed that on this Fourth of July we are gathered to . . .

5.2.12 Inclusive numbers. Inclusive numbers may be written with a hyphen:

Repeated testing yielded measurements of 6-0 volts.

The Russo-Finnish War was fought during the winter of 1939-1940.

5.2.13 Indefinite and round numbers. Indefinite and round numbers are usually spelled out:

As I said before, "A thousand times no!"

Thanks a million.

They say that upward of fifty thousand people were at the concert.

In a good year he sells between four and five hundred head of cattle.

Exceptions: Some cases call for numerals plus the words million or billion:

The population of the United States is 250 million.

Our planet earth is at least 4.5 billion years old.

5.2.14 Large numbers. Large numbers are best written as numerals. Except in some scientific publications which use a space, commas separate three-digit segments written to the left of the decimal point:

16,475 (or 16 475 in some scientific publications)

1,212

15,062.73

Exceptions:

binary numbers: 0010110

page numbers: page 1233

serial numbers: 346177715

5.2.15 Numbers in dialogue. In narrative or in dialogue, words and not numerals are normally used.

The director said that the staff meeting begins at half past nine.

"Dinner will be served at seven," the hostess announced.

"Give me four bucks," I said.

5.3 Ages, Dates, Times, and Years

5.3.1 Ages. The style of writing ages follows these examples:

son six years old	seventh birthday
six-year-old son	76th birthday
25 years old	109th birthday

5.3.2 Dates. No punctuation is necessary when a date is written only as a month and year:

Someone will be appointed to arrange the May 1987 convention.

When a day of the month is added, a comma separates the day from the year:

The society's next convention will convene on May 21, 1987.

When a complete date—month, day, and year—is written into a sentence, the question arises whether to place a comma after the year. Either style shown in the next two examples is acceptable, as long as the same style is followed throughout:

The May 21, 1987, convention has been rescheduled.
The May 21, 1987 convention has been rescheduled.

Four different styles of writing dates are now in use:

May 21, 1987—Order is month, day, year. A comma and a space separate the day from the year. This is the traditional American method of showing a date.

21 May 1987—Order is day, month, year. Internal punctuation is not used. This style of writing dates is used in the military and in some scholarly and scientific publications.

1987-05-21—Order is year, month, day. Hyphens are

used between year and month and between month and day. Used in some
computer applications, this style *always*
uses 10 keystrokes. Months and days of
less than two digits must have a zero
placed in front of them to make 10
keystrokes, as in 1987-01-01 (January 1,
1987).

5/21/87—Order is month, day, year. Slant bars
are used to separate internal elements.
Use is limited to informal correspondence.

5.3.3 Time. Clock time is usually expressed as numerals, especially when the exact minute is important. A
colon with no space on either side of it separates the
hour from the minutes. The abbreviations "a.m." and
"p.m." may be lowercased or capitalized and are punctuated with periods but no internal space:

Flight 647's departure time is 3:19 p.m.
Today's staff meeting begins promptly at 9:30 A.M.
All participants completed testing in 2 hr. 27 min.

No punctuation is used when referring to the 24-hour
clock, nor are "a.m." and "p.m." used:

Flight 647's departure time is 1519.
Today's staff meeting begins promptly at 0930.

5.3.4 Time span and the apostrophe. The apostrophe
is used with time span in constructions like these:

Some people expect two weeks' pay for one day's
work.
This plaque is presented in honor of Santiago Perre-
ira's twenty-five years' service to the company.

5.3.5 Years. Years are best expressed as numerals.
When the abbreviations "B.C." or "A.D." are used,
they are capitalized. A space is placed between the year
and the abbreviation. The abbreviations themselves are
punctuated with periods but not spaces. Note that
"B.C." follows the year; "A.D." comes before:

Our best year was 1976.
Gaius Caesar, a grandson of Augustus, was born in 20 B.C. and died in A.D. 4.

However "A.D." may appear after the time period in this type of construction:

Disease struck the village in the second century A.D.

5.3.6 Abbreviations of years. Use an apostrophe to form the shorter form of a year:

The class of '80 held its five-year reunion late.
Paine exemplified the spirit of '76.

5.3.7 Prefixes with years. Use a hyphen to join a prefix to a year:

Her novel was definitely a pre-1950 epic.

5.3.8 Combining successive years. Successive years should be combined with a hyphen, not a slant bar:

Congress was late in acting on the budget for the 1980-81 fiscal year.
Several blizzards struck during the winter of 1978-79.

5.3.9 Decades and centuries. When writing decades and centuries, use numerals in constructions like these:

Events of the 19th century seemed bound to repeat themselves.
Even though his feet were firmly planted in the 1970s, he was a serious student of the Gay '90s.

Spell out numbers in constructions such as these:

Nothing happened on the continent for four centuries.
He devoted the last three decades of his life to the project.

5.4 Numbers in Scientific and Technical Uses

5.4.1 Binary numbers. Binary numbers are written without commas or any other internal punctuation:

100001

5.4.2 Decimals. Use a zero to the left of the decimal point if no value applies. Use a zero to the right of the decimal point only to show exact measurement:

measured height of 16.0 feet	1.35 inches
But: .50-caliber bullet	0.35 inches

In some scientific publications, spaces separate three-digit segments to the right of the decimal point. Accordingly, "pi" is written as 3.141 59.

5.4.3 Degrees of measurement. Punctuation with degrees of measurement is as shown below:

36°30′N (no space between degrees, minutes, and symbols)
20°C (no period after C) or 20 degrees Celsius
an angle of 16° or an angle of 16 degrees
50 million degrees Fahrenheit

5.4.4 Dimensions and sizes. When writing dimensions and sizes, the usual practice is to write numbers as numerals while spelling out units of measurement:

6 feet 2 inches tall
a 6-foot-2-inch man
7 meters wide by 18 meters long
4 x 4 matrix
size 10 dress
size 38 regular
8½-by-11-inch paper
3-by-5 cards or, more precisely, 3″ x 5″ cards or 3-inch-by-5-inch cards

5.4.5 Distances and speeds. When writing distances or speeds, use a hyphen if the value is a compound adjective:

journey of 10 miles
a five-mile trip
the 12-mile limit
velocity of 1,600 feet per second
a 15-knot wind
speed of eight miles per hour

5.4.6 Fractions. Use a hyphen to form spelled-out fractions as shown below. Also use a hyphen when you prefix a fraction to a word or form a compound word of a fraction.

In addition, spell out a fraction when it is followed by *of a* or *of an*:

a ½-inch pipe   one-half of an inch
as many as 3¼ times   two two-hundredths
cut in one-half   twenty-five one-thousandths

5.4.7 Frequencies. When a frequency consists of four or more digits, use a comma between the third and fourth digit counting from the right:

20,000 hertz

Exception: 1610 kilocycles

5.4.8 Percentages. Use numerals to write percentages. The word *percent* is usually preferred in text in place of the symbol (%). The symbol is preferred in tables and equations.

A space goes between the numeral and percent; no space is placed between the numeral and the symbol:

11 percent; 11%
0.5 percent; 0.5%
3 percentage points
range of 50 percent to 70 percent; 50% to 70%

5.4.9 Proportions. Proportions are expressed as numerals and are written out:

Use 1 cup of flour to ½ cup of milk.

5.4.10 Ratios. Ratios are expressed as numerals and punctuated with a colon. No space is used on either side of the colon:

gear ratio of 3.73:1
calculated ratio of 1:53,000

5.4.11 Serial numbers. A serial number is the number of an item in a series of items produced. The items might be books, the parts of a book, or amendments to the Consitution.

Representative serial numbers are shown below. The punctuation of the original is retained. Numerals are preferred except for more formal uses:

First Amendment   page 6
10th Amendment   subsection II.1
Sociology 10-A   treatment protocol 10
chapter 2   Document 95

5.5 Money

The writing of money is as shown in the examples below. Cents are carried to two decimal places when there is a need to be specific. In addition, when you spell out the number, also spell out the unit of currency:

$3.25 $4.00 worth of candy
$0.87 or 87 cents $410 net loss
five dollars $300,000

Amounts of money of a million dollars or more are partly spelled out. The reason is to avoid excessive strings of zeros. Note that the dollar sign comes before the numeral and not where the word *dollars* would fall:

Investments totaled $11 million for the year, and sales amounted to $6 million.

The company's net worth is $1.25 billion.

5.6 Scores, Betting Odds, and Handicaps

Sports items such as scores, betting odds, and handicaps are written as numerals joined by a hyphen. The word *to* is seldom necessary, but when it is used it should be hyphenated:

The final score was 6-2 in favor of the Giants.
Or The final score was 6-to-2 in favor of the Giants.
    Or The final score was Giants 6, Cubs 2.
Odds of 5-4 were posted at the start.
She plays with a 3-stroke handicap.

Appendix 6
Capitalization

Cross-reference: For the capitalization of abbreviations, see Appendix 7, Section 2.

6.1 Capitalization—General

To capitalize means to capitalize—to write as uppercase—the first letter of a word.

Words in several categories are capitalized. One category consists of first words, words that begin sentences, quotations, lines of poetry, lists, and outlines. Another category consists of proper nouns, words that name particular persons, places, or things. Also capitalized are proper adjectives, words that take their descriptive meanings from proper nouns. In addition, the pronoun *I* should always be capitalized.

Capitalization lends emphasis and importance to a word. Accordingly, capitalization should be used sparingly, to lend emphasis and importance only when it is needed. Otherwise, when too many capitals are used and when too many words stand out, none stand out.

6.2 Capitalization of First Words

6.2.1 Sentence beginnings. Capitalize the first word of a sentence whether complete or incomplete:

The general decided on a plan.
How fast can this car go?
Unbelievable!
Really?
When were you last home? Yesterday? Two days ago?

In most cases, capitalize the first word of a sentence that begins within a sentence:

My rule is, When in doubt, go shopping.
The question is, What happened to the $5 million that disappeared from the governor's special fund?

Or, less formally

Okay, what's the problem here?

Capitalize the first word of a sentence in parentheses outside of another sentence:

Collisions between the classes of the old society furthered the development of the proletariat. (There were many such collisions.)

Do not capitalize the first word of a complete sentence that appears in parentheses or dashes inside another sentence.

Collisions between the classes of the old society (there were many such collisions) furthered the development of the proletariat.

Collisions between the classes of the old society—there were many such collisions—furthered the development of the proletariat.

A complete sentence appearing after a colon may be capitalized, or it may begin with a lowercase letter.

The general pondered this question: Should we attack at dawn?

Or, less formally

Silently, the general reviewed the situation to himself: dawn would be a good time to attack.

6.2.2 Quotations. Capitalize the first word of a quotation:

To the general's command, "We'll attack at dawn," the soldiers said, "Nuts."

If a quotation is interrupted in midsentence, the second part does not begin with a capital letter:

"Our troops are ready," the general said, "and we'll attack at dawn."

Do not capitalize the first word of a quotation introduced with the word *that*:

The general said that "we'll attack at dawn."

6.2.3 Lists and outlines. Capitalize the first word of each line in a vertical list:

• Minerals form the bulk of the earth's crust.
• Minerals are found in hundreds of varieties.
• Minerals may be reusable.
• Minerals are never renewable.

Short items in a list need not be capitalized:

a. twenty   c. forty
b. thirty   d. all of the above

Capitalize the first words of complete sentences in run-in lists:

This is the things-to-do list for tomorrow:
(1) Do laundry.   (2) Cut the grass.   (3) Take the dog
to the vet.   (4) Go to grocery store.

Do not capitalize the first words of incomplete sentences
in run-in lists:

Here is the agenda for the meeting: (1) call to order,
(2) minutes of last meeting, (3) treasurer's report, (4)
new business, (5) discussion.

Capitalize the first word of each item in an outline:

Introduction
  I. Previous research in this area
  II. Methods and materials
  III. Findings
  IV. Conclusions and recommendations

In lists in legal matter and minutes, capitalize introductory matter such as *Whereas* and *Resolved*. Also capitalize the first word following the introductory matter:

Resolved, That . . .
Whereas, After twenty years of service . . .

6.2.4 Poetry. In general, capitalize the first word of
each line in a poem:

Theirs not to make reply,
Theirs not to reason why,
Theirs but to do and die.
    "The Charge of the Light Brigade," Alfred, Lord
Tennyson

But follow the style of the author:

Humanity i love you because
when you're hard up you pawn
your intelligence to buy a drink.
    "Humanity i love you," E. E. Cummings

6.2.5 Correspondence. Capitalize the first word of a
letter's salutation or closing:

Dear John,   Sincerely yours,

But Ladies and Gentlemen:

Capitalize the first word and all major words following the "SUBJECT" and "TO" lines in a memo heading:

SUBJECT: Meeting Agenda
TO: All Committee Members

6.3 Capitalization of Proper Nouns and Proper Adjectives.

Proper nouns and proper adjectives are capitalized, but the definition of "proper" is not all that cut and dried.

In almost all cases, personal names are capitalized as are *official* names and titles of places and things. Otherwise, little standardization exists when it comes to capitalizing or lowercasing shortened or popular versions of names and titles.

Accordingly, your best courses of action are these:

- Follow the style manual used by the publication that you are writing for.
- Have handy a dictionary or encyclopedia for checking the capitalization of terms not covered in the following guidelines and examples.

6.3.1 Abstract terms. An abstract term may be capitalized to add importance to the term, even though meaning is clear without such capitalization:

Was there ever a time when Truth ruled the land?
Knowledge is Power.

6.3.2 Academic degrees. Names of academic degrees are capitalized when they follow a person's name. Abbreviations of names of degrees are always capitalized:

Melvin Law, Doctor of Divinity
S.O. Krateeze, Ph.D.
He earned an M.A. in English.

When not associated with a particular person, the name
of the degree may be capitalized or lowercased, according to individual preference:

He earned a Master of Arts degree.
or
He earned a master of arts degree.

General terms such as *bachelor's*, *master's*, or *doctorate*
are not capitalized.

6.3.3 Awards and honors. Names of awards and honors are capitalized. Descriptive terms that are not part
of the award are lowercased:

Academy Award	Nobel Peace Prize
Nobel Prize in physics	Rhodes scholar
Medal of Honor	Silver Star

6.3.4 Buildings and rooms. Capitalize the names of
buildings and rooms:

Oval Office	Empire State Building
White House	Room 212

6.3.5 Derived terms. A term derived from a capitalized
expression is usually capitalized itself, especially if the
term is used in its primary sense. However, if the derived
term has taken on a meaning of its own, the term is
usually lowercased:

Roman law	roman numbers
an Americanism	french fries
Victorian dress	manila envelope

6.3.6 Directions and compass points. Directions such
as *south* are not capitalized, but a word such as *South* is
capitalized when referring to a part of the country.

They lived in the South until drought struck; then they pulled up stakes and traveled west.

Nouns and adjectives that refer to specific regions are usually capitalized:

the Eastern establishment   Westerners

the Midwestern climate   Southern accent

Words such as *city, county*, and *state* are capitalized after a noun but not before it.

New York City; the city of New York
Washington State; the state of Washington
   Rogers County; the county of Rogers

However, legal style would sometimes capitalize *city, county*, and *state* regardless of where they occur:

the State of Washington; the State

6.3.7 Events. The full name of an event is capitalized. Short forms are frequently lowercased.

the Battle of the Little Bighorn; the battle
the San Francisco Earthquake; the earthquake
the Bonus March of 1932; the march; the marchers

6.3.8 Family relationships. Words of family relationship are capitalized when they precede a person's name or are used in place of a person's name:

Grandfather Bates   Aunt Bess
I know when Father's birthday is.

A word of family relationship may be lowercased when used as part of a noun phrase in place of a name:

I know when my mother's birthday is.

6.3.9 Groups of people. Capitalize the names of specific national, racial, or similar groups:

Cheyenne Indians	Jews
Mormons	Hispanics
Negroes	Italians
Taiwanese	Alabamians

Do not ordinarily capitalize names based on color: *black, redneck, white*. However, this general rule is often ignored by writers who capitalize *Black*.

In a class by itself is *Native American*—not *native*—for American Indian.

6.3.10 Hyphenated compounds. Capitalize the elements of hyphenated compounds if they are proper nouns or proper adjectives:

Tay-Sachs disease	Arab-Israeli pact
Afro-American descent	Sino-Soviet conflict

Lowercase any word in a hyphenated compound that is not a proper noun or proper adjective:

anti-American sentiments
Thirty-fourth Street
post-World War II negotiations

The word *pan* is usually capitalized when prefixed to a proper noun:

Pan-American efforts   Pan-African Congress

6.3.11 Imaginative names and nicknames. Imaginative names and nicknames are capitalized:

the Establishment	Big Brother
the First Lady	Boom Boom Mancini
the Big Blue (IBM)	

A nickname is frequently placed in parentheses or quotation marks or both when used with the person's name:

Dennis (Oil Can) Boyd; Dennis "Oil Can" Boyd;
Dennis ("Oil Can") Boyd

6.3.12 Numerical designations. Capitalize a noun in front of a numerical reference:

Flight 647	Form 2700EZ
Table 3	Chapter 5

Minor designations are usually lowercased:

page 16	mile 8.5

6.3.13 Official titles. Capitalize an official title when it comes immediately before a personal name; in that situation, the title is viewed as part of the name and is capitalized as the name would be.

Do not capitalize an official title when it stands alone or when punctuation separates the title from the name. In those situations, the title is viewed as being separate from the name. It would not be wrong to capitalize a title that stands alone or appears after a name, and some writers, especially those in government, frequently do capitalize such titles.

General Norman Schwarzkopf; Norman Schwarzkopf, general; the general
President George Bush; the president of the United States, *or* the President of the United States; the president, *or* the President
Chairman of the Board Lee Iacocca; Lee Iacocca, the chairman of the board; the chairman
Pope John Paul II; the pope

Do not capitalize generic occupational titles such as *executive, secretary, engineer.*

6.3.14 Organizations. The full official name of an organization is capitalized. Short forms are usually written as lowercase.

American Medical Association; the association
Hudson's Bay Company; the company
United States Congress; the Ninety-ninth Congress; congressional
World Wildlife Fund; the fund

the Ku Klux Klan; the Klan
California Department of Transportation; the department
National Security Council; the council
General Motors Corporation; the corporation
the Reagan Administration; the administration
the Communist Party; the Communist party
the U.S. Air Force; the Air Force; air force planes
First Battalion; the battalion

The practice in many organizations is to always upper-case any reference to the organization's own name:

National Security Council; the Council

6.3.15 Periods of time. Named periods of time are capitalized:

the Stone Age   the Christian Era
the Reformation   the Roaring Twenties

Numerically designated periods are not capitalized: *the nineteenth century, the sixties.*
   A day (*Sunday*) is capitalized as is a month (*January*). A season (*spring*) is not capitalized.

6.3.16 Personal names. Capitalize names and initials of persons:

Gloria Steinem   T. S. Eliot
JFK   Jean-Paul Sartre
St. Thomas Aquinas   Mary of Burgundy
Ludwig van Beethoven   Martin Van Buren

Lowercase uncapitalized particles of names unless the particle is not preceded by a name or title:

That was the policy of Frederik Willem de Klerk.
That was President de Klerk's policy.
De Klerk's policy was to . . .
That was De Klerk's policy.

The best way to treat a person's name—in terms of capitalization and spelling—is to write the name exactly as the person does.

For guidance concerning the capitalization of names of famous people, consult *Webster's New Biographical Dictionary*, *Who's Who*, and *Who's Who in America*.

Note: Every once in a while there comes along a writer like E. E. Cummings (1894–1962). Cummings generally disregarded the rules of grammar and punctuation and spelled his name as e e cummings. However, the tendency among editors today is to treat Cummings' name according to the standard practices for capitalizing names.

6.3.17 Place names. Nouns that name places are capitalized.

> the Arctic Ocean
> Baja California
> Middle West; Midwest
> Down Under (Australia)
> South Bend, Indiana

Shortened forms that refer to places areas are usually lowercased.

> Lake Michigan; the lake
> Lakes Mead and Powell; the lakes
> Mississippi and Missouri rivers; the rivers
> Ninth Judicial District; the district
> he San Diego Zoo; the zoo

Popular place names are capitalized:

the Big Apple   the Twin Cities

A generic term that accompanies a place name is not capitalized:

the California coast   the Nile delta

6.3.18 Religious terms. Capitalize all references to the Deity:

God is the One who sustains us.

Expressions such as these are also capitalized

Allah	Holy Ghost
Jehovah	Son of God
Yahweh	Christ

The Bible and its books are capitalized:

Acts	I. Kings

6.3.19 Scientific and technical terms. For the capitalization of scientific and technical terms, including terms in medicine and data processing, consult a current dictionary or specialized reference work.

6.3.20 Terms of address. In direct address or when referring to a named person, capitalize the person's title:

He went to see Doctor Sitha.
Have the troops stand at ease, Sergeant.
That's where Ms. Jones lives.

In indirect reference or when a person is not named, do not capitalize the person's title:

He went to see the doctor.
I'll have the sergeant tell the troops to stand at ease.

6.3.21 Titles of works. The expression "titles of works" refers to titles of articles, books, essays, plays, poems, stories, and the like. Titles of works should be capitalized according to these guidelines:

Capitalize the first and last word of a title and all other words except articles (*a, and, the*); prepositions (words such as *to, in, with, through*); and coordinating conjunctions (words such as *for, and, but*). Capitalize any word that begins a subtitle, even if the word is an article, preposition, or conjunction.

Treaty of Versailles
Border Beagles, A Tale of Mississippi

The Sea-Wolf
Porgy and Bess

The style of some publications is to italicize a title or to put it in quotation marks. When that style is followed, titles of complete works are italicized, and titles of parts of works are put in quotatoin marks.

The Unknown Country (book)
"The Men in Sheepskin Coats" (chapter)
Appendix 3, "The Testing of Usability"

6.3.22 Trademarks. Trademarks and service marks are capitalized according to the style used by the owner of the mark. To identify a trademark or service mark, see if it is accompanied by the word "Registered" or the letters *R*, *SM* or *TM* in a circle. Reference guides that list thousands of trademarks are *The Trademark Register of the United States* and *Brands and Their Companies* (formerly *Trade Names Dictionary*).

Appendix 7
The Writing of Abbreviations

7.1 Abbreviations—General

An *abbreviation* is any shortened form of a word. For ease of reference here, abbreviations are sorted into three types—*acronym, initialism*, and *abbreviation*.

An *acronym* is made up of the initial letters of all the words or sometimes just the principal words of an expression. An acronym is read or spoken as a word rather than letter by letter. The word *laser* (*l*ight *a*mplification by *s*timulated *e*mission of *r*adiation) is an acronym, as is the U.S. Postal Service's *ZIP* (*Z*one *I*mprovement *P*lan).

An *initialism* is also composed of the initial letters of an expression but is pronounced letter by letter rather than as a word. Examples of initialism are *rpm* (*r*evolutions *p*er *m*inute) and *GNP* (*g*ross *n*ational *p*roduct).

Any shortened form that doesn't fall into the above categories can be called an *abbreviation*. Examples that occur under this definition are *Dr.* (Doctor) and *Calif.* (California).

7.2 Capitalization of Abbreviations

A shortened form of a word is capitalized just as the spelled-out form would be:

Brit. (British)   Jan. (January)

An abbreviation is usually written in all capital letters when the abbreviation is formed from the first letters of what is being abbreviated, even if the spelled-out term is lowercased:

ETA (estimated time of arrival)
FYI (for your information)
NFL (National Football League)
OPEC (Organization of Petroleum Exporting Countries)

However, some popular abbreviations are written as lowercase:

aka (also known as)   dba (doing business as)

In addition, abbreviations that have become words in their own right are often lowercased:

laser (light amplification by stimulated emission of radiation)
scuba (self-contained underwater breathing apparatus)

7.3 Plurals of Abbreviations

7.3.1 Single word. A single word is abbreviated by shortening the word and ending it with a period: *building* become *bldg*. The plural is formed by adding *s* before the period:

bldg. *becomes* bldgs.
no. *becomes* nos.
vol. *becomes* vols.
Dr. *becomes* Drs.

7.3.2 Phrase. When a phrase is formed into an abbreviation, the abbreviation can be either punctuated or unpunctuated.

A *punctuated* abbreviation of a phrase or compound

expression can be pluralized by adding *s* or *'s* after the
last period:

	M.B.A.s	M.D.s	Ph.D.s.
or	M.B.A.'s	M.D.'s	Ph.D.'s

If the abbreviation is *unpunctuated* and written in all
capital letters, the apostrophe is usually not necessary:

CEOs	CPUs	ICBMs	IOUs
IQs	PTAs	VIPs	YMCAs

However, readability can be improved in some instances
by using the *'s*:

SOS's, *not* SOSs

7.3.3 Single letter. An abbreviation formed by a single
letter is often pluralized by repeating the letter:

p. *becomes* pp. (pages)
l. *becomes* ll. (lines)

7.3.4 Internal word plurals. When an internal word of
an abbreviated phrase is a plural, a small *s* is occasionally
added to the end of the shortened form. An apostrophe
is sometimes used before the *s*. Thus "runs batted in"
may be written as *RBI* or *RBIs* or even *RBI's*.

Strictly speaking, it doesn't make much sense to say
or write *RBIs*, for that literally stands for "runs batted
ins"; "runs" makes sense, but what about "ins"? However, ballplayers use "*RBIs*," and many writers do the
same so that their writing will sound natural.

Whether to use an apostrophe with the plural of an
abbreviation defies logic. In current use are expressions
such as *snag* (sensitive *n*ew *a*ge *g*uy, pluralized without
an apostrophe as *snags*) and *rpm's* (revolutions *p*er *m*inute, pluralized with an apostrophe).

Usually the apostrophe isn't necessary, and its presence may contribute to confusion. That is, the apostrophe may allow the shortened form to be interpreted as
a contraction, a possessive, or a plural.

7.4 Punctuation of Abbreviations

The trend is toward unpunctuated abbreviations, that is, no periods between the letters. As an example, EPA instead of E.P.A. for Environmental Protection Agency.

In addition, units of measurement are sometimes abbreviated without an ending period: six ml instead of six ml., for six milliliters.

Appendix 8
Useful Tables

8.1 Chemical Elements and Symbols

Table 8.1 shows the style of writing the names of the chemical elements and their symbols. The table is based on these sources: Janet Dodd, ed. *The ACS Style Guide* (Washington, D.C.: American Chemical Society), 1986; and *Pure and Applied Chemistry*, June 1984, in Roger Grant and Claire Grant, *Grant and Hackh's Chemical Dictionary*, 5th ed. (New York: McGraw-Hill Book Company), 1987.

Table 8.1
Chemical Elements and Symbols

ELEMENT	SYMBOL
actinium	Ac
aluminum	Al
americium	Am
antimony	Sb
argon	Ar
arsenic	As
astatine	At
barium	Ba
berkelium	Bk
beryllium	Be
bismuth	Bi
boron	B
bromine	Br
cadmium	Cd

ELEMENT	SYMBOL
calcium	Ca
californium	Cf
carbon	C
cerium	Ce
cesium	Cs
chlorine	Cl
chromium	Cr
cobalt	Co
copper	Cu
curium	Cm
dysprosium	Dy
einsteinium	Es
erbium	Er
europium	Eu
fermium	Fm
fluorine	F
francium	Fr
gadolinium	Gd
gallium	Ga
germanium	Ge
gold	Au
hafnium	Hf
hahnium	Ha
helium	He
holmium	Ho
hydrogen	H
indium	In
iodine	I
iridium	Ir
iron	Fe
krypton	Kr
lanthanum	La
lawrencium	Lr
lead	Pb
lithium	Li
lutetium	Lu
magnesium	Mg
manganese	Mn
mendelevium	Md
mercury	Hg
molybdenum	Mo
neodymium	Nd

ELEMENT	SYMBOL
neon	Ne
neptunium	Np
nickel	Ni
niobium	Nb
nitrogen	N
nobelium	No
osmium	Os
oxygen	O
palladium	Pd
phosphorous	P
platinum	Pt
plutonium	Pu
polonium	Po
potassium	K
praseodymium	Pr
promethium	Pm
protactinium	Pa
radium	Ra
radon	Rn
rhenium	Re
rhodium	Rh
rubidium	Rb
ruthenium	Ru
rutherfordium	Rf
samarium	Sm
scandium	Sc
selenium	Se
silicon	Si
silver	Ag
sodium	Na
strontium	Sr
sulfur	S
tantalum	Ta
technetium	Tc
tellurium	Te
terbium	Tb
thallium	Tl
thorium	Th
thulium	Tm
tin	Sn
titanium	Ti
tungsten	W

ELEMENT	SYMBOL
uranium	U
vanadium	V
xenon	Xe
ytterbium	Yb
yttrium	Y
zinc	Zn
zirconium	Zr

8.2 U.S. Postal Service State Abbreviations

Table 8.2 shows names of the states and other areas of the United States. Postal Service two-letter abbreviations are also shown. *Source*: U.S. Postal Service, *National Five-Digit ZIP Code and Post Office Directory* (Washington, D.C.: U.S. Government Printing Office), 1990.

Table 8.2
U.S. Postal Service State Abbvreviations

STATE OR AREA	ABBREVIATION
Alabama	AL
Alaska	AK
American Samoa	AS
Arizona	AZ
Arkansas	AR
California	CA
Colorado	CO
Connecticut	CT
Delaware	DE
District of Columbia	DC
Federated States of Micronesia	FM
Florida	FL
Georgia	GA
Guam	GU
Hawaii	HI
Idaho	ID
Illinois	IL
Indiana	IN
Iowa	IA
Kansas	KS

STATE OR AREA	ABBREVIATION
Kentucky	KY
Louisiana	LA
Maine	ME
Marshall Islands	MH
Maryland	MD
Massachusetts	MA
Michigan	MI
Minnesota	MN
Mississippi	MS
Missouri	MO
Montana	MT
Nebraska	NE
Nevada	NV
New Hampshire	NH
New Jersey	NJ
New Mexico	NM
New York	NY
North Carolina	NC
North Dakota	ND
Northern Mariana Islands	MP
Ohio	OH
Oklahoma	OK
Oregon	OR
Palau	PW
Pennsylvania	PA
Puerto Rico	PR
Rhode Island	RI
South Carolina	SC
South Dakota	SD
Tennessee	TN
Texas	TX
Utah	UT
Vermont	VT
Virginia	VA
Virgin Islands	VI
Washington	WA
West Virginia	WV
Wisconsin	WI
Wyoming	WY

8.3 Metric Conversions

Tables 8.3 and 8.4 provide factors for converting frequently used measurements to and from metric measurements. Table 8.3 shows conversions *to* metric units. Table 8.4 shows conversions *from* metric units.

Table 8.3
Conversions *to* Metric Units

WHEN YOU KNOW	MULTIPLY BY	TO FIND
miles	1.609	kilometers
yards	.914	meters
feet	.3048	meters
feet	30.48	centimeters
inches	2.54	centimeters
inches	25.40	millimeters
square miles	2.59	square kilometers
acres	.405	hectares
cubic yards	.765	cubic meters
cubic feet	.028	cubic meters
cubic inches	16.387	cubic centimeters
square yards	.836	cubic meters
square feet	.093	square meters
square inches	6.451	square centimeters
short tons (2000 lbs/ton)	0.907	metric tons
long tons (2240 lbs/ton)	1.016	metric tons
pounds (avoirdupois)	.453	kilograms
ounces (avoirdupois)	28.349	grams
gallons	3.785	liters
quarts	.946	liters
pints	.473	liters
temperature (Fahrenheit)	5/9 after subtracting 32	Celsius temperature

Table 8.4
Conversions *from* Metric Units

WHEN YOU KNOW	MULTIPLY BY	TO FIND
kilometers	.621	miles
meters	39.378	inches
meters	3.281	feet
meters	1.094	yards
centimeters	.033	feet
centimeters	.3937	inches
millimeters	.039	inches
square kilometers	.386	square miles
hectares	2.471	acres
cubic meters	1.308	cubic yards
cubic meters	35.71	cubic feet
cubic centimeters	.061	cubic inches
square meters	1.196	square yards
square centimeters	.155	square inches
metric tons	2204.623	pounds
metric tons	1.102	short tons (2000 lbs/ton)
metric tons	.984	long tons (2240 lbs/ton)
kilograms	2.205	pounds (avoirdupois)
grams	.035	ounces (avoirdupois)
liters	.264	gallons
liters	1.057	quarts
liters	2.114	pints
temperature (Celsius)	9/5 then add 32	Fahrenheit temperature

There's an epidemic with 27 million victims. And no visible symptoms.

It's an epidemic of people who can't read.

Believe it or not, 27 million Americans are functionally illiterate, about one adult in five.

The solution to this problem is you... when you join the fight against illiteracy. So call the Coalition for Literacy at toll-free **1-800-228-8813** and volunteer.

Volunteer Against Illiteracy. The only degree you need is a degree of caring.